Communications
in Computer and Information Science 1895

Rationale

The CCIS series is devoted to the publication of proceedings of computer science conferences. Its aim is to efficiently disseminate original research results in informatics in printed and electronic form. While the focus is on publication of peer-reviewed full papers presenting mature work, inclusion of reviewed short papers reporting on work in progress is welcome, too. Besides globally relevant meetings with internationally representative program committees guaranteeing a strict peer-reviewing and paper selection process, conferences run by societies or of high regional or national relevance are also considered for publication.

Topics

The topical scope of CCIS spans the entire spectrum of informatics ranging from foundational topics in the theory of computing to information and communications science and technology and a broad variety of interdisciplinary application fields.

Information for Volume Editors and Authors

Publication in CCIS is free of charge. No royalties are paid, however, we offer registered conference participants temporary free access to the online version of the conference proceedings on SpringerLink (http://link.springer.com) by means of an http referrer from the conference website and/or a number of complimentary printed copies, as specified in the official acceptance email of the event.

CCIS proceedings can be published in time for distribution at conferences or as post-proceedings, and delivered in the form of printed books and/or electronically as USBs and/or e-content licenses for accessing proceedings at SpringerLink. Furthermore, CCIS proceedings are included in the CCIS electronic book series hosted in the SpringerLink digital library at http://link.springer.com/bookseries/7899. Conferences publishing in CCIS are allowed to use Online Conference Service (OCS) for managing the whole proceedings lifecycle (from submission and reviewing to preparing for publication) free of charge.

Publication process

The language of publication is exclusively English. Authors publishing in CCIS have to sign the Springer CCIS copyright transfer form, however, they are free to use their material published in CCIS for substantially changed, more elaborate subsequent publications elsewhere. For the preparation of the camera-ready papers/files, authors have to strictly adhere to the Springer CCIS Authors' Instructions and are strongly encouraged to use the CCIS LaTeX style files or templates.

Abstracting/Indexing

CCIS is abstracted/indexed in DBLP, Google Scholar, EI-Compendex, Mathematical Reviews, SCImago, Scopus. CCIS volumes are also submitted for the inclusion in ISI Proceedings.

How to start

To start the evaluation of your proposal for inclusion in the CCIS series, please send an e-mail to ccis@springer.com.

use of wearable sensors in a healthcare learning environment to understand collaboration patterns [5]; group dynamics over a multi-session ill-structured problem-solving activity [6]; and cross-cultural collaboration and identity in a multi-session STEM-based resource creation program [7, 8]. Programming experience in introductory programming was used as a lens onto novice/expert behaviors in debugging in one paper [9]. Reflecting a current topical concern, [10] analyzed student comments in a student-targeted news space to understand perceptions regarding the regulation of AI chatbots (such as chatGPT) in schools.

Finally, a paper in animal behavioral science that is the first of its kind at ICQE which analyzes behavioral data in chimpanzees to understand the range and development of behaviors seen [11].

Society, Culture, Identity, and Justice

A further set of contributions addressed themes around Society, Culture, Identity, and Justice. These papers explored Narratives and Identities in Education, as well as approaches to Modeling Identities and Narrative in a wider context, and QE as a lens onto Speech and Culture, with a strand of papers investigating applications of QE in Equity and Social Justice.

These papers include wider issues in education regarding effective science communication [12] and motivational language in commencement speeches [13]; and investigation of representation and curriculum through the analysis of scholarly literature as a lens onto representation of Asian students pre/post-COVID-19 [14]; expression of intersectional identities by Pakistani and US high-school students [15]; issues of intersectionality, narrative, and identity from interview data with pre-service teachers of color [16]; analysis of interview data relating to post-colonial education [17]; and narratives in history textbooks [18]. In a broader societal context, papers provided investigation through analysis of political discourse on social media [19]; issues of Justice, Equity, Diversity, and Inclusion in the cultural sector, through data from Instagram [20]; analysis of identity and representation in narrative from interviews with Latinx immigrants [21]; probing of diagnostic modeling issues in the DSM through analysis of interview transcripts with psychiatric patients [22]; and interview data regarding cultural integration in business contexts [23].

Advances in QE Methodologies

Finally, a set of papers specifically targeted Advances in QE Methodologies, sometimes drawing on data from learning contexts to do so. Topics in this theme included Comparing and Combining Modeling Tools, Innovations in Coding Tools and Coding Approaches, and Teaching QE.

These papers included investigation of measurement models in problem-solving tasks that are customized to context [24], developing methods for multimodal interaction data [25], a comparison of coding approaches for online asynchronous discussion [26], and of interaction around data and its analysis [27]. Another set of papers explored

Preface

This volume represents the proceedings of the Fifth International Conference on Quantitative Ethnography (ICQE 2023), and the first event in Australasia, following the inaugural North American event (Madison, ICQE 2019), two online years, and a European event (Copenhagen, ICQE 2022). The conference, alongside the International Society for Quantitative Ethnography (ISQE), has continued to foster an open community, aiming to invite new and returning scholars, and disciplines, into community discussion around the data, methods, and uses of approaches that unify qualitative and quantitative analyses.

A core goal of ISQE, and the wider community, is to foster discussion regarding Quantitative Ethnography (QE), and key concerns regarding making meaning from rich sets of, often large, and often digital, data.

ICQE 2023 received 39 submissions as full papers, evaluated by two expert reviewers and a meta-reviewer using a double-blind model; 33 full papers were accepted. Reflecting the interest in this new methodology, of these full papers, 20 were 'student paper' submissions. Alongside contributions in these published proceedings, the conference included 10 Doctoral Consortium applications, 29 Posters, 2 Workshops, 2 Symposia, and 23 Research Agenda Development (RAD) proposals. These submissions are available in the ICQE 2023 Supplementary Proceedings available via the ISQE website. RAD submissions were accepted for the first time at ICQE 2023, to provide a forum at the conference for discussion regarding future research directions across the field, and its theoretical and methodological underpinnings, while facilitating international and interdisciplinary collaborations.

The paper topics, data, contexts, and implications reflect the interdisciplinarity of QE as a method, its application across contexts, and the scholarly community it engages. These proceedings organize papers against three core themes, although many submissions made contributions against multiple themes.

Learning and Learners

Approximately a third of the papers focused on understanding learning and learners, through Modeling Learners' Perspectives and Knowledge, Behavior and Multi-Modal Analyses, and applications of QE in STEM Education and Games and Digital Spaces for learning.

Papers in this section use a range of data, including interviews, game log-data, and wearable sensors, to consider issues in design for learning. They do this through investigation of: adaptive scaffolding in academic writing in relation to self-regulated learning [1]; game design implications arising from relationships between prior knowledge and game behavior [2], and reasons for unsuccessful game-level completion [3]; and student language structures and their relationship to design of conversational agent language [4]. These contributions also investigated: collaborative learning contexts, including through

Editors
Golnaz Arastoopour Irgens 🆔
Clemson University
Clemson, SC, USA

Simon Knight 🆔
University of Technology Sydney
Ultimo, NSW, Australia

ISSN 1865-0929   ISSN 1865-0937 (electronic)
Communications in Computer and Information Science
ISBN 978-3-031-47013-4   ISBN 978-3-031-47014-1 (eBook)
https://doi.org/10.1007/978-3-031-47014-1

This Springer imprint is published by the registered company Springer Nature Switzerland AG
The registered company address is: Gewerbestrasse 11, 6330 Cham, Switzerland

Paper in this product is recyclable.

Golnaz Arastoopour Irgens · Simon Knight
Editors

Advances in Quantitative Ethnography

5th International Conference, ICQE 2023
Melbourne, VIC, Australia, October 8–12, 2023
Proceedings

 Springer

approaches to developing and applying codes, including automated discovery and interpretation of codes [28], their selection [29], refining of codes [30], automated regex creation for code development [31], and intelligent co-rating as an approach to coding [32]. One paper also investigated the teaching of QE as an approach to Data Science Education [33].

ICQE: Conference and Community

ICQE provides a community forum for sharing and developing work in QE. The scope of QE's impact is reflected in the range of areas of application, forms of data, disciplinary contexts, and contributions in the submissions, both full papers and broader. It is perhaps unsurprising, reflecting current wider interest, that a set of papers used emerging generative AI and other computational innovations largely to investigate ways to support the coding process [28, 30–32], with one investigating perceptions of chatGPT regulation in schools [10].

Reflecting on the community, using the author 'country' data, the ICQE 2023 authors were based in twenty countries. Data represented in ICQE 2023 is largely drawn from online data sources (including public datasets and social media data), or US-based projects; we identify data drawn from research in nine additional countries (Norway, Finland, Kenya, Japan, Pakistan, Australia, Brazil, Cameroon, Namibia), with a single paper [7] involving four of these. Authors have analyzed a wide range of contexts, of those in education approximately half discuss school-based learning, and half university-level, with other foci including use of public datasets, sometimes to exemplify the potential for a particular analytic approach.

We would like to thank all the authors, and continue to invite researchers into the QE community, previous authors and new. We would also like to thank the reviewers, program committee members, and others in the QE community who have supported the conference. The program chairs would like to acknowledge support from ISQE and the National Science Foundation in the USA. We are particularly grateful to the local chairs and organizers for their work in planning the conference and welcoming ICQE to Melbourne.

September 2023   Golnaz Arastoopour Irgens
                                                                                  Simon Knight

References

1. Li, T., Lin, J., Iqbal, S., Swiecki, Z., Tsai, Y.-S., Fan, Y., Gašević, D.: Do learners appreciate adaptivity? An epistemic network analysis of how learners perceive adaptive scaffolding. In: Arastoopour Irgens, G. and Knight, S. (eds.) Advances in quantitative ethnography: Fifth international conference, ICQE 2023. pp. 3–17. Springer / International Society for Quantitative Ethnography (ISQE), Melbourne, Australia (2023)
2. Zambrano, A.F., Barany, A., Ocumpaugh, J., Nasiar, N., Hutt, S., Goslen, A., Rowe, J., Lester, J., Wiebe, E., Mott, B.: Cracking the code of learning gains: Using ordered network analysis to understand the influence of prior knowledge. In: Arastoopour Irgens, G. and Knight, S. (eds.) Advances in quantitative ethnography: Fifth international conference, ICQE 2023. pp. 18–33. Springer / International Society for Quantitative Ethnography (ISQE), Melbourne, Australia (2023)
3. Liu, X., Hussein, B., Barany, A., Baker, R.S., Chen, B.: Decoding player behavior: An epistemic network analysis of the reasons for player quitting using log data from the puzzle game baba is you. In: Arastoopour Irgens, G. and Knight, S. (eds.) Advances in quantitative ethnography: Fifth international conference, ICQE 2023. pp. 34–48. Springer / International Society for Quantitative Ethnography (ISQE), Melbourne, Australia (2023)
4. Li, H., Cai, Z., Wang, G., Cheng, F., Marquart, C.: Impact of agent language on student language in the structures of language connections. In: Arastoopour Irgens, G. and Knight, S. (eds.) Advances in quantitative ethnography: Fifth international conference, ICQE 2023. pp. 49–65. Springer/International Society for Quantitative Ethnography (ISQE), Melbourne, Australia (2023)
5. Yan, L., Tan, Y., Swiecki, Z., Gašević, D., Williamson Shaffer, D., Zhao, L., Li, X., Martinez-Maldonado, R.: Characterising individual-level collaborative learning behaviours using ordered network analysis and wearable sensors. In: Arastoopour Irgens, G. and Knight, S. (eds.) Advances in quantitative ethnography: Fifth international conference, ICQE 2023. pp. 66–80. Springer / International Society for Quantitative Ethnography (ISQE), Melbourne, Australia (2023)
6. Kaliisa, R., Dane, J.O., Sánchez, D., Pratt, J., Damsa, C., Scianna, J.: Understanding group dynamics during synchronous collaborative problem-solving activities: An epistemic network approach. In: Arastoopour Irgens, G. and Knight, S. (eds.) Advances in quantitative ethnography: Fifth international conference, ICQE 2023. pp. 81–95. Springer / International Society for Quantitative Ethnography (ISQE), Melbourne, Australia (2023)
7. Akumbu, R., Lux, K., Schulz, D., Espino, D., Hamilton, E.: Cultural impact on a global virtual STEM project. In: Arastoopour Irgens, G. and Knight, S. (eds.) Advances in quantitative ethnography: Fifth international conference, ICQE 2023. pp. 96–111. Springer / International Society for Quantitative Ethnography (ISQE), Melbourne, Australia (2023)
8. Espino, D., Hamilton, E., Lux, K., Lee, S.: From We to Me: Moving towards an examination of self identity in an online, global, collaborative, learning environment. In: Arastoopour Irgens, G. and Knight, S. (eds.) Advances in quantitative ethnography: Fifth international conference, ICQE 2023. pp. 112–124. Springer / International Society for Quantitative Ethnography (ISQE), Melbourne, Australia (2023)
9. Pinto, J., Liu, Q., Paquette, L., Zhang, Y., Fan, A.: Investigating the relationship between programming experience and debugging behaviors in an introductory computer science course. In: Arastoopour Irgens, G. and Knight, S. (eds.) Advances in quantitative ethnography: Fifth international conference, ICQE 2023. pp. 125–139. Springer / International Society for Quantitative Ethnography (ISQE), Melbourne, Australia (2023)

10. Famaye, T., Adisa, I., Arastoopour Irgens, G.: To ban or embrace - students' perceptions towards adopting advanced AI chatbots in schools. In: Arastoopour Irgens, G. and Knight, S. (eds.) Advances in quantitative ethnography: Fifth international conference, ICQE 2023. pp. 140–154. Springer / International Society for Quantitative Ethnography (ISQE), Melbourne, Australia (2023)

11. Andres-Bray, T., Barany, A., Gonder, M.K.: Using epistemic network analysis to explore flexibility and development of termite fishing techniques in nigeria-cameroon chimpanzees (pan troglodytes ellioti). In: Arastoopour Irgens, G. and Knight, S. (eds.) Advances in quantitative ethnography: Fifth international conference, ICQE 2023. pp. 155–169. Springer / International Society for Quantitative Ethnography (ISQE), Melbourne, Australia (2023)

12. Mulholland, K., Arastoopour Irgens, G.: Examining the discourse of effective science communicators using epistemic network analysis. In: Arastoopour Irgens, G. and Knight, S. (eds.) Advances in quantitative ethnography: Fifth international conference, ICQE 2023. pp. 187–201. Springer / International Society for Quantitative Ethnography (ISQE), Melbourne, Australia (2023)

13. Seol, Y.: Examining motivating language in commencement speech using epistemic network analysis. In: Arastoopour Irgens, G. and Knight, S. (eds.) Advances in quantitative ethnography: Fifth international conference, ICQE 2023. pp. 173–186. Springer / International Society for Quantitative Ethnography (ISQE), Melbourne, Australia (2023)

14. Sun, J., Nguyen, C.: Asian american education literature before and after covid-19. In: Arastoopour Irgens, G. and Knight, S. (eds.) Advances in quantitative ethnography: Fifth international conference, ICQE 2023. pp. 202–214. Springer / International Society for Quantitative Ethnography (ISQE), Melbourne, Australia (2023)

15. Mallikaarjun, V., Mahmud, U., Ravitch, S.: Examining student conceptualizations of intersectional identities across global contexts via epistemic network analysis (ENA). In: Arastoopour Irgens, G. and Knight, S. (eds.) Advances in quantitative ethnography: Fifth international conference, ICQE 2023. pp. 215–229. Springer / International Society for Quantitative Ethnography (ISQE), Melbourne, Australia (2023)

16. Goldstein, A., Remillard, J.: Using epistemic network analysis to understand the intersectional experiences of teachers of color in white-dominated education institutions (updated). In: Arastoopour Irgens, G. and Knight, S. (eds.) Advances in quantitative ethnography: Fifth international conference, ICQE 2023. pp. 230–243. Springer / International Society for Quantitative Ethnography (ISQE), Melbourne, Australia (2023)

17. Akumbu, R.: Conceptualizing theoretical frameworks for post-colonial education for Kisii K-12, Kenya. In: Arastoopour Irgens, G. and Knight, S. (eds.) Advances in quantitative ethnography: Fifth international conference, ICQE 2023. pp. 244–260. Springer / International Society for Quantitative Ethnography (ISQE), Melbourne, Australia (2023)

18. Kim, J., Barany, A., Liu, X., Zambrano, A.F.: The stories we tell: Uncovering hidden narratives in history textbooks through epistemic network analysis. In: Arastoopour Irgens, G. and Knight, S. (eds.) Advances in quantitative ethnography: Fifth international conference, ICQE 2023. pp. 261–274. Springer / International Society for Quantitative Ethnography (ISQE), Melbourne, Australia (2023)

19. Hamilton, E., Hurford, A., Williamson, M.: Theory and tool-building for a science of dysfunctional political discourse. In: Arastoopour Irgens, G. and Knight, S. (eds.) Advances in quantitative ethnography: Fifth international conference, ICQE 2023. pp. 275–289. Springer / International Society for Quantitative Ethnography (ISQE), Melbourne, Australia (2023)

20. Espino, D., Keene, B., Green, S., Werbowsky, P.: Leveraging epistemic network analysis (ENA) to identify focus areas for justice, equity, diversity and inclusion (JEDI) efforts in museum workplace contexts. In: Arastoopour Irgens, G. and Knight, S. (eds.) Advances in

quantitative ethnography: Fifth international conference, ICQE 2023. pp. 290–303. Springer / International Society for Quantitative Ethnography (ISQE), Melbourne, Australia (2023)

21. Rivera-Kumar, S., Zambrano, A., Barany, A.: Envisioning latinx narratives: Exploring mexican and honduran immigrant perspectives using epistemic networks by geospatial location. In: Arastoopour Irgens, G. and Knight, S. (eds.) Advances in quantitative ethnography: Fifth international conference, ICQE 2023. pp. 304–315. Springer / International Society for Quantitative Ethnography (ISQE), Melbourne, Australia (2023)

22. Kovács, S.D., Mulholland, K., Condon, L., Koncz, Z., Zörgő, S.: Interaction of diagnostic criteria in the narratives of patients with borderline personality disorder. In: Arastoopour Irgens, G. and Knight, S. (eds.) Advances in quantitative ethnography: Fifth international conference, ICQE 2023. pp. 316–329. Springer / International Society for Quantitative Ethnography (ISQE), Melbourne, Australia (2023)

23. Mackey, S.: Leveraging epistemic network analysis in monologic interviews to explore cultural integration in global organizations. In: Arastoopour Irgens, G. and Knight, S. (eds.) Advances in quantitative ethnography: Fifth international conference, ICQE 2023. pp. 330–345. Springer / International Society for Quantitative Ethnography (ISQE), Melbourne, Australia (2023)

24. Ruis, A., Tan, Y., Brohinsky, J., Yang, B., Wang, Y., Cai, Z., Williamson Shaffer, D.: Thin Data, Thick Description: Modeling Socio-Environmental Problem-Solving Trajectories in Localized Land-Use Simulations. In: Arastoopour Irgens, G. and Knight, S. (eds.) Advances in quantitative ethnography: Fifth international conference, ICQE 2023. pp. 349–364. Springer / International Society for Quantitative Ethnography (ISQE), Melbourne, Australia (2023)

25. Wang, Y., Shah, M., Jimenez, F., Wilson, C., Ashiq, M., Eagan, B., Williamson Shaffer, D.: Developing nursing Students' practice readiness with patient first: A transmodal analysis. In: Arastoopour Irgens, G. and Knight, S. (eds.) Advances in quantitative ethnography: Fifth international conference, ICQE 2023. pp. 365–380. Springer / International Society for Quantitative Ethnography (ISQE), Melbourne, Australia (2023)

26. Moraes, M., Ghaffari, S., Luther, Y., Folkestad, J.: Combining automatic coding and instructor input to generate ENA visualizations for asynchronous online discussion. In: Arastoopour Irgens, G. and Knight, S. (eds.) Advances in quantitative ethnography: Fifth international conference, ICQE 2023. pp. 381–394. Springer / International Society for Quantitative Ethnography (ISQE), Melbourne, Australia (2023)

27. Scianna, J., Liu, X., Slater, S., Baker, R.S.: A case for (Inter)Action: The role of log data in QE. In: Arastoopour Irgens, G. and Knight, S. (eds.) Advances in quantitative ethnography: Fifth international conference, ICQE 2023. pp. 395–408. Springer / International Society for Quantitative Ethnography (ISQE), Melbourne, Australia (2023)

28. Fang, Z., Yang, Y., Swiecki, Z.: Automated code discovery via graph neural networks and generative AI. In: Arastoopour Irgens, G. and Knight, S. (eds.) Advances in quantitative ethnography: Fifth international conference, ICQE 2023. pp. 438–454. Springer / International Society for Quantitative Ethnography (ISQE), Melbourne, Australia (2023)

29. Árva, D., Jeney, A., Dunai, D., Major, D., Cseh, A., Zörgő, S.: Approaches to code selection for epistemic networks. In: Arastoopour Irgens, G. and Knight, S. (eds.) Advances in quantitative ethnography: Fifth international conference, ICQE 2023. pp. 409–425. Springer / International Society for Quantitative Ethnography (ISQE), Melbourne, Australia (2023)

30. Zambrano, A.F., Liu, X., Barany, A., Baker, R.S., Kim, J., Nasiar, N.: From nCoder to ChatGPT: From automated coding to refining human coding. In: Arastoopour Irgens, G. and Knight, S. (eds.) Advances in quantitative ethnography: Fifth international conference, ICQE 2023. pp. 470–485. Springer / International Society for Quantitative Ethnography (ISQE), Melbourne, Australia (2023)

31. Cai, Z., Marquart, C., Eagan, B., Xiao, Y., Williamson Shaffer, D.: A lightweight interactive regex generator for qualitative coding in quantitative ethnography. In: Arastoopour Irgens, G. and Knight, S. (eds.) Advances in quantitative ethnography: Fifth international conference, ICQE 2023. pp. 455–469. Springer / International Society for Quantitative Ethnography (ISQE), Melbourne, Australia (2023)

32. Cai, Z., Eagan, B., Williamson Shaffer, D.: Negative reversion: Toward intelligent co-raters for coding qualitative data in quantitative ethnography. In: Arastoopour Irgens, G. and Knight, S. (eds.) Advances in quantitative ethnography: Fifth international conference, ICQE 2023. pp. 426–437. Springer / International Society for Quantitative Ethnography (ISQE), Melbourne, Australia (2023)

33. Ohsaki, A.: Teaching quantitative ethnography as data science education: How novices learned in using epistemic network analysis. In: Arastoopour Irgens, G. and Knight, S. (eds.) Advances in quantitative ethnography: Fifth international conference, ICQE 2023. pp. 486–500. Springer / International Society for Quantitative Ethnography (ISQE), Melbourne, Australia (2023)

Organization

Program Chair

Golnaz Arastoopour Irgens   Clemson University, USA

Program Co-chair

Simon Knight   University of Technology Sydney, Australia

Conference Chair

Mike Phillips   Monash University, Australia

Program Committee

Ishari Amarasinghe	Universitat Pompeu Fabra, Spain
Janine Arantes	Victoria University, Australia
Aneesha Bakharia	University of Queensland, Australia
Simon Buckingham Shum	University of Technology Sydney, Australia
Linda Corrin	Deakin University, Australia
Cynthia D'Angelo	University of Illinois at Urbana-Champaign, USA
Srecko Joksimovic	University of South Australia, Australia
Vitomir Kovanović	University of South Australia, Australia
Kamila Misiejuk	University of Bergen, Norway
Marcia Moraes	Colorado State University, USA
Valentina Nachtigall	Ruhr-Universität Bochum, Germany
Luc Pacquette	University of Illinois at Urbana-Champaign, USA
Natasa Pantic	University of Edinburgh, UK
Vitaliy Popov	University of Michigan, USA
Karoline Schnaider	Umeå Universitet, Sweden
JooYoung Seo	University of Illinois at Urbana-Champaign, USA

Conference Committee

Ibrahim Oluwajoba Adisa	Clemson University, USA
Cinamon Bailey	Clemson University, USA
Amanda Barany	Drexel University, USA
Brendan Eagan	University of Wisconsin-Madison, USA
Danielle Espino	Pepperdine University, USA
Tolulope Famaye	Clemson University, USA
César Hinojosa	University of Wisconsin-Madison, USA
Y. J. Kim	University of Wisconsin-Madison, USA
Caitlin Lancaster	Clemson University, USA
Katherine Mulholland	Clemson University, USA
Deepika Sistla	Clemson University, USA
Ian Thompson	Clemson University, USA
David Williamson Shaffer	University of Wisconsin-Madison, USA

Additional Reviewers

Jonathon Sun
Jennifer Scianna
Letitia Lee
Ayano Ohsaki
Stephanie Rivera-Kumar
Sabrina Gao
Shen Ba
Sheri Mackey
Tongguang Li
Amanda Peel
Juhan Kim
Mamta Shah
Hendra Agustian
Dorottya Árva
Adina Goldstein
Liv Nøhr
Zachari Swiecki
Virginia Clark
Juan Pinto
Andy Stoiber
Yeyu Wang
Andrew Ruis
Zhiqiang Cai
Theerapong Binali
Xiner Liu
Anggi Irawan

Szilárd Kovács
Seung Lee
Zheng Fang
Jennifer Kornell
Jamie Boisvenue
Tyler Andres-Bray
Aziz Awaludin
Eric Hamilton
Yujung Seol
Ward Peeters
Ruth Akumbu
Rogers Kaliisa
Mariah Knowles
Krirk Nirunwiroj
Haiying Li
Luis Felipe Martinez-Gomez
Kristina Lux
Jae Han
Jade Pratt
Amalia Dache
Vinay Mallikaarjun
Sadaf Ghaffari
Andres Zambrano
Yuanru Tan
Jun Lu

Contents

Understanding Learners and Learning

Do Learners Appreciate Adaptivity? An Epistemic Network Analysis
of How Learners Perceive Adaptive Scaffolding 3
*Tongguang Li, Jionghao Lin, Sehrish Iqbal, Zachari Swiecki,
Yi-Shan Tsai, Yizhou Fan, and Dragan Gašević*

Cracking the Code of Learning Gains: Using Ordered Network Analysis
to Understand the Influence of Prior Knowledge 18
*Andres Felipe Zambrano, Amanda Barany, Jaclyn Ocumpaugh,
Nidhi Nasiar, Stephen Hutt, Alex Goslen, Jonathan Rowe,
James Lester, Eric Wiebe, and Bradford Mott*

Decoding Player Behavior: Analyzing Reasons for Player Quitting Using
Log Data from Puzzle Game Baba Is You 34
*Xiner Liu, Basel Hussein, Amanda Barany, Ryan S. Baker,
and Bodong Chen*

Impact of Agent Language on Student Language in the Structures
of Language Connections 49
*Haiying Li, Zhiqiang Cai, Grace Wang, Fanshuo Cheng,
and Cody Marquart*

Characterising Individual-Level Collaborative Learning Behaviours Using
Ordered Network Analysis and Wearable Sensors 66
*Lixiang Yan, Yuanru Tan, Zachari Swiecki, Dragan Gašević,
David Williamson Shaffer, Linxuan Zhao, Xinyu Li,
and Roberto Martinez-Maldonado*

Understanding Group Dynamics During Synchronous Collaborative
Problem-Solving Activities: An Epistemic Network Approach 81
*Rogers Kaliisa, Jai Oni Dane, Daniel Sanchez, Jade Pratt,
Crina Damsa, and Jennifer Scianna*

Cultural Impact on a Global Virtual STEM Project 96
*Ruth V. Akumbu, Kristina Lux, Dante Schulz, Danielle Espino,
and Eric Hamilton*

From We to Me: Moving Towards an Examination of Self Identity
in an Online, Global, Collaborative, Learning Environment 112
    Danielle P. Espino, Eric Hamilton, Kristina Lux, and Seung B. Lee

Investigating the Relationship Between Programming Experience
and Debugging Behaviors in an Introductory Computer Science Course 125
    *Juan D. Pinto, Qianhui Liu, Luc Paquette, Yingbin Zhang,
    and Aysa Xuemo Fan*

To Ban or Embrace: Students' Perceptions Towards Adopting Advanced
AI Chatbots in Schools 140
    *Tolulope Famaye, Ibrahim Oluwajoba Adisa,
    and Golnaz Arastoopour Irgens*

Using Epistemic Network Analysis to Explore Flexibility and Development
of Termite Fishing Techniques in Nigeria-Cameroon Chimpanzees (*Pan
troglodytes ellioti*) 155
    Tyler Andres-Bray, Amanda Barany, and Mary Katherine Gonder

Society, Culture, Identity, and Justice

Examining Motivating Language in Commencement Speeches Using
Epistemic Network Analysis 173
    Yujung Seol

Examining the Discourse of Effective Science Communicators Using
Epistemic Network Analysis 187
    Katherine Mulholland and Golnaz Arastoopour Irgens

Asian American Education Literature Before and After Covid-19 202
    Jonathon Sun and Chi Nguyen

Examining Student Conceptualizations of Intersectional Identities Across
Global Contexts via Epistemic Network Analysis (ENA) 215
    Vinay R. Mallikaarjun, Usama Mahmud, and Sharon M. Ravitch

Using Epistemic Network Analysis to Understand the Intersectional
Experiences of Teachers of Color in White-Dominated Education
Institutions 230
    Adina Goldstein and Janine Remillard

Conceptualizing Theoretical Frameworks for Post-colonial Education
for Kisii K–12, Kenya 244
    Ruth Vitsemmo Akumbu

The Stories We Tell: Uncovering Hidden Narratives in History Textbooks
Through Epistemic Network Analysis 261
   Juhan Kim, Amanda Barany, Xiner Liu, and Andres Felipe Zambrano

Theory-Building and Tool-Building for a Science of Dysfunctional
Political Discourse 275
   Eric Hamilton, Marguerite Williamson, and Andrew Hurford

Leveraging Epistemic Network Analysis (ENA) to Identify Focus Areas
for Justice, Equity, Diversity and Inclusion (JEDI) Efforts in Museum
Workplace Contexts 290
   Danielle P. Espino, Samuel Green, Bryan C. Keene,
   and Payten Werbowsky

Envisioning Latinx Narratives: Exploring Mexican and Honduran
Immigrant Perspectives Using Epistemic Networks by Geospatial Location 304
   Stephanie Rivera-Kumar, Andres Zambrano, and Amanda Barany

Interaction of Diagnostic Criteria in the Narratives of Patients
with Borderline Personality Disorder 316
   Szilárd Dávid Kovács, Katherine Mulholland, Lara Condon,
   Zsuzsa Koncz, and Szilvia Zörgő

Leveraging Epistemic Network Analysis in Monologic Interviews
to Explore Cultural Integration In Global Organizations 330
   Sheri L. Mackey

Advances in QE Methodologies

Thin Data, Thick Description: Modeling Socio-Environmental
Problem-Solving Trajectories in Localized Land-Use Simulations 349
   A. R. Ruis, Yuanru Tan, Jais Brohinsky, Binrui Yang, Yeyu Wang,
   Zhiqiang Cai, and David Williamson Shaffer

Developing Nursing Students' Practice Readiness with Shadow Health®
Digital Clinical Experiences™: A Transmodal Analysis 365
   Yeyu Wang, Mamta Shah, Francisco A. Jimenez, Cheryl Wilson,
   Muhammad Ashiq, Brendan Eagan, and David Williamson Shaffer

Combining Automatic Coding and Instructor Input to Generate ENA
Visualizations for Asynchronous Online Discussion 381
   Marcia Moraes, Sadaf Ghaffari, Yanye Luther, and James Folkesdtad

A Case for (Inter)Action: The Role of Log Data in QE 395
   Jennifer Scianna, Xiner Liu, Stefan Slater, and Ryan S. Baker

Approaches to Code Selection for Epistemic Networks 409
  Dorottya Árva, Anna Jeney, Diána Dunai, David Major,
  Annamária Cseh, and Szilvia Zörgő

Negative Reversion: Toward Intelligent Co-raters for Coding Qualitative
Data in Quantitative Ethnography 426
  Zhiqiang Cai, Brendan Eagan, and David Williamson Shaffer

Automated Code Discovery via Graph Neural Networks and Generative AI 438
  Zheng Fang, Ying Yang, and Zachari Swiecki

A Lightweight Interactive Regular Expression Generator for Qualitative
Coding in Quantitative Ethnography 455
  Zhiqiang Cai, Cody Marquart, Brendan Eagan, Yaxuan Xiao,
  and David Williamson Shaffer

From nCoder to ChatGPT: From Automated Coding to Refining Human
Coding 470
  Andres Felipe Zambrano, Xiner Liu, Amanda Barany, Ryan S. Baker,
  Juhan Kim, and Nidhi Nasiar

Teaching Quantitative Ethnography as Data Science Education: How
Novices Learned in Using Epistemic Network Analysis 486
  Ayano Ohsaki

Author Index 501

Understanding Learners and Learning

Do Learners Appreciate Adaptivity? An Epistemic Network Analysis of How Learners Perceive Adaptive Scaffolding

Tongguang Li[1]([✉]) [iD], Jionghao Lin[1,2] [iD], Sehrish Iqbal[1], Zachari Swiecki[1], Yi-Shan Tsai[1], Yizhou Fan[3], and Dragan Gašević[1] [iD]

[1] Faculty of Information Technology, Monash University, Clayton, Australia
`tongguang.li@monash.edu`
[2] Human-Computer Interaction Institute, Carnegie Mellon University, Pittsburgh, PA, USA
[3] Graduate School of Education, Peking University, Beijing, China

Abstract. Self-regulated learning (SRL) is a critical skill for learners to acquire, and academics have designed and implemented SRL scaffolding to support learners in developing their SRL and use of learning strategies. Adaptive scaffolding is believed to be more effective in promoting SRL, but limited studies have explored how different learners perceive the adaptivity of scaffolding to their personal needs in relation to the strategies they use. This study recruited 22 undergraduate learners who were given an online learning task and provided with adaptive scaffolding. Post-task interviews were conducted to understand their learning strategies and how they perceived the adaptivity of the scaffolds. We used epistemic network analysis (ENA) to understand the associations among learning strategies and perceived adaptivity, and to examine whether these associations differed according to task performance. Results indicate that learners' adoption of learning strategies is associated with their perceived adaptivity of scaffolding, and the association differed between high- and low-performing learners. Learners who adopted a strategy consistent with the scaffolding design expressed a stronger appreciation of its adaptivity and demonstrated higher task performance.

Keywords: Adaptive scaffolding · Adaptivity · Self-regulated learning · Learning strategies · Learning performance · Epistemic network analysis

1 Introduction

Self-regulated learning (SRL) describes a process in which learners are cognitively, metacognitively, and motivationally engaged [7]. In this process, learners employ effective cognitive strategies and tactics while metacognitively monitoring, searching, and adjusting their cognitive processes to achieve learning goals [27]. Given that the adoption of SRL strategies is positively correlated

G. Arastoopour Irgens and S. Knight (Eds.): ICQE 2023, CCIS 1895, pp. 3–17, 2023.
https://doi.org/10.1007/978-3-031-47014-1_1

with academic outcomes [5], there has been growing interest among scholars in exploring ways to effectively support learners' acquisition and development of SRL [3,9,15] through scaffolding—processes that aim to support and enhance effective learning skills until independent performance is attained [17].

In the current literature, SRL scaffolding can be categorised into either fixed or adaptive scaffolding. Fixed scaffolding delivers identical scaffolds to a large cohort of learners, while adaptive scaffolding aims to tailor the content, timing, or format of scaffolding to address individuals' learning needs. For instance, Bannert et al. [4] invited learners to co-design their own scaffolding (i.e., self-directed scaffolds), which is posited to be more adapted to their learning needs and effective in developing their individual SRL repertoire. However, previous studies evaluating the effectiveness of adaptive scaffolding revealed inconsistent findings [2,3,14,15,18], leading academics to investigate individual differences that may impede learners from utilising the benefits of adaptive scaffolding. As explained by Jivet and colleagues [10], variability in the effectiveness of scaffolding may be related to learners' unique individual characteristics, their ability to make sense of scaffolding, and learning to utilise the scaffolding in different ways.

To date, numerous studies have examined the extent to which individual factors, such as goal orientation, tendency to engage and enjoy thinking (i.e., need for cognition), reading aptitude, and verbal intelligence, affect the effectiveness of scaffolding [6,15,18,23]. For example, Pieger et al. [18] found that learners' reading and verbal intelligence moderate the effects of scaffolding on learning performance. Nevertheless, the majority of these studies have employed quantitative analyses based on process data, such as trace and think-aloud data, with few studies exploring learners' self-reported experiences from receiving scaffolding. As Lim et al. [13] argues, even if the instructional design is adapted according to learners' individual learning data (i.e., log file data), this does not guarantee that the adaptive scaffolding can effectively address individual learning needs. Moreover, given that learners' engagement plays a vital role in mediating the effectiveness of instructional supports [12], studies evaluating the effectiveness adaptive scaffolding should shift their focus solely from *quantitative* evaluations to examining how learners *subjectively* perceive adaptive scaffolding. By gaining more insights from learners' perspectives, researchers can further inform the adaptivity of scaffolding that takes into account learners' individual needs.

As the trend of implementing adaptive scaffolding in promoting learners' SRL continues to grow and few studies have considered how learners perceive adaptivity of scaffolding, the present study examined the extent to which learners perceive an adaptive scaffolding approach empowered by learning analytics. To this end, we conducted one-on-one interviews with learners who completed an academic writing task in which adaptive scaffolding designed to promote SRL processes was implemented. Subsequently, we used epistemic network analysis (ENA), a method designed to analyse connections among cognitive elements, to provide a compact representation and integrated understanding of how different learners may perceive the adaptive scaffolding in different ways. The findings showed that the adaptivity of scaffolding was perceived differently by learners employing different learning strategies, and this association differed between high- and low-performing learners.

2 Background

2.1 Perceived Adaptivity of SRL Scaffolding

To date, some studies have investigated how learners responded to the SRL scaffolding [12,13,16,21]. For example, Pardo et al. [16] found a positive association between the provision of adaptive feedback and learners' satisfaction with feedback quality. In a similar study, Lim et al. [13] used ENA to analyse the relationships among learners' perceptions of the usefulness of adaptive feedback, their emotional response to the feedback, and their motivation to learn. They found that the majority of learners reported positive perceptions of feedback, as they felt cared for by the instructor and received task-focused suggestions.

While insightful, these studies were focused on the provision of feedback after the learning session, rather than scaffolding triggered in real-time in response to learner actions. To the best of our knowledge, few studies have considered how learners responded to the real-time scaffolding, and there is a scarcity in understanding how learners perceive differently to the adaptivity of scaffolding. For example, Siadaty et al. [21] implemented a post-task questionnaire and investigated how learners perceived the usefulness of SRL scaffolding. However, this study is limited in two important ways. First, it was situated in the context of workplace learning instead of a formal education context that is our primary focus, and second, its focus was on the perceived general usefulness of scaffolding, rather than the extent to which learners perceive the scaffolding was adaptive to their learning needs. As effective scaffolding should take into account that learners are different [1], more studies are expected to understand how different learners may perceive the adaptive scaffolding in different ways.

2.2 Perceived Adaptivity and Learning Strategies

Different learners may adopt different learning strategies, and it is believed that scaffolding should be adapted to the learners' adoption of learning strategies [1]. A learning strategy refers to the actions and thoughts that a learner employs with the intention of impacting their learning process [24], and learners enact their agency on a given learning task and determine what learning strategies will be adopted [27]. Previous studies have shown that learners who adopted different learning strategies would respond to scaffolding in different ways. For example, Lim et al. [12] posited that learners may be reluctant to adopt the suggested learning strategies from personalised feedback because the suggestions are very much different from their adopted strategies. This can be explained by the fact that suggesting strategies that are unfamiliar to learners would require more cognitive load (i.e., load on working memory) to implement, and it is believed that effective instructional design should mitigate unnecessary use of cognitive load to free cognitive capacity for other learning-related activities [11]. Despite the existing research on learning strategies and scaffolding, few studies have evaluated the extent to which rule-based adaptive scaffolding is effective in encouraging learners to accept and adopt suggested learning strategies. Moreover, insufficient studies have examined the association between adopted learning strategies and perceived adaptivity of scaffolding. Our study thus seeks to explore this association from the angle of learners' perspective so as to inform improvements on the design and implementation of adaptive scaffolding tools.

2.3 Perceived Adaptivity, Learning Strategies, and Academic Performance

Previous research on the effectiveness of scaffolding in relation to academic performance has yielded inconsistent findings. Some studies have demonstrated that adaptive scaffolding improves learners' knowledge levels [2], transfer performance [3,4,23], and engagement with tasks [15]. In contrast, other studies have reported that adaptive scaffolding has no direct impact on learning performance [14,18]. This may be caused by the fact that each learner carries unique individual characteristics, leading them to perceive and make sense of scaffolding in different ways [10]. For example, Sitzmann et al. [22] evaluated the effectiveness of SRL scaffolding on learning performance and found that learners' cognitive abilities and self-efficacy moderate the effect of SRL scaffolding on learning performance. This finding raised the consideration of aptitude-treatment interaction, which emphasises that the differences in learner characteristics may result in different reactions to the scaffolding. In another example, Duffy et al. [6] found that learners' dominant achievement goal interacted with SRL scaffolding. Specifically, for learners who received scaffolding, those who were predominantly performance-oriented demonstrated higher learning performance than those who were predominantly mastery-oriented. Building on this finding, they further hypothesised that learners with different learning characteristics (e.g., different goal orientations) might perceive the scaffolding differently, and this difference could be associated with their willingness to deploy suggested learning strategies, ultimately leading to varying learning performance. However, the current literature lacks an integrated understanding of whether perceived adaptation of scaffolding is associated with the adoption of learning strategies, and whether this association differs among learners with different levels of performance. Understanding the interplay between learners' learning strategies, how they perceive the adaptivity of scaffolding, and the subsequent impact on learning performance is essential, as researchers and instructional designers will be informed to develop more adaptive scaffolding that caters to the diverse needs and preferences of learners. Therefore, the current study aimed at understanding not only how learners perceive the adaptivity of scaffolding in different ways based on the learning strategies they employ but also how these varying connections are associated with learning performance. Accordingly, two research questions were proposed:

- **RQ 1.** Are self-reported learning strategies associated with perceived adaptivity of scaffolds to personal needs?
- **RQ 2.** Does the association between self-reported learning strategies and perceived adaptivity differ between high and low performing learners?

Given that this study is aimed at understanding the associations proposed in the research questions, we used ENA to explore the potential co-occurrence of perceived adaptivity and strategies as self-reported by learners in interviews, and tested whether these co-occurrences are associated with task performance.

3 Method

3.1 Study Context and Design

This study involved graduate learners from a research-oriented university who participated in an academic writing course designed to improve non-native English speakers' academic writing skills. The 16-week course consisted of ten modules. As part of the course, participants were required to complete a two-hour writing task to assess their reading comprehension and academic writing skills. A total of 253 learners participated in the two-hour learning session, all of whom were unpaid. Following the writing task, 94 learners were invited for an interview, with 22 agreeing to participate. These interviews were conducted in a semi-structured format during the first week after the completion of the writing task. Each interview took place individually over the phone.

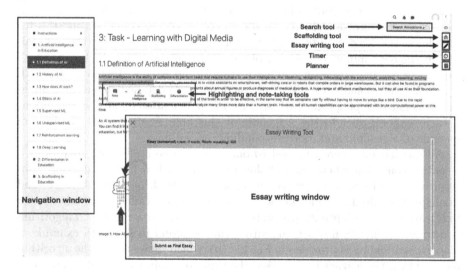

Fig. 1. A screenshot of the technological-enhanced learning platform.

The writing task was conducted on a technology-enhanced learning platform based on the Moodle environment [19]. The platform offered learners various

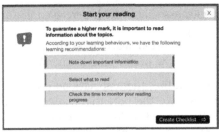 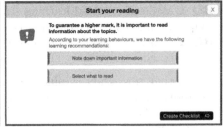

(a) example of the fixed scaffolding   (b) example of the adaptive scaffolding

Fig. 2. A comparison of scaffolding design.

instrumentation tools to support their reading and writing processes, including a timer, annotation tool, highlighter, planner, and essay-writing tools (as illustrated in Fig. 1). During the learning session, the learners were provided with reading material that focused on three main topics – Artificial Intelligence (AI), Differentiation, and Scaffolding. Based on the reading material, they were asked to write a 300–400 word essay discussing their understanding of the three topics and how these concepts could be applied to the future of education.

During the writing task, scaffolds were employed to support participants to use effective SRL strategies. A total of five scaffolds were created and triggered at designated times throughout the session, and each scaffold served different purposes, including comprehending the task (the 1st scaffold, at the 5th minute), starting to read (the 2nd scaffold, at the 17th minute), monitoring the reading process (the 3rd scaffold, at the 40th minute), commencing writing (the 4th scaffold, at the 52nd minute), and monitoring the writing process (the 5th scaffold, at the 88th minute). This scaffolding design aligned with the learning task (i.e., essay writing based on reading material) and is consistent with the SRL cycle [25]. Additionally, each scaffold included three detailed suggestions nudging learners to adopt specific SRL actions. For information on all the suggestions in each scaffold, refer to the Appendix at this link. Figure 2 - (a) provides an example of a scaffold and its corresponding suggestions.

All participants were assigned to one of the three scaffolding conditions – a control condition where no scaffolds were provided, a fixed scaffolding condition where all learners received identical scaffolds throughout the task, and an adaptive scaffolding condition where the content of scaffolds was adaptive to each learner. The adaptivity was implemented based on a rule-based algorithm (a detailed explanation of the algorithm can be found in [19]). An example of adaptive scaffolding is provided in Fig. 2 – (b), which shows that if the algorithm detected that the learner had checked the time to monitor the reading progress, then unlike the fixed scaffold (as shown in Fig. 2 – (a)), then the specific suggestion would be hidden from the learner (as shown in Fig. 2 – (b)).

3.2 Data Collection and Analysis

Interview and Qualitative Coding. All interviews were arranged and conducted within one week after the completion of the learning task. As understanding how learners perceived the adaptivity of scaffolding was the main focus of the current study, only participants assigned to the adaptive scaffolding group were invited for the interview, and all interviews were audio-recorded and manually transcribed. Prior to conducting the study, ethical approval was obtained from the university where the writing course was offered. Learners were asked for consent for audio-recording before each interview.

The coding scheme we applied consisted of six codes, including four codes that relate to overall learning strategies adopted in the learning task, and two codes related to learners' perceived adaptivity of scaffolding (see Table 1 for the descriptions and examples of the codes). The four learning strategies were selected as they were emerged from the interview data, which were therefore included in the coding scheme. The interview transcripts were segmented by turn of talk (i.e., conversational turn-taking) and coded by two researchers. Inter-rater reliability was reached using a social moderation process [20] in which both researchers agreed upon the coding for each turn of talk. The interviews were conducted in Mandarin and transcribed into Chinese. The two researchers involved in the coding process are native Mandarin speakers. For presentation in this paper, the interview questions, coding scheme, and all cited responses from interviews were translated from Chinese to English. Without altering the original meanings, some translations may involve minor adjustments to ensure readability.

Task Performance. Essay scores were used to represent learners' task performance, and they were based on a scoring rubric. The rubric was made up of four key aspects. The first focused on learners' comprehension of the three key concepts – AI, Differentiation, and Scaffolding – and learners would be awarded nine marks if all three concepts were discussed in terms of definition, explanation, and application. The second aspect evaluated learners' ability to integrate the three concepts in their own vision, and they would be awarded six marks. The third aspect evaluated learners' ability to think innovatively and apply the concepts to the future of education (maximum of three marks). Lastly, a maximum of 3 marks were awarded if the number of words fell within the range of 300 to 400. In sum, the full mark that a learner could receive was 21. The essay marking was done manually by two researchers, who marked the essays equally. An inter-rater reliability test was conducted. Respectively, the kappa results were 0.88 for AI, 0.83 for Differentiation, 0.89 for Scaffolding, 1.00 for the vision integration, 0.94 for future education, and 1.00 for word count.

For this study, the essay scores for those who were interviewed were included. The mean score was $\bar{x} = 12.95$ ($\sigma = 3.99$) and the median was 13 ($Q_1 = 9.75$, $Q_3 = 16.5$), based on which they were grouped into low- and high-performing groups – learners who scored 13 or higher formed the high-performing group and those who performed under 13 formed the low-performing group.

Table 1. Qualitative codes, descriptions, and examples.

Code	Description	Example
Read first then write	Describe a strategy for allocating time for reading first and then writing as a whole, mostly according to task requirements, without special plan	*"I didn't think too much about it at first, I just planned to read for an hour and write for an hour"*
Write while reading and taking notes	The three modules of reading, comprehension (sometimes reflected in note-taking) and writing do not have clear boundaries, but gradually cycle forward	*"While reading, I wrote down some of my own thoughts. These thoughts may be what I want to write in the next article, and they are also some key points, and then I slowly put the article together"*
Speed Reading–Intensive Reading–Focus on Writing	Describe a three-stage learning strategy. First, quickly scan the outline of the reading content to know what you are reading. Then, spend a certain amount of time intensively reading the parts you think are useful. Finally, write everything up	*"I'll go through the table of contents quickly to see what's there, then maybe skip the first part I'm familiar with and focus on the next two, and then I'll start and focus on writing"*
Guided reading and writing with article ideas	The description of the overall learning process focuses on the leading role of article writing, and emphasises that reading serves writing	*"After reading the task description, I thought about the context of the article. When reading, I read it with the article idea in mind. When I saw something useful, I immediately excerpted it to the writing box"*
Not perceived as adaptive	When it comes to scaffolding that doesn't particularly fit learners' needs	*"It doesn't feel like it fits my needs well"*
Perceived as adaptive	When it comes to scaffolding that fits learners' needs	*"Some of the suggestions are really helpful and feel like they fit my needs."*

Epistemic Network Analysis. To address our first research question, we constructed an ENA model with participant ID as the unit of analysis and the conversation selection. Interviewer networks were removed from the model such that it only distinguished between interviewees. We chose the "whole conversation" stanza option, meaning that any codes that co-occurred within the interview could be considered as connected. This decision was made due to the interview structure. Questions pertaining to learning strategies tended to come at the beginning of the interviews, while questions pertaining to the perceived adaptivity of scaffolding tended to come some minutes later. Thus, identifying connections between these concepts necessitated a large stanza window.

As our first research question concerned our sample of interviewees overall, the orientation of the ENA space was not relevant. To simplify the visualisation, we used the optimised unit circle node orientation. Meanwhile, to address our second research question, we used the same model specifications except that we added a grouping variable for the essay score (high vs. low). As we wished to compare groups, we used the means rotation option in ENA such that the metric space maximised the difference between the two groups. We visually compared the groups using a network subtraction and statistically compared them using a Mann-Whitney U test on the means rotated dimension.

4 Results

4.1 Are Self-reported Learning Strategies Associated with Perceived Adaptivity of Scaffolds to Personal Needs?

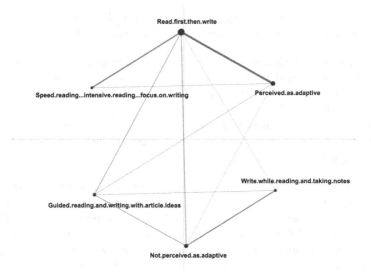

Fig. 3. Network of associations between self-reported learning strategies and perceived adaptivity of the scaffolding.

To address the first research question, we constructed an ENA model (Fig. 3) that included the codes of 'Perceived as adaptive', 'Not perceived as adaptive', and the four self-reported learning strategies. Thicker lines equate to stronger associations. As seen in Fig. 3, all of the self-reported learning strategies were associated with being perceived as adaptive to personal needs except for **write while reading and taking notes**. The strongest association with being perceived as adaptive was with the **read first then write** strategy. Relatedly, all strategies were associated with not being perceived as adaptive except for **speed reading–intensive reading–focus on writing**. The strongest association with not being perceived as adaptive was with the **write while reading and taking notes** strategy.

The results for the strongest associations are clearly reflected in our interview data. For example, when one of the learners was asked about their adopted learning strategy, they referenced a **read first then write** strategy, stating:

"Basically, I spend an hour going over and reviewing the material, and then I spend another hour writing."

Later, describing how they perceived the adaptivity of scaffolding, they added:

"About an hour, a pop-up message appeared saying not to read everything, and suggested that I only read the parts I want. I thought it made sense. It is indeed better to only read the parts we need."

When they were asked about what had been learned from the scaffolding (pop-up window), they responded:

"I think the scaffold had suggested a valid point. Later on, I felt that the time was tight, so I didn't read everything thoroughly afterwards."

In other words, the learner referenced thoroughly reading the material before writing their essay, and they perceived the scaffolding they received as being adaptive to their needs—"I thought it made sense", "I think the scaffold had suggested a valid point".

In contrast, some learners were less positive about their experience with the scaffolds. For example, when one learner was asked whether they followed the scaffolds, they responded:

"At first, I did, but later I found out that I couldn't keep up with the speed of the pop-up window, so I decided to ignore it. Also, it's suggesting things that relatively experienced readers would do, but I'm not one of them. What I did is actually different from what it suggests; I read and write at the same time, going back and forth in a very inefficient process. However, the pop-up seems to be from a very experienced person. For example, it's already starting to make a summary, while I've only written half of it."

And when they were specifically asked if the scaffolds **did not** meet their needs, they added:

"Yes, they are much better than me."

This learner mentioned that they adopted the **write while reading and taking notes** strategy—"I read and write at the same time". However, they clearly did not perceive the scaffolding they received as adaptive to their needs. They saw the scaffolding as not being for them—"it's suggesting things that relatively experienced readers would do, *but I'm not one of them"*—and being more suited to better writers—"[the scaffolds] are much better than me".

4.2 Does the Association Between Self-reported Learning Strategies and Perceived Adaptivity Differ Between High and Low Performing Learners?

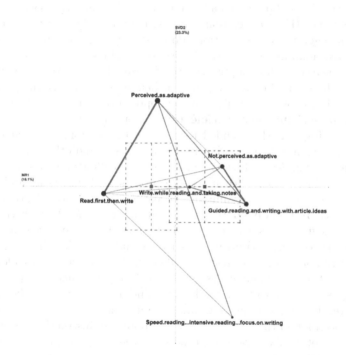

Fig. 4. ENA subtraction between low (red) and high (blue) performers on the essay task. (Color figure online)

To address our second research question, we compared the ENA networks of high and low performers as indicated by their essay scores. The results suggest that learners who followed the **read first then write** strategy and perceived that the scaffolding was adaptive to their needs performed better (as indicated by the

strong connection between "Perceived as adaptive" and "Read first then write").
Learners who adopted the **guide reading and writing with article ideas**
strategy had comparatively lower performance, with some perceiving the scaffolding as adaptive and some not. In addition, learners who reported using the
speed reading – intensive reading – focus on writing strategy also tended
to perform lower, although mostly they perceived the scaffolding as adaptive to
their needs. A Mann-Whitney test revealed a significant difference between high-
and low-performing groups on the first dimension of the ENA space ($p < .01$,
$U = 98.00$) with a moderately strong effect size ($r = 0.63$). However, for the
second dimension, the difference was not significant ($p = 0.57$, $U = 69.00$) and
had a weak effect size ($r = 0.15$) (Fig. 4).

5   Discussion and Conclusion

This study used ENA to analyse the associations between learners' self-reported
learning strategies and perceived adaptivity of scaffolding to personal needs, and
explored whether these associations differed between high and low performers.
The results suggest that associations do exist between self-reported strategies
and perceived adaptability and that these associations vary with performance.
Specifically, learners who adopted the **read first then write** strategy tended
to perceive the scaffolding as adaptive to their needs and performed better on
the essay task. In contrast, learners who adopted other strategies (e.g., **guided
reading and writing with article ideas**) demonstrated lower performance
on the task. However, they tended to perceive the scaffolding in mixed ways,
with some perceiving them as adaptive to their needs and others not.

As mentioned in Sect. 3.1, the main idea of the scaffolds was to prompt learners to first read and monitor their reading process, and then write and monitor
their writing process. When examining the learners' self-reported learning strategies, the **read first then write** strategy aligns most closely with the overall
scaffolding design. Because the results of RQ1 show that the strongest association
is between the **read first then write** strategy and perceiving the scaffolding as
being adaptive, our results suggest that when the learning strategies adopted are
consistent with the scaffolding design, learners are more likely to perceive the
scaffolding as adaptive to their needs. This finding aligns with earlier research
that explored how learners perceive adaptive instructional supports. For example, it has been found that learners tend to appreciate instructional suggestions
when they adopt similar strategies; otherwise, they may exhibit defensive reactions, become reluctant to change their learning strategies, and remain committed to their existing strategy [12,13].

The findings from RQ2 suggest that the alignment between strategy, perceived adaptivity, and scaffolding design is positively associated with task performance. Those that did not report using the **read first then write** strategy and
did not perceive the scaffolds as adapted to their needs performed worse. Learning strategies can be understood as cognitive tools, and according to Winne [26],
effective tool use requires four conditions: recognising the existence and value of

the available tools, choosing a tool that matches the task, skillfully using the tool, and being metacognitively engaged in the tool use. Winne [26] further argued that instructional supports (e.g., scaffolding) should be designed to guide learners in making successful choices and using effective cognitive tools. Our results suggest that learners who were able to choose and adopt effective cognitive tools demonstrated an awareness of the availability and usefulness of the tools. Relatedly, some learners perceived that the scaffolding was not adapted to their needs, implying that they may have been unable to perceive the value and usefulness of the suggested tools. Hence, one way to improve the acceptance of adaptive scaffolding may be to guide learners to understand the value of suggested cognitive tools. This can be achieved by providing adaptive content to those who do not perceive the value of suggested tools—for instance, scaffolding could include explanations of the potential benefits of using the suggested tools, rather than merely prompting learners to adopt them without a justified reason.

The results of RQ2 also suggest that alignment between strategy and perceived adaptivity alone is not enough—some learners perceived the scaffolding as adaptive to their needs, but nevertheless still under-performed. This may be attributed to their understanding of the value of the suggested tools and the purposes they serve, while still being unable to choose and skillfully use the tools. The design of learning tasks and adaptive scaffolding could address these learners' situations by, for example, conducting targeted training sessions that teach learners how to effectively use various tools. By addressing these concerns, we can support learners in making informed decisions regarding the adoption and use of effective learning strategies. Subsequently, through training and practice, SRL can be well learned and improved [22].

Our study has several limitations. First, the analysis and findings presented in this paper are based on learners' self-reported data collected through interviews. While self-report data can provide valuable insights into how learners perceive adaptivity, it is important to note that self-reported data is limited in capturing the dynamic and situational information on learning processes [28]. Future studies are therefore suggested to utilise both self-reported data, which provides information on context-specific strategy use [8], and trace data, which collects temporal and situational information of the learning task [28]. This approach would potentially offer a more fine-grained and accurate reflection of the learning process and yield more robust and comprehensive findings. Additionally, the learning context from which the findings were derived is a two-hour academic writing task, limiting the applicability of the results to similar learning contexts. Consequently, it would be valuable to replicate this study in different learning environments and assess whether the findings remain valid across various learning contexts.

Apart from these limitations, this study offers valuable insights into how learners perceive the association between adaptivity and learning strategies, and how this association differs among learners with different levels of performance, which guides and warrants further developments in the adaptivity of scaffolding.

References

1. Aleven, V., McLaughlin, E.A., Glenn, R.A., Koedinger, K.R.: Instruction based on adaptive learning technologies. Handb. Res. Learn. Instruct. **2**, 522–560 (2016)
2. Azevedo, R., Cromley, J.G., Moos, D.C., Greene, J.A., Winters, F.I.: Adaptive content and process scaffolding: a key to facilitating students' self-regulated learning with hypermedia. Psychol. Test Assess. Model. **53**(1), 106 (2011)
3. Bannert, M., Reimann, P.: Supporting self-regulated hypermedia learning through prompts. Instr. Sci. **40**, 193–211 (2012)
4. Bannert, M., Sonnenberg, C., Mengelkamp, C., Pieger, E.: Short-and long-term effects of students' self-directed metacognitive prompts on navigation behavior and learning performance. Comput. Hum. Behav. **52**, 293–306 (2015)
5. Broadbent, J.: Comparing online and blended learner's self-regulated learning strategies and academic performance. Internet High. Educ. **33**, 24–32 (2017)
6. Duffy, M.C., Azevedo, R.: Motivation matters: interactions between achievement goals and agent scaffolding for self-regulated learning within an intelligent tutoring system. Comput. Hum. Behav. **52**, 338–348 (2015)
7. Greene, J.A., Azevedo, R.: A theoretical review of Winne and Hadwin's model of self-regulated learning: new perspectives and directions. Rev. Educ. Res. **77**(3), 334–372 (2007)
8. Hadwin, A.F., Winne, P.H., Stockley, D.B., Nesbit, J.C., Woszczyna, C.: Context moderates students' self-reports about how they study. J. Educ. Psychol. **93**(3), 477 (2001)
9. Jansen, R.S., van Leeuwen, A., Janssen, J., Conijn, R., Kester, L.: Supporting learners' self-regulated learning in massive open online courses. Comput. Educ. **146**, 103771 (2020)
10. Jivet, I., Scheffel, M., Specht, M., Drachsler, H.: License to evaluate: preparing learning analytics dashboards for educational practice. In: Proceedings of the 8th International Conference on Learning Analytics and Knowledge, pp. 31–40 (2018)
11. Jovanović, J., Gašević, D., Pardo, A., Dawson, S., Whitelock-Wainwright, A.: Introducing meaning to clicks: towards traced-measures of self-efficacy and cognitive load. In: Proceedings of the 9th International Conference on Learning Analytics & Knowledge, pp. 511–520 (2019)
12. Lim, L.A., et al.: Students' sense-making of personalised feedback based on learning analytics. Australas. J. Educ. Technol. **36**(6), 15–33 (2020)
13. Lim, L.A., et al.: Students' perceptions of, and emotional responses to, personalised learning analytics-based feedback: an exploratory study of four courses. Assess. Eval. High. Educ. **46**(3), 339–359 (2021)
14. Lim, L., et al.: Effects of real-time analytics-based personalized scaffolds on students' self-regulated learning. Comput. Hum. Behav. **139**, 107547 (2023)
15. Milikić, N., Gašević, D., Jovanović, J.: Measuring effects of technology-enabled mirroring scaffolds on self-regulated learning. IEEE Trans. Learn. Technol. **13**(1), 150–163 (2018)
16. Pardo, A., Jovanovic, J., Dawson, S., Gašević, D., Mirriahi, N.: Using learning analytics to scale the provision of personalised feedback. Br. J. Edu. Technol. **50**(1), 128–138 (2019)
17. Pea, R.D.: The social and technological dimensions of scaffolding and related theoretical concepts for learning, education, and human activity. J. Learn. Sci. 423–451 (2018)

18. Pieger, E., Bannert, M.: Differential effects of students' self-directed metacognitive prompts. Comput. Hum. Behav. **86**, 165–173 (2018)
19. Rakovic, M., et al.: Using learner trace data to understand metacognitive processes in writing from multiple sources. In: LAK22: 12th International Learning Analytics and Knowledge Conference, pp. 130–141 (2022)
20. Shaffer, D.W., Ruis, A.R.: How we code. In: Ruis, A.R., Lee, S.B. (eds.) ICQE 2021. CCIS, vol. 1312, pp. 62–77. Springer, Cham (2021). https://doi.org/10.1007/978-3-030-67788-6_5
21. Siadaty, M., Gašević, D., Hatala, M.: Associations between technological scaffolding and micro-level processes of self-regulated learning: a workplace study. Comput. Hum. Behav. **55**, 1007–1019 (2016)
22. Sitzmann, T., Bell, B.S., Kraiger, K., Kanar, A.M.: A multilevel analysis of the effect of prompting self-regulation in technology-delivered instruction. Pers. Psychol. **62**(4), 697–734 (2009)
23. Sonnenberg, C., Bannert, M.: Discovering the effects of metacognitive prompts on the sequential structure of SRL-processes using process mining techniques. J. Learn. Anal. **2**(1), 72–100 (2015)
24. Weinstein, C.E., Mayer, R.E.: The teaching of learning strategies. In: Innovation abstracts, vol. 5, p. n32. ERIC (1983)
25. Winne, P.H.: Experimenting to bootstrap self-regulated learning. J. Educ. Psychol. **89**(3), 397 (1997)
26. Winne, P.H.: How software technologies can improve research on learning and bolster school reform. Educ. Psychol. **41**(1), 5–17 (2006)
27. Winne, P.H.: Learning strategies, study skills, and self-regulated learning in post-secondary education. High. Educ.: Handb. Theory Res. **28**, 377–403 (2013)
28. Zhou, M., Winne, P.H.: Modeling academic achievement by self-reported versus traced goal orientation. Learn. Instr. **22**(6), 413–419 (2012)

Cracking the Code of Learning Gains: Using Ordered Network Analysis to Understand the Influence of Prior Knowledge

Andres Felipe Zambrano[1]([✉]) [iD], Amanda Barany[1] [iD], Jaclyn Ocumpaugh[1] [iD], Nidhi Nasiar[1] [iD], Stephen Hutt[2] [iD], Alex Goslen[3] [iD], Jonathan Rowe[3] [iD], James Lester[3] [iD], Eric Wiebe[3] [iD], and Bradford Mott[3] [iD]

[1] University of Pennsylvania, Philadelphia, PA, USA
azamb13@upenn.edu
[2] University of Denver, Denver, CO, USA
[3] North Carolina State University, Raleigh, NC, USA

Abstract. Prior research has shown that digital games can enhance STEM education by providing learners with immersive and authentic scientific experiences. However, optimizing the learning outcomes of students engaged in game-based environments requires aligning the game design with diverse student needs. Therefore, an in-depth understanding of player behavior is crucial for identifying students who need additional support or modifications to the game design. This study applies an Ordered Network Analysis (ONA)—a specific kind of Epistemic Network Analysis (ENA)—to examine the game trace log data of student interactions, to gain insights into how learning gains relate to the different ways that students move through an open-ended virtual world for learning microbiology. Our findings reveal that differences between students with high and low learning gains are mediated by their prior knowledge. Specifically, level of prior knowledge is related to behaviors that resemble wheel-spinning, which warrant the development of future interventions. Results also have implications for discovery with modeling approaches and for enhancing in-game support for learners and improving game design.

Keywords: STEM Education · Game-based Learning · Ordered Network Analysis · Epistemic Network Analysis

1 Introduction

Digital games are increasingly prevalent in STEM education [1–3], given their design affordances for engaging learners in authentic scientific processes and STEM experiences that are not otherwise accessible [4–7]. To maximize these benefits, however, game experiences should meet (and where possible, adapt to) diverse student needs and contexts (e.g., prior knowledge). One way to understand such needs is to map student behavior to learning outcomes, a first step in differentiating between a student who is persisting productively and one who might be wheel-spinning [8].

© The Author(s), under exclusive license to Springer Nature Switzerland AG 2023
G. Arastoopour Irgens and S. Knight (Eds.): ICQE 2023, CCIS 1895, pp. 18–33, 2023.
https://doi.org/10.1007/978-3-031-47014-1_2

Prior research has explored factors that influence user experiences in virtual environments such as prior knowledge [9], self-regulation [10], interest in the topic of the game [11], and digital literacy [12]. Other studies have examined the in-game experiences of learners through filtered time series analyses [13] and graph theory techniques [14], while comparing students' pathways with an expert problem-solving trajectory [13]. However, new techniques for quantifying learners' trajectories through educational games could help us to better understand how students who are learning more differ in behavior and experiences over time from those who learn less.

This work aims to bridge this gap by employing Epistemic Network Analysis (ENA) [15] to investigate the differences between students' in-game behaviors and their learning gains. We do so in the context of a game developed for microbiology education [16], where rich logfiles of students' actions are explored in conjunction with measures of prior knowledge. We specifically employ an Ordered Network Analysis (ONA), a method derived from ENA that takes into account the temporal order of connections between codes [25]. With this approach, we aim to answer two main research questions: (1) What paths through the game are associated with learning gains? and (2) How does prior knowledge influence these paths?

2   Related Work

Understanding differences in how actions in an educational game are enacted over time by those with higher and lower learning gains is an important component of successful game design. Prior research in this area has applied filtered time series analysis to students' log data [13, 17]. This method uses principal component analysis (PCA) [18] to filter a multivariate time series (defined by a set of constructs coded in the log files data) to a univariate time series [13]. Using PCA as a filtering strategy allows for context-specific analyses about timing, but likely eliminates nuance about which actions are most useful. This is perhaps evidenced by conflicting results in the literature. Researchers have shown that higher rates of student actions in virtual worlds are positively associated with learning in a game-based environment about ecosystems [17], but negatively associated with learning in a game-based environment for microbiology [13], indicating that a more nuanced analysis about students' interactions is required to understand effective learning strategies.

Previous research has used graph theory analysis to examine the locations students visited during gameplay in a science learning environment [14]. Trajectories through virtual locations were compared using metrics of density and similarity among networks. Their results showed that student exploration of the environment might be more beneficial for learning than more efficient pathways focused solely on game completion [14]. However, the employed networks compared transitions completed by at least 50% of the students in each of the two groups (based on high or low learning gains). While this approach highlighted variance in student behaviors related to learning gains, it still used a categorical threshold (transitions done by 50% of students) for defining a binary graph instead of a weighted graph, overlooking the repetitions or weights of those common pathways.

The work reported in this paper builds on this previous research by applying a new method for understanding student trajectories through a virtual world. Specifically, we use Ordered Network Analysis [25], a method derived from Epistemic Network Analysis (ENA) [15]. ENA measures the relationships between coded elements by quantifying their co-occurrences [15], and then representing them in a network diagram that illustrates the weights of these connections [19]. Each coded element, or unit, is represented as a single point on the Cartesian plane, meaning that the diagram's unit means can be used to determine statistical differences between them [19]. The ability to quantify the connections between codes and determine statistical differences makes ENA a valuable complement to prior methodologies examining learners' game experiences.

In the context of game-based learning and virtual worlds, ENA was first used in previous research on language data to investigate identity exploration [20], scientific practices [21], and student goals [22], but has also been applied to trace data of student interactions with virtual environments. For example, Karumbaiah et al. [23] applied ENA to clickstream data to uncover the trajectories that lead to quitting behaviors in a learning game called Physics Playground. Similarly, Scianna and Knowles [24] used ENA on player log files to identify how they responded differently to game events during second playthroughs of a video game, showing improvements in student planning skills. These initial examples demonstrate the valuable potential of traditional quantitative ethnographic techniques such as ENA (which typically models patterns in complex discourse data) with detailed log files of player actions.

Ordered Network Analysis (ONA) [25] uses the same principles as ENA but takes directionality of connections between codes over time into account. We do so in order to understand how different trajectories through a virtual game relate to differences in learning gains. Specifically, we are interested in finding ways to identify students who are productively exploring the game in ways that improve their learning, as opposed to those who might be wheel-spinning, a phenomenon that occurs when students become stuck because they lack the prerequisite knowledge necessary to advance [26, 27].

3 Methods

The goal of this work is to identify potentially productive problem-solving actions in a game-based learning environment called CRYSTAL ISLAND [16]. We employ Ordered Network Analysis (ONA) [25], which has been used to offer a more nuanced understanding of complex cognition and behavior across contexts (e.g., [25, 28]), and holds particular promise in problem-solving contexts, particularly those such as CRYSTAL ISLAND in which the orders of certain actions may contribute to in-game success, learning, or stagnation. As with ENA, the ONA algorithm uses a *moving window* to identify connections between lines in students logfile data (e.g., in-game actions or locations) within the recent temporal window. However, ONA accounts for the order in which connections might occur in the data by constructing an asymmetric adjacency matrix for each unit. That is, it calculates both the strength of associations between students first completing Action A (e.g., Reading) and then completing Action B (e.g., Moving) as well as Action B followed by Action A. In this way, the conventional visualization of an ENA model is expanded to include bi-directional edges between each pair of connected nodes. These edges denote the strength of these ordered associations, offering a more nuanced view of students' problem-solving behaviors within the game environment.

3.1 Dataset

We analyzed data from 92 students from an urban school in the southeastern United States (i.e., from [29]) who used an inquiry-based game to learn microbiology. In CRYSTAL ISLAND [16], players adopt the role of a researcher tasked with diagnosing the cause of a disease outbreak affecting an island-based research team. To successfully complete the game, players must explore several locations, interact with non-player characters (NPCs), collect information from in-game reading materials, and test their hypotheses using laboratory equipment. Players are provided with a concept matrix to help them organize the information obtained from the readings, as well as a worksheet to organize their hypotheses and results. The game interface, including the "golden pathway" (i.e., the most efficient path to game completion) proposed by [13], is presented in Fig. 1.

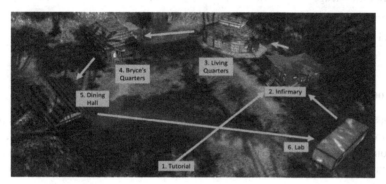

Fig. 1. Overview of CRYSTAL ISLAND with the expert "golden pathway" for game completion as operationalized by [13].

3.2 Learning Measures

To evaluate students' knowledge of microbiology, identical pre- and post-tests were administered. Normalized learning gains were calculated based on the equation proposed in [30]. This approach compares differences between post- and pre-test scores with potential improvements students could achieve based on their initial scores. Data from 26 students with incomplete test responses were excluded, leaving a total of 66 students for the current analyses.

3.3 Unit Variables and Other Divisions

The *unit variables* (i.e., the variables that organize the dataset into meaningful groups for comparison and visualization) for ONA in this study were based on student learning gains and prior knowledge. Specifically, we segmented and unitized the students into two groups based on learning gains because the difference models of ONA do not handle further division. We analyzed the data from students with high and low prior knowledge separately. Both learning gains and prior knowledge groupings were generated using median values (*Mdne* = 8 for pretest or prior knowledge and *Mdn* = 0.15 for learning gains).

We present comparative ordered network difference models for high and low learning gain groups for each prior knowledge group to identify potential variations in behaviors that may lead to differences in learning. We also conducted a correlation analysis (spearman) to assess the impact of these behaviors on learning. Table 1 shows the distribution of students based on learning gains and prior knowledge.

Table 1. Distribution of students based on learning gains and prior knowledge.

	Low Learning	High Learning	Subtotal
Low Prior Knowledge	16	14	30
High Prior Knowledge	18	18	36
Subtotal	34	32	66

3.4 Codes

Two sets of codes were applied to the log files of students used for the analyses in this study: location codes ($N = 7$) and actions codes ($N = 7$). Action codes were selected based on student behaviors that have proven relevant in previous work [13]. Location codes correspond to the 7 sites on the virtual island in the game. Both are automatically

Table 2. Definition of codes (Actions).

Code	Definition
Movement	The **action** of moving from one location to another is logged if the student performed an action in the new location *or* spent at least 10 s there
NPC Interaction	Talking with an NPC. Each message is counted as one **action**
Reading	Observing a book or research article (found in several game locations) for at least 5 s. Each minute of reading is counted as one **action**
Concept Matrix	Each submission of a concept matrix (where students summarize what they just read) counts as one **action**
Object	Picking up an object that would be used for testing a hypothesis in the future. Each object counts as one **action**
Hypothesis Testing	Scanning an object using laboratory equipment to determine if it contains the virus or bacteria the student hypothesized is affecting the island. Each scan counts as one **action**
Diagnosis Worksheet	Providing an entry in the game's worksheet, which helps students to systematize the hypothesis testing process. Each entry counts as one **action**

recorded in Crystal Islands log files. Given the small number of classifications and their direct and unambiguous nature, it is unnecessary to report IRR for these codes.

Table 2 provides an overview of the action codes which were extracted from each line of the interaction logs. Although individual lines of data in the interaction logs do not account for the duration of each action, many actions have a relatively fixed duration that is consistent across students. For instance, hypothesis testing in the lab typically takes around 5 s. For other actions that lack a fixed duration, we employ a repetition strategy for considering the duration. For example, when students interact with NPCs, we consider each message they sent as a separate action, rather than grouping the entire interaction as a single data line. Thus, students who exchange more messages with the same NPC will have more lines representing this action. Similarly, in the case of reading and movement, if the student spends more than a minute on a particular page or moving between two locations, we duplicate the line to indicate that the student was engaged in that action for a longer duration.

Table 3 shows the location codes that were extracted from the students' interaction logs. In this study, location changes were coded either when the player performed an action other than "Movement" in the new location or spent at least 10 s there. This threshold differentiates between locations where the student was actively engaged and those where the student was simply moving between locations. Similarly, the code "Outside" was reserved for students who spent more than 10 consecutive seconds outside, suggesting deliberation or uncertainty about where to go next.

Table 3. Definition of codes (Locations).

Code	Definition
Tutorial	Students begin the game at this **location** (a beach), where they receive initial instructions, interact with an NPC, learn how to pick up objects, and are introduced to the concept matrix. They are instructed to go to the infirmary at the end of the tutorial
Infirmary	Students are instructed to go to this **location** after the tutorial to receive the only additional instructions in the game. These come from an NPC (the nurse), but they can also interact with NPC patients. They return later to provide the suggested treatment for the disease
Laboratory	Students bring objects to this **location** to test them for contamination with a virtual scanner (i.e., with the virus or bacteria causing the island inhabitants to get sick). They can also read research articles at this location. Because they can only carry 3 objects at the same time, students often require multiple visits to this location to solve the game
Living Quarters	In this **location**, students can acquire information by interacting with NPCs and reading disciplinary content

(continued)

Table 3. (*continued*)

Code	Definition
Bryce's Quarters	Students who enter this **location** can interact with NPCs and read pages and articles associated with microbiology. This location has more disciplinary content than any other individual location in the game
Dining Hall	**Location** where students can find most of the objects to scan, including the one necessary for solving the mystery
Outside	This **location** composes the largest region of the game. All students must move through this area to get from one location to another, but it contains no additional information or objects to test. Therefore, it is only analyzed if the student spends at least 10 s without entering another location

In the current analysis, action codes and location codes are presented in separate difference models. While actions and locations are meaningfully connected, we took this approach for two reasons. First, in some cases, actions are bounded by location, which would artificially inflate the appearance of certain action/location connections. Second, ordered and epistemic networks become practically and visually overwhelming with higher numbers of codes present, often necessitating techniques to make existing models more parsimonious (e.g., [31]). In this case, presenting two separate models of different code sets avoids both issues and provides two corresponding perspectives on student experience.

3.5 Segmentation and Stanza Selection

ENA models complex systems by creating a series of adjacency matrices that connect the codes applied to one line to codes in prior lines (in this case, a moving window). *Conversation variables* serve as boundaries for these calculations by grouping data into stanzas across which associations are not calculated (e.g., all data associated with student 1 in one stanza and student 2 in separate stanza). For this study, we set student play sessions as the conversation variable. Extant research using non-linguistic data has used conversation variables such as game level [23] or complete playthrough [24]. Because the duration of CRYSTAL ISLAND play was short ($Avg = 65.1\ min, SD = 13.5$) and no natural break points were observed, we refrained from segmentation into more fine-grained stanzas.

To define the *moving window* length (which defines how far back codes in one line are associated with codes applied to prior lines) we drew on previous studies applying ENA to log files [23, 24]. In these cases, wider moving windows were needed to capture the contexts of fine-grained log data [32]. In Karumbaiah and colleagues' [23] work on a level-based game with a limited action set, authors set the moving window to encompass approximately 20 s of gameplay that represented how far back a player might routinely connect a single in-game action to prior actions.

In CRYSTAL ISLAND, the duration of different actions varies widely; reading an article, for example, may take more time than picking up an object. To account for this, we set the moving window width based on the average number of actions performed by students in two consecutive locations. This approach ensures that the associations in the networks are based on meaningful stanzas of gameplay, while also accounting for variations in the length of actions. It also aligns with the design of the game, in which sets of problem-solving actions are situated in specific in-game locations and students must choose to move between them in certain orders to access actions that can complete in-game goals [13, 17].

Students performed an average of 188.3 actions ($SD = 45.9$) and 22.5 visits to locations ($SD = 8.1$) throughout the gameplay. On average, students conducted 8.3 actions ($SD = 2.5$) during each visit to a given location before moving on to the next. In line with prior work on this topic [14], we connected the actions performed in one location to those in the following location, defining a moving window size of two times this average number of actions during each visit (17). We opted for this choice instead of the infinite stanza, as the initial actions were similar among all players, and recent actions are more relevant to current actions than the earlier ones. Moreover, we apply a threshold at |0.02| in the visualization of connections to ensure interpretability of the models.

4 Results

As discussed above, we divide the students in these analyses into high and low prior knowledge groups. We then consider, separately, how trajectories through different locations, and trajectories through different actions are associated with learning.

4.1 Low Prior Knowledge Students

This work explores differences between students who demonstrated high and low learning gains in both the high and low prior knowledge groups. For the low prior knowledge group, Mann-Whitney U tests showed significant differences ($alpha = 0.05$) between those with high and low learning gains for both: (1) location patterns ($U = 192.00, p < 0.001, r = -0.71$) and (2) action patterns ($U = 22.00, p < 0.001, r = 0.80$). Goodness of fit, measured using both Pearson and Spearman correlation indexes, was greater than 0.82 for both axes in each model. The ordered networks shown in this study only display connections with a weight higher than 0.02. We employ this threshold to prevent the figures from being overloaded with additional connections among codes that do not correspond to the most substantial differences between the compared groups.

Figure 2a and b displays the difference models between students with high (blue) and low (red) learning gains for the low prior knowledge group. We have tailored all the ONA model visualizations in this study to enhance the readability of transitions between nodes using the visualization software Diagrams.net, and strategically omitted line weights for visual clarity (see below). While our ONA visualizations deviate from the formats common to prior studies, the node positioning and arrow line weights are analogous to the ordered networks generated in R for this data. In these visualizations, the size of each node signifies the frequency of each action or location, and which group (high or low learning gains) undertakes that action or visits that location more often.

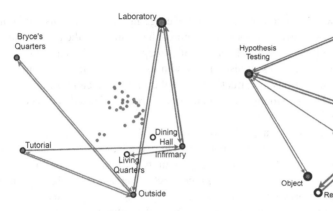

a. Location-based difference model.   **b.** Action-based difference model.

Fig. 2. Location-based and action-based difference models between students with high learning gains (blue) and low learning gains (red) for *low prior knowledge* students. Line weights below |0.2| are omitted for visual clarity.

Students with higher learning gains in the low prior knowledge group were observed to engage in more transitions between testing hypotheses and filling out the worksheet with the corresponding results of the tests (*normalized line weight, lw = 0.048*), indicating a greater emphasis on understanding and framing the test results within the context of the game's goal. Additionally, students with higher learning gains were observed to transition more frequently between movement and hypothesis testing (*lw = 0.050*). This pattern of movements might be related to the ultimate goal of discovering the solution for the game, rather than seemingly undirected movement among locations.

The patterns of locations visited by students in the high learning gain condition also show similar results. Students with higher learning consecutively visited the laboratory (the place for hypothesis testing) and infirmary (the place where students receive game instructions and interact with patients suffering from the disease) more than students in the low learning group (*lw = 0.040*). This result aligns with a positive correlation between the number of hypotheses tested and learning gains for the low prior knowledge group (*rho = 0.404, p = 0.027*). Similarly, students with higher learning gains transition directly from the tutorial to the infirmary, a place where they receive more productive information.

Students in the high learning group tended to visit the living quarters after visiting the infirmary more often than the low learning students (*lw = 0.028*). Overall, learning gains are positively correlated with the connection between interactions with NPCs and reading material (*rho = 0.340, p = 0.066*), which can be completed in the infirmary and living quarters. These types of actions tend to be performed more often by students who understand the game's dynamics. The total number of actions, which are also associated with a better understanding of the game's logic, are correlated with learning gains for the low prior knowledge group (*rho = 0.328, p = 0.077*). This aligns with the results shown by the actions-based difference model (Fig. 2b) for this group, where students who learned more tend to have more connections between actions than their peers in the low learning gain condition, explaining why the line omission procedure resulted in a difference model that only showcases higher learners' higher rates of action. These results suggest that students may require the instructions provided in the infirmary to effectively learn from the disciplinary content taught in the living quarters.

In contrast, students in the low learning gain group tended to move between the tutorial and outside locations more often compared to their high learning gain peers (*lw* = *0.036*). Low learning is also associated with Bryce's Quarters. This seems surprising, given that this is the location where most of the educational reading materials can be found. Although, as observed in Fig. 2b, the students with lower learning gains are not engaging more in the actions that can be conducted in Bryce's quarters than their peers who are learning more.

4.2 High Prior Knowledge Students

Statistical differences were also found among the high prior knowledge group, where a third and fourth Mann-Whitney tests revealed that the behavior of students with high learning gains (*Mdn* = −0.10, *N* = 18) was significantly different from the behavior of the students in the low learning gain group in terms of the visited locations (*Mdn* = 0.10, *N* = 18, *U* = 288.00, *p* < 0.001, *r* = −0.78), and their actions (*U* = 231.50, *p* = 0.003, *r* = −0.43) at the alpha = 0.05 level. The goodness of fit, calculated with both Pearson and Spearman correlation indexes, was greater than 0.86 for both axes.

Figure 3a and b shows the difference models between students with high (blue) and low (red) learning gains for the low prior knowledge condition. The behavior of students with high prior knowledge substantially differs from those with low prior knowledge. Results from Fig. 3a suggest that the transitions related to the infirmary are conducted

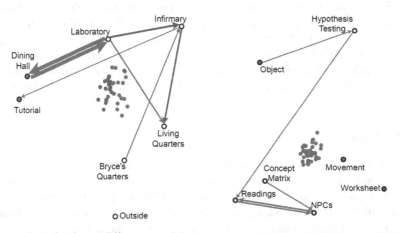

a. Location-based difference model.   **b.** Action-based difference model.

Fig. 3. Location-based and action-based difference models between students with high learning gains (blue) and low learning gains (red) for *high prior knowledge* students. Line weights below |0.2| are omitted for visual clarity.

more by the high learning group in the high prior knowledge condition. However, transitions having this place as starting point do not suppose a substantial difference between the two learning groups, as observed in the low prior knowledge case. Although some students with high prior knowledge and low learning gains tend to return from the infirmary to the tutorial ($lw = 0.022$), this connection is weaker than the observed back and forth between the tutorial and outside, in the low prior knowledge students.

For the high prior knowledge group, visits to the living quarters from the laboratory instead of the infirmary were also more common for the low learning gain group ($lw = 0.029$). Notably, while the laboratory was mainly visited by students in the high learning gain group for the low prior knowledge condition, the strongest connection observed in this study appeared between the laboratory (where testing occurs) and the dining hall (where most of the testable objects are located) for the low learning gain group among the high prior knowledge learners ($lw = 0.082$). Some students in this group may be repeatedly moving between the laboratory and the dining hall to obtain more objects, test more hypotheses, and solve the challenge quickly without engaging in reading or deeper understanding. This result aligns with a negative significant correlation between learning gains and the number of objects picked up by students in the high prior knowledge group ($rho = -0.375, p = 0.024$).

The ordered network analysis for the high prior knowledge students also reveals a notable connection starting from hypothesis testing to readings for the low learning gain group ($lw = 0.022$), indicating that students in this group tend to read the disciplinary content after testing the hypothesis. This is the opposite of the desired order of these two actions and was also observed in the negative significant correlation between learning gains and the number of transitions from testing a hypothesis to reading ($rho = -0.332, p = 0.048$).

Furthermore, as shown in Fig. 3b, students with lower learning gains also show a stronger connection between readings and interactions with NPCs (the two alternatives they have in the game to receive disciplinary content; $lw = 0.042$) than their high-learning peers. These students might be returning more to these two activities after picking an object and rejecting a hypothesis in the lab to receive more insights about other possible solutions. Although they are engaging more in these two activities, this does not imply that they are reflecting on this information, and therefore, they would not be learning as much as their peers.

5 Discussion

Understanding the relationship between prior knowledge and students' in-game behavioral patterns is an important step for developing new ways to support struggling learners, especially in an open-ended learning environment. While it is perhaps not surprising that students with lower prior knowledge likely need different learning experiences than those who come in with higher domain knowledge, understanding how to quantify those experiences has historically been challenging in such open-ended environments. This study uses an ordered network analysis (ONA) to better understand the trajectories of students in a middle-school science game and to gain insight into which behaviors are more likely to lead to learning (e.g., productive persistence, as opposed to wheel-spinning) even if they do not reflect the most efficient route through the game.

Results from this ONA show that overall, students with low prior knowledge require more location visits and actions in order to learn, while those with high prior knowledge are the opposite. It seems likely that this might extend to other learning contexts as well (e.g., [33]). That is, we should expect students with low levels of prior knowledge to have different questions and to require a higher level of repetition than students who already know quite a bit about the domain.

Beyond these differences, we also see that the same trajectories can be associated with the opposite effects on learning among high and low prior knowledge learners. Such results have important implications for supporting learners, whether through larger changes to the game design or through detector-driven prompts that are delivered when a student appears to be struggling.

Game design changes might explore ways to mitigate the ways in which the layout of the game influences student behavior. For example, ONA suggests that students with low learning gains may sometimes ignore the instructions to go directly to the infirmary (which is farther away from the tutorial than some of the other buildings in the game). While major game changes (e.g., moving the location of the infirmary closer to the tutorial) might be antithetical to the self-regulation the game is designed to foster, it might be useful to prompt students who have ignored these instructions a second time. Likewise, students who are ignoring reading materials in favor of what they think is a more efficient strategy (e.g., the loop of picking up new objects and testing them) might be prompted to make better use of the available resources in much the same way that a resident at a hospital might have a supervising physician suggest they read relevant articles. Finally, students might also be asked to externalize their hypotheses and their rationale for selecting the objects to scan before testing to see if they are relying on prior knowledge or disengaging from the educational material.

Other game design changes might be more subtle. For example, we currently see a strong pattern among high prior knowledge students with low learning gains. Many of these students seem to be looping between the dining hall (where most of the testable objects are) and the laboratory (where tests can be performed). It is possible that a more even distribution of testable objects and reading material throughout the game, might increase the chances that a student comes across (and makes use of) these resource articles. However, we note that this same looping behavior (between the dining hall and the laboratory) leads to higher learning gains for students with low prior knowledge. Therefore, any game redesigns should be carefully prioritized and tested among students with both high and low prior knowledge, which could be operationalized by integrating the pre-test into the game's adaptability algorithms.

Another possible solution is to implement wheel-spinning detectors (e.g., [8, 34–36]), and features based on the results of this ONA might help us to better predict this construct. For example, features related to multiple trips to the tutorial or excessive amounts of time wandering outside might be important indicators that a student does not have the skills to move forward even if they have not fully disengaged from the system. Likewise, we might develop features related to students who are testing without reading or reading but not leveraging that information to go to the next most productive location. Such detectors have been implemented in a range of learning software, but it can be more challenging to detect unproductive behaviors in less-linear systems. The results here, however, suggest a path forward for such research using features discovered with ONA, akin to the discovery with models approach used in previous research [37].

6   Conclusions and Future Work

We have shown that ONA, a particular derivation of ENA, of student log files illustrates important patterns in open-ended learning environments, but this work is not without limitations. A potential limitation of this approach is that an ONA collapses a large number of student trajectories across time. That is, while ONA offers the advantage of directionality (compared to more traditional ENA methods) it does not show the specific moment when these connections occur during the student's game trajectory. Future work could work to address this limitation, either through data segmentation that could provide more nuanced insights into the trajectory of student behavior over time [38], or by supplementing ONA results with other techniques that examine time-series data. Future work might also leverage this approach to examine player differences based on other learner metrics such as content-related interest or in-game affect.

We have also shown that learning trajectories differ considerably among high and low prior knowledge learners, but future research should consider other student-level characteristics, since disciplinary content is not the unique factor that influences students' understanding of game dynamics. A few characteristics that may be especially important include prior game literacy [39] as well as reading skills and visual attention [40]. Students who are unaccustomed to exploration-based games or who struggle to comprehend written instructions (and written content in general) may encounter greater difficulty in engaging with and persisting in the game. Both lines of inquiry have the potential to yield valuable insights for improving game design, and supporting students' learning.

In summary, we envision the visualization and quantification capabilities of ONA as a significant contribution to closing the interpretation loop when examining the interactions between students and open-ended, game-based learning environments. Combining this analysis with a range of other data on student characteristics and in-game behaviors can yield a broad range of insights for game designers and educators to enhance game-based learning environments. In particular, it would be good to use these insights as part of a discovery with models approach [37] to better capture potential features for modeling differences between students who are wheel-spinning versus those that are persisting productively.

Acknowledgments. This work was funded by a grant from the National Science Foundation (NSF Cyberlearning #2016943). We would also like to thank Kristy Boyer for access to this data and Yuanru Tan for developing the ONA package used in this analysis. Andres Felipe Zambrano thanks the Ministerio de Ciencia, Tecnología e Innovación and the Fulbright-Colombia commission for supporting his doctoral studies through the Fulbright-MinCiencias 2022 scholarship.

References

1. Clark, D.B., Sengupta, P., Brady, C.E., Martinez-Garza, M.M., Killingsworth, S.S.: Disciplinary integration of digital games for science learning. Int. J. STEM Educ. **2**(1), 2 (2015)
2. Gao, F., Li, L., Sun, Y.: A systematic review of mobile game-based learning in STEM education. Educ. Tech. Res. Dev. **68**, 1791–1827 (2020)
3. Saricam, U., Yildirim, M.: The effects of digital game-based STEM activities on students' interests in STEM fields and scientific creativity: minecraft case. Int. J. Technol. Educ. Sci. **5**(2), 166–192 (2021)
4. Shaffer, D.W., Gee, J.P.: How Computer Games help Children Learn. Palgrave Macmillan, New York (2006)
5. Annetta, L.A., Minogue, J., Holmes, S.Y., Cheng, M.T.: Investigating the impact of video games on high school students' engagement and learning about genetics. Comput. Educ. **53**(1), 74–85 (2009)
6. Anderson, J., Barnett, M.: Using video games to support pre-service elementary teachers learning of basic physics principles. J. Sci. Educ. Technol. **20**, 347–362 (2011)
7. Kanematsu, H., Kobayashi, T., Barry, D.M., Fukumura, Y., Dharmawansa, A., Ogawa, N.: Virtual STEM class for nuclear safety education in metaverse. Procedia Comput. Sci. **35**, 1255–1261 (2014)
8. Owen, V.E., et al.: Detecting wheel spinning and productive persistence in educational games. In: Proceedings of the 12th International Conference on Educational Data Mining, pp. 378–383 (2019)
9. Aleven, V., Stahl, E., Schworm, S., Fischer, F., Wallace, R.: Help seeking and help design in interactive learning environments. Rev. Educ. Res. **73**(3), 277–320 (2003)
10. Nietfeld, J.L., Shores, L.R., Hoffmann, K.F.: Self-regulation and gender within a game-based learning environment. J. Educ. Psychol. **106**(4), 961 (2014)
11. Zhang, J., et al.: Investigating student interest and engagement in game-based learning environments. In: Artificial Intelligence in Education: 23rd International Conference, AIED 2022, Durham, UK, July 27–31, 2022, Proceedings, Part I, pp. 711–716. Springer International Publishing (2022)
12. Steinkuehler, C.: Video games and digital literacies. J. Adolesc. Health. **54**(1), 61–63 (2010)
13. Sawyer, R., Rowe, J., Azevedo, R., Lester, J.: Filtered Time Series Analyses of Student Problem-Solving Behaviors in Game-Based Learning. International Educational Data Mining Society (2018)
14. Nasiar, N. et al.: It's good to explore: investigating silver pathways and the role of frustration during game-based learning. In: Wang, N., Rebolledo-Mendez, G., Dimitrova, V., Matsuda, N., Santos, O.C. (eds.) Artificial Intelligence in Education. Posters and Late Breaking Results, Workshops and Tutorials, Industry and Innovation Tracks, Practitioners, Doctoral Consortium and Blue Sky. AIED 2023. Communications in Computer and Information Science, vol. 1831. Springer, Cham (2023). https://doi.org/10.1007/978-3-031-36336-8_77
15. Shaffer, D.W., et al.: Epistemic network analysis: a prototype for 21st-century assessment of learning. Int. J. Learn. Media **1**(2), 33–53 (2009)
16. Rowe, J.P., Shores, L.R., Mott, B.W., Lester, J.C.: Integrating learning, problem solving, and engagement in narrative-centered learning environments. Int. J. Artif. Intell. Educ. **21**(1–2), 115–133 (2011)
17. Reilly, J.M., Dede, C.: Differences in student trajectories via filtered time series analysis in an immersive virtual world. In: Proceedings of the 9th International Conference on Learning Analytics and Knowledge, pp. 130–134 (2019)

18. Abdi, H., Williams, L.J.: Principal component analysis. WIRs: Comput. Stat. **2**(4), 433–459 (2010)
19. Shaffer, D.W., Collier, W., Ruis, A.R.: A tutorial on epistemic network analysis: analyzing the structure of connections in cognitive, social, and interaction data. J. Learn. Analytics **3**(3), 9–45 (2016)
20. Barany, A., Foster, A.: Examining identity exploration in a video game participatory culture. In: Eagan, B., Misfeldt, M., Siebert-Evenstone, A. (eds.) ICQE 2019. CCIS, vol. 1112, pp. 3–13. Springer, Cham (2019). https://doi.org/10.1007/978-3-030-33232-7_1
21. Bressler, D.M., Bodzin, A.M., Eagan, B., Tabatabai, S.: Using epistemic network analysis to examine discourse and scientific practice during a collaborative game. J. Sci. Educ. Technol. **28**, 553–566 (2019)
22. Bressler, D.M., Annetta, L.A., Dunekack, A., Lamb, R.L., Vallett, D.B.: How STEM game design participants discuss their project goals and their success differently. In: Advances in Quantitative Ethnography: 3rd International Conf., ICQE 2021, Virtual Event, November 6–11, 2021, Proceedings 3, pp. 176–190. Springer International Publishing (2022). https://doi.org/10.1007/978-3-030-93859-8_12
23. Karumbaiah, S., Baker, R.S., Barany, A., Shute, V.: Using epistemic networks with automated codes to understand why players quit levels in a learning game. In: Eagan, B., Misfeldt, M., Siebert-Evenstone, A. (eds.) Advances in Quantitative Ethnography. ICQE 2019. Communications in Computer and Information Science, vol. 1112. Springer, Cham (2019).https://doi.org/10.1007/978-3-030-33232-7_9
24. Scianna, J., Gagnon, D., Knowles, B.: Counting the game: visualizing changes in play by incorporating game events. In: Ruis, A.R., Lee, S.B. (eds.) Advances in Quantitative Ethnography. ICQE 2021. Communications in Computer and Information Science, vol. 1312. Springer, Cham (2021). https://doi.org/10.1007/978-3-030-67788-6_15
25. Tan, Y., Ruis, A.R., Marquart, C., Cai, Z., Knowles, M., Shaffer, D.W: Ordered network analysis. In: Damşa, C., Barany, A. (eds.) Advances in Quantitative Ethnography: Fourth International Conference, ICQE 2022. Springer International Publishing (2022). https://doi.org/10.1007/978-3-031-31726-2_8
26. Wan, H., Beck, J.B.: Considering the Influence of Prerequisite Performance on Wheel Spinning. International Educational Data Mining Society (2015)
27. Palaoag, T.D., Rodrigo, M.M.T., Andres, J.M.L., Andres, J.M.A.L., Beck, J.E.: Wheel-spinning in a game-based learning environment for physics. In: Micarelli, A., Stamper, J., Panourgia, K. (eds.) ITS 2016. LNCS, vol. 9684, pp. 234–239. Springer, Cham (2016). https://doi.org/10.1007/978-3-319-39583-8_23
28. Fan, Y., et al.: Dissecting learning tactics in MOOC using ordered network analysis. J. Comput. Assist. Learn. **39**(1), 154–166 (2023)
29. Min, W., et al.: Multimodal goal recognition in open-world digital games. Proc. AAAI Conf. Artif. Intell. Interact. Dig. Entertainment **13**(1), 80–86 (2021)
30. Vail, A.K., Grafsgaard, J.F., Boyer, K.E., Wiebe, E.N., Lester, J.C.: Predicting Learning from student affective response to tutor questions. In: Micarelli, A., Stamper, J., Panourgia, K. (eds.) ITS 2016. LNCS, vol. 9684, pp. 154–164. Springer, Cham (2016). https://doi.org/10.1007/978-3-319-39583-8_15
31. Wang, Y., Swiecki, Z., Ruis, A.R., Shaffer, D.W.: Simplification of epistemic networks using parsimonious removal with interpretive alignment. In: Ruis, A.R., Lee, S.B. (eds.) ICQE 2021. CCIS, vol. 1312, pp. 137–151. Springer, Cham (2021). https://doi.org/10.1007/978-3-030-67788-6_10
32. Arastoopour Irgens, G., Shaffer, D.W., Swiecki, Z., Ruis, A.R., Chesler, N.C.: Teaching and assessing engineering design thinking with virtual internships and epistemic network analysis. Int. J. Eng. Educ. **32**, 1492–1501 (2015)

33. Beck, J.E., Gong, Y.: Wheel-spinning: Students who fail to master a skill. In: Artificial Intelligence in Education: 16th International Conference AIED 2013, Memphis, TN, USA, July 9–13, 2013, pp. 431–440. Springer, Berlin Heidelberg (2013)
34. Yang, J.C., Quadir, B.: Effects of prior knowledge on learning performance and anxiety in an English learning online role-playing game. J. Educ. Technol. Soc. **21**(3), 174–185 (2018)
35. Kai, S., Almeda, M.V., Baker, R.S., Heffernan, C., Heffernan, N.: Decision tree modeling of wheel-spinning and productive persistence in skill builders. J. Educ. Data Min. **10**(1), 36–71 (2018)
36. Botelho, A.F., Varatharaj, A., Patikorn, T., Doherty, D., Adjei, S.A., Beck, J.E.: Developing early detectors of student attrition and wheel spinning using deep learning. IEEE Trans. Learn. Technol. **12**(2), 158–170 (2019)
37. Baker, R.S., Yacef, K.: The state of educational data mining in 2009: a review and future visions. J. Educ. Data Min. **1**(1), 3–17 (2009)
38. Brohinsky, J., Marquart, C., Wang, J., Ruis, A.R., Shaffer, D.W.: Trajectories in epistemic network analysis. In: Ruis, A.R., Lee, S.B. (eds.) ICQE 2021. CCIS, vol. 1312, pp. 106–121. Springer, Cham (2021). https://doi.org/10.1007/978-3-030-67788-6_8
39. Squire, K.D.: Video-game literacy: A literacy of expertise. In: Handbook of Research on New Literacies, pp. 635–669. Routledge (2014)
40. Kress, S., Neudorf, J., Borowsky, B., Borowsky, R.: What's in a game: video game visual-spatial demand location exhibits a double dissociation with reading speed. Acta Physiol. (Oxf) **232**, 103822 (2023)

Decoding Player Behavior: Analyzing Reasons for Player Quitting Using Log Data from Puzzle Game Baba Is You

Xiner Liu[1]([⊠]) [iD], Basel Hussein[2] [iD], Amanda Barany[1] [iD], Ryan S. Baker[1] [iD], and Bodong Chen[1] [iD]

[1] University of Pennsylvania, Philadelphia, PA 19104, USA
xiner@upenn.edu
[2] University of Minnesota, Twin Cities, MN 55455, USA

Abstract. In this paper, we study the reasons for unsuccessful level completion in *Baba is You*, a puzzle-based video game, using Epistemic Network Analysis (ENA). The study focuses on student cognition, which can be inferred through an in-depth examination of in-game actions and decisions recorded in log data from complex, contextualized game levels. To build epistemic networks around video game log data, chronological log records of player levels were set as codes. Epistemic networks of player actions paired with interpretive examinations of the context of each level offer insights into why students may quit levels in *Baba is You*. Findings suggest that (1) inadequate acquisition of knowledge from the previous level, (2) premature focus on winning at the earlier stage without engaging in distributed exploration and experimentation, and (3) over-reliance on undoing actions may all play a role in unsuccessful level completion. The goal of this work is to support the design of future game-based interventions that can address context-specific quitting and foster student engagement within the game.

Keywords: Digital Game · Quitting Behavior · Epistemic Network Analysis · Automated Codes · Interaction Log

1 Introduction

In the field of education, digital games, whether commercial or serious, have emerged as useful tools for creating engaging learning experiences for students [23, 29]. However, to support persistence and learning, game designers often face the challenge of creating a level of difficulty that is "pleasantly frustrating" – challenging players without discouraging them [10]. When the difficulty level is high, some players may encounter setbacks and manage them in productive ways [4], while other players may quit due to inadequate understanding of the concepts or mechanics, ineffective puzzle-solving strategies, or lower levels of academic achievement [8, 15, 24]. Given this context, a comprehensive understanding of the drivers of player quitting is crucial for promoting more universally effective and engaging learning environments in games, informing timely interventions, and preventing frustration-induced stopout.

© The Author(s), under exclusive license to Springer Nature Switzerland AG 2023
G. Arastoopour Irgens and S. Knight (Eds.): ICQE 2023, CCIS 1895, pp. 34–48, 2023.
https://doi.org/10.1007/978-3-031-47014-1_3

In this paper, we investigate what patterns of in-game decisions and actions precede unsuccessful completions within the syntax-based problem-solving game *Baba is You*. Specifically, we focus on players' spatial reasoning decisions through game log data, with cognition inferred from their interactions within the complex, contextualized game levels. To achieve this objective, we visualize player interactions using Epistemic Network Analysis (ENA) [21], a quantitative ethnographic technique that can visualize patterns of connections between concepts or behaviors in large-scale, complex datasets. Our work builds on prior research that has used epistemic networks of in-game log data to explore players' in-game actions and understand how learning and decision-making emerge (e.g., [14]). Our work examines students' actions contextualized by the unique attributes of specific game levels, with the goal of examining specific reasons for players quitting related to that particular level.

The research questions guiding this study are: 1) How do patterns of game behaviors differ between students who quit and those who do not, and 2) What insights can these differences provide us regarding why students quit? Through this research, we hope to contribute to the understanding of how players interact with complex puzzle games and provide insights into how game designers and educators can create effective and engaging learning environments.

2   Literature Review

Digital games provide students with access to immersive and authentic learning experiences in specific content areas in STEM [26], offering opportunities for developing critical skills such as problem-solving [18], decision-making [5], and communication [3]. High-quality game design has been linked to the development of intrinsic motivation in players around targeted content areas. This, in turn, can be valuable to learning, as motivated learners are more likely to engage deeply with the content, persist through challenges, and seek out additional learning opportunities on their own [1, 9].

Given the learning benefits associated with games, understanding player cognition in games has become an increasingly popular research topic among scholars from diverse fields such as psychology [2], neuroscience [6], and computer science [27]. One specific area of interest revolves around inferring players' cognitive processes based on their in-game behaviors. For example, Hou [11] found that learners' behavior and exploration patterns while they are playing in the simulation game *Perfect PAPA II©* may often be influenced by cognitive processes such as memory retrieval and alignment. Owen and colleagues [20] constructed prediction models based on features of behavior patterns to detect both unproductive persistence and wheel spinning behaviors, which are often associated with frustration or reduced motivation, among students using the adaptive game-based learning system *Mastering Math*. Similarly, Leduc-McNiven et al. [17] utilized player action data to infer cognitive processes such as strategy learning, retention, and recall in a serious game *WarCAT*. These examples demonstrate the potential of game-based activities as a means of investigating cognitive processes.

Our work aims to contribute to the existing research by providing insight into students' cognition within the puzzle-based video game, *Baba is You*, leveraging the fine granularity of interaction logs. A growing body of work within the QE community has demonstrated the utility of interaction logs for studying fine-grained behaviors across different contexts and over time in human-computer interactions. For example, Karumbaiah et al. [14] used clickstream data from the educational game *Physics Playground* to analyze students' quitting behavior. Karumbaiah and Baker [13] extended applications of ENA to investigate affect dynamics when students solve problems on ASSISTments, while Wu and colleagues [28] used ENA to explore the metacognitive aspect of math learning in the context of self-regulated learning (SRL) in CueThink. Drawing on the insights gained from previous studies, we studied the relationships between the events logged by the game *Baba is You* to determine the possible reasons for quitting in learning games, as well as to provide insights into phenomena such as how learners apply concepts across levels and players' exploration patterns in the game between those who complete the game and those who quit.

3   Context

In this study, we explored and compared patterns of in-game actions and behaviors enacted by players who quit and complete levels in the commercial video game *Baba is You*. In the game, players complete levels by solving complex puzzles that involve manipulating push-able text objects on the game board to create, break, or modify rules [25]. The rules consist of three distinct types of text objects: nouns (e.g., BABA, WALL, and FLAG), operators (e.g., IS and AND), and properties (e.g., WIN and STOP). When the three text objects are aligned vertically or horizontally, the rule becomes activated, assigning the specified property to the noun associated with said rule. For example, as shown in Figure 1, the rule WALL IS STOP signifies that walls possess the property of obstructing players from traversing through them. However, if any of the three text objects constituting the rule are displaced from their original position, the rule becomes nullified, rendering walls ineffective in stopping players or possessing any properties.

The primary objective of each level is for players to create a winnable rule, i.e., [OBJECT] IS WIN, and guide the player-controlled character, typically Baba—a sheep-like avatar—to touch this winnable element. Across levels, the player is presented with unique combinations of obstacles and rule sets that can be manipulated in different ways to reach the win state. Participants have the option to 'undo' their actions or 'restart' the level entirely at any time, thereby reverting the puzzle to its original state.

Despite the absence of hints or scaffolding by design, the early levels of the game serve as a platform for players to familiarize themselves with the game mechanics as well as the conditions necessary to complete a level. For example, in level 1 (See Fig. 1), players can gradually deduce that pushing any text object within the rule WALL IS STOP would break the rule and render the walls permeable. Once the player passes through the previously blocked wall, they can establish the rule FLAG IS WIN and then touch the flag object in order to complete the level. At the onset of each level, players may not see viable paths to victory, necessitating exploration of each level's context to devise, test, and apply possible winning strategies.

For this study, we examined player quit behavior on two levels. *Lonely Flag* (level 02 in the sub-world Rocket Trip) was selected as a context in which players must apply iterative, cross-level knowledge to achieve success (and avoid quitting), while *Walls of*

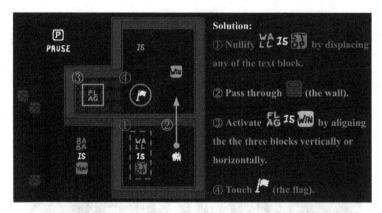

Fig. 1. Design of the first level, *Where Do I Go?*, in *Baba is You*

Gold (level 09 of the subworld Temple Ruins) serves as a later-game example of a level with a more complex win state, in which quitting is more common.

Level *Lonely Flag* and the preceding level *Empty* are purposefully linked together by the designer to challenge players to learn and apply the new concept in the game. In the first level (*Empty*), players are introduced to the special noun referred to as EMPTY, which functions differently depending on its usage. Assigning an object with the property of EMPTY causes that object to permanently disappear from the game board. However, when EMPTY is used as a noun, such as in EMPTY IS FLAG, it transfers all unoccupied cells on the game board to the object that EMPTY represents (in this case, the FLAG). Players can use EMPTY as either a property or a noun to solve the level *Empty*. However, in the next level, *Lonely Flag*, players must use EMPTY as both a property and a noun in order to win. Given the relative rarity of multi-use nouns such as EMPTY in the game, player use of EMPTY as a noun in the prior level (though not required for success) may prime players for subsequent completion of *Lonely Flag* (Fig. 2).

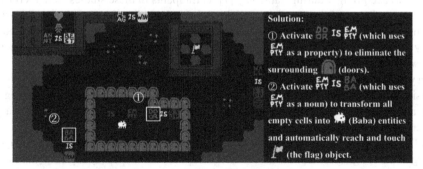

Fig. 2. Design of the level *Lonely Flag*. Players must first create DOOR IS EMPTY (property) to eliminate surrounding doors and then form EMPTY IS BABA (noun) to transform empty spaces into BABA entities that automatically reach and touch the FLAG object.

38   X. Liu et al.

The level *Walls of Gold* (See Fig. 3) does not introduce new objects but is a game level with multi-stage win states designed to challenge players to demonstrate a comprehensive understanding of multiple game elements. Similar to other advanced levels in the game, *Walls of Gold* offers a more intricate challenge that requires players to explore and experiment with different strategies to find a solution.

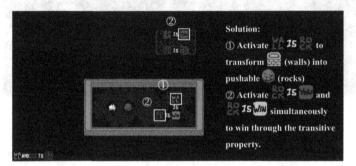

Fig. 3. Design of the level *Walls of Gold*. Players must first create the rule WALL IS ROCK to transform the walls into pushable rocks to break free from the obstruction. Subsequently, they must configure the rules ROCK IS WIN and ROCK IS YOU, using the YOU text situated in the top-right corner of the screen, and complete the level through the transitive property.

4 Method

This work is part of a larger research project that seeks to improve our understanding of how players solve problems in *Baba is You*. Prior studies have examined how players notice deviations (situations when the outcomes of their goal-oriented actions deviate from their expectations), generate causal explanations, and adjust their problem-solving strategies accordingly during gameplay [7]. Participants in these studies were recruited through email advertisements circulated through local middle schools and around a large public university in the United States. Once individuals were enrolled, they installed a copy of the game on their device and were instructed to play for approximately one hour per week over a period of three weeks. As players completed their gameplay sessions, data was uploaded to a secure server and preprocessed for analysis. The complete dataset consisted of player interactions from 184 middle-school and college students, with ages ranging from 10–31. The sample consisted of 49% identifying as male, 43% as female, 5% as non-binary, and 3% preferring not to respond.

The log data was structured to provide (1) player ID, (2) keyboard inputs as the player navigated through game space, (3) the timestamp of each move, (4) any changes made to the game state (e.g., creation or breaking of a rule), and (5) location of each object in x:y coordinates. Using this data, our team was able to track player interactions with specific rules and objects of interest, which were relevant to measuring player behaviors. For this paper, we draw from the complete dataset, but sample 11 players who played *Lonely Flag* and 26 players who played *Walls of Gold* – the levels best suited for our analysis. Although we observe variation in player ages across both levels, our analysis using Pearson's correlation coefficient revealed no statistically significant correlation between age and performance ($r = 0.12$, $p = 0.45$). In other words, the findings provide no evidence to suggest that older players consistently outperform younger players or that younger players are more prone to quitting.

4.1 Participant Sampling

Out of the 11 players who attempted and passed the level *Empty*, 7 players applied EMPTY as a property in the prior level, while 4 players opted to use EMPTY as a noun in their win condition. Out of the 11 players, 8 were able to correctly apply EMPTY as both a noun and property in the subsequent level, *Lonely Flag*, while 3 quit before identifying a solution. It is possible that using EMPTY as a noun during the first level can ultimately assist players in completing the second level. Therefore, to examine the potential influence of players' prior learning on their subsequent performance, we analyzed the click-stream data in *Lonely Flag* and categorized the 11 participants into "Noun" and "Property" groups based on their strategies in completing Level *Empty*, and into "Quit" and "Complete" groups based on their success whether they succeeded in solving *Lonely Flag*. The outcome of the categorization yielded three exclusive groupings, specifically denoted as "Complete (Property)", "Complete (Noun)", and "Quit (Property)", with 4, 3, and 4 instances, respectively, in Figure. 4. These groups were used as unit variables to generate ENA visualizations.

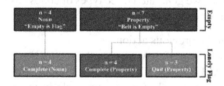

Fig. 4. The categorization of players in *Empty* and *Lonely Flag*

In the second level, *Walls of Gold*, 15 out of the 26 players (we excluded two players out of the initial 28 players from the analysis so that the remaining players have adopted the same solution) were able to successfully complete the level, resulting in a quitting percentage of 42.30%. To complete this level, players must achieve a two-stage goal of first breaking the wall and then forming winning conditions for victory. Therefore, to study player's activities and the cognitive processes involved during different stages of gameplay, we segmented players' activities into "Part-1" when players must free themselves from the walled prison, and "Part-2" when players exit to the exterior where they can access the final win state. Players are also organized into "Quit" and "Complete" groups. The detailed decomposition of the players is represented in Figure 5. One player in the Quit group did not manage to enter the second stage. These groups were used as unit variables to generate ENA visualizations.

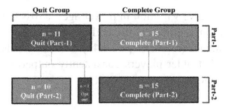

Fig. 5. The categorization of players in *Walls of Gold*

4.2 Epistemic Network Analysis

Our investigation focuses on identifying the differences in the interrelations of events between players who completed a game level and those who did not, seeking to explore the reasons why some players may quit, while others may persevere. To achieve this objective, we generated epistemic network visualizations to map the patterns of different player groups' behaviors over time in each level.

To gain a more comprehensive understanding of players' cognitive processes, we used different unit variables for each level, owing to their distinctive structural attributes. Unit variables for *Lonely Flag* grouped player data into Complete (Noun), Complete (Property), and Quit (Property) groups. Unit variables for *Walls of Gold* grouped player data into Complete (Part-1), Quit (Part-1), Complete (Part-2), and Quit (Part-2) groups. The secondary unit variable for each model groups the play data by individual-level attempts. Since our objective is to analyze the interrelated actions and choices of individual players in the game, we generated three types of codes based on pre-coded events in the click-stream data for each level, as outlined below:

1. *Undo*: the reversal of the previous action
2. *Add < Rule >*: the creation of new rules in the game. For example, the activity of forming the rule "WALL IS ROCK" is coded as "Add < Wall is Rock >"
3. *Remove < Rule >*: the removal of an existing rule in the game. For example, the activity of breaking the rule "WALL IS ROCK" is coded as "Remove < Wall is Rock >"

The numbers of codes generated for each level are as follows: *Lonely Flag* (30 codes; 15 from rule creation and 14 from rule removal), and *Walls of Gold* (30 codes; 15 from rule creation and 14 from rule removal).

Other features of network structures remain consistent for both examinations. We segmented the data based on each player's attempt at a level (conversation variables: Player ID, Restart), as we consider each player's single attempt a suitable unit for the analysis of interconnected behaviors. Given the frequency of the selected logged events in *Baba is You*, with an average rate of one event every two seconds, we used a relatively wide moving window size of 10 actions. This window size corresponds to an average gameplay duration of 20 s, providing an appropriate temporal context to identify relevant co-occurrences of events. This decision was informed by the fine-grained nature of the event logs, which require a relatively high moving window size compared to many previous ENA analyses [16, 19, 22].

In generating epistemic networks for each level, we utilized the ENA Web Tool, which transformed the temporally sequenced one-hot encodings of the events into a network representation, allowing us to identify relevant patterns of co-occurring events that can provide insights into the temporarily interrelated behaviors of the players during gameplay.

5 Results

5.1 Lonely Flag

We used epistemic network visualizations to map the interconnection of events in the level *Lonely Flag* among players classified into the above-mentioned categories (See Fig. 4). Figure 6 presents the difference networks between Complete (Noun) and Quit (Property) groups (left) and networks between Complete (Noun) and Complete (Property) groups (right). In constructing the epistemic networks, we included all 30 codes, but excluded edges with weights less than 0.1 and labeled only the nodes related to the use of EMPTY to enhance visual clarity. Along the X-axis (dimension 1 after means rotation), a two-sample t-test assuming unequal variance showed that group Complete (Noun) was statistically significantly different from group Quit (Property) with an effect size of d = 2.26 (t(4.34) = −3.19, p = 0.03*), and from group Complete (Property) with an effect size of d = 2.28 (t(3.93) = −3.41, p = 0.03*). The difference is not statistically significant between Complete (Property) and Quit (Property) (t(4.99) = 0.22, p = 0.84), which precluded the need for a difference network. In the following section, we explicate two key themes that have shed light on the transfer of learning across levels, as well as the underlying factors that account for quitting behaviors.

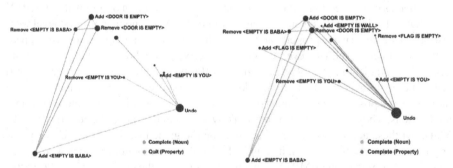

Fig. 6. The difference networks between Complete (Noun) and Quit (Property) (*left*), and the difference networks between Complete (Noun) and Complete (Property) (*right*)

Undoing as a Persistence Strategy for Property Groups
The networks indicate a contrast in the association between Undo and other game events among players in the Property and Noun groups. Specifically, we found a stronger connection between Undo and other events in players from the Property groups, whereas fewer connections to Undo were observed in the Noun group. This behavioral pattern,

characterized by the formation or breaking of rules without meaningful connections to other events other than Undo, indicates repeated attempts to solve the puzzle without making progress that aligns with the objective. For example, believing that EMPTY is key to solving the puzzle, players in the Property group may repeatedly form EMPTY IS YOU, and immediately Undo their actions after realizing that Baba is no longer a controllable character.

One possible explanation for this behavior is the phenomenon of "wheel spinning," which occurs when players engage in prolonged gameplay without achieving significant progress, leading to frustration and ultimately, giving up on the level [20]. On the other hand, the fragmented actions and frequent backtracking of progress in the Property group during their exploration of the level may also reflect a lack of confidence in their decisions or an inability to comprehend the extent to which their current actions contribute to achieving ultimate success. In contrast, the Noun group demonstrates a more cohesive approach to leveraging game objects to solve the level, with their actions being more logically connected. These patterns may signify greater clarity in comprehending the connection between their actions and the win condition, leading to a more efficient and successful level completion.

Transfer of Learning Across Levels

Successful completion of *Lonely Flag* required the creation of the DOOR IS EMPTY, which causes the surrounding door to disappear, testing the player's ability to use EMPTY as a property. In the difference network shown on the right in Figure 6, the Complete (Property) group displayed a stronger association between the Add <DOOR IS EMPTY> action and the Undo, signifying the transfer of knowledge on the application of EMPTY as property across levels. Similarly, the Complete (Noun) group demonstrated robust connections between Add <DOOR IS EMPTY> and several other in-game activities, whereas no connections were found concerning the addition or removal of EMPTY IS DOOR. This indicates players who employed EMPTY as a noun in the first level were also able to perceive it as a property and deduce the method of making the doors disappear in the subsequent level. However, the Quit (Property) group did not exhibit such strong associations, indicating that players in the Quit (Property) group may have encountered difficulties in transferring their acquired knowledge to subsequent levels, which could be indicative of a possible lack of understanding of the concept of EMPTY and its variable applications. They were, however, more likely to add and remove the rule EMPTY IS YOU, but these actions would have no effect on the game board since YOU is a property rather than an object. Thus, it is unlikely that these exploratory actions would have facilitated learning of the EMPTY concept as a noun for players in the Quit (Property) group, which might be one of the reasons that they did not ultimately complete this level.

To conclude the second part, players must formulate the rule EMPTY IS BABA using EMPTY as a noun. As evidenced by the networks, a much stronger connection was observed between Add <EMPTY IS BABA> and other actions in the Complete (Noun) group as compared to the other two groups. Players who used EMPTY as a noun in the first level demonstrate a more extensive comprehension of its dual nature as both a noun and a property. Conversely, those who opt for an alternative strategy may be more likely to experience difficulties when solving the second level, even if they ultimately achieve success. Those players transferred knowledge about the use of EMPTY as a property from the previous level, which may have had an unintended negative impact on their performance. Their attachment to what they had learned previously, rather than considering new approaches, might have hindered their progress to some extent.

The results of our analysis indicate that there was no statistically significant difference between the two Property groups, and their networks showed a high degree of similarity. Nevertheless, when each Property group was compared to the Noun group, there were discernible statistical and visual differences. This suggests that variance in player actions in the second level primarily results from the strategies used in the first level, namely, the decision to use EMPTY as either a Property or a Noun. The choice may reflect their comprehension of the newly introduced concept. However, players in the Complete (Property) group may compensate for a lack of knowledge by engaging in a more distributed exploration of various activities in the second level, particularly those related to using EMPTY as a noun, such as Add <EMPTY IS WALL>, thus successfully completing this level. By contrast, the Quit (Property) group tended to explore fewer possibilities in the game. A lack of exploration and a possible inability to transfer learning from the previous level to the current one could be the reasons why those players ultimately quit the current level.

5.2 Walls of Gold

We proceed to present the findings for the second level, *Walls of Gold*. Figure 7 shows the difference networks between Complete (Part-1) and Quit (Part-1) (left) and networks between Complete (Part-2) and Quit (Part-2) (right). We created epistemic networks based on all 30 codes, but excluded edges weighted less than 0.05 to improve visual clarity. The networks for both stages illustrate notable differences in both the cognitive processes and behaviors of players who completed the level versus those who quit. Along the X-axis, a two-sample t-test assuming unequal variance showed that group Complete (Part-1) was statistically significantly different from group Quit (Part-1) with an effect size of d = 1.00 (t(21.74) = -2.52, p = 0.02*); Complete (Part-2) was statistically significantly different from group Quit (Part-2) with an effect size of d = 1.72 (t(22.01) = 4.39, p < 0.01*). Our results reveal three themes related to players quitting at different stages of the gameplay for *Walls of Gold*.

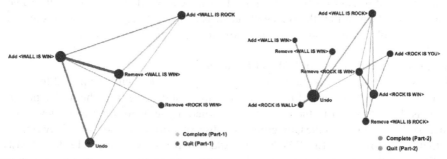

Fig. 7. The difference networks between Complete (Part-1) and Quit (Part-1) (*left*), and the difference networks between Complete (Part-2) and Quit (Part-2) (*right*).

Undoing as a Persistence Strategy for Quit Groups

Networks in Figure 7 suggest that players in the Quit groups exhibit a greater tendency to undo their actions during both stages of gameplay compared to players in the Complete group, a pattern also seen in *Lonely Flag*. Specifically, in the first stage, stronger associations were found between Undo and Add <WALL IS WIN> and Remove <ROCK IS WIN>. In the second stage, stronger associations were found between Undo and Add <WALL IS WIN>, Remove <ROCK IS WIN>, and Add <WALL IS ROCK>. The Complete group used the undo command less frequently in relation to other actions throughout the level, especially in the second stage where only two events are associated with Undo. As discussed in the analysis of *Lonely Flag*, favoring undo may indicate wheel-spinning or lack of confidence during the gameplay. The results may serve as a starting point for understanding the use of undo as a strategy for persistence as players explore actions to determine and eventually achieve the win condition.

Win-Seeking Behavior

As shown in the left network in Fig. 7, the associations between the activity Add < WALL IS WIN > and several other game actions were stronger for players in the Quit group. In contrast, we do not observe correspondingly strong associations between win-related events and other actions for players in the Complete group, with the exception of the connection between Remove < WALL IS WIN > and Add < WALL IS ROCK >, which are crucial preconditions for escaping the enclosed wall prison. These findings suggest that players who quit this level exhibit a stronger inclination to engage directly and repeatedly with the WIN object throughout gameplay, perhaps without first establishing a comprehensive understanding of the level design. Players who completed the level, on the other hand, are less likely to engage with the WIN object repeatedly; for instance, within this group, three players formed win-related rules on only two occasions throughout their gameplay, while two players engaged WIN solely at the point of level success. These patterns suggest that players who complete the level may have a more holistic strategy for success in mind at an earlier point in their play. As a result, these players are less likely to engage in hasty attempts to achieve victory before overcoming the initial level obstacle. The results suggest that the broader strategies adopted by players (e.g., engaging directly with WIN without a broader strategy) may play a key role in determining whether they successfully complete the level or quit. Players who prioritize understanding the level mechanics and solutions before attempting to win are more likely to complete the game, while those who prioritize the WIN without the backing of strategy and an understanding of level complexity may, somewhat paradoxically, be more likely to quit.

Strategic Abandonment and Object Fixation

The results of our analysis also suggest that players in the Quit group tend to repeat actions from the first stage of the game, prior to breaking free from the walled prison, even as they transition to the second stage, where these actions are less relevant for success. For example, in the Quit group, we observe a stronger association between the activities Remove <WALL IS WIN> and Add <WALL IS ROCK> and Add <WALL IS WIN> in the first stage of the level. In the second stage, these activities remain more connected to other actions for the Quit group but are now more strongly associated with Undo. This suggests that these players are repeating patterns of actions that led to recent success again with an unclear or incorrect strategy in mind for how these actions will lead to level completion (this combination of actions cannot result in a win). While such actions could indicate player exploration and "testing" of the level mechanics with the goal of eventually identifying a winning strategy, repeated attempts could also be associated with frustration or confusion, such as the case of one player who attempted "Add <WALL IS ROCK>" 72 times before ultimately quitting the level.

In contrast, the networks for the Complete group in both stages exhibit marked differences from one another. Unlike the Quit group, the Complete group was more likely to strategically abandon objects (as evidenced by their weaker associations to part 1 actions) that previously helped them progress in the level, which suggests greater flexibility in their thinking to identify innovative strategies for success. As indicated by the number of visible connections to each action, players who eventually quit this level engage in slightly more explorations in the beginning stage of the game, with these activities persisting throughout the second stage of the game. In contrast, students who successfully solve the level initially start with limited actions and progressively expand their search for possible actions to win the level.

6 Discussion

The aim of this research paper was to explore possible reasons for players quitting in the puzzle-based video game *Baba is You*, by analyzing and visualizing player interactions using Epistemic Network Analysis (ENA). In constructing the network, we used codes from the automatically generated events recorded in the game's interaction log and applied epistemic network analysis to gain further insights into the players' cognition. The analysis was conducted on two game levels that (1) require cross-level knowledge to achieve success and (2) feature a more complex win state with higher rates of quitting.

Our analysis suggests that insufficient acquisition of specific knowledge components from previous levels (e.g., application of spatial reasoning mechanics such as the use of objects as nouns or properties) may be an important reason why players quit. Moreover, we found that players who prematurely engage with the final win condition without prerequisite strategies for success, who reapply objects or rules they initially encountered when they no longer lead to success, and who engage in less distributed exploration and experimentation may be more likely to quit. In both levels we analyzed, we observed that students who quit are more likely to engage in repeated or redundant actions, which may indicate a lack of confidence in their actions or a limited capacity to understand how their current actions contribute (or don't contribute) to level completion. These findings highlight the potential benefit of targeted interventions that address the specific knowledge gaps and gameplay behaviors that may contribute to a player quitting. With this in mind, initiatives to design on-demand or tailored experiences, prompts, and supports for students could prove valuable. Leveraging metrics or behavior patterns such as those identified in our analysis, educators and game designers can better identify at-risk players and provide them with targeted interventions that help to address their individual needs and promote sustained engagement. In the case of *Baba is You*, cognitive scaffolds could be built into the *Lonely Flag* level that shows learners who only used EMPTY as a property previously that it can also function as a noun. Targeted hints could encourage more experimentation and exploration of the game mechanics in *Walls of Gold* for players who over-engage with the WIN object. Finally, an expansion of support for players resorting to Undo as part of level engagement, through hints or tutorials, could help players pass disengaging roadblocks. Though the primary aim of this work is a preliminary examination of player quitting behaviors, a limitation of this iteration of the work is the smaller sample size of students, especially for the level *Lonely Flag*, which only had 11 players. Additionally, it is also important to note that other external factors beyond players' interactions, and social or cultural influences [12], may also impact students' motivation and confidence levels, leading them to potentially disengage from the game. Future research should study a broader range of levels and students to understand what aspects of the findings generalize, and account for other external factors that could impact player retention with the game.

These results suggest that the application of Epistemic Network Analysis (ENA) to investigate player behavior in video games and other learning environments holds promise for enhancing our understanding of how students learn and interact with complex systems. Utilizing automatically generated events as codes, ENA provides a window for examining constructs related to student learning, engagement, and experience, not only in games but also in other learning contexts featuring well-designed event-based logging mechanisms. Although exploratory in nature, the insights obtained from this study could potentially inform the development of targeted interventions that address specific gameplay behaviors and knowledge gaps in games like *Baba is You*, ultimately fostering sustained engagement and success. Future research will expand the scope of this inquiry by examining additional samples and contexts to further comprehend in-game learning experiences and behaviors. Our hope is that this applied example could inspire further research that explores log data as a source of rich, contextualized discourse for quantitative ethnographic investigations.

References

1. Allen, D.: Desire to finish college: an empirical link between motivation and persistence. Res. High. Educ. **40**(4), 461–485 (1999)
2. Ang, C.S., Zaphiris, P., Mahmood, S.: A model of cognitive loads in massively multiplayer online role playing games. Interact. Comput. **19**(2), 167–179 (2007)
3. Bailey, C., Pearson, E., Gkatzidou, S., Green, S.: Using video games to develop social, collaborative and communication skills. In: Proceedings of World Conference on Educational Multimedia, Hypermedia and Telecommunications 2006, pp. 1154–1161. AACE, Chesapeake, VA (2006)
4. Cao, L., Jacobson, M.J., Markauskaite, L., Lai, P.K.: The use of productive failure to learn genetics in a game-based environment. In: Paper presented at the Annual Meeting of the American Educational Research Association, San Francisco, CA (2020)
5. Chow, A.F., Woodford, K.C., Maes, J.: Deal or no deal: using games to improve students learning, retention and decision making. Int. J. Math. Educ. Sci. Technol. **42**(2), 259–264 (2010)
6. Dale, G., Joessel, A., Bavelier, D., Green, C.S.: A new look at the cognitive neuroscience of video game play. Ann. N. Y. Acad. Sci. **1464**(1), 192–203 (2020)
7. DeLiema, D., et al.: Playful learning following deviations: a mixture of tinkering, causal explanations, and revision rationales. In: Chinn, C., Tan, E., Chan, C., and Kali, Y. (eds.) Proceedings of the 16th International Conference of the Learning Sciences, pp. 1421–1424 (2022)

8. Franzwa, C., Tang, Y., Johnson, A.: Serious game design: motivating students through a balance of fun and learning. In: 5th International Conference on Games and Virtual Worlds for Serious Applications (VS-GAMES), pp. 1–7. IEEE (2013)

9. Gambrell, L.B.: What we know about motivation to read. In: Flippo, R.F. (eds.) Reading Researchers in Search of Common Ground, pp. 129–143. International Reading Association, Newark, DE (2001)

10. Gee, J.P.: Learning by design: Good video games as learning machines. E-Learn. Dig. Media **2**(1), 5–16 (2005)

11. Hou, H.T.: Integrating cluster and sequential analysis to explore learners' flow and behavioral patterns in a simulation game with situated-learning context for science courses: a video-based process exploration. Comput. Hum. Behav. **48**, 424–435 (2015)

12. Isik, U., et al.: Factors influencing academic motivation of ethnic minority students: a review. SAGE Open **8**(2), 1–8 (2018)

13. Karumbaiah, S., Baker, R.S.: Studying affect dynamics using epistemic networks. In: Ruis, A.R., Lee, S.B. (eds.) Advances in Quantitative Ethnography: Second International Conference, ICQE 2020, Malibu, CA, USA, 1–3 Feb 2021, Proceedings, pp. 390–405. Springer, Cham (2021)

14. Karumbaiah, S., Baker, R., Barany, A., Shute, V.: Using epistemic networks with automated codes to understand why players quit levels in a learning game. In: Eagan, B., Misfeldt, M., Siebert-Evenstone, A. (eds.) Advances in Quantitative Ethnography: First International Conference, ICQE 2019, Madison, WI, USA, 20–22 Oct 2019, Proceedings, pp. 106–116. Springer, Cham (2019)

15. Kazimoglu, C., Kiernan, M., Bacon, L., Mackinnon, L.: Developing a game model for computational thinking and learning traditional programming through game-play. In: ELearn: World Conference on E-Learning in Corporate, Government, Healthcare, and Higher Education, pp. 1378–1386. Association for the Advancement of Computing in Education (AACE), San Diego, CA (2010)

16. Knight, S., Arastoopour, G., Williamson Shaffer, D., Buckingham Shum, S., Littleton, K.: Epistemic networks for epistemic commitments. In: Polman, J.L., et al. (eds.) Learning and Becoming in Practice: The International Conference of the Learning Sciences, vol. 1, pp. 150–157. Boulder, CO (2014)

17. Leduc-McNiven, K., Dion, R.T., Mukhi, S.N., McLeod, R.D., Friesen, M.R.: Machine learning and serious games: Opportunities and requirements for detection of mild cognitive impairment. J. Med. Artif. Intell. **1**, 1–1 (2018)

18. Mathew, R., Malik, S.I., Tawafak, R.M.: Teaching problem solving skills using an educational game in a computer programming course. Inform Educ. **18**(2), 359373 (2019)

19. Melzner, N., Greisel, M., Dresel, M., Kollar, I.: Using process mining (PM) and epistemic network analysis (ENA) for comparing processes of collaborative problem regulation. In: Eagan, B., Misfeldt, M., Siebert-Evenstone, A. (eds.) Advances in Quantitative Ethnography: First International Conference, ICQE 2019, Madison, WI, USA, 20–22 Oct 2019, Proceedings, pp. 154–164. Springer, Cham (2019)

20. Owen, V.E., et al.: Detecting wheel-spinning and productive persistence in educational games. In: Desmarais, M.C., Lynch, C.F., Merceron, A., Nkambou, R. (eds.) Proceedings of the 12th International Conference on Educational Data Mining, pp. 378–383. International Educational Data Mining Society, Montréal, Canada (2019)

21. Shaffer, D.W., Collier, W., Ruis, A.R.: A tutorial on epistemic network analysis: analyzing the structure of connections in cognitive, social, and interaction data. J. Learn. Anal. **3**(3), 9–45 (2016)

22. Shah, M., Siebert-Evenstone, A., Moots, H., Eagan, B.: Quality and safety education for nursing (QSEN) in virtual reality simulations: a quantitative ethnographic examination. In:

Wasson, B., Zörgő, S. (eds.) Advances in Quantitative Ethnography: Third International Conference, ICQE 2021, Virtual Event, 6–11 Nov 2021, Proceedings, pp. 49–65. Springer, Cham (2022). https://doi.org/10.1007/978-3-030-93859-8_16

23. Shute, V.J., Ventura, M., Ke, F.: The power of play: the effects of Portal 2 and Lumosity on cognitive and noncognitive skills. Comput. Educ. **80**, 58–67 (2015)

24. Tärning, B., Haake, M., Gulz, A.: Off-task engagement in a teachable agent based math game. In: Proceedings of the 19th International Conference on Computers in Education (ICCE-2011), 28 (2011)

25. Teikari, A.: Baba is You [PC version]. Hempuli Oy, Finland (2019)

26. Wang, L.H., Chen, B., Hwang, G.J., Guan, J.Q., Wang, Y.Q.: Effects of digital gamebased STEM education on students' learning achievement: a meta-analysis. Int. J. STEM Educ. **9**, 26 (2022)

27. Westera, W.: How people learn while playing serious games: a computational modelling approach. J. Comput. Sci. **18**, 32–45 (2017)

28. Wu, M., Zhang, J., Barany, A.: Understanding detectors for SMART model cognitive operation in mathematical problem-solving process: an epistemic network analysis. In: Damşa, C., Barany, A. (eds.) Advances in Quantitative Ethnography: Fourth International Conference, ICQE 2022, Copenhagen, Denmark, 15–19 Oct 2022, Proceedings, pp. 314–327. Virtual Event, 6–11 Nov 2021, Proceedings, pp. 49–65. Springer, Cham (2023)

29. Young, M.F., et al.: Our princess is in another castle: a review of trends in serious gaming for education. Rev. Educ. Res. **82**(1), 61–89 (2012)

Impact of Agent Language on Student Language in the Structures of Language Connections

Haiying Li[1]($\boxtimes$) (ID), Zhiqiang Cai[2], Grace Wang[3], Fanshuo Cheng[4], and Cody Marquart[2]

[1] University of Pennsylvania, Philadelphia, PA 19014, USA
haiyli@upenn.edu
[2] University of Wisconsin, Madison, WI 53706, USA
{zhiqiang.cai,cody.marquart}@wisc.edu
[3] University of Southern California, Los Angeles, CA 90007, USA
graceywa@usc.edu
[4] University of Iowa, Iowa City, IA 52242, USA
fanshuo-cheng@iowa.edu

Abstract. This study explores the impact of conversational agent language (formal vs. informal) on student language in an intelligent tutoring system (ITS). Unlike previous studies that analyzed language features in isolation, we utilized the epistemic network analysis (ENA) approach to investigate the structure of language connections in five dimensions, including non-narrativity, word abstractness, syntactic complexity, referential cohesion, and deep cohesion, in summaries written before and after the intervention. Visualizations of the ENA networks revealed differences in language connection structures between pretest and posttest in both formal and informal groups. Specifically, in the informal group, the connection between non-narrativity and word abstractness was stronger in the posttest network. In the formal group, the connection between non-narrativity and referential cohesion was stronger in the posttest network. Additionally, the connection between deep cohesion and syntactic complexity shifted from significant on pretest networks to insignificant on posttest networks. This study has implications for the design of conversational agent language and sheds light on the potential of combining ENA and Coh-Metrix components to analyze the differences in the structure of language connections, rather than individual language features in isolation.

Keywords: AutoTutor ARC · Coh-Metrix · Conversational agent · Epistemic Network Analysis · Formality · Intelligent tutoring system · Summary writing

1 Introduction

Mastery of academic language skills and the ability to write in an academic style are essential requirements for K-12 students to demonstrate their knowledge and enhance their understanding [1, 10]. However, meeting these standards is often challenging for students [20]. While summary writing, a reading-to-write or source-based writing task [12], is increasingly used to evaluate students' deep reading comprehension, the role of

G. Arastoopour Irgens and S. Knight (Eds.): ICQE 2023, CCIS 1895, pp. 49–65, 2023.
https://doi.org/10.1007/978-3-031-47014-1_4

academic language skills in summarization remains inadequately investigated [3, 4]. A recent study examining the impact of agent language on student language in summarization found no significant difference in the language used in summaries written by students before and after receiving summarization interventions [15]. However, further research is needed to explore the relationship between academic language skills and summarization, as the challenge of meeting academic language standards persists for K-12 students.

Past research on teacher/agent-student language focused on individual language and discourse features in isolation. However, language comprises multiple levels, ranging from words and sentences to larger structures such as cohesion and genre [7]. While each feature has its own unique contribution to language, none of them can fully capture the intricacy of language use. Therefore, it is imperative to investigate teacher/agent-student language by examining the associations of language connections. This study utilizes the epistemic network analysis (ENA) approach [23] to investigate how conversational agent language (formal versus informal) affects student language through a summarization intervention using an intelligent tutoring system (ITS), the AutoTutor for Adult Reading Comprehension (ARC).

This study contributes to the research on teacher/agent-student language in two significant ways. Firstly, the ENA approach is advantageous as it can reveal subtle differences that may go unnoticed when analyzing isolated features. Secondly, the study is the first to incorporate both the ENA approach and multi-level language features using automated text analysis tools, such as Coh-Metrix, to compute language features, and *rENA* in *R* to visualize language associations. This methodology has the potential to advance language-related research.

1.1 Summarization and Academic Language

Summary writing is utilized to assess students' reading comprehension skills required for success in post-secondary education and the workforce. Compared to traditional reading comprehension measures like multiple-choice (MC) tests, summary writing provides a more accurate assessment of a student's ability to identify and write the main ideas of a text, integrating and uniting them into a coherent whole [4, 11]. Summary writing is established on the Construction-Integration (CI) model of text comprehension [14, 26] and the developmental model of writing [13]. It involves comprehension of the source text and the skills to represent the ideas in the source text accurately using academic language [4, 22]. Academic language refers to the language forms that are pre-planned, well-organized, precise, and coherent and are used in both spoken and written communication within academic and professional communities [15, 16, 21, 24]. Unlike everyday language, which is spontaneous, less organized, and more disjointed, academic language is not dependent on context or shared understanding among participants.

Generating a summary of an expository science text requires a range of skills, including decoding the text at the surface level, language comprehension at the textbase level, and higher-order skills (e.g., synthesis and reproduction). Summary writing requires conveying abstract ideas in academic contexts, and academic language affects the performance in summarizing scientific expository texts [4]. For instance, mature writers, either L1 or L2, demonstrated more syntactic complexity and adversative connectors in written summaries than less mature writers, whereas only L1 writers used more phrasal elaboration and richer, more diverse vocabulary [22]. They also found that many measures of syntactic complexity were inextricably linked with connector use. However, the role of academic language skills in summarization has not been adequately investigated, which is within the scope of the present study.

1.2 Teacher Language and Agent Language

Early research on teacher language primarily focused on theoretical frameworks and related theories. One such framework, the pragmatics-based framework, represents a comprehensive perspective on teacher language and proposes measures for various language levels, including linguistic and cognitive features [24]. These features encompass interpersonal stance, information load, organization of information, lexical choices, representational congruence, genre mastery, command of reasoning or argumentative strategies, and disciplinary knowledge. Teacher language has been found to be significantly associated with students' language development [2, 17] in English [5], Chinese [25], French [22], Spanish [19], etc.

Researchers have used the pragmatics-based framework [24] to conduct empirical correlational studies on specific levels of teacher language, including lexical, syntactic, and text-based levels. For example, Gámez and Lesaux [6] found that students' vocabulary skills were positively associated with teachers' use of sophisticated academic vocabulary and complex syntax. However, manipulating teacher language has been a challenge in these studies. This challenge can be addressed through the manipulation of conversational agent language in the ITS to investigate the causal relationship between agent language and student language [15, 16].

For example, Li and Graesser [15, 16] developed a conversation-based ITS to manipulate agent language to investigate the impact of agent language on student language in written summaries at multiple levels of language. They utilized Coh-Metrix formality scores and its five major components of discourse, including word abstractness, syntactic complexity, referential cohesion, deep cohesion, and non-narrativity, to analyze agent and student language. The Coh-Metrix tool is developed based on a multilevel theoretical framework, which includes textbase, situation model, genre, rhetorical structure, and pragmatic communication [8]. Coh-Metrix allows for computing most language features listed in the pragmatics-based framework [24] and multilevel theoretical framework [8]. These components were derived through a principal components analysis using a corpus of texts that individuals are exposed to the texts from kindergarten to the early years of college [9]. Table 1 displays the definition and examples of these five primary Coh-Metrix components.

Academic language and conversational language are at opposite ends of the formality continuum, with academic language being formal and conversational language being informal. Academic language is associated with high scores in all five components, while conversational language is associated with low scores. Prior studies did not find a significant effect of agent language, formal, mixed, or informal, on student language in written summaries measured by five Coh-Metrix components [16].

This study utilized the ENA approach to investigate whether conversational agent language (formal versus informal) affects student language by examining the differences in language associations rather than individual language features in isolation. We aim to answer the following research question: *How does the formality level of conversational agent language impact the structure of language connections in students' written summaries?*

Table 1. Five primary Coh-Metrix components

Component	Definition	Example
Word Abstractness (Inverse: Word Concreteness)	Use of abstract words that lack mental imagery (which are harder to comprehend than concrete, meaningful, and imagery-evoking content words)	*Moral* (more abstract), *butterfly* (more concrete)
Syntactic Complexity (Inverse: Syntactic Simplicity)	Use of unfamiliar syntactic structures (e.g., high noun-phrase density and left-embedded syntax), which are challenging and difficult to process	Complex: *Two of the most destructive hurricanes hit the U.S. in recent years* Simple: *Two hurricanes are the most dangerous. They hit the U.S. in recent years*
Referential Cohesion	An overlap of words and ideas across sentences and throughout the text helps the reader connect the text	Two hurricanes are the most dangerous. They hit the U.S. in recent years ("*Hurricanes*" and "*They*" constructs an argument overlap)
Deep Cohesion	Use of connectives or conceptual ideas that contribute to a more explicit and coherent understanding of the text at the level of a situation model	Causality (e.g., *affect*), causal verb (e.g., *because*); intentional verb (e.g., *talk*)
Non-Narrativity (Inverse: Narrativity)	Lack of storytelling components such as familiar characters, events, places, and things, related to everyday oral conversation	Less narrative: *A hurricane is a powerful storm with strong winds and heavy rain, causing destruction*; More narrative: *The hurricane arrived, bringing strong winds and heavy rain that damaged windows of homes*

2 Method

2.1 Participants and Procedures

We recruited individuals from Amazon Mechanical Turk (AMT) who expect to improve their English summary writing skills. These participants were compensated with $30 for a three-hour intervention [15, 16]. After the screening process, we randomly assigned participants to one of two groups, and only 122 completed the experiment due to the technical issues: formal ($N = 57$) and informal ($N = 65$). The participants had an average age of 33.25 ($SD = 8.43$), with 41.8% females, 86.9% language learners, and 61.5% from India. On average, the language learners had studied English for 17.62 years ($SD = 8.02$) and had spent 10.22 years ($SD = 8.75$) in a foreign country. Among the participants, 39.3% held a master's or higher degree, 43.4% had a B.A., and 17.2% had less than four years of higher education.

For this study, participants were given eight texts—four comparison texts and four causation texts—with an average of 260.13 words each ($SD = 63.47$) to read and then write the summary. From these eight texts, two of the comparison texts (*Walking and Running, Kobe and Jordan*) and two of the causation texts (*Effects of Exercising, Diabetes*) were randomly selected for the intervention, while the other two comparison texts (*Butterfly & Moth, Hurricane*) and two causation texts (*Floods, Job Market*) were used for the pretest and posttest, with one comparison text and one causation text on each test. A balanced 4 × 4 Latin-square design was used to control for the order effect. The difficulty of the texts was fit for upper middle school students and high school students [15, 16].

The participants were assessed for their proficiency in summary writing before and after receiving a summarization intervention. A trialogue-based ITS was used to develop a one-hour summarization intervention. Two computer agents, a tutor agent and a peer agent, interactively guided participants to learn a summarization strategy. The intervention started with a brief lecture, followed by participants reading four expository texts. During the lecture, the agents used text maps to introduce text structures and their corresponding signal words, such as "*likely*" for similarities in comparison texts and "*therefore*" for effects in causation texts. After reading each text, participants completed five MC questions to test their ability to identify text structure and main ideas and distinguish important information from minor details. Participants received personalized feedback and scaffolding for the MC questions. For each text, participants also wrote a summary and evaluated it, but they did not receive feedback or scaffolding for these two tasks. Participants also evaluated peers' summaries, for which they received personalized feedback. On the pretest and posttest, participants wrote and evaluated summaries without receiving feedback, or scaffolding.

Participants were instructed to use their own words to summarize the text and utilize signal words and topic sentences to highlight the main ideas and important supporting information. The written summaries were then analyzed using Coh-Metrix version 3.0. This tool computed five primary Coh-Metrix components with percentile scores, which included narrativity, word concreteness, syntactic simplicity, referential cohesion, and deep cohesion [15, 16]. To ensure consistent measurements of academic language, the first three components' scores were inversed to represent non-narrativity, word abstractness, and syntactic complexity (see Table 1). Finally, each of these five components was standardized using z-scores for the final analysis.

2.2 Agent Language Manipulation

The Expectation and Misconception-Tailored (EMT) dialogue mechanism [7] was used to design agents' conversations. The tutor initiated the conversation by asking the learner a challenging question with an expected correct answer. To lead the learner towards the correct answer, a five-step tutoring frame was utilized: (1) the agent asked the question, (2) the learner provided the initial response, (3) the agent provided brief feedback on the learner's response, (4) the agent used hint-assertion dialogue moves to guide the learner to the expected answer, and (5) the conversation is wrapped up.

A natural language discourse expert generated the agents' conversations, which were then modified into formal and informal language considering five levels of discourse: word, syntax, referential cohesion, deep cohesion, and genre [9, 15, 16]. The formal conversations used more complex words (e.g., *clarification* vs. *show*) and sentence structures (e.g., subordinate clauses vs. simple subject-verb), more content word overlapping resulting in higher cohesion (e.g., repeating content words), more connectives (e.g., *additionally*), and a non-narrative style (e.g., impersonal articles vs. 1st- and 2nd-person pronouns). Another expert confirmed that these conversations were natural and appropriate. Below are two examples of agent language in formal and informal language, where the tutor agent provided feedback on a student's rating of a peer's summary:

Formal language: Morgan's summary is rated as medium level by the experts, because it states the major similarities between walking and running, with the signal word in a topic sentence.

Informal language: Morgan's summary is at the medium level. She points out the main idea in a topic sentence. It tells us how walking and running are similar.

The study used formal and informal conversations to create two groups of formality: (1) formal, where both the tutor agent, Christina, and the peer agent, Jordan, used formal language; and (2) informal, where both agents used informal language. The formality of each group was evaluated using Coh-Metrix formality scores [9, 15, 16]. Conversations in the formal group had a mean score of 4.70 ($SD = 1.89$), and conversations in the informal group had a mean score of -2.00 ($SD = 0.82$). These scores were consistent with experts' perceptions of formality [15, 16].

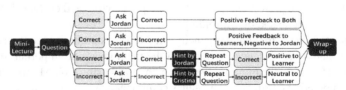

Fig. 1. Dialogue moves during the intervention. *Note.* Dark green boxes indicate manipulated agent language. Light green boxes indicate participants' responses.

3 Results

3.1 ENA Analyses

To answer our research question, we utilized the *rENA* package in *R* [18] to generate language networks within a one-moving summary window and examined the variation in associations among the five Coh-Metrix components: non-narrativity, word abstractness, syntactic complexity, referential cohesion, and deep cohesion. The units and conversations were the test (pretest and posttest), condition (formal and informal), and individual students. The model was generated using endpoints and weighted by square root. The rotation direction was from pretest to posttest, maximizing the variance between the means of the pretest and posttest, with the left side of the plot representing strong co-occurrence of language on the pretest, and the right side representing strong co-occurrence on the posttest. In each of the two networks (superimposed and subtracted networks of pretest and posttest), the placement of nodes is in fixed positions, allowing for a meaningful comparison of connection patterns and interpretation of the projection space [23]. The larger the node, the stronger the connection with other Coh-Metrix components, with lines representing the co-occurrence of these components. Darker, thicker lines indicate stronger connections, while lighter, thinner lines indicate weaker connections. Each red dot on the pretest and blue dot on the posttest represents an individual learner in the ENA plot. The square at the center of each coordinate represents the means, and the dotted line represents the 95% confidence interval (Conf. Int.).

Figures 2a and b illustrate the superimposed and subtracted networks in the informal condition. The visualization displays a difference in the structure of language connections, namely, a stronger connection between word abstractness and non-narrativity in the posttest network. Figures 2c and d depict a different pattern of connection structures in the formal condition. The connection between deep cohesion and syntactic complexity was stronger in the pretest network, whereas the connection between non-narrativity and referential cohesion was stronger in the posttest network (Fig. 2).

Although network projections can visually demonstrate the differences in language connection structures, it is hard to tell whether the difference is statistically significant or not, especially when the connection line is slightly light and thin. Therefore, we calculated the mean positions of pretest and posttest scores in both the formal and informal groups to further explore whether the language structure differences are statistically significant. Results of one-way ANOVA indicated a significant effect of agent language on student language with a small effect size in the informal group, $F(1, 125) = 5.63$, $p = 0.019$, $\eta^2 = 0.04$. Post hoc comparison with the Tukey HSD test indicated that the rotation of the means was significantly higher on the posttest ($M = 0.07$, $SD = 0.23$) than on the pretest ($M = -0.02$, $SD = 0.23$) in the informal condition. This result suggested that conversational agents who spoke informal language elicited students to make more gains in language use.

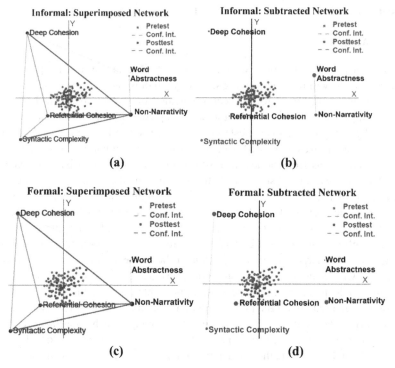

Fig. 2. Superimposed and subtracted networks.

The results of the formal group also revealed a significant effect of agent language on student language with a small effect size, $F(1, 111) = 4.36$, $p = 0.039$, $\eta^2 = 0.04$. Its post hoc comparison showed that the rotation of the means was significantly higher on the posttest ($M = 0.02$, $SD = 0.22$) than on the pretest ($M = -0.07$, $SD = 0.21$). This finding indicated that conversational agents who spoke formal language also prompted students to make more gains in language use.

To identify where differences existed, one-way ANOVA analyses were performed on 10 line weights that represent the associations between each two of the five Coh-Metrix components within each group (see Table 2). Within the informal group, only the connection between non-narrativity and word abstractness was significantly different with a small effect size, $F(1, 125) = 7.01$, $p = 0.001$, $\eta^2 = 0.05$. Post hoc comparisons revealed that this connection was significantly higher on the posttest ($M = 0.26$, $SD = 0.16$) than on the pretest ($M = 0.19$, $SD = 0.16$). This finding confirmed the ENA visualization that conversational agents who spoke informal language influenced students to achieve more learning gains in language. Specifically, when learners wrote more non-narrative summaries, they tended to use more abstract words.

Table 2. Descriptives and ANOVA results of 10 line weights

Language	Test	Formal ($F(1, 111)$)				Informal ($F(1, 125)$)			
		Mean	SD	F	η^2	Mean	SD	F	η^2
Non-Narrativity * Word Abstractness	Post	0.20	0.15	1.58	0.01	**0.26**	**0.16**	**7.01****	**0.05**
	Pre	0.17	0.13			**0.19**	**0.16**		
Non-Narrativity * Syntactic Complexity	Post	0.37	0.16	0.16	0.001	0.36	0.15	0.11	0.001
	Pre	0.38	0.20			0.35	0.15		
Non-Narrativity * Referential Cohesion	Post	**0.38**	**0.16**	**5.02***	0.04	0.37	0.13	0.16	0.001
	Pre	**0.32**	**0.11**			0.38	0.14		
Non-Narrativity * Deep Cohesion	Post	0.39	0.17	0.11	0.001	0.40	0.16	0.85	0.01
	Pre	0.38	0.19			0.37	0.14		
Word Abstractness * Syntactic Complexity	Post	0.13	0.11	0.01	0.00	0.16	0.11	3.14†	0.02
	Pre	0.13	0.10			0.12	0.10		
Word Abstractness * Referential Cohesion	Post	0.13	0.09	0.74	0.01	0.15	0.10	0.15	0.001
	Pre	0.11	0.10			0.14	0.12		
Word Abstractness * Deep Cohesion	Post	0.17	0.14	0.07	0.001	0.20	0.13	0.34	0.003
	Pre	0.16	0.12			0.18	0.14		
Syntactic Complexity * Referential Cohesion	Post	0.32	0.17	0.02	0.00	0.28	0.15	2.47	0.02
	Pre	0.31	0.17			0.33	0.16		
Syntactic Complexity * Deep Cohesion	Post	**0.25**	**0.13**	**5.54***	**0.05**	0.25	0.14	1.25	0.01
	Pre	**0.31**	**0.14**			0.28	0.14		
Referential Cohesion * Deep Cohesion	Post	0.29	0.17	1.45	0.01	0.28	0.15	1.78	0.01
	Pre	0.33	0.18			0.32	0.16		

Note. **, $p < .01$; *, $p < .05$; †, $p < .10$, which apply to all the tables.

This pattern was not observed in the formal group. In the formal group, the connection between non-narrativity and referential cohesion was significantly different between the pretest and posttest with a small effect size, $F(1, 111) = 5.02, p = 0.027, \eta^2 = 0.04$. Post hoc comparisons showed that this connection was significantly higher on the posttest ($M = 0.38, SD = 0.16$) than on the pretest ($M = 0.32, SD = 0.11$). This finding confirmed the ENA visualization that conversational agents who spoke formal language influenced students to achieve more learning gains in language. Especially when learners wrote more non-narrative summaries, they tended to use more referential cohesion.

Additionally, another connection between syntactic complexity and deep cohesion was also significantly different between the pretest and posttest in the formal condition with a small effect size, $F(1, 111) = 5.54, p = 0.020, \eta^2 = 0.05$. Post hoc comparisons indicated that this connection was significantly lower on the posttest ($M = 0.25, SD = 0.13$) than on the pretest ($M = 0.31, SD = 0.14$). This finding confirmed the ENA visualization that before the intervention, learners tended to use higher deep cohesion when they generated complex sentence structures, but this difference disappeared after they learned summarization strategies with the conversational agents who spoke the formal language.

3.2 Traditional Analyses

We conducted one-way ANOVA analyses on the original five Coh-Metrix components (see Table 3) but did not find an effect of agent language on student language in the formal group. However, there was a significant effect on non-narrativity in the informal condition, $F(1, 250) = 9.45, p = 0.002, \eta^2 = 0.04$. Post hoc comparison revealed that non-narrativity was significantly higher on the posttest ($M = 0.79, SD = 0.16$) than on the pretest. This finding suggests that conversational agents who spoke informal language influenced students to use more non-narrative language in their summaries on the posttest compared to the pretest.

We conducted additional one-way ANOVA analyses to compare the impact of agent language on student language, using the means rotation of the five Coh-Metrix components. The results showed a significant effect of informal agent language on student language in the informal condition, $F(1, 250) = 8.32, p = 0.004, \eta^2 = 0.03$. Post hoc comparison revealed that the rotation of the means was significantly higher on the posttest ($M = 0.01, SD = 0.34$) than on the pretest ($M = -0.11, SD = 0.32$). However, no significant effect was found in the formal condition, $F(1, 224) = 3.84, p = 0.051, \eta^2 = 0.02$ (pretest: $M = -0.13, SD = 0.35$; posttest: $M = -0.05, SD = 0.31$). These findings suggest that conversational agents who used informal language led to higher means rotation in student language on the posttest compared to the pretest. In contrast, the use of formal language by conversational agents did not impact student language.

Table 3. Descriptives and ANOVA results of five Coh-Metrix components.

Language	Test	Formal ($F(1, 224)$)				Informal ($F(1, 250)$)			
		Mean	SD	F	η^2	Mean	SD	F	η^2
Non-Narrativity	Post	0.77	0.18	3.62†	0.02	**0.79**	**0.16**	**9.45****	**0.04**
	Pre	0.71	0.23			**0.72**	**0.20**		
Word Abstractness	Post	0.30	0.28	0.80	0.004	0.38	0.30	3.15†	0.01
	Pre	0.27	0.26			0.31	0.30		
Syntactic Complexity	Post	0.58	0.33	0.72	0.003	0.54	0.30	1.19	0.005
	Pre	0.62	0.31			0.58	0.29		
Referential Cohesion	Post	0.60	0.32	0.19	0.001	0.58	0.32	2.74†	0.01
	Pre	0.59	0.32			0.65	0.33		
Deep Cohesion	Post	0.59	0.38	1.75	0.01	0.62	0.38	0.46	0.002
	Pre	0.66	0.37			0.65	0.36		

4 Discussions and Conclusions

This study investigates how conversational agent language affects student language in written summaries using the ENA approach and evaluates its effectiveness by comparing it with traditional approaches. The ENA visualization and one-way ANOVA analyses on ENA means rotation and line weights revealed differences in the structures of language connections in written summaries between the pretest and posttest within each formal and informal group. Specifically, we found that conversational agents using informal language led students to use more abstract words in their non-narrative summaries on the posttest. On the other hand, those using formal language elicited learners to use more referential cohesion in their non-narrative summaries. Interestingly, in the formal group, the language connection between deep cohesion and syntactic complexity was strong on the pretest, but not on the posttest.

To evaluate the effectiveness of the ENA approach, we compared it to the traditional approaches, namely ANOVA on five Coh-Metrix components and their means rotation. Our comparison showed that the ENA approach was more effective in detecting differences in the structure of language associations than individual language features in isolation or their means rotation. Specifically, the traditional approaches only identified differences in one language feature of non-narrativity or in a means rotation in the informal group, and they failed to detect any difference in the formal group. Moreover, the ENA approach revealed the difference in language association rather than individual language features [7, 24]. These findings demonstrate that the ENA approach, which highlights the difference in the structure of connection, is more effective than the traditional approaches that examine individual language features in isolation due to the identification of subtle differences.

To better illustrate the differences in the connection structures between the pretest and posttest networks, we provided examples for each case. These findings have significant implications for understanding the impact of conversational agents on student language in written summaries and for using the ENA approach in discourse analyses. This approach is aligned with the characteristics of language, which integrate multiple levels of features, rather than considering individual language features in isolation [7, 24].

4.1 Informal Language Facilitates Learning

This study found that when conversational agents spoke in informal language, students tended to use more abstract words in their written summaries for non-narrative styles. To illustrate this finding, we provided two excerpts of student responses, one generated on a posttest and the other on a pretest, with high non-narrativity but differing levels of word abstractness. Example 1 contained more abstract words, such as "destruction," to summarize the general primary information presented in the original text, while Example 2 contained more concrete words, such as "winds measured 175 miles," to describe specific destruction and damage. Considering this difference was not significant in the formal condition, the informal language used by the conversational agents may have made it easier for learners [7] to understand the intervention strategies and apply them to summary writing, resulting in using more abstract words to deliver main ideas and general information in their informational summaries. This aligns with previous research that suggests that informal language is easier for learners to comprehend.

Example 1 (Posttest): High Non-Narrativity $= 0.93$, Word Abstractness $= 0.97$

> *The most destructive and worst hurricanes in US in recent years are Andrew in 1992 and Katrina in 2005. They led to massive destruction and damage. Hurricane Andrew is a category 5 hurricane. it caused extensive damage in property and causalities. The estimated property damage is 25 billion dollars. But compared to Andrew Katrina was not that strong. But in terms of destruction Katrina is far more destructive and deadly. There was flooding 80 of the city with more than 1800 people are dead and property damage of worth 81 billion.*

Example 2 (Pretest): Non-Narrativity $= 0.99$, Word Abstractness $= 0$

> *Deadly Hurricanes. Two mot destructive hurricanes hit US in 1992 and 2005. Hurricane Andrew hit in 1992 which was strongest category. Its winds measured 175 miles per hour, damaged property worth 25 billion and killed 26 people. Hurricane Katrina struck Mississippi and Louisiana cost at a speed of 120 miles per hour. It caused more damage than Hurricane Andrew because of its path was through New Orleans. The property damage was about 81 billion and 1800 people died. It flooded 80 of the city.*

4.2 Formal Language Facilitates Language Assimilation

The conversational agents who used formal language influenced students to incorporate high referential cohesion in their informational summaries while weakening the co-occurrence between deep cohesion and syntactic complexity on the posttest. Examples 3 and 4 had high non-narrativity, but the former, written on the posttest, contained high referential cohesion that overlapped words such as "butterfly" and "moth" or their pronouns across the summary to form explicit threads that connected the text for easier understanding. The latter, on the other hand, written on the pretest, had low referential cohesion and used more pronouns (e.g., "both") to refer to previously mentioned nouns, making it more difficult to understand due to fewer connections tying the ideas together during information processing. This finding suggests that students who learned with conversational agents who used formal language tended to imitate their language and repeatedly utilized nouns rather than pronouns to explicitly deliver meanings while using a more non-narrative style to generate summaries. This demonstrates that learners imitate the language of the agents in their summary writing.

Example 3. Formal, Posttest: Non-Narrativity = 0.98, Referential Cohesion = 0.96

Butterfly and moths are large winged insects with two long antennae and four stage life cycles. They belongs to lepidoptera and three body parts-head, thorax and abdomen. Both have long tongue and have tiny colored scales covering their wings. But butterflies are active in day and moths are active in night. The body of the butterflies are slender and smoother than moths. Butterflies have colorful wings than moths.

Example 4. Formal, Pretest: Non-Narrativity = 0.96, Referential Cohesion = 0.04

Butterfly and moth are both insects from group lepidoptera, both have large wings, antennae and four stages lifecycle metamorphosis, etc. Mainly they have three main body parts head, thorax and abdomen. Both have tongue known as proboscis. Their main differences are buteerflies are diurinal, have slender and smooth body, antennae have thick knobs and its larva forms chrysalis and hangs from tree branch whereas moth are nocturnal, much harier then butterflies, and larva usually spins silk cocoon and lies on ground or debris.

Examples 5 (posttest) and 6 (pretest) demonstrate that the connection between syntactic complexity and deep cohesion weakened on the posttest. Both examples used more complex syntax, such as longer sentences and complex sentence structures (e.g., *which/if* clauses, *by observing*). On the pretest, the summary contained high deep cohesion, as evidenced by the use of causal connectives (e.g., affect, cause, reason), resulting in a focus on causal explanations. However, the original text focused on scientists' predictions regarding floods in different groups, not the causal explanations of floods. The overuse of causal explanations in summaries [22] may have led to a misunderstanding of the main ideas of the text. This finding suggests that, after the intervention, students tended to reduce the use of causal connectives when generating summaries with more complex sentences. This reduction in causal connectives indicates that students were better able to identify the main ideas accurately and use connectives more effectively on the posttest than on the pretest.

Example 5. Formal, Posttest: Syntactic Complexity = 0.99, Deep Cohesion = 0.06

Flooding is second commonest natural disaster, which can do lots of damages and even death. Scientist can improve the ability to predict the flooding by observing and judging condition of the deep snow melting, sudden warming weather, still frozen ground, heavy raining, weak dam. The combined estimation will help the scientists to better predict the flooding and prevent the damages at best.

Example 6. Formal, Pretest: Syntactic Complexity = 0.99, Deep Cohesion = 0.98

Flood is most common in all disasters, Its affect every area in world, the cause of flood is excessive rain in some part of the world . Other reason is deep snow melt on mountain due to climate change, when snow is melt river over flow if heavy rain occur, its require a lot of research to reduce the damage due to potential flooding.

In summary, these findings suggest that informal and formal language used by conversational agents have different effects on learner language. Informal language is more easily understood and helps students apply summarization strategies effectively, resulting in the use of more abstract words to provide general information in their summaries. On the other hand, formal language influences learners to imitate the language used by agents in their summaries, leading to the repetition of nouns instead of using pronouns. Additionally, formal language assists learners in accurately identifying main ideas and using correct connectives to convey important information in their summaries.

4.3 Advantages of ENA

This study compares the ENA approach and the traditional approach, such as individual language features in isolation and their rotation of means. The results suggest that the ENA approach has two major advantages over other methods. Firstly, the ENA visualization displays the differences in the structure of language connections between the pretest and posttest within each formal and informal group, while the traditional methods only identified differences in one language feature in the informal group. This indicates that the ENA approach allows for identifying more subtle differences in the association of connections than the traditional methods using features in isolation. Secondly, ANOVA analyses for ENA line weights between language features provide fine-grained analyses for each of the 10 language combinations in each condition. The statistical analyses, combined with the visualization of networks, provide more information about the pattern of association than the mere presence of these features in isolation. Therefore, the ENA method shows promise in teacher-student language research for identifying interactive variations between language features compared to traditional approaches. This is particularly relevant to the study of language, which is a multilevel structure that requires multiple perspectives for a comprehensive examination [7, 24]. The empirical evidence provided by this study supports the promising approach of the ENA in discourse analyses and the design of conversational agents for academic writing interventions.

5 Implications and Future Directions

The study investigated how conversational agent language affects student language in written summaries using the ENA approach. The results showed that the language used by conversational agents affected students' use of language in their written summaries, with those exposed to informal language using more abstract words and those exposed to formal language using more referential cohesion when students wrote more informational summaries. The ENA approach was found to be more effective than traditional approaches in detecting differences in the structure of language associations rather than individual language features in isolation. Overall, the findings support that the ENA approach is effective for discourse analyses due to its alignment with the characteristics of language that integrate multiple language levels. Examples were provided to better illustrate the differences in language connection structures in the pretest and posttest networks.

Although the present study investigated the structure of language connections in overall networks of summaries, focusing on the pretest and posttest, there are additional factors that could be considered to better understand the differences in language connections. Specifically, text structures and the quality of summaries could influence the choice of language, and therefore, the structure of the network may differ. Future studies should consider conducting a more fine-grained analysis that considers different text structures, such as comparison texts and causation texts, to reveal the differences that exist between them. Additionally, exploring the differences in the structure of networks between summaries of varying quality levels, such as good and poor summaries, could better inform the instruction of summary writing in both classroom settings and intelligent tutoring systems. By examining these factors, future studies can provide a more comprehensive understanding of the role of language connections in summary writing. Finally, future research should replicate this study to explore the generalizability of the findings. Investigating how the results may vary if the formality of conversational agent language is manipulated could provide valuable insights. These findings will inform researchers on the design of the conversational language that aligns with the goals of academic writing instruction.

Acknowledgements. This research was supported by IES Grant #R305C120001.

References

1. Common Core State Standards Initiative: Common Core State Standards for English language arts and literacy in history/social studies, science, and technical subjects http://www.corest andards.org/ELA-Literacy/ (2010). https://doi.org/10.2139/ssrn.1965026
2. Fillmore, L.W., Snow, C.E.: What teachers need to know about language. In: Adger, C.A., Snow, C.E., Christian, D. (eds.) What Teachers Need to Know about Language, pp. 7–54. CAL (2003). https://doi.org/10.21832/adger0186
3. Galloway, E.P., Uccelli, P.: Modeling the relationship between lexico-grammatical and discourse organization skills in middle grade writers: insights into later productive language skills that support academic writing. Read. Writ. **28**(6), 797–828 (2015). https://doi.org/10.1007/s11145-015-9550-7
4. Galloway, E.P., Uccelli, P.: Beyond reading comprehension: exploring the additional contribution of core academic language skills to early adolescents' written summaries. Read. Writ. **32**, 729–759 (2019). https://doi.org/10.1007/s11145-018-9880-3
5. Gámez, P.B., Lesaux, N.K.: The relation between exposure to sophisticated and complex language and early-adolescent English-only and language minority learners' vocabulary. Child Dev. **83**(4), 1316–1331 (2012). https://doi.org/10.1111/j.1467-8624.2012.01776.x

6. Gámez, P.B., Lesaux, N.K.: Early-adolescents' reading comprehension and the stability of the middle school classroom-language environment. Dev. Psychol. **51**(4), 447–458 (2015). https://doi.org/10.1037/a0038868
7. Graesser, A.C., Li, H., Forsyth, C.: Learning by communicating in natural language with conversational agents. Curr. Dir. Psychol. Sci. **23**(5), 374–380 (2014)
8. Graesser, A.C., McNamara, D.S.: Computational analyses of multilevel discourse comprehension. Top. Cogn. Sci. **3**, 371 (2011). https://doi.org/10.1111/j.1756-8765.2010.010 81.x
9. Graesser, A.C., McNamara, D.S., Cai, Z., Conley, M., Li, H., Pennebaker, J.: Coh-metrix measures text characteristics at multiple levels of language and discourse. Elementary Sch. J. **115**(2), 210–229 (2014). https://doi.org/10.1086/678293
10. Graham, S.: Strategy instruction and the teaching of writing: a meta-analysis. In: MacArthur, C.A., Graham, S., Fitzgerald, J. (eds.) Handbook of Writing Research, pp. 187–207. Guilford, New York, NY (2006). https://doi.org/10.1111/j.1467-873x.2008.00423.x
11. Graham, S., Harris, K.R.: Common core state standards and writing: introduction to the special issue. Elem. Sch. J. **115**(4), 457–463 (2015). https://doi.org/10.1086/681963
12. Graham, S., Harris, K.R.: Reading and writing connections: how writing can build better readers (and vice versa). In: Ng, C., Bartlett, B. (eds.) Improving Reading and Reading Engagement in the 21st Century, pp. 333–350. Springer, Singapore (2017)
13. Kim, Y.S.G., Schatschneider, C.: Expanding the developmental models of writing: a direct and indirect effects model of developmental writing (DIEW). J. Educ. Psychol. **109**(1), 35–50 (2017). https://doi.org/10.1037/edu0000129
14. Kintsch, W.: Text comprehension, memory, and learning. Am. Psychol. **49**(4), 294–303 (1994). https://doi.org/10.1037/0003-066x.49.4.294
15. Li, H., Graesser, A.C.: Impact of conversational formality on the quality and formality of written summaries. In: Bittencourt, I., Cukurova, M., Muldner, K., Luckin, R., Millán, E. (eds.) Artificial Intelligence in Education: 21st International Conference, AIED 2020, Ifrane, Morocco, July 6–10, 2020, Proceedings, Part I, pp. 321–332. Springer International Publishing, Cham (2020). https://doi.org/10.1007/978-3-030-52237-7_26
16. Li, H., Graesser, A.C.: The impact of conversational agents' language on summary writing. J. Res. Technol. Educ. **53**(1), 44–66 (2021). https://doi.org/10.1007/978-3-030-52237-7_26
17. Lucero, A.: Teachers' use of linguistic scaffolding to support the academic language development of firstgrade emergent bilingual students. J. Early Child. Lit. **14**(4), 534–561 (2014). https://doi.org/10.1177/1468798413512848
18. Marquart, C.L., Zachar, S., Collier, W., Eagan, B., Woodward, R., Shaffer, D.W.: rENA: Epistemic Network Analysis. https://cran.rproject.org/web/packages/rENA/index.html (2018)
19. Meneses, A., Uccelli, P., Valeri, L.: Teacher talk and literacy gains in chilean elementary students: teacher participation, lexical diversity, and instructional non-present talk. Linguistics Educ. **73**, 101145 (2023). https://doi.org/10.1016/j.linged.2022.101145
20. NAEP: 2015 Reading Assessment [Data file]: http://nces.ed.gov/nationsreportcard/subject/publications/stt2015/pdf/2016008AZ4.pdf (2015)
21. Nagy, W., Townsend, D.: Words as tools: Learning academic vocabulary as language acquisition. Read. Res. Q. **47**(1), 91–108 (2012). https://doi.org/10.1002/rrq.011
22. Rivard, L.P., Gueye, N.R.: Syntactic complexity and connector use in the summary writing of L1 and L2 Canadian students. J. Fr. Lang. Stud. **33**(2), 197–226 (2023)
23. Shaffer, D.W., Collier, W., Ruis, A.R.: A tutorial on epistemic network analysis: analyzing the structure of connections in cognitive, social, and interaction data. J. Learn. Anal. **3**(3), 9–45 (2016). https://doi.org/10.18608/jla.2016.33.3
24. Snow, C.E., Uccelli, P.: The challenge of academic language. In: Olson, D.R., Torrance, N. (eds.) The Cambridge Handbook of Literacy, vol. 121, pp. 112–133. Cambridge University Press, Cambridge (2009). https://doi.org/10.1017/CBO9780511609664.008

25. Sun, H., Verspoor, M.: Mandarin vocabulary growth, teacher qualifications and teacher talk in child heritage language learners. Int. J. Biling. Educ. Biling. **25**(6), 1976–1991 (2022)
26. Van Dijk, T.A., Kintsch, W.: Strategies of discourse comprehension, pp. 11–12. Academic Press, New York (1983). https://doi.org/10.2307/415483

Characterising Individual-Level Collaborative Learning Behaviours Using Ordered Network Analysis and Wearable Sensors

Lixiang Yan[1]([✉]), Yuanru Tan[2], Zachari Swiecki[1], Dragan Gašević[1],
David Williamson Shaffer[2], Linxuan Zhao[1], Xinyu Li[1],
and Roberto Martinez-Maldonado[1]

[1] Monash University, Clayton, VIC 3108, Australia
jimmie.yan@monash.edu
[2] University of Wisconsin-Madison, Madison, WI, USA

Abstract. Wearable positioning sensors are enabling unprecedented opportunities to model students' procedural and social behaviours during collaborative learning tasks in physical learning spaces. Emerging work in this area has mainly focused on modelling *group-level* interactions from low-level x-y positioning data. Yet, little work has utilised such data to automatically identify *individual-level* differences among students working in co-located groups in terms of procedural and social aspects such as task prioritisation and collaboration dynamics, respectively. To address this gap, this study characterised key differences among 124 students' procedural and social behaviours according to their perceived stress, collaboration, and task satisfaction during a complex group task using wearable positioning sensors and ordered networked analysis. The results revealed that students who demonstrated more collaborative behaviours were associated with lower stress and higher collaboration satisfaction. Interestingly, students who worked individually on the primary and secondary learning tasks reported lower and higher task satisfaction, respectively. These findings can deepen our understanding of students' individual-level behaviours and experiences while learning in groups.

Keywords: Collaborative Learning · Learning Analytics · Educational Data Mining · Ordered Network Analysis · Stress · Satisfaction

1 Introduction and Related Work

Recent studies in the emerging area of multimodal learning analytics (MMLA) are promoting the use of sensing technologies to model students' activity in the physical places where collaborative learning occurs [3]. These sensor-based innovations have shown the potential to capture students' physical and physiological data traces with high granularity and automation, enabling new opportunities

G. Arastoopour Irgens and S. Knight (Eds.): ICQE 2023, CCIS 1895, pp. 66–80, 2023.
https://doi.org/10.1007/978-3-031-47014-1_5

to explore students' perceived experiences (e.g., stress and satisfaction) of collaborative learning in authentic settings [18]. Understanding these experiences is critical for pinpointing the potential impact of the learning design on students' cognitive and affective processes and creating mechanisms to support reflection [16,30]. In contrast, studying such physical and physiological aspects of collaborative learning using traditional data collection methods (e.g., survey, interview, and direct observation) can be labour-intensive and intrusive [14].

1.1 Wearable Sensors

Wearable positioning sensors have been increasingly used to model student behaviour that demonstrates knowledge or effective collaboration skill development (i.e., procedural and social behaviours, respectively) during co-located collaborative learning tasks [21,30]. Hall's [11] seminal work on *proxemics theory* has been used as the theoretical foundation for modelling students' interactions with other individuals and different spaces of interest from their positioning trace data captured in maker spaces [2], the classroom [22], the library [21] and open learning spaces [29]. For example, a zone-based model consisting of multiple spaces of interest (e.g., patient bed site and medical trolley) was developed to model students' within-group movements from positioning traces [5]. Based on such a model, social and epistemic network analyses have been used to unpack students' interpersonal interaction and spatial transition during collaborative learning [7]. Teachers have demonstrated a profound interest in using such evidence to support reflective practices [30].

1.2 Collaborative Learning Behaviours

However, most of the aforementioned works have only focused on capturing *group-level* dynamics. Little work has explored whether wearable positioning sensors can also capture evidence about *individual-level* procedural and social behaviours in co-located collaborative learning, limiting the potential to support personalised feedback and individualised reflective practices. Additionally, while prior studies have investigated the behavioural differences between groups with different performance (evaluated by teachers) [28,30,33], more work needs to be done to understand the associations between individual students' procedural and social behaviours (e.g., task prioritisation and collaboration) and their perceived experiences (e.g., stress and satisfaction) in collaborative learning. Understanding these associations could reveal valuable insights about whether students have demonstrated behaviours in accordance with teachers' learning design intentions and whether students' subjective experiences of their behaviours are in line with the intended learning objectives. For example, collaboration has been perceived as a potential mitigation strategy that adult learners would adopt to reduce their personal stress level [13]. Likewise, working with others has also shown positive impacts on students' affective states and learning satisfaction [4]. Thus, it is essential to identify whether students have collaborated to resolve the learning tasks or merely to reduce their perceived stress and enhance their personal learning satisfaction. Such insights could help teachers to identify potential dissonance between their learning designs and students' perceived learning experience, contributing evidence to support post-hoc reflective practices.

1.3   Ordered Behavioural Connections

Prior MMLA studies on collaborative learning behaviours have often used epistemic network analysis (ENA), a widely used network analysis technique for the modelling of learning phenomena [1,23,24,26], to capture relationships between different behaviours. For example, ENA has been used to differentiate between low-performing and high-performing groups in clinical simulations based on the co-occurrence of their socio-spatial behaviours [30] and verbal communication behaviours [32] across different learning scenarios and phases. While ENA can uncover valuable insights regarding the structure of connections among different behaviours, it does not account for the order of these connections. Such orders may be important for understanding individual students' procedural and social behaviours as this directional information can significantly alter the meaning behind individuals' behaviours. For example, students moving from working individually on the primary task to working collaboratively on the secondary task could potentially signal distraction by others, whereas the opposite behaviour could potentially represent successful identification of the primary objective. Therefore, adopting a method that can capture ordered connections among different behaviours, such as ordered network analysis (ONA; further elaborated in Sect. 2.4), can potentially provide additional insights for unpacking individual students' procedural and social behaviours in co-located collaborative learning.

1.4   Research Questions and Contributions

We address the gaps in the literature identified above by characterising the differences in individual students' procedural and social behaviours based on their perceived experiences in collaborative learning using ONA and wearable positioning sensors. Specifically, we address the following research questions:

- **RQ1)** To what extent do students' procedural and social behaviours, modelled from positioning data, differ based on their perceived stress?
- **RQ2)** To what extent do students' procedural and social behaviours differ based on their perceived collaboration satisfaction?
- **RQ3)** To what extent do students' procedural and social behaviours differ based on their perceived task satisfaction?

The current study used wearable positioning sensors and a novel network analysis approach to characterise students' individual-level procedural and social behaviours during a co-located collaborative learning activity. The x-y positioning data of 124 students were collected from 31 healthcare simulations using wearable positioning sensors. These data were mapped into eight different procedural and social behaviours that were expected by teachers according to their learning design. Three ordered network analyses were conducted to identify key differences between students' individual-level behaviours according to their perceived stress, collaboration satisfaction, and task satisfaction. The findings from this study contribute empirical evidence to support the use of ordered network analysis and sensing technologies in capturing evidence about individual students' procedural and social behaviours in co-located collaborative learning. Such evidence could advance our understanding of students' behavioural strategies, provoke evidence-based student reflections, and empower the assessment of the learning designs' potential cognitive and affective impacts on students.

2   Methods

2.1   Study Context

The current study was conducted in a face-to-face clinical simulation unit. The simulations took place in a technologically-hybrid classroom equipped with authentic medical devices (e.g., oxygen masks) and high-fidelity patient manikins with measurable vital signals (e.g., controllable heart rates, pulses, and respiration rates). The patient manikins were voice-played and controlled by teaching staff from a control room that could directly observe the classroom through a one-way mirror. Each simulation consisted of a group of four students, with two taking on the role of the graduate nurses who entered the classroom at the beginning of the simulation. The other two ward nurses waited outside the classroom and could be called in by the graduate nurses for help. Students were often unaware of the multiple events that would unfold and were expected to demonstrate several critical behaviours, including familiarising themselves with the situations, evaluating the priority of different tasks, and distributing their attention among these tasks efficiently. The high complexity of the tasks also demands students to work collaboratively with other group members to achieve shared goals.

The *primary task* of the simulations involved students working collaboratively to resolve the medical emergency of a clinically deteriorating patient after being assigned several *secondary tasks* (e.g., completing a pre-operation check and an intravenous delivery). They also needed to deal with a patient relative (role-played by teaching staff) who impatiently demanded completing her husband's patient release process (the distraction task). The simulation was livestreamed in a debriefing room to students who were not currently participating as a part of the simulation unit. As this study focused on unpacking individuals' procedural and social behaviours during the simulations, we focused on analysing these behaviours when all four students were in the classroom.

2.2   Apparatus and Data Collection

The Pozyx Creator Kit [19] was used to capture participants' indoor positioning traces inside the simulation classroom. Each participant was assigned a wearable

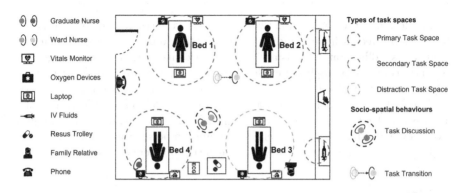

Fig. 1. Floor plan of the learning spaces divided into different task spaces.

Ultra-Wideband tag that transmitted signals at 60 Hz to five anchors, affixed to the side walls of the simulation classroom. Pozyx's proprietary engine automatically computed these signals into real-time x-y coordinates using wireless Two-Way Ranging algorithms. Positioning data was only available when participants were located inside the simulation classroom. Participants also completed a post-survey (Table 1) containing three single-item measures to capture their perceived task, collaboration satisfaction, and stress after the simulation, each with a seven-point bipolar Likert scale, ranging from *strongly disagree* (1) to *strongly agree* (7). The positioning and survey data of 208 students across 52 simulations were captured with their informed consent and under the ethical approval of [Anonymised] University (Project ID: [Anonymised]). This study focused on analysing the 124 students who participated in the same simulation scenario, where the learning design emphasised task prioritisation and collaboration as they were required to actively identify and attend to the primary task while handling the distraction and secondary tasks. Whereas the other 84 students participated in a different scenario that was less complicated and more straightforward.

Table 1. Items on students' perceived task (S1), collaboration (S2), and stress (S3).

Item	Details	M	SD
S1	I am satisfied with my task performance during the simulation	4.49	1.37
S2	I am satisfied with the collaboration performance of my group	5.67	1.20
S3	I felt high levels of stress during the simulation	5.97	1.15

2.3 Feature Extraction

A total of eight different procedural and social behaviours behavioural features were modelled from students' positioning traces to inform on their task prioritisation and collaboration (Table 2). The learning space was first divided into three different spaces of interest based on their related learning tasks and the inputs from the simulation unit coordinator, including primary, secondary, and distraction task spaces (Fig. 1). A student was registered as in a given task space if located within 1.5 m (large circles) or 1 m (small circles) from the centre of the task space (euclidean distance) for more than ten consecutive seconds to reduce the likelihood of misidentifying students' walking behaviours as working on the related tasks [10]. The students were registered as working collaboratively if two or more students were in the same task space. Together, these two conditions were used to model the first six procedural and social behaviours in Table 2. The remaining two procedural and social behaviours were modelled from positioning traces outside of the task spaces (circles) either by themselves (*task_transition*) or within one-meter proximity of other students for more than ten consecutive seconds (*task_discussion*). These proximity thresholds were based on prior studies [17,33] and were validated by experienced teachers.

Table 2. Procedural and social behavioural features.

Label	Procedural and social behaviours
primary_ind	Students working individually on the primary tasks
primary_col	Students working collaboratively on the primary tasks
secondary_ind	Students working individually on the secondary tasks
secondary_col	Students working collaboratively on the secondary tasks
distraction_ind	Students working individually on the distracting tasks
distraction_col	Students working collaboratively on the distracting tasks
task_discussion	Students discussing with others outside of the task spaces
task_transition	Students transiting from one task space to another

2.4 Ordered Network Analysis

We used ONA to analyse the differences in individual students' procedural and social behaviours based on their perceived stress (RQ1), collaboration (RQ2), and task satisfaction (RQ3) of the simulation. ONA was chosen in this study because previous work has demonstrated its analytical and visual affordance in identifying key differences between individuals' learning behaviours [6,27].

We used the ONA R package to conduct the analysis [15]. The ONA algorithm follows similar computational procedures implemented in ENA with an additional set of functions to account for the order. As in ENA, we first binary coded each student's actions in the simulations using the eight procedural and social behaviours (Table 2) as codes, where 1 and 0 represented the presence or absence of a given behaviour, respectively. The connection and unit of analysis are within each individual student, so each activity only contains the behavioural codes of one student at a given time (within 10 s). With the coded data set, the ONA algorithm used a sliding window to accumulate code connections for each student, showing how their current behaviours were connected to the behaviours that occurred within the *recent temporal context* [25], defined as a specified number of lines preceding the current line in the data. In this study, we defined the recent temporal context as being six lines, each line plus the five previous lines. This decision was made because six lines in the data represent a sixty-second time interval in the simulation, as most behaviour engagement for a given line, was contained within a one-minute window. After the connection accumulation stage, each student's connection counts were represented as a high-dimensional vector, where the connection strength and connection direction between each pair of codes were recorded. The ONA algorithm then performed a dimensional reduction to project those high-dimensional vectors onto a two-dimensional metric space. Each group's average network was summarised as a mean point (represented as a square in network visualizations) in the space and each individual student's network was summarised as a point, or ONA point, (represented as dots in network visualizations). For the dimensional reduction in this study, we used a technique that optimises the differences between the mean of two groups called Means Rotation (MR) [1] – in this case, students in high and low perceived stress (RQ1), collaboration (RQ2), and task satisfaction (RQ3). We applied MR on each of the three groups to compare the high and low conditions within each group. The groups were created based on teachers' recommendations, where students with a rating of 1–4 and 5–7 were categorised into the low and high groups, respectively, for each item in Table 1. The resulting two-dimensional space highlighted the differences between groups (if any) by placing the means of the group as close as possible to the X-axis of the space (see [27] for details).

To answer our three research questions, we created three ONA subtracted plots. For each plot, a two-sample Mann-Whitney U test was conducted to test whether the differences in directed connections between the two conditions were statistically significant. We chose to use the Mann-Whitney U test because the Intraclass Correlation Coefficient (ICC) scores for the outcome variable (i.e., ONA points) are all below 0.3 across all three conditions (i.e., perceived stress groups, collaboration, task satisfaction), indicating that a substantial amount of the variance in students' ONA networks is due to variation between groups, rather than variation within groups. Therefore, the Mann-Whitney U test is a more appropriate choice to compare the two groups. In ONA subtracted plots, both the node size and the edge thickness were proportional to the frequency of behaviour occurrence. Between each pair of nodes, a chevron was placed on the edge side with relatively heavier weights. The coloured circle within each node represented directed connections made from one code to itself, also known as self-transition. The larger the coloured circle was, the more self-transition that code had made to itself. We used a blue-red colour coding scheme across all three subtracted plots, where blue represented the high-group and red represented the low-group.

3   Results

3.1   RQ1: Perceived Stress

The Mann-Whitney U test revealed significant differences in the directed connections of procedural and social behaviours between low-stress (N = 32, Mdn = −0.12, Q1 = −0.18, Q3 = 0.21) and high-stress students (N = 92, Mdn = 0.01, Q1 = −0.18, Q3 = 0.21) among the x-axis (U = 1876, p = 0.02, r = 0.54). As shown in Fig. 2, low-stress students were strongly characterised by their focus on collaboration despite the task priority. For example, they demonstrated high self-transition in *primary_col*, *distraction_col*, and *task_discussion*, which are all procedural and social behaviours related to collaboration but for different task types. We also observed more directed connections toward working collaboratively in low-stress students, as they were more likely to transit to *primary_col*, *secondary_col*, and *distraction_col* from working either collaboratively or individually on other tasks. On the other hand, high-stress students were strongly characterised by both frequent self-transitions and directed connections to *primary_ind* from other behaviours, suggesting that these students spent the majority of their time working individually on the primary task despite their prior procedural and social behaviours. Such findings were expected as students who were left alone working on the primary tasks could experience higher pressure when trying to resolve the medical emergence of the deteriorating patient, whereas having others to help with this stressful task or collaborating on other less stressful tasks could potentially mitigate their perceived stress.

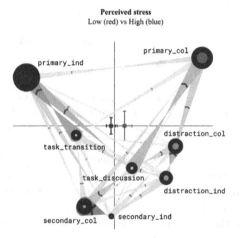

Fig. 2. The differences in directed connections between students with low (red) and high (blue) perceived stress (Color figure online)

3.2   RQ2: Collaboration Satisfaction

Although the Mann-Whitney U tests showed that the differences in the directed connections of procedural and social behaviours between low collaboration satisfaction (N = 20, Mdn = 0.11, Q1 = −0.06, Q3 = 0.29) and high collaboration satisfaction students (N = 104, Mdn = −0.04, Q1 = −0.24, Q3 = 0.15) were not significant on either axis ($p = 0.059$, $r = 0.21$ on the x-axis, $p = 0.082$, $r = 0.18$ on the y-axis), visually investigating the subtraction plot (Fig. 3) still revealed some insights.

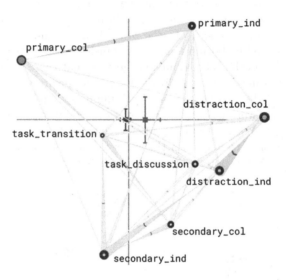

Collaboration satisfaction
Low (red) vs High (blue)

Fig. 3. The differences in directed connections between students with low (red) and high (blue) perceived collaboration satisfaction (Color figure online)

The high collaboration satisfaction students were characterised by their focus on working collaboratively on the primary (*primary_col*) and distraction task (*distraction_col*), and the directed connections that lead toward *primary_col*, such as the triadic connections between *task_transition*, *secondary_ind*, and *secondary_col*. Whereas the two directed connections from *distraction_col* to *distraction_ind* and from *distraction_ind* to *secondary_ind* characterised the procedural and social behaviours of low collaboration satisfaction students. These findings were expected as more collaboration was consistent with higher self-rated collaboration satisfaction, and more directed connections toward working individually on different tasks could lead to lower collaboration satisfaction.

3.3 RQ3: Task Satisfaction

We found significant differences in the directed connections of procedural and social behaviours between low task satisfaction (N = 57, Mdn = 0.11, Q1 = −0.27, Q3 = 0.57) and high task satisfaction students (N = 67, Mdn = −0.12, Q1 = −0.40, Q3 = 0.06) among the x-axis ($U = 1305$, $p = 0.002$, $r = 0.48$). As shown in Fig. 4, low task satisfaction students were strongly characterised by working individually on the primary task (*primary_ind*) and working collaboratively on the secondary tasks (*secondary_col*). The directed connections from *primary_ind* to *task_transition* and from *primary_col* to *primary_ind* further suggested that low task satisfaction students were stuck to the primary task by themselves, despite having other students come to help occasionally and transiting in and out of the primary task spaces. This finding is interesting as these students were prioritising the right task (primary task) but felt they did not perform well, task-wise. One potential explanation is that these students were unsatisfied with their task because they felt overwhelmed by the primary task as they were working on it mostly by themselves, whereas this task was designed for at least two students.

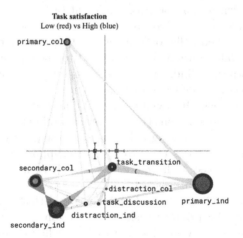

Fig. 4. The differences in directed connections between students with low (red) and high (blue) perceived task satisfaction (Color figure online)

On the other hand, high task satisfaction students were characterised by their focus on working individually on the secondary tasks (*secondary_ind*), the directed connections from *secondary_col* to *task_transition* and then to *secondary_ind*, and working collaboratively on the primary task (*primary_col*). The later finding (*primary_col*) was expected from students. The first two findings were unexpected, as these students were satisfied with their task despite prioritising the secondary task and working individually for an extensive duration. A potential explanation of such findings is that these students may not have deliberately focused on the secondary task but were assigned to these tasks during team discussion and responsibility delegation. Consequently, their high perceived task satisfaction could originate from completing the secondary tasks, which follow a more straightforward procedure than the primary tasks. Additionally, they may also have felt that they were less responsible for the primary task.

4   Discussion

This study characterised the differences in individual students' procedural and social behaviours based on their perceived stress, collaboration, and task satisfaction in co-located collaborative learning using wearable positioning sensors and ordered network analysis. For the first research question (RQ1), we identified that students who prioritised and worked on the primary task alone were associated with higher post-simulation stress than those who focused on collaborating with others despite task prioritises. This finding resonates with prior literature on the potential effects of collaboration as a mitigation strategy for reducing students' personal stress levels [13]. While this strategy could benefit collaborative learning tasks with a clear goal, the current finding further illustrated that it could potentially distract students from the primary task in learning contexts requiring them to identify and prioritise different tasks.

Similar findings were also uncovered in the second research question (RQ2), where students' perceived collaboration satisfaction was characterised by their social behaviours (collaboration) but unrelated to their procedural behaviours (prioritisation). Both these findings (RQ1&2) suggest that, in complex collaborative learning settings with multiple tasks and uncertain goals, merely capturing evidence of students' social behaviours might be insufficient to support student reflection. Additional evidence on students' procedural behaviours is also needed for a holistic view of their learning behaviours. Consequently, educational technologies and learning analytics tools that aim to support student reflections in collaborative learning need to have context-sensitivity instead of relying on a fixed set of features and measurements [8].

For the third research question (RQ3), we found that low task satisfaction students focused on the primary task alone. In contrast, students with high perceived task satisfaction were characterised by collaborating on the primary task (as expected) but even more by working individually on the secondary tasks. While such findings were unexpected based on the learning design, where students who focused on the primary task were expected to have higher task satisfaction as they were prioritising the right task, these findings resonate with prior literature on the socio-emotional connections between belonging and satisfaction [4]. For example, students who worked individually on the primary task may have felt unsupported by other group members, leading to lower task satisfaction. The high task satisfaction in students who worked individually on the secondary tasks resonates with prior findings on the positive association between self-efficacy and student satisfaction [20]. As the secondary tasks were more straightforward than the primary task, where students already knew the required actions, they could potentially have higher self-efficacy and more success in completing these simpler tasks, resulting in higher task satisfaction. These findings revealed some unexpected associations between the learning designs and students' collaborative learning behaviours and experiences, which teachers may need to address during post-hoc reflections to ensure that students have a clear understanding of the learning tasks and objectives.

Implications and Ethical Considerations. The findings have several implications for future quantitative ethnography and learning analytics research. Specifically, combining quantitative ethnography approaches (e.g., ENA and ONA) with novel data streams (e.g., physical and physiological data) could potentially reveal valuable insights regarding the temporal dynamics of individuals' learning behaviours. As our findings show, wearable positioning sensors combined with ordered network analysis can capture and unpack students' procedural and social behaviours in physical classrooms. Such sensor-based approaches could potentially empower future studies that aim to gain deeper insights into the cognitive process behind students' collaborative learning strategies [9], for example, uncover behavioural features for distinguishing between productive and unproductive collaboration. This potential could fuel the development of educational technologies that aim to automate the process of systematic observation in physical classrooms. Such technologies could potentially reduce teachers' workloads, generate behavioural evidence to support reflective practices, and make formative assessments in physical classrooms more sustainable [31]. As we only used wearable positioning sensors, future studies can combine other wearable sensors to capture multimodal behaviour traces (e.g., physiological and verbal behaviours [12]), providing further opportunities to unpack and triangulate students' cognitive and affective process during collaborative learning [3]. Additionally, sensor-based approaches could contribute to the advancement in learning space and design research as individualised evidence regarding students' interaction with the physical environments can be captured with minimum intrusion and automatically, potentially benefiting further longitudinal research. However, such data-driven approaches could also elicit potential ethical and privacy concerns, such as data misuse and unintended surveillance. Educational stakeholders must be aware that even simple x-y positioning data can contain critical information (e.g., learning behaviours) besides spatial coordinates when analysed with contextual information. Future studies must consider these ethical implications before deploying sensor-based systems in physical classrooms [31].

Limitations and Future Directions. The current approach has limitations as we characterised students' procedural and social behaviours based on their proximity to the different task spaces instead of whether they have demonstrated such behaviours. Although this approach is valid in our study as the task spaces were purposely designed for the corresponding tasks, future studies conducted outside of such confined learning contexts (e.g., in open learning spaces [29]) should validate if students are engaged in certain behaviours based on proximity, especially when multiple tasks can unfold in a same physical location. Finally, providing a qualitative interpretation of the raw data is difficult in the context of a static paper, given that the data is dynamic and position-based. In future work, we will explore representations that afford these kinds of descriptions.

5   Conclusion

This study illustrates the potential of combining wearable positioning sensors and ordered network analysis in characterising students' individual-level procedural and social behaviours based on their experiences during collaborative learning in physical classrooms. The findings emphasised the potential value of quantitative ethnography approaches and wearable sensors in supporting systematic observation and investigating the potential impacts of the learning designs on students' learning experiences.

Acknowledgements. This research was funded partially by the Australian Government through the Australian Research Council (project number DP210100060). Roberto Martinez-Maldonado's research is partly funded by Jacobs Foundation.

Conflict of Interest. The authors have declared no conflicts of interest.

Ethics Statement. Ethics approval was obtained from Monash University (Project ID: 28026).

Data Availability Statement. The data that support the findings of this study are available from the corresponding author upon reasonable request. The data are not publicly available due to privacy or ethical restrictions.

References

1. Bowman, D., et al.: The mathematical foundations of epistemic network analysis. In: Ruis, A.R., Lee, S.B. (eds.) ICQE 2021. CCIS, vol. 1312, pp. 91–105. Springer, Cham (2021). https://doi.org/10.1007/978-3-030-67788-6_7
2. Chng, E., Seyam, M.R., Yao, W., Schneider, B.: Using motion sensors to understand collaborative interactions in digital fabrication labs. In: Bittencourt, I.I., Cukurova, M., Muldner, K., Luckin, R., Millán, E. (eds.) AIED 2020. LNCS (LNAI), vol. 12163, pp. 118–128. Springer, Cham (2020). https://doi.org/10.1007/978-3-030-52237-7_10
3. Cukurova, M., Giannakos, M., Martinez-Maldonado, R.: The promise and challenges of multimodal learning analytics. BJET **51**(5), 1441–1449 (2020)
4. Delahunty, J., Verenikina, I., Jones, P.: Socio-emotional connections: identity, belonging and learning in online interactions. A literature review. Technol. Pedag. Educ. **23**(2), 243–265 (2014)
5. Echeverria, V., Martinez-Maldonado, R., Power, T., Hayes, C., Shum, S.B.: Where is the nurse? Towards automatically visualising meaningful team movement in healthcare education. In: Penstein Rosé, C., et al. (eds.) AIED 2018. LNCS (LNAI), vol. 10948, pp. 74–78. Springer, Cham (2018). https://doi.org/10.1007/978-3-319-93846-2_14
6. Fan, Y., et al.: Dissecting learning tactics in MOOC using ordered network analysis. J. Comput. Assist. Learn. **39**, 154–166 (2022)
7. Fernandez-Nieto, G.M., Martinez-Maldonado, R., Kitto, K., Shum, S.B.: Modelling spatial behaviours in clinical team simulations using epistemic network analysis: methodology and teacher evaluation. In: LAK 2021, pp. 386–396 (2021)

8. Gašević, D., Dawson, S., Rogers, T., Gasevic, D.: Learning analytics should not promote one size fits all: the effects of instructional conditions in predicting academic success. Internet High. Educ. **28**, 68–84 (2016)
9. Giannakos, M., Cukurova, M., Papavlasopoulou, S.: Sensor-based analytics in education: lessons learned from research in multimodal learning analytics. In: Giannakos, M., Spikol, D., Di Mitri, D., Sharma, K., Ochoa, X., Hammad, R. (eds.) The Multimodal Learning Analytics Handbook, pp. 329–358. Springer, Cham (2022). https://doi.org/10.1007/978-3-031-08076-0_13
10. Greenberg, S., Boring, S., Vermeulen, J., Dostal, J.: Dark patterns in proxemic interactions: a critical perspective. In: DIS 2014, pp. 523–532 (2014)
11. Hall, E.T.: The Hidden Dimension, vol. 609. Doubleday, Garden City (1966)
12. Järvelä, S., Dindar, M., Sobocinski, M., Nguyen, A.: Multimodal research for studying collaborative learning in higher education. In: Handbook of Digital Higher Education, pp. 199–210. Edward Elgar Publishing (2022)
13. Kinkead, K.J., Miller, H., Hammett, R.: Adult perceptions of in-class collaborative problem solving as mitigation for statistics anxiety. J. Contin. High. Educ. **64**(2), 101–111 (2016)
14. Luciano, M.M., Mathieu, J.E., Park, S., Tannenbaum, S.I.: A fitting approach to construct and measurement alignment: the role of big data in advancing dynamic theories. Organ. Res. Methods **21**(3), 592–632 (2018)
15. Marquart, C., Tan, Y., Cai, Z., Shaffer, D.W.: Ordered network analysis (2022). https://epistemic-analytics.gitlab.io/qe-packages/ona/cran/
16. Martinez-Maldonado, R., Echeverria, V., Fernandez Nieto, G., Buckingham Shum, S.: From data to insights: a layered storytelling approach for multimodal learning analytics. In: CHI, pp. 1–15 (2020)
17. Martinez-Maldonado, R., Echeverria, V., Schulte, J., Shibani, A., Mangaroska, K., Buckingham Shum, S.: Moodoo: indoor positioning analytics for characterising classroom teaching. In: Bittencourt, I.I., Cukurova, M., Muldner, K., Luckin, R., Millán, E. (eds.) AIED 2020. LNCS (LNAI), vol. 12163, pp. 360–373. Springer, Cham (2020). https://doi.org/10.1007/978-3-030-52237-7_29
18. Martínez-Maldonado, R., Yan, L., Deppeler, J., Phillips, M., Gašević, D.: Classroom analytics: telling stories about learning spaces using sensor data. In: Gil, E., Mor, Y., Dimitriadis, Y., Köppe, C. (eds.) Hybrid Learning Spaces. Understanding Teaching-Learning Practice, pp. 185–203. Springer, Cham (2022). https://doi.org/10.1007/978-3-030-88520-5_11
19. Pozyx: Unleash the power of real-time location solutions (2022). https://www.pozyx.io/. Accessed 21 Nov 2022
20. Prifti, R.: Self-efficacy and student satisfaction in the context of blended learning courses. Open Learn. **37**(2), 111–125 (2022)
21. Riquelme, F., et al.: Where are you? Exploring micro-location in indoor learning environments. IEEE Access **8**, 125776–125785 (2020)
22. Saquib, N., Bose, A., George, D., Kamvar, S.: Sensei: sensing educational interaction. PACM IMWUT **1**(4), 1–27 (2018)
23. Shaffer, D.W., Collier, W., Ruis, A.R.: A tutorial on epistemic network analysis: analyzing the structure of connections in cognitive, social, and interaction data. J. Learn. Anal. **3**(3), 9–45 (2016)
24. Shaffer, D.W., et al.: Epistemic network analysis: a prototype for 21st-century assessment of learning. IJLM **1**(2), 33–53 (2009)
25. Siebert-Evenstone, A.L., Irgens, G.A., Collier, W., Swiecki, Z., Ruis, A.R., Shaffer, D.W.: In search of conversational grain size: modeling semantic structure using moving stanza windows. J. Learn. Anal. **4**(3), 123–139 (2017)

26. Swiecki, Z., et al.: Assessment in the age of artificial intelligence. Comput. Educ.: Artif. Intell. (2022). In press
27. Tan, Y., Ruis, A.R., Marquart, C., Cai, Z., Knowles, M.A., Shaffer, D.W.: Ordered network analysis. In: Damşa, C., Barany, A. (eds.) Advances in Quantitative Ethnography. Communications in Computer and Information Science, vol. 1785, pp. 101–116. Springer, Cham (2022). https://doi.org/10.1007/978-3-031-31726-2_8
28. Vrzakova, H., Amon, M.J., Stewart, A., Duran, N.D., D'Mello, S.K.: Focused or stuck together: multimodal patterns reveal triads' performance in collaborative problem solving. In: Proceedings of the Tenth International Conference on Learning Analytics & Knowledge, pp. 295–304 (2020)
29. Yan, L., et al.: Footprints at school: modelling in-class social dynamics from students' physical positioning traces. In: LAK 2021, pp. 43–54 (2021)
30. Yan, L., et al.: The role of indoor positioning analytics in assessment of simulation-based learning. Br. Educ. Res. J. (2022). In press
31. Yan, L., Zhao, L., Gasevic, D., Martinez-Maldonado, R.: Scalability, sustainability, and ethicality of multimodal learning analytics. In: LAK 2022, pp. 13–23. Association for Computing Machinery, New York (2022)
32. Zhao, L., et al.: METS: multimodal learning analytics of embodied teamwork learning. In: 13th International Learning Analytics and Knowledge Conference (2023). In press. https://doi.org/10.1145/3576050.3576076
33. Zhao, L., et al.: Modelling co-located team communication from voice detection and positioning data in healthcare simulation. In: LAK 2022, pp. 370–380 (2022)

Understanding Group Dynamics During Synchronous Collaborative Problem-Solving Activities: An Epistemic Network Approach

Rogers Kaliisa[1]([⊠]) [iD], Jai Oni Dane[2] [iD], Daniel Sanchez[1] [iD], Jade Pratt[2] [iD],
Crina Damsa[1] [iD], and Jennifer Scianna[3] [iD]

[1] Department of Education, University of Oslo, Oslo, Norway
rogers.kaliisa@iped.uio.no
[2] Graduate School of Education and Psychology, Pepperdine University, Malibu, CA, USA
[3] Department of Curriculum and Instruction, UW Madison, Madison, WI, USA

Abstract. Collaborative problem-solving (CPS) is important in today's fast-paced and interconnected world. However, assessing and supporting CPS skills and actions in online and co-located collaborative settings is challenging for researchers and teachers. To identify individual and group CPS behavioral patterns, this study employs epistemic network analysis (ENA) in analyzing, modeling, and visualizing the collaborative discourse patterns of legal students working on an ill-structured problem in a semester-long course. The results showed that individual students' CPS strategies differed across the two meetings, and demonstrated varying standards for cognitive and metacognitive regulation processes. We provide implications for researchers and teachers working in CPS environments and underscore the need for multimodal datasets to understand students' CPS strategies clearly.

Keywords: Collaborative Problem Solving · Epistemic Network Analysis · Asynchronous Collaboration · Self-Regulated Learning

1 Introduction

This paper presents an epistemic network analysis (ENA) of students' collaborative problem-solving (CPS) processes in the context of legal training to model and visualise students' discourse at the individual and group levels. While there are existing studies that used ENA to study CPS [10, 11], some of the studies are neither based on authentic settings nor tightly connected to a theoretical perspective relevant to CPS. In this study, we apply ENA to a context of legal students working on an ill-structured problem, leveraging self-regulated learning (SRL) [12], a well-known theoretical perspective, to identify relevant collaborative actions. In this paper, we investigate how CPS strategy usage can be identified between group members and within the group over time. These insights, if provided to students and teachers promptly, may support students' reflection on their own collaboration process, group dynamics, and provide teachers with an informed and timely understanding of students' CPS discourse to support the collaborating groups.

© The Author(s), under exclusive license to Springer Nature Switzerland AG 2023
G. Arastoopour Irgens and S. Knight (Eds.): ICQE 2023, CCIS 1895, pp. 81–95, 2023.
https://doi.org/10.1007/978-3-031-47014-1_6

2 Background

Collaboration, problem solving, communication, and effective teamwork are key skills for employability in the twenty-first century [1]. Employers across different industrial sectors require that most school and university graduates understand domain-specific concepts well. Yet, studies indicate that graduates are often ill-equipped to deal with novel, complex, real-world challenges [2]. CPS is a complex process that requires practice, awareness of group dynamics, and learning from feedback on previous activities [3]. During CPS activities, teachers are expected to monitor group processes and provide feedback to group members about the collaborative process to facilitate meaningful collaboration. In practice, however, identifying students' collaborative actions and related group dynamics (e.g., who is doing what, how teams plan and resolve conflicts) may be impractical and unsustainable in contemporary educational scenarios [4]. In particular, in conventional face-to-face and blended learning situations, the heavy workload and limited teacher time make it difficult to monitor students' behaviours. This affects the quality of support and feedback teachers can provide students [5]. Moreover, another challenge is assessing the contributions of individual students while accounting for how they relate to the contributions of other members over the course of a collaborative task [6].

The literature suggests that the most common methods of providing feedback to students during CPS are summative assessments, debriefing sessions, and relatively simple self or peer ratings of CPS performance [7]. However, such approaches rarely allow teachers to record all the key moments they wish to discuss during debriefings and consider the redesign of courses. This is particularly problematic in co-located settings, where evidence of events during a group activity is invisible and difficult to log [8]. In addition, while these approaches improve upon our understanding of CPS processes, the techniques used (e.g., observer ratings or self-reported surveys) tend to treat students' individual actions as isolated and independent. Yet, individual students' contributions during a CPS task are part of the entire group's discourse and might affect the dynamics of the entire group since CPS is characterized as an interactive and synergistic phenomenon [6, 9].

A promising way to approach this challenge could be leveraging analytical approaches that make it possible to capture the interactive and dynamic collaborative behavioral patterns of students working in teams to generate comprehensible, actionable insights to support team reflection [5].

3 Theoretical Background

Collaborative problem solving (CPS) is a key competency in today's fast-paced and interconnected world. CPS refers to the coordinated attempt of two or more people to share their skills and knowledge to construct and maintain a unified solution to a problem [13]. In this sense, the collaborating students are required to solve complex, ill-structured, and sometimes well-formed problems without fixed answers to achieve the goal of collective knowledge co-construction [13]. However, the CPS process is a *multimodal, dynamic,* and *synergistic* phenomenon where interactive, cognitive, regulative, behavioral, and socio-emotional aspects of collaboration happen and might affect the outcome of collaborative activity [6, 9]. While all the different collaboration aspects are important, in this paper, we focus on the regulative dimension, highlighted in previous studies [14] as critical in a successful CPS process. The regulative dimension of CPS seeks to explore how students plan, negotiate, set goals, reflect, and monitor their collaborative tasks.

According to [15], SRL is a social cognitive process achieved in cycles of (i) planning (i.e., task analysis, goal setting, and planning), (ii) performance (i.e. execution of the learning task and progress monitoring), and (iii) self-reflection (i.e., self-evaluation of outcomes and the effectiveness of their learning strategies) [16, 17]. Self-regulated learners make decisions not only about what, when, and where to study but also set and adjust goals, choose fitting learning strategies, monitor their progress, and evaluate the learning outcomes and the effectiveness of their learning strategies [12]. In this study, we present the results of our investigation of students' collaborative patterns during CPS in an online, synchronous collaboration environment. Using SRL as the lens to interpret CPS, we code and analyze students' online video meetings through ENA to identify collaborative patterns and how they relate to and inform each other. The following research questions guide this study:

1. *How do students engage in CPS strategies in a group setting OR/as a group over the course of two online synchronous collaboration sessions?*
2. *How do students contribute individually in meaningful ways, with regard to CPS strategies, over the course of two online synchronous collaboration sessions?*

4 Methodology

4.1 Participants and Context

This study is part of a larger project at a research-intensive university in Norway. It aims to study how CPS can be guided by providing automated feedback to student teams about their teamwork during and after CPS in online and co-located environments. The data was selected from a group of students undertaking a master-level legal technology course called Legal Technology: Artificial Intelligence and Law. This is an elective course (approximately 77 students) that is run both online (using Microsoft Teams) and face-to-face (e.g., boot camps and physical lectures). The course is intended to explore current trends and future possibilities of using technology, software and computer analytics to provide legal services and justice. Four teachers and four mentors facilitated the course and the group projects. As part of the course assessment, students were asked to work on an ill-structured and open-ended problem related to the course content (e.g., Legal Technology: Artificial Intelligence and Law). A subset of all students enrolled in the course were recruited to participate in the research objectives. These students comprised four groups. The students agreed upon the work mode (e.g., how to meet, the resources to use, the type of task to choose, etc.) and had 11 weeks to work on the project. For this initial investigation, we chose to investigate data from one group, which was composed of four female exchange students. As part of the course project, the group worked on the topic called *GDPR Fine Calculator*. The project's goal was to create a legal technology solution as an application that can predict the amount of a *GDPR Article 83 administrative fine*. The group had two online meetings, which lasted approximately 3.5 h. This data was utilized after obtaining informed consent from all the group members and gaining approval for the TeamLearn project from the National Ethics/Scientific Committee in Norway.

4.2 Data Processing and Coding

Video data were transcribed verbatim, and later, researchers converted it into a qualitative data table, where each row contained one student's turn of talk. Metadata was added by including the meeting number and the timestamps representing the start and end of an utterance. To code the transcribed video data for use in ENA, we used a hybrid approach where codes were inductively developed by looking at the data to identify aspects relevant to CPS and deductively developed based on the three stages of SRL theory: (i) Planning/forethought, (ii) performance, and (iii) self-reflection [15]. Based on this hybrid approach, we identified ten codes in the data: *task analysis, role allocation, goal setting, monitoring, questioning, subject matter knowledge, contribution, affirmation/confirmation, socio-emotional, and reflection* (see Table 1 for explanations and examples). Social moderation was used to code the data with four raters coding it manually using a spreadsheet and meeting several times to compare the results of their respective codes and settle any discrepancies. The entire dataset was composed of 480 utterances/turns of talk. It is important to note that during the coding, one sentence/turn of talk could include multiple codes (e.g., representing planning but also subject matter knowledge). In this case, multiple codes were assigned.

Table 1. The qualitative coding table illustrating codes, explanations, and data examples

SRL Dimension	Code	Explanation	Data Example
Planning	Task analysis	Statements where students discuss instructions and requirements of the group task	Yes, to me, I guess we have to like to add what we talked about during lectures like legal design and all that, but they weren't really precise on what we should do (S2)
	Goal-setting	Statements where students discuss what the group needs to do during the session or at home to accomplish the task or set milestones to accomplish the group task	Should we make a goal or something for next week (S3, week 1)
	Task allocation	Statements where students distribute roles amongst each other	Does someone want to take responsibility for emailing them? (S3)

(continued)

Table 1. (*continued*)

SRL Dimension	Code	Explanation	Data Example
Performance	Contribution	Student poses a potential solution; a new idea or next step	Should we just try for, like, the presentation or whatever, to have a kind of like a homepage for the quiz, like with our name on the top corner and the quiz with like boxes you can like check, you know. Yeah, that's why I want to use Neota because there you can just do that (S1)
	Monitoring	At the moment, checking in on the progress of the task	Yeah, for the code, yeah, I'm still stuck. But yeah, it's getting better. Before, I had like three different boxes with three different elements, and now I'm trying to write it in only one box. Hence, it looks kinda like one long code and not like three (S3)
	Subject matter knowledge	Utterances or statements where students use subject-specific concepts or literature during their discussions	Yeah. So, Sweden doesn't have any guidelines but actually I would have to Now, I compared the max fine to the actual fine; the more interesting thing is maybe the annual turnover in comparison to the fine. So, yeah, then you also have to go into the case to find the annual turnover. And look at this one got 40% of the max fine. Wild. All of these ones (S3)

(*continued*)

Table 1. (*continued*)

SRL Dimension	Code	Explanation	Data Example
Self Reflection	Reflection	Statements where students discuss if the group has reached its goals, how the group solved a task, the kinds of feelings the task aroused and discuss the challenges in the group's performance	Yes. Yeah, no, we, like I said last time, we already made the biggest effort and work. We don't have much to do anymore, we have all the information we just have to well, but it's in a nice way. That's it. (S2)
Other CPS-related codes	Socio- emotional	Statements where students discuss or share feelings of motivation, positive or negative feelings towards the collaboration or the task	Yeah, but so for our paper for Legaltech, I mean, I don't really know how much time we need to spend on it. And since we're this week and next is like a flexible week. Right. I'm not worried anyways (S1)
	Confirming / Affirmation	Statements where students are adding on an agreement or voice support for actions, plans, Validation of others and Revoicing of others	Yeah, right (S3)
	Questioning	Statements where students are trying to figure out what to do with the task in the moment	Yeah. Is there something more we could get help with, from the lovdata? (S3)

4.3 Data Analysis

4.3.1 Analysis of Code Frequencies

The analysis started with exploring the code segments within student discussions across the two group meetings. We began our analysis with a quantitative count of code occurrences to ensure how often students participated in CPS strategies individually and across the meetings. Frequency distribution was calculated for each code occurrence across meetings and individual students (see Table 2).

4.3.2 An Epistemic Network Analysis Approach

Once we determined differences in the frequency of the codes, we sought to understand how the CPS behaviors were employed in connection with one another across the two sessions. For this purpose, we use ENA to visualize the co-occurrence of codes within the collaborative sessions. To form the ENA models, we used the ENA web software (https://www.epistemicnetwork.org/). The ENA model we constructed used a conversation segment based on the meeting students were in and employed a moving window of 4 lines to limit connections to discourse occurring too far outside the recent temporal context [18, 19]. This decision was based on the assumption that when students are working in teams, their actions or responses could be influenced by what their peers say within the moment or micro-context, which in turn forms the chronological sequence of the recent dialogue segments [18, 19]. The model is based on an adjacency matrix generated by aggregating across all lines for each unit of analysis in the model. In our case, we made two models to address the group dynamic vs. individual student question. The first model used units of analysis defined as meetings composed of students to compare how students behaved within the two meetings; meetings 1 and 2 had 3 and 4 student units, respectively. The second model reversed this orientation, comparing students who each had two units, one of which represented their behavior in each meeting.

Model 1 included the following codes: *Reflection, Goal Setting, Task Allocation,* and *Task Analysis.* This allowed for the exploration of the planning behaviors across meetings. To further facilitate the comparison of meetings, the ENA model used a means rotation comparing first and second meetings along the x-axis. Model 2 was more concerned with individual student actions within the planning process, including the following codes: *Subject Matter Knowledge (SMK), Monitoring, Contribution, Feedback, Questioning, Affirmation, Confusion,* and *Socio-emotional.* We drew this distinction because the latter codes, like *Questioning,* are more based on individual contributions to the discourse. We wanted to be able to infer how students were contributing to the larger goals of planning through these behaviors. Because we were primarily concerned with differences between individual students, we used the evenly spaced, unit circle ENA plot, which relies on the strength of code connections and disregards spatial representations for codes. Both ENA models defined conversations as all data lines associated with a single value of Meeting and used a moving window of 4 lines.

5 Results

We began our analysis using counts of code occurrence to consider how often students participated holistically in CPS strategies across the meeting times and as individuals. When we consider the meetings as a whole, it seems that the group dynamic engages more in particular behaviors, *Task analysis, Subject matter knowledge,* and *Confirming/Affirming* in the first meeting. In contrast, the second meeting sees an influx of *Monitoring* and *Socio-emotional* engagement. This indicates a potential transition point between meetings that we explore further using ENA. Students also take on different roles when we consider counts of the number of times they engage in CPS strategies. Student 3, for example, is more likely to use *Subject-Matter Knowledge* than any other students, and Students 1 and 3 are more likely to engage in *Task Allocation* than Students 2 and 4. In part, this may be because Student 4 was only active during a portion of Meeting 2, thus missing opportunities to divide labor within these meetings. Their absence also accounts for the reduced amount of coded lines for them (See Table 2).

Table 2. Counts of code occurrence between Meeting 1 and 2 and across student participation in both meetings.

Code	Meeting		Student			
	1	2	1	2	3	4
Task analysis	66	13	22	25	29	3
Goal-setting	19	9	7	6	14	1
Task allocation	21	23	18	8	14	4
Contribution	38	15	12	13	21	7
Monitoring	9	23	12	8	10	2
Subject matter knowledge	35	8	11	9	23	0
Reflection	8	8	2	7	5	2
Socio-emotional	10	24	9	12	13	0
Confirming / Affirmation	112	67	63	55	55	4
Questioning	32	19	21	18	12	0
Total	393	229	200	180	214	26

Given the discrepancies in CPS strategy usage across meetings and between students, we sought to understand better how these differences manifest in coordination with one another. To do this, we use ENA to quantify and visualise the connections between CPS strategies as students engage as individuals and as a group over the course of the two online synchronous collaboration sessions.

First, we look at Model 1, which compares participation in Meetings 1 and 2 using a means rotation to maximize group differences (Fig. 1). This model yielded Pearson correlation values of 0.97 (X-axis), demonstrating that the model itself is a visually accurate representation of the underlying data. The model explained 0.52 of the variance on the X-axis. Along the X axis, a two-sample t-test assuming unequal variance showed that Meeting 1 (mean $= -1.56$, SD $= 1.08$, N $= 4$) was statistically significantly different at the alpha $= 0.05$ level from Meeting 2 (mean $= 1.56$, SD $= 0.55$, N $= 4$; t(4.47) $= -5.14$, p $= 0.01$, Cohen's d $= 3.63$).

In meeting one, the SRL planning dimension of *Task Analysis* is central to several other group CPS behaviors, *Goal Setting, Monitoring,* and *Monitoring.* Meeting 2 shows stronger connections between *Task Allocation, Monitoring,* and *Reflection. Task Allocation* was expected to be prominent in the early weeks as students are sorting out a strategy for project responsibilities, but the occurrence counts demonstrate its presence across the two sessions. However, when visualized with the comparison plot (Fig. 1), it is clear that the role of *Task Allocation* shifts from Meeting 1 to Meeting 2. In Meeting 2,

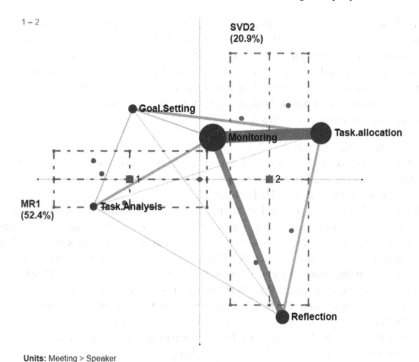

Units: Meeting > Speaker
Conversation: Meeting

Fig. 1. The comparison plot between meeting 1 (red) and meeting 2 (blue) illustrates the overall CPS discourse for meetings 1 (red) and 2 (blue) for the entire group. In meeting 1, task analysis and Goal Setting are central to several other group CPS behaviors. In meeting two, there is a shift to task allocation, monitoring, and reflection as the primary SRL dimensions.

students are both reprising roles that they have as well as *Monitoring* and *Reflecting* on the progress within their roles. This result is less surprising given that as the group progresses with the task, they are expected to concentrate on checking on the task's progress and identify any issues to address (*Monitoring*) other than planning. For example, Student 1 says, *"So basically, (Student 4), what we all said, I don't know about you, but we were all working on our cyber security papers, so we didn't really do much."* Here, they are discussing where they have gotten in their own work (*Monitoring*) in relation to the *Task Allocation* of everyone's current job. This connection does not exist in Meeting 1. However, while the findings highlighted some connection to *Task Allocation*, the groups' discourse revealed that the group did not have assigned leaders and task allocation was not done explicitly. S1 highlighted this by making the following comment: *"Also.... I feel like we didn't really assign any. Like we didn't say, 'Okay, you're responsible for this' and 'you're responsible for that'. We're just working on everything a bit together".*

A similar issue was identified in meeting 2, where student 4 was wondering how the group would proceed with the task:

"Yeah, so I uploaded the two things I did, which was the template. I was just sort of thinking through everything that we needed to include. I'm not sure if I'm missing anything out; you can just add that in. And then I just did a mockup of the design, which was somebody did a paper mockup of the design, so I just put that into a computerized format. But other than that, I was just wondering when you wanted to start with the writing and if I should just start with that, whether we're doing it all together and how that works".

In this response from student 2, we can see the relationship of *Questioning* to the *Task Allocation* code; as they surface their own wondering about the process, they allow their fellow students to chime in on what the next steps should be. For this reason, we focus on the more individual codes for Model 2.

Model 2 focuses on individual students' behaviors across the performance codes. The model yielded a Pearson correlation of .91 and .53 across the X and Y-axes. This indicates that the horizontal axis is well fit and an accurate visual representation of the data, while the vertical axis may not be. The two-plotted dimensions can be described as moving from the pragmatics of CPS, like *Subject Matter Knowledge (SMK) and Clarification,* to the more uncertain behaviors, like *Questioning* and *Confusion.* We use an evenly distributed unit circle plot to better visualize the students in relation to all of the codes (Fig. 2). From these plots, students 1–3 are similar in the types of connections they are making within the group work for CPS strategies. However, Student 4 is quite different in their network, likely due to them missing key planning elements in Meeting 1.

We can further observe differences between meetings in this plot. For each student, the units in the upper left are from Meeting 1, and the units further to the bottom right are from Meeting 2. Student 4 only has one node representing the mean because they did not participate in Meeting 1. Thus, their mean is equivalent to Meeting 2. There is no statistically significant difference between the students on either axis.

However, although no statistical differences were observed, the analysis showed differences in how students contributed to the group discussions. For example, as illustrated in Fig. 2, in meeting 1, student 1 (red) was strongly associated with *Affirmation, Contribution,* and *Questioning* behaviors. In contrast, student 2 (blue) was connected to *Affirmation, Contribution, Questioning,* and *Socio-Emotional* behaviors. Student 3 (purple) connected similarly to student 2 (e.g., *Affirmation, Contribution, Questioning,* and *Socio-Emotional* behaviors). It was observed that *SMK* was equally distributed among the students. In contrast, given that student 4 missed the first meeting and joined the second meeting late, their connections were different from the other students. For example, although student 4 had connections between *Affirmation, Contribution,* and *Questioning,* these were weakly connected. Moreover, student 4 has no connection to the codes of *SMK* and *Clarification.* This can be attributed to several things: Student 4 was not familiar with the group dynamics or things discussed before the meeting, which is crucial when working with a group. However, although Student 4 joined late, they tend to connect contributions to both socio-emotional and questioning more often than any of the other students. One possible explanation is that when Student 4 joined, they wanted to make up for their absence to hit the ground running and contribute quickly.

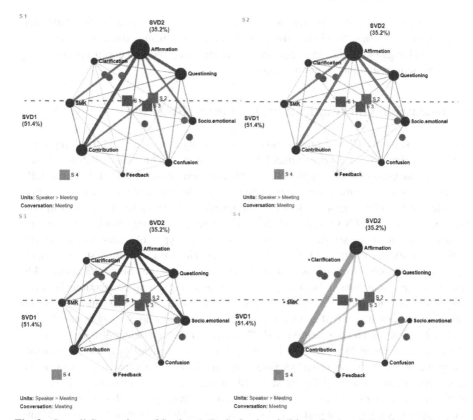

Fig. 2. Overall Comparison of Student 1 (Red), Student 2 (Blue), Student 3 (Purple), and Student 4 (Green).

In addition, among all four students and between both meetings, *Affirmation* is an important behavior that tends to connect to all other codes. The robust interconnection between affirmation and most CPS-related codes in both meetings (see Fig. 2) is likely attributed to the presence of uncertainty towards the task, which in both meetings was often demonstrated through expressions such as "I think", "I don't know" or "I'm not sure.". For example, students 1, 2, and 3 were engaged in the following discussion during meeting 1.

"I think if we because I was wondering about that as well, but if we stick to the company, it could be used for both. I don't know".

"I also, I don't know if we get more information about the paper from class because I think we're talking about the project and the planning, but they don't give us much about the paper». «Does someone know the word limit? Actually. I don't remember".

"I don't know".

[20] highlighted that such expressions not only convey the speaker's uncertainty but also implicitly request validation from the listener. As a result, students engage in a mutual exchange of validation, reciprocally seeking and providing confirmation during their interactions and interventions with peers.

6 Discussion and Implications for Future Research

Identifying students' CPS strategies and related group dynamics (e.g., who is doing what, how teams plan and assign roles) may be impractical in synchronous collaboration settings [4]. The present study supports the potential of leveraging data from students' CPS activities (e.g., online meetings) to understand how students engage in CPS strategies as individuals and as a group. Model 1 demonstrates that there are differences in how students engage in CPS strategies at the different stages of group work. Furthermore, model 2 demonstrates students 1–3 are similar in the types of connections they are making within the group work for CPS strategies. However, although students' CPS actions were relatively similar across the two observed sessions, Student 3 appeared to dominate the discussions in both meetings, demonstrating strong connections between *Subject-matter knowledge*, *Task analysis*, and *Goal setting*. Moreover, Student 4 stood out as an outlier with limited connections to CPS actions such as *Subject-matter knowledge*, *Clarification*, and *Socioemotional*. This is likely due to student 4 missing the key planning elements in Meeting 1 and arriving late for the second meeting. In addition, group members likely possessed varying levels of skillset and knowledge towards the task, hence demonstrating different standards for metacognitive monitoring [21]. This implies that collaborative teams could benefit from structured protocols embedded within the learning design or collaborative tasks, explicitly highlighting expectations regarding participation and contribution to the group task.

While the findings highlighted some connection to *Task Allocation*, the groups' discourse revealed that the group did not have assigned leaders and *Task Allocation* was not explicit. The lack of clear *Task Allocation* during the collaborative activity suggests that the students may not have been aware of the expected roles in the group activity. In such a case, if teachers identify such a situation early enough, teachers can promote role distribution by explicitly asking students to assign roles and providing opportunities to practice and reflect on their roles. Teachers can also provide feedback to students on their collaborative skills and strategies and help them develop metacognitive strategies to improve their learning.

Moreover, the findings also showed that students rarely engaged in *Reflection*. Yet, it is a crucial component of CPS and self-regulation, as it helps students consolidate their learning and identify areas for improvement [14]. In practice, if teachers are presented with information about such discourse (e.g., limited reflection), teachers can support reflection by asking students to share their thoughts and providing meta-cognitive scaffolding such as prompts and guidelines for self and group monitoring to support their problem-solving endeavors [15].

Moving towards considerations of research question 2, on modeling CPS within groups and across individuals, we have demonstrated through this analysis that ENA allows for differentiating patterns across meetings and between students, even when students are not present for each meeting. That being said, questions arise for the best parameters for such a model. For example, in such a small group, window size may have a larger impact on how students are perceived in making connections in the model. They may receive inflated connections between two codes even if they only engage in one manner just because of the frequency of the other code. We addressed this in this paper by focusing on the comparison between meetings and students, so sheer presence was not the focus.

7 Limitations and Directions for Future Work

There were three main limitations in the current study. First, the analysis was based on one group of four students and video data from meetings. While this could provide insight into students' CPS processes, a detailed dataset with more groups and data sources that capture students' learning processes could improve the interpretation of students' CPS behaviors. For example, from the analysis of the discourse, students referred to information that seemed to belong to other sources other than the video data transcribed. For example, student 3 asked other group members in meeting one to 'do some things from the to-do list.' This means that relying on one data source to understand students' CPS processes may not be adequate. In this regard, future research could consider multiple groups and leverage multimodal data sources (e.g., digital traces, assignment drafts, and revision history) to understand the complexity of CPS in asynchronous settings better. Second, this study used Zimmerman's [15] SRL framework as the lens to identify and model CPS strategies. While this framework is relevant and widely used, we found it more oriented towards the cognitive aspects of regulation and focusing more on individuals other than group-level regulation. Since CPS involves multiple people and is inherently a dialogical process, future work can consider frameworks that consider the cognitive, meta-cognitive, and social aspects of regulation. Lastly, although ENA revealed patterns and the nature of discourse individual students were engaged in during the group meetings, it was difficult to establish the interactional, emotional, and temporal patterns of students' collaborative process. Future research can overcome this challenge by using approaches that account for the recent temporal context, such as ordered network analysis [10] and combining ENA with other analytical approaches, such as social network analysis and sequence mining, to detect social interactions and CPS sequences and how they evolve over time at an individual and group level.

8 Conclusion

In this paper, we sought to identify the kind of collaborative actions manifested during CPS activities at an individual and group level in an online synchronous collaboration environment. Using ENA and SRL as the theoretical perspective to identify evidence of CPS actions, the results showed differences in discourse between students at different stages of the CPS process. Moreover, models showed specific SRL actions less prevalent in students' discourse (e.g., reflection). While the current study is at an exploratory level whose findings cannot be used to draw strong conclusions about CPS actions, the insights presented in this paper point to the potential of ENA in modeling individual and group behaviors during CPS. This information could be employed by educators as a basis for providing timely feedback and adapting learning design to support CPS processes.

References

1. OECD: What is collaborative problem-solving? In: PISA 2015 (vol. V): Collaborative Problem Solving. OECD, Paris (2017)
2. Haste, H.: Ambiguity, autonomy and agency: Psychological challenges to new competence. In: Defining and Selecting Key Competencies, pp. 93–120. Hogrefe & Huber (2001)
3. Littleton, K., Miell, D., Faulkner, D.: Learning to Collaborate, Collaborating to Learn: Understanding and Promoting Educationally Productive Collaborative Work. Nova Science Publishers Inc. (2004)
4. Cukurova, M., Luckin, R., Millán, E., Mavrikis, M.: The NISPI framework: analysing collaborative problem-solving from students' physical interactions. Comput. Educ. **116**, 93–109 (2018)
5. Pardo, A., Poquet, O., Martínez-Maldonado, R., Dawson, S.: Provision of data-driven student feedback in LA & EDM. In: Lang, C., Siemens, G., Wise, A., Gasevic, D (eds.) Handbook of Learning Analytics. Society for Learning Analytics Research (SoLAR), pp. 163–174 (2017)
6. Swiecki, Z., Ruis, A.R., Farrell, C., Shaffer, D.W.: Assessing individual contributions to collaborative problem solving: a network analysis approach. Comput. Hum. Behav. **104**, 105876 (2020)
7. Kyllonen, P.C., Zhu, M., von Davier, A.A.: Introduction: innovative assessment of collaboration. In: von Davier, A.A., Zhu, M., Kyllonen, P.C. (eds.) Innovative Assessment of Collaboration, pp. 1–18. Springer International Publishing, Cham (2017). https://doi.org/10.1007/978-3-319-33261-1_1
8. Echeverria, V., Martinez-Maldonado, R., Buckingham Shum, S.: Towards collaboration translucence: Giving meaning to multimodal group data. Paper presented at the Proceedings of the 2019 CHI Conference on Human Factors in Computing System (2019)
9. Stahl, G., Hakkarainen, K.: Theories of CSCL. In: Cress, Ul., Rosé, C., Wise, A.F., Oshima, J. (eds.) International handbook of computer-supported collaborative learning. CCLS, vol. 19, pp. 23–43. Springer, Cham (2021). https://doi.org/10.1007/978-3-030-65291-3_2
10. Tan, Y., Ruis, A. R., Marquart, C., Cai, Z., Knowles, M.A., Shaffer, D.W.: Ordered network analysis. In: Advances in Quantitative Ethnography: 4th International Conference, ICQE 2022, Copenhagen, Denmark, 15–19 Oct 2022, Proceedings, pp. 101–116. Springer Nature Switzerland, Cham (2023)
11. Wang, Y., Ruis, A.R., Shaffer, D.W.: Modeling Collaborative Discourse with ENA Using a Probabilistic Function. In: Advances in Quantitative Ethnography: 4th International Conference, ICQE 2022, Copenhagen, Denmark, 15–19 Oct 2022, Proceedings, pp. 132–145. Springer Nature Switzerland.- check paper, Cham (2023)
12. Zimmerman, B.J., Martinez-Pons, M.: Student differences in self-regulated learning: relating grade, sex, and giftedness to self-efficacy and strategy use. J. Educ. Psychol. **82**(1), 51 (1990)
13. Roschelle, J., Teasley, S.D.: The construction of shared knowledge in collaborative problem solving. In: O'Malley, C. (ed.) Computer Supported Collaborative Learning, pp. 69–97. Springer Berlin Heidelberg, Berlin, Heidelberg (1995). https://doi.org/10.1007/978-3-642-85098-1_5
14. Malmberg, J., Järvelä, S., Järvenoja, H.: Capturing temporal and sequential patterns of self-, co-, and socially shared regulation in the context of collaborative learning. Contemp. Educ. Psychol. **49**, 160–174 (2017)

15. Zimmerman, B.J.: Self-regulated learning and academic achievement: an overview. Educ. Psychol. **25**(1), 3–17 (1990)
16. Jivet, I., Wong, J., Scheffel, M., Valle Torre, M., Specht, M., Drachsler, H.: Quantum of Choice: how learners' feedback monitoring decisions, goals and self-regulated learning skills are related. In: LAK21: 11th International Learning Analytics and Knowledge Conference, pp. 416–427 (2021)
17. Zimmerman, B.J., Schunk, D.H.: Handbook of Self-Regulation of Learning and Performance. Routledge/Taylor & Francis Group (2011)
18. Siebert-Evenstone, A.L., Irgens, G.A., Collier, W., Swiecki, Z., Ruis, A.R., Shaffer, D.W.: In search of conversational grain size: Modeling semantic structure using moving stanza windows. J. Learn. Anal. **4**(3), 123–139 (2017)
19. Shaffer, D.W., Collier, W., Ruis, A.R.: A tutorial on epistemic network analysis: analyzing the structure of connections in cognitive, social, and interaction data. J. Learn. Anal. **3**(3), 9–45 (2016)
20. Johansen, S.H.: A contrastive approach to the types of hedging strategies used in Norwegian and English informal spoken conversations. Contrastive Pragmatics **2**(1), 81–105 (2020)
21. Winne, P.H.: Self-regulated learning: In: International Encyclopedia of the Social & Behavioral Sciences, pp. 535–540. Elsevier (2015)

Cultural Impact on a Global Virtual STEM Project

Ruth V. Akumbu[✉], Kristina Lux, Dante Schulz, Danielle Espino, and Eric Hamilton

Pepperdine University, Malibu, USA
ruthakumbu@gmail.com

Abstract. This paper examines discourse patterns of adolescents from five countries collaborating on STEM-related projects through online videoconferencing and the impact of culture on the program. Epistemic network analysis was used to analyze cross-cultural collaboration and interactions among learners from Brazil, Cameroon, Kenya, Namibia, and the United States while participating in the International Community for Collaborative Content Creation. Guided by the transfer and adoption of universal principles theory and intergroup contact theory, the research results show evidence of cultural sensitivity as it pertains to practices, heritage, and local STEM projects in June 2017, as well as values and language in August 2020, as learners engaged in STEM-related content creation.

Keywords: Culture · STEM · Intercultural Interactions · Virtual Learning · Africa · Diversity · Decolonization · Curriculum

1 Introduction

This paper examines the intercultural interactions of adolescent leaders in an international virtual learning community and how culture impacted the research project. In the formation stages of collaborative teams, research shows some participants are apprehensive about intercultural interaction [1, 2]. This apprehension can often hinder cross-cultural groups from interacting or initiating conversations, resulting in weak outcomes or missed opportunities. For younger populations, anxiety communicating cross-culturally among learners often impedes asking questions or withdrawal from a conversation. Overcoming this anxiety through exposure to a richer and more satisfying cross-cultural experience can benefit children in STEM-related fields in a global digital learning space [3, 4]. Researchers believe that increasing intercultural interactions can enhance learners' ability to process interactions, predict misunderstandings, and then adapt their own behavior in multicultural situations [5, 6]. Furthermore, these intercultural interactions can spark an active desire within a young learner to understand a culture outside one's own to create heightened intercultural experiences and curiosity, thus facilitating appreciation, empathy, and respect for other cultures. Recommendations are to further understand the potential impact of intercultural experiences on young learners by examining the overall development of cross-cultural competence for learners in the United States [7]. By focusing on the U.S., this study adds to the body of knowledge

G. Arastoopour Irgens and S. Knight (Eds.): ICQE 2023, CCIS 1895, pp. 96–111, 2023.
https://doi.org/10.1007/978-3-031-47014-1_7

and rationale for U.S. institutions to integrate intercultural and cross-cultural exchanges between learners from diverse backgrounds in curricula that could result in cultural capacity building for U.S. learners.

1.1 Diversity in the United States and Beyond

The diversity index in the U.S. in 2015 was 0.49 [8] and increased to 0.61 in 2020 [9], indicating that the country is increasingly diverse. Generally, diversity in the U.S. can be observed in urban regions as people from different backgrounds converge in search of work. Therefore, children from the U.S. participating in global STEM communities are not devoid of experience interacting with children with diverse cultural backgrounds, but they should be encouraged to understand and value the cultural differences when interacting with children outside the U.S. because no group is completely homogenous.

Significant differences exist between American children and children in Africa, such as language, beliefs, values, practices, and norms [10]. For example, regarding the cultural element of language, Africa has an estimated 2,143 developing literal traditions, which means that children from the continent speak and write in languages other than English, thus promoting literacy in the local language [10, 11]. In the past, oral tradition was the main form of transferring knowledge. Language is only one example of the significant differences within countries. An understanding of the diversity of learners in a global learning community could lead to program designers creating more culturally conscious curricula. It could also result in students learning from peers' cultural competencies, which could be beneficial for future collaboration with people from diverse societies. Teaching STEM learners in a global community with significantly diverse backgrounds and colonial histories opens the doors to conversations about decolonizing curricula.

1.2 Decolonization of the Curriculum

Most education systems serving multicultural and Indigenous societies are grounded in Eurocentric and colonial-era worldviews. Eurocentric ideas have "shaped the boundaries of thought and behavior for individuals and institutions globally," as far back as the 14th century [10 p. 11], [12]. Decolonization is a call to address or reverse the negative impacts of colonialism on Indigenous peoples and their communities at all levels of education [13, 14]. Calls to decolonize the curriculum show that Indigenous communities desire their children's education to reflect local culture and context [15]. Creating culturally relevant curricula in the U.S. is as critical as revising curricula of nations such as Cameroon, Kenya, Namibia, and Brazil. These are countries that are significantly different from the U.S. but share similarities in the representation of Indigenous peoples in their curriculums. These countries' education systems did not prioritize the local culture for centuries.

Curricula that integrate learners' cultures can motivate and encourage engagement and heighten the learners' self-esteem, as it is believed the differences in learning across cultures can be decreased when the cultural background of the learner is taken into consideration [10, 16, 17]. Even though this topic is larger than the scope of this study, it is relevant because STEM programs with learners from diverse cultural backgrounds often prioritize hard skills and put very little emphasis on the local culture and context of the learner. Therefore, the need to create culturally relevant content is not limited to urban areas such as Nairobi, the capital of Kenya, where learners come from diverse backgrounds or regions. Integrating culture into education creates culturally relevant education and culturally conscious learners [10, 15].

Research shows that education in the Kisii tribe of Kenya is not culturally relevant, even though Kenya has made great strides in integrating local cultures into the curricula, underscoring the need for continuous efforts toward augmenting or decolonizing the curriculum [10, 18]. Conducting research, creating culturally relevant curricula, and creating content that prioritizes the local culture and context of the learners by integrating elements from their culture into the curriculum are steps toward the decolonization of education for learners from countries with colonial backgrounds [10, 13]. This can also result in a decolonized mindset where the learners can apply information from their culture and context to STEM learning, thus respecting their cultural ways of being and allowing them to experience and share their authentic selves with others in a global learning community [12, 18].

1.3   The International Community for Collaborative Content Creation (IC4)

The IC4 project was established in 2017. The research examined the changes that occur in students' learning when international collaborative teams in a virtual community function, as teachers helped students better understand one another and their STEM topics. IC4 clubs sought willing and open-minded U.S. participants ages 12–17 to build cross-cultural collaboration skills by interacting with students globally in an online community. Students from Brazil, Cameroon, Kenya, Namibia, and the U.S. interacted and collaborated in a digital maker space environment to create and share STEM-focused projects [19]. The IC4 program encouraged the exchange of ideas through collaborative projects and intercultural interactions.

The intercultural interactions of learners who participated in the IC4 program were examined. Guided by the transfer and adoption of universal principles (TAUP) model, and intergroup contact theory, epistemic network analysis (ENA) was applied to compare the transcriptions collected from two global meetups, one in June 2017 and one in August 2020. The TAUP model is an emerging framework that was applied to this research for validation.

2   Theory

2.1   Intergroup Contact Theory

Intercultural contact is any form of connection between people from different cultures, resulting in intergroup contact. Allport's [20] intergroup contact theory holds that interaction between members of diverse groups enhances outcomes when guided by situational equality, mutual goals, intergroup cooperation, support from leadership, and friendship [21]. During intergroup contact, also called cross-cultural collaboration or intercultural interactions of students from diverse backgrounds, positive learning outcomes can be hindered by apprehension.

In the forming stages of collaborative teams, research shows participants are apprehensive about intercultural communication, resulting in negative cultural adaptation [1, 2]. Apprehension can stop individuals in cross-cultural groups from interacting or initiating conversations essential for project completion, thus resulting in weak outcomes and missed opportunities [2]. Missed opportunities refer to instances in which learners are too anxious to ask questions, engage in dialogue, or provide their opinions. An important skill in intercultural interactions is overcoming anxiety for a rich and satisfying cross-cultural experience [2–4]. Intercultural interaction also enhances individuals' ability to process interactions, predict misunderstandings, and adapt their behavior in multicultural situations [2, 5, 6]. An active desire to understand a culture outside one's own can create better intercultural experiences, curiosity, appreciation, empathy, and respect for the others' culture [5, 7].

Societies' interconnectedness and multicultural nature require programs designed to develop intercultural competence. Perry and Southwell [7] asserted that more studies examining the development of intercultural competence for K–12 learners are essential. The IC4 research team facilitated intergroup interactions aimed at learning STEM skills in a cross-cultural context for learners from diverse sociocultural and economic backgrounds. The program encouraged the participants to exchange ideas and intercultural interactions through collaborative content development by diverse teams within the IC4 learning community.

2.2 Decoloniality

Conversations about decolonizing the curriculum often follow a decoloniality theory, which is generally viewed as removing all colonial influences from the curriculum which is not feasible in 21st-century societies in which globalization is the norm [21]. Today's societies are interconnected through access to global communication tools, creating a reality with extreme ideological or cultural positions in almost every area of life, including education [22]. Technology has made working and learning across cultures easier, and students can learn, interact, and influence each other, which is critical for learners to understand and interact with learners from Eurocentric worldviews. Césaire [23] suggested that advocates of decolonization learn and understand the past and use that information to improve the present and the future.

In a more realistic sense, decoloniality encourages and prioritizes culturally relevant intellectual pursuits by integrating cultural factors, such as spirituality, values, norms, and beliefs into teaching and learning [10]. This perspective aims to diminish the effects of Eurocentric worldviews on Indigenous learners. Knowledge shared irrespective of the local culture of the learner can lead to the mimicry of western ways of being and culture and a low self-reference or fractured identity [10, 13]. Learners who can apply information taught in class to their local cultural context are able to be authentic, recall information faster, and have better understanding and confidence, resulting in a sense of self and identity [12, 13, 24]. When students learn about histories, places, and things that are not part of their environment such as snow and apples, it is harder to conceptualize and create a barrier to learning [10]. For a more equitable and relevant education that preserves the learner's identity, it is necessary to integrate culturally relevant frameworks into the learning process that support learning for children from colonial and Indigenous communities.

2.3 The Transfer and Adoption of Universal Principles (TAUP)

The TAUP model was designed to support learning for students from countries with colonial and Indigenous backgrounds or in a multicultural environment. The model encourages a symbiotic relationship between a learner, their local cultural context, and a culture different from their own [10]. In this relationship, knowledge adopted or acquired is implemented outside the learning community, and knowledge acquired outside supports classroom learning (see Fig. 1). This means that learning is influenced by teachers, parents, students, school systems, local culture, local context, and the school system or curriculum.

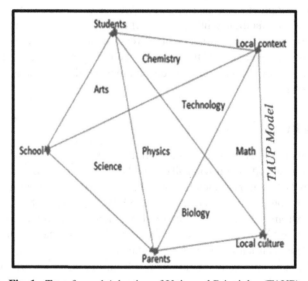

Fig. 1. Transfer and Adoption of Universal Principles (TAUP)

The TAUP model is grounded in social learning, and situated cognition developed following ethnographic research in the Kisii tribe of Kenya using focus group interviews with 60 participants ages 12–70. The research data were collected using semistructured interviews of eight focus groups comprised of teachers ($n = 17$), students ($n = 17$), parents ($n = 14$), administrators ($n = 6$), and cultural experts ($n = 6$). A thematic analysis indicated nine elements of cultural relevance for Kisii K–12 schools: (a) rite of passage or initiation, (b) language, (c) heritage, (d) oral traditions, (e) beliefs, (f) values, (g) reward and punishment, (h) local STEM, and (i) practice over theory [10]. The ENA tool was used to analyze the data further, and the nine elements from the thematic analysis were used as codes to create visualizations of the relationships and structure of connections in the data. Figure 2 shows the nine elements from the thematic

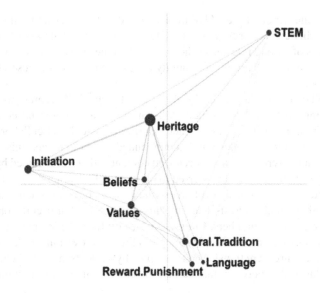

Fig. 2. Sample Relationship Between Codes

analysis and provides an example of the connections made by the codes, modeling what is expected in the analysis section of this paper.

A key component of the TAUP model is the requirement that learners process information through the lens of culture. In the case of Kisii, the nine cultural elements represented in Fig. 3 are integrated into the education process using the cultural integration and augmentation (CIA) framework [10]. It provides a model of the cultural elements suggested for teaching and learning for Kisii K–12 schools.

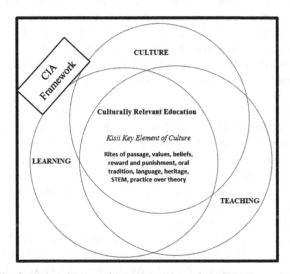

Fig. 3. Cultural Integration and Augmentation (CIA) Framework

The CIA framework and the TAUP model were developed in the Kisii research for adaptation for other education communities. Other tribes can repeat the same research to find the elements of culture relevant to the group. The nine elements can be used with or without adaptation to the learning community or research project because of the broad definition of codes.

In Fig. 3, STEM is referred to as "local STEM." Local STEM represents alternative ways of thinking about STEM or hard skills in the local culture and context while encouraging cultural sensitivity and capacity during cross-cultural collaborations [10, 25]. Building upon the nine elements recommended by participants, this framework encourages learners to create culturally relevant content and projects guided by universal STEM principles, which can be transferred to or adopted by learners. Learning through the lens of culture, a continuously evolving social construct, requires active and diverse participants with mutual interests learning through cross-cultural collaboration with support from community members. Cultural sensitivity from the learners' perspectives in addition to seven of the nine cultural elements in Fig. 3 were examined. It was assumed that elements of culture were transferred or adopted by students in the IC4 clubs through a symbiotic relationship between the learner, the classroom, the local culture, and the local context.

3   Methods

3.1   Sampling

The intercultural interactions of learners in the IC4 program were examined in this quantitative ethnography research. The discourse data in this study are from the 2017 group of six students from Kenya, Namibia, and the U.S. and the 2020 meetup of seven learners from Brazil, Cameroon, Kenya, and the U.S. IC4 participants ranged in age from 12–17, were either enrolled in middle school or high school, and opted into the IC4 program based on their own personal interest in STEM. Projects on STEM topics allowed IC4 participants to think critically about how to resolve issues within their local communities and then translate their methodology and thinking into language commonly understood by the other global participants when presenting at weekly IC4 meetups. This study focused on cultural elements transferred and adopted by students during two meetups.

The IC4 project recruited from the participating nations and video-recorded meetups during the program from 2017 to 2022, and the participants for this research were selected in the years 2017–2020. Participants enrolled in the program mainly through the secondary or high schools they attended. IC4 facilitators in the countries of origin aided recruitment through their professional networks. Forms were sent via e-mail to the facilitators for schools', students', and parents' consent. Students without signed consent forms were excluded from the program. The students interested in the program required access to the internet, a computer, or a mobile device for content creation and video conferencing. Participants were expected to be interested in STEM and complete STEM assignments in the IC4 program. Students who faced technical issues logging in to meetup sessions were encouraged to post a prerecorded video or PowerPoint presentation on Slack, an instant messaging program. Peers were encouraged to review the posting and provide feedback. The data for this research were selected from meetups.

3.2 Data Collection and Analysis

The meetups were approximately one hour, and recordings were transcribed. An utterance, or turn of talk by each learner, was represented by one line of data. Each turn of talk was coded independently by two raters using a codebook (Table 1) consisting of eight constructs organized around two categories: (a) soft skills transferred or adopted and (b) hard skills transferred or adopted. The codebook was developed from the nine elements of culture for teaching and learning in K–12 schools and supported by the TAUP model for augmenting the education of children from diverse cultural or colonial backgrounds [10]. Culture consists of universal principles or constructs, such as beliefs, values, and language, which have a broad meaning generally understood by all people but differing in application or attributes to people in different communities. They can create diverging views in multicultural learning environments. For instance, Christians and Muslims all believe in God, but their practices and names for the deity differ. Belief and the rest of the codes are, therefore, universal and unifying principles with unique inferences based on the ascribed meaning and cultural context of the learner.

Table 1. Codebook of Constructs Included in the Analysis

Category	Code	Description
Soft Skills Transferred or Adopted	Beliefs	Beliefs connected to spirituality, religion, life after death, and taboos: *("Abagusii, we have a lot of beliefs that does not go with other tribes."* *For instance, the belief that if a woman "climb up the roof and start putting the iron sheets. It is a bad omen," and she will be barren.")*
	Values	Respect, hard work, discipline, morality, unity, love, courage, trust: *("The child is now a grown-up and should behave with uttermost respect ..." "There was a lot of love among the children... Sharing the same Skins.")*
	Practices	Practices are norms and customs, ways of being such as caning, rewards: *"Pupils need something material"* as an incentive to *"keep working hard...")*

(continued)

Table 1. (*continued*)

Category	Code	Description
	Heritage	Food, cooking, location, names, clothing styles, history: (*"I'm a Kisii because I eat the Ugali from millet."*)
	Oral Traditions	Songs, proverbs, stories, music, dance: (*"At school, they should integrate the Kisii stories as a refreshment when we are bored, mix stories with chemistry."*)
	Language	Intercultural communication, speaking in a language other than English: (*"You can use that language that a kid understands better."*)
	Cultural Sensitivity	Awareness, knowledge, respect of the other, and understanding [14]
Hard Skills Transferred or Adopted	Local STEM	Local ways of thinking about STEM or local resources and material: (*"In Kisii culture, you know we had people who were experts performing surgery. They will just open your head without going into hospital and somebody survives."*)

The codebook comprised the codes: (a) beliefs, (b) values, (c) practice, (d) heritage, (e) oral traditions, (f) language, and (g) local STEM from the CIA framework. They were used to study the soft and hard skills transferred and adopted and the evidence of cultural sensitivity following intergroup interactions [5, 10, 20, 21, 25]. Two raters agreed on the codebook and final coding of research data through a social moderation process [26]. Social moderation by two raters ensured that there was consistency in coding the turns of talk before utilizing the ENA software. Raters also agreed on the interpretation of the results from the analysis, increasing the confidence level of the finding.

3.3   Epistemic Network Analysis (ENA)

ENA is a quantitative ethnographic tool that measures the structures of connections in data and creates visualizations of the relationships between the elements of culture or codes in learners' discourse [27]. ENA was used to model the co-occurrences and connections between the codes by quantifying their co-occurrences in the recent temporal context [28]. For this analysis, a unit of analysis was defined as a turn of talk taken by an IC4 participant. A moving window of size 7 was used to model the co-occurrences of codes between a given line and six preceding lines in the same conversation. ENA simultaneously analyzes all networks and creates a set of networks that can be compared visually.

4 Results

Figure 4 shows the mean positions for all data sets. Findings show high confidence levels and strong positive correlations of 0.99 (Pearson) and 0.85 (Spearman) for the first dimension, and 0.94 (Pearson) and 0.69 (Spearman) for the second dimension. A Mann-Whitney test shows that data sets are statistically significantly different at the alpha $= 0.05$ level at the X axis and Y axis.

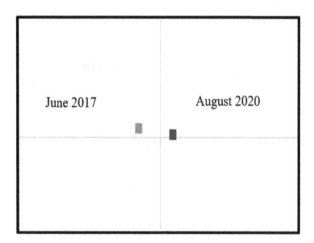

Fig. 4. Mean Position for Data Set Visualization

Discourse provides evidence of cultural sensitivity, language, practices, heritage, and values, which are positive results of the connection between the learners from diverse cultures as they interacted, collaborated, transferred, and adopted cultural elements and STEM knowledge [10, 20].

4.1 IC4 Global Meetup June 2017

The first analysis consisted of a meetup in 2017. Figure 5 presents the ENA model reflecting the discourse pattern of learners as they engaged in and shared their STEM-related projects. Strong connections were visible among the codes of heritage and local STEM. Strength in the connections between local STEM and heritage suggests that learners expressed STEM concepts and ideas through the lens of their personal cultural experiences. An example of this discourse was captured by a Kenyan learner regarding soil enrichment: "I just have that passion about making a video about this so that's all that I considered." Triangulation among the codes local STEM, heritage, and cultural sensitivity further suggests that learners were aware of the cultural differences and diversity among them as they interacted. An example of this discourse was captured between U.S., Kenyan, and Namibian learners as they shared where they were from:

Kenyan Learner: I'm from Kenya

U.S.: I'm from U.S.A.

Kenyan Learner: I'm from St. Aloysius Gonzaga in Kenya.

Namibian Learner: I'm joining you guys from Okahandja. Yeah, I'm schooling at [Namibia].

Discourse data show triangulation among local STEM, cultural sensitivity, and practices expressed by learners who spoke of local cultures and practices, as indicated in the presentations specific to their country. Connections of beliefs, oral traditions, language, and values were nonexistent, and participants made no references to these codes in the discourse, as seen in Fig. 5.

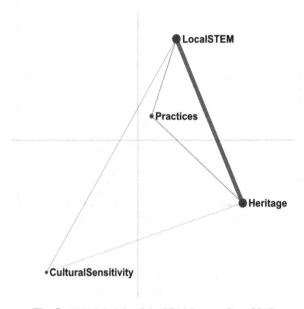

Fig. 5. ENA Models of the IC4 Meetups June 2017

4.2 IC4 Global Meetup August 2020

The second analysis consisted of a meetup in 2020. Figure 6 presents the ENA model reflecting the discourse pattern of the learners as they engaged and shared STEM-related projects about three years later. None of the students from June 2017 participated in the August 2020 meetup. A strong connection between language and local STEM can be seen.

This connection shows that non-English speaking participants of IC4 communicated about STEM-related content through an English translator and facilitator. This connection is significant as it suggests that, as the IC4 program matured, non-English speaking

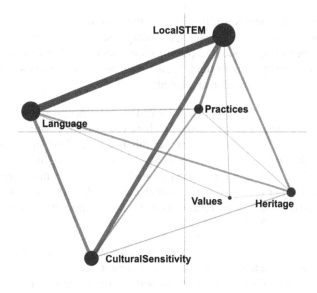

Fig. 6. ENA Models of the IC4 Meetups August 2020

learners were confident participating in the IC4 program and contributing to the conversations within the meetup. In addition, both English and non-English speakers elected to translate their presentations into writing for all to understand. An example of this discourse can be seen in the following utterances between a learner from Cameroon and the translator:

> Cameroonian Learner: "Those who are the Portuguese, we have the translation. If they want to know more, they can read it below."
>
> Translator: "[They] really loved your guys' presentation, and they really appreciate you guys having also translated into Portuguese once again. So, thank you so much."

The thick edges between local STEM and cultural sensitivity are much more pronounced when compared to Fig. 5, suggesting the IC4 participants acknowledged the presence of other cultures, allowing for cultural interactions to be more prominent as the program matured. Students applied their learning to the local context through the STEM projects they created. A learner from Cameroon shared about the importance of medical plants having gathered information from online resources:

> So, to conclude, medicinal plants are inseparable from local livelihoods because they have long been collected, consumed, and managed through local customs and knowledge. Management of traditional therapies is urged because the therapies are empirical and knowledge that is often culturally inherited. However, traditional therapies are currently being eroded due to changing lifestyles, perceptions, social transformation, and acculturation.

The students from Cameroon utilized Zoom conferencing software to transfer knowledge about a local fruit, which they had previously discussed in another project. Even though this was outside this meetup's presentation content, the learners understood the need for peers, especially those in the U.S., to visualize the materials they used in their projects. A learner from Cameroon explained:

So last week, we talked about bitter cola, and so some people don't know what bitter cola is. So today we just decided to show you how bitter cola looks as you can see, this is bitter cola. As you can see this is a fruit. When it bends, this is how it looks like. When you open it now, you will see the fruit inside. When you remove the bitter cola inside, you need to wash it. When you finish washing it, you will dry it. After drying it, this is how the bitter cola looks like after drying. When you...When you peel the bitter cola, it is white inside and has some nuts, so it is one that is good. You can eat it now.

While coded utterances of beliefs and oral traditions were absent again in Fig. 5, codes of values and language did surface, suggesting a deeper cultural experience as the IC4 program matured and learners continued to experience various cultures in the virtual setting. The relationships between cultural elements in Fig. 5 are local STEM, heritage, practices, and cultural sensitivity, and in Fig. 6, local STEM, language, cultural sensitivity, heritage, values, and practices made connections.

The difference between the strength of the connections or thickness of the edges in Fig. 6 indicates increased intercultural contact and students' ability to collaborate cross-culturally while transferring cultural knowledge and information from their local contexts. Codes that made no significant connections are hidden from Figs. 5 and 6. In Fig. 5, these codes are beliefs, values, language, and oral transition, while in Fig. 6 the codes consist of beliefs and oral traditions.

4.3 Discussion

In the 2020 meeting (Fig. 5), learners expressed cultural sensitivity to other global learners by translating their projects. Namibia and U.S. learners discussed differences in technology and ideas for cross-cultural collaboration without the help of facilitators. A U.S. student stated, "We could talk about how our video equipment differs being in the different countries that we are in," but a learner from Namibia had the confidence to say, "So I have an idea. ...[We] can work on a photography project, maybe." This learner showed no sign of apprehension, which often hinders the learner from initiating conversations.

A learner in the 2020 meetup indicated a desire for inclusivity and accomplishing a mutual goal by asking other participants in the group the question, "Is there anything the rest of you guys would be interested in taking pictures of if we chose photography?" This question also shows the desire to engage in a project that was enjoyable as well as culturally relevant.

Following the TAUP model, learners applied universal STEM principles and knowledge from the IC4 project in their local communities while highlighting their cultural values by solving an issue in the community. For example, in 2020, in a conversation with a Brazilian student, a Kenyan learner stated, "We [are] still giving them to the most vulnerable. [In a] few months, we will start selling them out at a very cheaper price." This is evidence that participants were applying skills from IC4 to solve problems in their communities.

Comparing the 2017 and 2020 virtual global meetups, cultural sensitivity was more prominent as the IC4 program matured due to a stronger presence of cultural knowledge, projects that prioritized the local context, and learners' confidence when interacting with others outside their own culture. The 2020 utterances showed no apprehension as participants easily discussed future projects, observed through the discourse of IC4 learners as they interacted and initiated conversations. Learners selected projects based on their interests and their local cultural context, referred to as local STEM. Students also translated their content into Portuguese or English to enable a better understanding of their presentations by peers.

5 Conclusion

Intercultural interactions of participants in the IC4 program had positive outcomes for learners in the global virtual STEM learning community. Findings show high confidence levels and strong positive correlations between variables, with the data sets statistically significantly different at the alpha $= 0.05$ level. Positive relationships were evidenced by the codes (a) language, (b) values, (c) heritage, (d) practices, (e) cultural sensitivity, and (f) local STEM. This finding supports Allport's [19] intergroup contract theory, which states that intercultural contact occurs and enhances outcomes when people from diverse cultures connect with mutual goals and intergroup cooperation [22].

The data also show that learners from diverse cultural backgrounds adopted and transferred elements of culture and local STEM knowledge, validating the TAUP model and the CIA framework, evident in the strong connections between local STEM, language, and cultural sensitivity (Fig. 5). Learners augmented their projects by integrating elements of culture, such as values and practices (Fig. 6) from their local context, thus creating more culturally relevant STEM content. The strong connections between elements of culture transferred or adopted by learners provide evidence of the impact of culture on IC4, a global virtual STEM project.

These findings imply that U.S. institutions should integrate intercultural and cross-cultural communication and collaborations into curricula to enhance learners' experiences and develop cultural capacity. Cross-cultural collaboration can also provide U.S. learners with alternative methods of solving STEM-related problems. These can enable U.S. learners to better interact with and learn from diverse people.

A limitation and bias of the study appeared in the lack of uniformity in the data sets. Even though learners in the selected data sets attended more than one meetup, students in the 2017 group were different from those in the August 2020 group. This study, therefore, did not measure an increase or decrease in the cross-cultural competence of the learners over time. Students in the study were exposed to the cultures of others through collaboration, but further research is necessary to determine the long-term impact of the cultural knowledge transferred and adopted by peers and whether any evidence exists of learners applying the competencies after leaving the program.

Acknowledgment. The authors wish to acknowledge the generous support of the US National Science Foundation (#2109443) for support of the research that this paper presents. The views expressed in this paper are those of the authors and not of the National Science Foundation.

References

1. Beom, K.: The influence of internet and intercultural communication apprehension on socio-cultural adaptation. In: Paper presentation. The International Communication Association, San Diego, CA, United States (2003)
2. Neuliep, J.W.: The relationship among intercultural communication apprehension, ethnocentrism, uncertainty reduction, and communication satisfaction during initial intercultural interaction: an extension of anxiety and uncertainty management (AUM) theory. J. Intercult. Commun. Res. **41**(1), 1–16 (2012). https://doi.org/10.1080/17475759.2011.623239
3. Bedwell, W.L., Wildman, J.L., DiazGranados, D., Salazar, M., Kramer, W.S., Salas, E.: Collaboration at work: an integrative multilevel conceptualization. Hum. Resour. Manag. Rev. **22**(2), 128–145 (2012). https://doi.org/10.1016/j.hrmr.2011.11.007
4. Salazar, M., Salas, E.: Reflections of cross-cultural collaboration science. J. Organ. Behav. **34**(6), 910–917 (2013). https://doi.org/10.1002/job.1881
5. Bennett, J., Bennett, M.: Developing intercultural sensitivity: an integrative approach to global and domestic diversity. In: Landis, D., Bennett, J.M., Bennett, M.J. (Eds.) Handbook of intercultural training, pp. 147–165. SAGE Publications (2004). https://doi.org/10.4135/978 1452[23]1129.n6
6. Herrington, T.K.: Crossing global boundaries: beyond intercultural communication. J. Bus. Tech. Commun. **24**(4), 516–539 (2010). https://doi.org/10.1177/1050651910371303
7. Perry, L.B., Southwell, L.: Developing intercultural understanding and skills: models and approaches. Intercult. Educ. **22**(6), 453–466 (2011). https://doi.org/10.1080/14675986.2011. 644948
8. Luiz, J.: The impact of ethno-linguistic fractionalization on cultural measures: dynamics, endogeneity and modernization. J. Int. Bus. Stud. **46**(9), 1080–1098 (2015). https://doi.org/ 10.1057/jibs.2015
9. United States Census Bureau: The chance that two people chosen at random are of different race or ethnicity groups has increased since 2010. (2021)https://www.census.gov/library/stories/2021/08/2020-united-states-population-more-racially-ethnically-diverse-than-2010. html
10. Akumbu, R.V.: Culturally relevant elements for K–12 education in Kisii. Order No. 29323485. Doctoral dissertation, Pepperdine University. ProQuest Dissertations Publishing (2022)
11. Amfo, N.A.A., Anderson, J.: Multilingualism and language policies in the African context: lessons from Ghana. Curr. Issues Lang. Plan. **20**(4), 333–337 (2019). https://doi.org/10.1080/14664208.2019.1582945
12. Gatimu, M.W.: Rationale for critical pedagogy of decolonization: Kenya as a unit of analysis. J. Crit. Educ. Policy Stud. **7**(2), 66–97. https://eric.ed.gov/?id=EJ868821
13. Charles, M.: Effective teaching and learning: decolonizing the curriculum. J. Black Stud. **50**(8), 731–766 (2019). https://doi.org/10.1177/0021934719885631
14. Etieyibo, E.: Why decolonization of the knowledge curriculum in Africa? *Africa Today, 67*(4), 74–87 (2021). https://www.muse.jhu.edu/article/794678
15. Hammond, Z.: Culturally Responsive Teaching & the Brain: Promoting Authentic Engagement and Rigor Among Culturally and Linguistically Diverse Students. Corwin (2015)

16. Biraimah, K.L.: Moving beyond a destructive past to a decolonised and inclusive future: the role of Ubuntu-style education in providing culturally relevant pedagogy for Namibia. Int. Rev. Educ. **62**(1), 45–62 (2016). https://doi.org/10.1007/s11159-016-9541-1
17. Irvine, J.J.: Culturally relevant pedagogy. Educ. Digest **75**(8), 57–61 (2010). https://eric.ed.gov/?id=EJ880896
18. Nashon, S.M.: Decolonizing science education in Africa: curriculum and pedagogy. In: Abdi, A.A., Misiaszek, G.W. (eds.) The Palgrave Handbook on Critical Theories of Education, pp. 449–464. Springer International Publishing, Cham (2022). https://doi.org/10.1007/978-3-030-86343-2_25
19. Espino, D.P., Lee, S.B., van Tress, L., Baker, T.T., Hamilton, E.R.: Analysis of U.S., Kenyan, and Finnish discourse patterns in a cross-cultural digital makerspace learning community through the IBE-UNESCO global competences framework. Res. Soc. Sci. Technol. **5**(1),86–100 (2020). https://files.eric.ed.gov/fulltext/EJ1265479.pdf
20. Allport, G.W.: The Nature of Prejudice. Addison-Wesley (1954)
21. Pettigrew, T.F.: Intergroup contact theory. Annu. Rev. Psychol. **49**(1), 65–85 (1998). https://doi.org/10.1146/annurev.psych.49.1.65
22. Fernández, J.S., Sonn, C.C., Carolissen, R., Stevens, G.: Roots and routes toward decoloniality within and outside psychology praxis. Rev. Gen. Psychol. **25**(4), 354–368 (2021). https://doi.org/10.1177/10892680211002437
23. Adler, N.J., Aycan, Z.: Cross-cultural interaction: what we know and what we need to know. Annu. Rev. Organ. Psych. Organ. Behav. **5**(1), 307–333 (2018). https://doi.org/10.1146/annurev-orgpsych-032117-104528
24. Césaire, A.: Discourse on Colonialism. Pinkham, J. trans. Monthly Review Press (2001)
25. Maffly-Kipp, J., Mccredie, M.N., Morey, L.C.: The self-reference effect as a behavioral indicator of identity disturbances associated with borderline personality features in a non-clinical sample. Borderline Personal. Disord. Emot. Dysregulation **9**(1) (2022). https://doi.org/10.1186/s40479-022-00189-7
26. Foronda, C.L.: A concept analysis of cultural sensitivity. J. Transcult. Nurs. **19**(3), 207–212 (2008). https://doi.org/10.1177/1043659608317093
27. Herrenkohl, L.R., Cornelius, L.: Investigating elementary students' scientific and historical argumentation. J. Learn. Sci. **22**(3), 413–461 (2013). https://https://doi.org/10.1080/10508406.2013.799475
28. Shaffer, D.W.: Quantitative Ethnography. Cathcart (2017)
29. Siebert-Evenstone, A., Arastoopour Irgens, G., Collier, W., Swiecki, Z., Ruis, A.R., Williamson Shaffer, D.: In search of conversational grain size: modeling semantic structure using moving stanza windows. J. Learn. Anal. **4**(3), 123–139 (2017). https://doi.org/10.18608/jla.2017.43.7

From We to Me: Moving Towards an Examination of Self Identity in an Online, Global, Collaborative, Learning Environment

Danielle P. Espino$^{(\boxtimes)}$ ⓘD, Eric Hamilton, Kristina Lux, and Seung B. Lee ⓘD

Pepperdine University, Malibu, CA 90263, USA
`danielle.espino@pepperdine.edu`

Abstract. This paper reflects on previous work using QE to examine patterns of discourse of adolescent learners in a virtual, global, collaborative informal learning setting. The collective impact of involvement in the project on participants' experiences was observed in various reflective interviews over the last five years. The deep reflection of this work resulted in a research shift from the general impact on the participants to a shift towards examining how such experiences shape self-identity, such as recognizing identity congruence, relational self, and overcoming negative identity fostered by master narrative frameworks. An initial examination of pre-assessment interviews indicates that younger students are still negotiating their self-understanding, leaving the potential for involvement in the project environment to develop a more thorough understanding of self.

Keywords: Community · Collaboration · Learning · Global · Virtual · Online · STEM · Makerspace · Discourse

1 Introduction

This paper reflects on the use of quantitative ethnography (QE) in an education research project over several years, and its impact on the evolution of research thinking and trajectory as a result. Initially beginning at the end of 2016, the project entailed the engagement of adolescent learners from the U.S. with learners from other countries in a virtual setting for collaborating on the development of STEM-focused media artifacts as a way to foster STEM learning. The project, also called the International Community for Collaborative Content Creation (IC4), began with participants from the U.S., Kenya, and Finland. The IC4 project's theoretical base had emerged from an amalgamation of the maker movement, the rise of user-created video, the psychological dynamics of self-explanation [1], the growth of peer teaching [2], and the changes that technology and social media were precipitating [3] that reversed many traditional classroom roles. Educators were vividly aware that students often were more capable with digital tools both to create and to store knowledge. Contemporary literature, NSF investment directions, and precursor projects all contributed to a rationale for explicitly positioning students as "participatory teachers" – that is, they were to serve as creative agents, generating

G. Arastoopour Irgens and S. Knight (Eds.): ICQE 2023, CCIS 1895, pp. 112–124, 2023.
https://doi.org/10.1007/978-3-031-47014-1_8

instructional content, by which they would learn STEM content more deeply under the mentorship of their school teachers, and develop rich collaboration skills that could serve them well in Global South – Global North collaboration [4]. The construct of participatory teaching and the related construct of help-giving in an international context became the most salient element of planning and central to efforts to win federal support.

Initially intended to focus on asynchronous means of collaboration, the energetic engagement from students when meeting synchronously on video conference calls quickly became the core interest of the project and main source of data collection. These video calls, or global meet-ups, became the source of rich discourse among participants as they shared presentations about STEM topics, provided feedback on artifacts, asked questions and reflected on things they learned.

One of the initial project aims was to develop cultural competence among the participants, and by extension, a tool to assess such competency. However, defining cultural competence for adolescents became an arduous endeavor, due to the layers involved in understanding culture. Rather, there was the realization that the project was more than just attempting to understand and embrace cultural differences, but recognize how the creation of a neutral space for learning can be one where all ways of knowing can be valued.

One of the most notable anecdotal examples of this took place early on in the project at a meet-up in 2017. A female learner from Kenya shared a science presentation about the use of eggshells. While she initially discussed the scientific composition of eggshells, she began to discuss the various benefits and uses for eggshells in her daily life activities which were unfamiliar yet enlightening to her Western counterparts. This example came up as an eye opening presentation for U.S. participants, as well as the researchers, in realizing how valuable other ways of knowing can be. There have been various examples of this since, where students are able to bring aspects of themselves beyond classroom knowledge into the project's learning space, and to enrich learning among peers [5]. While anecdotal accounts tug at heart strings, the need for formal analysis of the data to help convey these accounts became more and more pressing.

1.1 Developing a QE Scholarly Voice

Included in its funding proposal in 2016, the IC4 project sought to utilize a relatively new methodological approach, quantitative ethnography (QE), as its primary technique for analysis. While the project was pushing forward, understanding the use of QE in the data analysis was a moving at a much slower pace. With a limited understanding of how to operationalize QE using epistemic network analysis (ENA), the first research team effort examining reflective interviews was submitted in summer 2018 [6]. In this paper, the researchers sought to "zoom in" on the ENA models of individual participants and how they contributed to collective ENA model representing groups of students. This direction came from a desire to demonstrate that QE had potential for sharing stories from interview data. Shortly after this submission, the researchers participated in an intensive workshop at the lab at the University of Wisconsin-Madison which led to a better understanding of using ENA that would grow with time. The first paper directly following the workshop focused on how the participants in the project developed a shared sense of community over time [7], which began an interest in an analysis of discourse from the global meet-up data to the collective identity of participation in the project environment.

This led not only to recognition of the richness of data contained in discourse data of adolescent youth from various countries engaging in collaborative STEM learning, but the understanding that ENA could allow for the analysis of the same data from multiple angles depending on the research question. In lieu of pre and post assessments, shifts and changes among participants over time could be better visualized. With the expectation for constant dissemination that comes from a federally funded research project, this became an empowering realization that led to the effort of multiple "short term" papers using QE to analyze discourse data from both global meet-ups and school year end reflective interviews, each contributing something unique to the growing understanding of the dynamics taking place in the project. Overall, these works focused on certain group behavior within the project environment, such as examination on participation level, geographic location (country), and level of prompted discourse [8–10].

While initially led by the core researchers, papers became more led by research assistants as their understanding of using QE also developed to tell the stories they saw emerging in the growing collection of data. This included a longitudinal analysis on a long-term collaboration, revisiting community formation in a maturing project environment, and the student development of emotional intelligence [11–13]. These various papers, focused on analyzing discourse from global meet-ups and post-experience interviews to draw out findings about groups within the project learning setting, led to gradual reflection on the collective results among the studies.

1.2   Reflecting on Various QE Results to a Shift in Thinking

At the project start, the researchers were aware of the dynamics by which adolescents might see themselves differently through their participation in instruction related activities with peers [14]. When the authority figure of the teacher seeks help from the student, the student sees herself or himself differently. The teacher sees that student differently. Peers see that student differently. And the student sees peers differently. Participatory teaching through digital media creation, coupled with the plainly humane and salutary effects of students helping each other, promised to tap into and recruit powerful socio-affective and cognitive mechanisms that were underdeveloped in education research literature.

The actual sequence by which IC4 unfolded and then gave way to the current project, Asset-Based Learning Environments (ABLE), was both unexpected and, in retrospect, enormously reasonable. The expectation that students would focus on creating lessons for their peers in geographically different locations turned out differently in that students focused on doing projects of their own interest and sharing them. In a sense, the students reified the evolution of pedagogical theory, from teacher-centered to student-centered. The researchers expected that students would gravitate readily to the teachers' role, and readily embrace their sanctioned role as instructional helpers or mentees of professional teachers. The reality represented a slight shift, whereby students found ways to explore their own topics of interest and share those projects simply by sharing about them in the global meetups.

At first approximation, this seems less centered around the help-giving initially aspired to provide and more around indulging a desire by students to share their personal interests. Yet the meet-ups actually intensified the sentiments of help-giving. Students truly did, in both quiet and explicit ways, celebrate the opportunity to come alongside peers in other parts of the world, especially when there was a national income differential. Students from low-income countries eagerly crossed the invisible boundary or working with peers from wealthy countries, and vice-versa. In that process, they wound up continually evidencing deep appreciation for each other and a willingness to learn from one another, though the actual effort was less about teaching each other than about sharing with each other. Among the consistent themes of IC4 identified from meet-up data was the routine generosity students extended to each other after sharing, and the routine pleasure that students shared simply to work alongside one another. The researchers struggled as project leaders with many aspects of project selection, definition, and execution. But the students consistently lived out the project's aspirations to build a supportive community, which was originally and accurately identified as a help-giving community.

But sharing projects of interest differs substantially from directly creating teaching experiences under the rubric of participatory teaching. Meanwhile, the dynamics of adolescents seeing each other differently, seeing their peers differently, and seeing their teachers differently continually emerged in student reflections and in student interviews. Perhaps more than anything, pre-teens and teens reported developing poise and confidence through the collaborative exchanges through which they developed stronger STEM competencies. There were numerous event markers also, by which student STEM experiences appeared to transcend traditional stereotypes of under-resourced versus wealthy and that undermined traditional gender stereotypes. The IC4 project suggested to participants that unhealthy identity expectations -who they thought they were – did not conform to how they came to view themselves in a healthy, international collaborative experience. They continually report that the satisfaction and satisfaction of collaboration with peers from other countries shaped their sense of confidence, poise, and how they saw themselves in an international context.

The construct of participatory teaching and help-giving seemed a clever and compelling pursuit within IC4 project. In retrospect, the transactional component of students teaching one another way to the slight shift that focused on students sharing with each other. The emotional and intellectual energy of the sharing and support process seemed to convert to the dynamic the researchers had expected and hoped for from the outset – that students would see themselves, their peers, and their teachers differently. The participatory teaching construct had merits but the construct proved subordinate to the more pressing and important changes that were shaping how students envisioned themselves as "STEM" people in global collaboration. Realizing that this is where interactions and data took the project led simply to making that identity formation the primary research focus of the successor project.

1.3 Embarking on a New Research Direction

As a result of this deep reflection on various QE results, the researchers embarked on the aforementioned new project effort (ABLE) with a research focus on identity development. This intends to closely focus on individual shifts in how participants view themselves ("me"), alongside ongoing collective behavior observed in the project community ("we"). While aspects of the project remain the same, involving adolescent learners in a global, collaborative, informal STEM-focused learning environment, there are now some key design changes to build on the previous project. Primarily led by schools in the U.S (formerly led by just the researchers), participants will partake in not only co-creating STEM-focused media artifacts, but developing idea cards for other participants to consider responding to. Regarding composition of participants, there is a larger focus on the inclusion of learners from historically marginalized groups in the U.S. One of the key research aims is by participating in a global learning environment where different ways of knowing and understanding are embraced, students will overcome any negative identity associations and develop identity congruence both as STEM learners and as collaborative, global citizens.

The remaining sections of the paper provide an initial analysis of the pre-experience interviews of participants in the new ABLE program. While preliminary, this exemplifies the shift in focusing on how students see themselves, and how that can potentially develop with their involvement in the program.

2 Methods

The data analyzed in this section was collected through semi-structured pre-experience interviews with 22 ABLE participants in March and April 2023. The sample consists of learners spanning from grade school to high school from the countries of Kenya and the U.S., as shown in Table 1. The interview questions revolved around the learners' identity based on how they see themselves within their community. Learners were also asked questions pertaining to their interests, self-determined strengths and weaknesses in the STEM context, and their hopes or aspirations in the future. The interviews took place via Zoom, with each interview recorded and then transcribed.

Table 1. ABLE participants interviewed for this study

Participants from Kenya				Participants from US			
ID	Assumed Gender	Age	Grade Category	ID	Assumed Gender	Age	Grade Category
1	F	14	Secondary	11	M	13	Middle
2	F	14	Secondary	12	M	13	Middle
3	F	16	Secondary	13	M	13	Middle
4	F	11	Middle	14	M	13	Middle
5	F	15	Secondary	15	F	12	Middle
6	F	16	Secondary	16	M	11	Middle
7	F	16	Secondary	17	M	12	Middle
8	M	15	Secondary	18	M	12	Middle
9	M	11	Middle	19	F	17	Secondary
10	F	8	Elementary	20	M	12	Middle
				21	M	12	Middle
				22	F	12	Middle

A codebook from an iterative, grounded analysis of the data was generated and contained a total of 12 constructs, seen in Table 2. Each interview was independently coded by two raters using the codebook, who then came together in a process of social moderation to reach agreement on the final coding for 3,131 total utterances included in the dataset [15].

Table 2. ABLE Participant Analysis Codebook

Code	Definition & Sample Utterance	
Emotional Awareness	Definition:	Recognition of personal responses to situations, more focused on the self
	Sample:	"I am shy. I get nervous."
Social Awareness	Definition:	Recognition of other people's responses, more focused on others
	Sample:	[It's important to work with others, because] "the fact that it brings people together."
Technology Use	Definition:	Use of technology tools not just conceptual or subject
	Sample:	"I've made many PowerPoints about Mars and Jupiter, I presented to my whole class. Do you want to see?"
STEM Orientation	Definition:	Science, technology, engineering, math as subjects or concepts

(continued)

Table 2. (*continued*)

Code	Definition & Sample Utterance	
	Sample:	"I think, when I was in elementary like primary the science was like one subject, but it had all of these things to do with physics, maths, but we never really realized it."
Global/Cultural Awareness	Definition:	Recognition of differences that could arise based on culture, a global perspective
	Sample:	"My parents were immigrants from India and I was born here in America and I feel like learning to kind of not balance but understand my bi-cultural identity."
Collaborative Orientation	Definition:	Recognition of needing others to accomplish something, desire to work with others
	Sample:	"But then, I know it's a must to do it together that we can achieve something bigger. So yeah."
Independent Orientation	Definition:	Reliance of self rather than others in the accomplishment of something, self-reliant disposition
	Sample:	"But then I look at it and say, like, you know, I can figure this out and I can make it work."
Personality Attributes	Definition:	Individual identity, what I do or how I am, does not include future orientation
	Sample:	"Sometimes [I'm] a little funny and I'm kind."
Social Attributes	Definition:	Identification of a particular social construct grouping, social identity
	Sample:	"I also do Girl Scouts so that kind of helps definitely a lot with like leadership skills and things."
Self-efficacy	Definition:	Recognition of being exceptionally good at something
	Sample:	"I feel like I'm really strong in math and a little bit in science."
Challenge Awareness	Definition:	Recognition of not being good at something
	Sample:	"Maybe, like, sometimes I feel like I get distracted a bit easily."
Support Appreciation	Definition:	Acknowledging general help/support from a specific individual
	Sample:	"My teacher is really encouraging and really helped me along with that process."

After the social moderation process, models were generated using the ENA webtool. ENA, an approach operationalizing quantitative ethnography, creates visualization of data through the patterns of connections between constructs [16]. For this analysis, the speaker was identified as the unit of analysis and the response to a question within an interview was defined as the conversations in which connections were limited. The edge weights were scaled to 1.5 in order to better visualize the connections in the data.

3   Results

The resulting ENA network models are below, providing an overall pattern of the interviews, followed by an examination by country and school age group. Three constructs initially coded for (Collaborative, Global/Cultural Awareness, and Support Awareness) were removed from the models in order to focus the analysis on most relevant constructs.

For all the models, the nodes (dots) represent the different constructs that were coded for, and edges (lines) are the weighted connections between the constructs. Thicker lines indicate stronger connections, while thinner lines indicate less connection.

3.1 Overall Model

The overall pattern of interviews can be seen in Fig. 1, defined by Social Attributes at the top, Self-Efficacy and STEM-Orientation at the bottom and left, and Independent on the right. The strongest connections are on the bottom left constructs including Challenge/Deficiency with STEM Orientation and Self-Efficacy, which illustrates a part in the interview where participants reflect on how they see themselves in various roles. Overall, Personality Attributes are more connected than Social Attributes, indicating how students identify by their personality rather than the social in-groups they perceive themselves to be part of.

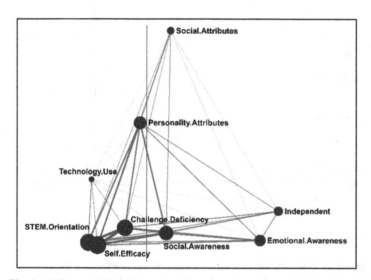

Fig. 1. ENA network model across all pre-experience interviews conducted.

3.2 Examination by Country

An examination of the interviews by country, Kenya and U.S., is see through a subtracted network model in Fig. 2. A means rotation was utilized to maximize the key differences between the two along the X axis. Participants from the U.S. had constructs more connected on the left side of the model, most prominently depicted between Technology Use, STEM Orientation, and Self-Efficacy. Participants from Kenya were mostly connected with constructs on the right, such as Independent and Personality attributes.

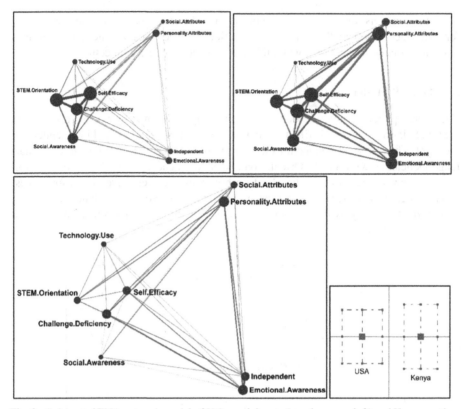

Fig. 2. Subtracted ENA network model of U.S. participants (purple, upper left) and Kenya participants (red, upper right) on the bottom left and their respective confidence intervals on the bottom right (Color figure online).

3.3 Examination by Grade Level

Figure 3 provides a subtracted network model of the interviews by grade level, with middle school in purple on the left and high school on the right. Similar to the results seen in Fig. 2, one group, the high school students, had a richer network model in general and were more focused on the right side of the model, including strong connections to Personality Attributes, Independent, Emotional Awareness, Challenge/Deficiency and Social Awareness. In comparison, the middle school group had less distinct connections, which were focused mostly on the lower left side of the model, with strong constructs connected to Technology Use and STEM Orientation.

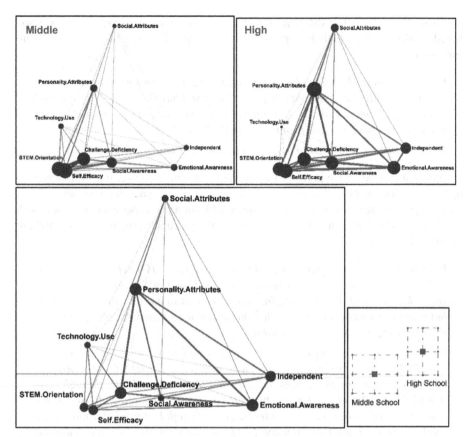

Fig. 3. Subtracted ENA network model (lower left) of middle school age participants (purple, upper left) and high school age participants (red, upper right) and their respective confidence intervals (right) (Color figure online).

4 Discussion

The examination of these pre-experience interviews provides an initial reporting of how participants currently see themselves, with the intent to track changes as a result of their participation in the ABLE project. In examining the comparison of construct patterns in the ENA models between countries (US and Kenya), students in Kenya reflected in a richer way compared to the students in the U.S., who had thinner connected models. A similar pattern was observed when examining the models by grade level, where middle school students had less rich connections, which were all focused on the lower left of the model, connecting between Technology Use, STEM-Orientation, Self-Efficacy and Challenge/Deficiency.

The parallel patterns of connection among the two subtracted models is not surprising, given that most Kenyan participants are high school age and most U.S. participants are in middle school The differences in the richness of their discourse can be illustrated by a comparison to their response to the same question, which asked about future aspirations:

> *Kenyan Student: The things I would mention I have aspirations. I aspire to be a botanist. I really got interested into plants lately so I have been doing my research since I got, I found out about this project. I wanted to find out what would happen, like whether it would assist me in some kind of way.*
>
> *U.S. Student: I would want to pursue engineering or engineering designs.*

While the more sparse network model can be attributed to age, it also indicates an opportunity for the project experience to have a lasting impact that can develop and affirm a positive sense of self. This is evidenced from a pre-experience interview with a U.S. high school student who participated in the precursor project, IC4, throughout middle school.

> *US Student: I've been a part of well, I had been a part of IC4 before it had ended, and I think I'd been part of it for seven years since I was in sixth grade up until last year when it ended. It helped me introduce me a lot to not only the science field, but how I can mix my interests with biological sciences and technology together, which I thought was really fascinating.*
>
> *Like academic was in like extracurricular wise and growing up, you know, I was a really big reader, so at first when I was younger, I was like, Oh, I really love literature and maybe this is something I want to pursue and then through clubs in middle school such as IC4 and two other technology related clubs and STEM clubs, I started realizing that my interests, even though I enjoyed literature, I was really intrigued by math and science. So I think that's why they're really important to me, and I'd like them to be an integral part of my future career and educational opportunities.*

This reflection illustrates the potential for how an experience in the ABLE project can strengthen a learner's sense of self identity over time. While the more sparse network model can be attributed to age, it also indicates an opportunity for the program experience to have a lasting impact that can develop and affirm a positive sense of self. A comparison with post-experience interviews will provide further insight into assessing these ideas.

The contribution of this paper is not merely in service of reporting on the results of an analysis of pre-experience interviews. Rather, this paper aims to illustrate is a result of "slow research" developing in parallel to the usual, urgent pace of dissemination [17, 18]. It takes the opportunity to reflect on and document the evolution of research thinking that came from ongoing reflection over time in using QE as a primary methodological approach. The precursor project allowed exploration into telling collective stories about groups of participants ("we"), leading to an interest in examining how the experience impacts an individual's shift in thinking about themselves ("me") in the current endeavor. In parallel to examining shifts of student participant thoughts about self, the researchers aim to continue reflecting on how to use QE to share the stories of their own shifts in thinking.

Acknowledgements. The authors want to recognize the efforts of their research team in coding the data included in the analysis, including Myron Fletcher, Julia Savoca Gibson, Samuel Green, Dante Schulz, and Haille Trimboli. The authors also gratefully acknowledge funding support from the National Science Foundation (#2215613) for the work this paper reports. Views appearing in this paper do not reflect those of the funding agency.

References

1. Chi, M., et al.: Eliciting self-explanations improves understanding. Cogn. Sci. **18**(3), 439–477 (1994)
2. Chi, M., et al.: Learning from human tutoring. Cogn. Sci. **25**(4), 471–533 (2001)
3. Roschelle, J.M., et al.: Changing how and what children learn in school with computer-based technologies. Future Child. **10**(2), 76–101 (2000)
4. Hamilton, E., et al.: A model and research agenda for teacher and student collaboration using pen-based tablets in digital media making in Sub-Saharan Africa. In: Hammond, T., Valentine, S., Adler, A. (eds.) Revolutionizing Education with Digital Ink. HIS, pp. 223–230. Springer, Cham (2016). https://doi.org/10.1007/978-3-319-31193-7_15
5. Moll, L.C., Amanti, C., Neff, D., Gonzalez, N.: Funds of knowledge for teaching: using a qualitative approach to connect homes and classrooms. Theory Pract. **31**(2), 132–141 (1992)
6. Lee, S.B., Espino, D.P, & Hamilton, E.R. (2019). Exploratory Research Application of Epistemic Network Analysis for Examining International Virtual Collaborative STEM Learning. American Education Research Association. Toronto, Canada
7. Espino, D., Lee, S., Eagan, B., Hamilton, E.: An initial look at the developing culture of online global meet-ups in establishing a collaborative, STEM media-making community. In: Lund, K., Niccolai, G.P., Lavoué, E., Gweon, C.H., Baker, M. (Eds.) A Wide Lens: Combining Embodied, Enactive, Extended, and Embedded Learning in Collaborative Settings, 13th International Conference on Computer Supported Collaborative Learning (CSCL) 2019, vol. 2, pp. 608–611. International Society of the Learning Sciences, Lyon, France (2019). https://doi.org/10.22318/cscl2019.608
8. Espino D.P., Lee S.B., Van Tress L., Hamilton E.R.: Examining the dynamic of participation level on group contribution in a global, STEM-focused digital makerspace community.In: Eagan, B., Misfeldt, M., Siebert-Evenstone, A. (eds) Advances in Quantitative Ethnography: First International Conference, ICQE 2019, Madison, WI, USA, October 20–22, 2019,Proceedings, pp. 55–65. Springer International Publishing, Cham (2019). https://doi.org/10.1007/978-3-030-33232-7_5
9. Espino, D., Lee, S., Van Tress, L., Baker, T., Hamilton, E.: Analysis of U.S., Kenyan, and Finnish discourse patterns in a cross-cultural digital makerspace learning community through the IBE-UNESCO global competences framework. Res. Soc. Sci. Technol. **5**(1), 86–100 (2020). https://doi.org/10.46303/ressat.05.01.5
10. Espino, D., Lee, S.B,, Hokama, M., Hamilton, E.: Examining prompted discourse patterns in an informal, online, global collaborative learning environment. In: Weinberger, A., Chen, W., Hernández-Leo, D., Chen, B. (eds.) Proceedings of the 15th International Conference on Computer-Supported Collaborative Learning – CSCL. International Society of the Learning Sciences, Hiroshima, Japan (2022)
11. Wright, T., OliveiraEspino, L.: Getting there together: examining patterns of a long-term collaboration in a virtual STEMmakerspace. In: Weinberger, A., Chen, W., Hernández-Leo, D., Chen, B. (eds.) Advances in Quantitative Ethnography: Third International Conference, ICQE 2021, Virtual Event, November 6–11,2021, Proceedings, pp. 334–345. Springer International Publishing, Cham (2022). https://doi.org/10.1007/978-3-030-93859-8_22

12. Orrantia, H., Espino, D., Tan, Y., Hamilton, E.R. Examining community development in an online, global, collaborative, learning environment. In: Damsa, C., Borge, M., Koh, E., Worsley, M. (eds.) Proceedings of the 16th International Conference on Computer-Supported Collaborative Learning – CSCL 2023. International Society of the Learning Sciences, Montreal, Canada (2023)
13. Hokama, M., Lowe, T., Tan, Y., Espino, D.P., Hamilton, E.: Personalized Learning and the Development of Emotional Intelligence: An Analysis of Students in a Global, Collaborative, STEM-focused Learning Environment. American Education Research Association, Chicago, Illinois (2023)
14. Spencer, M.B., et al.: Identity, self, and peers in context. In: Handbook of Applied Developmental Science: Promoting Positive Child, Adolescent, and Family Development Through Research, Policies and Programs, vol. 1, pp. 123–142 (2003)
15. Herrenkohl, L.R., Cornelius, L.: Investigating elementary students' scientific and historical argumentation. J. Learn. Sci. **22**(3), 413–461 (2013)
16. Shaffer, D.W.: Quantitative Ethnography. Cathcart Press, Madison, WI (2017)
17. Frey, K.: Keynote address. In: International Conference on Quantitative Ethnography, Copenhagen, Denmark, Oct 2022
18. Adams, V., Burke, N.J., Whitmarsh, I.: Slow research: thoughts for a movement in global health. Med. Anthropol. **33**(3), 179–197 (2014)

Investigating the Relationship Between Programming Experience and Debugging Behaviors in an Introductory Computer Science Course

Juan D. Pinto[1]([✉]), Qianhui Liu[1], Luc Paquette[1], Yingbin Zhang[2], and Aysa Xuemo Fan[1]

[1] University of Illinois Urbana-Champaign, Champaign, IL 61820, USA
jdpinto2@illinois.edu
[2] South China Normal University, Guangzhou Guangdong 510631, China

Abstract. Debugging is a challenging task for novice programmers in computer science courses and calls for specific investigation and support. Although the debugging process has been explored with qualitative methods and log data analyses, the detailed code changes that describe the evolution of debugging behaviors as students gain more experience remain relatively unexplored. In this study, we elicited "constituents" of the debugging process based on experts' interpretation of students' debugging behaviors in an introductory computer science (CS1) course. Epistemic Network Analysis (ENA) was used to study episodes where students fixed syntax/checkstyle errors or test errors. We compared epistemic networks between students with different prior programming experience and investigated how the networks evolved as students gained more experience throughout the semester. The ENA revealed that novices and experienced students put different emphasis on fixing checkstyle or syntax errors and highlighted interesting constituent co-occurrences that we investigated through further descriptive and statistical analyses.

Keywords: Computer Science Education · Debugging · Programming Experience · Epistemic Network Analysis · CS1

1 Introduction

Debugging is an important component of computer programming where students "find out exactly where the error is and how to fix it" [1]. Different from general programming ability, debugging skills cannot be immediately obtained from writing code [2] and thus deserve individual pedagogical attention [1]. Novice programmers often find debugging difficult for two main reasons. First, successful debugging requires a wide range of knowledge—including general programming expertise and knowledge of debugging methods—that novice programmers may not possess [3]. This deficiency of debugging knowledge and strategic skills often hinders students from controlling the programming process [4]. Second, the process of debugging often happens outside of class, so

G. Arastoopour Irgens and S. Knight (Eds.): ICQE 2023, CCIS 1895, pp. 125–139, 2023.
https://doi.org/10.1007/978-3-031-47014-1_9

instructors have limited opportunities to directly support students when they encounter difficulties and misconceptions [5].

Epistemic Network Analysis (ENA) is a technique that detects and measures associations between coded data elements and represents the associations through a dynamic network [6]. It allows researchers to visually and statistically compare different groups' networks. ENA can be applied to understand students' debugging processes by revealing the associations between debugging behaviors within a window slice and how these associations differ in student groups.

In this study, we used ENA in an introductory computer science (CS1) course to investigate the relationship between computer programming experience and debugging behaviors. To achieve this, we elicited what we called "constituents" of the debugging process—i.e., binary variables deduced from expert observations. Each constituent was operationalized based on how experts interpret students' debugging behaviors and was computed on the code submissions. We investigated debugging behaviors for two types of debugging episodes in which students attempted to fix different types of errors: syntax/checkstyle errors or test errors. ENA point plots and networks were created to explore the difference between students with and without prior experience, and to investigate how debugging behaviors evolved as students gained more experience over three different times periods of the semester. Our ENA highlighted interesting constituent co-occurrences that we investigated through further descriptive and statistical analyses.

Specifically, we asked the following research questions:

1. How does the use of ENA allow us to better understand students' debugging behaviors when solving computer programming problems?
2. How does the debugging behavior of students differ based on their prior computer programming experience?
3. How does debugging behavior evolve over the duration of the semester, as students gain more computer programming experience?

2 Related Work

2.1 Debugging

Students' debugging processes have been investigated through qualitative studies based on think-aloud transcriptions [7], grounded theory [8], interviews [9], and researcher coding [1]. These studies have identified insightful debugging challenges and concepts, such as barriers students encountered corresponding to different debugging phases [7] and debugging strategies articulated by students [8, 9] or experts [1].

Other studies have focused on revealing debugging behaviors with log data. Although programming processes have been modeled from different perspectives such as code updates [10] and program state transitions [11], limited studies have focused on specifically analyzing debugging processes using log data. Ahmadzadeh et al. [12] distinguished groups of good and weak debuggers based on how well they corrected logical bugs. While the study included statistical results, students' debugging behaviors were not analyzed quantitatively to explain differences in their performance. Jemmali et al. [13] considered both error states and programming actions in debugging sequence analysis. However, they only considered four levels of code modifications (no/small/medium/large change) and provided limited interpretations of debugging patterns. Since debugging involves a variety of knowledge and skills, debugging processes should be described with more detailed code-changing behaviors instead of simply how much the code has been changed.

2.2 ENA With Process Data

ENA has been applied to various types of educational process data [14], such as action logs [15, 16], coded discourse [17, 18], and affect observations [19]. Although the original ENA methods do not account for sequential order among learning events, they can extract features from process data that have predictive power on learning performance no worse than sequential analysis methods [18]. Recently, directed ENA has been developed to capture sequential information among learning events [20], and it has shown promise in dissecting MOOC learning tactics [21].

Many studies have used ENA to uncover the co-occurrence patterns among self-regulated learning behaviors [15–17] and to understand collaborative learning processes [17, 18]. Researchers have also utilized ENA in the field of computing education [22–24]. Particularly, Hutchins et al. [23] applied ENA to understand high school students' debugging process during block-based programming. Their result showed that a group characterized by tinkering and evaluation debugging strategies was better at integrating physics and computational thinking concepts than a group characterized by multiple code construction actions without testing.

3 Learning Context

In this study, we analyzed data collected from an undergraduate CS1 course in Java at a Midwestern public university. Students used an online auto-grading system to complete homework, quiz, and exam questions throughout the semester. The course included two large midterms, naturally dividing the semester into three periods. Homework was assigned almost every day, and students could submit unlimited attempts to the online system before the midnight deadline. For each submission, the system first checked if there were any syntax (incorrect Java code) or checkstyle (the code did not follow course specific formatting rules) errors. If so, the system would provide error messages. Otherwise, the platform ran a set of problem-specific test cases to evaluate the submission's correctness. The test cases returned information about the first encountered error or no error message if all cases passed.

3.1 Data

Submission log data of 745 students solving 69 homework questions was collected during the Fall 2019 semester. Each student made an average of 7.49 submissions per question. For each submission, the online learning system recorded the student's submitted code, submission time, and any syntax, checkstyle, or test error messages. Students also completed a pre-course survey providing demographic information and self-reported prior

128   J. D. Pinto et al.

experience in programming. Thirty-one percent of the students were female. We investigated two questions related to the students' prior programming experience. The first one asked which programming languages students were familiar with. We grouped the possible answers into four categories—Java, Java+ (Java and at least one other), other, or none—because we assumed that students with Java experience may learn differently in this introductory Java course. The second question asked students to self-rate their programming abilities on a range from 1 (lowest) to 5 (highest).

3.2 Eliciting Constituents

Process log data, such as code submissions, contain rich information that can be used to better understand students' debugging behaviors. However, log data first needs to be pre-processed to compute features that summarize debugging behaviors and filter out irrelevant information. To identify relevant and interpretable features, we elicited binary "constituents" of experts' interpretation of debugging behaviors, each operationalizing an element of debugging behavior that experts identified as meaningful.

We identified constituents using a similar method to the one used by Paquette, de Carvalho, & Baker [25]. The elicitation process involved conducting interviews with programming experts and extracting relevant components of their interpretation of students' code submissions. This section provides an overview of the expert interview process and describes how we identified a specific set of constituents for our study.

We recruited two programming experts, both computer science graduate students with a research focus on computer science education who also had prior teaching or tutoring experience. These experts were expected to possess a deep understanding of Java programming concepts and be familiar with common student misconceptions and debugging strategies. Both experts were presented with the same set of pre-selected examples of student problem solving submissions and were asked to comment on how students approached solving the problems and the debugging strategies they employed. In total, the first expert commented on 20 problems for a duration of 6.18 h, and the second expert commented on 24 problems for a duration of 9.82 h.

To identify key constituents of the experts' interpretations, we first constructed a flowchart representing their approach to interpreting code submissions, based on the recurring themes identified from the interview recordings. The flowchart was reviewed to identify missing components from the experts' interpretation approach, which lead to further review of the interviews. Through this iterative process, we generated a comprehensive list of constituents that captured the essence of the experts' interpretation. Finally, we computed these constituents from the code submission data.

Table 1 presents a list of all the constituents used in the analyses presented in this paper. These constituents represent various aspects of the debugging process, including changes to the submitted code and progress towards fixing errors. It is important to note that some of the elicited constituents, such as the use of print statements, were excluded from our analyses. While print statements can be used during debugging, some problems (especially early in the semester) required students to use print statements as part of the solution. The constituents were removed from the analyses to avoid confounding print statements that were part of the solution with those that were used for debugging.

Table 1. Debugging constituents based on the experts' interpretation.

Constituents	Operationalization
MASSIVE DELETION	The student deleted 4 or more lines of code, and at least 30% of all the lines from the previous submission were deleted
SUBMISSION UNDO	This is not the first submission, and the code is the same as a submission at least 2 submissions back
DELETED LINE W/ ERROR	At least one line with a checkstyle/syntax error from the previous submission was deleted
MODIFIED LINE W/ SYNTAX ERROR	At least one line with a syntax error from the previous submission was modified
CHANGED VAR NAME	The name of a variable was modified
REPEATED CHANGE	At least one identical change (deletion/addition/modification) was made on multiple lines. E.g., submission added the same word on two or more lines
IGNORED CHECKSTYLE BUT ADDRESSED SYNTAX	Lines with syntax errors in previous submission were altered but lines with checkstyle errors were not
REDUCED SYNTAX ERRORS	The current submission has less total syntax errors than the previous submission
REDUCED CHECKSTYLE ERRORS	The current submission has less total checkstyle errors than the previous submission
CHANGE IN TEST ERROR	The provided test error for the current submission is different than the test error that was provided from the previous submission
NEW ERROR	The current submission is not the first and has at least 1 error that was not present in the immediately preceding submission
REPEATED NEW ERROR	At least 1 error identified as new (NEW ERROR) is the same as one of the errors in the previous submissions

4   Epistemic Network Analysis

4.1   Methods

Data Preparation. To focus our analyses on how students debugged specific types of errors, we split our data into debugging episodes that exclusively kept submissions with either syntax/checkstyle errors or test errors. We settled on this approach after a pilot study revealed interpretation issues when keeping all error types together. This is due to the design of the learning platform, which only ran problem-specific tests when no syntax/checkstyle errors were present.

In addition, because debugging is a process that unfolds over multiple steps, students who solved problems in few attempts may not be provided with adequate opportunities to demonstrate their debugging process. As such, only episodes with a number of submissions in the 75th percentile or above were included, with a minimum submission threshold of 5 for syntax/checkstyle error episodes and 6 for test error episodes.

We calculated the constituents separately for each episode. We also included relevant grouping data to make our analysis possible: answers to survey questions about prior programming ability and experience with programming languages, as well as information about which third of the semester each problem was assigned to. For each set of episodes, we removed constituents that were not relevant to its type of error. For example, CHANGE IN TEST ERROR was not relevant to syntax/checkstyle errors, whereas REDUCED CHECKSTYLE ERRORS was not relevant to test errors.

Table 2. Number of debugging episodes for each grouping.

	Programming language (T1)				Prior ability (T1)					Time		
	None	Other	Java	Java+	1	2	3	4	5	T1	T2	T3
syntax/ checkstyle	832	954	520	1260	804	1357	1064	289	52	3576	4756	4439
test	174	491	237	273	209	413	403	133	17	1178	1485	3191

Epistemic Network Analysis. ENA was conducted using the rENA package [26]. We compared the networks obtained using two different window sizes (2 and 3) and found no meaningful differences. We therefore decided to use a window size of two for our analyses, which we reasoned would be easier to interpret as co-occurrences would be from either immediately adjacent submissions or from the same submission.

We created ENA point plots and networks for each type of debugging episode for each grouping dimension. We also created a separate mean epistemic network for each group, as well as plots showing the difference between pairs of mean group networks. Welch t-tests (Table 3) were conducted to identify statistically significant differences between networks. Table 2 provides detailed information about the number of data points included in each grouping. Since each of our grouping categories included more than two groups, we used singular value decomposition rather than means rotation.

When preparing the plots for prior programming ability and prior language experience groupings, we kept only problems that were part of the first third of the semester (T1). We reasoned that prior experience would have the most impact on debugging behaviors of students early on, but that this effect would decrease with in-course experience, which may equalize students with different prior levels of experience.

This series of plots allowed us to analyze the various co-occurrences between constituents, allowing us to answer our research questions on the impact of experience on

Table 3. Results of Welch t-tests for previously known languages (top), starting programming abilities (left), and semester time (right). In each cell, syntax/checkstyle debugging episodes are on top and test debugging episodes on bottom *in italics.* $^{*}p < 0.05$, $^{**}p < 0.01$, $^{***}p < 0.001$.

		Language						
		Java+	**Java**	**Other**				
2	1.34 / *0.58*	6.56*** / *1.48*	4.22*** / *1.04*	2.60** / *0.51*	**None**			
3	3.53*** / *0.23*	2.55* / *0.43*	0.86 / *0.16*	3.90*** / *0.97*	**Java+**			
4	4.28*** / *0.97*	3.61*** / *0.59*	1.96 / *0.89*	2.15* / *0.61*	**Java**	20.17*** / *3.25**	**T1**	Semester time
5	2.72** / *0.91*	2.39* / *1.12*	1.72 / *1.00*	0.85 / *1.31*	18.71*** / *4.10***	1.51 / *0.47*	**T3**	
	1	**2**	**3**	**4**	**T1**	**T2**		

(Ability labels on the left: 2, 3, 4, 5)

debugging practices. We also used ENA to identify follow-up questions that warranted further exploration of our data.

4.2 Results

Prior Experience. We compared the debugging-related actions in the first third of the semester (T1) of students with different levels of prior experience. We found that the epistemic networks for students subdivided by either previously known programing languages or self-reported experience level yielded very similar trends—that is, students with lower self-rated ability followed the same general debugging patterns as those with little or no prior knowledge of programming languages when compared with those who either rated their abilities higher or had more experience with languages such as Java. This raised the question of how often these two survey dimensions intersect, which we explored further in a second round of analysis (Follow-Up Question 1).

Debugging Syntax/Checkstyle Errors. The mean networks for syntax/checkstyle debugging episodes revealed that, along the x-axis, checkstyle-focused constituents were located on the left, whereas syntax-focused constituents were on the right, and constituents related to general code edits were closer to the center (Fig. 1, left). Overall, the epistemic networks for novice students were more heavily weighted on the right and more experienced students more on the left, across both starting ability level and previously known languages (Fig. 1, right). Together, these observations suggest that novice students showed more co-occurrences of debugging behaviors addressing syntax errors, whereas more experienced students showed more co-occurrences related to checkstyle errors.

We found further evidence of this when comparing the mean networks of students with different levels of prior ability (Fig. 1, left). Experienced students (self-reported

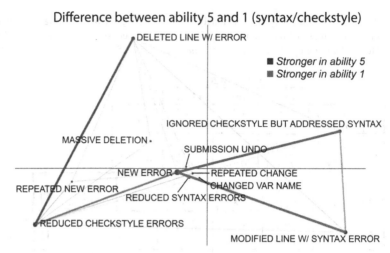

Fig. 1. Difference network between ability levels 5 and 1 in first third of semester (left); Means and confidence intervals across ability levels and prior know languages (right).

ability of 5) had stronger co-occurrences between NEW ERROR and REDUCED CHECK-STYLE ERRORS than novice students (self-reported ability of 1), as well as between DELETED LINE W/ ERROR and REDUCED CHECKSTYLE ERRORS.

One potential explanation is that experienced students may have simply encountered less syntax errors and, as such, encountered proportionally more checkstyle errors. Alternatively, experienced students could be addressing both syntax and checkstyle errors within the same submission. We decided to pursue these questions further in our second round of analysis (as Follow-Up Question 2) by exploring the distribution of checkstyle vs. syntax errors and the order in which students fixed checkstyle vs. syntax errors (checkstyle > syntax, syntax > checkstyle, or simultaneously).

With novice students, we found the opposite. They had many more co-occurrences between NEW ERROR and IGNORED CHECKSTYLE BUT ADDRESSED SYNTAX when both were present. Echoing some of our previous questions, this could be explained by experienced students simply making less syntax errors, giving them less opportunities for this constituent than novice students. There is some evidence for this in the fact that novice students had more co-occurrences between NEW ERROR and MODIFIED LINE W/ SYNTAX ERROR than experienced students.

Debugging Test Errors. We again found that the mean epistemic networks for less experienced students were more heavily weighted on the left and vice versa across the two dimensions of prior experience (self-rated ability levels and familiarity with various programming languages). There was one exception where the most advanced ability level (5) conspicuously did not follow this pattern (Fig. 2, right). However, given this group's much larger confidence interval, along with the consistency in the network graphs between the two experience dimensions aside from this group, we did not include the advance ability level further in our analyses at this stage, instead choosing to set its significance aside for later investigation as Follow-Up Question 3.

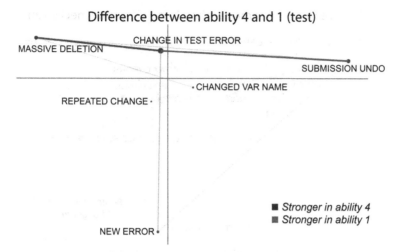

Fig. 2. Difference network between ability levels 4 and 1 for test error debugging (left); Means and confidence intervals across ability levels and prior know languages (right).

We found that experienced students had more co-occurrences between MASSIVE DELETION and CHANGE IN TEST ERROR than novice learners. A possible explanation is that experienced students are more confident in their abilities and make more changes to the code before submitting. However, this hypothesis should be verified in future studies.

As explained previously, one limitation of our dataset is that only a single test error can be identified in each submission, whereas all syntax/checkstyle errors are presented. This means that the NEW ERROR constituent is only measuring new syntax/checkstyle errors. In test error debugging episodes, this could only occur in the very last submission, indicating that a student's code had no more test errors but introduced new syntax/checkstyle errors. We found that novice students have more co-occurrences between this action and CHANGE IN TEST ERROR than experienced students. This may suggest that novices are more likely to make new syntax/checkstyle errors while debugging for test errors, though in this case we're only capturing that information at the very end of a test error debugging episode.

Changes Across Semester. Here we report on the variations in debugging patterns that we observed using ENA to compare students at the beginning (T1), the middle (T2), and the end (T3) of the semester, regardless of prior experience.

Debugging Checkstyle and Syntax Errors. Flipping the trend we observed earlier, where students with more prior experience showed more connections to checkstyle errors, it appears that, as the semester progresses and they develop more experience with programming and the expectations of the course, students increasingly spend more time on syntax errors and less on checkstyle errors. Figure 3 (left) reveals that the majority of co-occurrences between NEW ERROR and REDUCED CHECKSTYLE ERRORS take place during the first third of the semester. Figure 3 (right) further highlights how different the early part of the semester is from the latter two thirds.

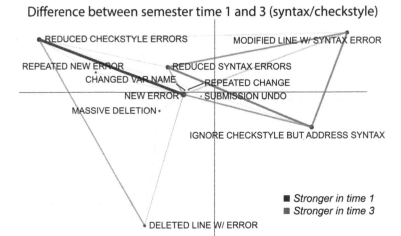

Fig. 3. Syntax/checkstyle debugging episodes. Difference network between semester time 1 and 3 (left); Means and confidence intervals across semester times (right).

The strong co-occurrences in the latter part of the semester with the constituent IGNORED CHECKSTYLE BUT ADDRESSED SYNTAX suggest that this may not simply be a case of students making less checkstyle errors, but rather of students consciously choosing to fix syntax errors first. We explore this further as Follow-Up Question 4.

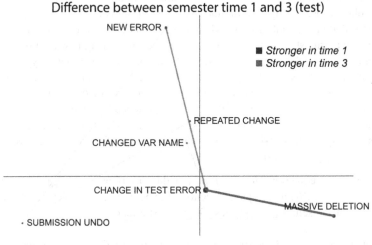

Fig. 4. Test debugging episodes. Difference network between semester time 1 and 3 (left); Means and confidence intervals across semester times (right).

Debugging Test Errors. With debugging for test errors, it is the last third of the semester that stands out as unique (Fig. 4, right). During these later weeks, students have many more co-occurrences between MASSIVE DELETION and CHANGE IN TEST ERROR. This is consistent with what we found among more experienced students during the early part of the semester, suggesting that experience leads to this debugging pattern.

The first two thirds of the semester included more co-occurrences between CHANGE IN TEST ERROR and NEW ERROR than the last third. This is similar to what we found among novice learners when compared with more experienced ones early in the semester, suggesting a consistent trend. Because of the nature of our data, this co-occurrence can be interpreted as students making new syntax/checkstyle errors while debugging a test error and either giving up or successfully solving the problem without making more test errors. We explored this further in Follow-Up Question 5.

5 Follow-Up Questions from ENA

The ENA analyses provided insights into the students' debugging behaviors. It high-lighted ways in which debugging behaviors varied based on prior programming expe-riences and how debugging behaviors evolved throughout the semester. However, it also raised questions that could not fully be answered by examining the co-occurrence networks by themselves. In this section, we investigate each of these questions.

Follow-Up Question 1. Through our use of ENA, we found that grouping debugging episodes using the two survey dimensions designed to measure experience provided very similar observations of debugging behaviors. We asked whether this was because students who self-rated as more capable were also those who listed prior knowledge of more programming languages. As part of a follow-up analysis, we calculated the Spearman's rank correlation between these two categories and found a moderate rela-tionship for student in both the syntax/checkstyle error dataset ($r_s = 0.63, p < 0.001$) and the test error dataset ($r_s = 0.63, p < 0.001$). A confusion matrix revealed, how-ever, that the majority of students—especially those with experience in Java and other languages—rated their abilities at the midpoint of 3 (Fig. 5). Because we are interested in comparing more vs. less experienced students, this neutral option makes it difficult to categorize students. We found that by removing all students in ability level 3, the Spearman correlation became stronger in both the syntax/checkstyle and the test error datasets ($r_s = 0.71, p < 0.001$ and $r_s = 0.71, p < 0.001$, respectively). For the rest of our follow-up analysis, we define experienced students as those with prior Java experience (*Java* or *Java+*) AND who rated their abilities as either 4 or 5. Similarly, we define novice students as those with either no prior known programming languages (*none*) or with only languages other than Java (*other*) AND who rated their abilities as either 1 or 2. This fits with how we analyzed these categories during our ENA as well.

Follow-Up Question 2. Another group of questions that arose during ENA were those regarding the connection between NEW ERROR and REDUCED CHECKSTYLE ERRORS. By looking at the frequency at which experienced students simultaneously fixed check-style and syntax errors (65 times) vs. performing these actions one after the other (310 times), we found that a certain trend we discovered via ENA—that experienced stu-dents placed more emphasis on checkstyle errors than syntax errors in comparison with novice students—was not simply a case of simultaneous debugging after all. We also found that experienced students had a ratio of checkstyle to syntax errors of about 1.71 (1.62 checkstyle and 0.95 syntax errors on average per submission), whereas novice students had a much smaller ratio of about 0.69 (0.99 checkstyle and 1.43 syntax errors on average per submission). Since the average number of syntax and checkstyle errors

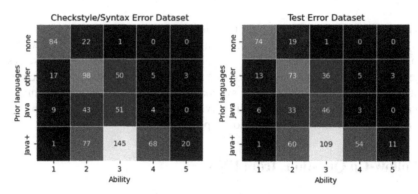

Fig. 5. Confusion matrix for prior ability and prior programming languages for both datasets: checkstyle/syntax and test debugging (T1 only). Lighter color indicates more instances.

per submission was similar between the groups (2.57 vs. 2.42), such a stark contrast in ratio seems to confirm that the trend we discovered was due to experienced students making more checkstyle errors while novices made more syntax errors.

Follow-Up Question 3. In our ENA, we found that students who self-rated their abilities as 5 (the highest) did not fit the trend set by the other ability levels. We investigated this and discovered that, as suspected, these students accounted for a disproportionally small subset of students (4%). As such, it is unclear whether the unexpected observation that high-ability students had more co-occurrences between SUBMISSION UNDO and CHANGE IN TEST ERROR than other students is simply due to the lower sample size.

Follow-Up Question 4. Some trends in our ENA led us to ask whether students made less checkstyle errors in the latter parts of the semester or if the proportion stayed the same, but they simply chose more often to ignore these and fix their syntax errors first. We found that the number of checkstyle errors per submission indeed decreased drastically after the first third of the semester, going from 1.18 to 0.43, and then only slightly increased to 0.73. We also found that the number of syntax errors per submission progressively increased from 1.27 to 1.67 and then to 2.07. These observations reveal a significant shift in the types of errors that students struggled with as they gained experienced. They also leave room for an acknowledgement of the shift in debugging strategy we observed in which students, as they gained experience, more often chose to focus on syntax errors first, even when they also had checkstyle errors present.

Follow-Up Question 5. Our ENA revealed that it was more common during the first two thirds of the semester for students to make a syntax/checkstyle error while debugging a test error and not receive any more test error messages in that problem. However, it was unclear if this was because students in these cases fixed both the new errors and the previous test error simultaneously, or if they simply gave up after the frustration of encountering a new type of error during the process of debugging. We found that in most cases—about 92%, regardless of the time in the semester—these students indeed solved the problem, indicating that they simultaneously fixed both types of errors.

6 Discussion and Conclusion

In this study, we elicited and calculated debugging constituents from episodes where students fixed syntax/checkstyle errors or test errors. We used ENA to compare the debugging behaviors of students based on their prior programming experience and to study how debugging behaviors evolved as students gained more programming experience throughout the semester. Results of our analyses showed how novices and experienced programmers put different emphasis on fixing checkstyle or syntax errors. The differences between co-occurrences of debugging patterns in the epistemic networks we generated raised further questions about the causes of such differences and about how debugging behaviors may shift as students gain more experience. We highlight our findings in the following paragraphs.

First, ENA for the two pre-course survey questions (self-rated programming ability level and previously known programming languages) showed similarities in the debugging behaviors of novice and experienced programmers in the first third of the semester. Experienced students placed more emphasis on fixing checkstyle errors while novice students focused more on syntax errors. An analysis of the distribution of syntax and checkstyle errors showed that this may largely be due to experienced students making less syntax errors (and proportionally more checkstyle errors). This may be related to the experienced students' greater familiarity with the Java language and its syntax and their lack of knowledge of the checkstyle rules specifically enforced in the course.

Second, as students gained more experience through the semester, they made significantly less checkstyle errors, causing them to focus more on fixing syntax errors. Even when they encountered checkstyle errors, they more often chose to tackle syntax errors first. This may be the result of an increase in problem complexity or the continuous introduction of new concepts with new syntax as the semester progressed. The change in programming concepts and problems can create more occasion for making syntax errors or encourage students to focus first on big problems (syntax errors) and worry about the details (checkstyle errors) later. During the constituent elicitation interviews, one of the experts explicitly commented on how students should ignore checkstyle errors until they fixed all syntax errors. As such, this may be evidence of students learning better debugging strategies with experience. Another potential factor could be the order in which errors are presented to students. Checkstyle errors are always put above syntax errors, so students might follow the displayed order to fix errors in earlier parts of the semester when still becoming familiar with the system. This suggests designing auto-grading systems to downplay less critical checkstyle rules so as to highlight the importance of addressing syntax and test errors first.

Third, similar debugging patterns for test errors appeared among more experienced students, whether they came to the class with more prior experience or gained additional experience throughout the semester. More experienced students more often performed massive deletions that led to changes in test errors. It is unclear why this is the case, as performing massive deletion doesn't appear, on the surface, to be an efficient debugging strategy. It may be evidence of increased confidence in deciding when to make significant—instead of incremental—changes to code. But further analyses will be required to better understand this phenomenon. More experienced students also finished their test debugging episodes attempting to fix syntax/checkstyle errors less often. While this didn't appear to prevent less experienced students from successfully solving problems, having to fix both types of errors simultaneously might slow down the debugging process. This suggests that it might be helpful to remind more novice students to focus primarily on test errors instead of being distracted by syntax/checkstyle errors.

While the use of ENA in this study revealed interesting findings about debugging patterns, existing limitations call for improvements in future work. First, the context in which our dataset was collected may have influenced the type of debugging behaviors that we observed. Unfortunately, the online homework that was used by the students was limited to displaying only one test error at a time. Because of this, it may have been difficult for students to assess whether they were making progress towards the correct solution when debugging test errors. It also limited us in our analyses of how much progress students were making towards the correct solution. Second, the self-reported survey data posed some difficulties in defining student experience groups. Students exposed to more programming languages did not consistently rate themselves at a higher ability level, as stated in Follow-Up Question 1. More objective measures of prior experience would help avoid such bias. Third, while ENA networks served as an insightful tool to explore debugging patterns in different student groups, the connection between constituents can only represent co-occurrence without showing which constituent comes before another. Given that debugging is a sequential process, this ambiguity caused difficulties in interpreting some behaviors and their causes. Directed ENA networks [20] could be applied to account for the sequential aspects of ENA. Fourth, additional qualitative analyses can be combined with ENA to explain the co-occurrence between constituents. For example, we found that the connection between massive deletion and a change in test error appeared more often for more experienced students. This result was unexpected because we would assume incremental changes to be more efficient during debugging, in most cases. Further analyses will be needed to qualitatively examine the submission log data and better understand this behavior.

References

1. Murphy, L., Lewandowski, G., McCauley, R., Simon, B., Thomas, L., Zander, C.: Debugging the good, the bad, and the quirky-a qualitative analysis of novices' strategies. ACM SIGCSE Bull. **40**(1), 163–167 (2008)
2. Kessler, C., Anderson, R.: A model of novice debugging in LISP. In: Proceedings of the First Workshop on Empirical Studies of Programmers, Ablex, Norwood, NJ (1986)
3. Begum, M., Nørbjerg, J., Clemmensen, T.: Strategies of novice programmers. In: Proceedings of the 41st Information Systems Research Seminar in Scandinavia (IRIS), Odder, Denmark (2018)
4. Perkins, D., Martin, F.: Fragile knowledge and neglected strategies in novice programmers. In: Soloway, E., Iyengar, S. (eds.) Empirical Studies of Programmers, pp. 213–229. Ablex, Norwood, NJ (1986)
5. Fitzgerald, S., et al.: Debugging: finding, fixing and flailing, a multi-institutional study of novice debuggers. Comput. Sci. Educ. **18**(2), 93–116 (2008)
6. Shaffer, D.W., Collier, W., Ruis, A.R.: A tutorial on epistemic network analysis: analyzing the structure of connections in cognitive, social, and interaction data. J. Learn. Anal. **3**(3), 9–45 (2016)
7. Liu, Z., Zhi, R., Hicks, A., Barnes, T.: Understanding problem solving behavior of 6–8 graders in a debugging game. Comput. Sci. Educ. **27**(1), 1–29 (2017)

8. Fitzgerald, S., Simon, B., Thomas, L.: Strategies that students use to trace code: an analysis based in grounded theory. In: Proceedings of the 2005 International Workshop on Computing Education Research (ICER'05), pp. 69–80. ACM, Seattle, USA (2005)

9. Fitzgerald, S., McCauley, R., Hanks, B., Murphy, L., Simon, B., Zander, C.: Debugging from the student perspective. IEEE Trans. Educ. **53**(3), 390–396 (2010)

10. Blikstein, P., Worsley, M., Piech, C., Sahami, M., Cooper. S., Koller, D.: Programming pluralism: using learning analytics to detect patterns in the learning of computer programming. J. Learn. Sci. **23**(4), 561–599 (2014)

11. Berland, M., Martin, T., Benton, T., Petrick Smith, C., Davis, D.: Using learning analytics to understand the learning pathways of novice programmers. J. Learn. Sci. **22**(4), 564–599 (2013)

12. Ahmadzadeh, M., Elliman, D., Higgins, C.: An analysis of patterns of debugging among novice computer science students. ACM SIGCSE Bull. **37**(3), 84–88 (2005)

13. Jemmali, C., Kleinman, E., Bunian, S., Almeda, M.V., Rowe, E., Seif El-Nasr, M.: MAADS: mixed-methods approach for the analysis of debugging sequences of beginner programmers. In: Proceedings of the 51st ACM Technical Symposium on Computer Science Education, pp. 86–92. ACM, Portland, OR, USA (2020)

14. Elmoazen, R., Saqr, M., Tedre, M., Hirsto, L.: A systematic literature review of empirical research on epistemic network analysis in education. IEEE Access **10**, 17330–17348 (2022)

15. Li, S., Huang, X., Wang, T., Pan, Z., Lajoie, S.P.: Examining the Interplay between self-regulated learning activities and types of knowledge within a computer-simulated environment. J. Learn. Anal. **9**(3), 152–168 (2022)

16. Paquette, L., Grant, T., Zhang, Y., Biswas, G., Baker, R.: Using epistemic networks to analyze self-regulated learning in an open-ended problem-solving environment. In: Proceedings of the 2nd International Conference on Quantitative Ethnography, pp. 185–201 (2021)

17. Melzner, N., Greisel, M., Dresel, M., Kollar, I.: using process mining (PM) and epistemic network analysis (ENA) for comparing processes of collaborative problem regulation. In: Proceedings of the 1st International Conference on Quantitative Ethnography (ICQE 2019), pp. 154–164. Springer, Cham, Madison, WI, USA (2019)

18. Swiecki, Z., Lian, Z., Ruis, A., Shaffer, D.: Does order matter? Investigating sequential and cotemporal models of collaboration. In: Proceedings of the 13th International Conference on Computer Supported Collaborative Learning (CSCL), pp. 112–119. ISLS, Lyon, France (2019)

19. Karumbaiah, S., Baker, R.S.: Studying affect dynamics using epistemic networks. In: Proceedings of the 2nd International Conference on Quantitative Ethnography, pp. 362–374. Springer, Malibu, USA (2021)

20. Fogel, A., et al.: Directed epistemic network analysis. In: Proceedings of the 2nd International Conference on Quantitative Ethnography, pp. 122–136. Springer, Malibu, USA (2021)

21. Fan, Y., et al.: Dissecting learning tactics in MOOC using ordered network analysis. J. Comput. Assist. Learn. **39**(1), 154–166 (2022)

22. Arastoopour Irgens, G., et al.: Modeling and measuring high school students' computational thinking practices in science. J. Sci. Educ. Technol. **29**, 137–161 (2020)

23. Hutchins, N.M., et al.: Analyzing debugging processes during collaborative, computational modeling in science. In: Proceedings of the 14th International Conference on Computer-Supported Collaborative Learning, pp. 221–224 (2021)

24. Xu, W., Wu, Y., Ouyang, F.: Multimodal learning analytics of collaborative patterns during pair programming in higher education. Int. J. Educ. Technol. High. Educ. **20**(1), 1–20 (2023)

25. Paquette, L., de Carvalho, A., Baker, R.: Towards understanding expert coding of student disengagement in online learning. In: Proceedings of the 36th Annual Meeting of the Cognitive Science Society, pp. 1126–1131, Québec City, Canada (2014)

26. Marquart, C., Swiecki, Z., Collier, W., Eagan, B., Woodward, R., Shaffer, D.W.: rENA (0.2.4) [R package] (2022). https://cran.r-project.org/web/packages/rENA/index.html

To Ban or Embrace: Students' Perceptions Towards Adopting Advanced AI Chatbots in Schools

Tolulope Famaye[(⊠)] [ID], Ibrahim Oluwajoba Adisa[ID],
and Golnaz Arastoopour Irgens[ID]

Learning Science, College of Education, Clemson University, Clemson, SC, USA
tfamaye@g.clemson.edu

Abstract. The launch of ChatGPT has caused a storm of reactions and debates in the academic community. These ongoing conversations have elicited mixed responses of enthusiasm, dissatisfaction, and apprehension among stakeholders in the academic spaces. However, student voices are yet to be heard. This paper analyses student responses to an opinion piece about ChatGPT published in The New York Times. Using the Theory of Reasoned Action, we interpreted students' perceptions and dispositions towards ChatGPT. We analyzed how students' beliefs, personal experiences with ChatGPT, and social expectations influenced their stance on adopting or banning ChatGPT in U.S. schools. We found that students perceived ChatGPT to be a valuable tool to support learning. However, they have several concerns about the potential for cheating, misinformation, and issues of fairness related to the use of ChatGPT.

Keywords: ChatGPT · Chatbots · AI Conversational Agent · Theory of Reasoned Action

1 Introduction

ChatGPT is an AI-based conversational system that uses advanced language models to understand and generate human-like text responses [1, 2]. It is designed to engage in natural language conversations with users, responding to their inputs in a way that simulates human conversation. The launch of ChatGPT in November 2022 elicited considerable debates among scholars and the public [11, 19, 20]. While some educators have expressed enthusiasm about the potential for ChatGPT to transform the educational landscape, others have voiced concerns regarding ethical considerations, data privacy, and academic integrity. One reason for the optimism about this particular AI chatbot is its capacity to facilitate personalized learning. On the other hand, there is growing concern and apprehension regarding upholding academic integrity within classrooms [10]. Critics have argued that the utilisation of AI chatbots such as ChatGPT may enable high-tech plagiarism and serve as a means of circumventing learning experiences.

© The Author(s), under exclusive license to Springer Nature Switzerland AG 2023
G. Arastoopour Irgens and S. Knight (Eds.): ICQE 2023, CCIS 1895, pp. 140–154, 2023.
https://doi.org/10.1007/978-3-031-47014-1_10

Given the possibility of implementing AI conversational agents like ChatGPT in academic settings, it is crucial to engage in discussions and consider the perspectives of various stakeholders within the academic community. Currently, much of the conversations exist among educators, administrators, and policymakers, but the perspectives of the learners themselves are lacking. Students are a crucial aspect of the educational ecosystem and, as such, may be directly and indirectly impacted by the policies implemented regarding adopting new technologies. Moreover, students are perceived as early adopters of new technologies and are often exposed to these tools outside their classrooms. Thus, student feedback is critical to successfully integrating intelligent chatbots within educational contexts, but few studies have looked closely at student data. This paper analyses high school students' responses to an online article published in the New York Times seeking students' opinions about the integration or ban of ChatGPT in U.S. schools. We answered the following research questions:

1. What are high school students' attitudes toward adopting ChatGPT in schools?
2. In what ways do high school students' experience with the AI chatbot ChatGPT influence their perceptions of the tool?

2   Theory of Reasoned Action (TRA)

The Theory of Reasoned Action (TRA) [3, 4] offers a suitable framework for understanding students' attitudes and opinions regarding adopting or banning ChatGPT in schools. Widely used in the fields of psychology, social psychology, and behavioural science [8, 9, 18], TRA suggests that behavioural intention, a predictor of behaviour, is directly influenced by personal and social variables [4] (Fig. 1). In TRA, attitude is theorized as a key determinant of behavioural intention, and it describes how people feel towards a particular behaviour, such as the degree of favourableness or unfavourableness towards an object. If an individual believes that a particular behaviour will result in a positive outcome, they are more likely to have a favourable attitude towards that behaviour. On the other hand, if they believe the behaviour will lead to a negative outcome, they are more likely to have a negative attitude toward it [3].

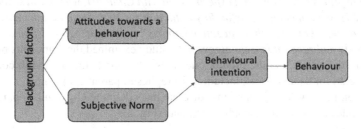

Fig. 1.   Theory of Reasoned Action (TRA)

The second key determinant of behavioural intention in TRA is subjective norm. It refers to an individual's perception of social pressure to perform or not perform a specific behaviour based on societal expectations and norms [3]. When individuals consider engaging in a behaviour, they consider the opinions and expectations of others, such as community, family, friends, or colleagues. If an individual believes society generally approves of a behaviour, then they are more likely to engage in that behavior. On the other hand, if they believe that society disapproves, they are more likely to avoid the behavior. Additionally, TRA acknowledges that background factors like beliefs, perceptions, personal experiences, and broader social factors influence attitudes and subjective norms. Based on the theoretical framing of this paper, an individual's intention to carry out a behaviour is based on two constructs: attitudes and subjective norms. Within the context of this paper, we investigate how students' attitudes and perceptions towards ChatGPT impact their opinion on the ban or adoption of ChatGPT.

3   Methods

3.1   Data collection and Coding

We used Quantitative Ethnography (QE) methodology [5, 21] to understand the phenomena under investigation comprehensively. Data used in this study consisted of high school students' comments to a Student Opinion post: *How Should Schools Respond to ChatGPT?* in the New York Times Learning Network dated January 24, 2023. The NY Times Learning Network section features articles that elicit students' viewpoints on diverse topics, predominantly those related to current events and issues (www.nytimes.com/column/learning-student-opinion). These articles are intended for a specific audience of middle and high school students, particularly students who are 13 years old or older. Responses undergo moderation by NY Times personnel, ensuring that only authorized contributions are made public. In the opinion piece, the author references a previously written article titled: *"Don't Ban ChatGPT in Schools. Teach With."* This article discusses the controversy surrounding the use of ChatGPT in schools. Students were prompted to read this hyperlinked article and share their opinion by responding to the following questions: *Have you experimented with ChatGPT, whether in school or on your own? How promising or useful do you think it is? Why do you think many educators are worried about it? What "negative impacts" can you imagine? Should teachers "thoughtfully embrace" this technology?* This study examined the comments posted in response to the article and the prompt questions. On March 15, 2023, 446 comments were collected for data analysis, including 79 replies to parent comments.

Each comment was segmented into discrete lines delimited by a full stop, resulting in 3,064 sentences derived from 446 comments (Fig. 2).

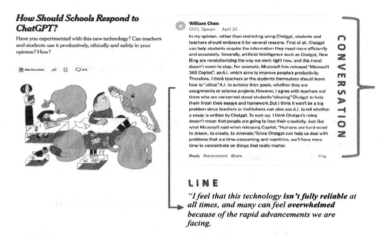

Fig. 2. Segmenting the data into lines (sentences) and conversations (a post and its responses)

We employed an inductive and deductive approach [14, 16] to analyze data, identifying twenty-two initial codes that were eventually grouped into seven final code categories (Table 1). The authors used nCoder [12] to calculate kappa and rho between the first coder (author 1), second coder (author 2), and the computer classifier (Table 2). The first coder trained the classifier using regular expression matching [17] on ninety tests set for each code. A second coder also coded the same sample.

Table 1. Codebook

Codes	Definition	Example	Sample Classifier Regex
Ethical Concerns	comments related to plagiarism, academic misconduct, fairness	*many students would most likely use it to cheat*	\b[Pp]lagiari \b[Cc]heat \bunfair
Control policies	Comments that suggest ways to adopt and manage the negative impact of ChatGPT	*schools should provide adequate training to teachers and students on how to use ChatGPT*	\b(detector?|detect(?:ion)?)\b \bregulated\b \bsupervis[eion]\b
Accept	references to accepting or using the ChatGPT	*I think ChatGPT should be allowed in school*	\ballowed\b
Perceived Limitation	Comments related to potential constraints or shortcomings of ChatGPT	*I doubt it could truly be capable of having the same thoughts a human could*	\bnot advanced\b \black the level of knowledge\b \bdoes not know\b
Apprehension	comments related to fear, anxiety concerning the use of the tool	*The scary thing...about chatgpt is that*	\bfear \bworried \bscary

(continued)

Table 1. (*continued*)

Codes	Definition	Example	Sample Classifier Regex
Perceived Usefulness	Comments that describe ChatGPT as valuable or beneficial	*I think it can be helpful to writers who struggle in certain ways*	\b(inspire|feedback|possibilities|beneficial|inspiration)
Negative Impact	Comments related to harmful outcome that may result from using ChatGPT	*AI would hinder students' ability to make a logical argument*	\bcause.{1,9}harm \b(negative|negatively)

Table 2. Kappa and Rho between the Human coders and classifier

Codes	Author 1 vs Author 2		Author 1 vs Classifier		Author 2 vs Classifier	
	Kappa	Rho	Kappa	rho	Kappa	rho
Ethical Concerns	0.94	0.01	0.97	0.01	0.93	0.03
Control policies	0.93	0.02	0.93	0.02	0.97	0.01
Accept	0.93	0.03	0.93	0.03	0.93	0.04
Perceived Limitation	1.00	0.00	1.00	0.00	0.97	0.00
Apprehension	1.00	0.00	1.00	0.00	1.00	0.00
Perceived Usefulness	0.97	0.00	0.97	0.00	1.00	0.00
Negative Impact	1.00	0.00	0.89	0.01	1.00	0.00

3.2 Data Analysis

Full Comment Sentiment Analysis

Sentiment analysis uses natural language processing, machine learning, and other computational techniques to identify subjective information from sources such as text, speech, or social media. This provides valuable insights into people's opinions, attitudes, and behaviours [13]. An initial sentiment analysis was done using the AFINN sentiment dictionary in the R programming language. Developed by Finn Årup Nielsen, AFINN is a list of English words rated for sentiment on a scale from -5 (negative) to + 5 (positive) and is often used as a baseline for sentiment analysis. AFINN provides a score for each word, and scores greater than 0 are considered positive, words with scores less than 0 are considered negative, and words with scores equal to 0 are considered neutral.

Considering that sentiment dictionaries may not accurately capture a word's sentiment in a specific context, we anticipated cases where words like *"cheating"* or *"worry"* are categorized as having a negative sentiment, even though the comment in question may have an overall positive connotation. For example, a statement such as *"I think that if teachers use it as a learning tool, it will show students how to use it to help their writing skills and decrease **cheating** levels…"* may be classified as negative due to the presence of the word *"cheating,"* even though the student is not using the term in a negative way. To verify the accuracy of the sentiment results generated by the AFINN sentiment dictionary, two researchers performed a hand coding of each comment (n = 446). We used these sentiment classifications of positive, neutral, and negative to create an *attitudinal sentiment* metadata group for each student comment. Table 3 provides a definition and examples of comments within each category.

Table 3. Attitudinal Sentiment Categories

Category	Definitions	Example
Positive	Comments that perceive ChatGPT as useful and should be embraced	*I feel that teachers and schools should embrace ChatGPT i would see this as a great learning experiment within schools because of the many things it can do for the students ...*
Negative	Comments that perceive ChatGPT as harmful and should be banned	*I overall think it is harmful to the English curriculum... it's hurting our learning and makes us take a step back... we need to figure out a way to pick up on it easier so that it's less used*
Neutral	Comments that appear to be in-between and makes no call to embrace or ban the use in schools	*..At this point we are forced to be okay with our new ways of life, someday an AI is all you will have, people will stop being creative and doing things on their own because AIs will know what we do, but better. This could be helpful right now... But no doubt, it will become an issue in the future*

Modelling Connections with ENA

In this study, we applied ENA [12, 21] to our data using the Web Tool (version 1.7.0) [12]. ENA is a technique in quantitative ethnography for modeling the structure of connections in data and assumes: (1) that it is possible to systematically identify a set of meaningful features in the data using codes, (2) that the data has local structure (conversations), and (3) that an important feature of the data is the way that Codes are connected to one another within conversations [21]. To model connections in the data, we decided to use a whole conversation window since all the students were making contributions to the same discussion prompts. For this study, we defined the units of analysis as all lines of data associated with a single value of *Attitudinal Sentiment Category* subsetted by *user id*. We were also interested in how students' experiences with the AI chatbot may influence students' attitudes and opinions toward the adoption of this technology in their schools. Thus, we coded each student's comment for *experience with ChatGPT*. From familiarity with the data, we grouped experience into three categories (Table 4). Then, we used a chi-square test of independence to examine the relationship between students' experience with ChatGPT and their perception of its adoption in schools.

Table 4. Experience with A.I chatbot

Experience	Definition	Example
No experience	Makes clear statements about having no experience using the app	*I have never used ChatGPT...*
First-person	Make clear statements about exploring the app	*...I have personally used the bot on my own time just messing around with it...*
Second-person	Make clear statements about having experience via observation	*In class, our teacher had ChatGPT create a marriage proposal*

In our ENA model, we aggregated networks using a binary summation in which the networks for a given line reflect the presence or absence of the co-occurrence of each pair of codes. The result was two coordinated representations for each unit of analysis: (1) a plotted point, which represents the location of that unit's network in the low-dimensional projected space, and (2) a weighted network graph. For the dimensional reduction, we used a singular value decomposition (SVD) [21] with independent dimensions to explain as much of the data's variation as possible using the first two dimensions.

The positions of the network graph nodes are fixed and determined by an optimization routine that minimizes the difference between the plotted points and their corresponding network centroids. Because of this co-registration of network graphs and projected space, the positions of the network graph nodes and the connections they define can be used to interpret the dimensions of the projected space and explain the positions of plotted points in the space. Our model had co-registration correlations of 0.88 (Pearson) and 0.86 (Spearman) for the first dimension and co-registration correlations of 0.92 (Pearson) and 0.93 (Spearman) for the second.

4   Results

4.1   RQ1: What are Students' Attitudes Toward Adopting ChatGPT in Schools?

Students with positive attitudes towards adopting ChatGPT

The ENA network model (Fig. 3a) revealed that students whose comments were classified as positive attitudes made the strongest connections with *perceived usefulness*, as indicated by the largest size of the node. These students generally made strong connections between the *AI* chatbot's *perceived usefulness and ethical concerns*. They advocated for schools to embrace and adopt the AI chatbot while considering the need for control policies or measures. An example of this result is evidenced in the data where one student states,

*"I feel that this technology **isn't fully reliable** at all times, and many **can feel overwhelmed** because of the rapid advancements we are facing, But, I think if we use this technology in **the right way,** people will be less overwhelmed and find it as more of a resource than a source, I think many teachers can **find this useful**, as AI can quickly identify complex questions one might have. I believe that there are many pros and cons to this, but if we **use** the technology **correctly**, it could **benefit us all."***

In the opening sentence of the comment, *"I feel that this technology isn't fully reliable at all times,"* the student expresses an underlying concern about the reliability of the technology (*perceived limitation*) but goes on to acknowledge the value of the tool, stating, *"if we use this technology in the right way, people will be less overwhelmed and find it as more of a resource."* This statement implies control policies and perceived value. Saying *"if we use this technology in the right way"*, implies the need for some measure of control applied to the use of the tool to enable people to be more comfortable with its use in the classrooms. Furthermore, the student gives an example (perceived usefulness) of how the AI chatbot can be used in the classroom. The student states, *"I think many teachers can find this useful, as AI can quickly identify complex questions one might have."* thereby highlighting another usefulness of the tool.

Another evidence of a similar connection was made by a student named Kora who strongly connects between *perceived limitation, perceived usefulness, control policies, and ethical implications* while also advocating for the use of Chat GPT in schools. In this comment, Kora explains:

*"Some people think that this website is **harmful** but I see it as a website that can and should **be used** in schools... teachers should let you be able to **use ChatGPT but only a certain amount of times** in a ... Also, **depending on what grade you're in** I think that should affect the use of this app... but **I don't think students should be able to if they're writing for assignment** that is a Summative because that is technically **cheating."***

Kora opened up the comment acknowledging the perceived limitation of the tool as **harmful** but proceeded to make a case for adopting the technology within the bounds of control, saying, *"teachers should let you be able **to use ChatGPT but only a certain amount** of times in a semester"* This statement suggests that teachers should allow students to use ChatGPT, as a resource in the classrooms. However, there should be a limit on the number of times a student can use ChatGPT during a semester. In other words, while students would have access to ChatGPT for assistance, it should be regulated to prevent excessive reliance or potential misuse of the tool. In a concluding statement, the student says, *"I don't think students should be able to if they're writing for assignment that is a summative because that is technically cheating."* This statement, *"technically cheating,"* suggests an ethical implication of using the tool for certain assignments, specifically summative assessments, which can be considered cheating from an ethical standpoint.

In these examples, we can see how students lend their voice to the ongoing conversations regarding adopting AI chatbots in schools by acknowledging the usefulness of the technology, raising ethical concerns, and recommending control measures to allow for using the technology in the classrooms.

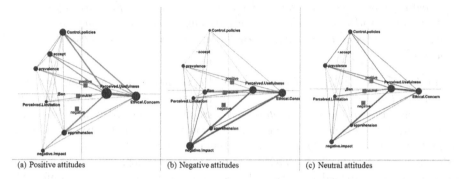

|(a) Positive attitudes|(b) Negative attitudes|(c) Neutral attitudes|

Fig. 3. Subtracted network models of students in positive and negative categories.

Students with Negative Attitudes Towards Adopting ChatGPT

The ENA network model (Fig. 3b) revealed that students whose comments were classified as negative attitudes made strong triadic connections among the nodes of *negative impact, perceived use,* and *ethical concern*. Their concerns about *negative impact* led them to generally connect with the node for a *ban* on the use of AI chatbots in schools (Fig. 3b). An example of this connection is evidenced in the data where one student commented,

> *"This new robot... is **impacting learning negatively**. ChatGPT is something that students in college and high school are **using to sabotage** the way they can actually learn. By getting bigger skills in writing, students use ChatGPT to turn in something, **not from their writing**. Students should not be able to use this robot because it shows no care of how students can give 100% but give maybe 5% in typing in a couple words to have a whole essay written..."*

In this example, the student argued that ChatGPT is causing undesirable consequences and hindering students learning experience. The student called out the "negative" impact of ChatGPT on learning and indicated the belief that the technology is disruptive to the learning process. This perception about the harmful nature of the technology is further emphasized in the sentence that follows, where the student states, *"ChatGPT is something that students in college and high school are using to sabotage the way they can actually learn."* In a concluding remark, this student recommends a ban on the use of AI chatbots, saying, *"Students should not be able to use this robot because it shows no care of how students can give 100% ..."* suggesting that the student believes the use of ChatGPT is allowing students to circumvent the effort required to complete assignments on their own, and is therefore undermining the value of their education. In this example, we see the student expressing a strong opinion that using the chatbot is harmful to learning and that students should not be allowed to use it. The statement

"Students should not be able to use this robot" suggests that the student believes there should be a policy to prohibit or restrict the chatbot use in educational settings.

Students with Neutral Attitudes Towards Adopting ChatGPT

The ENA network model (Fig. 3c and 4b) revealed that students whose comments were neutral had a more centralized position in the plot as they make strong connections between *negative impact, perceived usefulness, and ethical concern.* These students did not explicitly state whether to *adopt* or *ban* the technology. An example of this result is evidenced in the data where one student, Sam states,

> *"The whole world is beginning to bring more AIs to life, like making video games, having **AIs help with** homework and creating music or a job application all for you. At this point we are forced to be okay with our new ways of life, someday an AI is all you will have, **people will stop being creative** and doing things on their own because AIs will know what we do, but better. This could **be helpful right** now but no doubt, it will become an issue in the future.*

Sam's comment suggests a mixed perspective on AI. By saying, *"**AIs help with** homework and creating music or a job application all for you,"* the student acknowledges that AI can be beneficial. Yet, she also expresses concerns about the potential implications for the future, stating, *"it will become an issue in the future."* The student also raises concern about the prevalence of AI by saying, *"At this point, **we are forced** to be okay."* The comment implies that people may feel compelled to accept and adapt to the new ways of life driven by AI, and this reliance on AI could lead to a decrease in individual creativity and autonomy. Broadly speaking, students who fall into the neutral group did not explicitly make a case for either adopting or banning AI. Instead, they focused on acknowledging the usefulness of AI and expressed concerns about the negative impact of ChatGPT.

Statistical Differences between Positive, Negative, and Neutral Students

The ENA analysis revealed significant differences between students with positive attitudes and perceptions toward adopting ChatGPT in schools and those with negative attitudes and perceptions. As observed in the ENA network (Fig. 4).

This difference in the network is further substantiated by the statistical results that show that along the X axis, a two sample t test assuming unequal variance showed Positive (mean = 0.06, SD = 0.46, N = 230) was statistically significantly different at the alpha = 0.05 level from Negative (mean = -0.08, SD = 0.39, N = 120; t(278.98) = -2.94, p = 0.00, Cohen's d = 0.31). Along the Y axis, a two sample t test assuming unequal variance showed Positive (mean = 0.13, SD = 0.42, N = 230 was statistically significantly different at the alpha = 0.05 level from Negative (mean = -0.23, SD = 0.32, N = 120; t(299.95) = 8.90, p = 0.00, Cohen's d = 0.92). This statistical result is corroborated by the comparison plot (Fig. 4a) that revealed that students in the positive category have strong triad connections in their networks with *control policies, accept, perceived usefulness, and ethical concerns.* These connections primarily fall within the positive region of the Y-axis. While students within the negative sentiment category make strong triad connections with ban, ethical concerns, negative impact and perceived

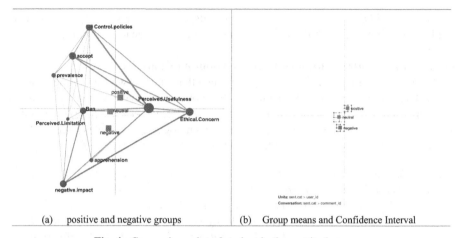

(a)   positive and negative groups   (b)   Group means and Confidence Interval

Fig. 4. Comparison plot of student in three attitude groups

usefulness of the technology the resulting networks primarily fall below the intersection point towards the negative region of the Y-axis. However, there are points of similarity observed between the positive and negative network groups. Both groups recognize the usefulness of the ChatGPT but have concerns related to the ethical implications of the use of the tool in the classroom. Figure 4a revealed points of connection at the thick nodes of perceived usefulness and ethical concern. This implies that despite any differences in sentiment or opinions between the two groups (positive and negative), both groups recognize the usefulness of ChatGPT and also express ethical concerns about the tool. This indicates that while both groups appreciate the value and benefits of ChatGPT, they raise questions or reservations about its ethical implications.

When comparing students in the neutral group with the students in the positive and negative attitudes respectively, the results showed statistically significant differences. Specifically, the plot revealed differences between the neutral and positive groups along the x and y axis. Along the X axis, a two sample t test assuming unequal variance showed Neutral (mean = -0.06, SD = 0.43, N = 74 was statistically significantly different at the alpha = 0.05 level from Positive (mean = 0.06, SD = 0.46, N = 230; t(131.57) = 2.05, p = 0.04, Cohen's d = 0.26). Along the Y axis, a two sample t test assuming unequal variance showed Neutral (mean = -0.03, SD = 0.36, N = 74) was statistically significantly different at the alpha = 0.05 level from Positive (mean = 0.13, SD = 0.42, N = 230; t(143.46) = -3.31, p = 0.00, Cohen's d = 0.41).

Comparing the neutral group with the negative group showed differences along the Y axis but no differences along the X axis. Statistical results showed along the X axis, a two sample t test assuming unequal variance showed Neutral (mean = -0.06, SD = 0.43, N = 74) was not statistically significantly different at the alpha = 0.05 level from Negative (mean = -0.08, SD = 0.39, N = 120; t(143.43) = -0.29, p = 0.77, Cohen's d = 0.04). Along the Y axis, a two sample t test assuming unequal variance showed Neutral (mean = -0.03, SD = 0.36, N = 74) was statistically significantly different at the alpha = 0.05 level from Negative (mean = -0.23, SD = 0.32, N = 120; t(143.10) = 3.83, p = 0.00, Cohen's d = 0.58).

4.2   RQ2: In What Ways do High School Students' Experience with the AI Chatbot ChatGPT Influence their Perceptions of the Tool?

Using the results of the sentiment analysis, we counted the occurrences of positive and negative perceptions towards ChatGPT for each experience groups and used the result to perform a Chi-square test of independence for the groups. For this analysis, we excluded the both the neutral sentiments and the population of students who did not indicate whether they have had any experience with ChatGPT or not. As such, our Chi-square analysis of negative or positive perception towards ChatGPT is limited to the population of students who explicitly indicated in their comment that they have either (1) firsthand experience, (2) secondhand experience, or (3) No experience.

Table 5. Chi-square Test and Descriptive Statistics for perception by Type of Experience

	Experiences			Total
Perception	First-person	Second-person	None	
Negative	6 (20%)	9 (30%)	**15 (50%)**	30
Positive	**39 (46%)**	15 (18%)	31 (36%)	85
Total	45	24	46	115

$X^2(2, N = 115) = 6.432$, p $= 0.0401$* Numbers in parentheses indicate row percentages.

Chi-square results (Table 5) show a statistically significant difference in students' perceptions of ChatGPT among the three experience groupings $X^2(2, N = 115) = 6.43$, p $= .0401$. Students who had a positive perception were more likely to have firsthand experience with the AI chatbot, while students who had a negative perception were more likely to have no experience with the AI chatbot. Our qualitative findings also supported this result and showed that students with first-person experience using ChatGPT tended to express more positive opinions about the tool and generally favored its adoption and use in school. For example, a user commented:

> *"I have seen others use and have used ChatGPT myself, as a strong study tool. It is very useful for summarizing information and generating examples that relate to what I'm working on. I think it's very helpful, though I always make sure to check and see if the information that I'm being provided is accurate, or else I'd be learning the wrong thing. Used the correct way, ChatGPT is very helpful, very effective, and can aid learning, knowledge and creativity."*

This student used ChatGPT for *"summarizing information and generating examples"* related to their work. Their firsthand interaction with ChatGPT allowed them to explore the affordances of the tool and its limitation, as evidenced by their comment about how they often ensure to "check and see" if the information provided by the tool is accurate. Based on their practical understanding of how ChatGPT works, how it can be used, and its potential for error, this user concluded that ChatGPT was a *"very helpful and very effective"* tool that supports creativity. Another user commented on how *"ChatGPT is quite flawed ... [and] unable to truly understand the complexities of speech"* however, they believed that the tool would continue to improve and could surpass humans' writing skills in the near future. Finally, this user considered AI tools like ChatGPT as an effective *"aid"* rather than an independent problem solver. Several other users with firsthand experience with the tool shared similar perspectives about the effectiveness of the tool and expressed optimism and excitement about its potential to "aid" students' learning. Other users' made similar comments such as *"I've checked it out and it gives a great step stool for a better piece of writing,"* and *"I believe schools should not ban ChatGPT but use it to further our learning ... I have used Chat GPT for many things such as emails, and also for just pure enjoyment."*

5 Discussion and Conclusion

The results of the study are consistent with the Theory of Reasoned Action, [3] which suggests that attitudes towards a behaviour are determined by subjective norms and perceived behavioural control. The results showed that students with positive attitudes towards the adoption of AI chatbots in schools were influenced by their perceived usefulness and perceived value of the technology, as well as their beliefs about the need for control measures to regulate its use. Furthermore, the students' recognition of the potential usefulness of AI chatbots for teachers reflects the influence of subjective norms on attitudes towards the technology. Students who held negative perceptions towards the adoption of ChatGPT in schools generally did not believe that this technology should be embraced by schools. The attitudes of these students may be influenced by the subjective norms present within their school environment. Some students have reported that their school had banned ChatGPT, and they agree with this ban.

The findings in this study revealed that students with a positive attitude perceived AI chatbots as valuable tools that can improve their educational experiences and make their academic lives easier. However, these students were also concerned about the potential risks associated with their use. They recognized that AI chatbots are not without their limitations and may present risks such as data privacy and security concerns, and they were more likely to advocate for the implementation of control measures to ensure the responsible use of AI chatbots and protect their personal information. Students with negative attitude perceived ChatGPT as harmful and unsafe to learners and, as such, advocated for a ban. The implications of these findings are that when given a platform, high schools students can engage in debates about the ethical use of AI in education and develop complex, multi-faceted arguments based on their lived experiences. Although discussions about ethical implications of AI chatbots in education typically exist among educators, administrators, and policymakers, students should also be included in these discussions as such decisions directly impact them and their lives.

Moreover, because many AI technologies are now widely available, students may experiment with such tools outside of school settings. As the findings revealed, students who had positive perceptions of the AI chatbot were more likely to have had firsthand experience with the tool. In contrast, those with negative perceptions were more likely to have had no experience with the tool. Those students with positive perceptions and firsthand experience provided sophisticated arguments that acknowledged the other side of the debate about how people may be resistant towards such technologies. These students also acknowledged the limitations of the tools, and although they were overall in favor of using AI Chatbots, many provided constraints on their usage. Based on these findings, we advocate for educators and parents to encourage high school-aged students to explore AI chatbots before drawing conclusions about their usage in education.

The goal of this study is not to generalise these claims to all high school students but rather to provide a thick description of a dataset of students who posted their opinions to this particular article. These findings suggest that this group of young people developed contrasting and complex arguments for and against the use of AI chatbots based on their lived experiences. Thus, we argue for engaging with students and addressing their ethical concerns transparently and openly to ensure that their opinions are heard and that they are actively involved in AI educational decision-making processes. By doing so, educators and policymakers can make informed decisions about the adoption or ban of such technologies in schools while also addressing the needs of students.

References

1. Kocaballi, A.B.: Conversational AI-Powered Design: ChatGPT as Designer, User, and Product. (February 2023) (2023). . Retrieved from http://arxiv.org/abs/2302.07406
2. Tlili, A., et al.: What if the devil is my guardian angel: ChatGPT as a case study of using chatbots in education. Smart Learn. Environ. **10**(1), 15 (2023). https://doi.org/10.1186/s40 561-023-00237-x
3. Ajzen, I., Fishbein, M.: A Bayesian analysis of attribution processes. Psychol. Bull. **82**(1975), 261–277 (1975). https://doi.org/10.1037/h0076477
4. Dolores, A., Ajzen, I.: Predicting and Changing Behavior: A Reasoned Action Approach. Prediction and Change of Health Behavior: Applying the Reasoned Action Approach, pp. 3–21. Lawrence Erlbaum Associates, Mahwah, NJ (2007)
5. Arastoopour Irgens, G., Eagan, B.: The foundations and fundamentals of quantitative ethnography. In: Damşa, C., Barany, A. (eds.) Advances in Quantitative Ethnography: 4th International Conference, ICQE 2022, Copenhagen, Denmark 15–19 Oct 2022, Proceedings, pp. 3–16. Springer Nature Switzerland, Cham (2023). https://doi.org/10.1007/978-3-031-31726-2_1
6. Conner, M., Sparks, P.: Ambivalence and Attitudes. Eur. Rev. Soc. Psychol. **12**(1), 37–70 (2002). https://doi.org/10.1080/14792772143000012
7. Fishbein, M.: A behavior theory approach to the relations between beliefs about an object and the attitude toward the object. In: Funke, U.H. (ed.) Mathematical Models in Marketing, pp. 87–88. Springer, Berlin, Heidelberg (1976). https://doi.org/10.1007/978-3-642-51565-1_25
8. Jalilian, F., Allahverdipour, H., Moeini, B., Moghimbeigi, A.: Effectiveness of anabolic steroid preventative intervention among gym users: applying theory of planned behavior. Health Promot Perspect **1**(1), 32–40 (2011). https://doi.org/10.5681/hpp.2011.002
9. Javadi, M., Kadkhodaee, M., Yaghoubi, M., Maroufi, M., Shams, A.: Applying theory of planned behavior in predicting of patient safety behaviors of nurses. Materia Socio Medica **25**(1), 52 (2013). https://doi.org/10.5455/msm.2013.25.52-55
10. King, M.R.: A conversation on artificial intelligence, chatbots, and plagiarism in higher education. Cell. Mol. Bioeng. **16**(1), 1–2 (2023). https://doi.org/10.1007/s12195-022-007 54-8

11. Marlo, M.: ChatGPT and the Death of Education. Harvard Independent. https://harvardindep endent.com/2023/02/chatgpt-and-the-death-of-education/ (2023). Retrieved 3 May 2023
12. Marquart, C.L., Hinojosa, C., Swiecki, Z., Eagan, B., Shaffer, D.W.: Epistemic Network Analysis (Version 1.7. 0) [Software] (2018). https://app.epistemicnetwork.org/login.html
13. Pang, Bo., Lee, Lillian: Opinion mining and sentiment analysis. FNT Inform. Retrieval 2(1–2), 1–135 (2008). https://doi.org/10.1561/1500000011
14. Saldana, J.: The Coding Manual for Qualitative Researchers. The Coding Manual for Qualitative Researchers, pp. 1–440. https://www.torrossa.com/en/resources/an/5018667 (2021). Retrieved 1 May 2023
15. Evenstone, A.L.S., Irgens, G.A., Collier, W., Swiecki, Z., Ruis, A.R., Shaffer, D.W.: In search of conversational grain size: modeling semantic structure using moving stanza windows. J. Learn. Anal. 4(3), 123–139 (2017)
16. Thomas, D.R.: A general inductive approach for analyzing qualitative evaluation data. Am. J. Eval. 27(2), 237–246 (2006). https://doi.org/10.1177/1098214005283748
17. Thompson, K.: Programming techniques: regular expression search algorithm. Commun. ACM 11(6), 419–422 (1968). https://doi.org/10.1145/363347.363387
18. Yadav, R., Pathak, G.S.: Determinants of consumers' green purchase behavior in a developing nation: applying and extending the theory of planned behavior. Ecol. Econ. 134, 114–122 (2017). https://doi.org/10.1016/j.ecolecon.2016.12.019
19. Yang, M.: New York City schools ban AI chatbot that writes essays and answers prompts. The Guardian. https://www.theguardian.com/us-news/2023/jan/06/new-york-city-schools-ban-ai-chatbot-chatgpt (2023). Retrieved 8 Apr 2023
20. Students using ChatGPT to cheat, professor warns. Retrieved May 3, 2023 from https://nyp ost.com/2022/12/26/students-using-chatgpt-to-cheat-professor-warns/
21. Shaffer, D.W.: Quantitative Ethnography. Cathcart Press, Madison, WI (2017)

Using Epistemic Network Analysis to Explore Flexibility and Development of Termite Fishing Techniques in Nigeria-Cameroon Chimpanzees (*Pan troglodytes ellioti*)

Tyler Andres-Bray[1,3](✉) ⓘ, Amanda Barany[2] ⓘ, and Mary Katherine Gonder[3,4]

[1] Department of Biological Sciences, Drexel University, Philadelphia, PA 19104, USA
tca38@drexel.edu
[2] Graduate School of Education, University of Pennsylvania, Philadelphia, PA 19104, USA
[3] Cameroon Biodiversity Protection Program, Yaoundé, Cameroon
[4] Department of Ecology and Conservation Biology, Texas A&M University, College Station, TX 77843, USA

Abstract. This work applies quantitative ethnographic techniques to a novel research context: animal behavior research in the field of biological sciences. Chimpanzee tool use is complex, culturally transmitted, and differs even between populations with similar ecological materials available. Tool use involves the flexible combination of behavioral elements to modify and utilize environmental materials and can expand an organisms' ecological niche by allowing access to otherwise inaccessible resources. Novel tool using behaviors and unique techniques (i.e., variations within a specific tool using behavior) can be innovated, transmitted from mothers to offspring, or spread among cohort members via observation. The ability to flexibly adjust one's behavior is vital to surviving new or changing habitats, but remains difficult to study empirically or quantitatively. In this study, we use Epistemic Network Analysis (ENA) to visualize and compare patterns of termite fishing behavioral elements – a ubiquitous tool-using behavior in chimpanzees – in a population of Nigeria-Cameroon chimpanzees (*Pan troglodytes ellioti*) in Mbam & Djerem National Park, Cameroon. We coded 87 videos representing over one hour of termite fishing observations of 12 individual chimpanzees of various ages (Adult: n = 6, Juvenile: n = 4, Infants: n = 2). Networks revealed variation in the combinations of termite fishing behavioral elements between age classes. Results suggest that flexibility in termite fishing is high in limited combinations with Infants, but overall flexibility increases with age and may be shaped by practice. Findings also highlight the utility of ENA in the study of behavioral flexibility and inform future research applications around cultural variation in chimpanzees.

Keywords: Nigeria-Cameroon Chimpanzee · Tool Use · Behavioral Flexibility · Epistemic Network Analysis

G. Arastoopour Irgens and S. Knight (Eds.): ICQE 2023, CCIS 1895, pp. 155–169, 2023.
https://doi.org/10.1007/978-3-031-47014-1_11

1 Introduction

1.1 Behavioral Flexibility and Survival

The Earth is currently experiencing a mass extinction event, with species disappearing at an alarming rate due to human activities [1]. Despite conservation efforts, the number of declining species exceeds those that have been saved [2]. Primates are particularly at risk, with 60% of primate species currently facing extinction [3]. With genetic adaptation occurring at a slow pace, behavioral flexibility is crucial for organisms to survive in changing and disturbed habitats.

Behavioral flexibility, or the ability to flexibly adjust behavior to local environmental conditions, can influence an individual's survival by allowing species to occupy variable environments [4, 5]. Environmental complexity has been linked to increased brain size in primates, and this increased brain size is associated with greater behavioral flexibility and innovation [6]. This suggests that primates with larger brains are better able to cope with resource scarcity, as greater innovative ability allows individuals to respond to novel or changing environments [6]. Great apes exhibit frequent innovation and a high degree of behavioral flexibility within and between populations [7].

Chimpanzees in particular are known for their behavioral flexibility, which has allowed them to adapt to a variety of environments and ecological niches [8]. Chimpanzees have a dynamic fission-fusion social system, where bonded communities of 20–150 individuals will split into smaller subgroups to forage [9]. This flexible social system may reduce the costs of travel and plays an important role in allowing chimpanzees to persist in their current habitats [10]. This social flexibility allows chimpanzees to maintain large groups relative to other great apes [9] and maximize protection in anthropogenic settings [10, 11]. In Bossou, Guinea, for example, chimpanzee groups will alter their positioning when crossing roads depending on the degree of risk and number of adult males present [10]. In Kibale, Uganda, foraging parties in human croplands vocalize less often than parties in the core of the range in response to greater potential risk of human detection [10].

Chimpanzees also respond flexibly to new or altered habitats through a variety of adaptations, although these presumed adaptations have not been directly linked variation in fitness or reproductive success. There is substantial evidence of chimpanzees altering behavior in response to climatic factors [12–14]. At Fongoli, Senegal, chimpanzees will rest in caves or soak in rivers to reduce heat stress associated with the dry, high temperature conditions [12]. In Issa Valley, Tanzania, chimpanzees will also alter nest architecture and materials based on local, overnight weather conditions [13]. Several chimpanzee populations also alter their nocturnal behavior, increasing activity at night when there are low rates of human activity or higher average daytime temperature [14]. Chimpanzees have also frequently been documented flexibly changing their foraging behaviors in response to environmental and anthropogenic factors [15, 16]. In Kibale, habitat destruction has led to some groups of chimpanzees exploiting croplands, with large raiding parties often including older individuals or nursing mothers [15]. Evidence comparing two chimpanzee groups at Bulindi, Uganda suggest that chimpanzees increase foraging adaptations to cultivated landscapes over time [16]. Overall, these cases exemplify the varied ways in which chimpanzees flexibly alter their behavior in response to their environment and anthropogenic context to influence their survival (e.g., acquire food, avoid heat exhaustion, contend with weather, etc.).

Behavioral flexibility assessments for chimpanzees have been conducted by observing wild chimpanzees and comparing behavior between different contexts (e.g., savanna chimp behavior at different times of day or temperatures [12–14]) or more directly in captive settings with experimental procedures that can be altered in order to quantify how quickly subjects can pivot from one behavior to another [17, 18].

1.2 Chimpanzee Tool Use

Tool use behaviors are highly flexible, innovative behaviors that often allow chimpanzees to access new dietary items [19, 20]. For example, termite fishing – where chimpanzees use modified plant probes to extract termites from mounds – has been documented in at least 15 chimpanzee communities across tropical Africa [7]. Termites can provide nontrivial amounts of important vitamins (e.g., B12), minerals (e.g., iron and manganese), and amino acids, and have higher comparative nutritional payoff due to their large colony sizes [21]. Additionally, tool use behaviors vary between chimpanzee populations based on genetic, cultural, and environmental differences [7, 22] Research suggests that food scarcity, increased exposure to tool using conditions, and/or the relative profitability of high-energy resources that can be obtained with tools have driven the development and maintenance of tool use in chimpanzees [20, 23]. However, studies have also found that genetic variation and behavioral variation between chimpanzee groups is highly correlated [22]. This suggests that genetic differences are also influencing variation in tool use behaviors, potentially via heritable traits like taste preference or dexterity [22]. Finally, increased diversity of behavior has been linked in chimpanzees to greater distance from their ancestral forest habitats during the Pleistocene glacial period, suggesting that behavioral flexibility has been important for chimpanzees surviving in new environments [24].

Ultimately, this implies that variation in cultural behaviors like tool use can influence chimpanzee evolution, as it is: (1) heritable [22], (2) differs within and between populations [7], (3) linked to environmental differences [23], and (4) provides fitness benefits [24]. These behaviors can also be transmitted socially between individuals through observation [25]. It is important to understand what factors promote behavioral flexibility in order to maintain behavioral variation in wild chimpanzee populations. Human influence has been related to sharp decreases in the diversity of chimpanzee behaviors [26]. As rates of human influence increase in and around chimpanzee habitats, preserving behavioral flexibility may be an important step in chimpanzee conservation.

Termite fishing is one of the most widely studied tool use behaviors in chimpanzees, with a large degree of variation in technical diversity between populations (Fig. 1) [7, 19, 27]. A recent study compared variation in termite fishing behavioral elements between 15 chimpanzee communities and identified 38 behavioral elements with community-specific combinations making up specific termite fishing techniques [19]. Tool use behaviors can serve as a useful measure of behavioral flexibility because they can be observed and quantified directly [28]. Therefore, termite fishing is a convenient method for studying behavioral flexibility, and a good foundation for comparing flexibility between chimpanzee populations.

Compared to other chimpanzee subspecies, termite fishing behaviors of the Nigeria-Cameroon chimpanzee (*Pan troglodytes ellioti*) remain relatively understudied. *P. t. ellioti* was identified as a separate subspecies relatively recently [29] and has no study populations habituated to human presence, making firsthand behavioral observations nearly impossible. *P. t. ellioti* is the most endangered chimpanzee subspecies, with the smallest population size and the smallest range [30]. The ability to quantify the behavioral flexibility of *P. t. ellioti* and understand how this flexibility may be shaped by its environment can be a powerful conservation tool for this endangered primate.

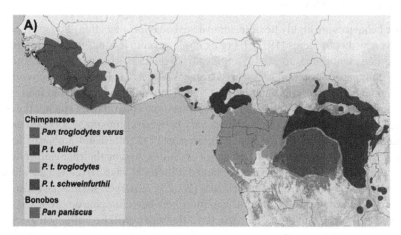

Fig. 1. Map of the distribution of chimpanzee subspecies. Present populations where termite fishing has been observed. Figure from [31].

1.3 Epistemic Network Analysis

Epistemic Network Analysis (ENA) is a quantitative ethnographic technique that visualizes patterns of associations across themes or elements in complex and often large-scale data [32]. Originally developed around the theoretical concept of epistemic frames, ENA is often used to model relationships between cognitive elements linked in a particular epistemology (i.e., a contextualized way of thinking) in human discourse. A common approach to building matrices of associations in ENA is the use of a moving stanza window, which connects binary codes applied to a single line of data to codes applied to prior lines within the recent temporal context [32, 33]. This framing aligns with existing understandings of technical combinations in chimpanzee tool use over time. Epistemic networks are also well-suited to the visual and statistical comparison of differences across unit groups (in this case chimpanzee age groups) through plotting of unit means and rotated network models in a single high dimensional space.

While used predominantly in the learning sciences, these features of ENA suggest that the technique has powerful potential applications in the study of animal behavior, particularly for visualizing the ways that chimpanzee connect complex and flexible behaviors over time as part of their tool use. ENA has recently shown promise in cross-disciplinary contexts as a technique to analyze (a) surgery trainees' operative performance during a simulated procedure [34]; (b) gaze coordination during collaborative work [35]; and (c) communication among health care teams [36]. We offer research on animal behavior as another valuable application of these approaches.

1.4 Research Questions

In this study, we use ENA to examine termite fishing behaviors in a group of *P. t. ellioti* in Mbam & Djerem National Park, Cameroon and address the following questions:

1. Do older chimpanzees exhibit greater flexibility in termite fishing behavior than younger chimpanzees?
2. Can ENA be used successfully to visualize behavioral flexibility and variation in termite fishing techniques in chimpanzees?

Given that termite fishing is socially transmitted and dexterously complex, we hypothesize that older chimpanzees will incorporate more behavioral elements than younger chimpanzees, and that younger chimpanzees will rely on fewer, more prototypical termite fishing techniques.

2 Methods

2.1 Study Site

This study was conducted along 10 2-km transects near Ganga Station in Mbam & Djerem National Park (MDNP), Cameroon. Ganga Station is located in the northeastern side of the park along the Djerem river in central Cameroon and is one of the only remaining continuous field sites studying *P. t. ellioti*. MDNP extends more than 4,165 km^2 and was created in 2000 [37, 38]. This region is part Guinea-Congolia/Sudania regional transition zone, where the Guinean rainforest, the Congolian rainforest, and the Sudania savanna intersect to create a mosaic ecotone of riparian forest, closed-canopy and gallery forest, and open grassland [38]. MDNP experiences an average annual rainfall of ~2000 mm and a wet season from April to October [37].

2.2 Video Collection and Coding

Camera traps were set up at seven termite mounds along transects near Ganga Station from February 2020 following an initial pilot study at one termite mound in May 2019. Camera traps were strapped to trees between 2–3 m from the termite mound and angled to show the entire mound structure. These camera traps use infrared motion detection and were programmed to record 1-min videos when triggered. Silica packets were placed on the camera screen to prevent damage from humidity. During this study, termite fishing was documented at four of the seven termite mounds. Every month, field assistants would swap out the SD cards and change the silica/batteries as needed.

Including the pilot data from May 2019, the camera traps recorded 254 videos of chimpanzee termite fishing from February 2020 to June 2021, totaling approximately

4 h of observation. Visitors to the mound were typically lone juvenile chimpanzees, or small family groups consisting of a single adult female and her dependent infants. In total, 12 chimpanzees were observed termite fishing during this period (Adults: n = 6, Juveniles: n = 4, Infants: n = 2). Random subsets of the videos of each chimpanzee subject were coded for analysis in this study for a total of 87 videos. Videos per subject ranged from 1 to 40 (mean = 7.25). This wide range is due to variation in representation for each chimpanzee subject. Chimpanzees with fewer than 6 videos of observation time had all of their videos coded, while all subjects who appear in more than 10 videos have at least 6 of their videos coded in this subset, chosen at random.

Videos were analyzed for behavioral elements using a comprehensive ethogram adapted from several ethograms of chimpanzee behavior and chimpanzee tool use [19, 39]. This comprehensive ethogram includes a total of 59 chimpanzee behaviors (Tool Making: n = 6; Tool Use: n = 30; Non-Tool Behaviors: n = 23). These elements are combined flexibly into techniques (e.g., wrist assisted probe), and these techniques may be contextually relevant to maximize termite fishing success. Each row of data represents a single behavioral element from a single chimpanzee in a single video, and includes data on the start time, body position, hand use, and other body parts utilized in the action. Start time for each behavioral element is recorded to the nearest quarter-second, and behavioral elements are considered to be mutually exclusive, meaning the start time of a particular behavioral element is also the end time of the previous one. This leads to a sequence of behavioral elements for each chimpanzee within each video, with each line representing only a single behavior, which demonstrates how the chipmanzees chain behaviors through time while using tools to termite fish. Subjects in this study generally exhibited between 20 and 60 behavioral elements per minute, with adults utilizing more behaviors than juveniles or infants on average.

All videos were coded by T. Andres-Bray. Fifteen of the 87 videos were also coded by a second observer to establish interrater reliability using Cohen's kappa [40]. The second observer underwent a period of training via co-coding with the primary observer before coding videos independently. Interrater reliability for all behavioral elements was $\kappa = 0.773$, which is considered very high [41].

2.3 Epistemic Network Analysis

We used Epistemic Network Analysis (ENA) [32] with the aid of the ENA Web Tool (version 1.7.0) [42] to analyze combinations of behavioral elements. Units of analysis were defined as all lines of data associated with a single chimpanzee age class subset by subject ID and video number. For example, a single unit in this study was all lines of data for the adult chimpanzee "Subject 1" from Video 1.

The ENA algorithm uses a moving window to construct a network model for each line in the data, showing how codes are connected within a recent temporal context [43]. In this case, the moving window for a particular line included that line and the 3 previous lines, within a given conversation (this window length was determined appropriate for self-referential tool use behaviors over time, as previous research has found termite fishing tool use in chimpanzees consists of combinations of approximately elements [19]). In this case, the conversation is defined as all lines of data for a given subject in a given video (e.g., all behavioral elements used by Subject 1 in Video 1). The resulting networks are aggregated for all lines for each unit of analysis in the model. In this model, we aggregated networks using a binary summation in which the networks for a given line reflect the presence or absence of the co-occurrence of each pair of codes.

Our ENA model included the following behavioral elements:

- Tool Making: 1) Reshape, using hand to straighten brush fibers of the tool; 2) Reduce, using hand or teeth to remove parts of the tool; and 3) Fray Bite, using teeth to create brush tip at the distal end of the tool.
- Tool Use: 1) Probe, inserting a tool into the mound; 2) Oscillate, moving the tool back and forth repeatedly within the mound; 3) Extract, remove the tool from mound; 4) Eat from Tool, consuming termite from the tool; 5) and Wrist Help, using the opposite wrist to guide tool to their mouth.
- Non-Tool: 1) Scratch Ground, using a finger to prepare an area for probing; and 2) Scan, visually search the surrounding area, typically considered vigilance behavior.

The ENA model normalized the networks for all units of analysis before they were subjected to a dimensional reduction, which accounts for the fact that different units of analysis may have different amounts of coded lines in the data. For the dimensional reduction, we used a singular value decomposition, which produces orthogonal dimensions that maximize the variance explained by each dimension [36].

Networks were visualized using network graphs where nodes correspond to the codes, and edges reflect the relative frequency of co-occurrence, or connection, between two codes. The result is two coordinated representations for each unit of analysis: (1) a plotted point, which represents the location of that unit's network in the low-dimensional projected space, and (2) a weighted network graph. The positions of the network graph nodes are fixed, and those positions are determined by an optimization routine that minimizes the difference between the plotted points and their corresponding network centroids. Because of this co-registration of network graphs and projected space, the positions of the network graph nodes—and the connections they define—can be used to interpret the dimensions of the projected space and explain the positions of plotted points in the space. Our model had co-registration correlations of 0.99 (Pearson) and 0.99 (Spearman) for the first dimension and co-registration correlations of 0.99 (Pearson) and 0.98 (Spearman) for the second. These measures indicate that there is a strong goodness of fit between the visualization and the original model.

3 Results

3.1 Age Class Comparison

Figures 2, 3, and 4 show connections between behavioral elements in the ENA model for Infants, Juveniles, and Adults respectively. The age class unit means are shown as colored squares (Infants: blue, Juveniles: purple, Adults: red). The strength of the connections for each age class is shown by the thickness of the lines (See Figs. 2, 3, and 4).

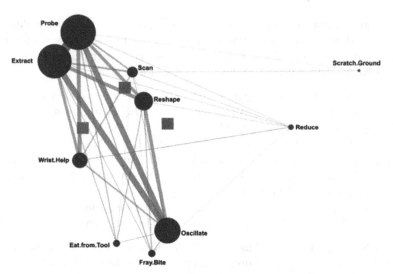

Fig. 2. Epistemic network of infant behavioral elements. This figure shows the connections between behavioral elements (circles) for infant chimpanzees. Stronger connections are represented by thicker lines. Variance explained by the x-dimension = 32.2%, Variance explained by the y-dimension = 14.7%. Squares represent unit means for each age class: infants (blue), juveniles (purple), and adults (red).

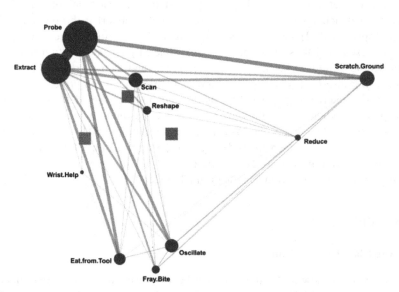

Fig. 3. Epistemic network of juvenile behavioral elements. This figure shows the connections between behavioral elements (circles) for juvenile chimpanzees. Stronger connections are represented by thicker lines. Variance explained and unit means are the same as Fig. 2.

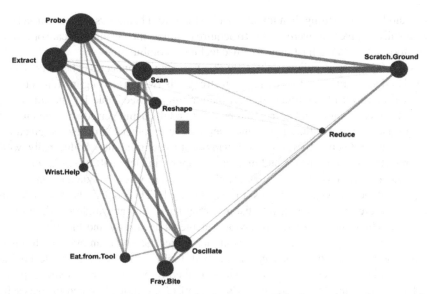

Fig. 4. Epistemic network of adult behavioral elements. This figure shows the connections between behavioral elements (circles) for adult chimpanzees. Stronger connections are represented by thicker lines. Variance explained and unit means are the same as Fig. 2.

The unit mean for Infants is pulled to the left in the space because of a triad of stronger connections between probe-oscillate-extract. This combination appears to be a modification of the prototypical probe-extract technique. Infants also have a stronger connection between wrist help and both probe and extract compared to Juveniles and Adults, indicating potentially more frequent use of the wrist help behavior (Table 1). The stronger connections between probe-oscillate-extract and the comparably strong connection with wrist help may indicate infants focus on a few specific combinations as they learn how to fish for termites. This fits with anecdotal evidence from our videos. The two infant subjects often employ fewer behavioral elements per video and perform these elements for longer. Additionally, they would repeat the same technical sequences of probe-extract or probe-oscillate-extract even if previous attempts were unsuccessful, suggesting they may not have completely mastered the techniques or perhaps are not experienced enough to know what other elements to employ to improve success rate.

Juveniles, on the other hand, maintain a stronger connection between probe and extract but lack the comparably strong connection with oscillate seen in Infants (Fig. 3). Additionally, while Juveniles have a comparably weaker connection between wrist help and both probe and extract, they show a stronger connection between probe and scratch ground than seen in Infants (See Table 1). This may indicate that with more experience, chimpanzees participate more in non-tool behaviors during termite fishing. As chimpanzees grow older, they may learn additional behavioral elements, like scratch ground, that do not involve the tool but can be combined with tool using elements to increase success. The juveniles in this study were generally more successful at termite fishing compared to infants. They tended to default to a scratch ground-probe-extract pattern but would be more willing than infants to adjust non-tool behaviors when unsuccessful. Anecdotally, if juveniles were unable to acquire termites, they would relocate or acquire a new tool rather than adjust their tool-use technical combinations.

The Adult mean is pulled to the right due to stronger connections between scratch ground and scan (Fig. 4). This connection strength is twice as strong in Adults than in Juveniles, and over fifteen times stronger than in Infants (See Table 1). The connection between scratch ground and scan could be due to adults using periods between termite fishing bouts to prepare the mound and keep an eye on other chimpanzees, given that adult females are generally present at mounds with young infants. Additionally, while the connection between probe and extract was approximately half as strong in Adults as compared to Infants and Juveniles, Adults have more varied, moderate connections among all of the behavioral elements (Fig. 2c) (Table 1). This could indicate that Adults, who have more experience termite fishing, may have a greater understanding of the context in which these different behavioral elements are useful and therefore employ them more precisely and flexibly. For example, Subject 1, who is an older adult female and prolific tool user, frequently multitasks with tool use and non-tool use techniques to acquire chimpanzees. She would switch frequently between probe-extract, probe-oscillate-extract, and picking termites directly off of the mound. When unsuccessful, she would modify the tool by reshaping the fibers or re-fraying the brush tip rather than seek out a new tool or location like juvenile chimpanzees, potentially suggesting an understanding of elements that can improve fishing success.

Table 1. Connection Strength Between Behavioral Elements. This table shows line weights for dyads of the behavioral elements (codes) from the ENA model where at least one of the three age classes had a connection value greater than 0.15.

Behavioral Dyads	Infant Value	Juvenile Value	Adult Value
Extract-Eat from Tool	0.05	0.16	0.10
Extract-Scan	0.11	0.15	0.04
Oscillate-Extract	0.34	0.13	0.16
Probe-Eat from Tool	0.06	0.18	0.06
Probe-Extract	0.54	0.55	0.31
Probe-Oscillate	0.33	0.17	0.15
Probe-Scratch Ground	0.01	0.23	0.16
Probe-Wrist Help	0.22	0.02	0.09
Reshape-Extract	0.21	0.09	0.12
Reshape-Oscillate	0.20	0.01	0.04
Reshape-Probe	0.19	0.08	0.14
Scratch Ground-Scan	0.02	0.13	0.31
Wrist Help-Extract	0.17	0.02	0.08

3.2   Behavioral Flexibility in ENA

Variation in connection strength between behavioral elements in the ENA model has the potential to be a useful measure of behavioral flexibility, as the strength of connection between behavioral elements is related to the frequency that those elements appear in the same moving window. An unbalanced model would indicate less flexibility as members of that age class would rely on a smaller number of technical combinations, while a more balanced model would indicate greater flexibility through the more varied use of different technical combinations.

Figure 5 compares the asymmetry in the models for all three age classes using 18 dyadic connections between behavioral elements. These dyads are all connections where at least one age class had a connection value of 0.05 or greater. These dyads were ranked from strongest to weakest connection within each age class and plotted to show the different models' asymmetry in connection strength. Thus, the dyad ranked 7 for Adults is not necessarily the same behavior pair as it is for Infants and Juveniles; rather, it is whichever dyad is the 9th strongest connection within each age class.

Adults had a more balanced model compared to both Juveniles and Infants (See Fig. 5). This suggests that Adults have more varied combinations of behavioral elements, which may imply that Adults utilize more flexible termite fishing techniques. Compared to Infants, the Juvenile model shows more diverse, though often less heavily weighted, connections across behaviors (See Fig. 5). This suggests infant chimpanzees show high flexibility with a limited number of behavioral elements, possibly as they vary combinations in a "guess-and-check" method. This is followed by a period of low flexibility where adolescent chimpanzees have a few techniques, with strong focus on those combinations. Finally, adult chimpanzees have had time to observe or innovate behavioral elements, and more experience in using more combinations, and this may explain the greater variation in moderate strength connections seen in Fig. 5.

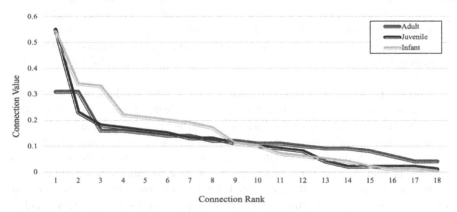

Fig. 5. Change in connection strength from strongest to weakest connections. This figure shows the diversity of different types of behavioral connections in each model by showing the connection values between behavioral elements in decreasing order within each age class. Note that the top ranked connection for adults is not necessarily the same as the top ranked connection for juveniles or infants, etc. (Table 1).

4 Discussion

Behavioral flexibility is an important trait that can aid organisms in accessing novel resources or survive in novel habitats [4, 7]. This trait becomes increasingly important as humans continue to alter natural habitats, as behavioral changes can occur faster than genetic adaptations to changing environments. Tool use is an important flexible behavior for chimpanzees, as it can be used to access nutrient-rich food items like social insects and can generalize strategies to acquire different resources [7]. The results of this study demonstrate that ENA is a valuable tool for quantifying behavioral flexibility in non-human animals and making behavioral comparisons.

The ENA model in this study was able to visualize differences in the ways chimpanzees of different age classes combined the same behavioral elements. These results suggest that Adults have a greater flexibility in the combinations of behavioral elements utilized to fish for termites, while both Infant and Juvenile chimpanzees show strong preferences for simpler, prototypical combinations (e.g., probe-extract). This is consistent with prior research which has shown: 1) a long developmental period required to master the different behavioral elements associated with tool use and to further combine them in functional sequences, and 2) the pattern of acquiring simpler combinations first before more complex patterns [44–46]. More varied analyses are needed to confirm this pattern, including an analysis of tool success and the sequential combinations of tools, but ENA has shown it is able to provide useful visual and conceptual information about chimpanzee tool use in Mbam & Djerem National Park, Cameroon.

There are several important drawbacks to ENA that are important to highlight in the context of this study. The model created here was limited to 10 behavioral elements, which is roughly one-sixth of the total behaviors present in the ethogram used in this project. More than 15 elements becomes cumbersome to visualize with ENA, and thus this analysis may miss out on some rare behavioral elements that could contribute to behavioral flexibility. Further, ENA can only show connections between pairs of behavioral elements and is unable to show if those combinations have directionality (e.g., probeextract vs. extractprobe). The sequence in which behavioral elements are utilized is an important part of tool use, and modeling methods that account for sequence (like Ordered Network Analysis [47]) may also be useful for this type of research.

However, ENA remains a powerful untapped analysis for non-human animal behavior research. Some of the greatest benefits of ENA include its flexibility and visualization ability. With enough metadata, ENA can easily model and visualize comparisons between a wealth of topics. In addition to age class comparison, ENA could be utilized to examine differences between different populations, sexes, tool characteristics, temporal or spatial locations, mound characteristics, and more. All of these potential topics could improve our understanding of factors that influence behavioral flexibility by providing a way to quantify flexibility and can ultimately benefit chimpanzee conservation. This could be particularly potent for long-term chimpanzee study sites (e.g., Goualougo Triangle [23], Gombe [45], or Ngogo [48]) that have a wealth of demographic and ecological data and also utilize behavioral videos. ENA would be an effective tool to compare behavioral patterns and behavioral flexibility between these well-known and well-studied chimpanzee communities.

References

1. Barnosky, A.D., et al.: Has the Earth's sixth mass extinction already arrived? Nature **471**, 51–57 (2011)
2. Hoffmann, M., et al.: The impact of conservation on the status of the world's vertebrates. Science **330**, 1503–1509 (2010)
3. Carvalho, J., et al.: Predicting range shifts of African apes under global change scenarios. Div. Distrib. **27**(9), 1663–1679 (2021). https://doi.org/10.1111/ddi.13358
4. Hockings, K.J., et al.: Apes in the Anthropocene: flexibility and survival. Trends Ecol. Evol. **30**(4), 215–222 (2015). https://doi.org/10.1016/j.tree.2015.02.002
5. Berger-Tal, O., Polak, T., Oron, A., Lubin, Y., Kotler, B.P., Saltz, D.: Integrating animal behavior and conservation biology: a conceptual framework. Behav. Ecol. **22**(2), 236–239 (2011)
6. LeFebvre, L., Reader, S.M., Sol, D.: Brains, innovations and evolution in birds and primates. Brain Behav. Evol. **63**, 233–246 (2004)
7. Whiten, A., et al.: Cultures in chimpanzees. Nature **399**, 682–685 (1999)
8. Stumpf, R.: Chimpanzees and bonobos: Inter-and intra-species diversity. In: Campbell, C.J., Fuentes, A., MacKinnon, K.C., Panger, M., Bearder, S.K. (eds.) Primates in Perspective, 2nd edn., pp. 340–356. Oxford University Press, UK (2010)
9. Mitani, J.C.: Demographic influences on the behavior of chimpanzees. Primates **47**(1), 6–13 (2006)
10. Hockings, K.J.: Behavioral flexibility and division of roles in chimpanzee road-crossing. In: Matsuzawa, T., Humle, T., Sugiyama, H. (eds.) The Chimpanzees of Bossou and Nimba, pp. 221–229. Springer, Tokyo (2011)
11. Wrangham, R., Wilson, M., Hauser, M.: Chimpanzees (*Pan troglodytes*) modify grouping and vocal behaviour in response to location-specific risk. Behaviour **144**(12), 1621–1653 (2007)
12. Pruetz, J.D.: Evidence of cave use by savanna chimpanzees (*Pan troglodytes verus*) at Fongoli, Senegal: implications for thermoregulatory behavior. Primates **48**(4), 316–319 (2007)
13. Stewart, F.A., Piel, A.K., Azkarate, J.C., Pruetz, J.D.: Savanna chimpanzees adjust sleeping nest architecture in response to local weather conditions. Am. J. Phys. Anthropol. **166**(3), 549–562 (2018)
14. Tagg, N., et al.: Nocturnal activity in wild chimpanzees (*Pan troglodytes*): evidence for flexible sleeping patterns and insights into human evolution. Am. J. Phys. Anthropol. **166**(3), 510–529 (2018)
15. Krief, S., Cibot, M., Bortolamiol, S., Seguya, A., Krief, J.M., Masi, S.: Wild chimpanzees on the edge: nocturnal activities in croplands. PLoS ONE **9**(10), e109925 (2014)
16. McLennan, M.R., Hockings, K.J.: Wild chimpanzees show group differences in selection of agricultural crops. Sci. Rep. **4**(1), 1–7 (2014)
17. Hopper, L.M., Kurtycz, L.M., Ross, S.R., Bonnie, K.E.: Captive chimpanzee foraging in a social setting: a test of problem solving, flexibility, and spatial discounting. PeerJ **3**, e833 (2015)
18. Manrique, H.M., Völter, C.J., Call, J.: Repeated innovation in great apes. Anim. Behav. **81**(1), 195–202 (2013)
19. Boesch, C., et al.: Chimpanzee ethnography reveals unexpected cultural diversity. Nat. Hum. Behav. **4**(9), 910–916 (2020)
20. Fox, E.A., Sitompul, A.F., van Schaik, C.P.: Intelligent tool use in wild Sumatran orangutans. In: Parker, S.T., Mitchell, R.W., Miles, H.L. (eds.) The Mentalities of Gorillas and Orangutans, pp. 99–116. Cambridge University Press, UK (1999)
21. Deblauwe, I., Janssens, G.P.: New insights in insect prey choice by chimpanzees and gorillas in southeast Cameroon: the role of nutritional value. Am. J. Phys. Anthropol. **135**(1), 42–55 (2008)

22. Langergraber, K.E., et al.: Genetic and 'cultural' similarity in wild chimpanzees. Proc. Royal Soc. B: Biol. Sci. **278**(1704), 408–416 (2011)
23. Sanz, C.M., Morgan, D.B.: Ecological and social correlates of chimpanzee tool use. Philos. Trans. R. Soc. B **368**, 20120416 (2013)
24. Kalan, A.K., et al.: Environmental variability supports chimpanzee behavioural diversity. Nat. Commun. **11**, 4451 (2020)
25. Lamon, N., Neumann, C., Gruber, T., Zuberbühler, K.: Kin-based cultural transmission of tool use in wild chimpanzees. Sci. Adv. **3**(4), e1602750 (2017)
26. Kühl, H.S., et al.: Human impact erodes chimpanzee behavioral diversity. Science **363**, 1453–1455 (2019)
27. Boesch, C., Boesch, H.: Tool use and tool making in wild chimpanzees. Folia Primatol. **54**, 86–99 (1990)
28. Reader, S.M., MacDonald, K.: Environmental variability and primate behavioural flexibility. In: Reader, S.N., Laland, K.N. (eds.) Animal Innovation, pp. 83–116. Oxford University Press, UK (2003)
29. Gonder, M.K., Oates, J.F., Disotell, T.R., Forstner, M.R., Morales, J.C., Melnick, D.J.: A new west African chimpanzee subspecies? Nature **388**(6640), 337 (1997)
30. Mittermeier, R.A., et al.: Primates in Peril: The World's 25 Most Endangered Primates 2022–2023. IUCN SSC Primate Specialist Group, International Primatological Society, Re:wild, Washington, DC (2022)
31. Mitchell, M.W., et al.: The population genetics of wild chimpanzees in Cameroon and Nigeria suggests a positive role for selection in the evolution of chimpanzee subspecies. BMC Evol. Biol. **15**(1), 3 (2015). https://doi.org/10.1186/s12862-014-0276-y
32. Shaffer, D.W.: Quantitative Ethnography. Cathcart Press, Madison, WI (2017)
33. Barany, A., Shah, M., Foster, A.: Connecting curricular design and student identity change: an epistemic network analysis. In: Ruis, A.R., Lee, S. B. (eds.) ICQE 2021. CCIS, vol. 1312, pp. 155–169. Springer, Cham (2021). https://doi.org/10.1007/978-3-030-67788-6_11
34. Ruis, A.R., Rosser, A.A., Quandt-Walle, C., Nathwani, J.N., Shaffer, D.W., Pugh, C.M.: The hands and head of a surgeon: modeling operative competency with multimodal epistemic network analysis. Am. J. Surg. **216**(5), 835–840 (2018)
35. Andrist, S., Collier, W., Gleicher, M., Mutlu, B., Shaffer, D.: Look together: Analyzing gaze coordination with epistemic network analysis. Front. Psychol. **6**, 1016 (2015)
36. Sullivan, S.A., et al.: Using epistemic network analysis to identify targets for educational interventions in trauma team communication. Surgery **163**(4), 938–943 (2017)
37. Abwe, E.E.: Linking behavioral diversity with genetic and ecological variation in the Nigeria-Camerioon chimpanzee. Dissertation: Drexel University, USA (2018)
38. Maisels, F.: Mbam Djerem National Park. Conservation status. In: Large mammals and human impact: Final report. WCS-Cameroon (2003)
39. Nishida, T., Kano, T., Goodall, J., McGrew, W.C., Nakamura, M.: Ethogram and ethnography of mahale chimpanzees. Anthropol. Sci. **107**(2), 141–188 (1999)
40. Cohen, J.: A coefficient of agreement for nominal scales. Educ. Psychol. Measur. **20**, 37–46 (1960)
41. Fleiss, J.L.: Statistical Methods for Rates and Proportions. Wiley, New York, NY (1981)
42. Marquart, C.L., Hinojosa, C., Swiecki, Z., Eagan, B., Shaffer, D.W.: Epistemic Network Analysis (Version 1.7.0). http://app.epistemicnetwork.org (2018)
43. Siebert-Evenstone, A., Arastoopour Irgens, G., Collier, W., Swiecki, Z., Ruis, A.R., Shaffer, D.W.: Search of conversational grain size: modelling semantic structure using moving stanza windows. J. Learn. Anal. **4**(3), 123–139 (2017)
44. Musgrave, S., Lonsdorf, E., Morgan, D., Sanz, C.: The ontogeny of termite gathering among chimpanzees in the Goualougo Triangle, Republic of Congo. Am. J. Phys. Anthropol. **174**(2), 187–200 (2021)

45. Lonsdorf, E.V.: Sex differences in the development of termite-fishing skills in the wild chimpanzees, *Pan troglodytes schweinfurthii*, of Gombe National Park, Tanzania. Anim. Behav. **70**(3), 673–683 (2005)
46. Lockman, J.J.: A perception–action perspective on tool use development. Child Dev. **71**(1), 137–144 (2000)
47. Tan, Y., Ruis, A.R., Marquart, C., Cai, Z., Knowles, M.A., Shaffer, D.W.: Ordered network analysis. In: Damşa, C., Barany, A. (eds.) Advances in Quantitative Ethnography: 4th International Conference, ICQE 2022, Copenhagen, Denmark, 15–19 Oct 2022, Proceedings, pp. 101–116. Springer Nature Switzerland, Cham (2023). https://doi.org/10.1007/978-3-031-31726-2_8
48. Watts, D.P.: Tool use by chimpanzees at Ngogo, Kibale National Park, Uganda. Int. J. Primatol. **29**, 83–94 (2008)

Society, Culture, Identity, and Justice

Examining Motivating Language in Commencement Speeches Using Epistemic Network Analysis

Yujung Seol[(✉)]

Ministry of Culture, Sports, and Tourism in Korean Government,
Sejong 30119, Republic of Korea
syj11977@korea.kr

Abstract. This research examines how speakers use language to motivate their audiences through an analysis of 15 Harvard University commencement speeches from 2007 to 2021. Motivating language theory classifies the data and interprets the result as a theoretical framework. This study modeled the language patterns employed by the speakers using Epistemic Network Analysis (ENA) and compared the ENA network model based on gender and time. Results indicate that meaning-making language serves as a dominant approach to motivating audiences. Particularly, the speakers mainly employed personal anecdotes or enlightenment, knowledge related to their own experience, and suggestion language to imply specific actions or ideas. Additionally, the differences in motivational language patterns between male and female speakers and between older and more recent speeches were found. These findings could help organizational leaders, who must communicate or speak to employees, motivate them to commit and engage with their work.

Keywords: Motivating Language · Commencement Speech · Epistemic Network Analysis (ENA)

1 Introduction

The language is employed by leaders in communicating with followers plays a vital role in leadership since it possesses the potential to influence the followers' attitudes and behaviors [1]. The leader's views and wisdom can be strategically conveyed depending on the language used, and so the language effectively encourages and inspires the followers [2]. Motivated workers are more likely to be engaged and productive on the job, which can result in enhanced performance and job satisfaction [3, 9]. Therefore, fostering individuals' motivation to engage in actions with enthusiasm via the language leaders use is considered a pivotal element in achieving good organizational management [2].

1.1 Motivating Language Theory

Motivation language theory explains how language use can significantly affect the motivation and behavior of individuals [1]. This theory asserts that motivational language

© The Author(s), under exclusive license to Springer Nature Switzerland AG 2023
G. Arastoopour Irgens and S. Knight (Eds.): ICQE 2023, CCIS 1895, pp. 173–186, 2023.
https://doi.org/10.1007/978-3-031-47014-1_12

plays a crucial role in fostering an environment that either increases or decreases the motivation of employees within an organization [6], increasing employees' job satisfaction and enhancing their quality of work life [7]. According to motivational language theory, motivational languages are classified into three languages: direction-giving language, empathetic language, and meaning-making language [9].

Firstly, direction-giving language is a language that decreases confusion by clearly presenting directions and guidelines linked to the job while an organization member does their job. It functions as a compass, informing members of the organization about their location and direction while doing their jobs [9]. This sort of leader talk demonstrates clarity of purpose and objective, influencing factors, considerations, problem-solving strategies, and previous work methods [8]. When leaders communicate a strategic essential in direction-giving, employees understand what must be done, including processes, time frames, and projected rewards [10].

Next, empathic language is used to boost employee morale by showing interest in, encouraging, and praising them [1]. This language demonstrates a leader's humanity and goes beyond a normal connection with employees [10]. A leader can engage in an empathetic conversation when he or she acknowledges or praises an employee's efforts or is sympathetic to the employee's difficulties. For instance, praise for achievement or effort, interest in individuals, and words promoting individual growth, for example, are all included [9]. Furthermore, language expressions expressing the leader's emotions may be incorporated since the language that can generate emotional disturbance in the employees may be included.

Lastly, meaning-making language recognizes the organization's culture, values, and expectations of members of the organization [1]. This type of language also conveys the meaning of work to validate employees' sense of self-worth and reinforce their commitment to the organization's goals. This type of language can be informal, for example, when referring to personal experiences, values, and wisdom [9]. If direction-giving language corresponds to "what" as a language that gives goals or directions, meaning-making language might be said to correlate to "why".

1.2 Gender Differences in Motivating Language

Numerous studies have investigated in depth the distinctions between female and male speech and language usage. These studies cover a range of research domains, from examining the language itself [11] to concentrating on communication styles [12, 13] and comparing the leadership styles of various leaders based on gender [14].

For instance, research into the differences in communication patterns between men and women has revealed that men tend to communicate with the goal of task completion in mind, using objective and direct language. In contrast, women prefer communication that focuses on establishing relationships with others and frequently employs emotional language [13]. In addition, research focusing on leaders in organizational contexts has revealed that male leaders are more likely to engage in conversations centered on goal achievement and performance outcomes. On the other hand, female executives emphasize conversations that motivate employees and result in perception shifts [14]. Therefore, this study also examined how the languages used in motivational speeches conducted to the public differ by gender.

1.3   The Use of Language in the Changing Times

Research investigating the evolution of language usage across time is being undertaken in diverse academic disciplines, including linguistics, political science, and leadership studies. The correlation between shifts in language usage and alterations in culture, society, and organization is a significant factor to consider.

In the field of linguistics, Pillar [15] has shown the transformations that have occurred in speech and language usage across different historical periods and cultural contexts. Chilton [16] conducted a study in political science wherein the researcher investigated the dynamic relationship between language and politics by analyzing political discourse. The study specifically focused on examining the shifts and transformations in language usage within speeches. Furthermore, within the realm of leadership, there has been a notable focus on examining leaders' language use and communication within organizations, particularly considering technological advancements and organizational transformations [17]. As such, the researcher concluded the change of language usage across time necessitates an investigation of the temporal variations in the motivating language in commencement speeches as well.

1.4   Purpose of Study

The study aims to explore leaders' language patterns for strategic speech delivering a valuable message to the public for motivation through ENA using the motivating language theory as a framework. Through an examination of 15 Harvard University's commencement speeches from 2007 to 2021, this study seeks to discover how speakers utilize language to effectively inspire and motivate audiences. In addition, the purpose of this research is to examine the differences in patterns of language based on gender and time of speech.

2   Method

2.1   Data Sources

The commencement speech is a collection of leaders' substantial and meaningful motivating languages to share their stories from their life experiences, explain what they learned from failures and struggles, and make graduating students inspire to reflect on the direction and meaning of life [4]. Commencement speeches are given by well-known speakers among the graduates, including journalists, artists, entrepreneurs, and politicians, who provide advice as seniors to juniors who graduate from university and plan their careers in society. Mainly, speakers devote significant effort to preparing flawless speeches. For instance, in the case of Bill Gates' commencement speech in 2007, he wrote it for six months and revised it six times to finish it [5].

Particularly, Harvard University invites commencement speakers who are always in the spotlight worldwide, namely world leaders. Thus, the Harvard commencement speech is incredibly enlightening and moving for students and the public, who value speakers. For example, influential media outlets compete to extract and introduce commencement speech messages; books are made by gathering graduation speeches; famous speeches are extensively disseminated on the Internet. For these reasons, the data used in this study was Harvard communication address manuscripts of 15 speakers from 2007 to 2021. The following Table 1 indicates the sample.

Table 1. Sample.

The number	Year	Speaker	Gender	Occupation
1	2007	Bill Gates	Male	Businessman
2	2008	J.K. Rowling	Female	Artist
3	2009	Steven Chu	Male	Scholar
4	2010	Jimmy Tingle	Male	Artist
5	2011	Amy Poehler	Female	Artist
6	2012	Fareed Zakaria	Male	Journalist
7	2013	Oprah Winfrey	Female	Artist
8	2014	Sheryl Sandberg	Female	Businessman
9	2015	Natalie Portman	Female	Artist
10	2016	Steven Spielberg	Male	Artist
11	2017	Mark Zuckerberg	Male	Businessman
12	2018	U.S. Rep. John Lewis	Male	Politician
13	2019	Angela Merkel	Female	Politician
14	2020	Martin Baron	Male	Journalist
15	2021	Ruth J. Simmons	Female	Scholar

2.2 Coding

In the coding phase, the data was segmented into sentences, resulting in a dataset containing 2,271 sentences that were then evaluated. The researcher employed an inductive coding approach to identify and extract semantic units, determining ten codes. Subsequently, the codes were classified into three distinct categories of motivational language—direction-giving language, empathetic language, and meaning-making language [1]. Consequently, multiple deliberations with a fellow researcher established and enhanced a codebook. Afterward, the final coding for each data line was established using a social moderation procedure [20]. Two raters independently coded all lines according to the prepared codebook and achieved consensus (Table 2).

Table 2. Codebook.

Categories	Codes	Definition	Examples
Direction-giving language	Suggestion	Suggesting to the listener to behavior or think or change	Trust yourself; you know what you should do
	Public Confidence	Stating personal previous achievements or quotes from prominent persons to enhance public confidence on his or her statement	Philip Randolph said, "we are all in the same boat now" and we must look out for each other and care for each other" From that moment, I worked day and night on this little extra credit project that marked the end of my college education and the beginning of a remarkable journey with Microsoft
	Question	Using the tone of a question as a means of emphasizing something or evoking interest, not as a question requiring a specific answer	So why do I talk about the benefits of failure?
	Repetitive Words	Repeating similar forms of words or phrases or sentence structures	As long as they have fewer and narrower educational opportunities, as long as they must fear for their safety every moment of every day of their lives
Empathetic language	Metaphors	Explaining a phenomenon or thing in comparison to another similar phenomenon or thing without directly explaining it	If you're constantly pushing yourself higher, higher the law of averages not to mention the Myth of Icarus predicts that you will at some point fall
	Inclusive We	Using first-person plural pronouns (we, us, ours, ourselves), including a speaker (1st) and audiences (2nd person pronouns)	We do not need magic to change the world, we carry all the power we need inside ourselves already: we have the power to imagine better
	Emotive Language	Using a language with words that reflect emotions rather than objective facts or reasoning	It could be exhilarating, intimidating, sometimes even discouraging, but always challenging
Meaning-making language	Personal Anecdotes	Sharing personal experiences or memories	Because, like most of you, I began college in my teens, but sophomore year, I was offered my dream job at Universal Studios, so I dropped out
	Wisdom	Mentioning a thoughtful and insightful way to make beneficial and correct decisions and judgments in thinking and acting in life	Failure is just life trying to move us in another direction
	Knowledge	Mentioning structured information from learning and experiencing	In 1980, the number of countries that were growing at 4 percent a year—robust growth —was around 60

2.3   Epistemic Network Analysis

The researcher utilized Epistemic Network Analysis (ENA), which is a tool to analyze qualitative data statistically and provide visualized network models [18]. ENA models relational patterns between codes by showing network graphs based on the weighted connection derived from code co-occurrence [19]. Additionally, ENA specializes in a comparative analysis between different results in a set of networks [19]. In a network graph obtained through ENA, nodes represent codes, and lines connecting nodes represent the relationship between codes. The more frequently codes and the relationship between codes appear in the data, the thicker the line and the bigger the node.

As for the ENA parameters, the speaker was defined as the unit of analysis, and an infinite moving window was utilized to model the connections between the codes. Since this is not a conversation but rather a speech delivered at a specific time during the commencement ceremony, the infinite moving window was chosen for data analysis. In this sense, the researcher interpreted that the speech was connected from the beginning to the end of the data because the speaker's arguments or contents were well-structured and meticulously prepared.

3   Result

3.1   Descriptive Findings

Fifteen speakers' speeches from 2007 to 2021 containing a total of 2,271 lines were analyzed. There were eight men and seven women, accounting for 53.2% and 46.8% of the dataset, respectively. There were seven speeches from 2007 to 2013 that were relatively old, accounting for 39.9% of the total data, and eight speeches from 2014 to 2021 that accounted for 60.1%. As for the occupations, Artists accounted for the most, with six, and 35.9% of the total utterances. Businessmen are three represented 26.8%, making them the second largest (Table 3).

Table 3. Descriptive Summary.

	The number of speeches	The number of utterances	Percentage (%)
All Speech	15	2,271	100
Male	8	1,209	53.2
Female	7	1,062	46.8
Old (2007–2013)	7	907	39.9
Recent (2014–2021)	8	1,364	60.1
Artist	6	815	35.9
Businessman	3	608	26.8
Journalist	2	337	14.8
Politician	2	255	11.2
Scholar	2	256	11.3

3.2   Overall Network Model

First, the researcher examined the leaders' speaking patterns as disclosed in the entire speech. PERSONAL ANECDOTES was the most crucial codes. PERSONAL ANEC-DOTES and SUGGESTION had the strongest association, and two connections showed the second strongest relationship equally with a connection value of 0.22: PER-SONAL ANECDOTES and PUBLIC CONFIDENCE, PERSONAL ANECDOTES, and KNOWLEDGE. The model's X axis represents variance (or SVD1) at the value of 36.3%, whereas the Y axis represents SVD2 at the value of 23.5%. Both the Pearson and Spearman correlations between the x and y axes in the model were 1. According to these metrics, the visualization closely matches the source model, indicating a strong goodness of fit (Fig. 1).

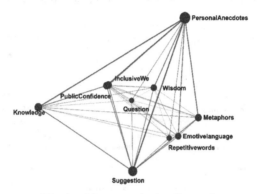

Fig. 1. ENA Networks for all speech.

3.3   Comparison of Group Network Models

Afterward, the researcher compared any differences in group models based on gender and time. The entire dataset was categorized by gender into men and women. Seven speeches from 2007 to 2013 were categorized as Old, while eight from 2014 to 2021 were categorized as Recent. Consequently, the subsequent analysis centered on comparing the male and female graphs (see Fig. 2) and the Old and Recent graphs (see Fig. 3).

Male and Female Speeches. The line between KNOWLEDGE and PERSONAL ANECDOTES is the strongest in the males, followed by the line between KNOWL-EDGE and SUGGESTION. In contrast, the strongest line in the women's group graph was between PERSONAL ANECDOTES and METAPHOR, and the second strongest relationship was between PERSONAL ANECDOTES and SUGGESTION. Upon combining the group models and examining the graph depicting significant differences between groups as opposed to the characteristics of each group, the male group was relatively more prominent in the characteristics mentioned above. In particular, the female group demonstrated relatively strong connections to PERSONAL ANECDOTES, EMOTIONAL LANGUAGE, and MATAPHOR. In this regard, ENA showed statistical differences between male and female groups. On the X axis (MR1), a Mann-Whitney test revealed that Male (Mdn = -1.07, N = 8) differed significantly from Female (Mdn = 0.99, N = 7 U = 4.00, p = 0.00, r = 0.86) at the alpha = 0.05 level.

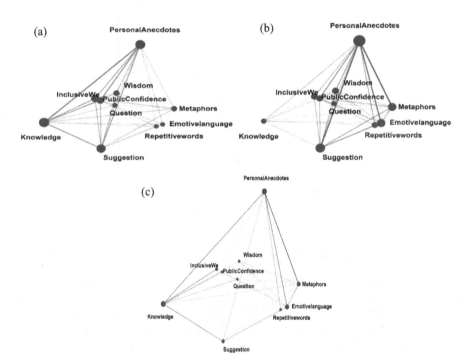

Fig. 2. ENA networks comparison based on gender. The upper left graph (a) is males' network model. The upper right graph (b) is females' network model. Below graph (c) is a subtracted network demonstrating the major differences between two groups.

Old and Recent Speeches. The graph (a) illustrates that the old model has a significant association between PERSONAL ANECDOTES and PUBLIC CONFIDENCE and KNOWLEDGE, whereas the graph (b) demonstrates that the recent model has the strongest association between PERSONAL ANECDOTES and SUGGESTION. In recent speeches, the relationship between PERSONAL ANECDOTES, REPETITIVE

WORDS, and SUGGESTION was more apparent than in earlier speeches. A Mann-Whitney test along the X axis (MR1) revealed that Old (Mdn = -0.18, N = 7) was statistically substantially different from Recent (Mdn = 0.68, N = 8 U = 9.00, p = 0.03, r = 0.68).

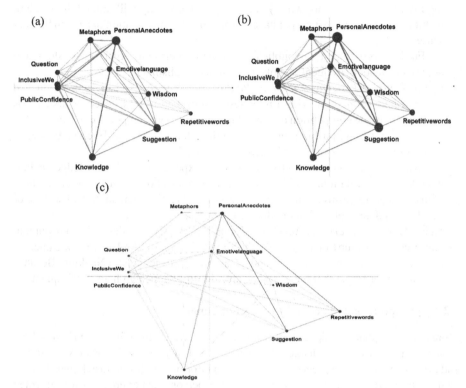

Fig. 3. ENA networks comparison based on time. The upper left graph (a) is the old speeches' network model. The upper right graph (b) is the recent speeches' network model. Below graph (c) is a subtracted network demonstrating the major differences between two groups.

4   Discussion

This research investigated motivational language patterns of prominent individuals in diverse fields at Harvard University Commencement speeches to learn more about the language these speakers use to inspire and encourage their audiences. Furthermore, this study analyzed how language patterns vary concerning speakers' gender and the time of day they speak.

4.1   Leaders' Motivating Language

When leaders wanted to motivate graduates and the public through graduation speeches, the most common method was to describe their experiences and memories. Additionally, the most frequently employed language was suggestion to change audiences' thoughts or behaviors. The subsequent examples illustrate this point in detail.

- *J.K. Rowling [Personal Anecdotes-Suggest]*: "Now you might think that I chose my second theme, the importance of imagination, because of the part it played in rebuilding my life, but that is not wholly so. Though I personally will defend the value of bedtime stories to my last gasp, I have learned to value imagination in a much broader sense."

   Furthermore, to give the public confidence in their own experiences, ideas, and arguments, leaders frequently spoke of their accomplishments.

- *Oprah Winfrey [Personal Anecdotes-Public Confidence]*: "And in 1986 I launched my own television show with a relentless determination to succeed at first. I was nervous about the competition and then I became my own competition raising the bar every year, pushing, pushing, pushing myself as hard as I knew. Eventually we did make it to the top and we stayed there for 25 years."

   In addition, leaders frequently connect their experiences with knowledge, including relevant information, significant events, and trends. For instance, it was a method of disseminating information to the public, consisting of an explanation of why he or she did it and an explanation of what he or she did.

- *Steven Spielberg [Personal Anecdotes-Knowledge]*: "My own desire to confront that reality compelled me to start, in 1994, the Shoah Foundation. And we're now gathering testimonies from genocides in Rwanda, Cambodia, Armenia, and Nanking. Because we must never forget that the inconceivable doesn't happen? it happens frequently."

4.2   Male and Female Leaders' Motivating Language

More frequently than female leaders, male leaders referred to their fact-based knowledge. Along with acquiring knowledge, there was a propensity to assert one's own opinions and to relate personal experiences to the acquired information. In contrast, female leaders were more likely than male leaders to share their personal experiences. It was affirmed that they used metaphorical language when describing their experiences, as well as more emotional than factual language. In this regard, both male and female leaders mainly use Meaning-making language. However, it was also found that men use more Direction-giving language, while women tend to use Empathic language more.

- *Mark Zuckerberg [Male: Knowledge-Personal Anecdotes-Suggestion]*: "But today, technology and automation are eliminating many jobs. Membership in communities is declining. Many people feel disconnected and depressed, and are trying to fill a void. As I've traveled around, I've sat with children in juvenile detention and opioid addicts, who told me their lives could have turned out differently if they just had something to do, an after school program or somewhere to go. To keep our society moving forward, we have a generational challenge—to not only create new jobs, but create a renewed sense of purpose."
- *Sheryl Sandberg [Female: Personal Anecdotes-Emotional Language-Metaphors]*: "My marriage fell apart within a year, something that was really embarrassing and painful at the time. And it did not help that so many friends came up to me and said, "I never knew that I Never thought that was going to work" or "I knew you two weren't

right for each other" No one had managed to say anything like that to me before I marched down an aisle when it would have been far more useful."

4.3 Old and Recent Leaders' Motivating Language

The difference in the language pattern between old and recent speeches was also prominent. In relatively recent years, leaders have used more direct language that suggests action or thought specifically as well as repeats the same sentence structure multiple times to emphasize meaning delivery. This characteristic was confirmed as well in the 2019 speech given by Angela Merkel. In this regard, it has been demonstrated that leaders are more likely to use direction-giving language today than in the past.

- *Angela Merkel [Recent: Personal Anecdotes-Suggestion-Repetitive Words]:* "As federal chancellor, I often have to ask myself, am I doing the right thing? am I doing something? Because it isn't right? Or simply because it is possible." That is something you two need to keep asking yourselves. And that is the third thought I wish to share with you today. Are we laying down the rules for technology or is technology dictating how we interact? Do we prioritize people as individuals with their human dignity and all their many facets?"
- *J.K. Rowling [Old: Personal Anecdotes-Wisdom-Metaphor]:* "Such knowledge is a true gift, for all that it is painfully won, and it has been worth more than any qualification I ever earned."

4.4 Conclusion

During commencement speeches, speakers often use language that imbues meaning to motivate and inspire their audiences. The speakers emphasized the credibility of their thoughts and arguments, employing personal anecdotes, highlighting their achievements, and establishing their validity by connecting pertinent material to their statements. Furthermore, it is recommended that the audience engage in proactive action or introspection regarding the subject matter in subsequent instances, drawing upon their personal encounters.

Female speakers employed a more significant amount of visceral and metaphorical language in comparison to their male counterparts. In recent years, there has been a shift in the content of leaders' motivating speeches, with an increased emphasis on meaning-making language. However, it is observed that leaders are today adopting a higher frequency of direction-giving language, characterized by exact expression and repeated emphasis on their points, compared to previous periods.

4.5 Implications

This research showed how Harvard commencement speakers use language to motivate their audiences. The findings of this study have the potential to contribute to our comprehension of language usage patterns, as well as the disparities in language between genders and throughout different time periods.

Primarily, it is crucial for leaders to underscore to employees the importance and worth of their work, along with the desired values of the organization. In essence, it would be advantageous for the leaders to articulate the reasons behind the significance and value of this endeavor, employing language that facilitates the creation of meaning [1, 9]. The method could encompass various approaches, such as the leaders providing a detailed account of their personal experiences, employing metaphoric expressions to draw parallels with other objects or situations, offering supplementary explanations rooted in relevant knowledge, or utilizing wise words to prompt employees to reassess the intended meanings subtly. Furthermore, the persuasiveness of leaders' arguments was enhanced when they effectively linked the knowledge and suggestions to their own personal experiences.

It is essential to utilize language that highlights the significance of a particular concept and that underscores specific obligations or guidance [9]. In addition, it can be beneficial to augment one's achievements that substantiate the significance and credibility of the subject matter a leader intends to communicate, drawing upon personal expertise and insights or referencing the statements of esteemed individuals who have achieved notable accomplishments. The assertion made by a leader can be reinforced by demonstrating that several individuals have achieved recognized triumphs and accomplishments by pursuing their desired values, so enhancing employees' confidence. Furthermore, while highlighting the importance or worth of work, effectively conveying the specific actions that employees ought to undertake and explicitly suggesting them can serve as an efficacious approach to foster a more realistic work drive.

In addition, consistent with the findings of Moran [14], as discussed earlier, this study's findings corroborate the notion that there is gender-based differences in the language spoken by leaders. There is a tendency for men to employ language that is grounded in factual knowledge or information, whereas women tend to utilize language that is comparatively more emotive and metaphorical. Thus, the result of this study implies when male leaders endeavor to apply a greater degree of emotional language, they might expect to elicit a higher frequency of favorable talks as a means of inspiring their colleagues. In contrast, it is anticipated by female leaders that employing goal-oriented language, along with a comprehensive understanding of the subject matter they seek to challenge, may facilitate their ability to engage in discussions with male subordinates effectively.

Lastly, the result of this study, like other research that has documented shifts in language patterns over time [15–17], which reveal differences in language used between old and recent speeches, could contribute to helping organizational leaders in understanding of changing speech trends and crafting more contemporary and practical addresses. It would help motivate employees by increasing the use of direction-giving language, characterized by future-oriented suggestions of specific ways to practice and using repeated exact expressions on their points.

4.6 Limitation and Future Study

The small sample size is a significant limitation of this study. The study utilized the speeches of 15 individuals, indicating that it may have been limited to generalizing all leaders' motivating language in commencement. Next, the study data included only Harvard University graduation speeches, which can act as a limitation to the generalization of the research results because speakers are selected to reflect the culture or characteristics of Harvard University. Furthermore, the target of the commencement speech is the public and graduates. Therefore, speeches and conversations intended for employees for specific objectives can be distinguished from those of word-wide leaders.

Thus, future research could also include speeches from other schools in addition to those from Harvard University. By incorporating speeches from schools in different regions, regional restrictions and specific cultural characteristics can be overcome, resulting in more trustworthy research findings. Additionally, to observe the pattern of motivational language use by company leaders, acquiring and analyzing data on the languages spoken by company leaders could also be a future research direction.

References

1. Sullivan, J.J.: Three roles of language in motivation theory. Acad. Manag. Rev. **13**(1), 104–115 (1988)
2. Jacqueline, R.M., Milton, R.M., Jerry, K.: Motivating language: exploring theory with scale development. J. Bus. Commun. **32**(4), 329–344 (1995)
3. Mayfield, J., Mayfield, M.: The relationship between leader motivating language and self-efficacy: a partial least squares model analysis. J. Bus. Commun. **49**(4), 357–376 (2012)
4. Gault, K.H.: The Development of a Genre: Commencement Addresses Delivered by Popular Cultural Icons. The Graduate Council of Texas State University, Texas (2008)
5. Robert, A.G.: The Speechmaker: How Bill Gates got ready for Harvard. The Wall Street J. (2007)
6. Mayfield, J.: Motivating language: a meaningful guide for leader communications. Dev. Learn. Organ. **23**(1), 9–11 (2009)
7. Conger, J.A.: Inspiring others: the language of leadership. Acad. Manag. Perspect. **5**(1), 31–45 (1991)
8. Mayfield, J.R., Mayfield, M.R., Kopf, J.: The effects of leader motivating language on subordinate performance and satisfaction. Hum. Res. Manage. **37**(3–4), 235–248 (1998)
9. Mayfield, J., Mayfield, M., Kopf, J.: Motivating language: exploring theory with scale development. J. Bus. Commun. **32**(4), 329–344 (1995)
10. Mayfield, J., Mayfield, M., Sharbrough, W.C., III.: Strategic vision and values in top leaders' communications: motivating language at a higher level. Int. J. Bus. Commun. **52**(1), 97–121 (2015)
11. Holmes, J.: Gendered talk at work: constructing gender identity through workplace discourse. Lang. Commun. **20**(1), 83–93 (2000)
12. Leaper, C., Robnett, R.D.: Free to be, you and me: connecting gender research on communication with gender studies. Sex Roles **64**(3), 238–252 (2011)
13. Myers, S.A., Sadaghiani, K.: Gender, communication, and leadership styles: a social role interpretation. J. Appl. Psychol. **95**(5), 1165–1174 (2010)
14. Choi, E., Rainey, H.G.: Gender and bureaucratic leadership: a contextual analysis. Public Adm. Rev. **70**(1), 121–130 (2010)
15. Piller, I.: Bilingual Couples Talk: The Discursive Construction of Hybridity. John Benjamins Publishing, Sydney (2002)
16. Chilton, P.: Analyzing political discourse: Theory and practice. Routledge (2004)
17. Avolio, B.J., Kahai, S.: Adding the e to e-leadership: how it may impact your leadership. Organ. Dyn. **31**(4), 325–338 (2003)
18. Shaffer, D.W.: Quantitative ethnography. Cathcart Press, WI (2017)

Examining the Discourse of Effective Science Communicators Using Epistemic Network Analysis

Katherine Mulholland[(✉)] ⓘ and Golnaz Arastoopour Irgens ⓘ

Clemson University, Clemson, SC 29634, USA
krfreem@clemson.edu

Abstract. Science communication, or the dissemination of scientific information to public entities, allows science communities to share ideas, impact policy, garner public support, and provide education. Recent calls have highlighted the need to move beyond the dominant models of science communication towards a model of explaining and viewing science communication as a form of social meaning-making or culture. Viewing science communication as a culture requires a systematic way to analyze and model the meaning-making to allow researchers to understand better how effective science communicators interact with the public to inform science communication training and education. We argue that quantitative ethnography (QE) and epistemic network analysis (ENA) are promising methodologies and tools to analyze and model science communication culture systematically. Our findings suggest that ENA networks can model how speakers employ science communication techniques and their interactions, the differences among speakers, and highlight how a speaker's presentation may change over time. Collectively, science communicators centered their TED Talks around the audience, attending to the audience's thoughts, feelings, and understanding of the topic.

Keywords: Epistemic Network Analysis · Science Communication · TED Talk · Discourse

1   Introduction

Science and scientific advancements have played a critical role in the development of most societies seen today. The discovery of the DNA structure by Rosalind Franklin, James Watson, and Francis Crick changed molecular biology and modern medicine [1]. More recently, advancements in machine learning technologies have created new avenues for transportation, such as automated driving [2]. As scientific advances continue, so does the need to understand how scientific information is disseminated to the public and how effective science communicators communicate to public audiences. Dissemination of scientific information to public entities allows science communities to share ideas, impact policy through laws and social programs, garner public support for scientific advancements, and educate others about the nature and limitations of science [3]. Over

G. Arastoopour Irgens and S. Knight (Eds.): ICQE 2023, CCIS 1895, pp. 187–201, 2023.
https://doi.org/10.1007/978-3-031-47014-1_13

the past several decades, practitioners and scientists have debated how to frame best practices in science communication, creating four prominent models to understand and make sense of science communication that mainly focus on knowledge transfer [4, 5]. More recently, researchers have argued to move beyond the four dominant models of science communication towards a model of explaining science communication as a form of *social meaning-making* or culture [4]. Viewing science communication as a culture requires a systematic way to analyze and model the culture of science communication to allow researchers to understand how effective science communicators interact with the public to inform science communication training and education.

The present study explores how epistemic network analysis (ENA) [6] can be leveraged as an exploratory tool to make sense of the different ways effective science communicators communicate. The research question addressed in this study is: *How did the top Science TED Talk speakers utilize communication techniques to create an experience for their audience?*

2 Background

2.1 Popularizing Science: TED Talks

TED (Technology, Entertainment, Design) Talks are one form of widespread science communication produced by the American Canadian non-profit TED [7, 8]. Traditional TED Talks are recorded as part of TED's annual international conference consisting of speakers from broad disciplinary fields, from medicine to politics to art, speaking about their content expertise. The speakers' presentations are video recorded and converted into a digital format. Select TED Talk videos are publicly available under a Creative Commons license and streamed over multiple platforms, including TEDTalks.com, YouTube, Netflix, and iTunes, which collectively receive over one million views daily [9]. TEDTalks.com categorizes and tags each video available on its website, with TED Talks' most popular categories being technology, entertainment, design, business, science, and global issues [7]. The popularization of TED Talks, particularly science TED Talks, lends the opportunity to examine the videos as a form of popular culture, specifically popular science culture.

2.2 Cultural Theories & Experiential Learning Theory

This study examines science communication as a form of culture, specifically popular culture. Popular culture can be viewed as the practices, beliefs, or objects recognized and consumed by a mass audience [10]. The framing of science communication as a form of popular culture challenges the current notions of viewing science communication through a lens of knowledge transfer and towards a view of collective meaning-making and significance within isolated experiences and over a continuum of experiences throughout one's life.

One way to examine science communication as a form of culture is through concepts of experience [4]. John Dewey's experiential learning theory can be used as a framework to understand how effective science communicators create an experience for their audiences. According to Dewey's experiential learning theory, an experience encompasses interacting with a meaningful entity and an individual's past and present lived experiences [11]. Experiences are personal and unique; however, the entities with which we have experienced are often shared in a social setting, such as through videos or presentations [4], creating multiple independent experiences or truths.

3 Methods

This study used quantitative ethnography (QE) [12] and epistemic network analysis (ENA) [13] to elucidate the culture of effective science communicators and how they create experiences for their audiences. Video transcripts analyzed in this study were the top ten most viewed traditional TED Talks tagged as "science" from TEDTalks.com. Traditional TED Talk videos were defined as videos that consisted of one speaker presenting information to an audience for less than 30 min. Several of the topmost viewed science TED Talk videos were excluded for not meeting the specified criterion, such as TED Ed videos. Most (80%) of the top ten science TED Talk speakers are New York Times bestselling authors, providing credibility for their effective science communicators status, millions of views, and thousands of likes on the speakers' TED Talk videos. Speakers' verbal discourse and actions, such as displaying a picture on the screen or referencing a prop, were transcribed using a combination of automated and manual transcription. Transcripts were segmented into lines based on a pause in the speakers' discourse or a change in subject. For example, if a speaker paused or used a transition word such as "so", this denoted the end of the subject and a transition to the next idea. The segmented data resulted in 591 lines.

Codes were developed using an inductive and deductive approach, deriving the codes from the data itself [14] and cultural and experiential learning theories (Table 1). The first author developed the codebook independently and hand-coded a randomly generated data set that contained a third of the lines (199). A second coder independently coded the test data set, and disagreements were mediated between the two coders. Cohen's Kappa was calculated for each code (Table 1), and the first author coded the remainder of the dataset.

As a final step in coding, a researcher created a metadata column as a higher-order segmentation [12] to model how the speakers created an experience for their audiences as the talk progressed and changed sections. For each line, the metadata column indicated the section of the talk (introduction, body, or conclusion). Sections such as the introduction, body, and conclusion are indicative of narrative or storytelling, techniques often used to deliver scientific content to nonexpert audiences, the public [15]. The section of the talk was determined by a change in the speaker's content and delivery [16]. For example, when transitioning to the conclusion, the speaker may summarize what was previously said.

Table 1. Codebook and Cade Validation

Codes (Cohen's Kappa)	Definition	Example Utterance
Including Audience (0.94)	Any instances of the speaker addressing the audience, including asking the audience questions, talking to the audience, or using *you* to speak to the audience. Does not include instances when the speaker uses *you* when talking about the collective *you*	*"**Which I'm glad you liked,** but they did not like that at all—silence on the phone. And into the silence, I said, "I'd be happy to speak at your school, but that's not a wellness week; that's a sickness week. You've outlined all the negative things that can happen but not talked about the positive."*
Connecting to Audience (0.95)	Any instances of the speaker using any personal information about them or their thoughts, feelings, beliefs, or past experiences to link themselves and their experiences to the audience and the current talk	*"There are also really big differences in how people think about time. So here **I have pictures of my grandfather at different ages**. And if I ask an English speaker to organize time, they might lay it out this way, from left to right. This has to do with writing direction..."*
Connecting Language (0.93)	Any instances when the speaker used language that connects to the audience as if they belong to the same group, such as the collective *we*, *us*, or *ours*. Does not include instances when the speaker uses, *we*, *us*, *you*, or *our* when talking about a specific group that does not include the audience	*"I am an energy being connected to the energy all around me through the consciousness of my right hemisphere. **We are energy beings** connected to one another through the consciousness of **our right hemispheres as one human family**. And right here, right now, **we are brothers and sisters on this planet**, here to make the world a better place. And in this moment, **we are perfect, we are whole, and we are beautiful.**"*
Support Tools (0.96)	Any instance when the speaker uses support tools and mechanisms to help deliver the message to the audience, including when the speaker references a support tool	***Screen reads: "But Is Synthetic Happiness Real?"* - Graph of % memory for owned Monet print of controls (~90%) and patients with amnesias (>50%)**
Audience Response (0.97)	Any instance of the audience responding to the speaker, including laughter, applause, groans, gasps, or other exclamations	*"This is a fact -- or, as we say in my hometown of Washington, DC, a true fact. **Laughter. Applause.**"*

The ENA [6] web tool was used to model the experience created by the top ten most viewed science TED Talk speakers for their audiences. Researchers visualized the co-occurrence of codes within a stanza using a sliding window [17] of five, which included the line of interest plus the previous four lines. The stanza size was determined by looking at the recent temporal context in the dataset, in which few speakers reference information over four lines of data. Table 2 contains the ENA models' parameters and goodness of fit correlations.

Table 2. ENA Model Parameters

	Model one	Model two
Unit of Analysis	Speaker	Speaker, Section
Conversational Unit	Speaker	Speaker
Moving Stanza Window Size	5	5
SVD1 variance	52.9%	35.5%
SVD2 variance	22.4%	24.3%
Pearson Correlation D1	1	1
Spearman Correlation D1	0.99	0.99
Pearson Correlation D2	0.98	0.99
Spearman Correlation D2	0.89	0.92

4 Results

4.1 Model 1

In the first ENA model, which modeled the discourse of all ten speakers, network analysis findings revealed that speakers created experiences for their audiences by (a) using *support tools* such as photos and *including the audience* in the speech and (b) *connecting to the audience* through personal stories while eliciting an *audience response* such as laughter.

4.1.1 Example 1: Support Tools to Include the Audience

The following excerpt highlights one speaker, Dan Gilbert, whose talk discusses the ideas of generating synthetic happiness. Dan's research examines the creation of happiness through how we view lived events, either naturally occurring or through synthetic generation. According to Dan, natural happiness is created when we achieve a goal or receive a desired item, achieving what we expect or want to occur. In contrast, synthetic happiness is generated from positive thoughts about an event that may have seemed negative initially, such as becoming a paraplegic. In the following excerpt, Dan used *support tools*, such as information displayed on a large screen for the audience to see, to *include the audience* in his talk by directly addressing the audience.

Line	Type	Utterance
7	Talk	Let's see how your experience simulators are working. Let's just run a quick diagnostic before I proceed with the rest of the talk. Here's two different futures that I invite you to contemplate. You can try to simulate them and tell me which one you think you might prefer. One of them is winning the lottery. This is about 314 million dollars. And the other is becoming paraplegic. Laughter
8	Media	Screen reads "Pop Quiz." – Below are two pictures, one of someone winning the lottery and the other is someone in a wheelchair (paraplegic)

(continued)

(*continued*)

Line	Type	Utterance
9	Talk	Just give it a moment of thought. Laughter. You probably don't feel like you need a moment of thought
10	Talk	Interestingly, there are data on these two groups of people, data on how happy they are. And this is exactly what you expected, isn't it? But these aren't the data. I made these up!
11	Media	Screen reads, "You Passed!" – Below is a false graph showing the happiness of lottery winners and paraplegics one year after the event – Lottery winners are at 60% while paraplegics are at 20%

In line 7, Dan poses an activity to the audience; he asks them to simulate an experience, to imagine if they would prefer to win the lottery or become a paraplegic. Here, Dan directly addresses the audience by asking them to participate in a thought activity during his presentation actively. Next, (line 8) Dan used a *support tool* to display the words "Pop Quiz" on the screen and used imagery to help the audience imagine the "simulation" as they engaged in the activity. Dan continues to use *support tools* to include the audience in his talk; for example, in line 11, Dan displays a graph on the screen depicting the happiness of lottery winners and people with paraplegia one year after their life event with the words "You Passed!" directly above the graph. As the graph is displayed on the screen, Dan addresses the audience again by asking them if the data displayed on the screen are the results they expected. Here, Dan uses language, such as "you," to *include the audience* in the speech in combination with the *support tools* to create an experience for the audience.

4.1.2   Example 2: Connecting to the Audience

For years, Jill Bolte Taylor was a neuroanatomist researcher who focused on studying how our brains understand and create reality. Jill's life drastically changed one morning when she woke up with a stroke, which took her eight years to recover fully. Now, Jill educates others about neuroplasticity through her position as the Harvard Brain Tissue Resource Center's National Spokesperson. In this example, Jill Bolte Taylor created an experience for her audience through *connecting to the audience* by immersing the audience in her thoughts and feelings the morning she had a stroke. While telling her story, Jill utilized other communication strategies, such as eliciting an *audience response* to facilitate the experience she was trying to create for her audience.

Line	Type	Utterance
33	Talk	So, I take the phone pad, and I put it right here. I take the business card, I put it right here, and I'm matching the shape of the squiggles on the card to the shape of the squiggles on the phone pad. But then I would drift back out into La La Land and not remember when I came back if I'd already dialed those numbers
34	Talk	So, I had to wield my paralyzed arm like a stump and cover the numbers as I went along and pushed them so that as I would come back to normal reality, I'd be able to tell, "Yes, I've already dialed that number."

(*continued*)

Line	Type	Utterance
35	Talk	Eventually, the whole number gets dialed, and I'm listening to the phone, and my colleague picks up the phone, and he says to me, "Woo woo woo woo." Laughter
36	Talk	And I think to myself, "Oh my gosh, he sounds like a Golden Retriever!" Laughter

In line 33, Jill *connected to the audience* by detailing the events that took place as she tried to phone for help the morning she woke up with a brain hemorrhage in her left hemisphere. Jill described finding the business card for her neuroscience research lab but being unable to register written numbers as numbers and drifting in and out of consciousness. Here, Jill *connected to the audience* by describing a personal and life-altering medical event in detail. Jill continued to *connect to the audience* in line 34, where she described struggling with paralysis on one side of her body. Next (line 35), Jill recounted the moment her colleague picked up the phone, but due to the hemorrhage, Jill could no longer understand human speech. To Jill, her colleague sounded like a "Golden Retriever" (line 36). Here, Jill continued to create an experience for her audience through immersing her audience in her personal thoughts and feelings by *connecting to the audience*. In the last two lines, Jill lightened the mood by recounting her experience with language that could provoke laughter, an *audience response*. In line 36, Jill described her lack of ability to understand speech as someone sounding like a "Golden Retriever," which provoked audience laughter. Here, Jill relied on humor and laughter to reduce the seriousness of her lack of ability to function.

4.1.3 Example 3: Audience Response: Eliciting laughter

One of the speakers, Mary Roach, is an established science writer with seven New York Times bestseller novels. Mary's talk centered on the information she learned while researching for her New York Times bestseller *Bonk: The Curious Coupling of Science and Sex*. In the following excerpt, Mary leveraged several communication strategies to create an experience for her audience, including *audience response, support tools,* and *connecting to the audience*. Similar to Jill, Mary described a past experience and relied on language to elicit laughter, an *audience response*, to reduce the tension when discussing the taboo subject of orgasms.

Line	Type	Utterance
7	Media	Screen reads: "2: You don't need genitals."
8	Talk	I think the most curious one that I came across was a case report of a woman who had an orgasm every time she brushed her teeth. Laughter
9	Talk	Something in the complex sensory-motor action of brushing her teeth was triggering orgasm. And she went to a neurologist, who was fascinated. He checked to see if it was something in the toothpaste, but no – it happened with any brand. They stimulated her gums with a toothpick, to see if that was doing it. No. It was the whole, you know, motion

(*continued*)

Line	Type	Utterance
10	Talk	And the amazing thing to me is that you would think this woman would have excellent oral hygiene. Laughter. Sadly – this is what it said in the journal paper – "She believed that she was possessed by demons and switched to mouthwash for her oral care." It's so sad. Laughter

In the seventh line, Mary used a *support tool* to display the number "2" and a brief description of the orgasm fact "You don't need genitals" she is currently addressing in her talk titled *Ten things you didn't know about orgasm*. Here, Mary used the *support tool* to tell the audience information without verbally speaking; she indicated to the audience that the talk was progressing to the next topic, topic #2. In line 8, Mary began talking about the second fact on orgasms by recounting a case study she discovered when researching for her novel. Mary never explicitly said, "you don't need genitals to have an orgasm," nor did she need to because of her use of *support tools*. Additionally, in line 8, Mary *connected to the audience* through sharing the reason she picked the case study described above to present during her TED Talk because she thought it was the most "curious one." Lastly, in line 8, Mary elicited an *audience response* by selecting a unique case study to present to the audience. Mary continued, line 9, recounting what she read in the case study regarding a woman who orgasmed when she brushed her teeth. In the last line of the excerpt, Mary once again connected to the audience and used language to elicit an audience response when she discussed her thoughts regarding the woman who orgasmed when she brushed her teeth. Mary's ability to elicit laughter, connect to the audience, and use support tools created a humorous experience for the audience when discussing a scientific topic that is usually not discussed in public spaces.

4.1.4 Co-occurrences of Codes Among All Speakers

The epistemic network analysis (ENA) web tool provided a visual model for the mean discourse network (Fig. 1) for the speakers and showed that the speakers collectively made connections among all codes during their TED Talks. However, the weight of these connections was not equally dispersed, as shown by the thicker line connecting *tools (support tools)* and *including audience (0.48)*. The more robust connection between these two codes indicates that the speakers used support tools to address the audience to include them in their talk. As shown above, Dan Gilbert, whose node (purple dot) is closest to the *tools* code, utilized both *support tools* and *included the audience* in his speech when asking the audience to partake in a thought activity, utilizing both his language and various media to create an experience for the audience.

The next strongest connections, as indicated by the thickness of the line and indicated weight of 0.33, are between *support tools* and *connecting language* and between *connecting language* and *including the audience*. The heavier weighted lines connecting *support tools* and *connecting language*, along with the connection between *connecting language* and *including audience*, indicated that the speakers used rhetoric to indicate they belong to a collective group when directly addressing the audience and using support tools.

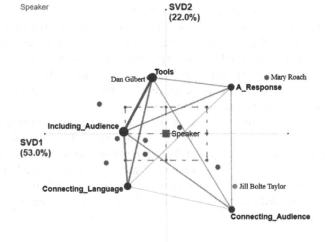

Fig. 1. Mean discourse network for top ten most viewed science TED Talk speakers. Three speaker examples, Dan Gilbert, Jill Bolte Taylor, and Mary Roach are labeled. The mean plotted point of speakers is at the center of the plot and represented by a red square. Confidence intervals are displayed.

Additionally, the placement of the unit nodes (speakers) in the ENA network directly correlated to that speaker's use of the codes, with the codes closer to the speaker nodes used more frequently. For example, the six speaker nodes to the left of the mean indicate that these six speakers made more connections to *connecting language, including audience* and *support tools*, in comparison to the mean. Alternatively, the placement of the four speaker nodes to the right of the speaker mean indicated that these four speakers *connect with the audience* and promote an *audience response* more than the other six speakers and the average. Here, the ENA was leveraged to visually represent the patterns of connection made by each speaker and collectively among all speakers.

4.1.5   Closer Examination of Individual Speakers

In addition to allowing researchers to model the co-occurrences of codes among all speakers visually, ENA can also provide a closer examination of individual speakers, like nodes that are further away from the average. Two speakers, Mary Roach and Jill Bolte Taylor, revealed a greater emphasis on *audience response* and *connecting language* as compared to the mean, as shown by the placement of their nodes in the mean network (Fig. 1). ENA subtraction networks were produced to visualize how speakers may create an experience for the audiences that differs from the mean network of all speakers. Figure 2 shows the ENA difference network for all speakers (red) and Jill Bolte Taylor (green), while Fig. 3 shows the ENA difference network for all speakers (red) and Mary Roach (blue).

Jill's use of *connecting to the audience* is shown in the ENA network through the weighted lines linking the *connecting to the audience* code to the other four codes. Although Jill's network revealed a connection between *connecting to the audience* and the other four codes, the weights are not evenly distributed, as shown by the thickness of the lines in the model. In comparison to the average, Jill's most robust connection was between the *connecting to the audience* and *audience response* codes. Therefore, the difference network revealed that Jill used her personal thoughts, feelings, and experiences to create an experience more than the other TED Talk speakers. Jill's use of *connecting to the audience* was seen in the excerpt above when Jill recounted attempting to call a colleague for help as she was experiencing a stroke.

In addition to highlighting Jill's use of *connecting to the audience* compared to the mean, Fig. 2 also reveals that Jill did not *utilize support tools* to include the audience in her TED Talk as frequently as the mean. This thin red line connecting the *support tools* code to the *included audience* code in the ENA model indicated that Jill used *tools* to *include the audience* in her talk less than the average. The thin weight of the line between these two codes revealed that there is not a large difference between the frequency of the co-occurrences of the codes between Jill and the average.

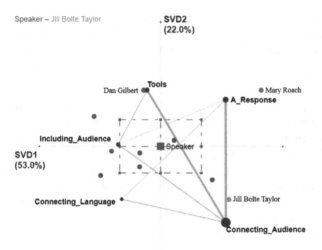

Fig. 2. Discourse network of the difference between mean ENA network for all speakers (red) and Jill Bolte Taylor (green). Mean plotted point of speakers is at the center of the plot and represented by a red square. Confidence intervals are displayed.

Like Jill, Mary Roach elicited an audience response to create an experience for her audience. Mary's strongest connection in the difference network is between *audience response* and *tools*, indicating that Mary used support tools to aid in delivering her TED Talk while also producing a positive audience response through provoking laughter. Although *audience response* is strongly connected with *support tools*, Mary did not use the *support tool* to elicit the audience's response; instead, the audience responded to what Mary said, as shown in the excerpt above. The strong connection between support tools and audience response is due to the codes frequently appearing together within the same context. Mary relied on humor and provoked an *audience response* more than the average to create a better experience for her audience by reducing the tension created when discussing sex and orgasms with a large crowd.

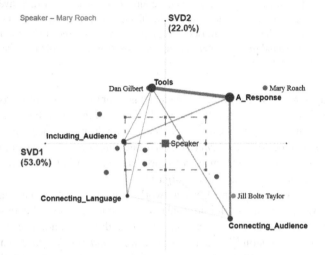

Fig. 3. Subtracted discourse network of mean ENA network of all speakers (red) and Mary Roach (blue). Mean plotted point of speakers is at the center of the plot and represented by a red square. Confidence intervals are displayed.

4.2 Model 2: Finer Grained Examination of Individual Speakers

The previous two sections have shown how ENA models the average discourse of all speakers as well as highlights individual speakers who may differ from the mean. In this section, we highlight how ENA can be used to model how speakers' communication may change according to the section of the talk: Introduction, Body, or Conclusion. The ENA Networks below (Figs. 4, 5 and 6) show the discourse networks for Mary Roach by section of the presentation. The introduction discourse network (Fig. 4) shows that Mary Roach only made connections between three of the five codes, *including audience, support tools,* and *audience response*. The lack of connections between the *connecting language* and *connecting to audience* codes indicates that these codes were not present in the introduction of Mary's talk, meaning she did not use connecting language or personal information to connect to the audience in the introduction of her TED Talk. The connections in the introduction were limited due to the lack of content in Mary's introduction, which consisted of one line, line 1. Mary began her talk using *support tools* to *include the audience* by displaying the title of her talk on the screen (line 1), shown as the thick blue line connecting *support tools* to *including the audience* in Fig. 4A, which directly addresses linguistically with the word "you." In line 2, Mary begins the body of her talk by discussing the first fact about orgasms.

Line	Type	Utterance
1	Media	Screen reads: "Ten things you didn't know about orgasm."
2	Talk	Alright. I'm going to show you a couple of images from a very diverting paper in The Journal of Ultrasound in Medicine. I'm going to go way out on a limb and say that it is the most diverting paper ever published in The Journal of Ultrasound in Medicine. The title is "Observations of In-Utero Masturbation." Laughter

In the body of Mary's TED Talk, she made connections between all five codes, as seen in Fig. 4B. In this section of her talk, Mary relied on multiple different communication techniques to create an experience for her audience, with the most robust ENA connection and the thickest line between *audience response* and *support tools.* An example of Mary using support tools and the audience's response can be seen in the expert above when describing the second of ten facts about orgasms.

Lastly, in the conclusion, the ENA network (Fig. 6) revealed that, similar to the introduction, Mary once again did not make a connection among all codes, refraining from using *support tools* or *connecting language* to address the audience. The strongest connection in the conclusion ENA network is between *audience response* and *including audience,* as shown by the thicker line between these two codes in the ENA network. In the conclusion, Mary used inclusive language to address the audience directly. Collectively analyzing the three ENA networks reveals that Mary consistently elicited an audience's response during all three sections of her talk.

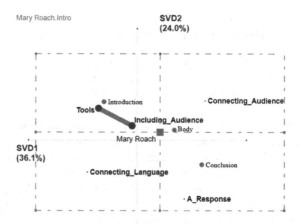

Fig. 4. Discourse network for Mary Roach by section of the TED Talk: introduction. Mary's mean plotted point is at the center of the plot and represented by a blue square.

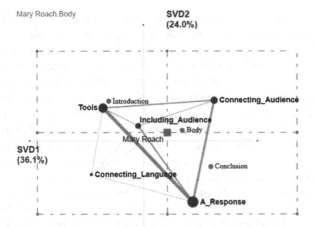

Fig. 5. Discourse network for Mary Roach by section of the TED Talk: body. Mary's mean plotted point is at the center of the plot and represented by a blue square.

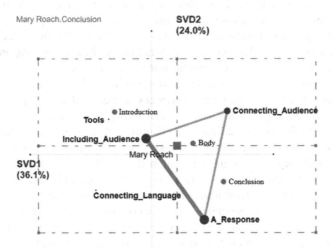

Fig. 6. Discourse network for Mary Roach by section of the TED Talk: conclusion. Mary's mean plotted point is at the center of the plot and represented by a blue square.

5 Discussion and Conclusion

Through the lens of cultural and experiential learning theory [4, 10, 11], this study analyzed the discourse of the top ten science TED Talk speakers to visualize and measure science communication best practices regarding creating an experience for an audience. Findings revealed that speakers created experiences for their audiences by (a) using *support tools* such as photos and *including the audience* in the speech and (b) *connecting to the audience* through personal stories while eliciting an *audience response*, such as laughter. These findings suggest that effective science communicators employ techniques to incorporate the audience into their talk, focusing on content delivery and audience involvement to create an immersive experience. Collectively, science communicators centered their talks around the audience, attending to the audience's thoughts, feelings, and understanding of the topic. More broadly, the results contribute to our understanding of the *culture* of effective science communicators as they negotiate how to present scientific information to create an experience for a large, diverse audience, which is an understudied area. The framing of science communication as a form of culture challenges the current notions of viewing science communication through a lens of knowledge transfer and, instead, moves towards a view of collective meaning-making and significance within isolated experiences and over a continuum of experiences throughout one's life.

In this study, we have identified four advantages of using ENA to examine the culture of effective science communicators. First, ENA allowed us to model the interactions between the codes for all ten TED Talk speakers selected for this study. The placement of the speaker nodes and mean plotted points provides the researcher with information about how all speakers used science communication techniques to center their talk around creating an experience for the audience. Second, the weight of the edges in an ENA network can indicate the codes that have a stronger relationship to one another, allowing the researcher to examine these interactions regarding the speakers, generating an understanding and involvement for the audience and *how* this involvement with the audience manifested. Third, subtracted ENA networks allow us to compare and contrast how speakers used science communication techniques and, in our case, to measure and visualize how much speakers differed from the mean. In this study, the difference networks highlighted that generating experiences are personal and unique and that science communicators leverage the shared social setting to create multiple independent experiences or truths for the audience [4]. Fourth, higher-order segmentation used in the second ENA model revealed how speakers' communication techniques changed over time, as referenced by the introduction, body, or conclusion section of their talk. Sections such as the introduction, body, and conclusion are indicative of narrative or storytelling communication techniques that are often used to deliver scientific content to nonexpert audiences and the general public [16]. For example, the finer grain analysis of one speaker, Mary, revealed that she did not utilize the same communication techniques in the three sections of her presentation, creating a designed differential experience for her audience over time.

In short, our findings suggest that quantitative ethnography (QE) and epistemic network analysis (ENA) can be leveraged to examine the culture of effective science. These results suggest qualitative methods alone are limited in their ability to model the complex interactions of effective science communicators and that ENA can be a powerful tool to discern the culture of effective science communicators. Moreover, these findings can help scientists disseminate their advancements more effectively to the public, allowing their work to impact policy, garner public support, and effectively facilitate public education about the nature and limitations of science [3].

References

1. Portin, P.: The birth and development of the DNA theory of inheritance: sixty years since the discovery of the structure of DNA. J. Genet. **93**, 293–302 (2014). https://doi.org/10.1007/s12 041-014-0337-4

2. Anderson, J., Rainie, L.: Artificial intelligence and the future of humans. Pew Research Center (2018). https://www.pewresearch.org/internet/2018/12/10/artificial-intelligence-and-the-future-of-humans/

3. Eagleman, D.M.: Why public dissemination of science matters: a manifesto. J. Neurosci.: The Off. J. Soc. Neurosci. **33**(30), 12147–12149 (2013). https://doi.org/10.1523/JNEURO SCI.2556-13.2013

4. Davies, S.R., Halpern, M., Horst, M., Kirby, D., Lewenstein, B.: Science stories as culture: experience, identity, narrative and emotion in public communication of science. J. Sci. Commun. **18**(05), A01 (2019). https://doi.org/10.22323/2.18050201

5. Tayeebwa, D.W., Wendo, D.C., Nakiwala, D.A.S.: Theories and Models of Science Communication. CABI Books. CABI International (2022). https://doi.org/10.1079/9781789249675. 0002.

6. Marquart, C.L., Hinojosa, C., Swiecki, Z., Eagan, B., Shaffer, D.W.: Epistemic Network Analysis (Version 1.7.0) [Software] (2018). www.app.epistemicnetwork.org

7. TED: About TED. http://www.ted.com/pages/about (2023)

8. Sugimoto, C.R., Thelwall, M.: Scholars on soap boxes: Science communication and dissemination in TED videos. J. Am. Soc. Inform. Sci. Technol. **64**(4), 663–674 (2013). https://doi. org/10.1002/asi.22764

9. Coe, J.: TED's Chris Anderson - Articles – Departures (2012). https://web.archive.org/web/ 20140426214919/http://www.departures.com/articles/teds-chris-anderson

10. Kidd, D., Kim, J., Turner, A.: Popular Culture. In: Korgen, K.O. (ed.) The Cambridge Handbook of Sociology: Specialty and Interdisciplinary Studies, pp. 284–292. Cambridge University Press (2017). https://doi.org/10.1017/9781316418369.030

11. Dewey, J.: Art as Experience. Perigree Press, New York, NY, USA (1938). Experience and education. Free Press, New York, NY, USA (1934)

12. Shaffer, D.W.: Quantitative Ethnography. Cathcart Press (2017)

13. Marquart, C.L., Hinojosa, C., Swiecki, Z., Eagan, B., Shaffer, D.W.: Epistemic network analysis software, version 1.7.0 (2018)

14. Walker, D., Myrick, F.: Grounded theory: an exploration of process and procedure. Qual. Health Res. **16**(4), 547–559 (2006)

15. Dahlstrom, M.F.: Using narratives and storytelling to communicate science with nonexpert audiences. Proc. Natl. Acad. Sci. U.S.A. **111**(supplement_4), 13614–13620 (2014). https:// doi.org/10.1073/pnas.1320645111

16. Telg, R.: Speech Writing and Types of Speeches1. https://journals.flvc.org/edis/article/dow nload/127037/126697/ (2011)

17. Siebert-Evenstone, A.L., Arastoopour Irgens, G., Collier, W., Swiecki, Z., Ruis, A.R., Shaffer, D.W.: In search of conversational grain size: modelling semantic structure using moving stanza windows. J. Learn. Anal. **4**(3), 123–139 (2017)

Asian American Education Literature Before and After Covid-19

Jonathon Sun[1]($\boxtimes$) (iD) and Chi Nguyen[2] (iD)

[1] University of Pennsylvania, Philadelphia, PA 19104, USA
Jonathonsun03@gmail.com
[2] The University of Arizona, Tucson, AZ 85721, USA

Abstract. Asian Americans have been stereotyped as "model minorities" and occupy a precarious racial position in U.S. racial hierarchy. At times in U.S. history, Asian Americans are touted as success stories of U.S. meritocracy; however, Asian American valorization often depends on broader social contexts. With the onset of the COVID-19 pandemic and its origins in China also came a wave of anti-Asian sentiment in the U.S. This shift in Asian American positionality became a focal point to scholars across fields and broadly shifted the discourse on Asian American issues. This study uses Epistemic Network Analysis (ENA) to build two models which thematically show differences across the literature before and after the onset of the COVID-19 pandemic. The first model focuses on Asian American issues, such as the perpetual foreigner and the model minority, and shows after the beginning of the COVID-19 pandemic; research focused much more on discrimination. The second model shows the relationship between Asian Americans and broader racial groups such as Black, Latinx, and White U.S. citizens, and found that before COVID-19, there was more discussion about the relationship between Black and Asian Americans; however, after the onset of COVID-19, there was a shift to White and Asian Americans.

Keywords: Epistemic Network Analysis · Literature Review · Asian American · Education

1 Introduction

Since the sterling Asian American "success stories" were projected in the mass media in the mid-1960s [1], scholars have paid great attention to how the image of Asian Americans has been socially constructed and shaped American society. Asian Americans are often stereotyped as intelligent, hardworking, high-achieving model minorities who have reached the "American Dream" academically and economically. However, Asian Americans are also viewed as perpetual foreigners, no matter how long their families have lived as citizens in the United States [2–4]. Despite being paradoxical, these racial stereotypes—the model minority and the perpetual foreigner myths—are identified as forms of racial discrimination.

Throughout history, global events have shifted perceptions of Asian Americans. In 1882, the Chinese Exclusion Act was passed due to anti-Chinese sentiment [4]. During

G. Arastoopour Irgens and S. Knight (Eds.): ICQE 2023, CCIS 1895, pp. 202–214, 2023.
https://doi.org/10.1007/978-3-031-47014-1_14

WWII, Japanese Americans were interned in concentration camps; and during the great depression, many Asian Americans were the targets of hate crimes like Vincent Chin [5]. More recently, we have seen the rise of hate crimes against Asian Americans with the onset of the COVID-19 pandemic and rhetoric around the pandemic, such as "Kung flu" [6]. As the COVID-19 pandemic has continued to persist, there has been a breadth of literature on Asian Americans' experiences, especially concerning their racial stereotypes [7–9].

However, there has yet to be a comprehensive examination of the shift in Asian American education scholarship published before and after the pandemic. Little is known about if and how COVID-19 has impacted Asian Americans' educational experiences and their perceptions in educational literature. Therefore, applying Epistemic Network Analysis (ENA) to Asian American education scholarship, our study seeks to understand (1) how Asian Americans have been framed concerning racial stereotypes and (2) how the COVID-19 pandemic has impacted the perceptions of Asian Americans.

2 Asian American Education Issues

2.1 The Model Minority and Perpetual Foreigner Myth

The model minority is currently the most prevalent stereotype of Asian Americans; historical-analytical studies revealed that the image of Asian Americans had changed drastically over time from negative to positive strands. Before the Black Power movement, Asian Americans were viewed as uncivilized, deviant "coolies," who were willing to work endless hours at low wages and in conditions that were unacceptable to White laborers [2, 10]. However, during the height of the Black Power Movement, the mass media in the U.S. started to project a positive image of Asian Americans in the mid-1960s. Being "skeptical" about the swift change of the Asian American image in American popular media, many scholars have explicated the historical development of the model minority myth and critiqued the grand political schemes behind the creation of the myth [4, 11–14]. These scholars have argued that it was no coincidence that a series of Asian American "success stories," led by Peterson's [1] article, were published amid the Black Power Movement. Rather, American politicians and White elites used the positive image of Asian Americans to suppress African Americans in their outspoken quest for equality, including civil rights protection and governmental assistance for minority groups. This narrative blamed African Americans, Latinos, American Indians, and poor Whites for their low academic and socioeconomic achievement [2, 4, 12].

Frank Wu called the perpetual foreigner stereotype "a twin" of the model minority myth. Despite being paradoxical, they work in tandem to form and perpetuate the prejudicial image of Asian Americans [4]. As the name suggests, Asian Americans are often stereotyped as perpetual foreigners, regardless of how many generations they have lived in the U.S. [3, 13]. While research studies have not been consistent in describing the historical development of the perpetual foreigner stereotype, most scholars posit that the stereotype was formed in the early history of Asian immigration, when Asian Americans were viewed as exotic, deviant, uncivilized "yellow perils" [4, 13]. This stereotype was reinforced during volatile historical periods, such as at the outbreak of World War II, during the Vietnam War, and at the end of the Cold War, when Asian immigrants from

Japan, Vietnam, and China, respectively, were considered suspicious and suspected of disloyalty and espionage [4, 13, 15].

In addition to the model minority myth, the perpetual foreigner stereotype is considered a form of racial discrimination that separates Asian Americans from other minority groups. It disconnects and silences the social struggles facing many Asian Americans in the mainstream political and racial discourses. From the lens of racial triangulation theory [16], the perpetual foreigner stereotype is interrelated with the model minority myth, in which Asian Americans are valorized as models for success in the American meritocracy and juxtaposed with African Americans who are often perceived as underachieving minorities despite their extended history, their 'insider status' in the U.S. [17].

2.2 Asian American Disaggregation

Since the inception of the model minority myth, scholars have called for a more nuanced approach to understand Asian Americans' experiences. Chun [18] critiqued the monolith by calling scholars to consider education, immigration, and occupational status. The American Council on Education [19] noted in their report that Asian American success had been frequently highlighted; however, this achievement has broadly masked the educational needs of the 28 other groups within Asian Americans. About a decade later, Chang and Kiang [20] would bring attention to the issue that Asian American data must be more nuanced, even more so because of the shifting demographics. Teranishi et al. [21] would also bring attention to this issue in their broad studies, which address challenges for Asian Americans in higher education. Finally, Museus [22] asserted that Asian Americans are arguably one of the most misunderstood populations, and as such more research is needed to understand this group. The literature is evident that, despite literature on Asian American educational achievement, there have been misunderstandings about Asian Americans because of how Asian American data can be disaggregated.

Scholars have also identified differences in the college application process for Southeast Asian American students (SEAA). SEAA economic and achievement outcomes differ considerably compared to the other Asian American Pacific Islander (AAPI) groups. SEAA has higher poverty rates, and 50% or more of the population has less than a high school education. Additionally, East Asian Americans and some South Asian American populations who enroll in higher education earn a bachelor's degree, and SEAA students' completion rates are broadly lower [23].

The model minority myth reduces the diversity of Asian American experiences into one narrative that does not accurately portray Asian Americans. Scholars have only begun to reveal the differences within the Asian American category. Whether it be how Asian American high schoolers navigate the model minority myth and their beliefs in education, how Southeast Asian Americans navigate the college application, or understanding generational status shapes college access knowledge. Therefore, it is essential to bring attention to the differences among Asian Americans to provide more equitable opportunities for the communities that may not have access to the same resources as high-achieving Asian American communities.

3   Theoretical Framework: Asian American Racial Positionality

Going "beyond Black and White" in the theoretical discourse about races in the U.S. frames Asian Americans as somewhere between Black and White. Multiple scholars over time have theorized Asian American racial positionality. Beginning with Kitano [24] who applies the middleman theory to Japanese immigrants in California and Hawaii to explain the development of Japanese Americans as the middleman minority. While the middleman minority possesses resources, politically and socially, the middleman minority is allowed very few privileges and often serve as scapegoats. Kitano concludes by taking the stance that the position of the middleman minority is paradoxically weak. While the middleman minority was a theory meant to apply to minority people in various countries, the application by Kitano shows Asian Americans occupying a middle space in U.S. social structures.

Later Kim [11] posits a theory of racial triangulation that considers the racial positions of Asian Americans relative to Whites and Blacks. Challenging a more common perception of racial hierarchy with Whites on the top, Blacks on the bottom, and other non-White groups in between [25, 26], Kim complicated this linear racial logic by looking specifically at the two axes (superior/inferior and insider/foreigner) that stratified racial groups [15, 16, 27]. Kim argues that Asian Americans have been racially triangulated vis-à-vis Whites and Blacks through two simultaneous, interrelated processes of "relative valorization" and "civic ostracism" [16]. In the former process, White opinion makers valorize Asian Americans as model minorities, placing them above Blacks on a superior/inferior axis. In the latter approach, White opinion makers construct Asian Americans as perpetually foreign and ostracized from politics, placing them below Blacks on an insider/foreigner axis [28]. Racial triangulation explains the social constructs of the model minority and perpetual foreigner stereotypes.

More recently, Zou and Cheryan [29] theorized a racial position model which captures groups' experiences with racial prejudice and their perception in U.S. society. This model explains the type of prejudice and discrimination each group faces and can be used to compare differing racialized experiences. While this model can be used to compare experiences, the authors state this model does not identify which groups are most oppressed. The authors theorize racial position on two axes. The first axis is measured on a binary of inferiority and superiority. The second axis is measured foreignness and Americanness. The authors found that Asian Americans were generally rated as superior to other groups; however, they were perceived as more foreign than racial groups such as Black Americans and Indigenous Americans.

Asian American racial position has been theorized, and we utilize the idea that Asian American racial positionality is consistently in flux. Thus, we use Asian Americans' ambiguous racial positioning to understand how Asian Americans are framed in U.S. society in relation to other racial groups. Further, we recognize the diversity of experiences within the Asian American panoply and attempt to differentiate Asian American experiences utilizing pan ethnic categories distinguishing between East Asian, Southeast Asian, South Asian, and Filipino experiences. The theory is also utilized to understand how COVID-19 shaped the relationships between racial positioning, the model minority myth, and the perpetual foreigner to create a more cohesive understanding of Asian Americans' perceptions and experiences in the U.S.

4 Methodology

4.1 Data Collection

The study analyzes education research on Asian Americans to understand how COVID-19 shaped Asian American racial dynamics in the U.S. In the first stage of the study, we collected titles and abstracts of peer-reviewed articles through four major electronic databases: Educational Resource Information Center (ERIC), Education Full Text, and JSTOR, using the following keywords: "Asian Americans," "Asian students," "stereotypes," "model minority myth," "perpetual foreigner," "education," "college access," and "schooling experience". In the second stage of the study, we applied inclusion and exclusion criteria to locate articles whose focuses align with the study's research questions concerning stereotypes and perspectives of Asian Americans students. In the third stage of the study, we divided our selected articles into two categories: (1) before COVID-19 with publications before 2020 and (2) after COVID-19 with publications after 2020.

In total, 160 articles were published before COVID-19, and 34 were published after COVID-19 using our search criteria. The difference between the number of studies before and after COVID-19 is due to the inclusion of all studies before 2020, in contrast to the two years in which studies have begun to address the impact of COVID-19 on Asian Americans. Titles and abstracts were then imported to the R statistical package for data analysis.

4.2 Development of Codes and Coding Process

We developed codes deductively based on the model minority, perpetual foreigner myth, and data disaggregation. The code model minority was used anytime the text included the phrase "model minority." Similarly, the perpetual foreigner was coded anytime the text included the phrase "perpetual foreigner." However, to capture the concept of data disaggregation Asian American was broken down into pan-ethnic groups: East Asian, Southeast Asian, South Asian and Filipino. The pan-ethnic East Asian includes the ethnic groups Japanese, Korean, and Chinese. These groups were developed based on theories of pan-ethnic development in the U.S. [30, 31] and challenges associated with pan-ethnic identities [32]. Although East Asian, Southeast Asian, and South Asian can be considered parts of Asian America, these codes were not aggregated. For example, it is possible for a study to address South Asians and not reference Asian Americans. The codes Black, White, and Latinx are included to reflect how Asian American racial position is contingent upon the concepts of Whiteness and Blackness in the U.S. Each code was coded to have any instance of the words.

The data was coded utilizing R studio. The R script searched the title and abstract for any indication of the codes and variations on the code. For example, for the code "model minority," R would search for the word "model minority." If the phrase was included in the text, then model minority would be indicated as present. For pan-ethnic groups such as East Asian, R would search for the words East Asian in addition to the ethnic groups categorized into East Asian such as Chinese, Japanese, and Korean. While this method allows for large amounts of text to be coded efficiently, limitations exist. Using R to search for keywords does not consider the broader context of how these statements are being used and assumes that if the keyword is in the text, the study addresses the conceptual framework.

4.3 Comparative Literature Review with Epistemic Network Analysis (ENA)

To understand the relationship between themes, we have chosen to use ENA, a quantitative ethnographic technique, to model the structure of data connections. ENA assumes: (1) it is possible to systematically identify a set of meaningful features in the data (Codes); (2) the data has a local structure; and (3) an essential feature of the data is the way codes are connected within conversations. This study is one of the few studies to use ENA to examine trends in comprehensive literature reviews and is a significant contribution to exploring themes from past literature. For example, one study used ENA to identify gaps in the literature and the semantic relationship between different themes [33]; however, this method is limited to modeling the relationship between keywords rather than its intended purpose of identifying and representing unique patterns and perceptual organization. Despite this limitation, ENA is beneficial for this study as it visually models the differences pre-COVID-19 and post-COVID-19.

For this comparative analysis, we used difference plots to highlight pre- and post-COVID-19 years rather than separate plots. The difference model shows the differences between pre- and post-COVID-19. For this study, we organized documents from the earliest to latest and selected an infinite stanza. The rationale for organizing studies by date is to reflect the idea that each of these studies is in conversation with one another. For example, a seminal study, such as Kim's theory of racial triangulation [16], can be referenced later in another study which can reflect a conversation. Using an infinite stanza assumes that each document is built upon similar concepts.

Figure 1 (see below) shows the Epistemic Network based on the text search and the codes developed. The model shows the relationships between the themes through the nodes' distance, size, and thickness. The red lines represent the general theme for articles before covid, while the blue lines represent the general themes for articles during covid. The size of the points indicates how frequently the themes occurred, while the thickness of the lines indicates the strength of the relationship between the two points. The placement of the gray points shows how semantically related each topic relates to each other. Finally, models' goodness of fit was checked using Pearson and Spearman, with values above 0.93.

5 Analysis and Findings

We built two networks to understand the relationship that Asian Americans had with other Asian ethnic groups (Fig. 1) and racial groups (Fig. 3). The themes were selected based on the deductive codes from the model minority myth, perpetual foreigner myth, and data disaggregation. The first model compares Asian American pan-ethnic groups and highlights how differing Asian American pan-ethnic categories have been addressed in the literature.

Often times when writing about Asian Americans there is an assumption that Asian American are East Asian American [32]. While Chinese, Japanese and Korean Americans are Asian American, there are many other Asian ethnic backgrounds such as Hmong,

Thai, Malaysian. The focus on East Asian Americans has led to other Asian American voices and needs being ignored. For example, while some Asian ethnic groups have very high bachelor's attainment rates, Taiwanese (72%) and Asian Indian (76%), this stands in stark contrast to Hmong (14%), Cambodian (13%), and Laotian (12%) communities [34].

The pan-ethnic categories attempt to reflect Asian American diversity and understand the relationship between them. The first model includes codes, Model Minority, Asian American, South Asian, discrimination, Southeast Asian, and perpetual foreigner. The second model focuses on the relationship that Asian Americans as a panethnic group have to other racial categories and includes: model minority, Latinx, Black, perpetual foreigner, White, Asian American, and discrimination. In addition to the models that show the overall mean. From each of these networks, two contrasting studies are selected to highlight the differences between the studies shown in Fig. 2, and Fig. 3.

5.1 COVID-19 and Perceptions of Asian Americans Panethnic Groups

Figure 1 shows the mean difference between Asian ethnic groups' themes before and after COVID-19. One finding from this graph shows before COVID-19, the literature focused on the relationship Asian Americans had with the model minority myth. Studies before COVID-19 addressed how the model minority did not accurately reflect the experiences of Asian Americans broadly [13, 35–37] and addressed how the model minority diminishes experiences of racism and structural problems [38]. After COVID-19, some studies discussed the veracity of Asian Americans as high-achieving model minorities [39]; however, one study addressed how Chinese transracial adoptees navigated being the model minority to being a perceived threat [9].

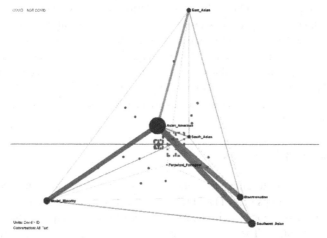

Fig. 1. Means difference network for panethnic Asian American literature before and after Covid-19

There is also a relationship between the model minority myth and broader panethnic categories such as Southeast Asians and East Asians. One exception to this analysis is the relationship the model minority myth has with South Asians, which has a more substantial relationship after COVID-19. This could be due to a shift in the field rather than related to COVID-19. After COVID-19, there seemed to be a shift in focus as there is a strong relationship between Asian Americans and discrimination. This is supported by Southeast Asians and East Asians having a connection to discrimination after COVID-19. This is contrasted against the code South Asian which found more instances of discrimination before the COVID-19 pandemic. This would be consistent with the increase in Asian American violence preceding the onset of the COVID-19 pandemic [7].

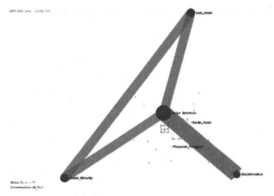

Fig. 2. Comparative means network for Park [40] and Kantamneni [41] using Panethnic Asian American model

Figure 2 shows the comparative network for two studies using the same network: Park [40] and Kantamneni [41]. Park's study was published in 2011 and directly addresses the role of the model minority in the lives of Korean immigrant students. It concludes that Korean immigrant students constructed their identities around those who were able to achieve the model minority status and those who were unable to achieve the status. Kantamneni's study was published in 2020 and describes how the COVID-19 pandemic affected different communities of color from a wide range of economic backgrounds, and particularly how the COVID-19 pandemic has increased discrimination against Asian Americans in society. Kantamneni then calls for a renewed research agenda around the COVID-19 pandemic. Park's study focuses on the model minority; while Kantamneni's study focuses on Asian American discrimination. The contrast in these two studies highlights the shift in topics before COVID-19 and afterward however, some studies continue to focus on discrimination, the model minority myth, and COVID-19. Misra et al. [42] calls upon addressing increasing stigmatization by examining research on mental health, stigma reduction practices, and federal policies to reduce anti-Asian racism. Some studies, such as Wing and Park-Taylor [9] contextualized the model minority within COVID-19 and recognized historically recurring anti-Asian sentiment like the yellow peril movement.

5.2 Asian American Framings and Covid 19

Figure 3 shows the relationships between different racial groups and Asian Americans. This differs from Fig. 1, by removing broad ethnic groups in Asian Americans and focusing on Latinx, Black, and White racial groups in addition to broad concepts such as the Model Minority and the Perpetual foreigner myth. With the addition of other racial groups, Asian American positionality becomes much more evident. For example, the position of Asian Americans to the White node is much closer than Black and Latinx. This would indicate that from the studies selected, there was a closer semantic distance for the White code than there were for other racial categories. Further, there is a strong thematic relationship between Asian Americans, White, and discrimination with the onset of COVID-19, which would be consistent with the shift in sentiment toward Asian Americans.

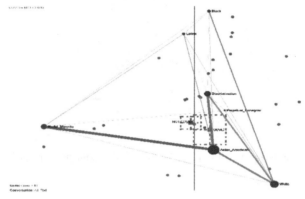

Fig. 3. Comparative network for Racial groups and Asian American literature before and after Covid-19

Using the size of the nodes as a comparison to indicate the frequency of occurrence, White has a higher frequency than Black or Latinx. This model provides examples of how other racial groups are framed in relationship to Asian American literature. For example, the relationship between all other racial groups seems stronger before COVID-19 than afterward. While all other racial groups share this commonality, they are semantically distant.

Figure 4 uses the network for Fig. 3 and compares two specific studies: Wing and Park-Taylor [9] and Wong and Halgin [14]. Wing and Park-Taylor's study was published in 2022, and they write about Chinese transracial adoptees who were adopted by White families and experience navigating the COVID-19 pandemic, finding the pandemic has significantly affected their physical and emotional well-being and their sense of belonging with their families. Wing and Park-Taylor conclude the model minority myth acts to minimize Asian American discrimination and conflicts in addressing Anti-Asian hate because of coinciding social justice issues such as Black Lives Matter. Wong and Halgin examine whether the model minority myth benefits or harms Asian Americans. They find the stereotype detrimental to Asian Americans because the label does not accurately reflect Asian Americans, pigeonholes Asian Americans, and may foster social

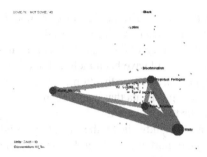

Fig. 4. Comparative means network for Wing and Park-Taylor [9] and Wong and Halgin [14] using the race model

indifference towards Asian American discrimination. Wong and Halgin' study focus particularly on Asian Americans as the model minority in relationship to White populations. At the same time, Wing and Park-Taylor's study attempts to grapple with how COVID-19 shifted how Asian Americans are perceived.

Figures 3 and 4 suggest Asian Americans occupy an ambiguous and fluctuating space within the racial hierarchy. There is a strong relationship in the studies that have examined Asian Americans explicitly mentioning White people or Whiteness. In contrast, few studies examine Asian Americans' relationship to Black and Latinx populations. This gap in Asian American issues relating to Black and Latinx populations was exacerbated during the COVID-19 pandemic, which emphasized focusing on anti-Asian crime. Some studies during the COVID-19 pandemic addressed the relationship between Asian Americans and other communities of color. For example, Pheng and Xiong [43] write about how as Southeast Asian researchers, they can produce anti-racist scholarship with their communities to benefit minoritized communities. In this study, COVID-19 was mentioned to contextualize anti-Asian racism and highlight how COVID-19 has been detrimental to Black, Indigenous, and People of Color (BIPOC). Similarly, Kantamneni [41] mentions how COVID-19 has disproportionality affected BIPOC communities and has stoked anti-Asian sentiments; however, the emphasis of the study was to address Asian American discrimination, rather than Pheng and Xiong [43], which shows how South East Asian scholars can work towards building solidarity and doing community education work.

6   Limitations and Next Steps

While ENA can be a powerful methodology for understanding broader discourse themes, this study has some limitations. The first limitation of this study is the body of text used. Abstracts are intended to provide summaries of studies; however, they often may not capture all aspects of the study. For example, Lee and Zhou's [44] abstract mentions the success frame with no mention of the model minority; however, in reviewing their complete work, the model minority becomes an essential component of their study. Rather than using abstracts, future studies may consider using full document texts. In addition to limitations by the abstract, similar limitations exist with how the data was coded using R. Because the data coded any instance of model minority and perpetual foreigner it is unclear how these frameworks were used.

Another limitation is the amount of data selected. This analysis used more than 160; however, many other studies could have been included to create a more comprehensive review of the field of Asian American education studies. This comprehensive review would need to include a coding schema that does not simply conduct a word search but rather understands the contexts of the word.

Despite the limitation, this study shows the first steps in how ENA can be used to compile literature and, more importantly, its usefulness in creating comparative literature networks. Future research using ENA for literature reviews can identify shifts in bodies of literature to show how the field has changed after a specific period or event by creating difference networks. Further, this method can compare different methods in selecting literature. For example, with the advent of A.I.-assisted research tools, a comparison could be conducted that compares A.I.-selected studies with human-selected studies.

7   Conclusion

This study uses two epistemic networks to show the shift in Asian American educational studies. Figure 1 broadly shows that before COVID-19, Asian American education research focused on Asian Americans and the model minority; however, after the COVID-19 pandemic, there was a stronger relationship between panethnic categorizations and Asian Americans. Figure 3 shows the relationship that Asian Americans had as a broad racial group to other racial groups, finding that before COVID-19, Asian American education literature addressed Black and Latinx studies; however, after COVID-19, there was a stronger relationship between Asian Americans and White studies.

ENA can be used to create a broad snapshot of the field's current state and allow scholars to understand the direction of the field. In the case of Asian American education research, more research needs to be done to connect how the COVID-19 pandemic relates Asian American populations to other communities of color, similar to the work of Pheng and Xiong [43]. Further research can also begin to understand how different Asian American panethnic groups are different.

References

1. Peterson, W.: Success Story: Japanese-American Style (1966)
2. Jo, J.-Y.O.: Neglected voices in the multicultural America: Asian American racial politics and its implication for multicultural education. Multicult. Perspect. **6**, 19–25 (2004)
3. Tuan, M.: Neither real Americans nor real Asians? Multigeneration Asian ethnics navigating the terrain of authenticity. Qual. Sociol. **22**, 105–125 (1999)
4. Wu, F.H.: Yellow: Race in America Beyond Black and White. Basic Books (2002)
5. Okihiro, G.Y.: American History Unbound: Asians and Pacific Islanders. University of California Press (2015)
6. Tavernise, S., Oppel Jr, R.A.: Spit On, Yelled At, Attacked: Chinese-Americans Fear for Their Safety (2020). https://www.nytimes.com/2020/03/23/us/chinese-coronavirus-racist-attacks.html

7. Walker, D., Anders, A.D.: "China Virus" and "Kung-Flu": a critical race case study of Asian American journalists' experiences during COVID-19. Cult. Stud. - Crit. Methodol. **22**, 76–88 (2022). https://doi.org/10.1177/15327086211055157

8. Wang, S.C., Santos, B.M.C.: "Go back to china with your (expletive) virus": a revelatory case study of anti-Asian racism during COVID-19. Asian Am. J. Psychol. (2022). https://doi.org/10.1037/aap0000287

9. Wing, H.M., Park-Taylor, J.: From model minority to racial threat: Chinese transracial adoptees' experience navigating the COVID-19 pandemic. Asian Am. J. Psychol. (2022). https://doi.org/10.1037/aap0000283

10. Takaki, R.: Strangers from a Different Shore: A History of Asian Americans. Little Brown (1998)

11. Kim, C.J.: Bitter Fruit: The Politics of Black-Korean Conflict in New York City. Yale University Press (2000)

12. Lee, S.J.: Behind the model-minority stereotype: voices of high-and low-achieving Asian American students. Anthropol. Educ. Q. **25**, 413–429 (1994). https://doi.org/10.1525/aeq.1994.25.4.04x0530j

13. Suzuki, B.H.: Revisiting the model minority stereotype: implications for student affairs practice and higher education. New Dir. Stud. Serv. **97**, 21–32 (2002). https://doi.org/10.1002/ss.36

14. Wong, F., Halgin, R.: The "model minority": bane or blessing for Asian Americans? J. Multicult. Couns. Dev. **34**, 38–49 (2006). https://doi.org/10.1002/j.2161-1912.2006.tb00025.x

15. Ng, J.C., Lee, S.S., Pak, Y.K.: Contesting the model minority and perpetual foreigner stereotypes: a critical review of literature on Asian Americans in education (chap. 4). Rev. Res. Educ. **31**, 95–130 (2007). https://doi.org/10.3102/0091732X06298015

16. Kim, C.J.: The racial triangulation of Asian Americans. Polit. Soc. **27**, 105–138 (1999). https://doi.org/10.1177/0032329299027001005

17. Tawa, J., Negrón, R., Suyemoto, K.L., Carter, A.S.: The effect of resource competition on Blacks' and Asians' social distance using a virtual world methodology. Group Process. Intergroup Relat. (2015). https://doi.org/10.1177/1368430214561694

18. Chun, K.-T.: The myth of Asian American success and its educational ramifications. IRCD Bull. **15**, 13 (1980)

19. Escueta, E., O'Brien, E.: Asian Americans in Higher Education: Trends and Issues. American Council on Education, Washington, D.C. (1991)

20. Chang, M.J., Kiang, P.N.: New challenges of representing Asian America students in U.S higher education. In: Smith, W.A. (ed.) The Racial Crisis in American Higher Education: Continuing Challenges for the Twenty-First Century, p. 22. State University of New York Press (2002)

21. Teranishi, R.T., Ceja, M., Antonio, A.L., Allen, W.R., McDonough, P.M.: The college-choice process for Asian Pacific Americans: ethnicity and socioeconomic class in context. Rev. High. Educ. **27**, 527–551 (2004). https://doi.org/10.1353/rhe.2004.0025

22. Museus, S.D.: Unpacking the complex and multifaceted nature of parental influences on southeast Asian American college students' educational trajectories. J. High. Educ. **84**, 708–738 (2013). https://doi.org/10.1353/jhe.2013.0031

23. Palmer, R.T., Maramba, D.C.: The impact of social capital on the access, adjustment, and success of Southeast Asian American college students. J. Coll. Stud. Dev. **56**, 45–60 (2015). https://doi.org/10.1353/csd.2015.0007

24. Kitano, H.H.L.: Japanese Americans: the development of a middleman minority. Pac. Hist. Rev. **43**, 500–519 (1974). https://doi.org/10.2307/3638430

25. Bonilla-Silva, E.: From bi-racial to tri-racial: towards a new system of racial stratification in the USA. Ethn. Racial Stud. **27**, 931–950 (2004). https://doi.org/10.1080/0141987042000268530
26. Okihiro, G.Y.: Margins and Mainstreams: Asians in American History and Culture. University of Washington Press (1994)
27. Kim, J.K.: Yellow over black: history of race in Korea and the new study of race and empire. Crit. Sociol. **41**, 205–217 (2015). https://doi.org/10.1177/0896920513507787
28. Kim, C.J.: Unyielding positions: a critique of the "race" debate. Ethnicities **4**, 337–355 (2004). https://doi.org/10.1177/1468796804045238
29. Zou, L.X., Cheryan, S.: Two axes of subordination: a new model of racial position. J. Pers. Soc. Psychol. **112**, 696–717 (2017). https://doi.org/10.1037/pspa0000080
30. Okamoto, D.G.: Redefining Race. Russell Sage Foundation (2014)
31. Le Espiritu, Y.: Asian American Panethnicity. Temple University Press (1992)
32. Nadal, K.L.: The brown Asian American movement: advocating for South Asian, Southeast Asian, and Filipino American communities. Asian Am. Policy Rev. **29**, 2–11, 95 (2019)
33. Sun, J., Barany, A.: Epistemic network analysis on Asian American college access literature. In: Damşa, C., Barany, A. (eds.) Conference Proceedings Supplemental, pp. 133–136. Denmark, Copenhagen (2022)
34. Museus, S.D.: Asian American Students in Higher Education. Routledge, Taylor & Francis Group, New York (2014)
35. Shih, F.H.: Asian-American students: the myth of a model minority. J. Coll. Sci. Teach. **17**, 356–359 (1988)
36. Lee, S.J.: Unraveling the "Model Minority" Stereotype: Listening to Asian American Youth. Teachers College Press, New York (2009)
37. Wong, P., Lai, C.F., Nagasawa, R., Lin, T.: Asian Americans as a model minority: self-perceptions and perceptions by other racial groups (1998)
38. Yu, T.: Challenging the politics of the "model minority" stereotype: a case for educational equality. Equity Excell. Educ. **39**, 325–333 (2006). https://doi.org/10.1080/10665680600932333
39. Chang, T.F., Shih, K.Y.: Are Asian American children and youth high achieving?: unpacking variations of educational achievement from an integrative ecological perspective. Asian Am. J. Psychol. (2021). https://doi.org/10.1037/aap0000252
40. Park, G.C.: Becoming a "model minority": acquisition, construction and enactment of American identity for Korean immigrant students. Urban Rev. **43**, 620–635 (2011). https://doi.org/10.1007/s11256-010-0164-8
41. Kantamneni, N.: The impact of the COVID-19 pandemic on marginalized populations in the United States: a research agenda. J. Vocat. Behav. **119** (2020). https://doi.org/10.1016/j.jvb.2020.103439
42. Misra, S., Le, P.T.D., Goldmann, E., Yang, L.H.: Psychological impact of anti-Asian stigma due to the COVID-19 pandemic: a call for research, practice, and policy responses. Psychol. Trauma Theory Res. Pract. Policy (2020). https://doi.org/10.1037/tra0000821
43. Pheng, L.M., Xiong, C.P.: What is social justice research for Asian Americans? Critical reflections on cross-racial and cross-ethnic coalition building in community-based educational spaces. Educ. Stud. - AESA (2022). https://doi.org/10.1080/00131946.2022.2033749
44. Lee, J., Zhou, M.: The success frame and achievement paradox: the costs and consequences for Asian Americans. Race Soc. Probl. **6**, 38–55 (2014). https://doi.org/10.1007/s12552-014-9112-7

Examining Student Conceptualizations of Intersectional Identities Across Global Contexts via Epistemic Network Analysis (ENA)

Vinay R. Mallikaarjun$^{(\boxtimes)}$, Usama Mahmud, and Sharon M. Ravitch

University of Pennsylvania, Philadelphia, PA 19104, USA
vinaym@upenn.edu

Abstract. Intersectional identity theory, also known as intersectionality, asserts that an individual's unique combination of identities both mediates and is mediated by their sociocultural contexts, and is thus a valuable theoretical framework for exploring identity. However, while intersectionality has been largely applied within USA contexts to explore intersections of race, gender, and class, its applicability to non-USA contexts remains largely unexplored. We interviewed high school students in the USA and Pakistan to understand their conceptualizations of intersectional identities with regard to their broader life experiences as well as within the context of their educational experiences. In this paper, we analyze ten of these interviews through a quantitative ethnographic-epistemic network analysis (QE-ENA) approach to identify connections made by participants between specific aspects of identity within their conceptualizations. Our results suggest that participants from different country groups emphasize and connect different aspects of identity and point towards the need to better contextualize intersectional identity theory for non-Western global contexts, alongside broader implications for applications of intersectionality within further global research as well as the efficacious nature of QE-ENA to analyze issues of intersectionality.

Keywords: Intersectionality · Student Identity · Global Research · Epistemic Network Analysis

1 Introduction

Educational experiences significantly influence children's cognitive abilities, academic achievement, and life outcomes, including their socioemotional and psychological development. Accordingly, educational settings must become more conducive to the optimal holistic development of children of all backgrounds, cultures, and social identities as an antidote to inequity and underdevelopment [1]. Intersectional identity theory asserts that individuals are impacted by multiple intersecting identity markers that serve as axes of oppression [2], such as gender, race, culture, religion, socioeconomic status, immigration status, education level, language, disability, and other such identity markers. Thus, intersectionality serves as a useful lens through which identity-based experiences can be examined.

© The Author(s), under exclusive license to Springer Nature Switzerland AG 2023
G. Arastoopour Irgens and S. Knight (Eds.): ICQE 2023, CCIS 1895, pp. 215–229, 2023.
https://doi.org/10.1007/978-3-031-47014-1_15

While discourse around educational inequities on the basis of identity are prevalent in the United States of America (USA), especially with regard to issues of race and gender inequities, most developing countries are yet to investigate how intersectional identities play out in educational settings in contemporary times [3]. In this study, we adopt a quantitative ethnographic approach and leverage epistemic network analysis [4] to examine the following questions:

1. Which aspects of identity are connected by high school students in the USA and in Pakistan when conceptualizing their own intersectional identities, both within and outside of their academic contexts?
2. What, if any, differences are present between high school students' conceptualizations of intersectional identity across the different country contexts of the USA and Pakistan?

We posit that intersectional identity theory is applicable across global contexts while noting that for intersectionality to be useful for non-Western populations, the theory itself must be iterated with precision by drawing upon the multidimensional lived experiences of non-Western populations. This study is our humble attempt to expand the boundaries of intersectional identity theory by foregrounding the lived experiences of students in non-Western contexts. To this end, we have utilized the emerging design philosophy of quantitative ethnography and its corresponding analytical approach of epistemic network analysis [4].

2   Theoretical Framework

2.1   Identity and Intersectionality

While there are a multitude of definitions for identity, we draw on Gee's [5] conceptualizations of identity which posit the existence of a more internal and intrinsic individual core identity as well as a number of external-facing identities that arise in response to different social contexts and pressures. We find this conceptualization of identity to be especially relevant to our study, which considers participants' identity both in their "core" state as well as the interplay between participants' identity and their educational experiences and contexts.

Intersectional thought has its roots in the work of Black feminist women activists and writers [6, 7]; intersectionality as a theory was first concretized by Crenshaw [2] as a legal framework for the purpose of gaining greater justice amidst systemic and institutionalized forces of oppression in the USA with a focus towards resisting racism and sexism. Accordingly, Crenshaw's [2] conceptualization of intersectionality focused on axes of race and gender, specifically the intersectional experiences of Black women, and challenged the paradigms of viewing oppression through a single-issue lens within a legal context.

The role of identity and intersectionality in educational experiences has been well-documented throughout the extant literature; educational experiences and learning outcomes for minoritized students are a function of their social identities, which shape their unequal access to quality resources and experiences [8]. Ethnic discrimination, for example, takes different forms and reflects deficit-based attitudes, expressed in explicit and implicit ways [9, 10]. These biases are often experienced as microaggressions or overt aggressions [11] and become institutionalized into systemic oppression, exacerbating educational disparities and causing disproportionate harm to minoritized students [12].

2.2 Country-Specific Applications of Intersectionality

Given the emphasis on identity as an analytical framework for understanding educational experiences, it is fitting that intersectionality has been propagated in a multitude of ways within the field of education research in the USA [13]. In the USA, Black, Latinx, and Native American students underperform relative to their White counterparts [9, 10]. Data reveal differences that map directly onto race and social class, i.e., the 2016 high school dropout rate for Hispanic versus White students [9]. In 2015, the percentage of students in grade 9–12 reported to have been in a physical fight in school within one year was higher for Black and Latinx students as compared to White students [14]. These statistics illuminate the diffusion effect of structural discrimination [9]. Accordingly, the use of intersectionality as a theory in education research typically gives emphasis towards identity markers of race, gender, socioeconomic status, and sexual orientation [13, 15–18]. However, it is important to note that these particular identity markers, while prominent within a USA context, may vary in their relevance when considering how to apply intersectionality as an epistemological lens for examining the experiences and identities of students within non-USA country contexts, thus underscoring the need for the present study.

Pakistan is one such context, possessing an abundance of multifaceted diversity that underscores the need for a contextually responsive iteration of intersectionality. 220 million people with 60% of the population below the age of 30 years form a range of intersectional identities [19]. Ethnically, Pakistan is diverse with Punjabi, Balochi, Sindhi, Pashtun, Kashmiri, Hazara, and Muhajir ethnicities and hosts a large refugee population, having absorbed 2 million refugees from Afghanistan [20]. As a Muslim majority nation with different religious sects, religious minorities include Christians, Hindus, and Sikhs. Linguistic and socioeconomic fault-lines are stark. These particular identity markers impact student experiences in educational settings across Pakistan. This is evident in learning levels, completion rates, and other education indicators which show a gap between historically marginalized and privileged segments of society. For example, students in the region of Balochistan have lower learning levels compared to the region of Punjab, completion rates for girls are lower in rural areas showing gender inequity, children with disabilities do not perform as well as peers, and religious minorities are unable to express themselves openly in educational spaces for fear of retribution and opportunity costs [21].

Thus, while structural inequities and oppressions are present within both Pakistan and the USA, their nature varies, and we thus hypothesize that the identities most affected and intersections thereof are different between the two countries. This signals the need for a theory of intersectional identity that has been fine-tuned in accordance with the specific identity-based contexts of a given country, whether that country be the USA, Pakistan, or otherwise. With such contextually specific adaptations, intersectionality could better inform the work of education practitioners by allowing them to gain a better sense of which identity aspects students give more or less emphasis towards, assisting them in improving the quality of educational experiences for students in a contextually responsive manner.

Lastly, given that the nature of intersectionality itself is one of interconnectedness, we find that there is great potential for the use of Quantitative Ethnography (QE), and specifically epistemic network analysis (ENA) in exploration and analysis of intersectional identity. Indeed, QE and ENA have been previously used to analyze certain conceptualizations of identity, particularly within the context of gaming communities [22, 23], but has not yet been applied to intersectional identity in ways similar to our analytic purview here.

3 Methods

3.1 Data Collection

We developed a semi-structured interview protocol to surface students' conceptualizations of their intersectional identities, in line with best practices for interview protocol development [24]. Data collection occurred from January through December 2022, wherein we conducted semi-structured interviews with 16 high school students throughout the Philadelphia and Los Angeles regions of the USA and 45 high school students across the Lahore, Kasur, Chinniot and Islamabad regions of Pakistan. Participants were selected through voluntary convenience sampling [24]. From our participant pool, we randomly selected five USA interviews and five Pakistani interviews for analysis in this paper.

While the interview protocol was kept consistent across countries, there was contextual-based variability in the frequency of and specific nature of interviewers' probes, a phenomenon that is inevitable when multiple researchers are conducting interviews [24]. One notable instance of this contextual variability was the interview language varying by country; the USA interviews were conducted in English and the Pakistani interviews were conducted in Urdu. Furthermore, our research team observed throughout the interview process that some questions varied in their applicability to different countries' participants based on researchers' understanding of the country's context. This created additional variability within the interview process, however, not to a degree where researchers had to abandon the protocol altogether. Any structural differences in interview applications were also considered as part of the interpretation of subsequent ENA models.

3.2 Data Cleaning, Organization and Selection

For the USA participants' interview data, automatically generated Zoom transcripts were cleaned manually, using the interview audio recording as a reference when necessary, and in-person interviews were manually transcribed. Data cleaning for the Pakistani participants' interview data was a lengthier process, as the research team manually transcribed interviews and then translated those transcripts from Urdu to English.

3.3 Data Analysis: Code Development and Coding Procedures

Codes were developed inductively through a collaborative process of thematic analysis [24] and then deductively applied to the data through a binary coding approach (See Table 1). Due to practical constraints, only one member of the research team engaged in coding of the data. This coder's positionality is that of a second generation Indian-American, Hindu, male, doctoral student. In line with single-coder criteria set forth by Shaffer & Ruis [25], the research team feels that this coder's positionality intersects with aspects of both countries' participants' experiences in ways that lend validity to his coding decisions, especially with respect to the USA participants. However, we do acknowledge that our coder's positionality is not a substitute for an emic Pakistani perspective in coding, which would have given our coding decisions even greater validity.

Table 1. Codebook.

Code	Definition
Family	Participant references their family
Education	Participant references their formalized education or academic identity
Emotional Affect	Participant references any experienced emotional state
Gender	Participant references their gender identity
Language	Participant references their written or spoken language
Location	Participant references their geographic location, whether macro or micro
Morality	Participant voices considerations of morality (i.e., "right," "wrong," etc.) in connection to an aspect of identity
Peer Interactions	Participant references interactions with their peers
Race	Participant references their race or ethnicity
Religion	Participant references their religion
Sexual Orientation	Participant references their sexual orientation

3.4 Epistemic Network Analysis

The coded interview transcripts were analyzed through Epistemic Network Analysis (ENA), as it is a valuable analytical method that gives structure to qualitative data while retaining contextual importance and allows for rich sensemaking of congruent themes in data through model visualization [26].

Each interview contains 40–60 coded lines of data on average. Each line of data is a participant utterance, separated by turn-of-talk between the participant and interviewer. Interviewer utterances were not coded or included in ENA models; however, those utterances were present in the transcript during coding to provide context for participants' utterances. This approach was intended to prioritize the visualization of patterns in participants' discussions of their own identities. Once a transcript was fully coded, interviewer utterances were removed due to our assessment that interviewer utterances were not indicative of surfacing participant identity.

ENA Modeling Decisions

The first-level unit variables are each country (the USA and Pakistan), with a second-level unit variable being each individual student and a third-level unit variable being each interview part. This second-level unit variable was the result of observations that questions #1–6 of the interview protocol ask the students to reflect on their identities in a more open-ended manner without calling particular attention to identity in the context of any social phenomenon (e.g., education); thus, we are referring to the responses from these first six questions as participants' conceptualizations of their intersectional identities at baseline. Though there can be no truly abstract baseline identity for any individual [5], given the sociocultural nature of the phenomenon, we use this term of baseline identity to distinguish participants' general conceptualizations of their intersectional identities from their conceptualizations of intersectional identities with regard to educational experiences and contexts. From Question #7 onwards marks a concrete shift in asking students to think about and reflect on how their educational experiences and school contexts have affected their identity.

The conversation variable is each individual student's interview. Lastly, our epistemic networks employ a moving stanza window of three lines, as the organization of each interview into two parts makes the data more suitable for a moving stanza window due to the natural flow of the discourse and self-reflection. We chose a stanza window of three lines due to line count in our interviews; interpretively, we noticed that participants were more often referring to their more immediate previous utterances.

Our ENA models are generated by the webENA tool. Coded data, along with the corresponding unit and conversation variables, are entered into and formatted in a spreadsheet according to standard ENA conventions in order for the webENA tool to generate a model [4]. The ENA models are made by the webENA tool looking for frequent co-occurrences of codes within every three line-window of data, bounded by the parameters set by our assignment of the unit variables, conversation variables, and stanza window [26]. The count of co-occurrences of every particular code combination for each three-line window within our data set is then aggregated into a matrix of values. These values are then normalized to account for different volumes of data between each interview, as no two interviews are exactly the same length. Finally, the connections between codes per each unit variable are visualized within an ENA model.

Once models were generated, we then engaged in parsimonious analysis to interpretively determine if any codes could be visually hidden from the models, to amplify visibility of emergent trends from the data. Accordingly, we decided that any code with no connections above a relative weight of 0.1 were excluded from the models. While this is not as systematic as approaches such as the Parsimonious Removal with Interpretive Alignment (PRIA) approach [27], we feel that this decision enhances the interpretive power of our models while maintaining thematic fidelity to the data.

4 Results and Discussion

Our results are organized with relation to our analysis of the two halves of the interview protocol as discrete entities, as discussed above. For each interview half, we discuss notable connections within each country group's models followed by a discussion of key differences seen within the respective comparison model and their broader implications. All models have a Pearson goodness of fit of 1.0.

4.1 Baseline Conceptualizations of Intersectional Identities

The ENA models for the first part of the interview (see Figs. 1, 2 and 3) visualize participants' baseline conceptualizations of their intersectional identities as unearthed through the first part of our interview protocol. In accordance with our methods, the codes of Morality and Socioeconomic Status were excluded from these models, as neither code formed any connections with any other codes above a relative weight of 0.1.

Within the USA students' conceptualizations of intersectional identities at baseline (see Fig. 1), a quartet of well-connected codes emerged from the model: Race, Gender, Peer Interactions, and Family, although the latter is the least strongly connected of the group. Race is the strongest connected code within the model with heavy connections to Gender (0.24[1]), Religion (0.19), and Peer Interactions (0.16). In addition to its connection to Race, Gender was most connected to Peer Interactions (0.21) and Religion (0.15), indicating that our USA participants may conceptualize their gender in relation to multiple other aspects of their identities. Evidencing the race-gender connection, one USA student said: "*I am a Black man, some people see us differently. They don't see us as equals sometimes.*" The results for the Race and Gender codes reinforce what we observed within the aforementioned literature on identity formation within the USA, which posits the importance of race and gender as key components of intersectional identity for this participant group.

Peer Interactions was strongly connected to Religion (0.18) and Family (0.14), in addition to its strong connections to Race and Gender. These connections ran counter to our expectations of Peer Interactions; extant identity-based literature often cognizes social phenomena as a mediator of identity as opposed to being a part of identity [28, 29], yet our results indicate that our USA participants conceptualize their interactions with peers as part of their baseline intersectional identities. Lastly, the Family code had a relatively strong connection to Education (0.21) and more moderate connections to Gender (0.13) and Peer Interactions (0.13), leading us to conclude that our USA participants' baseline conceptualizations of identity may be more likely to be shaped by their interactions and experiences with family members and within family contexts. One USA participant aptly describes this multidimensional connection when describing her baseline identity: "*Me and my friends try and go out just to have fun, because, like, school stresses us out sometimes...well, me and my friends have gotten really close this year. So, like, our families have met and stuff. So yeah, my mom really likes my friends.*" This participant fluidly connects aspects of her peer interactions, family experiences,

---

[1] All numbers within parentheses in this section refer to relative line weights as given by the webENA tool.

and academic identity with her broader notions of identity, demonstrating how these identity aspects intersect.

The ENA model of Pakistani students' highlights the prominence of the Education, Family, Language, Location, and Religion codes in their baseline conceptualizations of intersectional identities (see Fig. 2). Specifically, the Family code occupies a position of centrality through its stronger connections to Education (0.45), Language (0.27), Location (0.32), and Religion (0.21). The other four codes mentioned all have comparatively strong connections to each other; no connection among the group has a relative weight less than 0.22. Thus, this model provides us with a working understanding that our Pakistani participants conceptualize their identities primarily through their familial and education-related experiences, along with their regional, language, and religion-related identities.

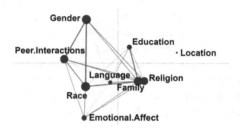

Fig. 1. ENA model of USA participants' baseline conceptualizations of intersectional identity. The line weight between Family and Religion (not visible) is 0.11.

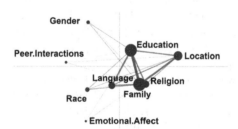

Fig. 2. ENA model of Pakistan participants' baseline conceptualizations of intersectional identity. The line weight between Family and Religion (not visible) is 0.21.

The comparison model (see Fig. 3) displays what our analysis of Figs. 1 and 2 tacitly builds towards: that our USA and Pakistani participants foreground different connections between different aspects of their baseline intersectional identities, and that these differences are stratified along country lines. For example, the prominent codes for our USA participants (Race, Gender, Peer Interactions) were less robustly connected to other codes among the Pakistani students' discussions of their baseline identities. The converse is also true of the more prominent codes for our Pakistani participants: while Family did have some connection to other codes for our USA participants (see Fig. 1), connections to Family among Pakistani participants are approximately twice as strong. The Education, Language, Location, Religion codes are more prominent within the model of our Pakistani participants but are more sparsely connected to other codes within the USA students' data. As one Pakistani participant described: *"What defines me, is my reason for studying. That's the main thing….the place I'm from, Kashmir, the level of education there is improving, but not from an Islamic point of view…I study here, with the support of this Islamic Trust, and…take what I learn here, from an Islamic point of view, when I go there,"* demonstrating these dynamic connections between academic, regional, and religious identities all at once.

Lastly, we note that the individual means of Pakistani student responses (visualized as dots in Fig. 3) are clustered closer together around the Pakistani mean, and the USA students are spread further from the USA mean, potentially indicating that our Pakistani participants' conceptualizations of baseline intersectional identity are more similar in terms of their patterns of connection-making than that of the USA participants.

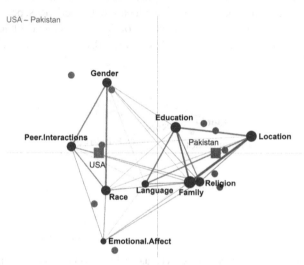

Fig. 3. ENA comparison model of relative differences between co-occurring aspects of identity for USA and Pakistan students. The line weight between Family and Religion (not visible) is 0.1.

We thus conclude that there is variability at the country level in how our participants conceptualize their baseline intersectional identity, as evidenced by the differences in specific code connections between the two groups. Both of these conclusions lead us to assert that theorists and researchers must account for contextual differences when seeking to utilize intersectionality as an epistemological lens, and that perhaps intersectionality in non-USA contexts must be treated as a grounded theory, to be generated and iterated upon in a highly emic manner.

4.2   Intersectional Identities and Educational Experiences

In analyzing the epistemic networks for the second part of the interview (see Figs. 4, 5 and 6), we first excluded Religion, Sexual Orientation, Socioeconomic Status, and Language codes based on our aforementioned criteria; none of these codes formed any connections with a weight of over 0.1. Next, we note that the prominence of the Education code in all models for this interview part is expected, given that the second part of our interview protocol is directly centered around students' educational experiences. What is notable to us, instead, are the connections made between the Education code and some codes over others, in addition to other particularly strong or weak code connections present.

As seen in Fig. 4, our USA participants more strongly associate their intersectional identities in the context of their educational experiences with Peer Interactions (0.55), followed by Emotional Affect (0.29). From this, we can posit that our USA participants were more likely to associate their education-related identity with peer interactions and emotional affect; this was reflected within the data. As one USA participant described in response to being asked about their identity in school, *"I was really immature in middle school, so I think I've definitely like, you know, opened up and just -- like I feel like everybody just has to be nice to everyone, I guess. Like, there's no reason to be mean,"* illustrating the connections made between her educational experiences, peer interactions, and emotional affect with regards to conceptions of nice versus mean. Other codes with less strong connections to Education included Gender (0.19), Race (0.12) Family (0.12) and Morality (0.1).

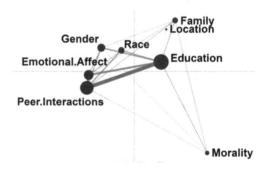

Fig. 4. ENA model of USA participants' conceptualizations of intersectional identity in educational contexts.

For our Pakistani participants (see Fig. 5), their strongest associations with the Education code were with Peer Interactions (0.48), Morality (0.27), Location (0.26), and Family (0.25). Gender was also associated with Education to a lesser degree (0.11).

When comparing the USA and Pakistani participants' themes from the second part of the interview (see Fig. 6), we are drawn to the similarities between both country groups in their strong association of Peer Interactions as part of their intersectional identities in the context of their educational experiences. This is the strongest and most consistent connection across both participant groups within either part of the interview. Perhaps this is because the highly social experience of being a student in school [30] is a commonality among all other country-based contextual differences with regard to educational experiences. Participants from both countries expressed their sentiments around the prominence of peer interactions in educational contexts. Speaking to a positive impact of peer interactions in educational contexts on their identity, one Pakistani participant describes that *"before coming to [school name] I would identify myself as*

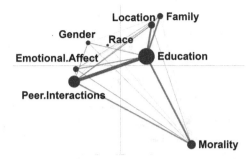

Fig. 5. ENA model of Pakistan participants' conceptualizations of intersectional identity in educational contexts.

someone who likes to stay on their own, gets angry easily, lacking patience and ability to understand others. But after coming to [school name] and interacting with many different people and also getting scolded a little, I changed and now I am a calmer, more accepting person." In comparison, one USA participant paints a more complicated picture of the intersections of peer interactions with their baseline identity: "*I think my identity shapes how my peers view me, because they see me as like, as somewhat of an outcast, they don't want to include you in something…But like, for the most part, kids, or the kids [at this school] are pretty cool. Like, they include you in stuff. They laugh and joke, and they'll talk to you. But sometimes there are people that stand out, and it just happens that they don't fit in with the group.*"

Additionally, another set of notable differences are that USA participants associate Emotional Affect (0.21) and Race (0.15) with Peer Interactions more than their Pakistani peers, whereas Pakistani participants associate Morality (0.14) and Location (0.12) with Peer Interactions more than the USA participants. Though the specific impacts of peer interactions on identity may differ by student, it is clear that peer interactions do intersect with identity heavily in the context of educational experiences.

Lastly, we note that the Education-Location connection (0.24) for Pakistani participants possesses the strongest difference of any code connection in this model. Interpretively, this is reflected in the data, as participants frequently discussed their region and location when asked about various aspects of their identity in relation to their educational experiences. As one Pakistani participant described: "*I like being around people who belong from different areas of Pakistan. I did not have to face any challenges in that aspect. Being the head boy of school has given me the leverage to manage people from different backgrounds, hence this has given me an opportunity to expand on my horizons.*" Again, while we cannot speculate as to the underlying reasons for these differences, these differences can be regarded as potential evidence that students in these different countries may place emphasis on different aspects of identity when engaging with their peers.

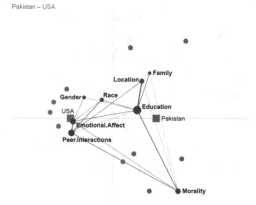

Fig. 6. Relative differences between co-occurring aspects of identity for USA and Pakistan students in the context of their educational experiences.

5 Conclusion

Our results have broader implications for the theory of intersectionality as an epistemological lens, as well as for global research design and for the QE-ENA approach.

As previously discussed, the dominant theoretical models of intersectionality are rooted within USA contexts, and applications of these models within education research thus largely focus on intersections of racial, gender, socioeconomic status, and sexual orientation identities [13]. Our Pakistani participants foreground aspects of identity that are not often considered by USA-based models of intersectionality, namely, academic identity, region-based identity, and family-based identity. For our USA participants, while they foreground connections between their racial and gender identities, socioeconomic and sexual orientation identities were more sparsely connected. Our USA participants also give greater prominence than expected to family identities and peer interaction-related identities, suggesting that there is more nuance to intersectional identities within the USA context that is yet to be uncovered. We thus conclude that further research is needed to understand these finer nuances, and to then utilize those nuances to create multiple emic, grounded theories of intersectionality that stem from participant experiences in an emic manner. At a theoretical level, we envision that these multiple theories of intersectionality, all operating from the same broad theoretical lens that identity is fundamentally intersectional, while simultaneously prioritizing contextually-based variability of which particular identities are intersected most and least, could then be used to better guide research on intersectional identities within non-USA contexts and even help to refine intersectional identity theories within the USA. Additionally, our findings also evince the need for identifying Pakistani-generated theories that can contribute to understanding intersectional identity in their specific context; such theories would be highly useful in achieving greater contextual sensitivity within future iterations of this work.

Our findings for how students conceptualize their intersectional identity within educational contexts are largely congruent with our aforementioned implication for intersectional identity theory; the differences between country groups with regard to the emphasized identity aspects within educational contexts support our implication that intersectionality must be adapted from and for specific participant groups when used as an epistemological frame for research with their contexts. However, one key theme from our findings on participants' identities within their educational contexts is the prevalence of the Peer Interactions code across both countries' participants. Participants from both countries conceptualize an aspect of their identities in relation to their interactions with their peers; furthermore, this peer interaction identity has the strongest connection to other codes within the context of participants' educational experiences. While peer-peer interactions are typically discussed in the literature as a social phenomenon and cognized as distinct from identity [28–30], our participants from both country contexts clearly foreground their identities in connection their peer interactions within educational contexts, perhaps indicating that there may be an aspect of individual identity that is derived mainly in relation to one's peer interactions.

Lastly, we note that the usage of QE-ENA as a research design and analytic approach is well-suited for investigating conceptualizations of intersectional identity; however, our application of QE-ENA to intersectional identity is relatively novel within the field of QE-ENA. While QE-ENA has been used to analyze identity, those studies had fundamentally different scopes of investigation as well as different conceptualizations of identity itself [22, 23]. The highly interconnected nature of intersectional identity itself makes it a natural phenomenon to be explored via QE-ENA, as the QE-ENA approach itself is ideal for visually surfacing and analyzing such interconnectedness at a fine grain and without sacrificing fidelity to participants' experiences and sociocultural contexts [4]. One specific future direction would be to use QE-ENA to analyze intersecting aspects of identity with regard to valence (i.e., positivity or negativity) to understand how students perceive their various aspects of identity, in addition to understanding which aspects students connect together more or less often. Additionally, we would like to engage methods of participatory QE-ENA in relation to this work to enhance the emic aspects of our methods and findings [31]; in future work, we can engage in participants in co-creation and modification of codes as well as soliciting their feedback on resultant ENA models. Meaningfully integrating participants' voices into our analysis through participatory QE-ENA methods would enhance the fidelity of our identity-related work. Thus, we hope to engage in further intersectionality-oriented research using QE-ENA, and hope that the QE-ENA field at large may find value in and expand upon our approach.

5.1 Limitations

We note four specific limitations with our study. Firstly, the epistemic network analysis within this paper is only applied to a small subset of our total participant group, limiting generalizability for implications of this work. Accordingly, we have been careful to analyze our results with respect to the subset of participants and without drawing broader inferences, and we thus state our implications in terms of potentialities as opposed to analytic certainties. Our next limitation concerns the translation of Pakistani participants' interview transcripts from Urdu to English. Though our team made every effort possible to ensure word-for-word accuracy within the translated transcripts, there is always room for error in fidelity that emerges when analyzing a translated interview transcript and is thus worth noting [24]. Next, we observed that there was what we consider to be a large amount of variability between interviewer styles. Though all interviewers were given the same semi-structured interview protocol and guidance on how to conduct interviews, we noticed that our USA interviewers tended to depart more readily from the protocol structure through the use of probing questions, whereas our Pakistani interviewers tended to follow the interview protocol more rigidly and with less probing questions. While interviewer variability is inevitable [24], such variability is still notable for its potential effects on participant responses and analysis thereof. Finally, we note the limitation of utilizing a single coder for the data without conducting test-retest reliability, as any potential biases on the part of the coder will have a greater impact upon the analysis with only one coder. The use of a single coder occurred due to practical constraints within our research team; for future work we will aim to utilize multiple coders with robust inter-rater reliability measures [32]. We will also aim to utilize coders that together possess emic perspectives of all contexts investigated within future work.

References

1. Pak, K., Ravitch, S.M.: Critical Leadership Praxis for Educational and Social Change. Teachers College Press, New York (2021)
2. Crenshaw, K.: Demarginalizing the intersection of race and sex: a black feminist critique of antidiscrimination doctrine, pp. 139–168. University of Chicago Legal Forum (1989)
3. Shakeir, R.Y.: An um kulthumist lens: an examination of Arab American Muslim women and the lived experience of higher education (2019)
4. Shaffer, D.W.: Quantitative Ethnography, 1st edn. Cathcart Press, Madison (2017)
5. Gee, J.P.: Identity as an analytic lens for research in education. Rev. Res. Educ. 25(1), 99–125 (2000)
6. Combahee River Collective: Combahee River Collective Statement (1977)
7. Moraga, C., Anzaldúa, G., Bambara, T.C.: This Bridge Called my Back: Writings by Radical Women of Color, 1st edn. Persephone Press, Watertown (1981)
8. Yosso, T.J.: Whose culture has capital? A critical race theory discussion of community cultural wealth. Race Ethn. Educ. 8(1), 69–91 (2005)
9. Aud, S.L., Fox, M.A.: Status and Trends in the Education of Racial and Ethnic Groups. U.S. Department of Education, Washington, D.C. (2010)
10. Khalifa, M.A.: Culturally Responsive School Leadership. Harvard Education Press, Cambridge (2018)
11. Sue, D.W.: Microaggressions in Everyday Life: Race, Gender, and Sexual Orientation. Wiley, Hoboken (2010)
12. McLaren, P.: Life in Schools: An introduction to Critical Pedagogy in the Foundations of Education. Routledge, New York (2015)
13. Davis, D.J.: Intersectionality in Educational Research. Stylus, Sterling (2015)
14. McFarland, J., et al.: The Condition of Education 2019. U.S. Department of Education. Washington, D.C. (2019)
15. Acevedo, N., Bejarano, C., Collazo, N.I.: A call for intersectionality in US schooling: Testimonios of Chicana students in high school. Harv. Educ. Rev. 90(2), 269–281 (2020)
16. Govinda, R.: Interrogating intersectionality: Dalit women, western classrooms, and the politics of feminist knowledge production. J. Int. Women's Stud. 23(2), 72–86 (2022)
17. Krause, K.H., Mpofu, J., Brown, M., Rico, A., Andrews, C., Underwood, J.M.: At the intersections: examining trends in experiences of violence, mental health status, and suicidal risk behaviors among US high school students using intersectionality, national youth risk behavior survey, 2015–2019. J. Adolesc. Health. 71(3), 293–300 (2022)

18. Taylor, K.: How We Get Free: Black Feminism and the Combahee River Collective. Haymarket Books, Chicago (2017)
19. Finance Division, Government of Pakistan: Pakistan Economic Survey 2018–2019. (2019)
20. UNHCR: UNHCR launches new appeal for Afghan refugees and hosts, urging partners to stay the course (2023)
21. Institute of Social and Policy Sciences: Punjab Education Sector Analysis 2018 (2018)
22. Barany, A., Foster, A.: Examining identity exploration in a video game participatory culture. In: Eagan, B., Misfeldt, M., Siebert-Evenstone, A. (eds.) ICQE 2019. CCIS, vol. 1112, pp. 3–13. Springer, Cham (2019). https://doi.org/10.1007/978-3-030-33232-7_1
23. Fan, Y., Barany, A., Foster, A.: Possible future selves in STEM: an epistemic network analysis of identity exploration in minoritized students and alumni. Int. J. STEM Educ. **10**(1), 22-15 (2023)
24. Ravitch, S.M., Carl, N.M.: Qualitative Research: Bridging the Conceptual, Theoretical, and Methodological, 2nd edn. SAGE Publications, Thousand Oaks (2021)
25. Shaffer, D.W., Ruis, A.R.: How we code. In: Ruis, A.R., Lee, S.B. (eds.) ICQE 2021. CCIS, vol. 1312, pp. 62–77. Springer, Cham (2021). https://doi.org/10.1007/978-3-030-67788-6_5
26. Shaffer, D.W., Collier, W., Ruis, A.R.: A tutorial on epistemic network analysis: analyzing the structure of connections in cognitive, social, and interaction data. J. Learn. Anal. **3**(3), 9–45 (2016)
27. Wang, Y., Swiecki, Z., Ruis, A.R., Shaffer, D.W.: Simplification of epistemic networks using parsimonious removal with interpretive alignment. In: Ruis, A.R., Lee, S.B. (eds.) ICQE 2021. CCIS, vol. 1312, pp. 137–151. Springer, Cham (2021). https://doi.org/10.1007/978-3-030-67788-6_10
28. Erozkan, A.: The effect of communication skills and interpersonal problem solving skills on social self-efficacy. Educ. Sci.: Theory Pract. **13**(2), 739–745 (2013)
29. Wentzel, K.R.: Social relationships and motivation in middle school: the role of parents, teachers, and peers. J. Educ. Psychol. **90**(2), 202–209 (1998)
30. Crosnoe, R.: Fitting In, Standing Out: Navigating the Social Challenges of High School to Get an Education. Cambridge University Press, New York (2011)
31. Vega, H., Irgens, G.A.: Constructing interpolations with participants through epistemic network analysis: towards participatory approaches in quantitative ethnography. In: Wasson, B., Zörgő, S. (eds.) ICQE 2021. CCIS, vol. 1522, pp. 3–16. Springer, Cham (2021). https://doi.org/10.1007/978-3-030-93859-8_1
32. Eagan, B., Brohinsky, J., Wang, J., Shaffer, D.W.: Testing the reliability of inter-rater reliability. In: Proceedings of the 10th International Conference on Learning Analytics & Knowledge, pp. 454–461. ACM, New York (2020)

Using Epistemic Network Analysis to Understand the Intersectional Experiences of Teachers of Color in White-Dominated Education Institutions

Adina Goldstein[✉] and Janine Remillard

University of Pennsylvania, Philadelphia, PA 19104, USA
goadina@upenn.edu

Abstract. This paper explores the experiences of preservice teachers of color completing teacher preparation historically white university. Drawing on critical race theory (CRT), this paper foregrounds intersectionality of participants' various and intersecting identities, using epistemic network analysis (ENA) to represent connections between participants' identities and senses of belonging within the context of their programs. ENA presents a unique opportunity to visually represent the connections between participants' experiences and multiple salient identities simultaneously, minimizing the risk of essentialism and tokenization. Results of this intersectional analysis of preservice teachers of colors' (PSTOC) experiences and implications for teacher education suggest that PSTOC experiences of belonging in teacher preparation can be understood through program interactions and that PSTOC social identities influence the ways they approach and make sense of their experiences. Further implications for the utility of ENA as a tool for understanding identity and intersectional experiences are offered.

Keywords: Epistemic Network Analysis · Teachers of Color · Teacher Education

1 Introduction

Schools and districts nationwide, as well as academics and policymakers, have voiced calls for a teaching force that reflects the growing diversity of American public school students – more than half of whom identify as a racial or ethnic minority [3]. However, teachers of colors' reflections on preparation programs indicate that preparation programs are often marginalizing and isolating spaces [1, 8, 12]. Consequently, teacher preparation programs have begun to reflect on racial dynamics present within their programs for PSTOC [1].

This paper explores PSTOC experiences in teacher preparation programs at historically white universities (HWI) using a dataset of 13 interviews conducted with graduates from three teacher preparation programs in HWI. This paper uses ENA to examine the questions:

G. Arastoopour Irgens and S. Knight (Eds.): ICQE 2023, CCIS 1895, pp. 230–243, 2023.
https://doi.org/10.1007/978-3-031-47014-1_16

1. How do PSTOC describe their experiences in teacher education programs in HWI?
2. How do PSTOC various social identities impact and influence their experiences in their teacher education programs in HWI?

2 Review of Literature

Ample literature about teacher of colors' (TOC) experiences in teacher preparation has revealed that, overall, they report experiences of marginalization and isolation [1]. Further investigation reveals that many university-based teacher preparation programs (and particularly those located within HWI) have been designed within normative white theoretical and pedagogical confines, and consequently fail to address the specific needs of the myriad and intersecting identities of PSTOC [2].

Developed by legal scholars in the 1970s, critical race theory has been extrapolated for its utility as a tool for understanding racial inequality across disciplines. One aspect of critical race theory is the centrality of race and racism as well as the ways that racism intersects with other social identities such as gender, class and more – often referred to as intersectionality [15]. Intersectional understandings of the lived experiences of minoritized communities positions people as complex beings who hold multiple social identities and are seen through those identities. Although some social identities may become more or less salient in particular circumstances, they can never be separated from an understanding of the person who holds them. This understanding guided an intentionally holistic and multifaceted analysis of interviews with participants that, while positioning race and racism as central to lived experience, did not limit itself to race as a singular social identity.

Theorized as part of the larger academic discourse in education on critical racial approaches to teaching and learning, culturally relevant pedagogy (CRP) advocates for culturally competent education which supports academic success while affirming and supporting students' cultural identities [10]. Affirmation and support of cultural identity tends to be subjective given that experiences of intersectionality may render individuals dominant in one social identity and marginalized in another simultaneously. The broadest possible manifestation of culturally competent education, then, is education that values and prioritizes the ways of knowing and experiences of communities of color. Research on culturally competency in teacher preparation reveals that a sense of belonging as reified in community construction is essential to honoring the strongly community-based forms of knowledge production in and values of communities of color [5, 9].

It is from this research that the decision was made to focus on the constructs of belonging and social identities and their roles within participants' teacher education experiences.

3 Methods

3.1 Study Design, Setting, and Participants

To begin to understand participants experiences in teacher preparation, we interviewed 13 recent (1–5 years) graduates of color from three graduate-level teacher education programs at HWIs in a large, poverty impacted city. In 2021, all graduates were offered a routine exit-survey soliciting program feedback. Those who self-identified as TOC were invited to participate in an interview about their experiences.

3.2 Data Collection and Organization Techniques

Interviews lasted between 30 and 60 min, followed a semi-structured interview protocol consisting of 17 questions and were video recorded and transcribed for analysis. Interviews took place via zoom and were conducted by graduate students who were not affiliated with any of the preparation programs. Variation in the number of questions per interview relates to the presence or absence of probing and conditional questions based on participant responses. During the transcription process, all names were deidentified. Anonymizing interviewees to protect the identity of participants was particularly important given researchers' proximity to the teacher education programs. For example, in some cases, members of the research team were professors, coaches or mentors in the program. The dataset consists of 13 interviews. Given the, at times, monologic nature of semi-structured interviews, only statements from the participant were included in the data set. Lines of data in the interview were segmented by the completion of a full thought as reviewed interpretively by members of the research team [16]. An advantage of the size of this dataset is that it was possible to segment data into lines by hand.

As part of a larger study in which epistemic network analysis was not originally considered, initial coding consisted of both traditional, qualitative coding, using deductive codes that looked broadly at identity and experiences in the program and flexible coding [3, 11]. Identity was coded according to conceptions of social identity, professional identity and personal identity. Experiences were coded based on whether they represented a structural, institutional, relational, or curricular experience. No inductive coding had yet been completed.

In accordance with the underlying ethnographic ideologies in quantitative ethnography, we left space to identify inductive codes after finalizing deductive coding [7]. It was here that the multitudes of social identities mentioned surfaced for us as noteworthy across several participants. We created codes based on the social identities mentioned by participants in interviews, and created additional codes based on emergent themes. At this stage, we had three parent codes, each of which had several child codes, and totaled 21 codes. After several rounds of iteration, we collapsed, changed and eliminated codes to reach a codebook that captured the most salient themes that emerged, and most directly related to the study's research questions. We were left with a set of codes that centered around social identities, interactions, and sense of belonging. Ultimately, we used sense of belonging and lack of belonging as a unit variable, so that both experiences could be easily isolated from one another, and analyzed in association with particular social identity and interaction codes. As such, sections of interviews were designated as pertaining to a sense of belonging, a lack of a sense of belonging, or, other, where the participant was not describing program experiences but instead giving background or contextual information. Like many quantitative ethnography studies, we used binary coding to indicate whether or not a code appeared in a given line. Each parent code had several child codes which served to categorize the nature of the relevant social identities, interactions, or experiences more specifically in any given statement. A codebook is included below (Table 1).

Table 1. Codebook

Parent Code: Social Identity Social identity codes were assigned when a participant made reference to a particular social identity that arose when describing themselves or while speaking about their experiences	
Age	Statements participants made in which they mentioned their age
Race	Statements participants made in which they mentioned their racial identity
Religion	Statements participants made in which they mentioned their religious identity
Gender	Statements participants made in which they mentioned their gender identity
Geography	Statements participants made in which they mentioned a hometown or other geographic location
SES	Statements participants made in which they mentioned their socioeconomic status
Sexual Identity	Statements participants made in which they mentioned their sexual identity

Parent Code: Interactions Interaction codes were assigned when a participant described an experience that included an interaction with another person who belongs to one of the categories described below	
Interactions with University Faculty/Staff	Statements participants made describing experiences in which they interacted with university faculty or other staff affiliated with the university or the program
Interactions with Fieldwork Adults	Statements participants made describing experiences in which they interacted with a colleague at a school-based fieldwork site (specifically, not a student at the site or a student's parent)
Interactions with People Outside the Program	Statements participants made describing experiences in which they interacted with anyone who was not affiliated with the program at all
Interactions with Peers	Statements participants made describing experiences in which they interacted with another person enrolled in the program
Interactions in Identity Subspaces	Statements participants made describing experiences in which they interacted with a peer specifically in a space defined by identity affinity, whether formally or informally formed

(*continued*)

(*continued*)

Parent Code: Interactions
Interaction codes were assigned when a participant described an experience that included an interaction with another person who belongs to one of the categories described below

Code: Experiences
An experience code denotes when a participant described a specific experience they had during the program, rather than when a participant gave context about themselves or talked broadly about the program

Coding first included presence or absence of the parent code. When a parent code was present, the statement was then coded for presence or absence of related child codes. For example, the following line was coded with a 1 in the parent code for social identities and the associated child codes of geography and socioeconomic status but received 0's for all other codes since no other social identities, specific interactions or program experiences were mentioned (Table 2).

"So I'm from a small. small town in western Pennsylvania. It's, it's a small town that's, you know not very not thriving very much and you know a lot of people in that town don't seek higher education."

Table 2. Coding Example

Social Identities	Age	Race	Religion	Gender
1	0	0	0	0
Interactions with…	Faculty & staff	Peers	Field-based colleagues	People outside the program
0	0	0	0	0

A more illustrative line of coding can be seen below, where the participant mentioned their racial identity as salient while describing a specific experience interacting with peers and faculty members (Table 3).

"Alpha: sure. I mean in no way, were they the best. I didn't feel like there were a lot of people of color that, you know, shared my same experiences. I really wanted a strong black community, and I was unable to find that in my Program. Some of my classmates were pretty intense and, excuse me, there was a number of diversity related experiences that happened, students making comments and classes that weren't necessarily checked by the professors. professors, not knowing. How to navigate those conversations when they came up."

Table 3. Coding Example

Social Identities	Age	Race	Religion	Gender
1	0	1	0	0
Interactions with...	Faculty & staff	Peers	Field-based colleagues	People outside the program
1	1	1	0	0

3.3 Data Analysis Techniques

Data analysis utilized ENA to examine the pattern of connections between the constructs in the codebook. For this study, there were three units of analysis. The first was the variable that categorized a statement as relating to belonging or lack of belonging (or neither), the secondary unit was the program in which participants were enrolled, and the third was the individual interview. Because the interview protocol asked questions about identity at the beginning of the interview and participants referenced those identities throughout, the decision to use an infinite stanza window allowed connections to identity to be captured in the analysis. To understand the impact of this decision on the proportion of connections in the middle of the interview, infinite stanza windows of four and eight lines were also tested. Neither led to significant changes. The individual interviews constituted the conversations.

4   Results

To interpret results and paint the most contextualized picture of participants' experiences, the connections established by epistemic network models and the words and descriptions offered by participants during their interviews are most effectively considered together. Pairing qualitative analysis of interviews with quantitative ethnographic analyses offers a way to triangulate interpretation of data in a thickly described and deeply contextual way. Qualitative analysis of interviews allows researchers to identify important focal points for further analysis. Epistemic network models allow for a more fine-grained investigation of the isolated focal points identified by qualitative analysis.

4.1   What are Teachers of Colors' Experiences of Belonging in Their Teacher Education Program?

Qualitative analysis surfaced themes of belonging and isolation as salient aspects of PSTOC experiences in programs. Numerous participants mentioned the impact of the pervasiveness of the normative vision of teachers as white, middle-class, mono-lingual women. Participants shared reflections on the ways this normative vision of teacher identity manifested within programs – from coursework likened to "diversity for white people," that amplified the experiences of "well-meaning white women," and ensured that "their voices were always present," to specific instances of individual white, women teachers perpetuating harmful narratives about families and students, "speaking about their experience, as if they're fact, or as if they're law" (Alpha; Kilo; Foxtrot). Experiences like these led some participants to question whether they belonged in their programs at all, or whether their admission or choice to enroll was a mistake. Engaging with the experiences that participants described during their interviews made clear the salience of belonging but left us with questions about where belonging and lack of belonging were felt most acutely.

ENA offers more fine-grained insights into participants' experiences with belonging as it allows us to put aspects of participants' experiences more directly in conversation with their experiences of belonging. One such aspect of participants' experiences we used ENA to understand more deeply in relation to belonging was the interactions that participants had within the program (Fig. 1).

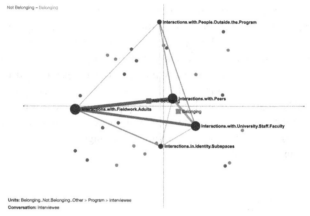

Fig. 1. A comparison plot of teachers of colors' experiences of belonging and not belonging as connected to program interactions. Because of the relatively strong connection between interactions with peers and interactions with faculty and staff in the belonging (0.79) and not belonging (0.74) groups, the line appears comparatively thin in the difference model above.

The model in the figure above shows that discussions around a lack of belonging had more overall connections to participants discussions of interactions with colleagues at fieldwork placements, while interactions with peers and interactions with university faculty and staff tended to drive discussions of both belonging and lack of belonging. The model highlights the potential impact that interactions – good and bad – had on participants' experiences, and in the case of interactions with peers and university faculty and staff, suggests that interactions can be positive or negative and were not categorically helpful or harmful to participants' experiences of belonging.

Indeed, this is corroborated by qualitative analysis of interviews, in which participants across all programs noted "a certain dismissiveness," "a certain coldness" or lack of sincerity palpable in interactions with faculty and staff (Kilo; Delta; Alpha). Speaking about interactions with faculty and staff, several participants noted feeling under supported. One participant shared how feeling under supported by faculty and staff, particularly in response to clear and direct requests for support, led that participant to question their belonging in the program, saying:

"All of my experiences in the program are the feedback that I'm receiving from the program so... not feeling heard by professors when I'm voicing concerns or, like, having difficulties with my school... all of this provides feedback to me that is telling me, you know, that maybe I made the wrong choice" (Alpha).

Participants also reflected on positive interpersonal experiences with faculty and staff that supported their senses of belonging within their programs. They shared experiences where their voices and critiques were heard by professors, and where they felt that professors saw them and were invested in their growth.

"[Two professor's names] are fantastic... I think that, um, where they are open to conversations about how things land or didn't land and how, like, they're willing to recreate pretty much on the spot" (Golf).

"I remember a lot of the people of color who were involved in the program were very sympathetic to me – they showed an interest in me and asked me about who I was and what I was about, so I always felt really great when I had professors that were really open and invested" (Delta).

"... every Black professor that I came in touch with, in contact, we had a great relationship" (Charlie)

Similarly, ENA inspired an investigation of participants' interactions with peers in their programs. Like interactions with faculty and staff, the epistemic network model pictured above suggests that peer interactions were not categorically positive or negative and contributed to both a sense of belonging and a lack of belonging for participants. This was also corroborated by a qualitative analysis of the interviews which revealed interactions between peers that fostered a sense of belonging and interactions between peers which isolated and marginalized participants.

Several participants mentioned negative interactions with white peers which emphasized, for them, the ways in which teachers of color felt marginalized and were made to feel marginalized within their programs. One participant, in particular, shared an experience where white peers made the teachers of color in the program feel actively excluded and erased, sharing that:

"Many of the white cohort members, um, pretty much did their own thing and kind of didn't really, like, talk to any of us or try to engage with any of us. It got to the point where they actually were invited to one of, one of the cohort member's, like, actual homes and like, their parents threw an all out dinner, and they posted it on social media ... not one person of color was, like, invited to that dinner gathering" (Echo).

Conversely, several participants also mentioned the healing and affirming powers of affinity spaces that consisted of peers of color.

"That kind of solidified our, like, affinity space of being, just, supportive of ourselves as people of color... Just by sheer necessity, we kind of just, stuck together." (Echo).

"I had a Black girls group chat and we were four young Black women… who are all English teachers… and yeah, I never felt alone in the program for sure" (Golf).

"I had a solid group of friends, who I still talk to now. Um, the reason why we're so solid is because we were the only people of color in the group…" (India).

Qualitative analysis of the data highlighted the salience of themes about belonging, while quantitative analysis of the data enabled a more focused examination of the themes of belonging and not belonging. Epistemic network analysis enabled a more detailed analysis of how sense of belonging and lack of sense of belonging were experienced by participants. Epistemic network analysis distilled interactions between participants and faculty and staff and between participants and peers as notable, which then guided further qualitative analysis of those interactions. Overall, epistemic network analysis of this data paints a picture of participants' positive and negative experiences in their teacher preparation programs and highlights how interactions that participants reflected on as positive and negative further influenced their own senses of belonging in their programs.

4.2 How do Teachers of Colors' Various Social Identities Impact and Influence Their Experiences in Their Teacher Education Program?

Using inductive codes that reflected the social identities that participants mentioned in interviews, epistemic network models that visualized connections between a sense of (and lack of a sense of) belonging and social identities was generated.

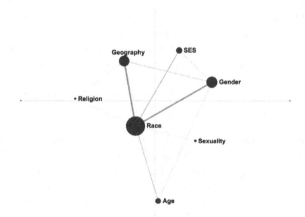

Fig. 2. Teachers of colors' experiences of belonging as connected to social identities.

Participant discussions coded for belonging tended to feature stronger patterns of associations between race, geography, and gender (see Fig. 2). A comparison plot (see Fig. 3) between belonging and not belonging discussions reveals that discussions around not belonging tended to have stronger code connections overall, specifically in terms of

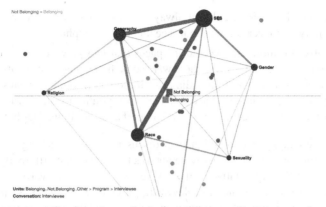

Fig. 3. A comparison plot of teachers of colors' experiences of belonging and not belonging as connected to their mentioned social identities.

participants' discussions of race and geographic affiliation (0.52), and race and socioeconomic status (0.33). Contextualizing these findings in relation to our understanding of the qualitative interview data suggests that race, socioeconomic status, and geographic affiliation presented points of tension which may have acted as barriers to feelings of belonging for participants.

The insights extrapolated from the epistemic network model guided a qualitative interpretation of the interviews with a specific focus on mentions of race, geographic affiliation and socioeconomic status. Qualitative analysis of the interviews elucidates the ways in which race and SES influenced a sense of belonging for participants. Participants connected race to feelings of not belonging.

"I was… canceled for asking a question in class to a student who was saying harmful things about Black parents, which means that they were also saying harmful things about Black communities… Before the incident in class, I felt that I could take on the world. Afterwards, after that incident, I realized that I should think carefully before I speak… I should think really, really hard about how my words will sound landing on white ears, and then, and then I usually decided not to say anything. I did not feel safe" (Bravo).

"I had a cohort of very… I guess… very expressive white people … and that felt hard because, you know, I was like, almost in a way defensive about, like, being in this… being… being in this program and being Black in this program. And um, like, being around white people in this program knowing that it was a program meant, you know, focused on urban teaching" (India).

"The white people in our program had their voices heard… because the program is tailored to their needs of, like, not understanding racism, not understanding classism, not understanding all of those things… I feel like they were heard more often because the program was structured for people like them, not for people like me" (Charlie).

Participants also connected SES to feelings of not belonging.

"… the voices of people of color, it always felt like those voices were missing. Um, especially in conversations about race and class" (Alpha).

"I think I also felt more empowered in spaces that had poor people in them, or people who had struggled. And so there were some first generation events that had happened that I went to and I immediately felt more comfortable because there's this hyper awareness that you have to have when you're a student who doesn't naturally fit in to this space, and it's good to let that armor down" (Juliet).

Although geography was mentioned in discussions of not belonging, interviews revealed that mentions of geography were approached somewhat differently than mentions of race or SES. A qualitative analysis revealed two primary ways in which geographic affiliation was mentioned as relevant to program experiences for participants. The first is as part of critiques of the program which surfaced that some participants found the narratives perpetuated about the local community to be problematic. One participant shared:

"I was also missing the voices of the Philadelphia natives because we spent a lot of time talking about Philly in ways that I wish were challenged or supported by the people who have the most to lose, you know, the residents of Philadelphia. And not the ones who are here for school or work, but you know, the ones who are here because they consider it to be home" (Alpha).

The other notable context in which geographic affiliation was mentioned as relevant to participants' program experiences was around how a participant's own geographic history (where they are from or where they have lived) impacted the way they engaged in the program. For example, one participant noted how their time living in the community inspired their professional ambitions, and also how their upbringing in a different geographic community impacted and influence the ways they carry themself professionally:

"I'm a long time Philadelphian. Um, I wasn't born here, but it definitely feels like home. I've been living and working in the city for about ten years and I feel that this has informed a lot about my professional trajectory. I like to be involved in things that benefit the city, and obviously, I'm a Black woman. I'm originally from the South. Southern hospitality – and I'm always constantly aware of that and what it means for my experiences in elite communities" (Kilo).

ENA enabled a more focused analysis of interview data by visually distinguishing potential connections of interest. Using ENA to distill the need for a more focused analysis of the particular social identities of race, socioeconomic status and geographic affiliation as related to discussions of belonging and not belonging enabled interpretation and meaning making around the ways that social identities impact and influenced participants' experiences in teacher preparation. Analysis and subsequent interpretation of interview data creates a compelling picture of PSTOC who are motivated by social identities such as race, geographic affiliation and socioeconomic status, and whose own experiences in teacher preparation are processed and interpreted through lenses of those social identities.

5   Discussion

This study's findings have potentially important implications for both these teacher preparation programs and for preparation of TOC more broadly. Most broadly, findings from this study reinforce the importance of teacher education research that centers teachers of color and their experiences in teacher preparation [6].

Findings around belonging, not belonging and program interactions have potential implications for university hiring and programmatic decisions around community building. Within the focal university, these findings imply that hiring faculty of color may have a positive impact on the experiences that preservice teachers of color have within the university's teacher preparation programs. Thus, if the university hopes to contribute to diversifying the teaching profession, ensuring that there are faculty and staff of color who relate to preservice teachers of color and see them fully, in ways that participants have described in this study, is important. Further, community building in affinity spaces may be important in establishing a sense of belonging for preservice teachers of color. Conversely, the potential that normative whiteness holds in disempowering preservice teachers of color in teacher preparation should also be considered.

Findings around the influence and impact of social identities on participants experiences in teacher preparation highlight the many salient social identities that are influence and impact the ways that participants made sense of their experiences. This has implications for the ways that this university's teacher education programs – and teacher education programs, broadly – maintain fidelity to the critical foundations of culturally relevant pedagogy. In particular, findings can be interpreted as making a case for the centrality of race and racism for teachers of color, as well as the ways that racism interacts with other social identities – both of which are central tenets of CRT. Foregrounding pedagogical approaches in the centrality of race and racism and in intersectional approaches necessitates culturally competent teacher preparation that honors the knowledge that is generated from teachers of colors' sensemaking processes that result from experiencing teacher preparation from the perspective of racialized and intersectional lenses.

5.1   ENA for Analysis of Identity and Intersectionality

Interpretation and analysis of interview data also gives way to rich discussions of ENA's utility in analysis of identity and intersectionality.

ENA was originally developed as a way of visualizing and modeling complex sociocultural systems. In particular, ENA was developed to model the skills, knowledges, identities, values and epistemologies within a particular cultural system or community of practice. Shaffer [13] argues that the different ways of knowing, of deciding what is worth knowing, and of adding to a collective body of knowledge and understanding for a community of practice constitutes a community of practice's epistemic frame. Further, Shaffer [14] views epistemic frames as the organizing principles for communities of practice and views learning as a process in which learners develop the ability to incorporate epistemic frames into their identities. It follows, then, that epistemic networks can be useful in modeling individuals' identities in relation to the epistemic frames of their communities of practice. In the case of this study, ENA offers a way to model connections between preservice teachers of colors' social identities and their senses of belonging or not belonging to a particular community of practice with a particular guiding epistemic frame. Epistemic network models, in this study, aid interpretation of insider and outsider identities and positionalities within the community of practice of professional teachers.

Further, ENA may offer a nuanced way to approach intersectional identities and their relative positionalities within communities of practice and their respective epistemic frames. Intersectionality positions people as complex beings who hold multiple social identities simultaneously. Thus, people bring multiple identities to the lenses through which they make sense within and experience the world. In short, while particular social identities may become more or less salient circumstantially, they can never be separated out from an understanding of the person who holds them, or that person's understanding of the world. ENA has potential value in showing how people are able to connect various intersecting pieces of their identities together. Indeed, in this study, it is of note interpretively that salient social identities were often mentioned together. For example, participants often mentioned their race in tandem with their gender or socioeconomic class, in addition to other combinations of social identities that came together to form a lens through which participants described experiences and understandings.

6 Conclusion

Findings suggest that TOC experiences of belonging in teacher preparation can be understood through the interactions they have as part of the program. In particular, findings suggest that, for the participants of this study, interactions between teachers of color and university faculty and staff, and interactions between teachers of color and their peers (of color and white peers) can meaningfully influence teachers of colors' experiences of belonging, both positively and negatively. Further findings suggest that TOC intersectional social identities influence the ways they approach teacher education experiences and impact the ways that they make sense of experiences.

Finally, findings suggest that ENA is a valuable tool for analyzing identity negotiation within the epistemic frames of communities of practice. More specifically, ENA may be useful in making sense of negotiation of multiple social identities within a community of practice's epistemic frame.

References

1. Brown, K.D.: Teaching in color: a critical race theory in education analysis of the literature on preservice teachers of color and teacher education in the US. Race Ethn. Educ. **17**(3), 326–345 (2014)
2. Chávez-Moreno, L.C., Villegas, A.M., Cochran-Smith, M.: The experiences and preparation of teacher candidates of color: a literature review. In: Handbook of Research on Teachers of Color and Indigenous Teachers, vol. 165 (2022)
3. Deterding, N.M., Waters, M.C.: Flexible coding of in-depth interviews: a twenty-first-century approach. Sociol. Methods Res. **50**(2), 708–739 (2021)
4. Frey, W.H.: The Nation is Diversifying Even Faster than Predicted, According to New Census Data. Brookings Institute (2020)
5. Gasman, M., Samayoa, A.C., Ginsberg, A.: Minority serving institutions: incubators for teachers of color. Teach. Educ. Q. **52**(2), 84–98 (2017)

6. Gist, C.D., Bristol, T.J. (eds.): Handbook of research on Teachers of Color and Indigenous Teachers. American Educational Research Association (2022)
7. Arastoopour Irgens, G., Eagen, B: The foundations and fundamentals of quantitative ethnography. In: Damşa, C., Barany, A. (eds.) ICQE 2022. CCIS, vol. 1785, pp. 3–16. Springer, Cham (2023). https://doi.org/10.1007/978-3-031-31726-2_1
8. Kohli, R.: Critical race reflections: valuing the experiences of teachers of color in teacher education. Race Ethn. Educ. 12(2), 235–251 (2009)
9. Lac, V.T.: A teacher action research study on critical hope in a teacher pipeline program for minoritized youth. In: Handbook of Research on Teachers of Color and Indigenous Teachers, vol. 67
10. Ladson-Billings, G.: Toward a theory of culturally relevant pedagogy. Am. Educ. Res. J. 32(3), 465–491 (1995)
11. Miles, M.B., Huberman, A.M., Saldana, J.: Qualitative Data Analysis: A Methods Sourcebook (2014)
12. Rodriguez-Mojica, C., Rodela, K.C., Ott, C.: "I didn't wanna believe it was a race issue": student teaching experiences of preservice teachers of color. Urban Rev. 52(3), 435–457 (2020). https://doi.org/10.1007/s11256-019-00546-x
13. Shaffer, D.W.: Pedagogical praxis: the professions as models for post-industrial education. Teach. Coll. Rec. 106(7) (2004a)
14. Shaffer, D.W.: Epistemic frames for epistemic games. Comput. Educ. 46(3), 223–234 (2006)
15. Solorzano, D.G., Bernal, D.D.: Examining transformational resistance through a critical race and LatCrit theory framework: Chicana and Chicano students in an urban context. Urban Educ. 36(3), 308–342 (2001)
16. Zörgő, S., Swiecki, Z., Ruis, A.R.: Exploring the effects of segmentation on semi-structured interview data with epistemic network analysis. In: Ruis, A.R., Lee, S.B. (eds.) ICQE 2021. CCIS, vol. 1312, pp. 78–90. Springer, Cham (2021). https://doi.org/10.1007/978-3-030-677 88-6_6

Conceptualizing Theoretical Frameworks for Post-colonial Education for Kisii K–12, Kenya

Ruth Vitsemmo Akumbu[(✉)]

Pepperdine University, Malibu, USA
ruthakumbu@gmail.com

Abstract. This research examined the relationship between the elements of culturally relevant education that might enhance learning for primary and secondary students in the Kisii tribe in Kenya. A mismatch exists between what and how Kisii children learn in school and at home. The study examined elements of culture that can be leveraged to enhance learning, focusing on mathematics. A total of 60 participants, divided into eight focus groups, were interviewed. The themes from the thematic analysis were used as codes in the epistemic network analysis, a quantitative ethnographic technique. This research confirms a mismatch is present between what and how Kisii children learn in school and at home. The epistemic network analysis showed connections between codes from the thematic analysis: initiation, language, heritage, oral traditions, values, beliefs, rewards and punishment, practical over theory, and local STEM. These analyses show elements of culture support learning and teaching for students in Kisii K–12 schools. This multilayered analysis contributes to the cultural integration and augmentation framework and the transfer and adoption of universal principles model.

Keywords: culture · mathematics · colonization · curriculum · education · STEM · Kenya · Africa

1 Introduction

1.1 Research Purpose

This research examined the relationship between the elements of culturally relevant education that support learning and teaching for K–12 students in the Kisii tribe in Kenya. Classroom education is relevant when it prioritizes the local culture and context of the learner, enabling the application of classroom knowledge outside of school [1]. Contextuality connects formal learning with external experiences, allowing learners to interpret situations based on prior knowledge and perceptions [2–5]. A child's experiences in Kisii should be based on their culture, and integrating culturally relevant elements into education could make learning, teaching, and the curriculum more effective, creating a deeper understanding in the learning process [6–10]. Culture and other previously learned content play a vital role in how and what the child learns and helps connect students' prior knowledge to new knowledge [11]. Marginalizing learners' culture causes cognitive dissonance as they struggle to adopt unfamiliar forms of consciousness and mental processes [12, 13].

1.2 Research Problem

Learning in primary and secondary schools in Kisii may be negatively affected by curriculum and pedagogies that are culturally irrelevant. In most African villages, education is community-based, relevant to the culture, and contextual. Children learn from their elders and the environment [14]. The colonial education system created knowledge gaps by failing to align with the knowledge children gain at home. Education is therefore an inherently flawed system if it prioritizes another's culture, system, and ideology—thus preparing the learner for a society other than their own. This dichotomy emphasizes the importance of culturally relevant elements of education to support optimal outcomes in teaching and learning in Indigenous communities, where the child's culture, context, and information processing are significant to learning [11, 15, 16]. The research suggests that learners' cultures can enable efficient connections between new knowledge and prior Indigenous knowledge, creating an emotionally safe space that impacts the learners' identity [2, 5, 17–19].

1.3 Background: Kisii Tribe and Kenyan Education Policy

The Kisii tribe is Bantu-speaking people in western Kenya with a population of about 1.1 million—predominantly farmers and herders—with a chieftaincy structure [20, 21]. The region has about 467 primary schools with 6,278 teachers and 334 secondary schools with 3,940 teachers [21]. Education is based on the British system, and the instructional language is English [22]. The English language priority stems from British colonialism that aimed to exert power over locals by transmitting their lifestyles, beliefs, values, and practices, which influenced the culture and political and educational systems [23, 24]. The government's policy is for children to start school by age six, but by that age children can speak and count in their mother tongue, and they have already been significantly shaped by their experiences, families, communities, and cultures in ways that strongly support cognitive development [17, 18, 25].

1.4 Divergence in Mathematical and Language

Mathematics can be affected by local cultural contexts. This highlights the need to consider contextual differences when integrating mathematical concepts into a new culture. When the language of instruction differs from the mother tongue, it can create a learning gap. Teaching mathematics in the mother tongue can bridge the language gap, potentially improving learning outcomes [26]. For instance, the English language has multiple groupings using a single terminology, but the TshiVenda language has no such emphasis causing students to group giraffes, goats, and cows based on their noncannibalistic relationship instead of an animal group [27]. It is important for educators to bridge the gap between learners' cultural knowledge and the content and concepts to be mastered by leveraging learners' lived experiences and the local context [16]. A deep understanding of the sociocultural context and language is crucial for the transfer and construction of knowledge, including universal principles of math, science, and language. This occurs between learners, educators, and the local environment. The symbiotic relationship found in mathematics buttresses students' connection with their schools and, as a result, lowers behavior problems while at the same time enhancing student learning outcomes [13].

1.5 Theory: Postcolonialism

A postcolonial framework supports understanding culture, linguistics, mathematics, etc. because of its relationship between colonial and current events [28]. Before World War II, western ideas defined the global boundaries for behavior and thinking for many individuals and institutions [29]. After the war, many subjugated nations sought independence from their colonial masters and initiated decolonization, including reversing political control and its impact on Indigenous people [24]. Many nations, such as Kenya, gained their independence, but it can be argued that coloniality—the impact of colonization on emotions, intellectual pursuits, and cultural factors—persists.

Scholars state that the education of subalterns and native learners from a European canon results in a state of nonbeing or insignificance, generally leading to a fractured existence or identity, which is evident in the mimicry of the West and previous colonial masters [29–32]. European systems of education have been replacing Indigenous educational systems from as early as the mid-14th century [33]. Such an education diminishes self-reference, forcing the learner to value the West over local ways of being. Postcolonial education theorists argue for culturally relevant education and sociopolitical consciousness, whereby learning is grounded in the native culture and context [18, 34]. Culturally relevant pedagogy, therefore, provides students with the ability to value and celebrate their cultures and that of others. Culturally relevant education aligns with postcoloniality theory. Postcoloniality empowers subalterns to shape their envisioned world by understanding past colonial relationships and current events, guided by African philosophies [29, 35].

Postcoloniality is supported by decoloniality, which aims for a colonialism-free identity and augments Eurocentric systems with local knowledge for a more equitable and relevant education system, instead of completely disposing of western education [28–31, 36]. In the search for ways to augment, Africanize the curriculum, or create a culturally relevant education for Kisii, there are significant aspects of western culture and structures of education that will remain. *Augmentation* of the curriculum is the process of making curriculum and teaching methods that are more relevant to the reality of Indigenous people such as the Kisii tribe [24, 37].

1.6 Research Questions

This research examined the following questions:

- RQ1: Culture: What are the elements of culture that might support learning and teaching for primary and secondary schools in the Kisii tribe in Kenya?
- RQ2: Learning: What are culturally relevant practices, strategies, and processes that enhance learning and teaching for Kisii students in primary and secondary schools?
- RQ3: Relationship: What are the relationships between the culturally relevant practices, strategies, and processes that support teaching and learning for Kisii students in primary and secondary schools?

2 Methods

2.1 Focused Ethnography (FE)

FE was used to identify, from the experiences of teachers, parents, learners, cultural experts, and school administrators, the culturally relevant elements that might support education in Kisii [38]. All participants responded to RQ1, while learners and teachers responded to RQ2. The first two RQs required a grounded research approach to determine the codes for answering RQ3. Ethnographic data collection techniques of recording audio and video of participants were used [39]. The data were transcribed, translated, thematically analyzed, and then analyzed with epistemic network analysis (ENA) to investigate the relationship between culturally relevant practices, strategies, and processes for teaching and learning in the Kisii tribe. A translator was used when necessary, and the transcribers also spoke the local language, enabling a second review of all translated quotes translations (Table 1).

Table 1. Codebook of Constructs Included in the Analysis

Code	Description	Example
STEM/Local STEM	Local ways of thinking about STEM or local resources and material	*"She counts up to 10; she puts a stick aside."*
Rites of passage	Birth, circumcision or initiation, marriage, death	*"We have the birth; circumcision; we have the marriage and death."*
Oral traditions	Songs, proverbs, stories, music, dance	*"If you are not taught at home, the world will teach you."*
Heritage	Food, names, clothing styles, history	*"I'm a Kisii because I eat the Ugali from millet."*
Language	Ekegusii, Gusii, Swahili, English	*"You can use that language that a kid understands better."*

(continued)

Table 1. (*continued*)

Code	Description	Example
Values	Respect, courage, discipline, morality,	*"the child is now a grown-up and should behave with uttermost respect."*
Beliefs	Spirituality, life after death, and taboos	*"we have a lot of beliefs that does not go with other tribes."*
Reward and punishment	Corporal punishment, gifts, motivation	*"Pupils need something material" as an incentive to "keep working hard."*
Practical over theory	Ways of learning outside of school	*"But in homes, we do practical. But in schools, it's just theory."*
Formal education system	Ways of learning in school	*But in schools, it's just theory Competency-based curriculum (CBC)*
Processes	Processes are the steps or list of activities. "how"	*"You go slaughter that hen, cut it into small pieces, put it into a sufuria*
Practices	Practices are norms and customs. "what"	*"if you're newly married, you will be sent to a kitchen [to] cook."*
Strategies	Strategies are short plans of action "how"	*"At school, they should integrate the Kisii stories as a refreshment when we are bored, mix stories with chemistry."*

2.2 Sampling

Participants were recruited through local contacts with a recruitment letter, and no remuneration was provided. Participants had the option to withdraw at any time. Sixty participants were interviewed using the recommended range of six to eight participants per focus group, and each interview lasted about 120 min per group to avoid burnout [40]. The participants from the Kisii community were predominantly natives, spoke the local language, and were aged 12 and older. The parents ($n = 14$), teachers ($n = 17$), students ($n = 17$), administrators ($n = 6$), and cultural experts ($n = 6$) brought the number of participants to $N = 60$.

2.3   Thematic Analysis (TA) and Epistemic Network Analysis

This research took an indirect approach to quantitative ethnography by first completing a qualitative ethnography. The data were analyzed for themes, codes, and elements of culture that can support learning and teaching for children in Kisii. Findings were grouped as elements of culture and then used as codes for studying existing connections and relationships in the discourse using ENA.

ENA is a quantitative ethnography (QE) analysis tool for measuring the structure of connections, creating visualizations of the relationships between the codes, and quantifying co-occurrences [41]. ENA simultaneously analyzes all networks and creates a set of networks that can be compared visually to provide a better understanding of the relationship between the content of discourse [41, 42]. Unit of analysis is defined as a turn of talk taken by participants. An Excel spreadsheet of the discourse and codes developed from the thematic analysis was used to code about 2,338 lines of dialogue. The reliability of codes was validated using social moderation, whereby two raters checked for the meaning of codes and accuracy of coding on 20% of the data collected. Differences were reconciled—a social moderation process or interrater reliability critical to QE [42–45].

3   Results

3A Thematic Analysis

Three major themes emerged from responses: (a) elements of culturally relevant education; (b) practices, strategies, and processes for enhancing learning in Kisii; and (c) practices, strategies, and processes for facilitating teaching in the Kisii tribe of Kenya. Frequency count for coded categories with the most codes for elements of culture to support learning and teaching for Kisii schools were identifying as a member of the Kisii tribe and culture ($n = 111$), teaching at school different from teaching at home and community ($n = 50$), learning at home different from learning at school ($n = 43$), and how to change or correct the teaching differences between home/community and school ($n = 32$). The categories that had coded responses from the most focus groups for elements of culture to support learning and teaching for Kisii schools were identifying as a member of the Kisii tribe and culture ($n = 8$), learned at home but not taught at school ($n = 8$), learning to speak Ekegusii or Kiswahili and other activities at home ($n = 6$), and learning at home different from learning at school ($n = 5$).

3.1   Elements of Culturally Relevant Education

For RQ1, focus group data were analyzed thematically to identify nine main categories under the theme of culturally relevant education elements: rites of passage, reward and punishment, the practice over theory, values, oral tradition, language, beliefs, heritage, and local STEM. Their responses provided context to the significance of the following.

Rites of Passage. This theme represents the Kisii rites of passage (birth, circumcision and initiation, marriage, death) and the formal and informal learning that appear after circumcision and initiation. An administrator noted, "We have the birth, even the naming;

even the circumcision; we have the marriage and death." A parent spoke about how circumcision signifies initiation into adulthood for boys: "In Kisii, especially for men, once you are circumcised, then we know you are now a man." Both male and female circumcision are critical to the identity of the Kisii tribe, as noted by a cultural expert: "So that was the thing that was making us Abagusii; that was making us distinct from the rest, but it is fading."

Reward and Punishment. The systems of reward and punishment reveal differences in learning at home and at school. This refers to practices such as caning, corporal punishment, giving gifts, motivation, and encouragement. Teachers and parents advocated for a form of reward and punishment: "Pupils need something material" as an incentive to "keep working hard." A cultural expert with teaching experience noted, "White man's... constitutions affect us in one way or another negatively." Another participant in the cultural group blamed this government action and the banning of caning on mimicking the West: "[You] know we are using the American Constitution purely."

Practical Learning over Theory. Practical learning over theory or the informal education system represents the largest gap in education in Kisii. "That new curriculum can never train you to be a perfect cook because yours is to watch what is done by your teacher." A teacher agreed: "But in homes, we do practical. For example, you go slaughter that hen, cut it into small pieces, put it into a *sufuria*. We light fire. We see with our naked eyes. But in schools, it's just theory."

Values. Many of the responses centered on the Kisii values of respect, hard work, discipline, morality, dressing properly after initiation, unity, and love. As one of the parents shared, "There was a lot of love among the children. Sharing the same skins which is obtained from the cow, and there was so much friendship between the children." Another parent mentioned the importance of dressing properly after circumcision as a sign of moral values, stating circumcision for a girl means "the child is now a grown-up and should behave with uttermost respect."

Oral Tradition. Oral tradition, including songs, proverbs, and stories, plays a vital role in preserving Kisii culture. Students expressed appreciation when their teachers integrated these elements into the curriculum, as it helped them feel more connected to their culture. One stated, "If you are not taught at home, the world will teach you." Students feel incorporating oral tradition into learning helps break up the monotony of education. "At school, they should integrate the Kisii stories as a refreshment when we are bored, mix stories with chemistry." A teacher noted that "western culture is creeping in more, and people are trading traditional culture in favor of western culture."

Language. Learning in Ekegusii, Swahili, and English offers the possibility of new communication pathways. Teachers recognize the value of using familiar language with students to illustrate difficult concepts or teach new words. One related, "You can use that language that a kid understands better. For example, you are talking about a plate," suggesting the teacher indicate or describe the plate. "From that, they can understand and know." However, students strongly recognized the value of learning multiple languages to communicate with members of other tribes and nations.

Heritage. The Kisii people share a common heritage, which is evident in their responses related to food, traditional cooking, names, history, clothing, and locations. Among these, food and cooking were the most frequently mentioned and significant codes in the heritage category. One parent shared how food connected her to her heritage: "I'm a Kisii because I eat the Ugali from millet." One of the teachers emphasized that cooking was so important to cultural identity that wives could be judged for bad cooking and even sent for retraining. A parent added that "if you're newly married, you will be sent to a kitchen, then you cook badly. For instance, you cook the Ugali, and it is soft," she can be sent back to her parents.

Local STEM. This theme examined how STEM activities are used outside of school or without formal education to solve complex problems and included references to STEM. Multiple focus groups mentioned that older generations demonstrated effective counting skills with local systems despite lacking formal education. A teacher gave an example of counting bananas for sale: "She counts up to 10; she puts a stick aside." Using this system, she calculates her profit faster than most students. Discussing education mismatch, a teacher noted: "[I ask] one over one [1/1] or two over two [2/2], and he tells me zero." Even though this sounds mathematically wrong, the teachers concluded that culturally the student is correct because once the child gives away the two items, there is nothing left to share. Cultural experts discussed how local experts conducted complex surgical procedures, and a teacher argued that "because of modernization and technology, we are copying other people's culture and throwing away our culture."

Kisii Beliefs. Kisii beliefs generally connect to the rites of passage (birth, circumcision and initiation, marriage, death) with examples such as life after death, taboos, and beliefs attached to naming. A female administrator from the cultural group noted that in addition to the beliefs and practices of naming, "We are the Bantu who migrated from the Congo Basin. Abagusii, we have a lot of beliefs that does not go with other tribes." For instance, the belief that if a woman "climb up the roof and start putting the iron sheets. It is a bad omen," and she will be barren. This means it is taboo for a woman to roof a house. An administrator talked about the uniqueness of names and rituals: "There are some other rituals done to those kids born on the road; if she is a lady, she is called Nyanchera and if he is a male is called Makori."

3.2 Practices, Strategies, and Processes for Enhancing Learning and Facilitating Teaching

The findings for RQ2, enhancing learning, are as follows: (a) integrating language as a strategy for better understanding, (b) integrating the local culture and context as a strategy for learning, (c) integrating practical learning over theory in the process of learning, (d) eliminating corporal punishments, and (e) integrating parents and elders to preserve the culture. The findings for RQ2 are language integration, cultural integration, practical learning, corporal punishment, involving parents and elders, and supporting the competency-based curriculum education process."

3B Epistemic Network Analysis Results

RQ3 was answered using ENA. Table 3 provides codes and descriptions used in the ENA applying a quantitative ethnographic technique that models the structure of connections in data. This analysis also measured the strength of connections between elements of culture in RQs 1–3 as codes: (a) STEM; (b) initiation, (c) oral tradition, (d) heritage, (e) language, (f) values, (g) beliefs, (h) reward/punishment, (i) Kisii education, (j) formal education, (k) process, (l) practices, and (m) strategies. These were used to code the data for ENA.

Figure 1 provides a visual of the mean representation of the data indicating statistically significant differences between all data sets except for parents and administrators. Along the x-axis, a two-sample t-test assuming unequal variance showed administrators (mean $= -0.14$, $SD = 0.31$, $N = 174$) was not statistically significantly different at the alpha $= 0.05$ level from parents (mean $= -0.12$, $SD = 0.35$, $N = 267$; $t(401.20) = -0.71$, $p = 0.48$, Cohen's $d = 0.07$).

The variance showing each axis of the model in Fig. 1, representing the entire discourse, is $x = 0.11$ and $y = 0.08$. Spearman's goodness-of-fit is $x = 0.79$ and $y = 0.87$. Pearson's goodness-of-fit is $x = 0.78$ and $y = 0.85$. These statistics are moderate, indicating the fit of correlated plot points to corresponding network centroids. The greatest spread is between students and cultural experts as can be observed in the mean position in Fig. 1. Figures 2 and 3 model subtractive graphs that compare findings using two ENA networks found within the same model. This was achieved by subtracting the edge weight of one network from another during the simulation, which shows the connections or relationships that exist between elements in different groups.

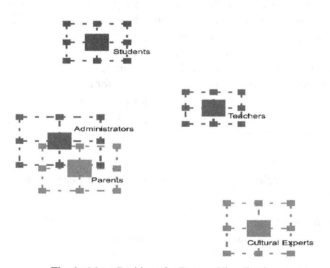

Fig. 1. Mean Positions for Dataset Visualization

In Fig. 2, the portion of network nodes that make up the ENA space for students along the x-axis on the top left quadrant are oral tradition, beliefs, reward and punishment, and Local STEM. These are interconnected by language, close to the y-axis, and at the very top. The bottom left quadrant is made up of initiation on the far left, followed by values and practices, and are interconnected by heritage in the teachers group. The top right quadrant comprises formal education, strategies with insignificant weight, and no obvious interconnects by language. The bottom left quadrant comprises process and Kisii education, both connected to heritage and initiation in the student group. Connections between elements were made in all the groups with varying strengths.

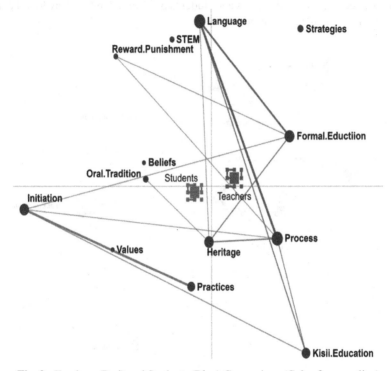

Fig. 2. Teachers (Red) and Students (Blue) Comparison (Color figure online)

In Fig. 3, along the x-axis on the top left quadrant are practices, processes, strategies, and reward and punishment. Belief on the x-axis shows weak connections within the cultural expert group. In the top right quadrant is Kisii education, which interconnects with processes. The bottom left quadrant comprises initiation, values, and oral traditions with weak connections and interconnection between cultural experts and students. The bottom right quadrant includes STEM, formal education, and language indicating strong relationships.

Figure 3 compares students to cultural experts, shows the widest gap of all the comparison models between the student and cultural expert groups, and presents the visualization of the discourse of students and cultural experts. The variance for Fig. 3 as indicated by each axis of the model is $x = 0.10$ and $y = 0.08$. Pearson's goodness-of-fit is $x = 0.93$ and $y = 0.79$, while Spearman's goodness-of-fit is $x = 0.93$ and $y = 0.79$. Along the x-axis, a two-sample t-test assuming unequal variance showed students (mean

$= 0.16, SD = 0.34, N = 313$) was statistically significantly different at the alpha $= 0.05$ level from cultural experts (mean $= -0.22, SD = 0.27, N = 218; t(517.27) = -14.43$, $p = 0.00$, Cohen's $d = 1.23$). Along the y-axis, a two-sample t-test assuming unequal variance showed students (mean $= 0.00, SD = 0.29, N = 313$ was not statistically significantly different at the alpha $= 0.05$ level from cultural experts (mean $= 0.00, SD = 0.37, N = 218; t(396.71) = -0.01, p = 0.99$, Cohen's $d = 0.00$). This difference could be the gap that exists between the education system and the local context and culture. The gap between the cultural experts and students is observed in Fig. 1 by looking at the visualizations of the mean positions.

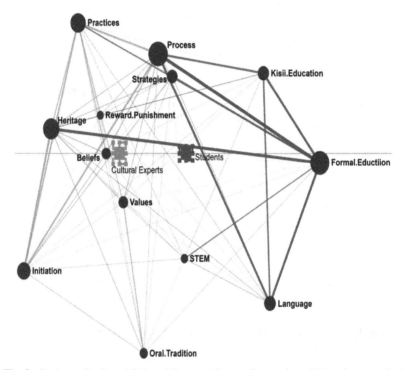

Fig. 3. Students (Red) and Cultural Experts (Green) Comparison (Color figure online)

4   Discussion

4.1   Thematic Analysis

The results from the thematic analysis led to nine cultural elements for enhancing the Kisii K–12 education system: (a) local STEM, (b) initiation or rites of passage, (c) oral tradition, (d) heritage, (e) language, (f) values, (g) beliefs, (h) reward/punishment, and (i) Kisii education. STEM was validated by its real-world applications. The study showed that the local context and culture are essential in educating children in Kisii. The local context comprises elders, parents, leaders, and more while the local culture embodies the nine elements of culture. Local STEM includes references to medicine, physics, and mathematics learned and taught outside of the classroom. All knowledge transferred and adopted outside of the classroom can be referred to as Kisii education.

Heritage, the most coded cultural element, encompasses artifacts, food, vegetation, animals, weather, history, and more. Participants took pride in discussing local food, their history, and their belief that they have the country's best climate. Heritage ties into oral tradition, and students noted that factors such as songs improved their learning. Students, compared to the rest of the participants, opposed caning as a form of punishment but encouraged all rewards that prioritize positive reinforcements [46, 47]. Most participants believe in consequences and noted that an alternative form of punishment is necessary.

A surprising finding is the passion for circumcision. The four rites of passage are birth, initiation/circumcision, marriage, and death. Circumcision is taught in school but lacks the necessary purpose and understanding, leading to dissatisfaction among parents and cultural experts. Discussions with elders strongly favored the Kisii education process during circumcision and other rites of passage. Circumcision, which happens in the early teen years, and death ceremonies are generally performed after the harvest season. A significant amount of the beliefs, values, norms, and more are transferred from the elders to the children during these activities and periods. The Kisii education system prioritizes practice over theory as children learn through observation and practice. Teachers and students found that integrating Ekegusii, the local language, into teaching enhances students' understanding and leads to cultural preservation. The thematic analysis provided the codes for the ENA.

4.2 Epistemic Network Analysis

Figure 2 compares the discourse of teachers and students and shows strong connections between language, process, and formal education for teachers. This means teachers used language in the process of teaching. Relationships in red are the perspectives of teachers and in blue are those of students. As indicated in earlier sections, the use of Ekegusii in the Kisii education code and food in the heritage code are the most frequently used elements in the process of formal learning and teaching. Interconnections occur lightly with elements such as initiation or rites of passage and Kisii education that prioritizes practical learning over theory. Discussion in the teacher and student groups also connects rewards and punishment with formal education where learners desire less punishment and more rewards, as stated earlier. The model shows no significant relationship between the teachers and learners as it relates to STEM, strategies, and beliefs. Even though groups discussed these independently, opinions from the groups are not connected. A teacher noted, "I teach physics, and there is a topic talking about centripetal force, and in the culture there is a [catapult or sling]." Students made no obvious mentions of teachers enhancing their learning in STEM-related classes but provided oral tradition examples: "At school they should integrate the Kisii stories as a refreshment when we are bored, mix stories with chemistry." The perspective of teachers and students indicates that in the process of teaching and learning, cultural elements such as (a) initiation, (b) oral tradition, (c) heritage, (d) language, (e) values, (f) reward/punishment, (g) Kisii education, (h) formal education, (i) process, and (j) practices can enhance learning.

Figure 3 compares cultural experts and students with the largest gap. Strong connections in the cultural expert group exist between initiation and heritage because the four rites of passage are linked by attributes such as food: "A lady [who] don't know how to cook, can be sent away from marriage," or "I'm a Kisii because I eat the Ugali from millet." The connections observed between processes and practices in relation to heritage and initiation result from discourse referencing activities such as cooking, circumcision, and burial practices. Elements of culture, such as beliefs, oral traditions, rewards, and punishment, show connections within the cultural expert group only compared to the formal education system, indicating a mismatch or divergence.

A relationship between cultural experts and students exists despite the divergence in opinions. The heritage code also shows strong interconnections with the formal education system as it relates to practices and procedures used for teaching in the community. The relationship is established through cooking and Ekegusii, the local language, and is used both in school and at home for teaching and learning. A stronger connection to strategy was seen in the use of the local language as a teaching mechanism in school, which a student suggested would "help those who do not understand English to make learning better." The connection between STEM, initiation, and process is weak but stronger between STEM and formal education codes. The connection to initiation results from references by cultural experts about marriages and traditional medicine, including different forms of treatment or local sciences. All codes made connections with varying strengths within each group with one significant interconnection between heritage and formal education already explained. Figures 1 and 3 provide visualizations of the mismatch between what and how Kisii children learn in school versus at home. This mismatch can be attributed to imposed elements in the education system: (a) English instead of Ekegusii; (b) formal school versus learning from parents and elders; (c) no caning and western-centric education, religion, names, and medicine as opposed to local names, religion, medicine, and education.

5   Conclusion

This research finds that there is a mismatch between what and how Kisii children learn in school versus at home. ENA analysis provides visualization of the gap and relationship between cultural elements. Thematic analysis resulted in nine cultural elements for enhancing the K–12 education system: (a) local STEM, (b) rites of passage, (c) oral tradition, (d) heritage, (e) language, (f) values, (g) beliefs, (h) reward/punishment, and (i) Kisii education. Findings also show a preference for practical over theoretical learning, which aligns with a community-based education often found in Indigenous communities, and culturally relevant and contextual learning [21, 32, 34, 43]. Integrating the nine elements of culture into classroom teaching and learning can improve understanding and make the education system more culturally relevant. Integrating the culture and local context shows respect for the community and can preserve the tribe's culture and identity.

5.1   Recommendations

This study led to the development of the cultural integration and augmentation (CIA) framework, also referred to as the cultural investigation, integration, and augmentation framework, and the transfer and adoption of universal principles (TAUP) model. The CIA framework investigates a group's cultural elements through research for integration into the desired system. In Kisii K–12 schools, the CIA framework holistically leverages elements from the learners' culture and context to be integrated into the formal education system. The framework could enable proper representation in the formal education system of the community, culture, and psychological wellbeing of the learner while accepting and acknowledging the validity of diversity in speech, attitude, learning, and thinking styles, which can result in better learning outcomes [48–51]. This research suggests that integrating cultural elements into education can impact the learner's cognition, identity, values, and skills.

The TAUP model represents the symbiotic relationship between teachers, learners, culture, and context in the teaching and learning process.

It aims to avoid the belief that all the concepts in STEM and the approach to teaching related subjects are universal and can be applied uniformly across cultural boundaries. The TAUP model is based on an understanding of learners' prior knowledge, sociocultural environment, and local context. In Indigenous communities such as Kisii, knowledge adoption and transfer should flow through the lens of the culture and local context, with constant collaboration between parents, community elders, learners, schools, and educators. The TAUP model is supported by situated cognition and social learning theory, placing significant value on the local context whereby learners spend long periods of time observing, thinking, describing, reflecting, and contextualizing information from their environment [6, 12, 46]. The key components of the TAUP model are: (a) processing information transferred or to be adopted through the lens of culture; (b) collaborating with all stakeholders in the transfer and adoption process; and (c) promoting the symbiotic relationship between learners, teachers, community, content, and culture. Assessment and evaluation of the TAUP model and CIA framework require further research, but for education systems it can be carried out in classrooms using the level two (learning) evaluation process that indicates what the student has or has not learned using discussions and group activities from inside and outside of the classroom [1, 2].

5.2   Implications and Future Research

The mismatch between children's home and school learning is a global problem. Children engage with only a small fraction of what they are taught in school, leading to disinterest and alienation. Even well-designed curricula, lesson plans, and books can be irrelevant to students if they are misaligned with their experiences. The implementation of formal education is a complex issue and a challenge for education systems. Further research is needed to determine the effectiveness of integrating Kisii cultural elements into education. Although the findings suggest that integration of Kisii cultural elements aligned with processes, practices, and strategies could enhance learning and make the current system more culturally relevant, further research is necessary to study their effectiveness in enhancing learning and academic achievement.

References

1. Kirkpatrick, J.D., Kirkpatrick, W.K.: Kirkpatrick's Four Levels of Training Evaluation. ATD Press (2016)
2. Hodell, C.: ISD from the Ground Up: A No-Nonsense Approach to Instructional Design, 4th edn. ATD Press (2016)
3. Im, E.-O., Page, R., Lin, L.-C., Tsai, H.-M., Cheng, C.-Y.: Rigor in cross-cultural nursing research. Int. J. Nurs. Stud. 41(8), 891–899 (2004). https://doi.org/10.1016/j.ijnurstu.2004.04.003
4. Nashon, S.M., Anderson, D.: Interpreting student views of learning experiences in a contextualized science discourse in Kenya. J. Res. Sci. Teach. 50(4), 381–407 (2013). https://doi.org/10.1002/tea.21078
5. Zimmerman, H.T.: Participating in science at home: recognition work and learning in biology. J. Res. Sci. Teach. 49(5), 597–630 (2012). https://doi.org/10.1002/tea.21014
6. Gay, G.: The what, why, and how of culturally responsive teaching: international mandates, challenges, and opportunities. Multicult. Educ. Rev. 7(3), 123–139 (2015). https://doi.org/10.1080/2005615x.2015.1072079
7. Hammond, Z.: Looking at sold through an equity lens: will the science of learning and development be used to advance critical pedagogy or will it be used to maintain inequity by design? Appl. Dev. Sci. 24(2), 151–158 (2020). https://doi.org/10.1080/10888691.2019.1609733
8. Kuhn, D., Arvidsson, T.S., Lesperance, R., Corprew, R.: Can engaging in science practices promote deep understanding of them? Sci. Educ. 101(2), 232–250 (2017). https://doi.org/10.1002/sce.21263
9. Marope, M.: Reconceptualizing and repositioning curriculum in the 21st century: a global paradigm shift. UNESCO International Bureau of Education (2019). http://www.ibe.unesco.org/sites/default/files/resources/reconceptualizing_and_repositioning.pdf?fbclid=IwAR3oOL6pkLL-j4VtLB4ClIFtuDP6fD2M5SAz2zvTKcsfe2NDg3_i0_nL-Ao
10. Penuel, W.R., Gallagher, L.P.: Preparing teachers to design instruction for deep understanding in middle school earth science. J. Learn. Sci. 18(4), 461–508 (2009). https://doi.org/10.1080/10508400903191904
11. Hanfstingl, B., Benke, G., Zhang, Y.: Comparing variation theory with Piaget's theory of cognitive development: more similarities than differences? Educ. Action Res. 27(4), 511–526 (2019). https://doi.org/10.1080/09650792.2018.1564687
12. Abrams, E., Taylor, P.C., Guo, C.-J.: Contextualizing culturally relevant science and mathematics teaching for indigenous learning. Int. J. Sci. Math. Educ. 11(1), 1–21 (2013). https://doi.org/10.1007/s10763-012-9388-2
13. Rosa, M., Orey. D.C.: Principles of culturally relevant education in an ethnomathematical perspective. Revista de Educação Matemática [Math. Educ. Perspect. J.] 17, 1–24 (2020). https://doi.org/10.37001/remat25269062v17id306
14. Mosweunyane, D.: The African educational evolution: from traditional training to formal education. High. Educ. Stud. 3(4), 50–57 (2013). https://doi.org/10.5539/hes.v3n4p50
15. Doolittle, P.E.: Complex constructivism: a theoretical model of complexity and cognition. Int. J. Teach. Learn. High. Educ. 26(3), 485–498 (2014). https://eric.ed.gov/?id=EJ1060852
16. Irvine, J.J.: Culturally relevant pedagogy. Educ. Digest: Essent. Read. Condens. Quick Rev. 75(8), 57–61 (2010). https://eric.ed.gov/?id=EJ880896
17. Babakr, Z.H., Mohamedamin, P., Kakamad, K.: Piaget's cognitive developmental theory: critical review. Educ. Q. Rev. 2(3), 517–524 (2019). https://doi.org/10.31014/aior.1993.02.03.84

18. Hammond, Z.: Culturally Responsive Teaching & The Brain: Promoting Authentic Engagement and Rigor Among Culturally and Linguistically Diverse Students. Corwin (2015)
19. Trester, E.F.: Student-centered learning: practical application of theory in practice. About Campus 24(1), 13–16 (2019). https://doi.org/10.1177/1086482219859895
20. Encyclopedia Britannica: Gusii. In Encyclopedia Britannica (2007). https://www.britannica.com/topic/Gusii. Accessed 2 Aug 2021
21. Kisii County Government: Education and Literacy (2021). https://www.kisii.go.ke/index.php/county-profile/socio-economics/item/1587-education-and-literacy
22. Encyclopedia.com: Gusii. In Worldmark Encyclopedia of Cultures and Daily Life (2018). https://www.encyclopedia.com/humanities/encyclopedias-almanacs-transcripts-and-maps/gusii-0. Accessed 2 Aug 2021
23. Githige, R.M.: The mission state relationship in colonial Kenya: a summary. J. Relig. Afr. 13(2), 110–125 (1982). https://doi.org/10.2307/1581206
24. Etieyibo, E.: Why decolonization of the knowledge curriculum in Africa? Afr. Today 67(4), 74–87 (2021). https://www.muse.jhu.edu/article/794678
25. Mandillah, L.: Kenyan curriculum reforms and mother tongue education: issues, challenges and implementation strategies. Educ. Change 23, 1–18 (2019). https://doi.org/10.25159/1947-9417/3379
26. Biraimah, K.L.: Moving beyond a destructive past to a decolonised and inclusive future: the role of Ubuntu-style education in providing culturally relevant pedagogy for Namibia. Int. Rev. Educ. 62(1), 45–62 (2016). https://doi.org/10.1007/s11159-016-9541-1
27. Muthivhi, A.E.: Development of verbal thinking and problem-solving among Tshivenda-speaking primary school children. Perspect. Educ. 31(2), 22–32 (2013). https://hdl.handle.net/10520/EJC145503
28. Burney, S.: Conceptual frameworks in postcolonial theory: applications for educational critique (chap. 7). Counterpoints 417, 173–193 (2012). http://www.jstor.org/stable/42981704
29. Weiss, T., Wilkinson, R. (eds.): International Organizations and Global Governance. Routledge Press (2018)
30. Césaire, A.: Discourse on Colonialism. (J. Pinkham, Trans.). Monthly Review Press (2001)
31. Fanon, F.: The Wretched of the Earth. (R. Philcox, Trans.). Grove Press. (Original work published 1961) (2004)
32. Kessi, S., Marks, Z., Ramugondo, E.: Decolonizing knowledge within and beyond the classroom. Crit. Afr. Stud. 13(1), 1–9 (2021). https://doi.org/10.1080/21681392.2021.192 0749
33. Gwanfogbe, M.: Changing Regimes and Educational Development in Cameroon. Spears Media Press (2018)
34. Ladson-Billings, G.: Toward a theory of culturally relevant pedagogy. Am. Educ. Res. J. 32(3), 465–491 (1995). https://doi.org/10.3102/00028312032003465
35. Odari, M.H.: The role of value creating education and "Ubuntu" philosophy in fostering humanism in Kenya. J. Interdiscip. Stud. Educ. 9(SI), 56–68 (2020). https://doi.org/10.32674/jise.v9is(1).1857
36. Fernández, J.S., Sonn, C.C., Carolissen, R., Stevens, G.: Roots and routes toward decoloniality within and outside psychology praxis. Rev. Gen. Psychol. 25(4), 354–368 (2021). https://doi.org/10.1177/10892680211002437
37. Brizuela-García, E.: The history of Africanization and the Africanization of history. Hist. Afr. 33, 85–100 (2006). http://www.jstor.org/stable/20065766
38. Rashid, M., Hodgson, C.S., Luig, T.: Ten tips for conducting focused ethnography in medical education research. Med. Educ. Online 24(1) (2019). https://doi.org/10.1080/10872981.2019.1624133
39. Creswell, J.W., Poth, C.N.: Qualitative Inquiry and Research Design: Choosing Among Five Approaches, 4th edn. Sage (2018)

40. Creswell, J.W., Creswell, D.J.: Research Design: Qualitative, Quantitative, and Mixed Methods Approaches, 5th edn. Sage (2018)
41. Siebert-Evenstone, A., Arastoopour Irgens, G., Collier, W., Swiecki, Z., Ruis, A.R., Williamson Shaffer, D.: In search of conversational grain size: modeling semantic structure using moving stanza windows. J. Learn. Anal. 4(3), 123–139 (2017). https://doi.org/10.18608/jla.2017.43.7
42. Shaffer, D.W., Collier, W., Ruis, A.R.: A tutorial on epistemic network analysis: analyzing the structure of connections in cognitive, social, and interaction data. J. Learn. Anal. 3(3), 9–45 (2016). https://doi.org/10.18608/jla.2016.33.3
43. Espino, D.P., Lee, S., Eagan, B., Hamilton, E.: An initial look at the developing culture of online global meet-ups in establishing a collaborative, STEM media-making community. In: Lund, K., Niccolai, G.P., Lavoué, E., Hmelo-Silver, C., Gweon, G., Baker, M. (eds.) A Wide Lens: Combining Embodied, Enactive, Extended, and Embedded Learning in Collaborative Settings, 13th International Conference on Computer Supported Collaborative Learning (CSCL) 2019, vol. 2, pp. 608–611. International Society of the Learning Sciences, Lyon, France (2019). https://doi.org/10.22318/cscl2019.608
44. Frederiksen, J.R., Sipusic, M., Sherin, M., Wolfe, E.W.: Video portfolio assessment: creating a framework for viewing the functions of teaching. Educ. Assess. 5, 225–297 (1998). https://doi.org/10.1207/s15326977ea0504_1
45. Herrenkohl, L.R., Cornelius, L.: Investigating elementary students' scientific and historical argumentation. J. Learn. Sci. 22(3), 413–461 (2013). https://doi.org/10.1080/10508406.2013.799475
46. Bandura, A.: Social Learning Theory. General Learning Press (1971)
47. Skinner, B.F.: The Behavior of Organisms: An Experimental Analysis. Prentice Hall (1938)
48. Acar-Çiftçi, Y., Gürol, M.: A conceptual framework regarding the multicultural education competencies of teachers. Hacettepe Üniversitesi Eğitim Fakültesi Dergisi [Hacettepe Univ. J. Educ.] 30(1), 1–14 (2015). https://www.researchgate.net/publication/279324029
49. Alismail, H.A.: Multicultural education: teachers' perceptions and preparation. J. Educ. Pract. 7(11), 139–146 (2016). https://files.eric.ed.gov/fulltext/EJ1099450.pdf
50. Le Grange, L., Ontong, K.: The need for place-based education in South African schools: the case of Greenfields Primary. Perspect. Educ. 33(3), 42–57 (2015). https://hdl.handle.net/10520/EJC178500
51. Ross, J.B.: Indigenous intergenerational teachings: the transfer of culture, language, and knowledge in an intergenerational summer camp. Am. Indian Q. 40(3), 216–250 (2016). https://doi.org/10.5250/amerindiquar.40.3.0216

The Stories We Tell: Uncovering Hidden Narratives in History Textbooks Through Epistemic Network Analysis

Juhan Kim(✉) [iD], Amanda Barany [iD], Xiner Liu [iD], and Andres Felipe Zambrano [iD]

University of Pennsylvania, 3700 Walnut St, Philadelphia, PA 19104, USA
jasperk@upenn.edu

Abstract. This study delves into the unique perspectives of authors of U.S. history textbooks on critical events, such as World War II, the Cold War, and the Vietnam War, employing quantitative ethnography (QE) and epistemic network analysis (ENA). These methodologies offer a lens through which divergent viewpoints can be analyzed, thereby revealing differences among documents sharing a common theme yet presenting varying narratives. The study presents the epistemic networks of two history textbooks and compares three shared events routinely discussed in each book. The findings emphasize the diverse patterns of perspective-taking by both the topic and the author, as evident in the connections drawn between common constructs of historical narratives. This research underscores the need to acknowledge the presence of multiple historical viewpoints and political perspectives, even within history textbooks from the same country. Exploring these perspectives is essential to fostering a more comprehensive understanding of historical events and promoting critical thinking and nuanced interpretations. The outcomes of this study suggest that applications of QE and ENA can be instrumental in critically examining how history is constructed and communicated, thereby advancing our understanding of the pedagogical implications in history education.

Keywords: History Textbook Analysis · Quantitative Ethnography · Epistemic Network Analysis · History Textbook · Textbook Analysis

1 Introduction

Educational systems frequently emphasize national history as they construct national identities around and within which individuals can situate themselves [1]. This has led authors of history textbooks to invest significant effort in presenting national historical accounts in a clear and accessible manner for learners. However, writing an entirely objective history text is challenging, if not impossible, due to the inherent subjectivity of both the authors' and broader societal perspectives. As a result, examining historical texts is vital to understanding the subjectivity and complexities present, as they reflect the ideological biases, dominant narratives, and values of the time and place they were written [2].

© The Author(s), under exclusive license to Springer Nature Switzerland AG 2023
G. Arastoopour Irgens and S. Knight (Eds.): ICQE 2023, CCIS 1895, pp. 261–274, 2023.
https://doi.org/10.1007/978-3-031-47014-1_18

This acknowledgment of embedded perspectives has given rise to the study of historiography, which scrutinizes historical writing and provides valuable insights into the practices of historians and assessments of the reliability and significance of their work [3]. Nonetheless, attaining a consistent understanding or interpretation of historical facts remains a challenging endeavor, even among people of the same country, let alone across nations. For instance, history texts routinely vary in both structure and content, depending on factors such as nationality, jurisdiction, publishing house, and authorial stance, which engender a plurality of perspectives in their narratives. As a media example, Dana Goldstein, in her article published in the New York Times, highlighted the prevalent variation in the content of history textbooks owing to the political polarization among states in the US [4].

These differences in the presentation may lead to distinct learning experiences and outcomes for student readers, particularly if they are applied differentially across student groups [5]. Although divergent perspectives are not inherently problematic, stakeholders involved in the learning process must develop awareness and make informed decisions regarding the implicit framing of historical media [6].

Consequently, scholars have advocated for developing standardized systems for analyzing historical texts [7, 8]. Grever and van der Vlies [9] proposed a focus on the content of different textbooks and the ways in which authors convey their perspectives through historical narratives rather than solely concentrating on fact-checking and identifying biases. However, this approach could be potentially challenging due to the number of historical writings that must be meticulously analyzed and compared. While the content analysis employed in Goldstein's work may aid in the identification of such discrepancies, its methodological approach tends to prioritize quantitative aspects of textbook data, such as the frequency of terms or concepts and the length of text allotted for descriptions, which may limit its capacity to offer more nuanced insight into the scope of these divergences in historical perspectives.

In this context, the field of quantitative ethnography (QE) and its associated technique, epistemic network analysis (ENA), appear as valuable tools for scholars. Research in QE using ENA has demonstrated the utility of the approach for examining divergent perspectives and revealing differences among documents that share a common theme but are written with varying perspectives [10]. Further, ENA's ability to quantitatively model connections between concepts in complex discourse data suggests potential utility for applying the approach to knowledge structure within different history textbooks [11]. Importantly, written text data, such as that in textbooks, can be conceptualized as a form of discourse, reflecting an ongoing narrative of historical events. In this setting, ENA can reveal the explicit differences in content and the often-implicit associations between concepts that shape an author's perspective on historical events. By analyzing these patterns, ENA can provide a deeper understanding of historical texts' underlying narratives and biases present in historical texts.

Moreover, ENA holds promising potential for streamlining the process of textbook analysis, rendering it a more practical and efficient solution for comparing multiple textbooks and addressing the extensive catalog of writings mentioned by Grever and van der Vlies [9]. The nature of ENA as a process of systematizing (typically) qualitative data allows the results to be replicable and comparable across different studies, thus contributing to a more standardized approach to history textbook analysis.

The current study employs ENA to conduct a comparative analysis of two US history textbooks obtained from online sources to address the following research question: How do authors connect common historical constructs to convey their unique perspectives in history textbooks? By addressing this research question, we aim to demonstrate the potential value of ENA as a tool for analyzing history textbooks. Although the study does not provide an expert-level historiographical analysis, it offers a systematic approach to assessing textbooks, aligning with the recommendations made by Grever and van der Vlies [9].

2 Methods

2.1 Data Collection and Preprocessing

This study utilizes US history textbooks [12, 13], concentrating on three historical events: World War II, the Cold War, and the Vietnam War. These events were selected based on their close chronological proximity and the varying outcomes for the United States. To offer a clearer understanding, we sourced two specific history textbooks for our analysis. Textbook 1 was published in NY in 2011 by a single author and comes from a relatively smaller publishing company, W. W. Norton & Company. Contrarily, Textbook 2, released in NY in 2015, was a collaborative effort by five authors and was published by the major firm, McGraw-Hill. Conducting ENA on history textbooks written in English, originating from different publications and authors, provides a starting point of appropriate scope that avoids potential misinterpretations associated with translating texts from multiple languages.

The methodological approach of this study involves using QE and ENA [11] to analyze two history textbooks with a focus on an objective to visualize and compare the authors' perspectives by examining patterns of connection-making between historical themes in their respective textbooks. Through analyzing the networks from each history textbook, the study seeks to uncover differences in the perspectives and narratives of authors in their writing [9].

It is important to note that history textbooks are typically composed of continuous narratives designed to convey a neutral tone, with each sentence conveying new, significant information [14]. However, descriptions of historical events are often divided into sections, indicated by headings or subheadings. Therefore, in this study, relevant chapters or sections from each textbook were selected to extract texts describing events of interest. This approach ensured that the dataset collected for analysis was directly relevant to the events of interest and aligned with previous research suggestions [7].

2.2 Method of Analysis

During the data analysis process, several methodological decisions were made to facilitate the use of ENA. Firstly, to address the research question, we identified the unit variables as *Textbook* and *Event*. Assigning *Textbook* as the primary unit variable, ENA generated comparable networks for both textbooks. The secondary unit variable, *Event*, allowed each textbook network to incorporate three events and calculate unit means for each event. This method allowed for a more detailed exploration of the distinctions and similarities in representing events across textbooks.

Conversation variables were set as *Section*, *Block*, and *Text* to segment the data hierarchically, allowing for a more granular analysis of the content. The *Section* variable organizes the text into broader thematic categories. In contrast, the *Block* variable breaks down the text into paragraphs or smaller subsections, facilitating a closer examination of the connections between concepts. Finally, the *Text* variable refers to individual sentences or phrases, which are the building blocks for constructing the epistemic networks. This methodological structure ensures that the analysis captures the intricacies of historical narratives and perspectives as organized by each book's authors and editors, providing a comprehensive understanding of the differences in the textbooks' content.

Secondly, the moving stanza window size was set to five sentences. This decision was based on the mean, median, and mode number of sentences in each paragraph converging to a value of five in the dataset. With these metrics in mind, the selected window size typically allows for associations within a single paragraph and back to one paragraph prior. The decision to use a moving stanza is based on the understanding that history textbooks, such as these, are constructed as organized, continuous narratives of historical events, with each sentence expected to continue the description from the preceding sentences [15].

2.3 Codes and Codebook

To ensure a comprehensive analysis of the textbooks, we employed nine codes in the ENA, each with a specific scheme encompassing relevant words or phrases. Drawing from Shemilt [16] and Zajda [17], we built a coding framework to discern how history textbooks guide national identity perspectives. Shemilt emphasized integrating multifaceted societal elements, such as economic systems, population dynamics, and political setups, while Zajda highlighted the forces influencing societal evolution. Although Shemilt proposed including technological advances, population dynamics, and religious practices, our coding merged these with other categories for clarity: technological advances as cultural artifacts within *Culture*, population dynamics within *Public Opinion/Atmosphere* due to their impact on societal sentiment, and religious practices also in *Public Opinion/Atmosphere*, reflecting group beliefs.

Indo-deductive code development was conducted to encompass the diverse criteria needed to comprehend the nuances of various history textbooks [18]. It is important to note that evaluating history through these constructs can be both contentious and subjective [18]. Hence, it's crucial to articulate the schemes or criteria for each code and rationalize their selection as constructs for history textbook analysis. The subsequent section will delve deeper into the rationale behind these code selections and elucidate the schemes employed to categorize words or phrases within the text under one of the nine designated codes.

These codes are intended to represent the fundamental constructs of historical narratives and how authors use them to (1) explain their interpretation of history and (2) relate historical events to the current shape of the United States, among other purposes. The nine codes and their coding schemes are defined and exemplified in Table 1.

Table 1. Codes, descriptions, and example sentences for each code.

Code	Description	Examples
Values/ Justice	Discussion of national values and justice as they pertain to a nation's historical actions and their impact on its present-day identity Terms: freedom, security, rights	"… President Roosevelt spoke eloquently of a future world order founded on the "essential human freedoms": freedom of speech, freedom of worship, freedom from want, and freedom from fear."
International Relations	Discussion of international relations, including relationships between the United States and other countries and relationships between countries other than the United States Terms: countries or regions (e.g., U.S., Europe), international organizations (e.g., United Nations	"These four powers would jointly occupy the German capital, Berlin, while an Allied Control Council supervised the national government."
Economic Impact	Discussion of economic conditions during a historical period, including indicators such as gross domestic product, industry success or failure, and employment rate Terms: gross domestic product, employment rate	"Despite the end of government wartime spending the gross national product fell less than 1 percent, and employment actually increased."
Politics	Discussion of political influences in the historical narrative, such as the political landscape during the text's depiction, including the political leadership and agendas Terms: political agendas, political regimes	"With the Democrats out of the White House for the first time since the Depression and with McCarthyites in retreat, Eisenhower did indeed seem to be leading the nation on a course "right down the middle.""
Public Opinion/ Atmosphere	Discussion of societal reactions and opinions towards events, including the depiction of broader societal implications and how they shape collective memory and identity Terms: public opinion, societal implications	"In the years immediately following World War II, the status of black Americans enjoyed a prominence in national affairs unmatched since Reconstruction."
Culture	Discussion of cultural artifacts and their significance in shaping American identity, including artwork, literature, and popular culture Terms: names or descriptions of cultural artifacts (e.g., Four Freedoms by Rockwell), other related terms (e.g., Zootsuit)	"Drawing on the lives of his Vermont neighbors, Rockwell translated the Four Freedoms into images of real people situated in small-town America."

(*continued*)

Table 1. (*continued*)

Code	Description	Examples
Figures	Discussion of historical figures mentioned in a text and their significant roles in shaping history Terms: Franklin D. Roosevelt, Harry S. Truman, Winston Churchill	"In Denver, Colorado, Rodolfo "Corky" Gonzales laid out a blueprint for a separatist Chicano society, with public housing set aside for Chicanos and the development of economically independent barrios."
Concepts/ Ideologies/ Terms	Discussion of newly emerged terms, ideologies, or concepts in a historical narrative and their impact on the broader intellectual and ideological frameworks of the United States during the depicted era Terms: Isolationism, and Anticommunism	"Riding a wave of anticommunism, fanatical patriotism, and anti-Semitism, Hitler's Nazi Party trumpeted similar fascist ideals, looking to unite all Germans in a Greater Third Reich."
Aggression/ Military Action	Discussion of military actions or conflicts, including strategies, tactics, motivations behind military operations, and their impacts Terms: World War II, military actions (e.g., invasion), military groups (e.g., army)	"In March Johnson ordered Operation Rolling Thunder, a systematic bombing campaign aimed at bolstering confidence in South Vietnam and cutting the flow of supplies from the North."

The data was coded independently by two graduate-level researchers. Inter-rater reliability (IRR) was assessed using Cohen's kappa and Shaffer's Rho. The agreement between the raters for 100 randomly selected lines for each construct was reasonably high, with Type I error rates: $\kappa > 0.85$ and $\rho(0.90) < 0.10$ (See Table 2). After establishing acceptable IRR thresholds, the full-scale dataset was coded for the nine constructs.

Table 2. Constructs and inter-rater reliability statistics.

Code	Cohen's Kappa (κ*)	Shaffer's Rho (ρ)
Values/Justice	0.87	< 0.05
International Relations	0.87	< 0.05
Economic Impact	0.95	< 0.05
Politics	0.89	< 0.05
Public Opinion/Atmosphere	0.89	< 0.05
Culture	0.85	0.09
Figures	0.96	< 0.05
Concepts/Ideologies/Terms	0.85	0.02
Aggression/Military Action	0.94	0.05

* *All the kappa values are statistically significant for $\rho(0.90) < 0.10$*

3   Results

3.1   Statistical Measures

In this study, the epistemic networks were generated using the open-access ENA tool to visualize and compare connections between inductive themes across two history textbooks. The epistemic networks demonstrated high precision, indicated by a goodness of fit value of 1 for both the X-axis and Y-axis. This value not only underlines the model's capability to accurately represent code networks, potentially offering insights into the authors' viewpoints, but also facilitates an extensive comparative analysis of units using plotted points, individual networks, and network difference graphs.

Networks for Textbooks 1 and 2 were found to be different to a degree of statistical significance. Each textbook was found to have a unique set of codes, leading to distinct narratives and contexts along the X-axis (MR1). To maximize the variance observed when comparing Textbook 1 and Textbook 2, a means rotation was performed for the visualization. A Mann-Whitney U test, conducted along the X-axis (MR1), indicated a statistically significant difference between the two textbooks, with a median value of 1.40 for Textbook 1 and -1.31 for Textbook 2 ($N = 3$, $U = 0$, $p = 0.10$, $r = 1.00$). In both dimensions, our model exhibited co-registration correlations of 1 for both Pearson and Spearman. This suggests a strong goodness of fit between the visualization and the original model.

3.2   Epistemic Network Analysis

To answer the question, "How do authors weave together common historical constructs to convey their unique perspectives in history textbooks?" The epistemic network graph of Textbook 1 is shown below in Fig. 1.

In the first textbook, certain codes had stronger associations, most notably between *Values/Justice* and *Public Opinion/Atmosphere* (lw = 0.31), as well as between *Politics and Figures* (lw = 0.31; see Fig. 1). The emphasis on these connections provides insights into the author's perspective on historical narratives and the factors deemed essential in shaping the representation of historical events.

One prominent connection in Textbook 1 is the link between *Values/Justice* and *Public Opinion/Atmosphere*, which illustrates the author's recognition of how values and justice influenced public opinion and the societal mood of the era. This connection is evident in the author's assertion,

> "The rights revolution completed the transformation of American freedom from a set of entitlements enjoyed mainly by white men into an open-ended claim to equality, recognition, and self-determination."

Through this statement, the author reveals the nation's fundamental values and their role in shaping the societal climate. This emphasis underscores the relationship between the United States' ethical and moral principles and public perception, which shape the wider historical narrative.

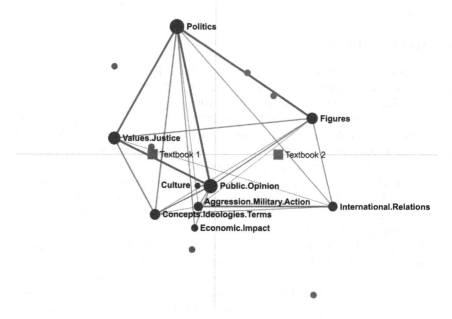

Fig. 1. An epistemic network model to describe historical events in Textbook 1.

The connection between *Politics* and *Figures* in Textbook 1 demonstrates the author's propensity to frame historical events around influential figures and their political actions. The statement below serves as an example:

> "Nixon ran for president in 1968 declaring that he had a 'secret plan' to end the war. On taking office, he announced a new policy, Vietnamization. Under this plan, American troops would gradually be withdrawn while South Vietnamese soldiers, backed by continued American bombing, did more and more of the fighting. But Vietnamization neither limited the war nor ended the antiwar movement."

In this quote, the author delivers a narrative that focuses on Nixon's public-facing political strategies. The author presents Nixon's campaign promise of a "secret plan" to end the war, and his implementation of Vietnamization, and the outcomes of these actions. The narrative here implies a critique of Nixon's policies, as it mentions that "Vietnamization neither limited the war nor ended the antiwar movement." It establishes a connection between Nixon's political actions and the continuation of the war, suggesting a gap between Nixon's promises and the results of his strategies (Fig. 2).

The authors of Textbook 2 also exhibited a high focus on connecting *Politics* and *Figures*(lw = 0.42), being slightly higher than the connection weight observed in Textbook 1 between these two codes. Additionally, there was a notable connection between *International Relations* and *Aggression/Military Actions* (lw = 0.37), among other connections between each code. This contrast in emphasis suggests that the authors of Textbook 2 may have approached the historical narrative with a different set of narrative priorities.

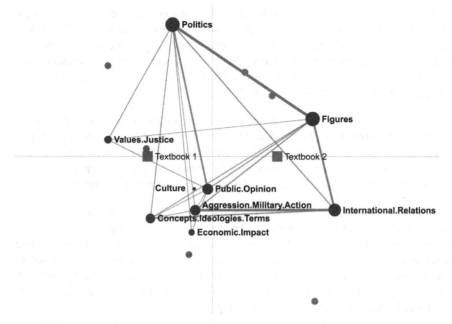

Fig. 2. An epistemic network model to describe historical events in Textbook 2.

The stronger connection between Politics and Figures in Textbook 2, similar to Textbook 1, showcases how the authors framed specific historical events around influential figures and their political actions play in shaping the historical narrative. The following example illustrates how the Vietnam War was framed around President Nixon's influence:

> "Nixon thus set two goals for his campaign: to distance himself from President Johnson on Vietnam and to turn Wallace's "average Americans" into a Republican majority. The Vietnam issue was delicate, because Nixon had generally supported the war. As he told one aide, 'I've come to the conclusion that there's no way to win the war. But we can't say that, of course. In fact, we have to seem to say the opposite.'"

The quote above offers a more nuanced and reflective look into Nixon's political motivations and strategies. It provides insights into Nixon's private thoughts and dilemmas about the war, contrasting with his public stance. The authors of Textbook 2 foregrounded Nixon's personal and political challenges, depicting him as a strategic politician in managing his public image and navigating the issues of the Vietnam War. This quote suggests a more complex connection between Nixon as a figure and his political actions, as it emphasizes the discord between his private beliefs and public activities. This focus enhances our understanding of the interplay between political dynamics and the actions of influential figures, offering readers a more anecdotal depiction of historical events.

On the other hand, the connection between International Relations and *Aggression/Military Action* in Textbook 2 reveals the authors' focus on the relationship between international relations and aggression or military actions between countries. This focus highlights the complex interdependence among nations and the role that military actions play in shaping the trajectory of global history. An example of this stronger connection emerges in the authors' discussion of WWII:

> "Before the war Americans seldom exerted leadership in international affairs. After it, the world looked to the United States to rebuild the economies of Europe and Asia and to maintain peace. Not only had World War II shown the global interdependence of economic and political systems, but it had also increased that interdependence. Out of the war developed a truly international economy."

The passage cited above offers an exemplary picture of how the United States, previously a relatively isolated player in international affairs, was propelled to a leadership role in the post-war era. The authors mentioned that the war exposed the inherent interdependence of global economic and political affairs and significantly increased this interdependence. From this passage, readers would learn that the war catalyzed the creation of a truly international economy, revealing the impact of military action on the world's political and economic landscape (Fig. 3).

Fig. 3. A comparative network model of nine codes employed to describe historical events in Textbook 1 and Textbook 2 is presented. In this model, only connections with a weight exceeding 0.1 are represented, as the primary objective of the comparative chart is to elucidate the distinct web of code constructions employed by the authors and highlight their differing approaches in narrating historical events.

The comparison chart further provides a visualization of the differences between the network maps for each textbook, highlighting the frequency with which specific pairs of codes were connected. In Textbook 1, there is a clear prominence of connections between the codes of *Values/Justice, Public Opinion/Atmosphere, Politics*, and *Concepts/Ideologies/Terms*. This recurring pattern indicates a thematic focus in the author's historical narrative.

An intriguing aspect of Textbook 1's approach is its distinct emphasis on the code of Values/Justice, which forms the centerpiece of many code connections. This is particularly apparent in the author's treatment of the Cold War era, as exemplified by the following passage:

> "...the anticommunist crusade had created a pervasive atmosphere of fear ... But anticommunism was as much a local as a national phenomenon ... States and localities required loyalty oaths of teachers, pharmacists, and members of other professions, and they banned communists from fishing, holding a driver's license, and, in Indiana, working as a professional wrestler."

In this narrative, the author depicts the pervasive fear that dominated the Cold War era, attributing it to the climate of mistrust and unease starkly contrasting with the democratic freedom of the US. This suggests the author's inclination to emphasize the role of values and justice in perceiving historical events. This concentration also reveals the author's interpretation of historical events. It serves as a reminder to readers that history is not merely a chain of events but a complex interweaving of *Values/Justice, Public Opinion/Atmosphere, Politics*, and *Concepts/Ideologies/Terms*.

Conversely, the most frequently mentioned codes in Textbook 2 were *International Relations, Aggression/Military Action, Figures*, and *Politics*. Additionally, Textbook 2 reveals that the connections of codes do not revolve around one particular code but are instead dispersed among several different codes. This observation suggests that the authors emphasized the interconnected nature of world events, emphasizing the relationships between various historical actors and their roles in shaping the global landscape. The authors' depiction below of the Cold War era illustrates this example:

> "Proposals for the international control of atomic energy fell victim to cold war fears ... But Truman chose Bernard Baruch, a staunch cold warrior, to draw up the recommendations to the United Nations in June 1946. Baruch's proposals ensured that the United States would dominate any international atomic agency."

In this passage, the authors outline the interwoven relationship between international relations, military actions, the figures involved, and their political decisions. The implications of Truman's decision, Baruch's role, and subsequent proposals are situated within the broader geopolitical context of the Cold War. These connections suggest the authors' emphasis on the interconnectedness of world events, historical actors, and their collective influence on the trajectory of global history.

4 Summary Discussion and Conclusion

In this study, we employed ENA to tackle the following research question: "How do authors weave together common historical constructs to convey their unique perspectives in history textbooks?" This preliminary investigation has highlighted the utility of ENA for analyzing discourse in history textbooks, as it helped uncover contrasting patterns in the two textbooks and highlighted the authors' differing viewpoints on historical narrative construction. Textbook 1, authored by a single individual, exhibited a pronounced linkage between *Values* and *Public Opinion/Atmosphere*, possibly reflecting the author's emphasis on the societal ramifications of historical events. In contrast, Textbook 2, a collaborative work by five authors, underscored the connections between *International Relations* and *Aggression/Military Actions*, suggesting a collective viewpoint rooted in global geopolitics. Importantly, a common thread across both textbooks is the emphasis on the relationship between *Politics* and *Figures*, which accentuates the universally acknowledged interplay between prominent individuals and their political actions. These observations enhance our comprehension of how the framework and origins of historical texts can influence their narrative. It's valuable to highlight these variances through an Epistemic Network Analysis (ENA) visualization. Historical narratives can be written from various perspectives, making it essential not only for publishers, authors, and instructors but also for students to be cognizant of these differing viewpoints. In sum, this exploratory analysis has broadened our understanding of how history is presented and interpreted within these textbooks.

One limitation of this study is that the codes and their schemes were developed indo-deductively, which could invite disagreement over their construct validity. In this paper, we acknowledge that the constructs set indo-deductively can be subjective. However, the reasons for not utilizing a clearer and more well-founded framework are twofold. First, upon examination, there isn't a pre-designed construct system suitable for QE research. Secondly, after reviewing history textbooks, we realized that there are instances where the same term aligns with more than one construct scheme. Additionally, we recognized no clear boundaries between distinct constructs and the terms appearing in the history text.

Another limitation of this study is that the coding process does not consider the order of connections between codes. Despite being aware of the limitations, this preliminary study proceeded with the specified methodological approach. According to our findings, this research explores a domain that hasn't been previously attempted. As a result, among the QE tools, ENA can provide the most basic yet definitive research outcomes. Moreover, the reason for not employing other tools, such as Ordered Network Analysis (ONA), is our belief that ENA is more suited to address the research question of this paper. This question pertains to how historical book authors connect the nine constructs and how they form different networks as a result of their perspective.

Future research could explore alternative coding schemes that highlight different facets of historical narratives to mitigate these challenges. To address the limitation regarding the order of code connections, researchers may consider the application of ONA [19].

An exciting prospect for future studies would be a transition towards a more evaluative approach, such as comparing each textbook against established social studies education standards. This would offer a more structured evaluation of the alignment of each textbook with recognized educational criteria.

Currently, this study is investigating themes and their interconnections within each textbook, along with the implications of these connections on the narrative approach of each work. The use of ENA, and potentially ONA, in history textbook analysis, could offer deeper insights into the product of historical narratives and perspectives. This systematic approach to assessing textbooks, especially within the context of history textbook analysis, could contribute to a more nuanced understanding of how history is presented and interpreted, thereby paving the way for richer and more diverse historical accounts.

Acknowledgements. We thank the research team for their invaluable contributions. We also acknowledge ChatGPT for enhancing the language clarity of our drafts, but human authors rigorously reviewed all content before submission.

References

1. Korostelina, K.V.: History education and social identity. Identity **8**(1), 25–45 (2008)
2. Loewen, J.W.: Lies My Teacher Told Me: Everything Your American History Textbook Got Wrong. The New Press (2018)
3. Becker, C.: What is historiography? Am. Hist. Rev. **44**(1), 20 (1938)
4. Goldstein, D.: Two States. Eight Textbooks. Two American Stories. The New York Times. https://www.nytimes.com/interactive/2020/01/12/us/texas-vs-california-history-textbooks.html. Accessed 28 Apr 2023
5. VanSledright, B.A., Kelly, C.: Reading American history: the influence of multiple sources on six fifth graders. Elem. Sch. J. **98**(3), 239–265 (1998)
6. Schusler, T.M., Decker, D.J., Pfeffer, M.J.: Social learning for collaborative natural resource management. Soc. Nat. Resour. **16**(4), 309–326 (2003)
7. Pingel, F.: UNESCO Guidebook on Textbook Research and Textbook Revision. UNESCO Publishing (2016)
8. Nicholls, J.: Methods in School Textbook Research. Int. J. Hist. Learn. Teach. Res. (Print) **3**(2), 11–26 (2003)
9. Grever, M., Van Der Vlies, T.: Why national narratives are perpetuated: a literature review on new insights from history textbook research. London Review of Education (2017c)
10. Ruis, A.R.: Quantitative ethnography of policy ecosystems: a case study on climate change adaptation planning. In: Advances in Quantitative Ethnography: 4th International Conference, ICQE 2022, Copenhagen, Denmark, 15–19 October 2022, Proceedings (pp. 414–428). Cham: Springer Nature Switzerland. (2023). https://doi.org/10.1007/978-3-031-31726-2_29
11. Shaffer, D.W., Collier, W., Ruis, A.R.: A tutorial on epistemic network analysis: analyzing the structure of connections in cognitive, social, and interaction data. J. Learn. Anal. **3**(3), 9–45 (2016)
12. Foner, E.: Give Me Liberty!: An American History. 3rd edn. W. W. Norton, New York, NY (2014)
13. Stoff, M.B., Davidson, J.W., Lytle, M.H., DeLay, B., Heyrman, C.L.: US: A Narrative History, Volume 2: Since 1865. 7th edn. McGraw-Hill Education, New York, NY (2014)
14. Crabtree, C., Nash, G. B.: National standards for united states history: exploring the american experience. Grades 5–12. Expanded Edition. Including Examples of Student Achievement. National Center for History in the Schools, University of California, Los Angeles, 10880 Wilshire Blvd., Suite 761, Los Angeles, CA 90024-4108 (1994)

15. Siebert-Evenstone, A., Irgens, G.A., Collier, W., Swiecki, Z., Ruis, A.R., Shaffer, D.W.: In search of conversational grain size: modeling semantic structure using moving stanza windows. J. Learn. Anal. **4**(3) (2017)
16. Shemilt, D.: History 13–16 evaluation study. Holmes McDougall (1980)
17. Zajda, J.: Discourses of Globalisation, and the Politics of History school textbooks. Springer eBooks (2022)
18. Thomas, D.: A general inductive approach for analyzing qualitative evaluation data. Am. J. Eval. **27**(2), 237–246 (2006)
19. Tan, Y., Ruis, A.R., Marquart, C., Cai, Z., Knowles, M.A., Shaffer, D.W.: Ordered network analysis. In Advances in Quantitative Ethnography: 4th International Conference, ICQE 2022, Copenhagen, Denmark, 15–19 October 2022, Proceedings, pp. 101–116. Cham: Springer Nature Switzerland. (2023). https://doi.org/10.1007/978-3-031-31726-2_8

Theory-Building and Tool-Building for a Science of Dysfunctional Political Discourse

Eric Hamilton[✉], Marguerite Williamson[✉], and Andrew Hurford[✉]

Pepperdine University, Malibu, CA 90263, USA
{eric.hamilton,marguerite.williamson}@pepperdine.edu,
andrewchurford@icloud.com

Abstract. This paper extends a developing analytic framework for political discourse that takes place over digital social media. Earlier presentations of the framework have furnished a rationale for applying the conceptual framework of epistemic frame theory and the tools of quantitative ethnography for political discourse analysis. They have provided early existence proofs of the viability of epistemic network analysis (ENA) for rudimentary models of social media threads that involve political content. The current theoretical paper moves significantly beyond this foundation. It summarizes and deepens the explanation of the constructs of discursive transactions, response grammars, and epistemic frames in political discourse. It proposes and supports three modeling tools for building a productive science of political discourse. The first modeling tool involves both ENA and a mathematical means for extending ENA's key explanatory and predictive potential to display dyadic connections between constructs. The second involves complex adaptive system (CAS) theory. The third involves the application of artificial neural networks. Each of these three tools provides valuable modeling affordances which the other two do not. Collectively, these three approaches hold promise to contribute to the science of political discourse by deepening our understanding and supporting potential repair of profoundly disturbing trends in political conversations that are unfolding globally.

Keywords: quantitative ethnography · epistemic network analysis · epistemic frames · political discourse · artificial neural networks · complex adaptive systems · parallax

1 Introduction and Purpose

This theoretical paper extends an analytic framework [1, 2] for political discourse that takes place over digital social media. It is intended as a prospectus for the challenge of building a more robust science of dysfunctional political discourse analysis. In the US and in other countries, dysfunctional or polarizing discourse has become a ubiquitous, ominous reality. Political discourse is a critical mediator for how a society sets priorities, deliberates over, and responds to urgent social issues. Yet especially when

G. Arastoopour Irgens and S. Knight (Eds.): ICQE 2023, CCIS 1895, pp. 275–289, 2023.
https://doi.org/10.1007/978-3-031-47014-1_19

conducted over social media, political discourse has fallen into widely-recognized dysfunction, characterized by increasing and self-reinforcing [3] anti-social norms of incivility, disgust, and polarization. That dysfunction sabotages the public policy processes that effective problem-solving and innovation require, imposing harsh, immeasurable setbacks to societal well-being and progress. Because dysfunctional discourse appears intractably resistant to obvious corrective measures, it merits serious analysis to uncover non-obvious patterns, connections, or structural properties. The goal of repairing political discourse seems only possible with the benefit of such targeted analyses.

Political discourse analytics have already found a growing niche in discourse analysis research more broadly, especially in the areas of narrative networks and bipartite analysis [4–6]. This paper adds to that broader literature by explaining how three interpretations, or modeling tools, of quantitative ethnography (epistemic network analysis, complex adaptive systems, and artificial neural networks) may separately and collectively yield explanatory and predictive models of political discourse, and may reveal tipping points beyond which productive discourse is statistically likely to worsen monotonically. As a theoretical paper, we offer it as a precursor to planned empirical and simulation studies that encompass myriad dynamic patterns and variables, studies designed to help build a productive science of dysfunctional political discourse.

Our primary goal in contributing to a science of dysfunctional discourse is to help foster discourse repair. Dozens of initiatives underway seek to do just that [e.g., cataloged in 7], through complementary approaches that address different aspects of what can be considered dysfunctional discourse pathology. Among such complementary approaches, this paper takes a theory-driven models and modeling perspective [8] to explore a view that humans, with views across political spectra, are highly vulnerable to false but avoidable polarization -- polarization that both a) sabotages the relational richness necessary to build social trust, and b) metastasizes by feeding on itself, thus iteratively catalyzing further depletion of social trust.

A possible foundational implication of visualizing the pathology of polarizing discourse is recognition that virtually every aspect of how individuals view others acrimoniously through the lens of political beliefs may be fundamentally unsound and flawed. That is the essence of the semantic parallax argument advanced in an earlier paper [2], that the meaning of *what* we see is distorted by the *ways* that we see – what we later refer to in this paper as our affect-intense epistemic frames. And because actions inexorably shape personal identity, *acting* on what we *think or believe* we see in one another can intensify the parallax, distorting us individually and collectively – unintentionally cultivating persona shifts that are artifacts of dysfunction but seem to validate negative views that political opposites have of one another. That parallax then recycles distortion to further damage social trust, collective identity, and national viability.

The modeling tools this paper suggests take on the difficult challenge to make such parallax and the dynamics it enmeshes visible in the following way. Models that can plainly depict polemics and response patterns used by different political groupings, and the subsequent divisions such patterns spawn in broader societal discourse, might illuminate unintentional but recurring traps – traps that misdirect discordant affect and attention, and thus subsequently erode civil discourse. We also expect to identify potential opportunities for repairing gaps in the verbal communication structure deployed by antagonistic participants engaged in hostile political dialog.

Each of the three types of modeling tools – epistemic network graphing, complex adaptive systems, and artificial neural networks – has different affordances and tradeoffs (summarized in Table 3) for making visible pathological aspects of dysfunctional discourse and its self-reinforcing nature. The next section outlines constructs that form a common language applicable to each of the three modeling approaches. The paper then reviews the potential viability of each approach and its tradeoffs.

1.1 Five Constructs: Epistemic Frames, Discursive Transactions, Response Grammars, Cognitive Appraisal, and High-Valence Activations

Five important constructs apply to each of the three tools the paper proposes for building a productive science of dysfunctional political discourse.

As noted elsewhere [1], the construct of **epistemic frames** [9] provides both language and a means to integrate important considerations underlying political discourse. Epistemic frames refer to "everything" that is involved in an individual's mindset – in this case, narrowed to a political mindset (qualifying that the term "mindset" includes considerations of emotion central to the study of dysfunctional discourse). The terms "political epistemic frame," "political point-of-view (POV)," or simply "epistemic frame" appear interchangeably here as a reference to an individual's political perspective. A political epistemic frame thus represents a holistic, dynamic, and multifaceted emotional and cognitive construct. It incorporates moral commitments, personal understandings, the impact of personal experiences, political interactions, prejudices, self-interest, and a sense of personal identity and identity protection – the totality of interconnected attitudes towards politically related attitudes and individuals. This theory-building and tool-building research centers around epistemic frames, how they are expressed. And how they change during socially-mediated political discourse.

Table 1. Sample Response Grammar Scenario

Representative X is attacked on social media by Candidate Y, running for the same office, for using taxpayer money to buy votes on a certain spending bill. In this example, X knows that by supporting the spending bill, s/he is doing exactly that - using taxpayer money to buy votes. X also knows that the spending bill will do some good – besides making it more likely s/he will get elected – an easy win-win situation. But X also believes that it may not be a very judicious use of taxpayer money, and it kicks the can down the road for resolving a looming fiscal crisis. X has a complex response that attacks Y by sarcastically belittling the original complaint, attempting to diminish Y's overall political philosophy, and raising questions about Y's suitability for office

How epistemic frames are expressed, and how they shift during discourse, leads to the next construct – a **discursive transaction** [1] (Fig. 1), defined as a sequence of steps in a political conversation that begins with reading or hearing an incoming message, followed by assessing the contents of that message and generating cognitive and affective responses. The final step of the discursive transaction is the reply. In epistemic graph practice, the reply phase of a discursive transaction is a codable utterance.

A **response grammar** refers to everything in a discursive transaction except the initial message or communication [1]. It thus includes **cognitive appraisal** of incoming messaging, emotional reaction to it, and reply (if any). Response grammars were originally referred to as emotional grammars [1], in recognition of a perceived underemphasis of the role that emotions play in the generation and analysis of polarized political discourse. Mathematically, a response grammar can be seen as a template based on probabilistic and acculturated norms that predict how an individual responds following an incoming communication in a conversation. A response grammar answers the question, "What is the most likely response, shaped by emotion, that might be expected to follow from a given input or provocation?" The response grammar for a compliment might involve a simple thanks. In contrast, the grammar for an insult might involve a retaliatory insult, anger, or alienation. Earlier papers [10] have enumerated relatively simple grammars or patterns of responses as they might appear in social media threads. The simplest (and most predictable) examples involve thanking someone for a compliment or responding with hostility to a directly offensive comment or insult.

But grammars more typically assume many (often competing) layers of complexity. For example, Table 1 furnishes a sample scenario with more layers than responding to a simple compliment or insult. It is referenced later in the description of the three modeling tools. For discussion purposes here, response grammars manage current relevant emotional factors, including those that relate to an individual's own perceived vulnerabilities. In the Table 1 scenario, several affective strata or factors contribute to the whole. One factor may be guilt (and fear of being exposed in an unfavorable light): X knows that Y is at least partially right. This realization may add anti-social incentive to belittle or to delegitimize Y to minimize the effect of the attack - Y has become an identity threat to X for telling the truth as Y sees it, and in a way that might plausibly garner voters' attention, to the detriment of X. Another potential emotional layer is quite different: X takes true and heart-felt satisfaction in the social good that the extra spending will produce. And X also enjoys *selfish* satisfaction in believing that the vote will help keep her or him in office. The active response grammar must manage multiple, affectively intense and sharply contrasting layers, some of which (as in this example) are attached to guilt, animus, humane benevolence, and self-interest – an unsurprising mix of both prosocial and antisocial factors. In whatever way Y then replies, the exchange has amplified the acrimony between them, as well as between their respective followers. The resulting epistemic frames shifted, perhaps only slightly, but now they incorporate the emotionally charged exchange and the polarizing feelings the exchange engendered.

The underlying public policy issue – i.e., whether the value of the spending merits passing the bill – has legitimate tradeoffs that constitute the critical public policy issues, but the tradeoffs never seem to get evaluated properly. Instead, they come shrouded in antagonistic charges and exchanges that result in hard feelings, anger, and unwillingness to treat an opposition's voice as valid. If legitimate public policy discussion represents "signal," the signal to noise ratio in this example might rhetorically be as little as 10%, and even that 10% is contaminated by the ill-will of the 90% noise. In this scenario, any next step that includes distortions, misinformation, or disinformation in the exchanges is critically important. When an individual perceives themselves falsely attacked in any context of consequence, the individual is likely to experience outrage and will retaliate with whatever tools might be available. An accusation perceived to be false is one of a handful of message categories that provoke high valence negative emotions such as intense outrage or fear in the response grammar, dual emotions that can then be propagated back into the discussion, or left to simmer, or both. In the realm of social media, this can include increased acrimony, sarcasm, or discord – and a natural polarization and delegitimizing of the other party. When these emotionally-charged messages go back into the discourse, they activate new response grammars with intense, similarly negative, emotional valence.

Fig. 1. Five phases of a Discursive Transaction. A primary thesis of this framework is that emotion exaggeration and cognitive deprivation in Phases 3–4 lead to dysfunctional discourse. The Response Grammar involves the final four phases.

What is the merit in breaking down an imaginary political exchange – the kind that can take place regularly over social media -- and how is it relevant to QE research methods? The intent in decomposing this fictitious exchange and fitting it with terms such as epistemic frames, discursive transactions, response grammars, and high-valence activations is to create a language of investigation that lends itself to political discourse models that can help to clarify the pathologies of dysfunction.

The ascent of social media has complicated those pathologies. It has significantly intensified the flow and variety of polarizing inputs which perpetuate simmering anger, disgust, and other emotion-rich responses, especially responses with high-valence outrage activations. This arises from several factors. For example, contemporary social media trigger still poorly understood physiological mechanisms of screen fascination and addiction [11]. Compounding the effect of those mechanisms, humans have evolved a retaliatory instinct that makes it difficult to step away from perceived aggression, antagonisms, or insults levelled by others; this retaliation trait, often fueled by anonymity, readily plays into cultivating fomenting discord on social media screens. Furthermore, as noted earlier, monetized algorithms and public figures alike intrinsically intensify parallax by fragmenting and distorting information flows [8]. The algorithms incite new polarizing angers and resentment because doing so increases clicks, readership and revenue [7]. The polarization feeds itself and expands with highly enmeshed pathologies.

2 Three Modeling Tools

Applying discourse modeling tools such as those below to help make these complex pathologies more visible will not undo the pathologies. Such models, though, can contribute to a kind of **explanatory relief** that validates rancor and the collective distortion it induces but also supplies alternative, prosocial, and accurate ways to make sense of the intransigence we see in one another. Even explanatory relief is not a sufficient condition for undoing the pathologies either, but is a necessary one and it is foundational for moving beyond a season of angry and injurious stalemate.

2.1 Modeling Tool 1: Epistemic Network Analysis, with Extension

Earlier papers have proposed and demonstrated the application of epistemic network analysis (ENA) for investigating limited forms of socially-mediated political discourse [1, 2]. The formulation of a codebook for political discourse included worked examples that modeled selected political commentary threads in online US newspapers between 2020 and 2022. These models showed patterns of both (a) acrimonious and civil discourse in political commentary, and (b) ENA subtraction models to depict differences between threads. The papers also introduced earlier versions of the constructs (e.g., epistemic frames and response grammars) appearing in the paper's previous section.

Discussions included in these earlier papers contributed to interpretive loops around dysfunctional discourse, and building arguments that contemporary political discourse in social media shows minimal evidence of intellectual humility (defined as the willingness to change one's mind when confronted with new information or perspectives). In the language of ENA, intellectual humility denotes a willingness, or capacity to shift one's epistemic frame upon encountering affectively or epistemically persuasive factors that support such shifting. Misunderstanding both the importance of and the value of intellectual humility may prove one of the most influential variables in developing dysfunctional discourse repairs.

The previous papers also suggested that a fundamental epistemic fallacy is often at play in political discourse, the fallacy that two apparently contradictory interpretations of events cannot be valid simultaneously. In reality, perceived opposites can simultaneously have validity for many reasons, but the flawed logic, especially in social media threads, incorrectly concludes that a position contrary to that held by an individual must be untrue and subscribers to it are thus intellectually inferior or morally defective.

Acting upon an epistemically flawed premise that someone who holds a different point of view is intellectually deficient or morally defective mistakenly invites and incites indignation and scorn, further escalating polarization. It prevents productive discourse that actually explores, compares, and contrasts the factors that can lead to different conclusions, and thus potential evolution of our collective thinking.

Constructive, collective discourse is marked by productive problem-solving, social trust, and collaborative satisfaction. The reductive logic outlined in the previous paragraph primarily produces alienation, ill-will, and mistrust, all of which then become recycled into the next round of discursive transactions. Earlier work [1] examining discursive transactions highlighted not only a lack of intellectual humility, but a related, and even more pronounced lack of gratitude for the respective contributions of those from other political perspectives. The ambient implication of any conversational context involving political discussions devoid of gratitude is that those of differing perspectives merit no more than civility, if that, and that their discursive inputs do not contribute to societal well-being. Yet mutual gratitude, when authentic, is one of the most powerful adhesives in social trust formation [12], or in the well-being of family units [13]. ENA graphs that map hostile discourse did not only find a lack of connections involving gratitude for those of differing political perspectives, they simply found *no* instances of gratitude at all.

Table 2. Coding for Four Sample Utterances

Construct	A	B	C	Number of segments the utterance produces
Utterance 1	1	1	0	One (AB)
Utterance 2	1	0	1	One (AC)
Utterance 3	0	1	1	One (BC)
Utterance 4	1	1	1	Three (AB, AC, BC)

Despite the strength of these findings, using ENA to model epistemic frames and socially-mediated political discourse has limitations. One of the most notable is the relatively small number of variables that can realistically fit into an ENA graph [14]. This limitation is inherent to any model visualization, and to the mathematics of variable decomposition that are foundational to representing complex discursive phenomena (such as political epistemic frames and socially-mediated political discourse). The proposed modeling tools of CAS theory and ANNs in the following sections present compelling tradeoffs. While they do not produce the ENA's powerful visual models, they may effectively reflect other informative system dynamics across myriad variables.

The use of CAS theory and ANNs may also enhance modeling of one aspect to which ENA has already made a signal contribution to quantitative ethnographies: *relationships between constructs.* Among ENA's most compelling affordances is visualization of the intensity of relationships between construct nodes. ENA not only depicts the existence of a connection, but its intensity by way of edge saturation. Yet one seemingly inherent limitation is that ENA network graphs only depict *dyadic* connections – edges, by definition, only appear between two constructs. Interpretations must rely on a holistic view of the aggregate structure of all visualized connections between constructs, but the dyadic nature of each edge can obscure possible important information in the following way: each utterance can be considered an n-tuple of 0s and 1s, where n is the number of constructs coded for the graph. The graph can depict the existence of ordered pairs of activated constructs (i.e., coded with a 1) embedded in the n-tuple. The ENA graph only depicts coded pairs, because edges connect only two points.

This means, for example, that connections between three constructs A, B, and C, can (a) appear separately in three utterances, or (b) appear in as few as a single utterance. Depending on segmentation, Utterances 1–3 in Table 2 will yield the same graph as Utterance 4. All four utterances in the same segment yield the same connections as Utterances 1–3 repeated, i.e., constituting double edge saturation. Yet Utterances 1–3 have a story that could differ substantially from the story behind Utterance 4, with no difference in the visual model. This could be relevant in multiple disciplines in which dyadic occurrences differ sharply from triadic (or quartic) occurrences. One practical path to distinguish AB, AC, BC combinations from ABC combinations is the use of color coding for the triads or higher order n-tuples. If color is not available, visual offsets (such as Fig. 1) are also possible.

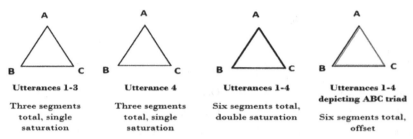

| Utterances 1-3 | Utterance 4 | Utterances 1-4 | Utterances 1-4 depicting ABC triad |
| Three segments total, single saturation | Three segments total, single saturation | Six segments total, double saturation | Six segments total, offset |

Fig. 2. Mapping Utterances from Table 1

What value might color-coding or visual offsets (such as the last triangle in Fig. 2) specific to 3-tuples (or n-tuples more generally) provide? Such techniques could identify the presence and intensity of co-occurrences of three or more constructs, and, similarly the absence of such combinations. Another possibility is to treat 3-tuples as connecting a set of nodes different from 2-tuples or ordered pairs (e.g., construct A is graphed as construct A ' if it appears in a 3-tuple or higher-level vector. Modifications of this type may extend the model's theoretical purchase in situations where ethnographies highlight not only co-occurrence of constructs, but distinctions in how the co-occurrences combine to change interpretations (e.g., where triadic or quartic connections require different interpretations than dyadic connections).

2.2   Modeling Tool 2: Complex Adaptive Systems (CAS) Theory

The second modeling tool involves complex adaptive systems (CAS) theory [15–17] as a means to analyze socially-mediated political discourse [18]. The theory and metaphors of CAS may provide a unique lens for understanding layers of dysfunctional discourse, and the self-propagating, downward spiral that dysfunctionality may induce. As the example in the Table 1 response grammar suggests, dysfunctional political discourse can be shaped less by the civic or social topics that are the focus of conversation, and more saliently by the social mediation of the conversation. To vary Marshall McLuhan's aphorism, the message becomes far less important than the medium.

In theory, and now quite likely in practice, social mediation of political conversation can become more prominent or salient than the putative topics of those conversations. The topics recede in importance or simply serve to seed escalating polarization before vanishing into the ensuing discordant communication. Giving the conversation and its rancor or other dynamics a higher priority than the underlying issues produces a reversal that not only obscures and prevents meaningful debate about central issues, but which currently seems structurally guaranteed to worsen if left unchecked. This reversal spawns in political conversation a matrix of natural signal suppression (a tendency to understate my weaknesses and my opponent's strengths) and amplification (a tendency to over-state my strengths and my opponent's weaknesses). It also can create opportunities for misrepresentation, misinformation, and outright disinformation.

This paper proposes to interpret political discourse as a CAS with certain definable and testable properties that can expose latent patterns that fuel dysfunction and therefore, merit broader recognition and scrutiny. The discussion positions classical CAS constructs (appearing in bold face below) in a discourse context in the following way: a **heterogenous population of autonomous agents** (individuals and political groups) in **dynamic, if intermittent engagement with one another** (in this context, through social media) in an **ecosystem defined by limited rule sets for agents' interaction** (including response grammars defined by individual epistemic frames, along with communication procedures defined by the medium), **feedback loops** (such as comment threads in social media and political developments and **self-modification of the overall system alongside discontinuous transitions** (e.g., new polarization, narratives, elections, or political events).

Every discursive transaction – that is, every instance of an incoming message, the cognitive appraisal and emotional reaction to it, and the response or feedback to it that ensues – modifies the complex system. Each discursive transaction encounters and modifies individual epistemic frames, and then introduces new feedback or encounters new responses into the complex system. These combine with responses that other individuals (agents) in the complex system then process through their own epistemic frames and response grammars, each in turn adding to the activity and polarizing evolution of the system. Using the constructs of response grammars, epistemic frames, and discursive transactions, a CAS interpretation may enable a realistic, microgenetic focus on the mechanics of polarization, and its ensuing escalation. CAS may incorporate emotion and cognitive appraisal theory as paramount tools for explaining dysfunctional patterns and examining how individuals contribute to increasing polarization, especially in accusatory or hostile discourse. A suggested explanation for the CAS interpretation employs the type of parallax of discerning an object in one location suggested by light refractions, when it is actually located elsewhere – as a metaphor to explain that both emotion and cognition are implicated in the misreading of and the responding to political discourse cues. The parallax mechanism distorts feedback loops in the complex system that continually escalate acrimonious dysfunction.

The paper argues that the cumulative effect of parallax-impaired feedback loops not only damages political conversation, but degrades it into a melee where each side (for example, left versus right) holds and expresses conviction that the other side poses obvious, existential risks to the nation. CAS theory helps explain why such convictions can become self-fulfilling: adaptive systems adjust and modify agents (humans and political factions) within the system in such a way as to make them more aligned with the system. The system's tendency toward conformity then causes people to trend into divergent polarities that (a) intensify misrepresentation, (b) create layers of misunderstanding, and (c) attenuate any ability to summon the collective wisdom required to face national shortcomings and crises. Finally, a CAS interpretation seeks to organize the nuanced, myriad factors inherent to political discourse into a novel, constructive, and holistic paradigm.

2.3 Modeling Tool 3: Artificial Neural Networks (ANNs)

Artificial neural networks (ANNs) mimic biological neural activity in ways that traditionally have helped to design pattern recognition systems and predictive algorithms [19]. They form the building blocks of the large language modeling (LLM) behind generative transformer model chat bots and future artificial general intelligence (AGI).

In contrast, the quite modest potential of ANNs in this paper's context involves modeling political discourse by conceptualizing an epistemic frame as a neural network, a network that can be represented with hundreds or thousands of nodes, each of which has a different weight and contribution to the other nodes, and to the overall epistemic frame. Components of the conceptualized epistemic frame can include: moral or ethical commitments, the enduring psychological effect of memorable experiences, acculturations, perceptions about political movements, knowledge (both accurate and inaccurate) about history and contemporary events, perspectives (wise or otherwise), and both emotional and cognitive dispositions. Each of these contributes to an overall, dynamic, epistemic frame that shifts, either slightly or substantially, with every discursive transaction, and with assimilation of new information that interactions with others entail.

Elements of a political perspective, or epistemic frame, are not intrinsically rational, or easy to describe. Financial or reputational self-interest, the ubiquitous human propensity to exert control over others, and threats to one's sense of identity, all contribute to an epistemic frame. ENA can model a relatively small number of nodes in an epistemic frame, with the general understanding that any single node can have a relationship with each of the other nodes. Use of neural networks to model epistemic frames maintains the same expectation, i.e., that each node (or neuron) might have a connection to every other neuron. The neural network interpretation can be tested with computer simulations that are theoretically more scalable than that of ENA simulations. The ENA graphing tool has the constraint of converting the model to a two-dimensional visual representation of nodes and edges. ANN modeling, however, accommodates thousands of neurons, or nodes, that connect with one another without requiring computational decomposition.

The value that might arise from informally cataloging the components that contribute to a political epistemic frame, and then treating them as heterogenous nodes (or neurons) in an artificial neural network model, is as follows. First, each node has a differential weighting, or prominence, in the frame. This feature of neural network theory corresponds to the universal tendency for political viewpoints to give higher prominence or priority to some issues over others. Theoretically, weightings may include cognitive or socio-affective commitments or dispositions, including variables associated with personal identity or security. Second, the nodes are interconnected, and can affect or shape one another. Third, the "learning" process associated with artificial neural network models entails multiple processing layers, yielding a new set of weights on each node, new weights that take form through processing response grammars and that result in a new epistemic frame.

In this interpretation, the epistemic frame constitutes the input architecture of a neural network model; a discursive transaction, operating under the rules of the response grammars, represents the learning or processing layers; the modified epistemic frame with different weightings for each of its nodes of neurons is the output. Note that the modified epistemic frame is only one result of the discursive transaction. A second, principal result is the actual response that the processing produces as the epistemic frame assimilates the message, and responds to it (i.e., the final phase of the discursive transaction in Fig. 1). That message then can activate new discursive transactions – i.e., the discourse or conversation continues (Fig. 3).

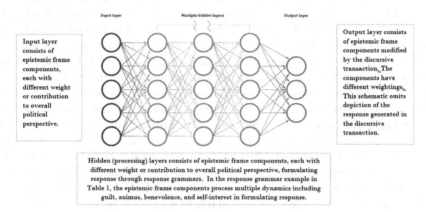

Input layer consists of epistemic frame components, each with different weight or contribution to overall political perspective.

Output layer consists of epistemic frame components modified by the discursive transaction. The components have different weightings. This schematic omits depiction of the response generated in the discursive transaction.

Hidden (processing) layers consists of epistemic frame components, each with different weight or contribution to overall political perspective, formulating response through response grammars. In the response grammar example in Table 1, the epistemic frame components process multiple dynamics including guilt, animus, benevolence, and self-interest in formulating response.

Fig. 3. Epistemic Frame Modification During Discursive Transaction – A Neural Network Interpretation image source: ibm.com/blog/ai-vs-machine-learning-vs-deep-learning-vs-neural-networks/

Discursive transactions that entail high-valence activations (such as those receiving false, but anger or rage-inducing accusations, reports of injustice or betrayal, or ominous news) can provoke learning layers that produce new weightings. New weightings that result from discourse with high-valence activations will likely result in new weightings with significantly stronger negative emotion towards and polarization away from the individuals and views that started the initial transactions. The re-weighted epistemic frame generates new messages that reflect – and induce – greater polarization.

Such a dynamic of self-fueling escalation of negative affect is at least one possible result of a neural network modeling approach. Testing such an approach initially would require analyzing sufficient data, both to structure an epistemic frame representation and to generate weightings for its nodes. The approach would need to detect shifts that discursive transactions, especially those with high-valence activations, would induce, followed by detection of the propagation shifts. Testing such a model empirically would likely prove prohibitive, but simulations could prove viable, with the goal of depicting whether the network produces inflection points, beyond which possible steps towards comity, compromise, gratitude towards others with differing views, or collaboration, become increasingly rare. Visual representation of those dynamics could depict the conjectured pathology of negative interactions that in turn feed increasingly negative interactions. Mapping this pathology is a critical aim of the modeling endeavor.

2.4 Why Building Blocks for a Science of Dysfunctional Political Discourse?

This paper relies heavily on the constructs of epistemic frames and response grammars to build a case for suggesting three tools to model dysfunctional political discourse.

The paper a) affirms the viability of ENA as a tool for modeling dysfunctional political discourse and suggests a dimensional enhancement (coloring selected n-tuples for n > 2) to display connections between nodes; b) maps ways that political discourse can be represented as a complex adaptive system (CAS); and c) suggests that neural networks can model microgenetic shifts in individual components and the total structure of an epistemic frame. Political discourse literature has already employed several quantitative modeling approaches [e.g., 4, 5], but none involve conceptual tools of epistemic frames or rule sets for political conversation. Epistemic frames and rule sets, however, are tools that lend themselves to (and require) a different level of theoretical traction. In doing so, they likely contribute to making the pathologies of dysfunctional discourse more visible. The epistemic frame construct represents a holistic network of myriad factors that comprise a political point of view. A response grammar identifies likely short-term ways that a political conversation shapes and is shaped by an epistemic frame. Each of the three proposed tools suggested in the paper offers different emphases for modeling these constructs, with the latter two of CAS and ANNs potentially able to model how discourse, with its dysfunctionalities unabated, can eventually become a self-fueling polarization spiral. Table 3 summarizes each of the three approaches in terms of affordances and tradeoffs, including reference to the critical role of response grammars in each.

2.5   Comparing and Contrasting the Three Tools: Summary Notes

Quantitative ethnography is often associated with the epistemic network graphing tool that co-evolved with the QE research community. While CAS and ANN do not seem to appear as modeling approaches in the QE literature, this paper suggests that they belong alongside ENA as a means to decompose a phenomenon quantitatively in order to augment our understanding of it. This paper suggests that the umbrella of quantitative ethnography should encompass what might be considered computational modeling, computational ethnography, or the application of more mathematized thinking, computational thinking, algorithms, and simulations of political discourse.

Terms such as quantitative ethnography reflect a powerful development in both academia and society more broadly, the realization that the constructs we apply to enable efficient organization of knowledge disciplines– chemistry, history, psychology, mathematics, etc. – may have great value in helping to generate knowledge, build universities, or make sense of the world. They are also inherently limiting, in the sense that there are few, if any, phenomena that do not reflect many disciplines. Terms such as multidisciplinary, interdisciplinary, or transdisciplinary reflect striving to decouple the knowledge-generating enterprise of understanding the world from the artificial boundaries of different disciplines [20] that have been an important conceptual device in building knowledge, but that are becoming increasingly outdated. Each modeling tool this paper relies on building blocks that are inherently heterogenous and consistent with interdisciplinary or transdisciplinary perspectives, including modeling that encompasses affective factors in addition to those traditionally referred to as epistemic.

Final Notes
The terminology of dysfunctional political discourse may tacitly convey the idea that political discourse has been functional, or at the very least less dysfunctional, in the

Table 3. Contrasting Three Tools for Modeling Dysfunctional Political Discourse

QE Tools →	Epistemic Network Analysis	Complex Adaptive Systems	Artificial Neural Networks
Description	• ENA models an individual's political perspective as an epistemic frame, emphasizing static or snapshot views of frames as ENA graphs.	• Political discourse is a definable, self-modifying CAS with properties not inherently related to underlying policy issues.	• "Learning" is a dynamic process of epistemic frame evolution through changing weightings on each node in the network.
Affordances	• Most straightforward tool for modeling empirical data. The underlying epistemic frame theory is applicable across all three tools. • Subtraction modeling highlights changes within individual or differences between groups.	• CAS approach partitions or separates discourse from the underlying issues that are the subject of discourse. • The self-modifying nature of CAS provides explanatory power for **collective** deterioration of discourse.	• Self-modifying nature of neural networks provides explanatory power for deterioration of discourse by **individual**. • Visual model depicts components of epistemic frame with weightings to emphasize components differentially.
Tradeoffs	• Difficult to model dynamic constructs such as discursive transactions. • Smaller number of nodes.	• Simulations are theoretically possible but visual CAS depictions are difficult.	• Difficult to model large number of nodes (epistemic frame elements) empirically.
Role of response grammars	• Furnish a probability rule-base for discourse that ENA models.	• Furnish a rule-base for system agents that can define simulations.	• Describes hidden layer interactions and activations of classical ANN theory.

past. This paper makes no such claim. Digital social media has helped produce and advance a chapter of global reckoning for profound systemic injustice and structural oppression. This represents immeasurable benefit to global society. But, like the worn comparison to the value and hazards faced upon the prehistoric discovery of fire, we again face tradeoffs – and those brought with the advent of social media are of extraordinary dimension.

It is almost impossible to imagine the benefits social media have brought, and are still likely to bring, to governance and its underlying political speech. It is, likewise, almost impossible to imagine the intense harm to humanity that social media can foster and inflict.

If the above comparison is apt, i.e., that extreme benefits and extreme hazards are possible, the solution path does not likely lie in reliance solely upon government or corporate shareholder regulatory mechanisms, but rather in building new practices and norms within the media realm. New practices and norms are not likely to reward any particular side in any political category, but that outcome, in itself, is not predictable. An overarching premise of this effort is that our forms of communication have so distorted not only our *perceptions* of others, but have distorted us as humans, both collectively and as individuals. In an improved realm where alienating communication, reactions, escalation, and mutual disgust give way to more salubrious, and attainable practices, how we view ourselves, and others, may no longer so closely resemble the fault lines and tribalism that define our contemporary political discourse. The aim of this paper is thus not ultimately simply to encourage civil conversation, nor to encourage compromise, nor to encourage more persuasive advocacy of perspectives. Its intention instead is to use discourse analysis to raise awareness that the present conditions of conversation are all wrong. We are at a point in history where the conditions of political conversation are severely damaging society collectively and its members individually, with social media acting as a rapid accelerant and key factor in that process. The paper thus seeks to contribute to conditions for resetting conditions of political conversation. That endeavor is neither as optional nor impossible as might be thought.

The modeling tools proposed in this paper, clarified and at full strength, may provide explanatory relief for why the polemics, advocacies, rhetoric, rage, and vilifications that fill our political web pages and that seem to tickle or please the like-minded are oddly ineffective in convincing or neutralizing others – and seem, instead, to intensify their resistance. The modeling tools are meant to clarify this pathology and to open up the idea that we have no idea of how much more effectively we would operationalize our moral commitments and perceive or interact with one another if the conditions of conversation were not so contaminated.

Initiatives are underway globally that seek to grapple with and change the conditions of conversation [7]. They are beyond the scope of this paper, and are of different flavors, methodologies, and political frameworks. They merit exploration and opportunities to flourish as the need to alter the dynamics of political discourse becomes recognized not as optional endeavor but as an existential requirement for maintaining free and fair democratic institutions and to recover from damage that has already been inflicted on them. That is an "emotional reset" [21] path that will ultimately entail shifts in the zeitgeist of political discourse in social media. Whether that reset occurs slowly or rapidly, peacefully or otherwise, is yet to be determined. The modeling tools proposed here, however, may help make clear that the current path is almost mathematically guaranteed to worsen until such a reset takes place.

References

1. Hamilton, E., Hobbs, W.: Epistemic frames and political discourse modeling. in advances in quantitative ethnography. ICQE 2021. Commun. Comput. Inf. Sci. **1312**. Springer, Cham (2021).https://doi.org/10.1007/978-3-030-67788-6_3
2. Hamilton, E., Hurford, A.: Political discourse modeling with epistemic network analysis and quantitative ethnography: rationale and examples. In: In Advances in Quantitative Ethnography: 4th International Conference, ICQE 2022, Copenhagen, Denmark, pp. 359–373. Springer, Cham, Switzerland (2023). https://doi.org/10.1007/978-3-031-31726-2_25
3. Anderson, A.A., et al.: Toxic talk: how online incivility can undermine perceptions of media. Int. J. Public Opin. Res. **30**(1), 156–168 (2018)
4. Leifeld, P.: Discourse network analysis. The Oxford handbook of political networks, pp. 301–326 (2017)
5. Ingram, M., Ingram, H., Lejano, R.: Environmental action in the Anthropocene: the power of narrative-networks. J. Environ. Planning Policy Manage. **21**(5), 492–503 (2019)
6. Takikawa, H., Sakamoto, T.: The moral–emotional foundations of political discourse: a comparative analysis of the speech records of the US and the Japanese legislatures. Qual. Quant. **54**, 547–566 (2020)
7. Hamilton, E.: Unpublished Catalog of US Depolarization Initiatives By URL (2023). http://bit.ly/depolarization-initiatives-2023
8. Lesh, R., Lester, F., Hjalmarson, M.: A models and modeling perspective on metacognitive functioning in everyday situations where problem solvers develop mathematical constructs. In: Lesh, R., Doerr, H.M. (eds.) Beyond constructivism: models and modeling perspectives on mathematics problem solving, learning, and teaching, pp. 383–403. Lawrence Erlbaum Associates, Mahwah, NJ (2003)

9. Phillips, M., et al.: Professional decision making: reframing teachers' work using epistemic frame theory. In: Advances in Quantitative Ethnography: Second International Conference, ICQE 2020, Malibu, CA, USA, 1–3 February 2021, Proceedings 2. Springer (2021). https://doi.org/10.1007/978-3-030-67788-6_18
10. Hamilton, E., Hobbs, W.: Epistemic frames and political discourse modeling. In: International Conference on Quantitative Ethnography (ICQE21). in review
11. Singh, R.: Perils of screen addiction. AKGEC Int. J. Technol. **13**, 40–44 (2022)
12. Zeng, Z.: The theories and effect of gratitude: a system review. J. Educ. Hum. Soc. Sci. **8**, 1158–1163 (2023)
13. You, S., Lee, J., Lee, Y.: Relationships between gratitude, social support, and prosocial and problem behaviors. Current Psychology, pp. 1–8 (2020)
14. Bowman, D., et al.: The mathematical foundations of epistemic network analysis. In: Advances in Quantitative Ethnography: Second International Conference, ICQE 2020, Malibu, CA, USA, 1–3 February 2021, Proceedings 2. Springer (2021). https://doi.org/10.1007/978-3-030-67788-6_7
15. Phelan, S.E.: What is complexity science, really? Emergence **3**(1), 120–136 (2001)
16. Sabelli, N.H.: Complexity, technology, science, and education. J. Learn. Sci. **15**(1), 5–9 (2006)
17. Hurford, A.: Complexity theories and theories of learning: Literature reviews and syntheses. In: Theories of mathematics education: Seeking new frontiers, pp. 567–589. Springer (2009)
18. Hamilton, E.: The Issue is not the Issue: a Complex Systems Approach to Political Discourse, in Annual Meeting of the American Political Science Association. Los Angeles, CA (2023)
19. Abiodun, O.I., et al.: Comprehensive review of artificial neural network applications to pattern recognition. IEEE Access **7**, 158820–158846 (2019)
20. Brodin, E.M., Avery, H.: Cross-disciplinary collaboration and scholarly independence in multidisciplinary learning environments at doctoral level and beyond. Minerva **58**(3), 409–433 (2020)
21. Zembylas, M.: Emotion and Traumatic Conflict: Reclaiming Healing in Education. Oxford University Press (2015)

Leveraging Epistemic Network Analysis (ENA) to Identify Focus Areas for Justice, Equity, Diversity and Inclusion (JEDI) Efforts in Museum Workplace Contexts

Danielle P. Espino[1]([✉]) [iD], Samuel Green[1], Bryan C. Keene[2], and Payten Werbowsky[3]

[1] Pepperdine University, Malibu, CA 90263, USA
danielle.espino@pepperdine.edu
[2] Riverside City College, Riverside, CA 92507, USA
bryan.keene@rcc.edu
[3] University of Wisconsin-Madison, Madison, WI 53706, USA

Abstract. The Change the Museum Instagram account launched in June 2020 to document instances of unchecked racism in US museums. When the posts are coded based on the prevailing identity categories of race, gender identity, sexual orientation, and positions of power, among other constructs, an Epistemic Network Analysis (ENA) model can be generated for each in order to visualize connections between individuals and the structural and systemic factors contributing to harmful work environments. The methodology of this study expands previous analyses of the first month and initial six months of posts by considering a full year of social media data. One goal in assessing this set of utterances is to contribute to policy change plans and decisions in this culture sector. Another aim is to demonstrate the shared, intersectional encounters with racism and other injustices as a roadmap for meaningful change.

Keywords: Museums · Workplace · Diversity · Racism · Microaggressions · Policy Change · Social Media

1 Introduction

Diversity, equity, inclusion, accessibility, anti-racism, and justice are aspirational pillars of mission, vision, and values across many public spheres in the United States, including the museum workplace. Abbreviations to signal such commitments vary, including DEAI, IDEA, or JEDI. Research and data have long shown that policies and practices that create an open, safe, and inclusive environment for employees from different backgrounds yields a more successful organization [1]. The concept of belonging or creating people-centered institutions further focuses these efforts on individuals. Such a lens considers the personal and communal relationships that people form during their work week or the feelings of welcome (or lack thereof) they experience in their job or while frequenting businesses or other public or online spaces.

G. Arastoopour Irgens and S. Knight (Eds.): ICQE 2023, CCIS 1895, pp. 290–303, 2023.
https://doi.org/10.1007/978-3-031-47014-1_20

The year 2020 was a watershed moment in these efforts with the combined factors of racism and injustice seen at the onset of the lockdowns associated with the Covid-19 pandemic and the murder of George Floyd and multiple other Black Americans. Examples of public outrage and calls for accountability of institutions and leaders increased exponentially online. There is a growing rise of discontent among those who examine the world through social media for the lack of accountability for organizations to make significant change to policies beyond performative allyship [2, 3]. Despite social media campaigns and other acts of proclaimed solidarity, there remains a level of stagnation to make institutional policy change thereby perpetuating discrimination in the workplace. Unfortunately, the evidence of this slow progress comes from the voices of marginalized groups who are impacted the most by bias, prejudice, and discrimination—people of color, women, and other historically underrepresented or under supported populations in the workplace. The challenge to implement change within organizations can be difficult if the clarion call is not led from (white) senior leadership or worse when it is perpetuated by them.

Museum staff have been at the forefront of calls for change. As repositories of cultural memory and hope, museums hold the responsibility to foster inclusion in society [4]. But the museum workplace has faced ongoing issues in the integration of inclusion practices. The American Alliance of Museums (formerly the American Association of Museums) has long been a leader in publishing studies about visitor experiences and workplace culture—since the 1980s and 1990s in fact. A report published in 2018 found that efforts towards inclusion had been in conversation for nearly 25 years, with the same recommendations shared over and over again, posing the question: why has there not been more change [5]?

The present study deepens an investigation of the Change the Museum (@changethemuseum) Instagram account, founded in June 2020 to record instances of unchecked racism in museums. The analysis addresses the ways in which individuals self-identify when experiencing racism or how they describe their witness of injustices in museum settings. These personal and observed accounts reveal relationships between workplace intersectionality (the multiple, interrelated identities of lived experiences with prejudice) and hierarchy, as senior leadership, management, and other positions of power often emerge as sources of ignorance, microaggressions, and bias.

This paper builds upon a previous analysis of Change the Museum posts [6, 7] by looking at a full year of data, from June 2020 – June 2021. The depth of experiences shared in these posts warrants examination from multiple angles in order to better understand the nuance of similarities and unique challenges faced by historically marginalized groups. The aim is to highlight how accounts such as these provide a roadmap for change. In a previous study examining the initial six months of posts, an overall summary of trends over time yielded insight into how highlighted concerns evolved each month and coincided with events taking place in society and in the field. Towards the end of that study, an examination of all posts that reported experiences of Black, Indigenous, People of Color (BIPOC) allowed authors to identify trends in the metadata for such posts. This paper further utilizes individual identity categories, notably ones that identify specific groups by race, gender, sexuality, and more to better reveal the issues that are relevant to each and where the related points of tension lie within the institution. This examination can provide insight to more specific action steps that might otherwise be lost when generalizing needs across all marginalized groups.

2 Methods

The study examined one full year of entries on the Change the Museum Instagram account (June 2020 – June 2021), which covers the most active period of posts. During the first year, the account shared a total of 641 posts. A breakdown by month seen below in Table 1. Submissions are anonymously sent by museum staff to the Change the Museum Instagram account, whose owners are also anonymous. Posts are not required to have formal attribution in order to protect the submitter, however certain institutions, locations, or individuals in leadership roles are often identified in the content of the post. The date posted was used initially to organize a review of the data. The text from each post was transcribed, and a codebook was developed through a carefully iterative process that was outlined in previous work [7]. With the additional 6 months of data included for this paper, it was determined that the existing codebook could still be applied without additional codes. While the full list of constructs appears in the previous paper [7], the list in Table 2 only includes the constructs most relevant to the results of this particular study.

Each post comprised multiple constructs, in order to capture the richness of the content as thoroughly as possible. The first 6 months (June 2020 – December 2020) were originally coded in the previous work, so the remaining 6 months (January 2021 – June 2021) were coded independently for the presence of each construct by two researchers. Agreement on the final binary coding for the posts was determined through a process of social moderation [8].

Table 1. Number of posts by month.

Month	Number of posts	Month	Number of posts
June 2020	30	January 2021	32
July 2020	171	February 2021	31
August 2020	86	March 2021	39
September 2020	61	April 2021	32
October 2020	50	May 2021	18
November 2020	42	June 2021	22
December 2020	27	Total	641

Once the binary coding process was complete, epistemic network analysis (ENA) was used to model the connections between the constructs in the data [9]. Each post was both the unit of analysis and the conversations in which connections were limited. In order to enhance visibility of the most salient connections, a minimum edge weight of .02 and .03 and scaling to 2.3 were applied.

Table 2. Codebook of constructs included in analysis.

Construct	Definition
Male	Directed toward or involves a person/people who are/identified as male
Female	Directed toward or involves a person/people who are/identified as female
LGBTQIA2 +	Lesbian, gay, bisexual, transgender, queer, intersex, asexual (sometimes ally), two-spirit, and other gender non-conforming identities or expressions of sexual couplings
Latinx	Directed toward or involves a person/people who are/identified as Latinx (Latino/a/e/x)
Black	Directed toward or involves a person/people who are/identified as Black
White	Directed toward or involves a person/people who are/identified as White
AAPI	Directed toward or involves a person/people who are/identified as Asian American or Pacific Islander
BIPOC	Directed toward or involves a person/people who are/identified as BIPOC (Black, Indigenous, People of Color), Indigenous/Native American, Brown, non-white, Bi-racial, or unclear intent but historically marginalized group
Donor, Board Member	Referring to donors, board members, VIPs, stakeholders
Senior (Leadership)	Referring to senior level of leadership, including President, VPs, Directors, "higher-ups," and Chief (C)-suite staff
Department Head, Supervisor	Referring to department heads, supervisors, managers, chief curators
Peers, Colleagues	Referring to peers, colleagues, curators
Front Facing	Referring to any front-of-house staff, security, visitor services, custodial, minimum-wage or entry-level position
Collections	Permanent collection, exhibitions, bilingual labeling, acquisitions, provenance, funding or money towards collection
Community	Community, neighborhood, city, region, or visitors
Harassment	Experience of detrimental physical or verbal harassment, includes exploitation, gaslighting, and anything warranting HR intervention
Inaction	No response or action after an incident has been reported or requested
Employment and Wages	Hiring, advancement, recruitment, wage disparity, internships, fellowships, contractors, limited-term staff, career advancement, COVID-19 conditions of employment, unionizing, diversity hires
Microaggression	Commonplace daily verbal, behavioral or environmental slights, whether intentional or unintentional, that communicate hostile, derogatory, or negative attitudes toward stigmatized or culturally marginalized groups; unconscious bias, has some understanding and can include discrimination
Ignorance	Explicit or intentional ignorance on an issue; explicit lack of care/empathy of issue; explicit lack of experience with an issue
Intent for Plan	Intent for IDEA plan/committee etc., but not necessarily follow through; also, the conducting of related IDEA training

ENA models are typically used to compare patterns of discourse between groups or to track changes over time in a way that allows the researcher to speak to statistical differences of those comparisons. For this study, the researchers are less concerned with identifying statistically significant differences than examining key patterns between constructs. Coded constructs that identified a historically marginalized group (including

BIPOC, AAPI, Black, Latinx, Female, and LGBTQIA2 +) were used as metadata to generate a separate ENA model. Since the presence of the construct was utilized as a unit for the model, it was not included as a code in the final model. With each model not having one of the codes included, the placement of the constructs are shifted for each model which does not allow for comparison across models. As mentioned, the intent for the study is the patterns themselves, rather than the ability to make statistically relevant comparisons.

3 Results

The ENA network models generated by using certain coded constructs as metadata are seen below. The dots (nodes) indicate the constructs included in the model, and the lines (edges) indicate the connections between constructs. The thicker the line, the stronger the connection between the constructs, and the opposite is true for thinner lines, which indicate weaker connections between constructs. While all codes (except for the construct code used as metadata) were included in the models, a minimum edge weight was applied and unconnected codes not shown, in order to better identify the strongest and most salient connections and constructs within that model. Because each model had one construct not included, the positioning of the nodes shift, and each model will be described separately.

3.1 Models of Constructs

BIPOC.   The overall model for posts that were coded for BIPOC is seen in Fig. 1. The strongest connections in the network models for posts coded for BIPOC (260 posts) were to White and other constructs, such as Ignorance, Microaggressions, Employment, Peers, Senior, Dept Heads, and Female; also strong were connections between Peers with Microaggressions, and Ignorance with Senior and Peers. There are strong associations unique to BIPOC-coded posts, including connections to Ignorance (such as with Exhibitions, Employment, Microaggressions, Senior) and Employment (Ignorance, Female, Front Facing). Posts connected to Ignorance tended to emphasize challenges with the intention of exhibitions, to the detriment of minorities, for example:

> *At the museum where I used to work, we were about to have a large-scale exhibition in our main gallery space by a Black artist who was commenting on gun violence against Black people in his work. Before the exhibition opened, we (the Education department, which was one of the only departments with a BIPOC) wanted to hire a facilitator to lead a museum-wide training. When we brought up this idea to the deputy director, he just said it was our "white guilt" talking and no one needs training to talk about race, racism, etc. The exhibition went on view with no front-line staff having any training (beyond the Education department), very little contextual information in the galleries, and no support for anyone who may have actually been affected by gun violence.*

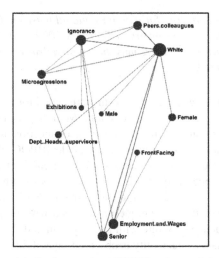

Fig. 1. ENA network models for the construct BIPOC, using a minimum edge weight of .03.

AAPI. Microaggressions ground the plot for posts that reference AAPI in Fig. 2, with the strongest connections to Peers/Colleagues, Senior, Ignorance, and White. On the left side of the model, there is a presence of Inaction, Employment and Wages, and Department Heads/Supervisors. Peers/Colleagues and Senior are on the edges of the network on opposite sides, with strong connections to other constructs. Also noted is the inclusion of Donors/Board Members and their association with Ignorance, Peers/Colleagues include connections to White, Ignorance, and Microaggressions. Senior is solely connected to Ignorance and Microaggressions, which could be interpreted as ignorance around microaggressions committed by people in positions of power against AAPI employees, as outlined in this example:

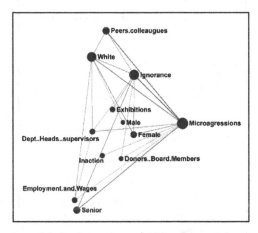

Fig. 2. ENA network models for the construct AAPI, using a minimum edge weight of .03.

I'm of Asian descent and work for a major regional museum. I had a 1:1 meeting with one of the senior staff members in February 2020, and she cut our meeting short and then remarked that there must be "coronavirus all over" the laptop she was using to write notes.

Black.   In examining the network for posts that are coded for Black (132 lines) seen in Fig. 3, the strongest connections involve White, Microaggressions, Employment and Wages, Senior, and Ignorance. The other strong connection is between Peers with Microaggressions. Other unique connections include BIPOC with Ignorance, White with both Department Heads and Female, and also Intent for Plan with Inaction, and Exhibitions with Ignorance. The prominent connections of White with Microaggressions, Senior, and Ignorance are common with other identity related constructs that were examined, however there is unique prominence with Employment and Wages, indicating that the influence of White with Employment and Wages is more prominent in posts that include Black. This reality is observed several times in the dataset:

I was part of the team that was looking to hire an education manager. A perfect candidate came in. She was black and a woman. The director and lead curator said "she will cause too many social and ethnic problems", so she was not hired. The job went to the white female curator who is now in charge of curation and education. This was in early 2020.

I work at the La Brea Tar Pits Museum in Los Angeles. Several years ago a management position for FOH staff became available. A Black staff member applied for the position. He was recommended by the exiting manager, had informally been working in a management capacity, was highly respected by his colleagues, and was a longtime staff member. Instead, the museum hired the white younger sister of another manager. She had been working at the museum for under a year.

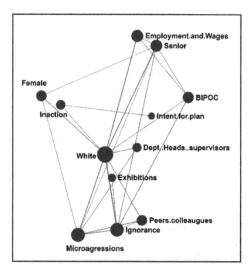

Fig. 3. ENA network models for the construct Black, using a minimum edge weight of .03.

Additionally, connections between Intent for Plan with Inaction occur more consistently in posts that include Black, as it highlights the appearance of wanting to create change for the institution, but falls short in practice. The other unique connection of Exhibitions with Ignorance highlights instances when exhibitions attempt to be inclusive, but are unaware of the contradiction they create, as seen in the example post:

> *One overhears a lot as a "white" person in a room of other white people who assume that everyone shares the same racial/ethnic identification and politics. I once witnessed a chief curator — one famous for showing and "supporting" Black artists; one who presents himself as an ally — suggest that another curator "just add one Black guy" to a show in order to make the exhibition "pass" as politically correct.*

Latinx. As seen in the ENA network model in Fig. 4, most prominent connections for posts related to Latinx were tied to Microaggressions from Peers and Colleagues, as well as Ignorance, White, Department Heads and Supervisors, Senior, Employment and Wages, and others. The other main connections for Latinx were to White and Ignorance. This occurrence is similar to other identity codes, although there is a distinct cluster of Ignorance, Department Head and Supervisor, Exhibitions, Community, and Microaggression. This cluster describes the ignorance Latinx museum employees faced from supervisors regarding exhibitions and community. This narrative is described many times by respondents:

> *When I was an intern at Museum of Fine Arts, Houston, the director was announcing recent acquisitions at an all staff meeting. And he stumbled while reading the name of an ancient Mexican maize God, so he laughed and said, "whatever, this is our new enchilada goddess."*
>
> *As a Latinx POC woman at SFMOMA, I was cleaning a shelf within my department. A white male manager from a different department walked up to me and asked me to clean his office next. I've never felt comfortable coming forward to my managers about it and do not feel comfortable especially around that individual.*

Female. The network model for posts that included the construct Female is seen in Fig. 5, which revealed the most significant connections focused on White to Employment/Wages, BIPOC, Microaggressions, Senior, and Ignorance. Conversely, the Exhibitions construct was not prominent enough to be included in the model at the minimum edge weight of .03, indicating this to not be a prominently connected construct compared to other models for BIPOC, AAPI, Black, and Latinx. Interestingly, there seems to be a differences highlighted in the experience of white females, even by white females, as illustrated in.

LGBTQIA2 +. While there were only a limited number of posts that included LGBTQIA2 + as a construct, in a study examining models based on marginalized groups, the researchers felt it necessary to include an examination of a model for LGBTQIA2 +, which is seen in Fig. 6. A lesser number of codes, which were generally less present in the

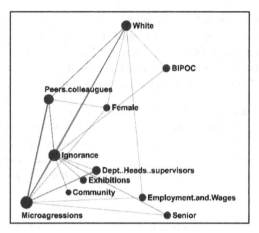

Fig. 4. ENA network models for the construct Latinx, using a minimum edge weight of .03.

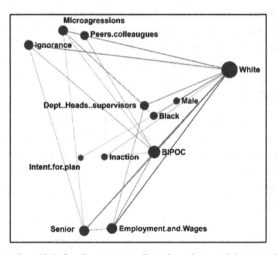

Fig. 5. ENA network models for the construct Female, using a minimum edge weight of .03.

posts including this construct, were included in the model in order to better understand where relevant connections formed with the more prevalent constructs.

The most prominent connections we see are connected to Senior, with connections to BIPOC, Ignorance, Microaggressions, Female, Employment and Wages, as well as others. Other prominent codes include Employment and Wages, Female, and Ignorance. These connections convey the idea that LGBTQIA2 + employees face ignorance and microaggressions from other employees, primarily those in senior positions. They are especially directed at BIPOC employees who identify as LGBTQIA2 +, as expressed in the data:

> *The former AVP of Education and Access terrorized staff the entire six-ish years*
> *he was on staff—his anger and work thievery was especially palpable for women,*

LGBT+, and POC staff, who he constantly belittled, often publicly. When brought to HR and the CEO's attention, he consistently received slaps on the wrist and excuses as to why he couldn't be reprimanded more harshly. When he was finally fired due to messing up a relationship with a significant donor and content partner, we had already lost significant great staff members who couldn't take it anymore. The saddest part is that none of us received any kind of remorse or apology from the CEO, who never took responsibility nor accountability for hiring and protecting a terrible hire over long term and high performing staff.

Over 10 years ago I was asked to organize a series of arts programs in the predominantly POC areas of Oklahoma as part of a new fully funded tourism project. I offered the names of several Black and Native American artists to head the programs instead of me (a white gay person). They said "no, we want you to do it because you're white." I declined again and offered more names of artists who were also POC. They said that the funding had been reduced unless I did it with white staff. I quit. They made antigay slurs at me as I headed for the door. Shortly after that I moved 2000 miles away from Oklahoma.

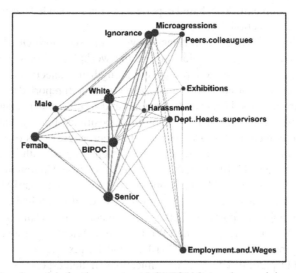

Fig. 6. ENA network models for the construct LGBTQIA2 +, using a minimum edge weight of .03.

4   Discussion

The benefit of this study is the ability to examine specific constructs and their connections by identity groups that constitute historically underserved communities and protected classes within museums. From the first QE study on Change the Museum, the researchers were asked to disaggregate the data in order to better show the fullest possible range of staff who have experienced racism in museums and to uncover the structures that perpetuate this harm through an epistemic network analysis. Examining constructs as metadata has revealed those shared and unique connections across the various different codes, an approach that reveals opportunities for measurable and meaningful action-based change in museums. By focusing on those recurring connections across the different models, we highlight the shared experiences of structural inequities. A look at the unique or less frequently occurring codes provides specific focus on the experiences, hopes, aspirations, and expectations of individual groups, effectively providing a roadmap for institutions committed to making change community by community.

Consider one example. When the model for Female is examined together with the categories of Black, Latinx, AAPI, and LGBTQIA2 +, we see clearly the intersectional relationships between the different identities that museum staff bring to work alongside the sources of microaggressions and harm that perpetuate racist environments and ultimately lead to turn over, specifically senior leadership, management, and others in positions of power. This approach intentionally moves beyond the types of metrics typically gathered by institutions, namely those focused on quantifying diversity through statistics presented by identity category. Such datasets may highlight salient identities, on the one hand, or quantify diversity as a check box, on the other, but may also risk overlooking the complexities of shared experiences or compounded harm inherent to the reality of living intersectional lives.

By disaggregating BIPOC as a category, we could see more clearly the concerns that individual communities of color face in the workplace. Microaggressions were experienced by each group, for example, but the strength of connections and placement or pull within the network varied: AAPI, Black, and Latinx staff reported microaggressions and ignorance from White Peers and Colleagues and from Senior managers, the last of which most often involves women in subordinate positions. Each group also shared a concern for employment and wages linked to the Microaggressions by the hierarchical category of Senior. The (lack of an) intent for a plan coupled with inaction appeared most clearly in accounts by Black staff, while Ignorance from Community, Exhibitions, and Department Heads affected Latinx workers, and Donors and Board Members played a role in the Ignorance and Microaggressions felt by AAPI individuals.

After coding a year of posts, we anticipated the codes that would occur most often in the different models. These included White, Senior, Microaggressions, and Male or Female forming networks with BIPOC (Black and Latinx specifically), Employment and Wages, and Departure. The types of connections matter, especially when reviewing individual posts, such as the examples provided above. Statistical data about museum leadership reveals that the majority of directors are white men, a reality also reflected in the Change the Museum data. The AAPI model was the most unique in the dispersal of codes and establishment of networks. A cluster of Male and Female around White, taken together with other utterances, demonstrates the dual work that Female undertakes here: Posts by Asian women often involved Microaggressions by Male colleagues, specifically White and Senior. Asian Female staff experiences associated these Microaggressions and Ignorance with concerns about Employment and Wages.

Across each of the models, a few codes appeared less frequently but are still important factors to address when advocating for change in museums. These include Hurt, Intent for

Plan, Resilience, and Call for Change. These codes express emotional care for museums or trauma from these spaces in ways that expand experiences of or feelings about racism and injustices in these sectors of culture and heritage. Additionally, the model for Black featured BIPOC as a pertinent code with various networks emerging that included White, Senior, Employment and Wages, and Ignorance. These connections suggest an expanded sense of community with other colleagues of color and similar experiences of racism from those in positions of power in ways that affect aspects of employment. In short, examining codes as metadata is a useful tool in both disaggregating large datasets and in modeling networks of intersectional relationships.

4.1 Future Opportunities

One action step from this study is to examine museum DEAI plans with ENA. As of 2020, only 16% of museums have a public DEAI statement, despite the fact that 90% state these priorities [10]. Numerous institutions issued statements in support of diversity and began gesturing toward a desire to create more inclusive environments beginning after the murder of George Floyd and a multitude of Black individuals in 2020 alone. Thus far we have begun discussing the statements and plans of institutions that have featured on the Change the Museum Instagram account: Cleveland Museum of Art; Getty Museum; The Solomon R. Guggenheim Museum and Foundation; Holland Museum; The Huntington Library, Art Museum, and Botanical Gardens; The Metropolitan Museum of Art; Minneapolis Institute of Art; The Morgan Library & Museum; National Gallery of Art; The Walters Art Museum.

   On July 1, 2020, the Association of Art Museum Curators (AAMC) hosted the webinar, "Beyond Statements: Taking Action," which focused on policy-based changes to dismantle the structural racism in museums [11]. In another venue, Americans for the Arts invited Angelique Power, president of the Field Foundation, to speak on equity. In her remarks, she stated, "Equity as a statement, an accessory, rather than a word that actually should create fear, is being used right now as a badge. And that is the death of the term 'equity [12].'" Three years later, the AAMC hosts, "Beyond Statements Revisited," a three-part program that will determine the types of changes that have been made and where institutions are at present [13]. The first session picks up from the 2020 webinar to address the advances or setbacks in DEAI efforts. The second considers belonging as part of the move toward inclusive workplaces (abbreviated DEAIB), with an acknowledgement of the burden placed on the individuals who lead these initiatives. The final session considers the studies, surveys, and analyses published on these topics in the field of museum studies. Each of the Change the Museum studies has been shared with the AAMC leadership in the hope that they will be considered by the curatorial spheres working in museums today.

   A brief survey of the state of museum DEAI or JEDI work suggests different paths forward. The Wellcome Institute, for example, provides a model for transparency in anti-racist work in cultural institutions. Their 2022 public study, "Evaluation of Wellcome Anti-Racism Programme Final Evaluation Report – Public," outlines the institution's goal of eradicating racism in its internal and external work, notes the limited progress made, and acknowledges the continues harm toward Black individuals and to people of color [14]. The report goes so far as to admit that the Wellcome has failed to meet its commitment and that it has allowed institutional racism to fester through both action and inaction. The American Alliance of Museums, by contrast, establishes DEAI momentum as part of their 2022–2025 strategic framework [15]. Their plan describes continuing to "engage partners, allies, and experts to champion an anti-racism movement across the museum field, catalyzing and supporting changemakers in museums and efforts to create more equitable outcomes in all aspects of their structures and programming" (pg. 9). While these sentiments are admirable, the actual implementation of such work is to be determined. The strategies are quite broad, including developing the five-year plan with a focus on intersectionality and equity, embedding DEAI into programs, benchmarking DEAI skills and resources, and celebrating and supporting professionals of color. In the case of both the Wellcome Institute and the AAM strategic plan, a focus on financials and the economic impact of DEAI or JEDI work is key. Both recommend or reveal the importance of contributing financial resources toward such work and to addressing the economic barriers already faced by people of color in the culture sector.

This study raises hypothetical questions about the economic impact of making change in museums and about advocating for policy changes that leadership and staff can commit to together. The Smithsonian Institution, for example, constitutes 19 museums – the largest museum network in the world. Of the individual properties devoted to a specific cultural group, the National Museum of African American History and Culture remains the most highly visited museum with an average of 1.2 million visitors, with another 1.1 million visitors to the American Art Museum. The latter museum featured on Change the Museum in a post highlighting the ways the institution responded to public criticism on social media over a post about Pocahontas. At the time of writing, there is an installation about Matoaka, also known as Pocahontas, with a dozen contextualizing objects that add an Indigenous-centered narrative to her story and legacy.

The digital turn in museums toward online virtual or hybrid programming, events, and collection presentations is another arena for demonstrating a commitment to DEAI or JEDI efforts, with a particular focus on accessibility. It is important to be conscious of the fact that equity in the digital sphere may or may not always reflect equity efforts on the ground in the galleries or in staffing situations. Mark Osterman notes that, "Museums that invest in removing barriers and expanding programs and missions can potentially increase avenues of revenue streams from digital programs. Redefining how museums serve their communities will help them continue to attract the necessary revenue, support, and funding needed to stay operational [16]."

Cultural spaces, such as museums, are much like dark forests—alluring and providing a sense of wonder to explore. There are also challenges to unpack, and in the effort to promote JEDI efforts, it can be easy to get caught in the underlying issues. But in this pursuit, there are opportunities for resilience, growth and change—which is the hope which motivates ongoing efforts much needed to see the possibility of an inclusive future in museum settings [17].

References

1. Stevens, F.G., Plaut, V.C., Sanchez-Burks, J.: Unlocking the benefits of diversity: all-inclusive multiculturalism and positive organizational change. J. Appl. Behav. Sci. **44**(1), 116–133 (2008)

2. Ekpe, L., Toutant, S.: Moving beyond performative allyship: a conceptual framework for anti-racist co-conspirators. In: Developing Anti-Racist Practices in the Helping Professions: Inclusive Theory, Pedagogy, and Application, pp. 67–91. Springer International Publishing, Cham (2022). https://doi.org/10.1007/978-3-030-95451-2_5

3. Wellman, M.L.: Black squares for Black lives? Performative allyship as credibility maintenance for social media influencers on Instagram. Soc. Media+ Soc. **8**(1), 20563051221080473 (2022)

4. American Alliance of Museums. Excellence and Equity: Education and the Public Dimension of Museums. (1992; 2008 revised edition). http://ww2.aam-us.org/docs/default-source/resource-library/excellence-and-equity.pdf

5. American Alliance of Museums. Facing Change: Insights from the American Alliance of Museums' Diversity, Equity, Accessibility, and Inclusion Working Group. (2018). https://www.aam-us.org/wp-content/uploads/2018/04/AAM-DEAI-Working-Group-Full-Report-2018.pdf

6. Espino, D.P., Keene, B.C.: Change the museum: initial analysis of social media posts reflecting on museum workplace experiences. In: ICQE21 Supplement, pp. 88–91 (2021)

7. Espino, D.P., Keene, B.C., Werbowsky, P.: Change the museum: examining social media posts on museum workplace experiences to support justice, equity, diversity and inclusion (JEDI) efforts. In: Damşa, C., Barany, A. (eds.) Advances in Quantitative Ethnography. ICQE 2022. Communications in Computer and Information Science, vol. 1785. Springer, Cham (2023). https://doi.org/10.1007/978-3-031-31726-2_23

8. Herrenkohl, L.R., Cornelius, L.: Investigating elementary students' scientific and historical argumentation. J. Learn. Sci. **22**(3), 413–461 (2013)

9. Shaffer, D.W.: Quantitative Ethnography. Cathart Press, Madison, WI (2017)

10. Garibay, C., Olson, J.M.: CCLI National Landscape Study: The State of DEAI Practices in Museums (2020). https://www.informalscience.org/sites/default/files/CCLI_National_Landscape_Study-DEAI_Practices_in_Museums_2020.pdf

11. The program featured the following curators: Sepake Angiama, artistic director of Iniva; Monica O. Montgomery, cultural consultant at Museum Hue; Sandra Shakespeare, museum and heritage consultant; and Sara Wajid, head of museum engagement, Museum of London and founding member of Museum Detox. Association of Art Museum Curators, "Beyond Statements: Taking Action," 1 July 2020. https://www.artcurators.org/page/beyondstatementstakingaction

12. Power, A.: "The Death of 'Equity'," Americans for the Arts (2020). https://www.youtube.com/watch?v=zhrklB9pFno

13. Association of Art Museum Curators, "Beyond Statements Revisited," 14, 21, and 28 June 2023. https://www.artcurators.org/page/BeyondStatementsRevisited

14. Evaluation of Wellcome Anti-Racism Programme Final Evaluation Report – Public (2022). https://cms.wellcome.org/sites/default/files/2022-08/Evaluation-of-Wellcome-Anti-Racism-Programme-Final-Evaluation-Report-2022.pdf

15. American Alliance of Museums (2021). 2022–2025 Strategic Framework. Retrieved from https://cms.wellcome.org/sites/default/files/2022-08/Evaluation-of-Wellcome-Anti-Racism-Programme-Final-Evaluation-Report-2022.pdf

16. Osterman, M.: Digital decisions to evolve, change, and adapt. In: Porter, J., Cunningham, M.K. (eds.), Museum Education for Today's Audiences: Meeting Expectations with New Models, (AAM, 2022), pp. 61–73 (2022)

17. Anderson, S.: On the importance of possibility and hope in Museum Studies. Medium (2022). https://medium.com/@NAEAMuseEd/on-the-importance-of-possibility-and-hope-in-museum-studies-9d430a32f5ea

Envisioning Latinx Narratives: Exploring Mexican and Honduran Immigrant Perspectives Using Epistemic Networks by Geospatial Location

Stephanie Rivera-Kumar$^{(\boxtimes)}$ (ID), Andres Zambrano (ID), and Amanda Barany (ID)

University of Pennsylvania, Philadelphia, PA 19104, USA
{sriverak,azamb13}@upenn.edu, amb595@drexel.edu

Abstract. This study delves into the expected demographic shift in the U.S., where Latinx immigrants are projected to comprise 29% of the total population by 2050, focusing on their economic and social influences in South Philadelphia, especially in the Italian Market area, a notable destination for various immigrant groups. Utilizing a blend of ethnographic semi-structured interviews with Latinx participants involved in entrepreneurial activities or working in the food and factory industries, the study probes their self-perceived impacts on this locale. The research employs a mix of geographic information system mapping and other spatial analyses, augmented by epistemic network analysis, to visually represent the nuanced relationships and experiences of these immigrants, surpassing the limitations of conventional mapping techniques. The investigation seeks to shed light on the various ways Latinx immigrants, primarily from Mexico and Northern Central America, shape the vitality of Philadelphia through their spatial, network, social, and economic engagements. The pivotal question this research seeks to answer is: How do Latinx immigrants express their contributions to the vibrancy of Philadelphia as a host community?

Keywords: Immigration · Urban Planning · Transnationalism · Epistemic Network Analysis · Geographic Information Systems

1 Introduction

By 2050, the Latinx population will reach 128 million, or 29 percent of the U.S. population, with "new immigrants and their descendants" accounting for seventy-four percent of the projected growth, which will eclipse the White population [1] Mexican immigrants, along with Northern Central American immigrants, are the largest immigrant group in the 21st century to inhabit Philadelphia [2]. The impacts of these demographic changes can be understood through an examination of the physical presence and the economic development Latinx immigrants generate in South Philadelphia, specifically around the Italian Market. This neighborhood serves as the designated location due to its high Latinx population, and it has historically served as a receiving community for immigrants of various nationalities [3]. In urban planning, a map can display the geographical

G. Arastoopour Irgens and S. Knight (Eds.): ICQE 2023, CCIS 1895, pp. 304–315, 2023.
https://doi.org/10.1007/978-3-031-47014-1_21

positions of participants within a city, but it falls short of expressing the significant links and relationships that are crucial in representing the real-life experiences of immigrants. To address this need, this project consists of ethnographic semi-structured interviews with Latinx immigrants residing in or with connections to South Philadelphia who work as entrepreneurs in the food industry or factory workers. By combining ethnographic interviews with epistemic network analysis, a geographic information system, and other spatial analyses, this study explores the network, spatial, social, and economic impacts of Latinx-driven economic development and population growth in South Philadelphia. In summary, this project seeks to answer the following research question: How do Latinx immigrants describe their actions and impacts on the vitality of Philadelphia, PA, as a receiving community?

2 Relevant Literature

Urban planning is a critical field that examines various aspects of our societal fabric, including migration and Latinx communities, entrepreneurship, community, and ethnicity [4]. Its expansive nature is evident in the wide range of topics it typically studies. For instance, research on Latinx communities often explores the relationships between migration patterns and urban development, as well as the influence of these patterns on local economies, receiving communities [5], which are the immigrants' destinations, and entrepreneurship [6]. In the context of community and ethnicity, urban planning scrutinizes how different ethnic groups interact with, shape, and are shaped by their urban environments [7]. The research methods employed in these studies are as diverse as the topics themselves. They often include data collection through surveys, interviews, observational studies, and a strong reliance on secondary data such as census reports and other public records [8]. Quantitative techniques like regression analyses are also common for interpreting these data sets [9]. Nonetheless, excessive dependence on statistics and secondary data in the quest for comprehending communities affords a constrained viewpoint that fails to accentuate or uplift community-centered interrelations and networks.

Epistemic Network Analysis (ENA), although less conventional, is an increasingly recognized method in urban planning research, which was initially explored through the development of the educational game *Land Science,* which led to students having an increased understanding of social and environmental issues and resulting in some of the students creating a "balanced urban plan" in response to their increased knowledge of networks [10]. ENA's power lies in its capacity to visualize and quantify connections in coded data, making it an ideal complement to traditional research methods. It can provide a nuanced understanding of complex social systems by revealing networks of relationships that might otherwise go unnoticed. As urban planning endeavors to unravel the intricate dynamics of migration, entrepreneurship, community, and ethnicity, the integration of ENA could prove to be a valuable asset for planning students, practitioners, and researchers [10].

3 Methods

3.1 Context

Alongside formal establishments and institutions in South Philadelphia exist vendors, many of whom are women who, through their informal entrepreneurship efforts, which can include selling artisanal items or homemade foods or other community activities, help preserve the Latinx culture among new and existing residents in the neighborhood. Upon further investigation, the names of women's groups, *Mercado de Latinas* and the *Comité* emerged as community anchors. Thus, the participants in the dataset are Latinx immigrant women who are members of the *Mercado de Latinas* (Market of Latinas) – a group of entrepreneurial Latinx immigrants, the *Comité* (Committee) – a group of Latinx immigrants who advocate for workers' rights as restaurant and domestic workers, or individuals who have a close connection to the South Philadelphia community. Before conducting interviews with participants, an introduction was made by a well-known community advocate who lives in the South Philadelphia neighborhood and has a personal conversation with one of the founders of the *Mercado de Latinas*. Background information, such as interview questions prepared in English and Spanish, was shared with the community advocate, who reviewed them for saliency. After connecting with the community advocate, participants self-selected whether they were interested in being interviewed, with the intervention consisting of semi-structured interviews held for approximately one hour. In summary, four women were interviewed, two from Mexico and the remaining from Honduras. The image below (See Fig. 1) uses a Geographic Information System to visualize participants' spatial locations in relation to their respective census tracts in Philadelphia, PA. The participants' locations represent census tracts experiencing a significant growth in Latinx immigrant populations [2]. These spatial locations served as a unit variable for model comparison for this quantitative ethnographic study.

3.2 Data Collection

Interviews with women associated with the *Mercado de Latinas* and the *Comite* resulted in discussions describing their journeys from Mexico and Honduras to the U.S, their tenure in Philadelphia, current and past employment, navigation of the city, interactions with nongovernmental organizations (NGOs) or community-based organizations, neighborhood involvement, and integration into the city. Additional aspects observed include the participants' future aspirations and their desires to remain in Philadelphia. Interviews with the participants were recorded on two separate recorders. After the interview, the interview data is uploaded to a secure folder, and the audio file is transcribed with the assistance of artificial intelligence, Rev [11]. In total, seventeen individuals indicated they were interested in being interviewed, fourteen interviews were scheduled, and thirteen interviews were completed.

The dataset was prepared by randomly selecting four participants to create a case study approach to the analysis. Given that one of the interviews is with the founder of the *Mercado de Latinas*, it is significant because its formation serves as a temporal marker of visibility and incorporation for the immigrant community in South Philadelphia. The

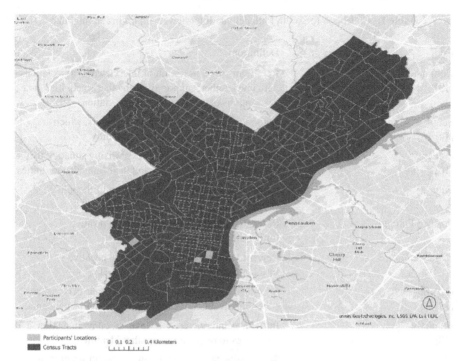

Participants' Locations
Census Tracts   0 0.1 0.2   0.4 Kilometers

Fig. 1. Participants' Locations across Philadelphia, PA Census Tracts

other women's interviews are equally important due to their roles as active community members in and around the South Philadelphia Latinx immigrant community who frequently share information or resources with recently arrived Latinx immigrants. Due to the author's research focus on urban planning, the conversation variables are Sending Community, which represents the participants' countries of origin [5], and Regional Connection, which describes their association with the *Mercado de Latinas* or the *Comité*. The dataset is organized into 1,538 lines, utilizing a moving stanza with a window size of four lines, unit variables which are Sending Community and Regional Connection, and the conversation variable Participant to closely analyze each participant's contribution to the discourse.

3.3 Theoretical Framework

The codes shown in Table 1 were developed as part of a process of inductive thematic analysis [12] as the result of the four semi-structured interviews. Inductive codes were then defined and connected to existing theoretical concepts in relevant disciplines, such as urban planning literature, to create the overarching theoretical framework for understanding the richness of Latinx immigrant discussions in the context of the study (See Table 1).

This study explores numerous themes; however, some are particularly key to understanding the study population and its relationship to urban planning. For instance, Lung-Amam (2017) argues that in the twenty-first century's first decade, "Half a century of

Table 1. Codebook for South Philadelphia Interviews with Latinx Immigrants

Code	Definition	
Community [13]	Represents the description of interviewees' associations with one another, support of each other's activities, and descriptions of other groups or associations	
Family [14, 15]	Refers to the mention of family members, which includes immediate and extended family	
Precarity [16]	Refers to any reference to a destabilizing situation that may personally affect them and their immediate families	
Future	Refers to interviewees' references to forthcoming activities	
Positive Future	Refers to interviewees' references to positive forthcoming activities	
Negative Future	Refers to interviewees' references to negative forthcoming activities	
COVID-19 [17]	Specifies interviewees' references to their personal and economic livelihoods during the coronavirus pandemic	
Ethnicity [18]	Introduces interviewees' awareness, communication, and references to their Latinx or other identities	
Migration [19]	Specifically captures interviewees' mentions of their journeys from their sending communities to Philadelphia or elsewhere in the U.S. en route to Philadelphia	
Transnationalism [20]	Represents all references to the activities, such as the import of goods or products, or behaviors that connect interviewees to their sending communities outside of the U.S	
Entrepreneurship [21]	Indicates the interviewees' references to forming businesses as part of the Mercado de Latinas, Market of Latinas, or the creation of other businesses	
Urban Areas	Refers to the mention of a geographic area	
Geography	Represents the mention of a spatial area that is not limited to a city or metropolis	

massive immigration and racial integration has fundamentally reshaped suburbia's spatial form and social makeup... Between 2000 and 2010, nearly half of the 100 largest metropolitan areas in the United States saw increases in their foreign-born populations of at least 50%" [22]. When discussing transnationalism and its relationship to the built environment, Glick Schiller et al. (1992) argue that transnationalism is the result of migrants "forging and sustaining multistranded social relations that linked their societies of origin and settlement" and "the emergence of a social process in which migrants establish social fields that cross geographic, cultural, and political borders" [20]. Whereas a straightforward definition of migration is "a change of residence that disrupts the basic ties with the local community and is a move that prevents commuting at least at any reasonable cost" [19]. However, the version of migration this study explores is more closely related to Borjas' (1989) economic theory of migration, which "analyzes the allocation of labor across international boundaries. The theory is based on the behavioral assumption that individuals migrate because it is in their benefit (either in terms of psychic satisfaction or income) to do so" [23].

Furthermore, in alignment with the economic motivations for migrating, immigrant populations frequently rely upon entrepreneurship as a form of employment, and there are multiple forms of entrepreneurship, not only the mainstream understanding but also informal entrepreneurship as part of the informal economy. For instance, Thai and Turkina (2014) argue that "informal commercial activities account for a sizeable share (over 30% on average) of economic activity around the world...[and] informal entrepreneurship takes place in all countries regardless of their level of economic development" [21].

3.4 Coding

Coding the interview data consisted of 0 to 1 binary deductive coding, with every instance of the Interviewer coded as 0. For instance, the following line is coded 1 for Migration: *"Pues, bueno, yo llevo casi 18 años viviendo aquí en Filadelfia. Me vine de muy chica,"* which in English translates to *"Well, I've been living here in Philadelphia for almost 18 years. I came when I was very young."* The author initially coded the first 100 lines, and then a native Spanish-speaking member of the research team assisted with the coding and data validation process. The coders selected social moderation [24] as their reliability measure to validate the dataset. The coders met for two sessions, discussing and consolidating codes applied to the remaining lines. This discussion resulted in creating and refining additional codes that better represent the discourse themes. The coding process is exploratory in nature, and the author operates as the primary coder due to sharing a cultural background with the participants, being a native Spanish speaker, and easily interpreting the participants' dialectical nuance.

3.5 Epistemic Network Analysis

In this study, the team applied epistemic network analysis [10, 25–27] to our data using the ENA Web Tool (version 1.7.0) [28]. In preparation for the ENA, unit variables consist of Participant, Gender, and Speaker. Additionally, we defined the units of analysis as all lines of data associated with a single value of Sending Community subset by Regional Connection. The ENA algorithm uses a moving window to construct a network model for each line in the data, showing how codes in the current line are connected to codes that occur within the recent temporal context [29], defined as four lines (each line plus the three previous lines) within a given conversation. The window size of four was selected due to the participants' tendency to speak at length about a particular topic until prompted with a different question. The resulting networks are aggregated for all lines for each unit of analysis in the model.

The ENA model includes the following codes: *Transnationalism, Ethnicity, COVID-19, Community, Entrepreneurship, Family, Urban Area, Geography, Migration, Precarity, COVID-19*, and *Future*. The data was segmented by participants without considering any additional segmentation within each interview. For instance, one conversation consisted of all the lines associated with the interview of the participant named Lucía.

4 Results

4.1 Epistemic Network Models

Networks were visualized using network graphs where nodes correspond to the codes, and edges reflect the relative frequency of co-occurrence, or connection, between two codes. The result is two coordinated representations for each unit of analysis: (1) a plotted point, which represents the location of that unit's network in the low-dimensional projected space, and (2) a weighted network graph. The positions of the network graph nodes are fixed, and those positions are determined by an optimization routine that minimizes the difference between the plotted points and their corresponding network centroids. The integration of network graphs and mapped space allows the locations of network graph nodes and the relationships they establish to be utilized to understand the dimensions of the mapped space and elucidate the locations of points plotted within it. The model exhibited co-registration correlations of 0.99 (Pearson) and 1 (Spearman) for the first dimension and correlations of 0.98 (Pearson) and 1 (Spearman) for the second. These metrics suggest a robust correlation between the visual representation and the original model.

ENA can be used to compare units of analysis in terms of their plotted point positions, individual networks, mean plotted point positions, and mean networks, which average the connection weights across individual networks. Networks may also be compared using network difference graphs. These graphs are calculated by subtracting the weight of each connection in one network from the corresponding connections in another. Additionally, the models' nodes are set equally spaced to maximize the visual appearance of differences between code associations.

Interviews with the Honduran participants (See Fig. 2) illustrate the strong connections between *Migration* and *Precarity, Precarity* and *Future, Migration* and *Geography*, and *Urban Area* and *Geography*.

The participants from Honduras did not demonstrate a strong relationship between *Entrepreneurship* and *Community* and *Entrepreneurship* and *Family* as seen for participants from Mexico (See Fig. 3). However, both sets of participants expressed strong connections between *Migration* and *Precarity* with an edge weight of 0.33 for Honduran participants and an edge weight of 0.25 for Mexican participants which support the onerous migration journeys expressed by the participants.

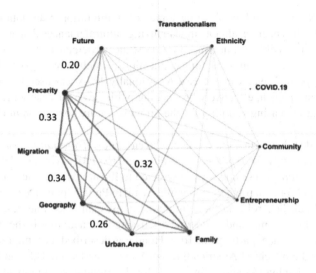

Fig. 2. ENA plot of participants from Honduras

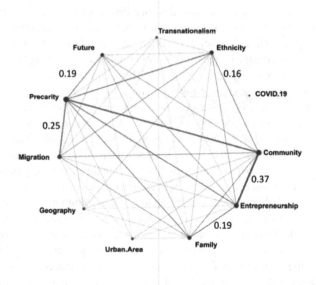

Fig. 3. ENA plot of participants from Mexico

5 Summary Discussion and Conclusion

Connecting ENA to the urban planning topics of immigration, transnationalism, and entrepreneurship has been invaluable in visualizing cultural nuances that are understood but are not spatially visible. While a map may illustrate participants' physical locations in a city, a map is limited in communicating connections, which prove impactful when documenting immigrants' lived experiences. Additionally, ENA was used to communicate data collected in Spanish, effectively broadening public awareness about Latinx immigrant issues and increasing visibility for the growing Latinx population in Philadelphia and across the U.S.

The networks shown in Fig. 4 reflect eleven codes: *Transnationalism, Ethnicity, COVID-19, Community, Entrepreneurship, Family, Urban Area, Geography, Migration, Precarity,* and *Future.* These codes were selected to illustrate the participants' multidimensional lives before, en route to, and while living in Philadelphia. Due to participants being asked about their roles in the community, they spent less time describing their immediate family dynamics and more time discussing their activities in the Philadelphia community. For instance, participants from Honduras described their migration experiences from Northern Central America through Mexico, across the U.S., and ultimately arriving in Philadelphia. As shown in Fig. 4, for the Honduran participants, there is a strong connection between *Migration* and *Geography*, reflecting an edge weight of 0.27. Interestingly, the Mexican participants demonstrate a strong connection between *Family* and *Community* and *Community* and *Entrepreneurship,* which has an edge weight of 0.37.

The stronger connections between codes (See Fig. 4) vary by the participants' Sending Communities. For the participants from Mexico, there is a strong connection between *Entrepreneurship* and *Family,* which reflects an edge weight of 0.19, *Entrepreneurship* and *Community* with an edge weight of 0.37, and finally, a connection between *Community* and *Ethnicity,* with an edge weight of 0.16. These connections support the discourse shared by the participants and the establishment of the *Mercado de Latinas,* a form of informal entrepreneurship. For instance, Lucía communicates her excitement by stating, "*Entonces este, pues dije no, pues vamos, vamos. Y empecé a a traer mercancía, contratar a mis hermanos, a mi hermana, mi hermana*" which roughly translates to "*Then um, well I said 'no' well let's go let's go. And I started bringing merchandise, employed my siblings, my sister, my sister.*" Here, Lucía is sharing the origin story of her storefront in South Philadelphia and how the demand for items from her home state of Chiapas in Mexico led her to collaborate with her sibling in Chiapas to import artisanal items to sell in her store. Consequently, city planning and migration literature support immigrants having a higher likelihood of becoming entrepreneurs because it is an atypical path to generating income without formal education or access to significant capital investments.

Separately, the connections for participants from Honduras demonstrate stronger connections between *Migration* and *Precarity,* which has an edge weight of 0.33, and *Migration* and *Geography,* which has an edge weight of 0.34. These connections reflect Rosa's and Ana's experiences reaching Philadelphia and their precarious work experiences. Rosa shares, "*Al siguiente día empecé a trabajar este me fui en la mañana como a las cinco la mañana pasaron por mí...pero trabajaba desde las cinco...de la mañana que llegaba el trabajo. Salí a veces 11, 12 de la noche todos los días. Yo no gastaba casi dinero porque lo que yo quería era pagar.*" In this excerpt, Rosa describes arriving in Philadelphia, working the next day, and working from 5 am to sometimes 11 pm or midnight every day to pay off a debt. Thus, the connections in Fig. 4 reflect the themes that emerged in the semi-structured interviews in the participants' discourse related to difficult or negative migration experiences.

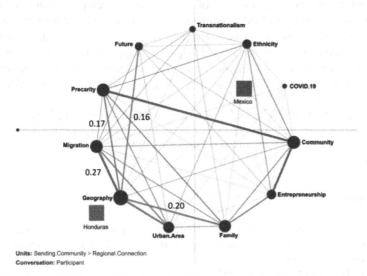

Fig. 4. Comparison ENA plot of Honduran participants represented by the blue network and the Mexican participants illustrated by the red network.

The limitations of the study include the use of data from only four interviews; however, forthcoming iterations of the study will consist of additional interview data from a larger sample of participants with diverse immigrant experiences. Moreover, while using artificial intelligence reduces costs associated with verbatim human transcription services, the transcriptions result in verbatim language processing versus contextually accurate transcriptions, which require additional interpretation when coding and greatly reduce the manual coding speed. Interpreting translations can reduce coding speed because transcriptions processed using artificial intelligence result in verbatim language, particularly when coding multiple interviews. Furthermore, Spanish-language speakers across different geographic regions utilize different dialects, which can also influence discourse interpretation, coding speed, and achieving reliability through social moderation for Spanish-language speakers.

In summary, the utilization of ENA presents a compelling avenue for increasing urban planners' understanding of the social and environmental issues affecting specific populations [10]. Moreover, ENA can aid in disseminating insights regarding the Latinx immigrant community's perceptions, as well as the intricate associations between diverse identities or concepts, their relationship to entrepreneurship, and immigrants' overall sense of belonging to a community [30, 31]. Acknowledging that immigrants possess a high level of motivation and desire to succeed can help reframe the negative narratives about immigrants and create a supportive community for all to thrive despite their economic limitations. Thus, an urban planning recommendation to planners, policymakers, financial institutions, educators, and community and immigrant rights advocates is to intentionally foster an inclusive and welcoming small-business community that increases access to capital and other resources through low-to-no-interest small-business loans, engages individuals with various levels of education and develops a mechanism for easily facilitating the sharing of information across all industries. For now, this group of Latinx immigrants relies on Carmen, who appropriately states, *"Igual, eh, organizar a la gente, comunicarles que hay nuevos recursos. Mm-hmm. Que hay nuevas oportunidades"* which translates to *"The same, eh, organizing the people, communicating to them that there are new resources. Mm-hmm. That there are new opportunities."*

Acknowledgments. Interview transcription services were supported by funds from the University of Pennsylvania Center for the Study of Ethnicity, Race and Immigration (CSERI) Turner Schulman Graduate Fellowship, awarded in December 2022.

References

1. Takenaka, A., Osirim, M.J. (eds.).: Global Philadelphia: immigrant communities Passel, J.S., D'Vera Cohn, D. (2008). US population projections, 2005-2050 (p. 20). Washington, DC: Pew Research Center (2010)
2. Vitiello, D.: The Sanctuary City (2022)
3. Takenaka, A., Osirim, M.J. (Eds.).: Global Philadelphia: Immigrant Communities Old and New. Temple University Press (2010)
4. Pendall, R.: Local land use regulation and the chain of exclusion. J. Am. Plann. Assoc. **66**(2), 125–142 (2000)
5. Jones-Correa, M., De Graauw, E.: Looking back to see ahead: unanticipated changes in immigration from 1986 to the present and their implications for American politics today. Annu. Rev. Polit. Sci. **16**, 209–230 (2013)
6. Huang, X., Liu, C.Y.: Immigrant entrepreneurship and economic development: a local policy perspective. J. Am. Plann. Assoc. **85**(4), 564–584 (2019)
7. Li, W.: Anatomy of a new ethnic settlement: the Chinese ethnoburb in Los Angeles. Urban studies **35**(3), 479–501 (1998)
8. Harris, T., Weiner, D.: Empowerment, marginalization, and" community-integrated" GIS. Cartograph. Geograph. Inf. Syst. **25**(2), 67–76 (1998)
9. Ewing, R., Park, K. (Eds.).: Basic Quantitative Research Methods for Urban Planners. Routledge (2020)
10. Shaffer, D.W.: Quantitative Ethnography. Cathcart Press, Madison, WI (2017)
11. Rev.com. (n.d.). Transcribe speech to text. Rev. https://www.rev.com/
12. Thomas, D.R.: A general inductive approach for qualitative data analysis (2003)
13. MacQueen, K.M., et al.: What is community? An evidence-based definition for participatory public health. Am. J. Public Health **91**(12), 1929–1938 (2001)
14. Sharma, R.: The family and family structure classification redefined for the current times. J. Family Med. Primary Care **2**(4), 306 (2013)
15. UNESCO, Mullatti L. "The changing family in Asia: Bangladesh, India, Japan, Philippines, and Thailand." Bangkok: Principal Regional Office for Asia and the Pacific (1992)

16. Biglia, B., Martí, J.B.: Precarity. In: Teo, T. (ed.), Encyclopedia of Critical (2014)
17. Coronavirus disease (COVID-19) pandemic. (n.d.). Accessed 20 Mar 2023. https://www.who. int/europe/emergencies/situations/covid-19
18. Definition of ethnicity—NCI Dictionary of Cancer Terms—NCI (nciglobal,ncienterprise) (2011). [NciAppModulePage]
19. Clark, W.A.: Human migration (2020)
20. Schiller, N.G., Basch, L., Blanc-Szanton, C.: Transnationalism: a new analytic framework for understanding migration. Ann. N. Y. Acad. Sci. **645**(1), 1–24 (1992)
21. Thai, M.T.T., Turkina, E.: Macro-level determinants of formal entrepreneurship versus informal entrepreneurship. J. Bus. Ventur. **29**(4), 490–510 (2014)
22. Lung-Amam, W.: Trespassers?: Asian Americans and the Battle for Suburbia. University of California Press, Berkeley, CA (2017)
23. Borjas, G.J.: Economic theory and international migration. Int. Migr. Rev. **23**(3), 457–485 (1989)
24. Eagan, B., Brohinsky, J., Wang, J., Shaffer, D.W.: Testing the reliability of inter-rater reliability. In: Proceedings of the Tenth International Conference on Learning Analytics & Knowledge, pp. 454–461 (2020)
25. Bowman, D., et al.: The mathematical foundations of epistemic network analysis. In: Ruis, A., Lee, S.B. (eds.), Advances in Quantitative Ethnography: Second International Conference, ICQE 2020, Malibu, CA, USA, February 1–3, 2021, Proceedings (pp. 91–105). Springer (2021). Shaffer, D.W., Collier, W., Ruis, A.R.: A tutorial on epistemic network analysis: analyzing the structure of connections in cognitive, social, and interaction data. J. Learn. Anal. **3**(3), 9–45 (2016)
26. Shaffer, D.W., Collier, W., Ruis, A.R.: A tutorial on epistemic network analysis: analyzing the structure of connections in cognitive, social, and interaction data. J. Learn. Anal. **3**(3), 9–45 (2016)
27. Shaffer, D.W., Ruis, A.R.: Epistemic network analysis: a worked example of theory-based learning analytics. In: Lang, C., Siemens, G., Wise, A.F., Gasevic, D. (eds.) Handbook of learning analytics, pp. 175–187. Society for Learning Analytics Research (2017)
28. Marquart, C.L., Hinojosa, C., Swiecki, Z., Eagan, B., Shaffer, D.W.: Epistemic Network Analysis (Version 1.7.0) [Software] (2018). http://app.epistemicnetwork.org
29. Siebert-Evenstone, A., Arastoopour Irgens, G., Collier, W., Swiecki, Z., Ruis, A.R., Williamson Shaffer, D.: In search of conversational grain size: modelling semantic structure using moving stanza windows. J. Learn. Anal. **4**(3), 123–139 (2017). https://doi.org/10. 18608/jla.2017.43.7
30. Deeb-Sossa, N., Méndez, J.B. (eds.).: Latinx Belonging: Community Building and Resilience in the United States. University of Arizona Press (2022)
31. Davis, M.: Magical urbanism: Latinos reinvent the US city. Verso (2001)

Interaction of Diagnostic Criteria in the Narratives of Patients with Borderline Personality Disorder

Szilárd Dávid Kovács[1]([✉]) [ID], Katherine Mulholland[2] [ID], Lara Condon[3] [ID],
Zsuzsa Koncz[1] [ID], and Szilvia Zörgő[4] [ID]

[1] Semmelweis University, Budapest 1089, Hungary
kovacs.szilard@phd.semmelweis.hu
[2] Clemson University, Clemson, SC 29634, USA
[3] University of Pennsylvania, Philadelphia, PA 19104, USA
[4] Maastricht University, 6200 MD Maastricht, The Netherlands

Abstract. The fifth edition of the Diagnostic and Statistical Manual of Mental Disorders requires the presence of at least five out of nine diagnostic criteria in order to diagnose borderline personality disorder. However, the manifestation, perception, and interaction of the diagnostic criteria differs in patients and with narrative focus. The objective of this study is to describe symptom co-occurrences in persons with borderline personality disorder vis-à-vis the focal points of their narrative. We utilized transcripts of interviews with borderline patients, which were coded by two raters, employing the diagnostic criteria as codes. We examined narratives across patients according to the narrative foci of the discussion (interviewee perceptions of self, others, and how others see them). We employed Epistemic Network Analysis to visualize the interaction of diagnostic criteria. Our study serves as a pilot for further research on mapping manifestations of diagnostic criteria of various mental disorders within patient lived experience. By encouraging future research employing this study design, our pilot aims to contribute to more personalized health care.

Keywords: Borderline Personality Disorder · Epistemic Network Analysis

1 Introduction

Personality disorders are persistent behaviors or inner experiences, which differ from the norm in an individual's sociocultural surrounding; they develop in puberty or young adulthood, and result in distress or impairment. Borderline Personality Disorder (BPD) is characterized as the widespread occurrence of prominent impulsivity and unstable interpersonal relationships, self-image, and affect. [1] The prevalence of BPD in random samples ranges from 0.5% to 0.7% [2–4], with 75% of the diagnosed patients being female [1]. In primary care samples, prevalence ranges from 4% to 6% [5, 6]. Individuals suffering from BPD may experience difficulties in maintaining relationships, fulfilling their role as a family member, friend, or marital spouse, maintaining financial resources,

G. Arastoopour Irgens and S. Knight (Eds.): ICQE 2023, CCIS 1895, pp. 316–329, 2023.
https://doi.org/10.1007/978-3-031-47014-1_22

academic achievement, and career success [7]. Likewise, family members, friends, and colleagues of a person living with BPD are also affected by the disorder, due to their mood shifts, self-damaging or self-destructive behavior, and uncertainty concerning how to relate to the person with BPD after becoming aware of their diagnosis [8].

In the fifth edition of the Diagnostic and Statistical Manual of Mental Disorders (DSM 5), BPD is diagnosed if at least five of the following nine diagnostic criteria (symptoms) are present: 1) Frantic efforts to avoid real or imagined abandonment, 2) A pattern of unstable and intense interpersonal relationships characterized by alternating between extremes of idealization and devaluation, 3) Identity disturbance, 4) Impulsivity in at least two areas that are potentially self-damaging, 5) Recurrent suicidal behavior, gestures, or threats, or self-mutilating behavior, 6) Affective instability due to a marked reactivity of mood, 7) Chronic feelings of emptiness, 8) Inappropriate, intense anger or difficulty controlling anger, and 9) Transient, stress-related paranoid ideation or severe dissociative symptoms [1]. Diagnosis requires the presence of multiple symptoms manifesting in constellations; thus, viewing symptoms in isolation is suboptimal because it is their interaction that constitutes the disorder. The DSM 5 also describes symptom co-occurrence in BPD patients, for example, efforts to avoid abandonment may co-occur with mood shifts, anger, and dissociative symptoms [1].

Previous studies have examined diagnostic criteria in patient narratives and in self-reported questionnaires. Qualitative studies provide insight into idiosyncratic manifestations of symptoms, as the study of Dammann et al., who conducted interviews with BPD patients regarding self-image, image of others, as well as their emotions and typical episodes [9]. However, the limitation of such studies is their focus on a single diagnostic criterion, identity disturbance in the above-mentioned article. As the diagnosis of BPD requires the presence of at least five diagnostic criteria, one could argue, investigating a single symptom is insufficient in describing the disorder. Furthermore, such idiosyncratic data is difficult to aggregate, and most qualitative studies, although working with small sample sizes, do not attempt to aggregate data systematically. Quantitative studies, generally employing self-reported questionnaires, also tend to scrutinize symptoms in isolation, as Koenigsberg et al. measured the dimensions of affective instability in patients with BPD and compared them to patients' with other personality disorders; again, solely investigating the manifestations of a single diagnostic criterion [10].

Research investigating symptom constellations has been conducted with quantitative methods. Klonsky employed structured interviews and a questionnaire on a subsample with a history of self-injury and a nonclinical subsample. The structured interviews measured the frequency of affect states in chronic feelings of emptiness before and after self-injury, while the questionnaire measured the co-occurrence of all nine diagnostic criteria, as well as anxiety, depression, suicidal ideations, and suicide attempts [11]. Albeit the study investigated possible co-occurrences among self-damage and other symptoms, participants were not screened for BPD, hence the results cannot accurately describe BPD patients. The interaction of all nine criteria in BPD patients was measured in Richetin et al.'s network analysis [12], yet the relationship among variables was computed across cases, yielding results regarding the whole sample, but compromising the ability to draw conclusions for individual patients (cf.: the ergodic fallacy [13]).

In addition to investigating the manifestation of all possible diagnostic criteria on an individual level, a further distinction may be clinically relevant on the level of narrative foci, i.e., whether the patient is describing themselves, others, or how they believe others see them. For example, Dammann et al. [9] distinguish such narrative foci as "self-description" and "description of others" in their study. The relevance of this differentiation is that patients' perceptions of others are also valid indicators of how they see themselves [14], and enable the investigation of transferential displacement, a defense mechanism in which unprocessed affect is projected onto another person or object to reduce associated anxiety [15].

Our first aim was to map the interaction among all diagnostic criteria in the narratives of persons diagnosed with BPD, thus facilitating diagnosis and individualized treatment. Our second aim was to distinguish the interaction of these criteria according to when patients speak about themselves, others, and how they assume others perceive them in order to investigate how code constellations change vis-à-vis these narrative foci. For this purpose, we utilized Epistemic Network Analysis (ENA), which allowed us to quantify and visualize connections among diagnostic criteria. This study aims to serve as a pilot for future studies intending to analyze corpora of patient narratives, especially in the context of practitioner – patient interaction on mental health issues.

2   Methods

All our materials, as well as our final, coded dataset is available in our project repository, available at: https://osf.io/5z624. Narratives were obtained from the YouTube channel Soft White Underbelly[1], containing interviews and portraits of the human condition by photographer, Mark Laita. We selected all interviews available with people living with BPD; two females (Grace and Shawna) and one male (Ernesto). Interviews lasted ca. 30-min each and were automatically transcribed by YouTube. Transcripts were scraped manually, placed into a text editor, and cleaned (timestamps and extra line breaks were removed). Transcripts lacked punctuation; to retain heuristics for creating sentences, the same researcher added punctuation marks to all transcripts.

Following an initial discussion on codes and segmentation, all researchers agreed the narratives should be coded on the level of sentences. Thus, text files were processed with the Reproducible Open Coding Kit (ROCK)[2] to create a spreadsheet where each sentence in the transcripts constituted a row. Our spreadsheet also had a column to indicate the case ID for each participant, specified on each row.

Code development was deductive; we adopted the nine diagnostic criteria and their descriptions listed in the DSM 5 [1], and supplemented the definitions with information from other chapters of the manual, such as defining anxiety and dysphoria according to the DSM 5's Glossary of Technical Terms. Our final codebook was reviewed and validated by a clinical psychologist in the team. Two researchers tested the applicability of our final codes on a subset of data (10% of total lines) and reached good percentage agreement (above 95% for each code), but because of the low base-rate of our codes,

---

[1] https://www.softwhiteunderbelly.com.

[2] https://rock.science.

we decided to compute Cohen's Kappa on the full dataset, not a subset (see below). Table 1 contains our simplified codebook; the complete codebook including examples is accessible through our repository (https://osf.io/audgb).

Table 1. Simplified codebook.

Code name	Code label	Simplified Definition
Avoiding abandonment	Avoid_aband	Acts to avoid real or perceived abandonment; Fear or anger by threat of abandonment
Unstable relationships	Unstab_relat	Idealizing, making demands, inappropriate intimacy; Expectation of "being there" in return for empathy
Identity disturbance	Id_disturb	Sudden shifts in self-image, goals, values, career plans, sexual identity; Self-perception: "bad", "evil"
Self-damaging	Self-dam	Self-damaging behavior not causing acute physical harm
Self-destructive	Self-destr	Suicidal gestures, threats, attempts, and self-mutilation
Mood reactivity	Mood_react	Episodes of dysphoria, irritability, anxiety, panic, despair
Emptiness	Emptiness	Feeling meaningless or purposeless, chronic visceral feeling in abdomen or chest; Easily bored
Anger	Anger	Intense, inappropriate, uncontrollable anger; Rage
Disconnection from reality	Disconnect	Episode of paranoid ideation or dissociation

Codes were applied by two researchers, both working independently in a spreadsheet that contained our data segmented by sentence and a column for each of our codes. If a code was identified in a given line, it was specified with a 1 in the correlating column; if the code was absent, it was indicated with a 0. When coding for the full dataset was complete, inter-rater reliability (IRR) was computed for the totality of lines. Table 2 shows the number of disagreements and Kappa values for the nine codes and two raters. IRR testing can serve the purpose of splitting data or splitting codes among coders, but in this case, it was employed solely as a measure of consistent application of codes and pinpointing differences in interpretation to be addressed in social moderation.

Following IRR testing, the two coders triangulated their work and resolved inconsistencies through social moderation to reach complete agreement. The clinical psychologist in the research team validated the final, coded dataset line-by-line. As a last step in coding, a researcher specified the narrative focus of each line in the final dataset by using a coding scheme of four inductively created categories and specifying these values in a separate column. Table 3 contains the narrative foci coding scheme. These narrative

Table 2. Number of disagreements and Cohen's Kappa values for two raters regarding nine employed codes.

Code	Number of disagreements	Cohen's Kappa
Unstab_relat	5	0.52
Id_disturb	10	0.89
Self-destr	5	0.83
Mood_react	11	0.75
Emptiness	4	0.84
Anger	3	0.89
Disconnect	2	0.50
Avoid_aband	5	0.73
Self-dam	13	0.82

foci served as a higher form of segmentation that provided meaningful context to code co-occurrences [16].

Table 3. Narrative foci coding scheme.

Code name	Code label	Definition
Perceiving others	Others	How interviewee perceives others around them
Others' perception	Them	How interviewee thinks others perceive interviewee
Perceiving self	Self	How interviewee perceives themselves
Miscellaneous	Miscell	Data that cannot be labeled with any other narrative focus

The final dataset was uploaded to the Epistemic Network Analysis web tool[3]. Detailed descriptions of how ENA generates networks can be found elsewhere [17–19], but succinctly: the tabular dataset containing code occurrences and metadata on segmentation and data provider was parsed according to "unit". A unit is the totality of lines associated with a given network in a model. We designated both narrative focus and data provider as our unit in a nested relationship. Code co-occurrence frequencies were computed with a weighted whole conversation stanza window method, which accumulated co-occurrences in the entire conversation in a weighted, as opposed to a binarized manner [20]. ENA aggregated these frequencies per unit to produce cumulative adjacency matrices of code co-occurrences, which were represented as vectors in high-dimensional space. Subsequent to normalization (to account for different amounts of narrative contained in the vectors), ENA performed a dimensional reduction procedure (singular value decomposition or SVD) to construct a two-dimensional space. These two dimensions form the axes along which the unit vectors are then projected as

---

[3] https://www.epistemicnetwork.org.

points (ENA scores) into the two-dimensional space. The scores each represent a unit's network in which the codes are nodes and the edges signify the relative frequency of co-occurrence between unique pairs of codes. Since the scores and networks are coordinated, the positions of the nodes can be used to interpret the dimensions forming the space and explain the positions of ENA scores. Table 4 contains the parameterization of our ENA model.

Table 4. Epistemic Network Analysis model parameters.

Parameters	Parameter values
Unit	Narrative focus > Case
Conversation	Narrative focus
Stanza window	Weighted Whole Conversation
SVD1	26.4%
SVD2	19.1%

Our model thus contained networks for each of our three interviewees in all four of our narrative foci, twelve in total. For our final analysis, we examined the mean network of our three narrative foci: how the interviewee perceives themselves ("Self"), how they perceive others ("Others"), and how they think others perceive them ("Them"). Analysis was performed by visually inspecting code co-occurrences (the thicker the edge, the higher the co-occurrence frequency) and by using the web tool to perform de- and re-contextualization for each code pair. In the following, diagnostic criteria code labels are indicated in italics, and participant narratives are in quotation marks.

3 Results

3.1 How BPD Patients View Themselves

As the mean network in Fig. 1 shows, when speaking about themselves, interviewees exhibited the strongest relationship among six of the nine DSM 5 diagnostic criteria: *avoiding abandonment, emptiness, mood reactivity, self-destructive, identity disturbance,* and *self-damaging.* Each of these six codes are connected to the other five, signifying that the interviewees made connections among these codes when referring to their past and present lived experiences, and shows how the diagnostic criteria interact to impact a patient's sense of self. One interviewee, Ernesto, described how the feeling of *emptiness* presented as intrusive and "[unwanted] thoughts that are coming in, are just constant and consistent that it became, like, unbearable". This ultimately led to his first suicide attempt at the age of 17, an example of self-destructive behavior. Grace, another interviewee, made connections between *identity disturbance* and *avoiding abandonment* when she described how she is "most afraid of ending up alone, like, in every aspect", because when she loves someone "it's easier for [her] to show [her] bad side". Here, Grace exhibited fears of abandonment because she perceived herself as "having a bad side", a negative self-image.

Disconnection from reality exhibited the weakest relationship with the other eight diagnostic criteria, indicating that included patients with BPD did not emphasize dissociative feelings, such as disconnecting from themselves or reality, regarding their sense of self or how they viewed themselves. One connection between *disconnection from reality* and *anger* was made by Shawna when she described "a really bad argument" with her boyfriend, during which she said she "just black[ed] out".

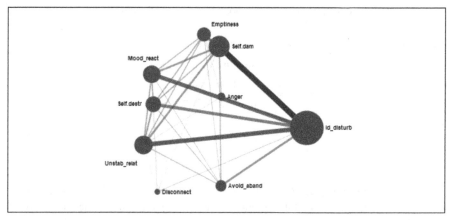

Fig. 1. Mean epistemic network for patients' narratives on themselves, showing the weighted structure of connections among the codes representing the diagnostic criteria of borderline personality disorder. The thickness and saturation of the edges (lines) indicate the relative frequency of co-occurrence between each pair of codes; the size of the nodes (black circles) indicates the relative frequency of each code within that group.

3.2   How BPD Patients Think Others View Them

The mean network for interviewees' perceptions on how others view them, displayed in Fig. 2, revealed a strong relationship between *self-damaging* and *identity disturbance*. This may indicate that interviewees thought others see them as unstable due to struggling with negative self-image and exhibiting self-damaging behavior, such as substance abuse or not taking prescribed medications. In her interview, Shawna described how family members and friends encouraged her to take her prescribed medication because "it'll help". However, Shawna avoided taking medications for no explicit reason: "I don't want to. I don't know why", displaying what may be interpreted clinically as self-damaging behavior. Later in the interview, when speaking about her relationship with her boyfriend, Shawna conveys a negative self-image, or *identity disturbance*, regarding her diagnosis with BPD: "I feel like it slows him down, or it holds him back". Here, Shawna thought her diagnosis of BPD, and ultimately her own person, are negatively impacting her boyfriend. Ernesto also made connections between *self-damaging* and *identity disturbance* when he described how he "feel[s] like a burden to people", which leads him to "reach out to people" or find himself "in, like, very questionable places [...] drinking during the day, going out". Ernesto thus perceived himself as a burden to the people around him, which led him to partake in self-damaging behavior, such as drinking during the day.

Emptiness was not connected to the other seven diagnostic criteria, indicating that although the interviewees experienced *emptiness* (Fig. 1), they did not think this was evident to others. Similarly to how interviewees view themselves, the code *anger* exhibited the weakest connection in the network visualizing how they think others view them.

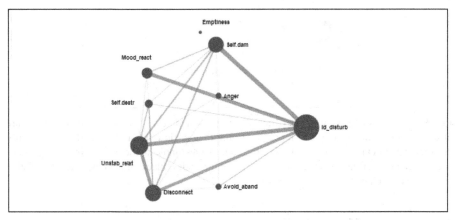

Fig. 2. Mean epistemic network for patients' narratives on how they assume others view them, showing the weighted structure of connections among the codes representing the diagnostic criteria of borderline personality disorder. The thickness and saturation of the edges (lines) indicate the relative frequency of co-occurrence between each pair of codes; the size of the nodes (black circles) indicates the relative frequency of each code within that group.

3.3   How BPD Patients View Others

When interviewees talked about their perceptions of others, displayed in Fig. 3, one of the strongest relationships in the mean network was between *unstable relationships* and *anger*. Ernesto connected *anger* and *unstable relationships* when he spoke about his relationship with his family, specifically his mother and brother. Ernesto remembered his brother having "anger issues for sure" and recalled when his brother would assault him: "he would just start, you know, punching me, smacking me, knocking me down, like it was, like, every other day". Ernesto saw his brother as a person who struggles with his anger. When speaking about his relationship with his mother, Ernesto recounted uncertainty, a characteristic of *unstable relationships*: "I would say I'm still close, it's just, um, I feel like she puts her beliefs before me a lot of the time, you know". Grace connected *unstable relationships* and *identity disturbance* when she spoke about her mother exhibiting similar behavior to herself: "My mom was the same kind of pattern where she would jump from things, she'd jump from partners, she'd jump from jobs". Here, Grace viewed her mother as having unstable relationships because she would experience challenges with commitment. This pattern is characteristic of *identity disturbance*: being unsure of who you are or what you want, exhibiting an unstable sense of self.

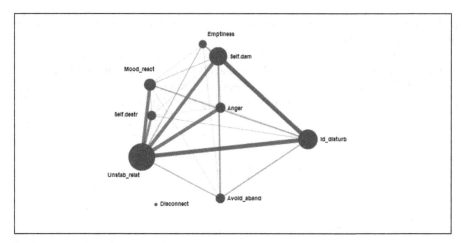

Fig. 3. Mean epistemic network for patients' narratives on others, showing the weighted structure of connections among the codes representing the diagnostic criteria of borderline personality disorder. The thickness and saturation of the edges (lines) indicate the relative frequency of co-occurrence between each pair of codes; the size of the nodes (black circles) indicates the relative frequency of each code within that group.

3.4 Comparing Mean Networks

The ENA projection space was constructed along two dimensions, SVD1 and SVD2, together explaining 45.5% of variance in the data (Table 4). Figure 4 displays the positions of the ENA scores (circles representing a network per narrative focus per person), and mean networks (squares; one for each narrative focus). The dashed lines around the means represent the 95% confidence intervals on the two dimensions. There were no significant differences among the mean networks, but there was a marked disparity between, on the one hand, how participants saw themselves and how they think others see them, and on the other hand, how they saw others.

The comparison plots in Fig. 5 highlight differences between the Self and Others (left), as well as the Them and Others mean networks (right). Codes *identity disturbance* and *mood reactivity* exhibited a strong connection in patient narratives on how they see themselves (purple) and how they think others perceive them (green), but connoted a weak connection in how they see others (teal). Codes *anger* and *unstable relationships* signified a marked connection in the network visualizing narratives on how they see others, while *anger* was the least connected node in the networks describing how BPD patients see themselves and how others see them.

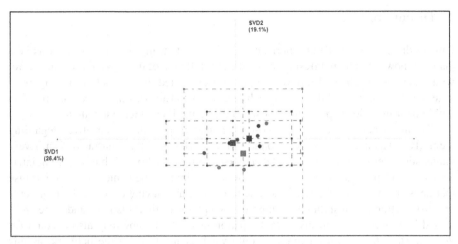

Fig. 4. Epistemic Network Analysis projection space constructed for three individuals living with borderline personality disorder with lines of data grouped according to three narrative foci. The colored circles show the network locations (ENA scores) of the networks generated for each narrative focus per person. The colored squares are the mean network locations (mean ENA scores) of each narrative focus, and the dashed lines around the means represent the 95% confidence intervals on each dimension.

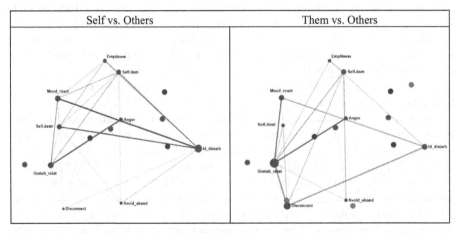

Fig. 5. *Left:* Comparison plot (subtracted graph) of mean epistemic networks highlighting the differences between how individuals living with borderline personality disorder see themselves (purple) versus how they see others (teal), with lines of data grouped according to three narrative foci. *Right:* Comparison plot of mean epistemic networks highlighting the differences between how individuals living with borderline personality disorder think others see them (green) versus how they see others (teal), with lines of data grouped according to three narrative foci. Black circles (nodes) represent our codes; the colored circles show the network locations (ENA scores) of the networks generated for each narrative focus per person (Color figure online).

4 Discussion

Patients diagnosed with BPD experience at least five of the nine diagnostic criteria of the disorder; however, the manifestation and the constellation of these symptoms may differ within patient narratives. Employing ENA, we examined the interaction of diagnostic criteria in the accounts of three persons living with BPD and distinguished narrative foci within their interviews: perception of self, others, and how others view them.

The mean network containing co-occurrences in participant narratives regarding themselves was the most densely connected network of the three narrative foci. Every diagnostic criterion, save *anger* and *disconnection from reality*, exhibited a strong interaction. As all participants were in therapy at the time of their interview, we surmise that dense network connectivity was due to participants having developed a high level of introspection and insight concerning the symptoms of their disorder and were well-versed in expressing themselves. Participation in active therapy may also account for *disconnection from reality* exhibiting only weak connections in the network, as this diagnostic criterion captures paranoid ideation and dissociation, phenomena that tend to decrease in frequency and intensity with ongoing psycho- and pharmacotherapy [21].

The mean network depicting co-occurrences in narratives on how participants think others view them exhibited a marked emphasis on *avoiding abandonment* and *emptiness*. These results may demonstrate that, according to patients, fear of isolation and aligned avoidance behaviors are not as overtly manifest as, for example, unstable identity and self-image. Other studies have shown that patients often feel that the effects of some symptoms of mental disorders are more underestimated by healthcare workers than others [22]. According to the patients included in our study, fear of abandonment connoted a BPD symptom that was de-emphasized by their social environment, compared to their more overt self-harming behavior. Discrepancies such as this one are noteworthy, as covert or unexpressed symptoms that go unnoticed by friends and family, or even by mental health professionals, may be the most dangerous ones [23].

Mean networks of patient narratives on themselves and how participants think others see them exhibited a similar structure of connections. When compared to the mean network depicting co-occurrences in narratives on how these patients view others, a marked distinction was the role of *anger*, especially its association to unstable relationships. According to a study by Dammann et al., BPD patients only saw aggressive tendencies in others, as opposed to observing anger in themselves [9]. Thus, anger signified the most prominent symptom that our participants cope with by transferential displacement. This aligns with previous studies indicating that anger is one of the most frequently displaced emotions in mental disorders [24].

Our study aimed to present a novel method of modelling the interaction of all nine diagnostic criteria of BPD, while also distinguishing among narrative foci in patient narratives to scrutinize these interactions in processed versus unprocessed affect. Anger represented a diagnostic criterion manifesting as lived experience chiefly through transferential displacement (projection onto others), which may indicate that this affect was least identified with, least integrated into perceptions of self, and therefore, patients exhibit little to no insight concerning their own anger. Dealing with such unprocessed affect for which the patient has not yet assumed ownership may require vastly different therapeutic approaches and strategies compared to their processed affective and behavioral counterparts. Differentiating among narrative foci enables modelling these domains separately, and can guide the clinician in developing a more tailored treatment plan.

5 Limitations

Our study design served as a proof-of-concept only; for this reason a small sample size sufficed, but our sample was not large enough to draw any clinically relevant conclusions, nor can we estimate the transferability of our results. Another limitation of our study concerned the use of categorical values (narrative foci codes) to delimit data segments. Although this technique is a viable option to group lines for code co-occurrence computation [16], there are challenges involved, such as how to address multiple categorical values exhibited in a single line of data (e.g., the sentence contains two narrative foci: Self and Others). Our coding decision was to employ chronological order, that is, apply the narrative foci code that appeared first in the sentence. This coding decision, as any methodological decision, affected our results; for example, if there was a tendency among our participants to emphasize perceptions of others in their sentences before they spoke about themselves, this would entail less lines of data included in the network displaying them describing themselves and false connections in the network displaying them describing others. Further studies based on our general design necessitate a more in-depth qualitative examination of these patterns and perhaps a different solution to this dilemma pertaining to categorical coding. Another limitation of our study is that ENA currently has no hypergraph capabilities, thus models display co-occurrences of unique pairs of codes (as opposed to triads, etc.).

6 Conclusion

The list of diagnostic criteria in the DSM-5 does not shed enough light on the combinatorial possibilities of each diagnostic criterion and their associated features idiosyncratic to a patient. Furthermore, diagnosis of personality disorders has evolved from a solely categorical ("present" or "absent") model to a more complex understanding in which individuals very rarely present with a 'pure' illness, but rather with a mixed personality disorder, comorbid with other disorders (e.g. mood disorders, addiction, etc.). We believe our study design may contribute to mapping case- and narrative focus-level interactions among diagnostic criteria and across multiple comorbidities, which may have the potential for more tailored and personalized healthcare.

Acknowledgements. This project received funding from the European Union's Horizon 2020 research and innovation program under the Marie Sklodowska-Curie grant agreement No. 101028644, as well as from University Fund Limburg/SWOL. The opinions, findings, and conclusions do not reflect the views of the funding agency, cooperating institutions, or other individuals.

References

1. American Psychiatric Association: Diagnostic and Statistical Manual of Mental Disorders 5th edn. American Psychiatric Publishing, Inc., Washington, DC (2013)
2. Samuels, J., Eaton, W.W., Bienvenu, O.J., Brown, C.H., Costa, P.T., Nestadt, G.: Prevalence and correlates of personality disorders in a community sample. Br. J. Psychiatry **180**, 536–542 (2002). https://doi.org/10.1192/bjp.180.6.536
3. Torgersen, S., Kringlen, E., Cramer, V.: The prevalence of personality disorders in a community sample. Arch. Gen. Psychiatry **58**, 590–596 (2001). https://doi.org/10.1001/archpsyc.58.6.590
4. Coid, J., Yang, M., Tyrer, P., Roberts, A., Ullrich, S.: Prevalence and correlates of personality disorder in Great Britain. Br. J. Psychiatry **188**, 423–431 (2006). https://doi.org/10.1192/bjp.188.5.423
5. Moran, P., Jenkins, R., Tylee, A., Blizard, R., Mann, A.: The prevalence of personality disorder among UK primary care attenders. Acta Psychiatr. Scand. **102**, 52–57 (2000). https://doi.org/10.1034/j.1600-0447.2000.102001052.x
6. Gross, R., et al.: Borderline personality disorder in primary care. Arch. Intern. Med. **162**, 53–60 (2002). https://doi.org/10.1001/archinte.162.1.53
7. Bagge, C., Nickell, A., Stepp, S., Durrett, C., Jackson, K., Trull, T.J.: Borderline personality disorder features predict negative outcomes 2 years later. J. Abnorm. Psychol. **113**, 279–288 (2004). https://doi.org/10.1037/0021-843X.113.2.279
8. Understanding and treating borderline personality disorder: A guide for professionals and families. American Psychiatric Publishing, Inc., Arlington, VA, US (2005)
9. Dammann, G., et al.: The self-image in borderline personality disorder: an in-depth qualitative research study. J. Pers. Disord. **25**, 517–527 (2011). https://doi.org/10.1521/pedi.2011.25.4.517
10. Koenigsberg, H.W., et al.: Characterizing affective instability in borderline personality disorder. Am. J. Psychiatry **159**, 784–788 (2002). https://doi.org/10.1176/appi.ajp.159.5.784
11. Klonsky, E.D.: What is emptiness? Clarifying the 7th criterion for borderline personality disorder. J. Pers. Disord. **22**, 418–426 (2008). https://doi.org/10.1521/pedi.2008.22.4.418
12. Richetin, J., Preti, E., Costantini, G., De Panfilis, C.: The centrality of affective instability and identity in borderline personality disorder: Evidence from network analysis. PLoS ONE **12**, e0186695 (2017). https://doi.org/10.1371/journal.pone.0186695
13. Speelman, C.P., McGann, M.: Statements about the pervasiveness of behavior require data about the pervasiveness of behavior. Front. Psychol. **11**, 594675 (2020). https://doi.org/10.3389/fpsyg.2020.594675
14. Whewell, P., Lingam, R., Chilton, R.: Reflective borderline group therapy: the patients' experience of being borderline. Psychoanal. Psychother. **18**, 324–345 (2004). https://doi.org/10.1080/14749730412331280948
15. Bennett, D.H., Holmes, D.S.: Influence of denial (situation redefinition) and projection on anxiety associated with threat to self-esteem. J. Pers. Soc. Psychol. **32**, 915–921 (1975). https://doi.org/10.1037//0022-3514.32.5.915
16. Zörgő, S., Brohinsky, J.: Parsing the continuum: manual segmentation of monologic data. In: Advances in Quantitative Ethnography. Communications in Computer and Information, pp. 163–181. Springer Nature, Cham Switzerland (2022). https://doi.org/10.1007/978-3-031-31726-2_12
17. Bowman, D., et al.: The mathematical foundations of epistemic network analysis. In: Advances in Quantitative Ethnography. Communications in Computer and Information Science Series, pp. 91–105. Springer Nature, Switzerland (2021). https://doi.org/10.1007/978-3-030-67788-6_7

18. Shaffer, D.: Quantitative Ethnography. Cathcart Press, Madison, WI (2017)
19. Shaffer, D., Collier, W., Ruis, A.: A tutorial on epistemic network analysis: analyzing the structure of connections in cognitive, social, and interaction data. J. Learn. Analytics **3**(3), 9–45 (2016). https://doi.org/10.18608/jla.2016.33.3
20. Zörgő, S.: Segmentation and code co-occurrence accumulation: operationalizing relational context with stanza windows. In: Advances in Quantitative Ethnography. Communications in Computer and Information Science, pp. 146–162. Springer Nature, Cham Switzerland (2022). https://doi.org/10.1007/978-3-031-31726-2_11
21. Barnow, S., Arens, E.A., Sieswerda, S., Dinu-Biringer, R., Spitzer, C., Lang, S.: Borderline personality disorder and psychosis: a review. Curr. Psychiatry Rep. **12**, 186–195 (2010). https://doi.org/10.1007/s11920-010-0107-9
22. Addington, J., Van Mastrigt, S., Hutchinson, J., Addington, D.: Pathways to care: help seeking behaviour in first episode psychosis. Acta Psychiatr. Scand. **106**, 358–364 (2002). https://doi.org/10.1034/j.1600-0447.2002.02004.x
23. Yamaguchi, T., Fujii, C., Nemoto, T., Tsujino, N., Takeshi, K., Mizuno, M.: Differences between subjective experiences and observed behaviors in near-fatal suicide attempters with untreated schizophrenia: A qualitative pilot study. Ann. Gen. Psychiatry, **14** (2015). https://doi.org/10.1186/s12991-015-0055-1
24. Plutchik, R., Kellerman, H., Conte, H.R.: A structural theory of ego defenses and emotions. In: Izard, C.E. (ed.) Emotions in Personality and Psychopathology, pp. 227–257. Springer US, Boston, MA (1979). https://doi.org/10.1007/978-1-4613-2892-6_9

Leveraging Epistemic Network Analysis in Monologic Interviews to Explore Cultural Integration In Global Organizations

Sheri L. Mackey[✉]

Oakland University, 275 Varner Drive, Rochester, MI 48309, USA
smackey2@oakland.edu

Abstract. This study responds to calls for pragmatic context-driven scholarship to evaluate the perceived need for cultural integration in global organizations. This paper aims to fill the gap between theoretical frameworks and contemporary phenomena with a grounded theory, quantitative ethnography study designed to explore the perceived need for cultural integration to improve business outcomes in global organizations, also evaluating the perceived need for a dedicated framework to develop cultural integration in global organizations. Data were collected through semi-structured interviews conducted with twenty global executives. Analysis of the dataset was done through thematic content analysis and epistemic network analysis. Research demonstrated that cultural integration, and its associated constructs, were perceived as critical to group and organizational success. Global executives and leaders confirmed the need for a dedicated framework for cultural integration to improve business outcomes. The current study addressed four research questions: (1) To what extent is there a perceived need for cultural integration in global organizations? (2) To what extent is cultural integration perceived relevant to business outcomes in global organizations? (3) To what extent do leaders perceive socio-cultural epistemic frames are malleable at the group level? (4) To what extent is there a perceived need for a dedicated framework to develop cultural integration to shift socio-cultural epistemic frames in global teams? This empirical study confirms that socio-cultural epistemic frames are malleable at the group level to develop cultural integration and there is a perceived need for a dedicated framework to develop cultural integration for improved business outcomes in global organizations.

Keywords: ENA · Cultural Integration · Global Organizations

1 Introduction

The rapid pace of globalization and the growing number of collaborative technology solutions has enabled virtual work practices to accelerate, while recent events, such as the recent pandemic, demand that organizations worldwide change the way they engage (Ladika, 2020). No longer is it viable for teams in global corporations to work in a central location and expect global objectives to be met. The demand for skills from

© The Author(s), under exclusive license to Springer Nature Switzerland AG 2023
G. Arastoopour Irgens and S. Knight (Eds.): ICQE 2023, CCIS 1895, pp. 330–345, 2023.
https://doi.org/10.1007/978-3-031-47014-1_23

around the world has made working across boundaries and borders a necessity. However, collaborative teamwork in global environments is not intuitive. It is far more than dealing with technology and time zones; it is about people and the value that collaboration across different cultures can bring to the organization.

Cultural differences in business have become a major source of frustration when employees of different nationalities do not share an implicit or explicit understanding of the world and how to get things done within it (House et al., 2004). It may be difficult and unproductive to compare cultures as superior or inferior, but there is almost always an overwhelming sense of the "right way" and the "wrong way" to do business, which at its root is often culturally driven. To overcome narrow worldviews, individuals must internalize and develop ways to work effectively with colleagues, partners, and customers who hold different worldviews (Adler & Aycan, 2018). While much is known about how to globalize corporations via technology, logistics management, and the like, few conclusive solutions exist for how to globalize people to meet these challenges (Javidan & Bowen, 2015) to deliver successful and sustainable global outcomes.

While historically, expatriate leaders were expected to integrate into the host nation culture to be successful, new global leadership competency requirements have emerged. Global leaders today are not only expected to succeed within the confines of a single host nation but are also expected to have the capacity to manage across multiple cultures simultaneously (Mendenhall et al., 2018). Today's reality suggests global corporations operate across many disparate cultures concurrently. Multicultural relationships are the day-to-day reality that define the efficiency of the multinational workforce (Fink & Holden, 2007). Global leaders and their teams need to understand the barriers to (and facilitators of) effective cross-cultural relationships.

Daily, people establish and maintain connections that by their very nature are multicultural and impact the organization's ability to succeed. If there are barriers to cultural integration in the global work environment, the effectiveness of the workforce is likely to drop exponentially due to obstacles to task realization. By contrast, effective multicultural interactions contribute to employees' learning and creativity, improve communications, and increase the satisfaction of personnel worldwide (Holden, 2002).

2 Problem Statement

Poor cross-cultural interactions often result in an inability to collaborate successfully across boundaries and borders. This frequently results in inconsistent global business results and poor financial performance. The significance of this problem is confirmed by the Economist Intelligence Unit (2016), indicating that 90% of executives from 68 countries report poor cross-cultural interactions to be a top issue in global operations. Asperion Global (2018) provided additional confirmation in reporting that 75% of all global initiatives fail to improve business results.

In addition, according to Culture Wizard's survey, Trends in Global Virtual Teams (Soloman, 2016), with respondents from 80 countries, 68% reported that cultural challenges are the biggest hurdle to global team productivity, and 58% of respondents indicated that global leaders are not adequately prepared to lead multicultural virtual teams. In alignment, the DDI Global Leadership Forecast (Ray & Sinar, 2018) reported that more than 70% of leaders who hold international team responsibility consistently do not meet their goals and objectives. These statistics indicate there may be a substantial, ongoing challenge working across cultures which frequently results in profoundly suboptimal outcomes for the individual, the team, and the company. Globalization and cultural diversity in all business operations dictate the necessity to achieve increasingly better outcomes and require global teams to become culturally integrated (Alizadeh & Chavan, 2016) to achieve strong, sustainable global business results.

As indicated above, designated methodologies have not been wholly successful as stand-alone solutions. Country-specific practices, orientations, assessments, and tools are all designed to help the global workforce acclimate to multicultural environments. However, these approaches focus on knowledge, skills, and attributes that appear to be the antecedents of cultural competence (Johnson et al., 2006) and do not necessarily create an environment for cultural integration. Without a cohesive approach to building out self and others simultaneously, global corporations are subject to the continually escalating failure rates that facilitate the unfortunate statistics seen in global business today.

3 Research Objectives

This grounded theory, quantitative ethnographic study was designed to empirically evaluate the need for cultural integration as a group phenomenon in global organizations. The purpose of this research was to evaluate whether there is a perceived need for cultural integration that impacts the sociocultural malleability in global teams at the group level to improve business outcomes. The study collected ethnographical data to analyze, synthesize, and understand leader views (Creswell & Creswell, 2018) in light of cultural integration.

In this study, quantitative ethnographical results were derived from ethnographical, semi-structured interviews with senior executive leaders and global/regional team leaders from two companies within the technology (Company Z) and supply chain (Company X) industries. The data collected were leveraged to identify specific malleable constructs that indicate the perceived need for cultural integration in global teams. The data were coded and analyzed for further ethnographical analysis. Epistemic Network Analysis was utilized to examine the strength of relationship between data elements to evaluate sociocultural frames that implicate cultural integration as a key factor toward improving global business outcomes. By combining methods for testing statistical significance with techniques to create deeper understanding, this grounded theory, quantitative ethnographic design enabled evaluation of the perceived need for cultural integration that impacts the sociocultural malleability in global teams at the group level to improve business outcomes in global organizations. Both qualitative and quantitative data were important to developing a complete understanding of the potential malleability of the underlying constructs in producing cultural integration in global teams. However, strategically merging these two approaches to harness the joint power of acquiring new insight required a way to provide thick descriptions of a significant population with the power of data analysis to truly integrate quantitative and qualitative approaches (Shaffer, 2018).

4 Research Questions

In the interest of evaluating if there is a perceived need for cultural integration that may impact the sociocultural malleability in global teams at the group level to improve business outcomes, this study addressed the following research questions:

RQ1: To what extent is there a perceived need for cultural integration in global organizations?
RQ2: To what extent is cultural integration perceived relevant to business outcomes in global organizations?
RQ3: To what extent do leaders perceive socio-cultural epistemic frames are malleable at the group level?
RQ4: To what extent is there a perceived need for a dedicated framework to develop cultural integration to shift socio-cultural epistemic frames in global teams?

5 Conceptual Framework

This study is significant because it evaluates the perceived need for cultural integration and the malleability of sociocultural frames to improve global business outcomes, however it also utilizes Epistemic Network Analysis in a previously unexplored application. It focuses on leveraging monologic interviews within the global corporate environment to collect the ethnographic data from key executives that was prepared and used in Epistemic Network Analysis.

This study contributes to understanding the sociocultural constructs that enable cultural integration and how they can be shifted for organizational success, as well as what could be a critical success factor enabling improved diversity and inclusion, using ENA as a constructivist tool to visualize and measure qualitative data collected from 20 global executives from two companies, across two different industries. The data was transformed and analyzed using quantitative ethnography for the development and validation of the need for cultural integration to enable diverse teams to scaffold learning and development to build upon existing knowledge and experience (Brown & Hirst, 2007). At the same time, ENA provided new constructs and knowledge to facilitate cultural integration resulting in long term learning and retention in the global workforce.

This grounded theory, quantitative ethnographical study extends the body of existing research, and explores a comprehensive, constructivist approach to significantly improve diverse interactions on a global scale to drive strong business outcomes. The goal of this research was to add to existing research, while also exploring the perceived need for flexibility in sociocultural constructs to develop cultural integration through an interdisciplinary framework enabling an intersubjective ecosystem that drives improved business outcomes in global organizations.

The goal of this research was to utilize quantitative ethnography to explore constructs that are malleable and contribute to the development of cultural integration in global organizations. In addition, this research provided a translational component to a multidisciplinary body of research by exploring the possibility of enabling a comprehensive network that drives improved business outcomes through the cultural integration of diverse, multicultural global teams. This study introduced the concept of a group phenomenon, cultural integration, and evaluated whether executives, global leaders, and their teams perceive a need for cultural integration that impacts sociocultural malleability in global teams to improve business outcomes.

6   Research Methods

This research presents a grounded theory, quantitative ethnographical approach aligning the evidence collected to the cultural phenomenon of interest (Shaffer, 2017), which was the perceived need for cultural integration to impact the sociocultural malleability in global teams at the group level to improve business outcomes. A grounded theory approach was chosen to provide a way to explore cultural integration through deep analysis of datasets. This methodology used guidelines that are systematic yet flexible for collecting and analyzing data. Charmaz (2006) explained that study populations bring their unique experiences, understanding, and points of view to the topic, and grounded theory is a construction of these realities. The objective of this study was to leverage the empirical data collected to better comprehend the need for cultural integration.

Quantitative ethnography (QE) was chosen because a typical mixed method approach would involve quantitative and qualitative methods running in sequence, with the idea that the results from one would inform the other. Where quantitative findings tend to be shallow but broadly applicable, qualitative findings tend to be detailed but narrowly focused (Creswell & Creswell, 2018). While the results include both techniques, the methods for this study were employed separately, limiting the research to evaluating and interpreting the results from differentiated vantage points (Shaffer, 2018). This approach brought together the power of statistics with the strength of an in-depth, ethnographic approach to examine data sets to better understand connections in culturally diverse human behavior.

Semi-structured interviews were conducted to explore the perceptions, experiences, and behaviors of executives and global team leaders, providing a thicker and richer description of the data as it yield quantifiable information about the network of discourse within the global organization. Shaffer (2004) proposed epistemic frame theory (EFT) to describe the pattern of association between skills, knowledge, and values that characterize groups of people who share similar ways of framing and solving complex problems. Each person filters information and builds frames that organize an understanding of the current situation based on sociocultural factors they bring to the global team (Phillips et al., 2021). Within a multicultural team context, these structures are frequently not consistent and cause challenges within the team that result in poor communications that lead to substandard outcomes. When team members engage, often on a virtual basis, actions are shaped by individual choices and beliefs about team members who are culturally diverse and unfamiliar. The approach and execution of work is significantly shaped by this cultural context. Given this premise, frames are the collections of both individual and social norms, values, and actions that form how culturally diverse members perceive the world, which often results in suboptimal outcomes for the individual, the team, and the organization. This study sought to determine whether sociocultural epistemic frames are malleable and can inform and develop cultural integration.

Using ENA, epistemic frames were analyzed to examine connections in discourse and to measure the co-occurrence of constructs within the semi-structured interviews.

ENA identifies and quantified connections between leaders, demonstrating where cultural integration was beneficial and the perceived impact on diverse member perceptions, experiences, and behaviors. An epistemic network—originally developed to model cognitive networks—represented the structure of connections and the strength of association among codes to determine if cultural integration was considered beneficial (Shaffer, 2017). To interpret specific events, codes were used to evaluate interview data (Shaffer et al., 2016).

QE provided the analytical tools to detect, describe, and better understand cultural integration in global teams, while also providing insight into the impact on the sociocultural constructs of the diverse study population. By combining methods for testing statistical significance with techniques to create deeper understanding, QE enabled the exploration of the need for cultural integration in global organizations. In addition, it brought to light the potential for cultural integration to impact business outcomes through the malleability of sociocultural epistemic frames at the group level, to provide evidence of the need for a dedicated framework for developing cultural integration. Through exploring the need for cultural integration in the study population, this quantitative ethnographical research illuminated a new path forward in developing effective global teams that have the capacity to drive successful outcomes for international organizations.

The population for this study was senior executives and global/regional leaders within two global organizations from the technology (company Z) and supply chain management (company X) industries, respectively. The team structure was characterized by a global leader residing in a single location, being responsible for regional leaders located across multiple regions. Global/regional leaders and teams were required to work together across multiple cultures simultaneously on a daily basis. Rep-resentative of the wider population, two levels of management within two international organizations from two different industries were leveraged to make a generalization about the broader population of teams working in the global marketplace. Purposive sampling was used to identify global executives prepared to engage in the research study and recommend leaders managing global and regional teams directly.

Data were collected via semi-structured interviews, with the protocol developed to evaluate the extent there is a perceived need for cultural integration in global organizations, but extended further to explore if global leaders perceived socio-cultural constructs may be malleable at the group level through cultural integration to impact business outcomes in global teams. After data collection was complete, transcripts of the interviews were analyzed, and the emerging codes were allocated into thematic categories. As codes developed, they were organized under the appropriate construct and interview questions were aligned to ensure a good representation of the data. Once the codes had emerged from the data, a codebook was developed and confirmed by the three-person coding team. Inter-rater Reliability using Cohen's κ was found to be $>.65$ and the master dataset, incorporating six interviews for each coder, was created. Once coding was complete, the three spreadsheets containing all eighteen interviews were combined into a master dataset to use for both ethnographical and quantitative analysis.

For qualitative investigation, thematic content analysis was used to establish overarching impressions of the data. Rather than approaching the data with a predetermined framework, common themes were identified through iterative data review to find common patterns across the data set. Following, data were uploaded into the ENA Webtool for quantitative analysis.

The analysis was conducted using the ENA webtool to create visualizations and quantitative data; however, ethnographical analysis informed the research by providing rich context and interpretation to the overall thematic discussion. A combination of these two methods provides a more complete view of the data set. Critical to the operationalization of these aspects of ENA was the segmentation of the data. This study leveraged the whole conversation stanza window, indicating the co-occurrence of codes exists in the lines contributed by a given unit in a conversation, then aggregated across all conversations in the data set. This approach equated conversation with stanza—thus, codes could co-occur anywhere in the conversation. Each question within the interview data, per single executive, was considered a conversation. This method was chosen to reflect the monologic nature of the data and importance of the entire response to each question. Sentences served as the smallest codable segments in this data set because the developed codes were most applicable to sentences (as opposed to e.g., smaller prosodic phrases or larger turns-of-talk) (Zorgo et al., 2021). Further, the intent was to present a concise amount of text on a level of granularity that would enable a fair number of co-occurrences to take place. While each sentence was considered an utterance, the segmentation reflected the gravity of the entire response to each question. Utterances in the monologic data were coded within the same code set. Co-occurrences of codes were then aggregated per unit for each unique pair of codes. Lastly, network models were generated manually to illustrate the strength of co-occurrences between codes and to inspect the differences in models produced for "all participants" versus "global/regional leaders" and "senior executives" separately.

Ethnographic, thematic analysis was conducted to mine rich contextual meaning from the data, while ENA was deployed to invoke strong visualization and statistical validity. Both methods were valuable as individual contributors to this body of research, but value increased exponentially as there was a distinct capability to pivot between the raw data, coded data, statistical models, and visualizations to identify preliminary assumptions, alternative or rival interpretations, and contextualized code interactions, thus closing the interpretive loop (Shaffer, 2017). Cultural integration, as the focus of this study, was a core construct from which all other codes were addressed. It became clear that cultural integration is a complex concept with many important linkages across the network. As such, each construct was evaluated as a subcategory linked to cultural integration. An overview is presented regarding the overall impressions and outcomes relative to the core construct of this study, and subsequent sections reflect the relationship between cultural integration and the associated codes, as determined by weight and density in the ENA model.

7 Findings

Cultural integration, as communicated to leaders, is a group phenomenon that enables culturally diverse teams to work better together despite perceived differences. Global leaders across both Company X and Company Z, as they answered the interview questions, became increasingly attuned to a different way of looking at existing challenges

(Fig. 1). The initial ENA visualization of all leaders indicated that while some edges may appear stronger than others, there are indisputable links to cultural integration within every code. Despite an unfamiliarity with cultural integration, there was an immediate connection point where leaders perceived this construct as an important component to success, yet realizing the intricacy of the construct. Figure 1 demonstrates the complexity of the network surrounding cultural integration, as was also reflected in the ethnographic data. It is important to note that while all nodes connect back to cultural integration, the co-occurrence of codes linking alternative codes strongly suggests that leaders are keenly interested in cultural integration as a mechanism to impact additional constructs, such as awareness of worldviews, business outcomes, effective teams, partnership and collaboration, and diversity of thought. However, a key limitation in the ENA software is that it currently does not have the ability to quantitatively hypergraph to evaluate co-occurrences that span multiple codes simultaneously, limiting multi-construct connectivity. However, in closing the interpretive loop, it becomes apparent that cultural integration may serve as key mechanism to improve overall results for the organization.

In consideration of cultural integration, leaders evaluated current challenges and made a strong connection between exhibited work methods, behaviors, and communications as demonstrated deficits to cultural integration. Multiple leaders spoke of having to "fill the gap" when working across cultures, equating accommodation to inadequate cultural integration to both time and money. They indicated frequent miscommunication and misalignment from team members having very different worldviews. The amalgamation of differing worldviews manifested through the exhibition of differing behaviors, patterns of speech, and work methods. These types of differences were repeatedly reported as causing incidents with varied levels of impact, such as minor frustrations or disagreements, missed deadlines, customer dissatisfaction, and even the loss of business.

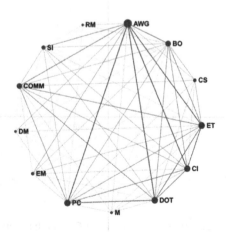

Fig. 1. Normative Sphere of Cultural Integration

Despite the challenges, leaders also considered the future, and indicated a potential for cultural integration to improve team effectiveness. While they understood currently there is little preparation for working with people who have different cultural backgrounds in either company, there was also a fundamental understanding that cultural integration has the capacity to change global team dynamics and provide a mechanism for teams to work together better. Leader 8 was optimistic in his assessment:

The reality of it is that cultural integration could really change team cohesiveness, but it could also be a great recruitment and retention tool. The team itself would benefit by understanding and connecting better, which leads to doing things better, faster, and cheaper. It could be a real enabler to increase productivity, but also to get people talking about their different ways so we can look for something like third, or fourth, or fifth best ways of doing things that lead to innovation. They stand to gain a lot.

There was clear recognition of the complex challenges faced daily when working across boundaries and borders, reflected in both the qualitative analysis and the visualization of the data set.

To further evaluate the interviews, leader data was segmented into two categories: senior executive (SrE) and global/regional leaders (GRL). In the SrE category there were six leaders representing ranks from the board of directors to heads of divisions, while the remaining 14 leaders represented leaders managing global or regional teams directly, ranking from director to vice president. The focus on this split-level analysis (Fig. 2) was to explore the two levels of leaders' perceptions regarding cultural integration and if there was variation in code pairings that could inform both the malleability of sociocultural epistemic frames and the perceived focus for the development of a dedicated framework for cultural integration in global organizations. ENA for split level analysis indicated that senior executives and global/regional leaders both indicated the need for cultural integration, but for different reasons.

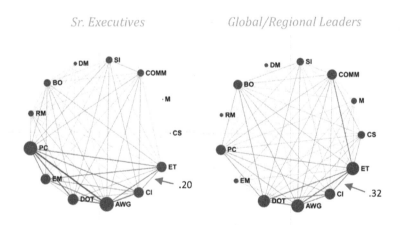

Fig. 2. Split Level Analysis for Cultural Integration

Senior Executives appeared to have an affinity for the psychological constructs of cultural integration, focusing more on awareness of worldviews, diversity of thought, partnerships, and empathy. While effective teams and business outcomes were prevalent in the qualitative data, there was also a sense of people being a high priority. This may have prompted senior executives to speak about cultural integration in terms of the human component, underlying the idea that by taking care of people, effective teams would emerge and result in improved business outcomes. It is also important to note that while ENA does not currently have the capacity to hypergraph, acknowledging the complexity of relationships in the data enabled the ability to visually perceive the notion that, for example, cultural integration is strongly aligned to partnership and collaboration. Collaboration is strongly connected to codes such as solutions and innovation, communications, and effective teams. From this data-driven perspective, it is important to infer further connections that implicate cultural integration in the overall network. Comparatively, global/regional leaders appeared to have greater alignment with behavioral and analytical constructs. The visual implication indicated strong alignment between cultural integration and communications, awareness of worldviews, solutions/Innovation, and effective teams. This could indicate a view closer to the ground as leaders of global and regional teams directly interface with those teams on a regular basis. While there is more variation in the visual data, it was important to note the leaders were very focused on the effectiveness of teams and business outcomes, understanding business outcomes for the organization are achieved through global teams. Similar to the Executive data, it is also important to note the inference of pathways across codes. Upon evaluation of the raw data, it became clear that there was strong alignment to partnership/collaboration, diversity of thought, customer satisfaction, and communications. However, in the visualized models these additional codes were not directly accessible via cultural integration.

Initially, awareness appeared to serve as an overall precursor to the ability to perceive cultural integration, as was evidenced when leaders began to see their business through a different lens. Although awareness is a code within the construct of cultural integration overall, findings indicated that awareness was central to the perception of global organizations' ability to address the challenge of cultural integration. Awareness bridged the gap to understanding cultural integration as a central construct. However, once made aware, leaders exhibited a strong belief that a lack of cultural integration is a critical explanatory factor for many challenges facing geographically dispersed global teams.

The ENA findings for cultural integration indicated awareness as a construct that spans the knowledge gap for both companies (Fig. 3), providing an initial starting point to help global teams work together effectively. When considering the visualization data, an edge of the all-participant data was 0.40 between cultural integration and awareness, which indicated exceptionally strong co-occurrence in the codes, depicting a substantial relationship. In addition, the large nodes for both awareness and cultural integration, alongside the associated utterances, indicated a level of acknowledgement and urgency associated to a lack of awareness and its potential to derail team outcomes. Split level analysis also indicated a strong relationship between awareness and cultural integration with both senior executives and global/regional leaders exhibiting a .48 weight in the edge. The node size per code indicates there was a high concentration of responses indicating awareness of worldviews to be a central point of interest. There was significant evidence in the qualitative data that awareness was not explicit within either organization, which was considered an indicator of the challenges inherent to the organizations.

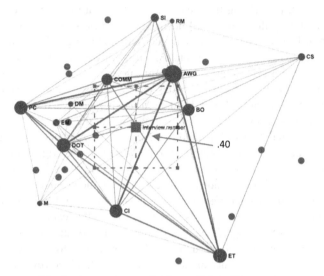

Fig. 3. Awareness as a Bridge to Cultural Integration

After the initial analysis of all participant data and the split-level analysis, the dataset was evaluated to determine the most prominent codes relative to this study for further exploration. Cultural integration, as the core construct for this study, was paired with codes determined to be the best fit in line with the visualization of key codes. To develop this model (Fig. 4), edges with a strength of less than .18 were eliminated from the visualization. The most prominent codes were determined by two factors: (a) the strength of the edge between pairings and (b) the size of the node relative to all codes. Upon close evaluation of the edges and nodes, it was determined that the key codes for the purpose of further evaluation were awareness of worldviews, effective teams, and business outcomes.

As the edges and nodes for the pairing cultural integration and effective teams were examined, there was a heavily weighted edge, and the nodes were quite big, indicating how prevalent the code pairing was in the networked ENA model. Although the data reflected a strong instance of co-occurrence (0.30), the qualitative data provided more depth of information. Examining the split-level data, the edges were quite strong for both executives, at .20 as well as leaders, at .32. While there was a strong edge connection and node size attributed to the cultural integration to effective teams pairing, further analysis revealed that both Company X and Company Z experience challenges in managing the cultural disparities on global teams, as was evidenced in boundary edges. From the opposite perspective, leaders also indicated significant opportunity in the challenges, communicating the strength and potential of the teams to leverage cultural integration to capture a unique form of competitive advantage in the global marketplace.

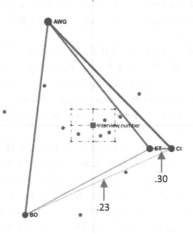

Fig. 4. Key Code Visualization

Closely aligned to effective teams was business outcomes. In turn, cultural integration is predicated on the global team's ability to work as a connected network, a system. In the visualization, the connection is noteworthy between cultural integration and business outcomes for all-participant data at .23. The node size for business outcomes is significant, indicating a substantial level of interest in the topic and a strong response to interview questions. When split level analysis of the visual data was done, there was a slight shift in the data, with senior executives being a bit less focused on business outcomes with an edge of .27, as compared to the global/regional leaders with an edge of .36. This was attributed to the distribution in the data set, as well as the leaders having direct responsibility for global and regional teams on the ground.

The broad spectrum of code connections to awareness may imply that cultural integration is accomplished through boundary-spanning, aimed at facilitating capacity development and dedication among multicultural team members towards culturally diverse practices (Roberts & Beamish, 2017). However, the node size per code also indicates that there was a high concentration of responses indicating awareness of worldviews to be a central point of interest.

Many leaders also considered awareness and cultural integration from the personal perspective of not knowing how to understand diverse cultures or what to do when they find themselves working alongside unfamiliar cultures. They inherently seemed to comprehend the team struggle in diverse environments, but did not know how to address the challenge. Despite the inability to hypergraph in the ENA webtool, the ethnographic data suggested many leaders had challenges when working across cultures. Upon reviewing the raw data, it was found that 78% of leaders spoke about their own experience, or that of their teams, in not understanding the real-world implications and challenges when working across cultures. Leader 3 suggested:

Today, I do not think people are given information about how other people might see different things, or how other cultures might interpret their words or actions, but it is necessary to success.

This perspective may explain the challenges in working within multicultural teams today. Ethnographic analysis of data indicated that, in general, leaders believed awareness of cultural diversity and its implications is low and often result in unintended consequences. There was strong belief that cultural integration is something that is not explicitly visible, and as a result, is not addressed directly, costing companies both money and time.

When considering the visualization data, an edge of the all-participant data was 0.40 between cultural integration and awareness, which indicated there was strong co-occurrence in the codes, depicting a substantial relationship. In addition, the large nodes for both awareness and cultural integration, alongside the associated utterances, indicated a level of acknowledgement and urgency associated to Awareness and its ability to derail team outcomes. Split level analysis also indicated a strong relationship between awareness and cultural integration with both senior executives and global/regional leaders exhibiting a .48 weight in the edge. Interview responses indicate there is a gap in knowledge on global teams regarding consideration and comprehension of diverse worldviews as a leverage point for awareness that can reduce or eliminate miscommunications and misalignment.

For this study, a two-sample t test assuming unequal variance was performed within the ENA software to determine if global/Regional Leaders were statistically significantly different from Senior Executives at an alpha of .05. While statistical significance indicated an effect existed, practical significance demonstrated the effect was large enough to be meaningful in the real world.

The ENA Webtool included a built-in utility that used the raw data in this study to calculate the t value. A significant t value of 5.29 indicated the difference between group mean was greater than the pooled standard error, indicating the two groups were statistically different from one another, while the p-value of .01 suggested evidence of statistical significance. While t test values indicated a significant difference in the study population outcomes between executives and leaders, a Cohen's d of 3.92 suggested a significant effect indicating outcomes may be meaningful in the real world.

This study examined the data from two separate perspectives, providing insight from a general leadership perspective, but also evaluating responses from a split-level angle, exploring the alignment between senior executives' and global/regional leaders' viewpoints and perceptions. In addition, data were analyzed through the lens of an interpretive loop to integrate the raw data and utterance of leaders to provide context to the visualizations. The overall analysis indicated strong support for cultural integration overall, with specific emphasis on awareness of worldviews, effective teams, and business outcomes. However, underlying each of these constructs, evidence suggests broad support for the additional coded constructs. This was powerfully reinforced in the individual utterances and was strengthened through network connections. The remaining coded constructs (motivation, customer satisfaction, partnership/collaboration, communications, decision-making, solutions/innovation, perspective/diversity of thought, empathy and risk mitigation) not only emerged as connections in the original network models, but were also discussed extensively throughout the interview process. The initial findings suggest:

1. Cultural integration is perceived as necessary in global organizations.
2. Cultural integration is highly relevant to business outcomes.
3. Leaders believe that sociocultural epistemic frames are malleable and can be shifted at the group level.
4. There is a perceived need for a dedicated framework to address cultural integration in global organizations.

In addition, when considering the overarching construct of cultural integration, there was a strong perception among leaders that cultural integration is an important strategic initiative for global organizations.

Cultural integration was a new concept for most leaders; however, there was an immediate recognition that it is something that is missing in global organizations today. Leaders repeatedly spoke of the concept as something that flows under the surface that greatly impacts the organization, but is not explicitly recognized. Once aware of the concept, leaders considered it a critical strategic imperative necessary to enabling a new approach to creating competitive advantage in the global marketplace.

8 Limitations

There were four primary limitations to this research: (a) small sample size, (b) limited industry exposure, (c) the inability to hypergraph (d) the inability to measure and quantify nodes in ENA.

Although the sample size was small, utilizing purposive sampling enabled a selection of best-fit participants from a small, geographically dispersed population to provide for a systematic investigation, leading to results highly relevant to the research proposed. In addition, by using purposive sampling the margin of error was reduced because the data sources were a close fit with the research context.

This study focused on two industries, the supply chain management and technology sectors. Although both Company X and Company Z were both highly representative of their respective industries, this study did not provide a view into the wide expanse of industries available. The goal of this initial research was to demonstrate that, irrespective of industry, cultural integration was perceived as necessary in global organizations. While both industries indicated the perceived need for cultural integration, it is not representative of a wide array of industries and further research must be done.

Because ENA had not been used in the corporate environment previously, it was challenging to discern how it would work and how the outcomes could be interpreted. In addition, there was a challenge with never having used the ENA webtool before and learning the tool from the ground up. As I did, limitations were discovered such as the tool not having the capacity to measure nodes, as well as an inability to hypergraph, which may have limited the insight from additional code connections.

9 Future Recommendations

Although all alternative hypotheses were confirmed, cultural integration, as a group phenomenon, is a new construct and in its infancy. It will be important to extend this research beyond its current borders, to explore quantitative ethnography in the corporate setting, as well as to expand to further industries and levels of organization. Many, if not most, leaders spoke of cultural integration as a strategic initiative which was described as one of the last great opportunities for competitive advantage in the global marketplace. As a new construct to global organizations, cultural integration needs to be deeply explored and evaluated. As a first of its kind study, utilizing quantitative ethnography in global corporations yielded substantive results and should be further explored to continue to explore and facilitate improved results in business environments. It would be useful to explore and evaluate ENA as a viable tool to evaluate monologic interviews in corporate environments as way to empirically understand global business leaders and how different constructs may impact global outcomes in organizations.

10 Conclusion

This study was the first to use ENA in a monologic setting in the global corporate environment, as well as confirming the need for a dedicated framework to support cultural integration in global organizations. There is much more work to do, however this research provided significant insight and opportunity for further research.

References

Adler, N.J., Aycan, Z:. Cross-cultural interaction: What we know and what we need to know. Ann. Rev. Organ. Psychol. Organ. Behav. **5**, 307–333 (2018). https://doi.org/10.1146/annurev-org psych-032117-104528. https://www.annualreviews.org/doi/pdf

Alizadeh, S., Chavan, M.: Cultural competence dimensions and outcomes: A systematic review of the literature. Health Soc. Care Commun. **24**(6), 117–130 (2016). https://doi.org/10.1111/hsc.12293

Brown, R., Hirst, E.: Developing an understanding of the mediating role of talk in the elementary mathematics classroom. J. Classroom Interact. 18-28 (2007). http://www.jstor.org/stable/23869444

Charmaz, K.: Constructing grounded theory: A practical guide through qualitative analysis. SAGE Publications (2006)

Creswell, J.W., Creswell, J.D.: Research design (5th edn). SAGE (2018)

Fink, G., Holden, N.J.: Cultural stretch: Knowledge transfer and disconcerting resistance to absorption and application. In: Pauleen, D. (ed.) Cross-Cultural Perspectives on Knowledge Management, pp. 65–80. Libraries Unlimited (2007)

Holden, N.J.: Cross-cultural management: A knowledge management perspective. Financial Times/Prentice Hall (2002)

House, R.J., Hanges, P.J., Javidan, M., Dorfman, P.W., Gupta, V.: Globe Associates. In: Culture, leadership, and organizations: The Globe Study of societies. Sage (2004)

Javidan, M., Bowen, D.: The global mindset: A new source of competitive advantage. Rotman Management (2015)

Johnson, J.P., Lenartowicz, T., Apud, S.: Cross-cultural competence in international business: Toward a definition and a model. J. Int. Bus. Stud. **37**(4), 525–543 (2006). https://doi.org/10.1057/palgrave.jibs.8400205

Ladika, S.: How the coronavirus pandemic will change the way we work. SHRM (2020)

Mendenhall, M.E., et al.: Global Leadership. Routledge (2018)

Phillips, M., Siebert-Evenstone, A., Kessler, A., Gasevic, D., Shaffer, D.W.: Professional decision making: Reframing teachers' work using epistemic frame theory. In: Ruis, A.R., Lee, S.B., (eds.) Advances in Quantitative Ethnography, vol. 1312, pp. 265–276. Springer International Publishing (2021). https://doi.org/10.1007/978-3-030-67788-6_18

Ray, R., Sinar, E.: Global leadership forecast 2018. The Conference Board (2018)

Shaffer, D.W.: Pedagogical praxis: using technology to build professional communities of practice. Assoc. Comput. Mach. (ACM) SigGROUP Bull. **24**(3), 39–43 (2004). https://doi.org/10.1111/j.1467-9620.2004.0038

Shaffer, D.W.: Quantitative ethnography. Cathcart Press (2017)

Shaffer, D.W:. Transforming big data into meaningful insights: Introducing quantitative ethnography. University of Wisconsin (2018)

Shaffer, D.W., Collier, W., Ruis, A.R.: A tutorial on epistemic network analysis: Analyzing the structure of connections in cognitive, social, and interaction data. J. Learn. Analytics, **3**(3), 9–45 (2016). https://doi.org/10.18608/jla.2016.33.3

Soloman, C.: Trends in global virtual teams. Rw3 Culturewizard (2016)

Zörgő, S., Swiecki, Z., Ruis, A.R.: Exploring the effects of segmentation on semi-structured interview data with epistemic network analysis. In: International Conference on Quantitative Ethnography, pp. 78–90. Springer, Cham (2021). https://doi.org/10.1007/978-3-030-67788-6_6

Advances in QE Methodologies

Thin Data, Thick Description: Modeling Socio-Environmental Problem-Solving Trajectories in Localized Land-Use Simulations

A. R. Ruis$^{(\boxtimes)}$ ⓘ, Yuanru Tan ⓘ, Jais Brohinsky ⓘ, Binrui Yang, Yeyu Wang ⓘ, Zhiqiang Cai ⓘ, and David Williamson Shaffer ⓘ

Wisconsin Center for Education Research, University of WI–Madison, Madison, WI 53706, USA
arruis@wisc.edu

Abstract. Many learning technologies are now able to support both user-customization of the content and automated personalization of the experience based on user activities. However, there is a tradeoff between customization and personalization: the more control an educator or learner has over the parameters that define the experience, the more difficult it is to develop learning analytic models that can reliably assess learning and adapt the system accordingly. In this paper, we present a novel QE method for automatically generating a learning analytic model for the land-use planning simulation *iPlan*, which enables users to construct custom local simulations of socio-environmental issues. Specifically, this method employs data simulation and network analysis to construct a measurement space using nothing but log data. This space can be used to analyze users' problem-solving processes in a context where normative measurement criteria cannot be specified in advance. In doing so, we argue that QE methods can be developed and employed even in the absence of rich qualitative data, facilitating thick(er) descriptions of complex processes based on relatively thin records of users' activities in digital systems.

Keywords: QE methods · data simulation · network analysis · learning analytics · problem solving · trajectory analysis · environmental education

1 Introduction

Learning technologies are increasingly designed to be *adaptable* to the needs of learners. This has generally taken two forms, often hybridized: (1) *customization*, in which educators can modify digital environments for their local contexts, learning objectives, and learner populations, or learners themselves can make modifications based on their interests or personal preferences; and (2) *personalization*, in which the technology adapts itself automatically, determining content and progression or providing formative feedback in real time [1–3].

Although adaptable educational technologies can have positive impacts on learning (e.g., [4, 5]), there is a tradeoff between customization and personalization: the more

G. Arastoopour Irgens and S. Knight (Eds.): ICQE 2023, CCIS 1895, pp. 349–364, 2023.
https://doi.org/10.1007/978-3-031-47014-1_24

customizable the educational experience is, the more difficult it is to design learning analytic models or other automated assessment systems that can be reliably used to measure learning. In other words, constructing normative assessments of learning in complex learning environments when neither the content nor the context is standardized presents significant challenges [6].

While this is generally true, it is especially so in environmental education, which often deals with *socio-environmental systems*: complex interactions among human (social, political, economic) and natural (biophysical, ecological, environmental) processes [7]. To make complex socio-environmental systems, such as land use, water quality management, or climate change, more accessible to learners, one effective approach is to *localize* them [8–10]. This situates authentic, real-world problems in a real place, one that students know and care about. For example, the online platform *iPlan* [11, 12] enables educators (or learners) to construct simulated land-use planning problems in which the location and the social and environmental issues are selected by the user. Some features are also non-deterministic, such that each simulated problem is different, even when the input choices are the same. While this enables educators to create localized simulations of realistic land-use problems that are well adapted to their curricula and contexts, it is particularly challenging to construct learning analytic models of student problem solving because each problem is unique and sufficiently complex to support manifold appropriate solution pathways.

Like most digital learning environments, *iPlan* records user activities in log files. This provides a large amount of data but a relatively low amount of information about learning and problem solving; that is, it is big data but not necessarily *thick* data. This presents further challenges to constructing learning analytic models, one that is too often solved by throwing all the data at a carousel of models in the pursuit of statistical significance.

In this paper, we present a pilot approach to modeling problem-solving processes in *iPlan* using only clickstream data. This approach leverages data simulation [13] and a novel network modeling method to create a normative measurement space that enables analysis of individual problem-solving trajectories. This method, which could inform the construction of assessment models for both *iPlan* and other highly customizable problem-solving spaces, makes it possible to produce interpretable representations of solution trajectories from click data. We argue that in the absence of richer ethnographic data, such as recordings of think alouds or interviews that can be used to assess how individuals develop solutions to complex problems, this approach enables construction of thick(er) descriptions from the relatively thin records of users' activities in digital systems.

2   Background

2.1   iPlan

iPlan [11] enables users to construct a realistic, localized land-use planning simulation for any location in the contiguous United States. The process of simulation construction is explained in detail elsewhere [14], but in brief, users (a) select a location using a

Google Maps interface and (b) choose five ecological and socio-economic indicators—measures of air and water pollution, greenhouse gas emissions, wildlife population levels, agricultural production, commercial activity, and housing—to include in the simulation. Based on the location and indicators selected, *iPlan* generates a land-use map of the selected region with at most 200 parcels and nine virtual stakeholders—business owners, activists, and concerned citizens—who advocate for different issues that the indicators reflect. *iPlan* uses a set of optimization routines to divide the selected region into parcels, assign an appropriate land-use class to each parcel, and set stakeholder thresholds—minimum or maximum satisfactory values—for the selected indicators. Collectively, this process results in localized, reduced-form simulations that are realistic and appropriately complex for non-specialists, who can use *iPlan* to explore some of the scientific and social challenges involved in land-use planning and management [12] (see Fig. 1 for an example of the map interface).

In *iPlan*, the goal is to produce a new land-use plan for the modeled region that satisfies as many stakeholders as possible. To do this, learners use a map interface to model the effects of specific land-use changes on the selected indicators. They then create *land-use scenarios* [15] and submit them to the virtual stakeholders for feedback. Learners have a limited number of feedback requests, so they are challenged to conduct experiments, or *stated preference surveys* [16], that help them determine with more precision the changes each stakeholder will accept.

Because the simulated stakeholders have different and often conflicting demands, learners must identify and negotiate trade-offs. For example, one stakeholder may advocate for an increase in jobs, which is easiest to accomplish by rezoning parcels for commercial or industrial use, but another stakeholder may want a decrease in greenhouse gas emissions, which will increase with commercial or industrial expansion. Thus, *iPlan* models not only the *effects* of land-use change on socio-economic and environmental indicators but also the *acceptability* of land-use change to various civic interest groups, and it is generally impossible to satisfy everyone simultaneously. That is, *iPlan* constructs simulations that help people learn about the scientific *and* civic practices through which land-use planning is managed and contested, helping them understand land-use management as a complex socio-environmental system.

2.2 Assessing Problem Solving in *iPlan* Simulations

Educators have found *iPlan* to be a useful pedagogical tool across a number of learning contexts [14], and localization of socio-environmental learning using simulation is a powerful technique for improving learning and civic engagement [9]. However, the complexity of the solution space in *iPlan* makes developing learning analytic models—and thus providing personalized scaffolding based on formative assessment—particularly challenging.

Each land-use simulation created by the *iPlan* system is a unique result of user selection (region, indicators) and non-deterministic optimization (parcelization, stakeholders' preferences), and there are no strong constraints on user actions. Moreover, there are many interaction effects: the impact of land use on indicators is determined by both the type of land use and the area (i.e., parcel size), and each land-use class influences multiple indicators.

Because of this, the simulations produced by *iPlan* present challenges to modeling problem-solving processes in two primary ways. First, while the division of the user-selected region into 200 parcels is not arbitrary—the boundaries are determined by Census boundaries—the parcels are formed based on an optimization algorithm that minimizes land-use assignment error and avoids significant asymmetries in parcel size. Thus, even if a user selected approximately the same region a second time, the resulting parcelized map may not be exactly the same. Moreover, learners can change any of 200 parcels to one of 10 other land-use classifications, resulting in 11^{200} possible land-use scenarios that can be constructed for a given land-use simulation. In other words, the problem space is large and relatively unbounded, and the exact features of any land-use map will not be available until it is created.

Second, the preferences of the virtual stakeholders are set such that the resulting land-use problem space is neither too simple nor too complex for teenagers and non-specialist adults. The system selects nine out of 57 possible stakeholders for each land-use simulation based on the indicators chosen and a prioritization algorithm, then runs an optimization routine to set the indicator threshold for each stakeholder. Because learners are trying to satisfy as many of the nine stakeholders as possible by making strategic land-use changes, and the thresholds determine *how much change* in the indicators is needed to satisfy each stakeholder, there are many possible solution pathways that cannot be specified in advance or even optimized mathematically.

As a result, it is difficult to assess user actions in the simulation. There are some universally useful strategies; for example, it is always helpful to begin by submitting the initial map, with no land-use changes, to all of the stakeholders in order to determine what the stakeholders want and to identify whether any of them are already satisfied. However, successful solution strategies will generally differ depending on the particular features of the simulation and the ways different learners negotiate the tradeoffs and challenges intrinsic to the problem.

In what follows, we present a method for automatically constructing a measurement space that accounts for the unique features of a given *iPlan* simulation and enables meaningful interpretation of the land-use scenarios that users construct and submit to stakeholders in that simulation. This method extracts information from log files that is otherwise inscrutable—that is, summary information about the type and amount of land-use changes made—and enhances understanding of both solution processes and outcomes. We then present two constructed cases to illustrate some affordances of the method and discuss future directions for this pilot work.

3 Methods

To model learners' problem-solving processes in *iPlan*, we developed an analytic procedure with three main components: (a) a *data simulation algorithm* that uses the features of a given *iPlan* simulation to construct a large and diverse set of land-use scenarios representative of the kinds of proposals that learners might submit to the virtual stakeholders; (b) a *measurement model* that uses the simulated data to construct a metric space into which learners' land-use scenarios can be projected, producing a summary measure of their decisions over the course of the simulation; and (c) a *coordinated visualization* that facilitates interpretation of learners' problem-solving trajectories. This process transforms unreadable click data into a meaningful, unified representation of learners' problem-solving approaches.

3.1 Data Simulation

Because the primary goal in *iPlan* is to construct a land-use scenario that pleases as many stakeholders as possible, it is important that the simulated data contain scenarios that cover all the stakeholders' preferences (and dispreferences). To do this, the data simulation algorithm produces 100 scenarios for each of the nine stakeholder, 50 that satisfy the stakeholder and 50 that do not. This set of 900 land-use scenarios is used as the input data for the measurement model.

Each stakeholder in *iPlan* is associated with one indicator, and their satisfaction or dissatisfaction with a given scenario is determined by whether that indicator is above or below their threshold. The effects of the 11 land-use classes on indicators are computed using a set of equations that take into account the area of each land-use class and the magnitude of the effect a given land-use class has on a given indicator per unit of area. In other words, for any given scenario submitted to the stakeholders, *iPlan* computes the indicator values and compares them to the stakeholders' thresholds to determine whether the stakeholders are satisfied or dissatisfied with that scenario.

To generate simulated scenarios that are likely to satisfy (or dissatisfy) a given stakeholder, the data simulation algorithm uses the features of the specific *iPlan* simulation— the area and initial land-use class of each parcel; the indicators selected and the models that relate land-use classes to those indicators in that location; and the stakeholders' preferences (thresholds and directionality) as inputs. Because the effects of each land-use on each indicator are known, for each indicator, we constructed two lists of land-use classes: the first list (List A) contains land-use classes with a large effect on the indicator; the second list (List B) contains land-use classes with a small or no effect on the indicator. In cases where a given land-use class has a moderate effect on the indicator, that land-use class is included in both lists. (For the purposes of data simulation and model construction, two of the land-use classes—*limited use* and *conservation*—are combined because they have identical effects on all indicators. Thus there are 10 land-use classes included in the lists.) These lists are constructed such that changing a parcel with a land-use class in List A to a (different) land-use class in List B will generally increase the value of the indicator, and making changes in the opposite direction (from land-use classes in List B to those in List A) will generally decrease the value of the indicator. Using this information as inputs, the algorithm used to generate 100 scenarios for each stakeholder is as follows:

1. A number, k, between 1 and 17 is randomly selected to determine the number of parcels whose land-use class will be changed. This range was selected because approximately two-thirds (64%) of the more than 1,300 scenarios submitted by users in a one-year period contained fewer than 18 land-use changes, and also because a secondary goal of the simulation is to maximize the number of stakeholders satisfied *while minimizing the amount of land-use change*.
2. The algorithm randomly chooses a land-use class from List A, randomly chooses a parcel with that land-use class, and changes it to a (different) randomly selected land-use class from List B. This process is repeated k times.

3. The value of the indicator that the stakeholder cares about is computed and compared against the stakeholder's threshold. If it is above the threshold, it is saved. If it is below, it is discarded.
4. Steps 1–3 are repeated until 50 scenarios are generated with indicator values above the stakeholder's threshold.
5. Steps 1–4 are then repeated in the opposite direction, that is, making land-use changes from List B to List A (Step 2) and saving scenarios with indicator values below the stakeholder's threshold (Steps 3–4).
6. Depending on whether the stakeholder wants the indicator to be below or above the threshold, one set of 50 scenarios represents satisfaction and the other represents dissatisfaction.

This process is conducted for each of the nine stakeholders, resulting in 900 scenarios.

Each land-use scenario is represented by a vector with 100 terms, where each term represents a unique ordered pair of 10 different land-use classes, and the value of each term is the total amount of area changed relative to the starting land-use map. Because there are a maximum of 17 land-use changes in any given scenario, most of the terms in the vectors are zeroes.

3.2 Constructing a Measurement Model

To construct a measurement model, we use the simulated data to parameterize a metric space into which learner-generated land-use scenarios can be projected. To do this, we (a) sphere normalize the 900 vectors generated by the data simulation algorithm; (b) construct nine dimensions, where each dimension maximizes the difference between the 50 scenarios that satisfy a given stakeholder and the 50 scenarios that dissatisfy that stakeholder; (c) perform a dimensional reduction using *singular value decomposition* (SVD); and (d) project the 900 scenarios into the reduced space formed by the first two SVD dimensions, which account for the most and second-most variance in the data, respectively. The details of this process are as follows.

Let M be a 900×100 matrix, where each row corresponds to a simulated land-use scenario, and each column corresponds to a dimension in the feature space, that is, a unique ordered pair of the 10 land-use classes. Each row is a vector, S, of length 100 that either satisfies ($S_i = 1$) or does not satisfy ($S_i = -1$) the corresponding stakeholder. The vectors are sphere normalized by dividing each term by the total map area, converting the raw areas into proportions of total area. This accounts for differences in length between vectors. The normalized vectors are then represented as points in a 100-dimensional space.

For each stakeholder j ($j = 1, 2, \ldots, 9$), the subset of points in the high-dimensional space where $S_j = 1$ ($n = 50$) and the subset where $S_j = -1$ ($n = 50$) are used to define a dimension. Specifically, the space is rotated (rigid-body rotation) so as to maximize the difference between the 50 points representing $S_j = 1$ and the 50 points representing $S_j = -1$. This results in nine dimensions, one for each stakeholder, each of which maximizes the difference between land-use scenarios that stakeholder likes and those they dislike.

An SVD is performed to construct a reduced set of dimensions that relate the type and magnitude of land-use change to stakeholder satisfaction across all nine stakeholders.

Each scenario is thus represented by a set of SVD scores, and the first two dimensions can be used to define a normative metric space into which other scenarios can be projected[1].

3.3 Visualizing and Interpreting Problem-Solving Trajectories

All 900 simulated land-use scenarios are represented as points in the two-dimensional space formed by the first and second SVD dimensions. The ten land-use classes are placed as nodes in the space using the *ordered semantic co-registration layout* (OSCL), the same layout used in ordered network analysis (ONA) [18]. (For more on the mathematics and affordances of co-registration, see [19].) Then, each land-use scenario can be visualized as an ordered network graph using the same visualization as ONA, and the nodes (i.e., the land-use classes) can be positioned in the space such that the centroid of each network corresponds with the location of the corresponding scenario in the reduced space. This results in two coordinated representations: (1) one in which each land-use scenario is summarized by a single point, and (2) one in which each land-use scenario is represented as a directed network graph that indicates the type and proportional magnitude of the land-use changes made.

This space can be interpreted not only based on the node positions, as in ENA or ONA, but also by where in the space different stakeholders are satisfied. The mean, 95% confidence interval, and range of the points representing land-use scenarios that satisfy each stakeholder can be computed, providing a mapping of the space based on stakeholder preferences. Stakeholder satisfaction is, in effect, sets of land-use changes that produce desired results, and so clustering points based on the stakeholders' preferences provides an additional means of interpreting the space.

Using the rotation matrix produced by the measurement model, other land-use scenarios produced under the same simulation, such as ones constructed by learners, can be projected into this space and interpreted by how they locate relative to the stakeholders' areas of satisfaction. Series of land-use scenarios produced by learners thus form trajectories through the space, providing insight into the problem-solving approach that learners take and facilitating meaningful interpretation of decision-making beyond what can be determined based on the outcome of each submission (i.e., which stakeholders were satisfied).

---

[1] For readers who may be wondering why we don't simply apply the SVD to the set of normalized vectors directly and omit the step involving the construction of a dimension for each stakeholder, this is in part because SVDs do not perform well on relatively sparse matrices, i.e., matrices in which many or most of the coefficients are zeroes [17]. Attempts to do this produced dimensions with low variance explained (generally < 3%) and poor co-registration (see §3.3). While there are many techniques specifically designed to decompose sparse matrices, we took an approach, inspired by means rotation in epistemic network analysis (ENA), that both addresses the sparse matrix problem and facilitates meaningful interpretation of the resulting space based on stakeholder preferences, which is useful given that the goal in *iPlan* is to maximize stakeholder satisfaction.

4 Proof of Concept

In what follows, we illustrate the method described above using one *iPlan* land-use simulation, and we show several constructed scenarios to demonstrate the affordances of the method.

4.1 Measurement Model of One *iPlan* Simulation

To construct a measurement model for evaluating problem-solving processes in *iPlan*, we developed a land-use simulation for Eugene, Oregon, in the northwestern United States. The simulation includes the indicators birds, runoff, greenhouse gas emissions, jobs, and population (see Fig. 1). This location was chosen because it exhibits a range of parcel sizes and land-use types, both developed and not. The central area contains mostly high-density housing, commercial, industrial, and recreation land, while the periphery contains mostly low-density housing, cropland, pasture, and land with limited human use.

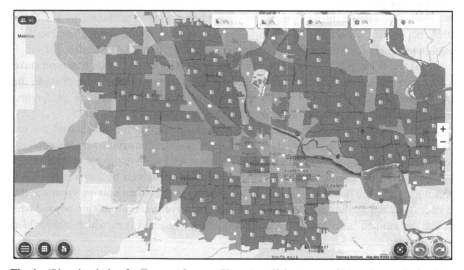

Fig. 1. *iPlan* simulation for Eugene, Oregon. Users can click any parcel(s) to change the land-use class, and the resulting effects on indicators (percentage change) are indicated at the top.

This simulation was used to construct the metric space shown in Fig. 2. The first (x) dimension accounts for 24% of the variance in the land-use scenarios, and the second (y) dimension accounts for 18% of the variance, indicating that the reduced space captures salient differences in the 900 land-use scenarios. The goodness of fit, or the correlation of the SVD scores with the corresponding network centroids, which is a measure of the extent to which the node positions can be used to interpret the space, is high: Pearson's and Spearman's $r > 0.95$ for both dimensions.

The first dimension generally distinguishes *low-intensity development* (low-density housing and recreation) from *high-intensity development* (commercial and industrial).

This is also the dimension that distinguishes the stakeholder who wants to increase bird populations (Grace) from the stakeholders who want to increase jobs (Ezra and Said). This makes sense, as commercial and industrial expansion significantly increases jobs, while low-intensity development, such as single-family homes, parks, and golf courses, provides ideal habitats for American robins (*Turdus migratorius*), the bird species that is modeled in *iPlan*.

The second dimension generally distinguishes *minimal development* (all of the land-uses in quadrant two) from *high-intensity development* (industrial, commercial, and high-density housing). This is also the dimension that distinguishes the stakeholders who want greenhouse gas emissions to decrease (Maya and Javier) from the stakeholders who want to increase jobs (Ezra and Said). This makes sense, as high-intensity development produces the most greenhouse gas emissions by area, while the lowest greenhouse gas emissions by area come from relatively undeveloped land.

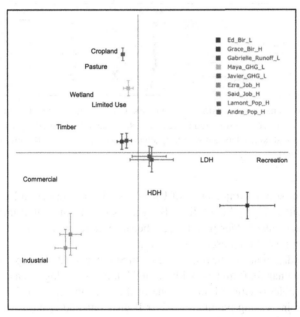

Fig. 2. Metric space for the Eugene, Oregon, *iPlan* simulation (Fig. 1). Colored squares with 95% confidence intervals are the mean locations of the scenarios that satisfied the associated stakeholders (key in upper right); the locations of the nodes (land-use classes) are labeled. HDH = High-Density Housing; LDH = Low-Density Housing; Limited Use includes Conservation

To evaluate the potential use of this modeling method as an assessment tool, we constructed two hypothetical cases using the Eugene simulation and projected the resulting land-use scenarios into the same metric space.

4.2   Case 1: Same Mountain, Different Paths

We constructed a set of submissions for each of two hypothetical *iPlan* users, User A and User B. Users A and B both adopt a similar, effective problem-solving strategy, but they carry out this strategy in distinct ways. Specifically, they both submit the initial map to gauge stakeholder preferences and then employ an *accretion strategy*, in which they attempt to make progressive land-use changes such that each submitted scenario contains all the changes from previous scenarios, the goal being to increase stakeholder support without losing any stakeholders who were previously satisfied. Both Users A and B have identical outcomes, in the sense that each scenario they submit satisfies exactly the same stakeholders (see Fig. 3). In other words, Users A and B employ the same basic strategy with the same outcome, but they make different decisions for each submission, which indicates different ways of thinking about the problem.

Fig. 3. Land-use scenario submission outcomes for User A and User B. Green indicates stakeholders satisfied with a submission, red indicates stakeholders dissatisfied with a submission, and blue boxes indicate stakeholders whose rating changed compared with the previous submission (Color figure online).

The problem-solving trajectories of Users A and B are shown in Fig. 4. (Note that the points are jittered to aid legibility.) Both users submit the initial map as their first scenario to gauge stakeholder preferences; because there are no land-use changes, the Submission 1 points of both users appear at the origin.

The biggest difference in the trajectories is in Submission 2 (see Fig. 5). User A made only one type of change, from land with limited human use to high-density housing, and as a result was able to satisfy Lamont, one of the stakeholders who is concerned with planning for an increasing population. User B also satisfied Lamont with Submission 2 by increasing high-density housing, but did so by proposing *infill*—replacing low-density housing with high-density housing rather than expanding to less developed land. In addition, User B also changed cropland to recreation. Given that this change has no impact on population, User B was most likely attempting to simultaneously satisfy Grace, the stakeholder who advocates for bird populations. While this attempt was not successful, it indicates that where User A may have preferred to focus on one indicator at a time, User B was likely attempting to satisfy multiple stakeholders across more than one indicator at once.

This case suggests that even when two users employ similar strategies and achieve identical outcomes, there are meaningful differences in their actions that an educator or the system itself could use as a basis for providing encouragement or additional scaffolding, or as an opportunity for broader discussions of land-use planning and civic

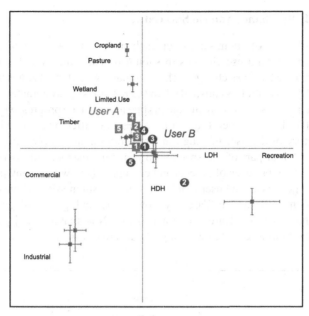

Fig. 4. Problem-solving trajectories of User A (yellow squares) and User B (green circles). The points are jittered to aid legibility (Color figure online).

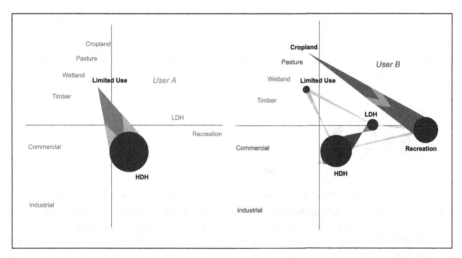

Fig. 5. Network graphs showing the land-use changes made by User A (left, yellow) and User B (right, green) for Submission 2 (Color figure online).

practices. For example, this one pair of submissions could spark a discussion of different planning strategies for addressing growing populations (e.g., infill vs. expansion) as well as broader discussions about complex problem solving when there are tradeoffs among indicators (e.g., the advantages and disadvantages of isolating one indicator at a time).

4.3   Case 2: If By Chance You Do Succeed...

We constructed a set of submissions for each of two hypothetical *iPlan* users, one who makes *random* land-use changes to submit to stakeholders and one who makes *systematic*, strategic land-use changes. The user making random changes finishes with a better result (6/9 stakeholders satisfied) than the user making systematic changes (5/9), and both sequences of submission outcomes appear to indicate progressive improvement (see Fig. 6, left). However, their trajectories reveal key differences (see Fig. 6, right).

The trajectory of the user making random submissions (purple squares) is erratic, moving to a different part of the space with each submission. This is indicative of a user simply clicking bunches of parcels and changing them without any particular goal in mind. The trajectory of the user making systematic submissions (blue circles) looks quite similar to that of User A in Case 1 (yellow squares in Fig. 4), with generally small-to-moderate changes and a clearer solution pathway. Note that both trajectories end in a similar place (Submission 5), but with slightly different results.

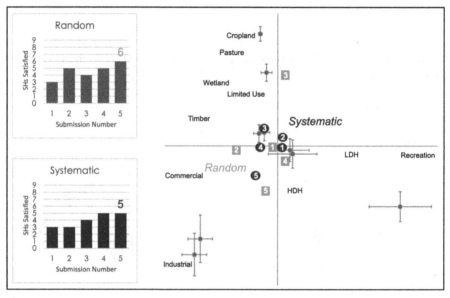

Fig. 6. Bar graphs (left) indicating the number of stakeholders satisfied by each scenario submitted and problem-solving trajectories (right) of two users: a user making *random* changes to construct land-use scenarios (purple squares) and a user making *systematic* changes (blue circles) (Color figure online).

This case suggests that the proposed method for modeling problem-solving trajectories could help educators and the system itself distinguish the activities of learners who are employing a good strategy but may require some additional scaffolding from the activities of learners who may be simply goofing around, even in cases when the outcomes do not disambiguate the two. That is, it can help distinguish those users who are trying unsuccessfully from those who are not trying but succeed anyway.

5   Discussion

At this point, you might be asking yourself if this study is actually quantitative *ethnography*: "Where is the *E* in QE?" While the proposed method for assessing problem-solving processes in a complex land-use simulation utilizes some of the mathematical and visual techniques commonly used in QE research, the only data come from log files, which in this case document the parameters and features of a given land-use simulation and record the land-use changes made and submitted to stakeholders by users. There is nothing that looks like a typical qualitative analysis, or even anything that looks like traditional qualitative data.

But while the data are, admittedly, thin, the clicks they represent are nonetheless a record of key decisions made and a latent reflection of the processes by which an individual attempts to solve a complex socio-environmental problem. The method we describe here enables a richer, *thicker* description of problem-solving activities to be constructed from data that are otherwise inaccessible to traditional qualitative analysis. That is, we use data simulation and modeling techniques to measure and visualize problem-solving trajectories by representing a key subset of the information captured in the log files in such a way that a meaningful story can be told about the behaviors they document.

Critically, we modeled only a very thin slice of the clickstream data, namely the land-use scenarios that users submitted to stakeholders. We omitted, among other things, the land-use changes users explored but didn't include in a submitted scenario, the use of the graphing tool to explore stakeholder preferences in more detail, and the resources that provide basic information about the land-use classes, indicators, and virtual stakeholders. While each of these data types could enhance understanding of learners' problem-solving strategies, they are more likely to occlude than clarify because it is harder to reliably link the digital record to a specific aspect of the problem-solving process. For example, a user could access a resource but not read it, read it but misunderstand it, or not access a resource yet still possess the knowledge it contains. All we know is whether they accessed a given resource, when, and for how long, and thus it is difficult to interpret the access records reliably enough for the purposes of understanding problem-solving strategies. In other words, without strong theoretical grounds or prior empirical work that would guide interpretation of this information, it is likely to add more noise than signal. Put another way, we gain more by pruning information than we do by adding it because this boosts the signal relative to the noise. This deep, theory-based engagement with the data, we argue, is a key feature of good quantitative ethnography and of good learning analytics [20]. And indeed, this entire modeling approach could only be developed because we have a deep understanding of *iPlan* and how it is used.

But this still leaves the question of how to close the interpretive loop; that is, how to warrant that the model is, indeed, well aligned with the original data and that re-interpretation of the original data in light of the model does not change the story. In this case, we didn't start with a qualitative interpretation of the data—that isn't often possible with clickstream data—but with a theory about different ways that a learner could solve the land-use problems simulated in *iPlan* and what that might look like as a series of submitted land-use scenarios. (And, because we constructed the case studies, we knew what users were trying to do.) Because our modeling process employs simulated data to construct the measurement space and projects real data into that space, closing the interpretive loop involves demonstrating both that the measurement space itself is aligned with the features of the specific *iPlan* simulation *and* that there is alignment between the model's representation of users' submission trajectories and the problem-solving strategies they represent. In this pilot study, we demonstrated that the data simulation and modeling process produces a sensible representation of the problem space based both on the node positions (land-use classes) and the locations of stakeholders in the space. We then showed that users' problem-solving trajectories were well aligned with the strategies they employed based on two constructed case studies: one comparing two users with similar strategies and identical outcomes, and one comparing two users whose outcomes may be misleading as indicators of effective problem solving. In both cases, the method was highly sensitive to key differences in problem-solving processes.

Because this is a pilot study, further work involving data from learners using *iPlan* in typical educational contexts and carefully designed studies that can link reported intentions and observed actions to model outputs will be needed to fully validate this approach. Such studies could also explore the inclusion of the other clickstream data types described above, or additional process data, by generating the theoretical basis for thoughtfully integrating that data with the submitted scenarios. Nonetheless, this initial study makes several contributions to QE methodology.

First, as Shaffer and Ruis have argued, QE is *not* just ENA [21]. While the method described here utilizes the ordered semantic co-registration layout from ONA [18] to generate directional network graphs that are co-registered with the metric space, the techniques used to accumulate connections and construct the metric space itself are novel and emerged from the specific challenges of analyzing decision-making and problem-solving in *iPlan*. This study thus adds to the growing methodological toolkit of QE research.

Second, this study provides an example of the use of data simulation in QE research, and indeed a use for data simulation beyond the four cases described by Swiecki and Eagan [13]. Learning technologies with highly customizable inputs and non-deterministic outputs can construct problems for which optimal solution pathways do not exist (or can't be reasonably derived). This means that norms cannot be established *a priori* for formative assessment of learner activities. Data simulation provides a mechanism for constructing a normative space into which learner activities can be projected and measured, providing the system with a basis to better scaffold learning, providing teachers with the information needed for just-in-time intervention and encouragement, and providing researchers with a powerful model for studying learning in a complex problem-solving context. While this is not the first example of such projection—Siebert-Evenstone, for example, projected planned and enacted curricula into a space constructed using the Next Generation Science Standards [22]—it demonstrates the utility of data simulation for constructing such spaces in contexts where prior data cannot be obtained.

Lastly, this study challenges, albeit indirectly, the assumption that more or richer data is necessarily better for modeling complex processes. The data used to model problem-solving in this study are quite thin, representing the types of land-use changes made and the amount of those changes at key points in the problem-solving process. That is, the data document only the decisions that users make when they submit land-use scenarios to stakeholders. But those data document arguably the most important decisions, and thus provide a good proxy for a learner's strategy. In other words, the model presented here was constructed based on a theory that links a key problem-solving behavior—choosing land-use scenarios to submit to stakeholders—to a broader problem-solving strategy. The choice of data—its thinness—was a strategic decision to minimize noise; that is, we discarded much of the information in the log files but also discarded most of the noise, leaving a high signal-to-noise ratio. In other words, we had less information, but it was more useful, and we argue that another key element of good QE research (and good learning analytics) is that every decision along the *primary modeling pathway* [20] is guided by theory about what to attend to and what to ignore.

This paper thus addresses a critical challenge in learning analytics and process modeling more broadly, namely the challenge of analyzing complex thinking or decision making in contexts where normative measurement criteria cannot be specified in advance. In doing so, we present a novel theoretical and methodological approach to generating thick descriptions from thin data.

Acknowledgements. This work was funded in part by the National Science Foundation (DRL-1661036, DRL-2100320, DRL-2201723, DRL-2225240), the Wisconsin Alumni Research Foundation, and the Office of the Vice Chancellor for Research and Graduate Education at the University of Wisconsin–Madison. The opinions, findings, and conclusions do not reflect the views of the funding agencies, cooperating institutions, or other individuals.

References

1. Dede, C.: Customization in immersive learning environments: implications for digital teaching environments. In: Dede, C., Richards, J., (eds.) Digital Teaching Platforms: Customizing Classroom Learning for Each Student, pp. 282–297. Teachers College Press (2012)
2. Matuk, C.F., Linn, M.C., Eylon, B.-S.: Technology to support teachers using evidence from student work to customize technology-enhanced inquiry units. Instr. Sci. **43**, 229–257 (2015). https://doi.org/10.1007/s11251-014-9338-1
3. Shemshack, A., Spector, J.M.: A systematic literature review of personalized learning terms. Smart Learn. Environ. **7**, 33 (2020). https://doi.org/10.1186/s40561-020-00140-9
4. Littenberg-Tobias, J., Beheshti, E., Staudt, C.: To customize or not to customize? exploring science teacher customization in an online lesson portal. J. Res. Sci. Teach. **53**, 349–367 (2016)
5. Zhang, L., Basham, J.D., Yang, S.: Understanding the implementation of personalized learning: a research synthesis. Educ. Res. Rev. **31**, 100339 (2020)
6. Barab, S.A., Luehmann, A.L.: Building sustainable science curriculum: acknowledging and accommodating local adaptation. Sci. Educ. **87**, 454–467 (2003)
7. Elsawah, S., et al.: Eight grand challenges in socio-environmental systems modeling. Socio-Environ. Syst. Model. **2** (2020)
8. Gruenewald, D.A.: Foundations of place: a multidisciplinary framework for place-conscious education. Am. Educ. Res. J. **40**, 619–654 (2003)
9. Siebert-Evenstone, A.L., Shaffer, D.W.: Location, location, location: the effects of place in place-based simulations. In: Lund, K., Niccolai, G., Lavoué, E., Hmelo-Silver, C., Gweon, G., Baker, M. (eds.) A Wide Lens: Combining Embodied, Enactive, Extended, and Embedded Learning in Collaborative Settings: 13th International Conference on Computer-Supported Collaborative Learning (CSCL) 2019, pp. 152–159 (2019)

10. Smith, G.A., Sobel, D.: Place- and Community-Based Education in Schools. Routledge (2014)
11. Ruis, A.R., et al.: iPlan (2020). https://app.i-plan.us/
12. Ruis, A.R., et al.: Localizing Socio-Environmental Problem Solving. In: Weinberger, A., Chen, W., Hernández-Leo, D., Chen, B., (eds.) International Collaboration toward Educational Innovation for All: Overarching Research, Development, and Practices: 15th International Conference on Computer-Supported Collaborative Learning (CSCL) 2022, pp. 459–462. International Society for the Learning Sciences (2022)
13. wiecki, Z., Eagan, B.R.: The Role of Data Simulation in Quantitative Ethnography. In: Damşa, C., Barany, A., (eds.) Advances in Quantitative Ethnography: Fourth International Conference, ICQE 2022, Copenhagen, Denmark, 15–19 October 2022, Proceedings, pp. 87–100. Springer (2023). https://doi.org/10.1007/978-3-031-31726-2_7
14. Ruis, A.R., et al.: Iplan: A Platform for Constructing Localized, Reduced-Form Models of Land-Use Impacts (2023)
15. Xiang, W.-N., Clarke, K.C.: The use of scenarios in land-use planning. Environ. Plan. B Plan. Des. **30**, 885–909 (2003)
16. Tagliafierro, C., Boeri, M., Longo, A., Hutchinson, W.G.: Stated preference methods and landscape ecology indicators: an example of transdisciplinarity in landscape economic valuation. Ecol. Econ. **127**, 11–22 (2016)
17. Duff, I.S., Erisman, A.M., Reid, J.K.: Direct Methods for Sparse Matrices. Oxford University Press (2017)
18. Tan, Y., Ruis, A.R., Marquart, C.L., Cai, Z., Knowles, M., Shaffer, D.W.: Ordered Network Analysis. In: Damşa, C., Barany, A., (eds.) Advances in Quantitative Ethnography: Fourth International Conference, ICQE 2022, Copenhagen, Denmark, 15–19 October 2022, Proceedings, pp. 101–116. Springer (2023). https://doi.org/10.1007/978-3-031-31726-2_8
19. Bowman, D., et al.: The mathematical foundations of epistemic network analysis. In: Ruis, A.R., Lee, S.B. (eds.) ICQE 2021. CCIS, vol. 1312, pp. 91–105. Springer, Cham (2021). https://doi.org/10.1007/978-3-030-67788-6_7
20. Shaffer, D.W., Ruis, A.R.: Theories all the way across: the role of theory in learning analytics and the case for unified methods. In: Bartimote, K., Howard, S., Gašević, D., (eds.) Theory Informing and Arising from Learning Analytics. In press. Springer (2023)
21. Shaffer, D.W., Ruis, A.R.: Is QE just ENA? In: Damşa, C., Barany, A., (eds.) Advances in Quantitative Ethnography: 4th International Conference, ICQE 2022, Copenhagen, Denmark, 15–19 October 2022, Proceedings, pp. 71–86. Springer (2023).https://doi.org/10.1007/978-3-031-31726-2_6
22. Siebert-Evenstone, A.: A qualitative analysis of connection-making in the NGSS. In: Wasson, B., Zörgő, S., (eds.) Advances in Quantitative Ethnography: Third International Conference, ICQE 2021, Virtual Event, 6–11 November Proceedings, pp. 105–123. Springer (2022). https://doi.org/10.1007/978-3-030-93859-8_7

Developing Nursing Students' Practice Readiness with Shadow Health® Digital Clinical Experiences™: A Transmodal Analysis

Yeyu Wang[1](✉), Mamta Shah[2], Francisco A. Jimenez[2], Cheryl Wilson[2], Muhammad Ashiq[1], Brendan Eagan[1], and David Williamson Shaffer[1]

[1] University of Wisconsin-Madison, Madison, USA
{ywang2466,ashiq,beagan}@wisc.edu, dws@education.wisc.edu
[2] Elsevier, Amsterdam, The Netherlands
{m.shah,f.jimenez,c.l.wilson}@elsevier.com

Abstract. This study applied Transmodal Analysis (TMA), a newly developed quantitative ethnographic approach, to examine whether and how virtual patient simulations can aid in educating undergraduate nursing students with competencies that exemplify practice-ready nurses. Multimodal transcripts capturing patient interactions, exam actions, and documentation were obtained from two students who used Elsevier's Shadow Health® Digital Clinical Experiences™ (DCE) in Fall 2022 and Spring 2023. Patient scenarios were situated in three content areas (Gerontology, Mental Health, and Community Health) and two assignment types (focused exam and contact tracing). In each scenario, similar patterns of engagement were observed for both students as they completed learning activities such as collecting patient data and establishing a caring relationship. These activities—guided by the instructional design of DCE—indicated how students practiced recognizing and analyzing cues, subjective assessment, diagnosing and prioritizing hypotheses, generating solutions, evaluating outcomes, therapeutic communication, and care coordination and management in relation to each patient's needs and conditions. A statistical difference was observed between competencies practiced while completing focused exam and contact tracing assignments. This study provides evidence for using simulations to facilitate competency-based education in nursing. Additionally, it provides motivation for using Transmodal Analysis combined with Ordered Network Analysis (T/ONA) to advance quantitative ethnography research in health care and health professions education.

Keywords: quantitative ethnography · transmodal analysis · nursing education · competency-based education · virtual patient simulations

1 Introduction

New graduates' insufficient practice readiness persists even as the demand for nurses is growing in the United States [1]. This is a multifaceted challenge since

G. Arastoopour Irgens and S. Knight (Eds.): ICQE 2023, CCIS 1895, pp. 365–380, 2023.
https://doi.org/10.1007/978-3-031-47014-1_25

nursing educators are faced with several paradigm shifts and competing gaps in preparing pre-licensure students for the profession. For instance, with the recent release of The Essentials: Core Competencies for Professional Nursing Education [2] and National Council of State Boards of Nursing Clinical Judgment Measurement Model (NCJMM) [3], nursing regulatory bodies have placed competency-based education at the forefront, prompting programs to transform teaching, learning and assessment practices. In addition, the Future of Nursing 2020–2030 report [4] has underscored the need for new nurses to be prepared to (a) treat patients that reflect diversity in social determinants of health and (b) promote health equity across communities. Furthermore, U.S nursing schools are having to turn away thousands of qualified applicants due to shortages of clinical sites, faculty, and resource constraints [5]. Lastly, nursing leaders are foreseeing a continued trend toward online/remote education. This pedagogical movement along with rapid digital transformation is likely to create new opportunities and challenges for nursing programs and regulations [6].

We believe that screen-based virtual simulations have the potential to cultivate students' practice readiness and aid nursing educators in addressing the aforementioned shifts and gaps in the discipline. Foronda and colleagues [7] concluded that utilizing virtual patient simulations (VPS)-a type of screen-based simulation- had a positive effect on multiple learning outcomes for nursing students. Eighty-six percent of studies in their review demonstrated that VPS were efficient at enhancing nursing students' knowledge acquisition, skill development, critical thinking, self-assurance, and satisfaction with learning. Recently, Cole [8] urged researchers to investigate learner performance as a direction for advancing simulation use for competency-based education.

Quantitative ethnography (QE) has enabled researchers and practitioners to investigate and illustrate complex patterns in human behavior in several domains. We build upon extant QE research, especially in nursing education, and apply Transmodal Analysis (TMA) for investigating students' interaction patterns in multimodal learning activities in Shadow Health® Digital Clinical Experiences™ (DCE). DCE is a type of VPS designed to cultivate nursing students' knowledge, skills, and attitudes for providing comprehensive and compassionate care to digitally standardized patients.

In what follows, we describe learning activities typically afforded by DCE, and provide an overview of DCE scenarios designed for gerontology, mental health, and community health content areas. Next, we describe the theoretical framework of this study, The Essentials [2], and delineate its application in this study. This is followed by a justification for using TMA to advance QE research on simulations in nursing education. Thereafter, we describe our methodological procedures and modeling decisions. This is followed by a report of findings for Rose and Roshni (pseudonyms) who completed two focused exams (End of Life scenario in Gerontology, Bipolar Disorder scenario in Mental Health) and one contact tracing assignment (HIV Diagnosis and with Contact Tracing scenario in Community Health) in DCE from 2022–2023. We conclude this paper by discussing the study findings and outlining implications for future research.

2 Shadow Health Digital® Clinical Experiences™ (DCE)

The DCE provides an array of standardized clinical scenarios across a comprehensive range of courses in undergraduate nursing education to guide learners in developing the knowledge, skills, and attitudes needed to care for diverse patients in a safe environment. Typically in a DCE scenario, learners can interact with virtual patients and ask questions to explore their medical and sociocultural backgrounds. Learners can also perform physical exams and document their findings in a simulated electronic health record (EHR). During the virtual exam, learners can also express empathy when the virtual patient shares emotional, physical, or experiential difficulties, and offer educational statements when the patient reveals gaps in their understanding of relevant medical topics. The virtual patients are programmed to recognize and respond to thousands of questions and statements related to the learning objectives covered in each scenario, making the conversation feel natural and realistic. As such, learners engage in a clinical reasoning process by completing patient care activities such as collections of history and physical examination data, therapeutic communication skills, and creations of care plans.

DCE simulations have been successful at increasing critical thinking, confidence, and satisfaction among undergraduate nursing students [9]. Students as early as in their first year of nursing education have demonstrated significant efficiency gains when it comes to gathering patient data, applying therapeutic communication, and creating care plans using DCE [10]. In addition, recent studies have shown that DCE scenarios can be an effective means of teaching nursing students about patient care issues that they may not encounter as part of their clinical education, such as fostering cultural competence and sensitivity when caring for transgender patients [11].

For this study, we focus on DCE scenarios from the following content areas in undergraduate nursing education: Gerontology, Mental Health, and Community Health. In Gerontology scenarios, students interact with a diverse range of older adult patients, gathering data to assess risk for geriatric syndromes and medication contraindications using Beers Criteria. They take complete health histories, perform problem-focused physical assessments and construct care plans. In Mental Health scenarios, students engage with a set of patients who are experiencing a variety of mental health conditions. They take complete health histories, perform mental status assessments, conduct problem-focused physical exams, and complete either care plans or Situation Background Assessment Recommendation (SBAR) handoffs. In Community Health scenarios, students explore a systems-view approach to healthcare- assessing community strengths and weaknesses, tracing the spread of disease, advocating for vulnerable populations, treating individual patients, and creating a care plan for the community.

3   Theoretical Framework

The Essentials [2] provides a competency-based education framework for guiding the development and revision of nursing curricula to prepare entry-level and advanced-level nurses. In addition, it outlines programmatic expectations for teaching, learning, and assessment at both levels. Competencies and sub-competencies are organized within 10 domains. These are applicable across all healthcare areas and diversity of patient populations. At the entry-level, learners should demonstrate attainment and integration of level 1 sub-competencies. Eight concepts (Clinical Judgment; Communication; Compassionate Care; Diversity, Equity, and Inclusion; Ethics; Evidence-based Practice; Health Policy; Social Determinants of Health) are central to professional nursing practice, integrated across the domains and competencies and included in The Essentials.

In this study, we examined competencies characterizing Domains 1 (Knowledge of Nursing Practice), 2 (Person-Centered Care), and 9 (Professionalism) described for entry-level programs. These included: Demonstrating clinical judgment founded on a broad knowledge base, Engaging with the individual in establishing a caring relationship, Communicating effectively with individuals, Integrating assessment skills in practice, Diagnosing actual or potential health problems and needs, Promoting self-care management, Providing care coordination, and Employing participatory approach to nursing care. For each of these competencies, we used select level 1 sub-competencies to guide our operationalization of the theoretical constructs we examined in this study (see Table 1 for codebook). We also used NCSBN Clinical Judgment Measurement Model Layer 3 [3] to guide our examination of learner performance in DCE.

At the entry-level, it is important for nursing students to be exposed to varied experiences in four spheres of care (Disease Prevention/Promotion of Health and Well Being, Chronic Disease Care, Regenerative/Hospice/Restorative Care, and Hospice/Restorative Care Palliative Care) with diverse populations and ages [2]. These guidelines along with the core concepts informed our choice of specific scenarios from the three content areas and two types of assignments (focused exam and contact tracing). We examined transcripts of students' interactions with three virtual patients; namely, Regina Walker from gerontology, Lucas Callahan from mental health, and Quan Tran from community health. Regina is a 69-year-old Black/African American, cisgender, and heterosexual woman. She is a retired family coach and program director at a non-profit. Regina is experiencing increased pain and decreased activity due to metastatic cancer. She needs recommendations for and discussion on hospice care. Lucas is a 25-year-old White cisgender and heteroflexible man who is currently unemployed. He is at risk of intentions to harm himself or others. Lucas needs education on symptoms common with a hypomanic state including lack of sleep. He also needs a care plan and recommendation for outpatient therapy. Quan Tran is a 52-year-old Vietnamese American man. He chooses not to disclose his sexual orientation and is employed as a manager at a trading company. Quan was recently diagnosed with HIV at a community center. The possible contacts of this communicable disease need to be traced using evidence-based guidelines. Quan and the contacts also need to be educated and cared for with empathy. Through these scenarios, students were exposed to patients needing Hospice/Palliative Care (i.e., Regina-End of Life), Chronic Disease Care (i.e., Lucas-Bipolar Disorder), and Prevention/promotion of Health and Wellbeing (i.e., Quan-HIV Diagnosis and Contact Tracing).

4   Quantitative Ethnography in Nursing Education Research

Quantitative Ethnography (QE) is an emerging field for understanding complex processes and discovering meaningful patterns in various disciplines such as education [12], and policy [13]. As a unified approach of qualitative and quantitative analyses, QE provides both thick descriptions and statistical warrants on a given analytic claim [14]. Recent studies in nursing education have applied QE methods to examine alignment of curricular content [15], trace student learning trajectories [16], model instructor facilitation and classroom interaction across pre-briefing, simulation, and debriefing phases for scenarios in fundamentals of nursing [16,17].

Nursing education by nature involves multiple modalities such as dialog, physical examinations, and documentation. However, existing work about nursing education in QE mainly relies on unimodal data. For example, Shah and colleagues [18] adopted epistemic network analysis (ENA) to investigate student learning trajectories based on discourse data collected from virtual reality simulation sessions. According to this study, ENA represented connections made among constructs derived from frameworks such as NCJMM and Quality and Safety Education for Nurses (QSEN). This study had two limitations: (1) ENA did not provide ordered relationships for the connections between any pair of constructs or self-references and, (2) ENA was not initially designed to analyze multimodal data and often requires a great deal of additional model parameterization. In ENA, it is not possible to assign different window sizes for different modalities, and as a result researchers often need to account for differences in the temporal influence of different data streams by manual adjustment in their model.

Current advancements in QE methods can help address these limitations. Specifically, Ordered Network Analysis enables researchers to represent self-references and ordered relationships of connections made during a learning activity such as a nursing simulation. Additionally, Transmodal Analysis enables researchers to model multimodal data by (a) specifying a function or functions that describe, for each data modality, how events interact and (b) using those functions to include multiple modalities in the same model [19]. As such, in this study, we implemented TMA combined with Ordered Network Analysis (T/ONA) [20] by specifying a different window size for each data modality. As described in further detail below, data was collected from students engaged in

DCE through conversations, virtual exams, and documentations. These modalities (dialog, click, documentation) are highly interactive and interwoven during the learning processes in DCE. Hence, we chose to use TMA to model the cross-modality interactions in complex thinking and activity in virtual patient simulations.

5 Methods

5.1 Participants and Settings

Purposive sampling was applied to identify two Bachelor of Science in Nursing (BSN) students from the same cohort at a public university in south central United States. The students were selected because they had completed the three scenarios at the time of the study. Rose and Roshni (pseudonyms) were enrolled in the Adaptation in Aging and Psychiatric-Mental Health Nursing courses in Fall 2022 where they completed the scenarios for Regina Walker and Lucas Callahan respectively. They completed Quan Tran's scenario in Spring 2023 as part of their Community Health Nursing course.

In this study, the interview guide was fully enabled by the instructor for all three assignments in DCE. The interview guide is meant to scaffold students' DCE as they engage in subjective data collection. The interview guide shows students the high-level outline for each section of the patient interview they will need to collect. Faculty may choose to (partially or fully) enable or disable the interview guide when assigning assignments to students. The full option allowed Rose and Roshni to see explicitly what subjective findings were scored in the interview (e.g. asked about chief complaint) before they uncovered them. This was the typical preference for faculty at the institution where the two students were enrolled.

5.2 Transcipts, Codebook, and Coding

We organized and examined a total of 1760 lines of timestamped utterances for the two students' (Rose and Roshni) transcripts from three scenarios (Regina, Lucas, Quan). The utterances included a variety of interactions (answer, clarification, exam action, feedback, greet, prompt, response, statement) logged between participants (student, patient, the system, and other virtual characters). These interactions characterized the nature of specific learning activities (e.g., objective data collection, subjective data collection, education, and empathy) students typically engage in DCE across three modalities (click, dialog, documentation) and distinct phases (assessment, care plan, contact tracing) in a scenario.

The nested nature of each utterance provided insight into the overall pedagogical structure of the simulation experience. For instance, the dialog data involved a conversation with the virtual patient for subjective data collection related to but not limited to the history of the patient's present illness, past medical history, review of systems, and social history. Dialog data also captured students' empathizing and educating their patients. The click data involved examining the patient, performing physical assessments, interpreting observations for any abnormalities, and practicing contact tracing. The documentation data involved the student summarizing and/or interpreting the state of the patient throughout the scenario. The temporal structure of the utterances was meaningful to understanding the sequence each student followed in a specific scenario and the amount of time they spent in each learning activity.

Table 1. Codebook

Code name	Definition	Example from Lucas Callahan's Scenario
Recognize Cues (RC)	Determining what client findings are significant, most important, and of immediate concern to the nurse (relevant cues)	Inspected right-left forearm, right-left wrist
Analyze Cues (AC)	Organizing and linking the relevant cues with client conditions/problems	Observations-Evidence of self-harm
Diagnosis + Prioritizing Hypothesis (DPH)	Ranking client conditions/problems according to urgency, complexity, and time. Diagnosing actual or potential health problems and needs	Diagnosis: Risk for injury
Generate Solutions (GS)	Identifying interventions that meet desired outcomes for the client; can include collecting additional assessment data	Short-term Goal-The patient will remain injury free until he can be evaluated by a psychiatric provider
Evaluate Outcomes (EO)	Comparing actual client outcomes with desired client outcomes to determine effectiveness of care	"[Patient] is writing poetry and reciting. That is not injurious to him. He is safe and free from injury"
Care-Management and Coordination (CMC)	Promoting self-care management and providing care coordination	Provide the patient with structured, solitary activities that do not present a risk for injury
Therapeutic Communication (TC)	Engaging with the individual in establishing a caring relationship. Communicating effectively with individuals. Employing a participatory approach to nursing care	"I am so sorry you feel that way. For your safety we will frequently check on you. We are moving you to a private room"
Subjective Assessment (SA)	Integrating assessment skills in practice	Have any other people noticed your mood or energy shifts?

We applied a combination of manual and automated approaches to code the dataset using the codebook above (See Table 1). Automated coding allows researchers to operate automatically and minimize human efforts; however, it is challenging to obtain high accuracy or other model evaluation (i.e. recall, Kappa, F-score, etc.) when coding affect-intensive complex constructs [21,22] and domain-specific jargons and terms [21,23]. In our study, considering the affordances and constraints of each coding method and our grounded understanding of the dataset used, we manually coded the constructs of Therapeutic Communication (TC), Subjective Assessment (SA), and Care-Management and Coordination (CMC) under social moderation [24]. These codes manifested in unique ways in students' transcripts based on the context of each scenario. Whereas, automation was applied to code students' actions for recognizing cues (RC), analyzing cues (AC), diagnosing and prioritizing hypotheses (DPH), generating solutions (GS) and evaluating outcomes (EO) because the conceptual definitions of these codes were consistent with procedural definitions (keyword matching) as captured by the DCE system. For example, logs were coded for an occurrence of RC when the student performed physical assessments using the exam action (e.g., assessed vitals). If the student correctly interpreted the result of their exam action (e.g., normothermic), this was coded as an occurrence of AC.

5.3 Model Construction and Research Questions

We applied T/ONA to represent patterns of student performance across the three scenarios in DCE. In particular, we specified different window lengths for learning events in different modalities. This is important to note because specifying different window lengths is an attempt to account for uneven data sizes and their varying temporal impacts in multimodal learning analytics. For instance, in a hypothetical context of collaborative problem solving where a student is involved in peer discussion and has access to resources in a system, chats may have a shorter window of impact on future learning events compared to searching and comprehending resources. That is, topics can rapidly change in a discussion, but engaging with a resource may have a longer influence on a student's connection-making compared to chatting.

In this study, we defined the smallest unit of analysis as students within learning activities. For each unit, ONA calculated and accumulated connections across eight codes (See Table 1) within recent temporal contexts. With learning events collected from three modalities, we operationalize recent temporal contexts for clicks, dialog, and documents respectively. That is, we configured unique window sizes for different modalities. Both patient interactions (dialog data) and exam actions (click data) have a strong temporal dependency and continuity due to interactivity between learners and the system. According to our qualitative analysis, we specified a window of five learning events for these two modalities. However, we selected a shorter window for the documentation modality, the length of two learning events, because each documentation is usually connected with the next action due to system design.

Using the methodological procedures and coding decisions described above, we developed and interpreted a combination of TMA and ONA (T/ONA) graphs to answer the two research questions (RQs):

1. *How do students engage in DCE scenarios?* We examined the alignment between learning patterns and guided instructional design across the three scenarios.
2. *Is there a difference in the connections of clinical competencies based on simulation assignment types in DCE?* We compared the patterns of connection-making across the focused exam and contact tracing scenarios.

6 Results

To answer each research, we describe the connection patterns visually and statistically and interpret the dimensions based on the node positions in respective T/ONA graphs. These are supported by qualitative examples from students' performance in DCE scenarios.

6.1 RQ1: How Do Students Engage in DCE Scenarios?

Figure 1 represents the grand mean connections (strength, self-referencing, direction) of learning patterns for Rose and Roshni across all scenarios. The thickness of edges indicates the strength of connections; arrows on edges indicate the main direction of connections; and the radius of the outer contour of a node indicates the total receiving degree, while the radius of the inner contour of a node indicates the degree of self-references.

According to the plot, students made self-references while practicing subjective assessment. That is, students spent a prolonged period performing a holistic assessment and obtaining a complete history of the patient. Self-referencing was also observed in students' practices of analyzing cues across the three scenarios. Students spent the bulk of their time in the scenarios interpreting patients' cues to relevant medical conditions/health problems. These activities preceded students' decision-making to foster patients' well-being. Therapeutic communication was central to Rose and Roshni's participation in the three scenarios. This allowed them to establish relationship-centered care, demonstrate empathy, practice humility and cultural sensitivity especially while engaging in subjective assessment and generating solutions for three different patients. Another pattern worth highlighting is students' practice of care management and coordination as a response to subjective assessment and generating solutions. Students were observed educating patients, promoting self-care, and facilitating continuity of care through coordination with family members and the healthcare team. Across the three scenarios, there was no significant difference between ONA scores for both students ($t(74.424) = 1.692$, $p = 0.095$, Cohen's $d = 0.378$). That is, both students practiced competencies related to clinical judgment, person centered-care, and professionalism in a similar manner as a result of using DCE. Below, we illustrate these connections to clinical competencies by drawing examples from Rose and Roshni's engagement in the gerontology scenario.

Students engaged in two phases in the end-of-life focused exam for virtual patient Regina Walker: assessment and care plan. During the assessment phase,

Rose and Roshni inquired about major health deviations. This included interacting with Regina about her chief complaint (increased pain), history of present illness (onset, duration, location, characteristics, aggravating factors, relieving factors, and severity of pain), past medical history (existing health conditions, general and medication allergies), social history (substance use), review of systems (head, eyes, ears, nose, throat, respiratory, cardiovascular, gastrointestinal, neurological, psychological). A big portion of their dialogue centered around Regina's functional status and geriatric syndromes for which older adults may be at risk. This included questions about depression, living environment, feeling safe at home, bathing, dressing, toileting, transferring, continence, ability to eat independently, sleeping habits, confusion, evidence of falls, gait and ambulatory aids, skin breakdowns, weight changes, weight loss, oral or dental problems, appetite changes, health, and social activity, perception of health, fatigue, ER visits or hospitalizations). Both students complemented this subjective data collection by performing exam actions and noting their observations for any abnormalities. This included (a) assessing vitals, IV bags, IV pump, IV site, and urine quality; (b) inspecting eyes, mouth, and skin; (c) auscultating carotids, breath sounds, heart sounds, and bowel sounds; (d) palpating abdomen, bladder; (e) testing cognition, skin turgor, and capillary refill. In a relatively brief but important part of this phase, Rose and Roshni discussed Regina's comfort and preference for hospice care, the family's need for health care services, and implications for health policy, financing, and service availability.

Their care plan focused on symptom management and advocacy for appropriate palliative/hospice care. Specifically, Rose and Roshni indicated their diagnosis for Regina (readiness for effective coping), identified signs and symptoms (interest in hospice care, increased home care needs outlined short-term goals), and recommended interventions (e.g., evaluate the patient's current understanding of coping strategies supporting their transition to hospice care), discuss the plan with the patient, and evaluate their own understanding of hospice care as a result of their simulated experience with Regina.

There were subtle differences in students' participation patterns. For instance, Rose engaged in a dialogue with Regina before performing exam actions. Roshni chose the opposite approach. Rose was also more compassionate in her communication during both phases; she (a) offered information about what to expect during the assessment phase, (b) provided reassurance during sensitive discussions, (c) expressed consideration for family and Regina while discussing an end-of-life transition plan. The following statements are an example:

> Rose: Ms. Walker, we are going to work on ways for you to cope with the upcoming changes you are about to face. This will help the transition be less demanding on you as well as your family. I know this is going to be hard on you all, so I am here for any questions or concerns. I want to know how much education you have on coping strategies, give you some supplemental strategies, and also give you referrals.

Roshini: "I will provide you and your family members a referral to the funeral service, spiritual support and financial assistance if that is ok with you.

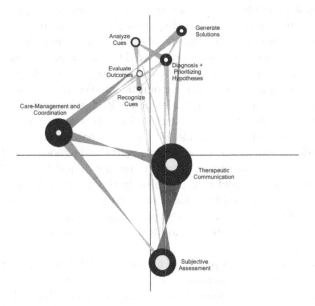

Fig. 1. Grand mean plot illustrating Rose and Roshni's patterns of engagement across the gerontology, mental health, and community health scenarios.

6.2   RQ2: Is There a Difference in the Connections Students Make to Clinical Competencies Based on Simulation Assignment Types in DCE?

Figure 2 depicts the differences in connections made by students in the two types of simulation assignments in DCE: focused exam and contact tracing. In this subtracted plot, edges and nodes are colored based on the stronger connections made by a certain scenario type (i.e., purple for focused exams and yellow for contact tracing). In the T/ONA space depicted in Fig. 2, competencies related to knowledge of nursing practice (Domain 1 of the Essentials) cluster on the negative side of the x-axis, while codes depicting person-centered care and professionalism (Domain 2 and 9 of the Essentials) cluster on the positive side. According to the t-test of ONA scores, there is a significant difference for connections made in the focused exams and contact tracing tasks ($t(76.471) = 11.3$, $p < .001$**, Cohen's $d = 1.985$). That is, the type of assignment in DCE participated in influenced the clinical competencies students practiced applying during learning activities in a scenario.

For connections made in focused exam scenarios, both care management, coordination, diagnosing, and prioritizing hypotheses were observed as common responses to analyzing cues. That is, after analyzing cues from the virtual patients, students tended to rank signs and symptoms, diagnose conditions, and provide care advice. Additionally, students made more connections from generating solutions to care management and coordination in focused exams. In other words, after generating solutions related to the virtual patients' conditions, Rose and Roshni offered corresponding care-management advice and coordination such as scheduling follow-up appointments. For the contact tracing scenario, students made more (1) self-references within subjective assessments, (2) self-references with therapeutic communication, (3) connections from subjective assessment to therapeutic communication, and (4) no connections to the clinical judgment codes (recognizing cues, analyzing cues, diagnosing and prioritizing hypothesis, generating solutions and evaluating outcomes) because there was no objective data collection and care planning in this scenario. Self-references and connections were influenced by a focus on conducting a comprehensive patient assessment, facilitating health literacy, preventing disease, and promoting well-being. Below, we illustrate Rose and Roshni's engagement in the community health scenario.

Students engaged in two phases of a contact tracing assignment for the virtual patient Quan Tran: assessment and contact tracing. During assessment, Rose and Roshni inquired about Quan's chief complaint (i.e., HIV diagnosis), history of present illness (testing history, prodrome), past medical history (vaccinations, allergies, past hospitalizations), social history (home life, support system, substance use, typical diet), medication (herbal supplements, antiretroviral prescription), sexual history (sexual partners), review of relevant systems (constitutional and mental health; integumentary, respiratory, and cardiovascular system), patient needs (goals and priorities), and social determinants of health (employment, health insurance, education). Once again there were subtle differences in Rose and Roshni's participation. For instance, Rose followed up with Quan when he reported not understanding how HIV infection is transmitted, taking an herbal supplement consisting of echinacea and goldenseal, and wanting to keep his diagnosis hidden from coworkers and family members. Roshni did not respond to Quan's lack of understanding of HIV transmission; she followed up on his use of herbal supplements and the reaction of others to HIV status. She also educated him when Quan reported unfamiliarity with his antiretroviral medication, and feeling anxious about his diagnosis.

Students were prompted and guided by the system during the second phase of the scenario to model the process of tracing contacts and notifying partners. This included asking contacts about the results of their sexually transmitted infection (STI) panel or offering assistance to identify a clinic that performs STI testing, underscoring the importance of treatment from an HIV specialist and an appropriate medication regimen, encouraging regular tracking of viral load, maintaining confidentiality, and promoting safe sex practices.

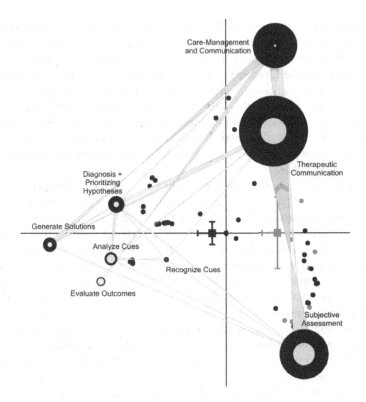

Fig. 2. Subtraction plot illustrating differences in connections made by Rose and Roshni in focussed exam (purple) vs contact tracing assignment (yellow). (Color figure online)

7 Discussion and Implications

Professional organizations and regulatory bodies such as the American Association of Colleges of Nursing (AACN) and National Council of State Boards of Nursing (NCSBN) are keen on helping nursing programs address the practice-readiness gap. An emphasis on competency-based education provides the opportunity to enhance interprofessional education, increase the use of simulation, and improve clinical judgment in new graduate and advanced practice nurses [25]. Virtual patient simulations provide a beneficial modality in which learners apply and practice their clinical reasoning and critical thinking abilities before interacting with real patients [26]. However, current research on simulations heavily relies on self-evaluations [8].

In this study, we examined two undergraduate students' performance in Elsevier's Shadow Health® Digital Clinical Experiences™ (DCE) and provided evidence for their practice of clinical competencies characterized in Domains 1 (Knowledge of Nursing Practice), 2 (Person-Centered Care), and 9 (Professionalism) for entry-level programs in The Essentials [2] and Layer 3 of NCSBN

Clinical Judgment Measurement Model [3]. We constructed a grand mean plot of two students' multimodal learning activities across three virtual patient scenarios and a subtraction plot to compare connection-making between focused exams and contact tracing assignments in DCE. The grand mean plot (Fig. 1) indicated that students practiced competencies in clinical judgment, person-centered care, and professionalism across the patient diversity and care needs represented in gerontology, mental health, and community health contexts. Additionally, the subtracted plot (Fig. 2) between focused exam and contact tracing indicated that the two assignment types afforded students to foreground specific competencies more than others.

There is a growing body of research in health care and health professions education that applies Quantitative Ethnography to investigate complex questions about professional enculturation and practice [27, 28]. However, few studies have used multimodal data and fewer exist in the nursing context [29]. This paper applied TMA to examine data obtained from three types of modalities (click, dialog, documentation) to make sense of students' engagement in collecting and interpreting patient data, synthesizing evidence, and promoting care that is suitable for each patient's condition (i.e., Disease Prevention/Promotion of Health and Well-Being, Chronic Disease Care, Hospice /Palliative Care). TMA allowed us to set and account for the impact of different window sizes for a variety of data types. For a complete discussion of both the mechanisms of TMA and its conceptual and theoretical underpinnings, please refer to a forthcoming paper [19].

In a previous study on DCE, researchers observed students practicing recognizing cues for a prolonged period and demonstrated the ways in which this clinical skill manifested in a pediatric and a geriatric patient scenario in the health assessment content area [30]. However, this self-referencing phenomenon could not be modeled using Epistemic Network Analysis (ENA). In this study, Ordered Network Analysis allowed us to not only capture the strength of connections among multiple clinical competencies that ENA typically allows, but also illustrate ordered relationship and self-referencing (Figs. 1 & 2) across two assignment types (focused exam and contact tracing) in three content areas (gerontology, mental health, community health).

Nursing programs are likely to continue their expanded use of virtual simulations even after the peak of the COVID-19 pandemic [31]. At the same time, extant QE research is providing valuable insight into the design and enactment of simulation-based learning in undergraduate nursing education (manikin-based, virtual reality, digital standardized patients) [15, 18, 30]. This study provides additional impetus for continuing the application of QE research methods in this discipline. In the future, researchers should broaden examinations using virtual patient simulations like DCE to include additional (a) foundational and specialty content areas in nursing, (b) clinical competencies, and (c) participants and sample sizes. Researchers should also consider deepening their examinations by investigating (a) students' performance in DCE scenarios where the interview guide is partially enabled or turned off, and (b) the impact of interaction types (e.g., questions, clarification) between participants (e.g., student, patient, system). Findings from these studies can yield recommendations on how nursing faculty and administrators can use virtual simulations systematically for fostering students' practice readiness.

Acknowledgments. This work was funded in part by the National Science Foundation (DRL-2100320, DRL-2201723, DRL-2225240), the Wisconsin Alumni Research Foundation, and the Office of the Vice Chancellor for Research and Graduate Education at the University of Wisconsin-Madison. The opinions, findings, and conclusions do not reflect the views of the funding agencies, cooperating institutions, or other individuals.

References

1. National Council of State Boards of Nursing: The NCSBN 2023 Environmental Scan: Nursing at a Crossroads–an Opportunity for Action: Nursing at a Crossroads: An Opportunity for Action. J. Nurs. Regul. **13**(4), S1–S48 (2023)
2. American Association of Colleges of Nursing: The Essentials: Core Competencies for Professional Nursing Education (2021)
3. Dickinson, P., et al.: NCSBN clinical judgment measurement model clarification. J. Nurs. Educ. **59**(7), 365 (2020)
4. Wakefield, M., et al.: The future of nursing 2020–2030: charting a path to achieve health equity (2021)
5. American Association of Colleges of Nursing: Data spotlight: The impact of insufficient clinical sites on baccalaureate program admissions (2022)
6. Alexander, M.: Nursing challenges continue into 2022. J. Nurs. Regul. **12**(4), 3 (2022)
7. Foronda, C.L., et al.: Virtual simulation in nursing education: a systematic review spanning 1996 to 2018. Simul. Healthc. **15**(1), 46–54 (2020)
8. Cole, H.S.: Competency-based evaluations in undergraduate nursing simulation: a state of the literature. Clin. Simul. Nurs. **76**, 1–16 (2023)
9. Turrise, S.L., et al.: Virtual simulation: comparing critical thinking and satisfaction in RN-BSN students. Clin. Simul. Nurs. **46**, 57–61 (2020)
10. Santarelli, T., et al.: Enhancing nursing student efficiency and efficacy in patient care through virtual patient simulation. MODSIM World 2022 (2022)
11. Altmiller, G., et al.: Impact of a virtual patient simulation on nursing students' attitudes of transgender care. Nurse Educ. 10–1097 (2022)
12. Carmona, G., et al.: Exploring interactions between computational and critical thinking in model-eliciting activities through epistemic network analysis (2022)
13. Siebert-Evenstone, A., et al.: Cause and because: using epistemic network analysis to model causality in the next generation science standards (2019)
14. Shaffer, D.W.: Quantitative ethnography (2017)
15. Shah, M., et al.: Alignment of content in simulation learning system to clinical judgement competencies. White paper. Elsevier Education (2023). https://evolve. elsevier.com/education/expertise/simulation-success/alignment-of-content-in-simulation-learning-system-to-clinical-judgment-competencies/
16. Shah, M., et al.: Student learning in simulation learning system with virtual reality: a quantitative ethnographic examination of a fundamentals of nursing scenario. White Paper. Elsevier Education (2022). https://evolve.elsevier.com/education/expertise/simulation-success/student-learning-in-simulation-learning-system-with-virtual-reality/

17. Shah, M., et al.: Modeling educator use of virtual reality simulations in nursing education using epistemic network analysis. In: 7th Conference of the Immersive Learning Research Network (iLRN), IEEE, pp. 1–8 (2021)

18. Shah, M., et al.: Quality and safety education for nursing (QSEN) in virtual reality simulations: a quantitative ethnographic examination. In: Third International Conference on Quantitative Ethnography, ICQE2021, Online, 8–11 November 2021, Conference Proceedings (2021)

19. Shaffer, D.W., et al.: Transmodal analysis (2023)

20. Tan, Y., et al.: Ordered network analysis. In: Damsa, C., Barany, A. (eds.) Advances in Quantitative Ethnography. ICQE 2022. CCIS, vol. 1785, pp. 101–116. Springer, Cham (2023). https://doi.org/10.1007/978-3-031-31726-2_8

21. Wallace, B.C., et al.: Computational irony: a survey and new perspectives. Artif. Intell. Rev. **43**, 467–483 (2015)

22. Gultchin, L., et al.: Humor in word embeddings: cockamamie gobbledegook for nincompoops. In: PMLR (2019)

23. Savova, G., et al.: Use of natural language processing to extract clinical cancer phenotypes from electronic medical records; natural language processing for cancer phenotypes from EMRs. Cancer Res. **79**(21), 5463–5470 (2019)

24. Herrenkohl, L.R., et al.: Investigating elementary students' scientific and historical argumentation. J. Learn. Sci. **22**(3), 413–461 (2013)

25. Lewis, L.S., et al.: Nursing education practice update 2022: competency-based education in nursing. Sage Open Nurs. (8) (2022)

26. Kononowicz, A., et al.: Virtual patient simulations in health professions education: systematic review and meta-analysis by the digital health education collaboration. J. Med. Internet Res. **21**(7) (2019)

27. Shah, M., et al.: Communicating QE: a two-part resource for quantitative ethnographers in health education and health care contexts (part 1 of 2). In: Fourth International Conference on Quantitative Ethnography: Conference Proceedings Supplement (2022)

28. Ruis, A., et al.: Communicating QE: a two-part resource for quantitative ethnographers in health education and health care contexts (part 2 of 2). In: Fourth International Conference on Quantitative Ethnography: Conference Proceedings Supplement (2022)

29. Buckingham-Shum, S., et al.: The multimodal matrix as a quantitative ethnography methodology. In: Eagan, B., Misfeldt, M., Siebert-Evenstone, A. (eds.) ICQE 2019. CCIS, vol. 1112, pp. 26–40. Springer, Cham (2019). https://doi.org/10.1007/978-3-030-33232-7_3

30. Shah, M., et al.: Understanding how undergraduate nursing students (learn to) recognize cues in digital clinical experiences: a transmodal analysis. In: Fourth International Conference on Quantitative Ethnography: Conference Proceedings Supplement (2022)

31. Harder, N., et al.: How the pandemic impacted simulation: where do we go from here? Clin. Simul. Nurs. **74**, 1–2 (2023)

Combining Automatic Coding and Instructor Input to Generate ENA Visualizations for Asynchronous Online Discussion

Marcia Moraes[1]([✉]) [iD], Sadaf Ghaffari[1] [iD], Yanye Luther[1] [iD], and James Folkesdtad[2] [iD]

[1] Department of Computer Science, Colorado State University, Fort Collins, CO 80523, USA
{marcia.moraes,sadaf.ghaffari,yanye.luther}@colostate.edu
[2] School of Education, Colorado State University, Fort Collins, CO 80523, USA
james.folkestad@colostate.edu

Abstract. Asynchronous online discussions are a common fundamental tool to facilitate social interaction in hybrid and online courses. However, instructors lack the tools to accomplish the overwhelming task of evaluating asynchronous online discussion activities. In this paper we present an approach that uses Latent Dirichlet Analysis (LDA) and the instructor's keywords to automatically extract codes from a relatively small dataset. We use the generated codes to build an Epistemic Network Analysis (ENA) model and compare this model with a previous ENA model built by human coders. The results show that there is no statistical difference between the two models. We present an analysis of these models and discuss the potential use of ENA as a visualization to help instructors evaluating asynchronous online discussions.

Keywords: ENA Visualization · Automated Coding · Unsupervised Learning · Instructor's Keywords

1 Introduction

Asynchronous online discussions are a common fundamental tool to facilitate social interaction in hybrid and online courses. They have been shown to improve students' critical thinking [10], knowledge construction [13], writing skills [2], and learning outcomes [24]. However, instructors lack the tools to accomplish the overwhelming task of evaluating asynchronous online discussion activities [14]. According to de Lima et al. [14], instructors reported struggling to assess students' contributions in forum activities due to difficulties in following the discussions, the lack of specific reports related to the subjects discussed, the students' contributions to those subjects, and the lack of visualizations to convey messages in a graphical format.

In order to address some of those difficulties, Epistemic Network Analysis (ENA) has been presented as learning analytics visualization tool to show the relationships among the different concepts students discuss in an asynchronous online discussion

---

M. Moraes and S. Ghaffari—These authors contributed equally to this work.

G. Arastoopour Irgens and S. Knight (Eds.): ICQE 2023, CCIS 1895, pp. 381–394, 2023.
https://doi.org/10.1007/978-3-031-47014-1_26

[16]. In this particular work [16], two human annotators manually coded the text data. In a more recent work [19], three different text mining approaches, namely Latent Semantic Analysis (LSA), Latent Dirichlet Analysis (LDA) and Clustering Word Vectors, were applied to automate code extraction from a relatively small discussion board dataset obtained from [16]. Based on the study presented in [16], we submitted a project proposal to our university's teaching innovation grant to investigate the application of ENA as a visualization tool to support instructors. Reviewers mentioned that instructors would like to have the visualizations but would not have time to be involved in the coding process, even if that process used nCoder [15]. However, the instructors would be willing to provide keywords that should be present in the codes. Based on the provided feedback, and unlike previous works, we not only looked into extracting codes from relatively small data using LDA but also illustrated how this can lead to generating ENA visualization without using nCoder [15] throughout the process.

This paper builds on those previous works by:

1. Using the automatically generated codes provided in [19] to code the same dataset used in [16].
2. Evaluating the quality of the automated coding with the human coding presented on [16] by interrater reliability.
3. Improving the automated code generation in order to reach a satisfactory interrater reliability between algorithm and human if necessary.
4. Applying the codes that were automatically generated in the creation of ENA visualizations.
5. Analyzing and evaluating those ENA visualizations with human coded ENA visualizations.
6. Validating both ENA visualizations with instructors.

In this paper we aim to answer the following research questions:

- **RQ1.** What is/are the difference(s) between the ENA visualizations generated using an automated coding process and a human coding process for the data presented in [16]?
- **RQ2.** How does an instructor evaluate the ENA visualizations generated?

The remainder of this paper is structured as follows. Section 2 summarizes prior research efforts on using ENA as a visualizations tool and on automated coding processes. Sections 3 and 4 describe the approach used in the study. Section 5 is dedicated to presenting the results obtained from our experiments. We discuss the results and outline directions for further work in Sect. 6. Section 7 presents the conclusion of this work.

2   Related Works

ENA has been used to support many facets of education and learning in several areas [4, 18, 21]. One use of ENA that is gaining more attention is its use as a visualization tool [22] to help instructors evaluate clinical team simulations [9], support teachers' interventions in students' virtual collaboration [12], evaluate teamwork [23], include participants in co-construction and co-interpretation of ENA representations [25], and unveil the conceptual connections that students are making in asynchronous online discussions [16]. All these studies utilized different coding strategies to code the data used in the ENA visualizations.

A recent work by Cai et al. [6] centered around nCoder where they investigated how close human created code words were to codes identified by topic models in two large datasets. Another work compared the performance of neural networks in a supervised learning manner with nCoder to assess which approach required the least human coding effort while achieving a sufficient and accurate classification [8]. In their comparison, they indicated nCoder had a higher accuracy. Although nCoder is a popular learning analytics platform used to develop coding schemes, it is not fully automated. In other words, it requires active human efforts to read through every item in the data and validate if the choice of coding is conceptually valid. It also suffers the low recall problem. Previous literature studies have identified ways to improve the problem of low recall or high false negative rate in nCoder. nCoder + [7] aims to improve low recall issue in nCoder through semantic component addition. However, as mentioned by the authors of nCoder +, the idea is still a prototype and is not a public tool yet. In another research effort, the use of Negative Reversion Set (NRS) sampling has been shown to improve the low recall for Regular Expressions based classifiers such as nCoder [5].

Our work has several distinctive features compared to prior works. First, we only take advantage of a Natural Language Processing (NLP) unsupervised learning technique to automate the code extraction, despite having a relatively small dataset without the use of nCoder. Second, we utilize coherence analysis [17] to identify the optimal number of topics in the discussion data, thus avoiding arbitrary selection of the number. Third, we use instructor keywords in addition to the LDA extracted keywords to generate the visualization.

3 Method

The main goal of our approach was to extract topic keywords from a relatively small online discussion dataset using Latent Dirichlet Allocation (LDA) [3], use those keywords to automatically code asynchronous online discussion data, and generate ENA visualizations based on that data. In this section, we describe how this process was automated.

3.1 Dataset Preprocessing

The data utilized to investigate the research questions comprised of online discussion posts from seven semesters: Fall 2017, Fall 2018, Fall 2019, Spring 2020, Fall 2020, Spring 2021, and Fall 2021. The data consisted of 2,648 postings collected from an online class for organizational leaders as part of a Masters of Education program at a Research 1 land-grant university. Table 1 represents prior codes in our dataset.

The problem of interest was based on code retrieval. This highlighted the importance of the preprocessing step in our setup. The preprocessing steps in our automatic extraction task consisted of tokenization, lowercasing, named-entity removal, stop words removal, in-document frequency filtering, and generating bigrams and trigrams since our interest was to retrieve the code containing two or three words.

Table 1. Priori Codes.

Code Name	Definition	Kappa (κ)
Retrieval practice, Spacing out practice, Interleaving	Retrieval practice is the act of recalling facts or concepts or events from memory and are also known as testing effect or retrieval-practice effect. Spacing out practice allows people to a little forgetting that helps their process of consolidation. Interleaving the practice of two or more concepts or skills help develop the ability to discriminate later between different kinds of problems and select the better solution	0.85
Illusion of mastery	Research have pointed out that students usually have a misunderstanding about how learning occurs and engage with learning strategies that are not beneficial for their long-term retention, such as rereading the material several times and cramming before exams	0.89
Effortful learning	Learning is deeper and more durable when it is effortful, meaning that efforts, short-terms impediments (desirable difficulties), learning from mistakes, and trying to solve some problem before knowing the correct answer makes for stronger learning	0.85
Get beyond Learning Styles	Researchers found that when instructional style matches the nature of the content, all learners learn better, regardless of their learning styles	0.86

3.2 Latent Dirichlet Analysis

We aimed to determine which codes are associated with each discussion post, i.e. in each document, and extract them. To accomplish this, we used LDA [3], a generative probabilistic model, to extract the codes from the online discussion data to help understand what topics were discussed in the course. In order to find high probability words within each topic, the number of topics was set to 5 to get the high topic coherence score [17, 19]. Table 2 shows the extracted words for each topic. In Table 2, Topic 1 code words are associated with Effortful learning code, Topic 2 code words are associated with Get beyond learning styles, Topic 3 code words are associated with Illusion of mastery, and Topic 4 code words are associated with Retrieval practice, Spacing out practice, and Interleaving. Only Topic 0 did not represent any codes.

Table 2. Five topics extracted by Latent Dirichlet Allocation.

Topic 0	Topic 1	Topic 2	Topic 3	Topic 4
lecture	desire	dyslexia	confidence	mass
solution	desire_difficulty	learn_style	feedback	mass_practice
classroom	plf *	individual	calibration	interleaving_practice
surgeon	resonate	learn_differ	confidence_memory	space_retrieval
acquire	parachute	disable	accuracy	tend
instruct	fall	intelligent	peer	day
learn_learn	land	prefer	answer	long_term
impact	jump	support	event	week
demand	parachute_land	dyslexia	state	myth
lecture_classroom	land_fall	focus	calibration_learn	practice_space

*Stands for Parachute Landing Fall.

4 Experiments

With the LDA extracted keywords for 4 topics, we conducted experiments with those keywords alone as described in 4.1, and along with the keywords identified by the instructor as described in 4.2 and 4.3.

4.1 Experiment 1

Following the results obtained from 3.2, we automatically generated a well-formatted table [20] in which each row consisted of: post entry number, user id, date and time for that post entry, actual discussion post data, and list of codes with 1's or 0's corresponding to the existence or no existence of the specific code in each post. The table was entered into the ENA webtool in an Excel format [1]. We then ran interrater reliability between the automated coding and the human coding provided by [16]. Table 3 presents the Cohen's kappa results for each code.

Table 3 shows the only code that had a Cohen's kappa moderate level of agreement [20] was the Get Beyond Learning Styles code. Illusion of Mastery had a weak level of agreement and the remaining codes had minimal level of agreement. In order to improve those numbers, we had asked the instructor, who manually coded the data, to provide us with keywords that we could include in the automatic process.

4.2 Experiment 2

After receiving the keywords from the instructor (Table 4), we combined extracted keywords from LDA and keywords from instructor and generated a new well-formatted data table containing the same elements present in the data table from Experiment 1. Table 4 demonstrates that some of the keywords provided by the instructor were very

Table 3. Interrater reliability between automated coding process and human coding process.

Code Name	Cohen's (κ)
Retrieval practice, Spacing out practice, Interleaving	0.36
Illusion of mastery	0.52
Effortful learning	0.23
Get Beyond Learning Styles	0.77

Table 4. Keywords provided by the instructor.

Codes	Keywords
Retrieval practice, Spacing out practice, Interleaving	retrieval practice, retrieval process, testing effect, test effect, recall knowledge, retrieval, actively retrieving, peri- odically testing, retrieval activity, retrieval activities, low stakes, effective retrieval must be repeated, flash cards, quizzing, practice and retrieval, quiz over time, continually retrieve the information, frequently quizzing, retrieval practice activity, retrieval practice activities, testing efforts, active retrieval, practice, testing for its benefit in the learning process, short quiz, active recall, process of retrieval, practice sessions, self testing, recall the information, RPA, RPAs, spacing out, spacing out practice, spaced practice, spacing practice, spaced out practice, spaced out, spaced retrieval, space retrieval, space practice, retrieval spaced, retrieve spaced, spaced application, spaced knowledge, space knowledge, spaced retrieval, retrieval practice is spaced, interleaving, interleaved practice, interleave, interleaved
Illusion of mastery	illusion of mastery, illusions of mastery, misunderstanding, illusion of knowing, illusions of knowing, illusion of learning, illusions of learning, re read, cram
Effortful learning	difficult, difficulties, mistakes, failure, effortful learning, desirable difficulty, desirable, effortful
Get beyond Learning Styles	instructional style, learning styles

similar to each other. In order to preserve the instructor's process, those keywords were not changed since they were used in the instructor's process of manually coding the data.

Table 5 presents the Cohen's kappa for the interrater reliability between the automated process with instructor's provided keywords and the human coding. Compared to simply using the automated extracted codes, the level of agreement increased. Effortful learning and Retrieval Practice, Spacing out Practice, Interleaving codes, which previously had minimal level of agreement increased to a moderate level of agreement. Illusion of Mastery which had a weak level also increased to a moderate level, and Beyond Learning Styles, which had a moderate level increased to a strong level of agreement.

Table 5. Interrater reliability between Automated + Human Keywords (A + HK) coding process and Human (H) coding process.

Code Name	Cohen's (κ)
Retrieval practice, Spacing out practice, Interleaving	0.79
Illusion of mastery	0.79
Effortful learning	0.70
Get Beyond Learning Styles	0.81

4.3 Experiment 3

The third experiment consisted of using the well-formatted data table produced from Experiment 2 and the well-formatted data table provided by [16] to create a joint well-formatted table that included an additional column, named source, to generate the ENA visualizations using the ENA webtool. All rows that contained data generated by the algorithm were labeled "algorithm" for the source column and all rows that contained human manual coding were labeled "human" for the source column.

We used the four codes produced by our approach described in Sect. 3.2. These codes were validated with the instructor to represent the concepts that the students were learning and therefore the concepts that the students should've connected in that online discussion. Those codes were Effortful Learning (represented simply as effort in ENA), Get Beyond Learning Styles (represented as beyondLS in ENA), Illusions of Mastery (represented as illusions in ENA), and Retrieval Practice, Spacing Out Practice, Interleaving (represented as retrieval-interleaving in ENA). As described in Experiment 2 and in Table 5, the interrater reliability using Cohen's Kappa reached at least $\kappa = 0.70$ for all the codes.

As we were interested in the individual student's network of concepts, both units of analysis and stanzas were students (i.e., all student messages) with an infinite stanza window. That configuration enabled us to visualize the connections between the codes for each student. To compare the model generated by the algorithm and the model generated by the human coder, the source column from our well-formatted data table was used.

5 Results

We analyzed the results produced by each data table to detect similarities and differences between the two models generated. After that, we had a meeting with the instructor to present the results to them and evaluate the two models produced. In this section we present the results from ENA generated using data from Experiment 3 and the evaluation process conducted by the instructor.

5.1 ENA Models

Figure 1a presents the group average network graph created using data from the automatic coding + human keywords (A + HK) process. The thickness of the lines between the codes indicates the strength of connections. Thicker lines indicate stronger connections, whereas thinner lines indicate weaker connections. The results indicated that for the A + HK process the strongest relationship was between the codes illusions and retrieval-interleave, followed by beyondLS and retrieval-interleave, and effort and retrieval-interleave. BeyondLS and illusions and effort and illusions had the same strength in relationship. The weakest relationship was between effort and beyondLS, as shown in Table 6.

Figure 1b presents the group average network graph created using data from the human coding process. Results show that the strongest relationships were between illusions and retrieval-interleave, followed by beyondLS and retrieval-interleave and effort and illusions. After that, the strongest relationships were between effort and retrieval-interleave and beyondLS and effort. BeyondLS and illusions connection had the weakest relation as we can observe from Table 6.

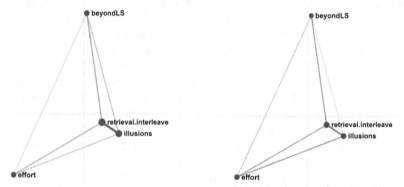

(a) ENA using data from A+HK coding process.

(b) ENA using data from H coding process.

Fig. 1. ENA Visualizations.

Table 6. Comparison of strength of connections between Automated + Human Keywords (A + HK) coding process and Human (H) coding process.

Connection	Strength (A + HK)	Strength (H)
illusions and retrieval-interleave	0.40	0.36
beyondLS and retrieval-interleave	0.32	0.28
effort and retrieval-interleave	0.30	0.27
beyondLS and illusions	0.27	0.18
effort and illusions	0.27	0.28
effort and beyondLS	0.21	0.22

As shown by Figs. 1a, b, and Table 6, both coding processes generated the same relationships between all the codes, with some differences between the strengths in the relationships. Figure 2 shows the difference between the A + HK model (named algorithm in the figure) and the human model, meaning that the A + HK made stronger connections between illusions and retrieval-interleave, beyondLS and retrieval-interleave, effort and retrieval-interleave, and beyondLS and illusions codes.

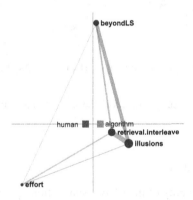

Fig. 2. Difference between ENA generated by the A + HK coding process and the H coding process.

Using the ENA webtool, we performed a statistical analysis to verify that the difference between the two models was significant. Along the X axis (MR1), a Mann-Whitney test showed that Human ($Mdn = -0.13$, $N = 25$) was not statistically significantly different at the $\alpha = 0.05$ level from algorithm ($Mdn = 0.13$, $N = 25$, $U = 206.00$, $p = 0.04$, $r = 0.34$). Along the Y axis (SVD2), a Mann-Whitney test showed that Human ($Mdn = -0.01$, $N = 25$) was not statistically significantly different at the $\alpha = 0.05$ level from algorithm ($Mdn = -0.01$, $N = 25$, $U = 318.00$, $p = 0.92$, $r = -0.02$). Therefore, there is no statistical difference between the model generated by the A + HK process and the H coding process.

Out of the 25 ENA visualizations generated, 12 of those (48%) had the same structure for both the A + HK process and human process. From those 12, 10 had the exact same strength in connections. One example can be seen in Figs. 3a and 3b. The remaining two had different strengths. In one of those two visualizations, the structure was the same but the A + HK process found stronger connections between retrieval-interleave and illusions code and the human found stronger connections between effort and illusions instead. In the other visualization, the human coding found stronger connections than the A + HK process for all codes (Figs. 4a and 4b).

The remaining 13 visualizations (52%) had a different structure. In 10 of those, the A + HK process found more connections than the human process. In the remaining three, the human found more connections that the A + HK process.

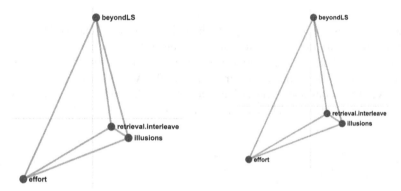

(a) User 142854 using A+HK coding process.   (b) User 142854 using H coding process.

Fig. 3. ENA visualizations with the same structure and strengths.

5.2 Instructor's Evaluation

In order to evaluate the quality of the ENA visualizations generated using the A + HK process, we met with the course instructor. The intention was to gain feedback regarding the correctness of the models generated in cases where the automated process found connections that weren't supported by human analysis, as well as cases where the automated process found relationships that were missed by the human coder. We presented the results described on Sect. 5.1 to the instructor who's familiar with Quantitative Ethnography and the ENA Web tool. Each one of the 25 visualizations were walked through with the instructor using the ENA Web tool.

First, all ENAs that had the same structure were analyzed. All the qualitative data extracts used to find the connections between the codes for the A + HK process and the human process were looked through. As expected, for the visualizations that had the same structure and same strengths of connections, both processes used the exact same data. For those two that had a different strength between connections, in one of them (125919 user as presented in 4c) the A + HK process found a relation that the human had missed, for the other (135030 user as presented in 4a), the A + HK process presented a false positive between retrieval- interleave and illusions codes. The automated process produced a false positive in this case because it identified a keyword. However, simply having that keyword present was insufficient for the human coder to establish a relationship between the two codes.

The next step was to analyze those 13 visualizations that had different structures between the A + HK and human processes. We started by analyzing the visualizations where the A + HK process found more connections between the codes than the human process. Out of those 10 cases, in seven cases the A + HK process found connections between codes that the human had missed. Only in three cases the A + HK process generated false positives connections. To evaluate the three cases where the A + HK process found less connections, we analyzed all the qualitative data and confirmed that the A + HK process missed those connections.

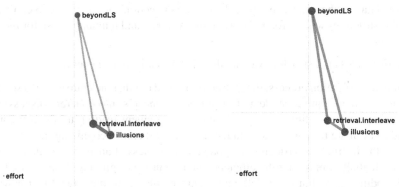

(a) ENA for user 135030 using A+HK coding process.

(b) ENA for user 135030 using H coding process.

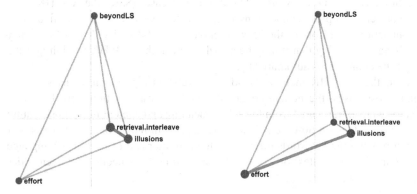

(c) ENA for user 125919 using A+HK coding process.

(d) ENA for user 125919 using H coding process.

Fig. 4. ENA visualizations with the same structure and different strengths.

6   Discussion

- **RQ1.** What is/are the difference(s) between the ENA visualizations generated using an automated coding process and a human coding process for the data presented in [16]?

As we can observe from Sect. 5.1 both the A + HK and the human processes generated the same structure for their network, with a small difference in the strength of some connections. The A + HK process found stronger connections between illusions and retrieval-interleave, beyondLS and retrieval-interleave, effort and retrieval-interleave, and beyondLS and illusions codes (Fig. 2). After running a statistical analysis, we observed that there was no statistical difference between the model generated by the A + HK and the human. This could potentially be a good indicator that an automated process that used combined LDA keywords and human keywords can contribute to generating ENA visualizations to help instructors in evaluating asynchronous online discussion data. Further tests need to be done in other sections of the course to confirm that similar structures will be found between the A + HK and human process for those new datasets.

- **RQ2.** How does an instructor evaluate the ENA visualizations generated?

During the evaluation process, the instructor pointed out that the course used a series of assignments that required students to synthesize concepts into coherent discussion posts. Consequently, grading those posts demanded frequent reading to identify concepts and to evaluate how well each student integrated them. Recognizing the grading challenges, the instructor considered the potential usefulness of an algorithm generated ENA for potentially improving the efficiency and accuracy of grading. Comparing the A + HK coding to the human coded equivalent, the instructor mentioned that it was impressive that the A + HK generated identical coding for 11 of the 25 students. Additionally, they noted it was encouraging to see that the algorithm found more connections in 11 additional cases. In other words, 22 out of the 25 cases (88%) the A + HK identified the correct conceptual connections in the written passages and identified more correct connections in 11 out of the 25 written passages (44%). The level of accuracy was promising, suggesting that it may be possible to use the A + HK to highlight the majority of the connections automatically.

However, the A + HK method found fewer relationships in three cases (12%). Examining those cases, the human coder identified accurate relationships, but those relationships were extrapolated from the subtle meaning and content in the post. Future work needs to be done on how to include those aspects in the automated process. For example, improving the keywords offered by the instructor and using Large Language Models to consider the context of words [11] for a stronger connection between codes discussed in a course.

7   Conclusion

In this paper we presented an approach that clustered topic keywords into meaningful categories from a relatively small online course discussion dataset using Latent Dirichlet Allocation (LDA) [3]. Those keywords and the instructor's keywords were then used to automatically code asynchronous online discussion data. Finally, ENA visualizations were generated based on the data. The visualizations were compared with the corresponding visualizations generated by human coding process, and both visualizations were evaluated by an instructor. Results indicated that there is no statistical difference between the model generated by the A + HK process and the human.

Overall, the result of the A + HK demonstrates significant potential to assist instructors in evaluating discussion-based assignments that demand the students' synthesis and integration of concepts, especially in larger classrooms. An automated method allows instructors teaching classes with hundreds of students to use discussion posts to promote these higher order learning outcomes. It is important to acknowledge that our approach is considered as a tool for instructors to enhance their evaluation process of asynchronous online discussions. Additional efforts need to be made in order to verify its applicability to other class settings such as different student populations and different course materials.

References

1. Ena web tool (2023). https://app.epistemicnetwork.org/login.html
2. Aloni, M., Harrington, C.: Research based practices for improving the effectiveness of asynchronous online discussion boards. Scholarsh. Teach. Learn. Psychol. 4(4), 271 (2018)
3. Blei, D.M., Ng, A.Y., Jordan, M.I.: Latent dirichlet allocation. J. Mach. Learn. Res. 3(Jan), 993–1022 (2003)
4. Bressler, D.M., Annetta, L.A., Dunekack, A., Lamb, R.L., Vallett, D.B.: How stem game design participants discuss their project goals and their success differently. In: Wasson, B., Zorgo, S. (eds.) Advances in Quantitative Ethnography, pp. 176–190. Springer International Publishing, Cham (2022). https://doi.org/10.1007/978-3-030-93859-8_12
5. Cai, Z., Eagan, B.C.M., Shaffer, D.: Lstm neural network assisted regex development for qualitative coding. In: Advances in Quantitative Ethnography: Fourth International Conference, International Conference on Quantitative Ethnography (2022). https://doi.org/10.1007/978-3-031-31726-2_2. https://par.nsf.gov/biblio/10354430
6. Cai, Z., Siebert-Evenstone, A., Eagan, B., Shaffer, D.W.: Using topic modeling for code discovery in large scale text data. In: Ruis, A.R., Lee, S.B. (eds.) Advances in Quantitative Ethnography: Second International Conference, ICQE 2020, Malibu, CA, USA, February 1-3, 2021, Proceedings, pp. 18–31. Springer International Publishing, Cham (2021). https://doi.org/10.1007/978-3-030-67788-6_2
7. Cai, Z., Siebert-Evenstone, Amanda, Eagan, Brendan, Shaffer, David Williamson, Xiangen, Hu., Graesser, Arthur C.: Ncoder+: a semantic tool for improving recall of ncoder coding. In: Eagan, Brendan, Misfeldt, Morten, Siebert-Evenstone, Amanda (eds.) ICQE 2019. CCIS, vol. 1112, pp. 41–54. Springer, Cham (2019). https://doi.org/10.1007/978-3-030-33232-7_4
8. Choi, J., Ruis, A.R., Cai, Z., Eagan, B.R., Shaffer, D.W.: Does active learning reduce human coding?: A systematic comparison of a neural network with ncoder. In: Advances in Quantitative Ethnography: Fourth International Conference, International Conference on Quantitative Ethnography (2022). https://doi.org/10.1007/978-3-031-31726-2_3 https://par.nsf.gov/biblio/10354410
9. Fernandez-Nieto, G.M., Martinez-Maldonado, R., Kitto, K., Bucking- ham Shum, S.: Modelling spatial behaviours in clinical team simulations using epistemic network analysis: Methodology and teacher evaluation. In: LAK21: 11th International Learning Analytics and Knowledge Conference, pp. 386–396. LAK21, Association for Computing Machinery, New York, NY, USA (2021). https://doi.org/10.1145/3448139.3448176

10. Garrison, D.R., Anderson, T., Archer, W.: Critical thinking, cognitive presence, and computer conferencing in distance education. Am. J. Distance Educ. **15**(1), 7–23 (2001)
11. Ghaffari, S., Krishnaswamy, N.: Grounding and distinguishing conceptual vocabulary through similarity learning in embodied simulations (2023). arXiv preprint arXiv:2305.13668
12. Herder, T., et al.: Supporting teachers' intervention in students' virtual collaboration using a network based model. In: Proceedings of the 8th International Conference on Learning Analytics and Knowledge, pp. 21–25. LAK '18, Association for Computing Machinery, New York, NY, USA (2018). https://doi.org/10.1145/3170358.3170394
13. Koh, J.H.L., Herring, S.C., Hew, K.F.: Project-based learning and student knowledge construction during asynchronous online discussion. Internet Higher Educ. **13**(4), 284–291 (2010)
14. de Lima, D.P., Gerosa, M.A., Conte, T.U., de, M., Netto, J.F.: What to expect, and how to improve online discussion forums: the instructors' perspective. J. Internet Serv. Appl. **10**, 1–15 (2019). https://doi.org/10.1186/s13174-019-0120-0
15. Marquart, C.L., Swiecki, Z., Eagan, B., Shaffer, D.W.: Package 'ncodeR' (2019). https://cran.r-project.org/web/packages/ncodeR/ncodeR.pdf, Accessed 18 May 2022
16. Moraes, M., Folkestad, J., McKenna, K.: Using epistemic network analysis to help instructors evaluate asynchronous online discussions. In: Second International Conference on Quantitative Ethnography: Conference Proceedings Supplement, pp. 19–22 (2021)
17. Newman, D., Lau, J.H., Grieser, K., Baldwin, T.: Automatic evaluation of topic coherence. In: Human Language Technologies: The 2010 Annual Conference of the North American Chapter of the Association for Computational Linguistics, pp. 100– 108 (2010)
18. Nguyen, H.: Exploring group discussion with conversational agents using epistemic network analysis. In: Wasson, B., Zörg˝o, S. (eds.) Advances in Quantitative Ethnography, pp. 378–394. Springer International Publishing, Cham (2022). https://doi.org/10.1007/978-3-030-93859-8_25
19. Saravani, S.M., Ghaffari, S., Luther, Y., Folkestad, J., Moraes, M.: Automated code extraction from discussion board text dataset. In: Advances in Quantitative Ethnography: 4th International Conference, ICQE 2022, Copenhagen, Denmark, 15–19 October 2022, Proceedings, pp. 227–238. Springer (2023). https://doi.org/10.1007/978-3-031-31726-2_16
20. Shaffer, D.W., Collier, W., Ruis, A.R.: A tutorial on epistemic network analysis: Analyzing the structure of connections in cognitive, social, and interaction data. J. Learn. Analytics **3**(3), 9–45 (2016)
21. Shah, M., Siebert-Evenstone, A., Moots, H., Eagan, B.: Quality and safety education for nursing (qsen) in virtual reality simulations: A quantitative ethnographic examination. In: Wasson, B., Zörgő, S. (eds.) Advances in Quantitative Ethnography, pp. 237–252. Springer International Publishing, Cham (2022). https://doi.org/10.1007/978-3-030-93859-8_16
22. Shum, S.B.: Qe visualizations as tools for thinking [powerpoint slides]. In: International Conference On Quantitative Ethnography 2021 Keynote Speaker (2021). https://simon.buckinghamshum.net/wp-content/uploads/2021/02/SBS_ICQE2020_Keynote.pdf
23. Swiecki, Z., Ruis, A., Shaffer, D.W.: Modeling and visualizing team performance using epistemic net-work analysis. In: Proceedings of the 7th Annual GIFT Users Symposium, pp. 148–156 (2019)
24. Thomas, M.J.: Learning within incoherent structures: The space of online discussion forums. J. Comput. Assist. Learn. **18**(3), 351–366 (2002)
25. Vega, H., Irgens, G.A.: Constructing interpretations with participants through epistemic network analysis: Towards participatory approaches in quantitative ethnography. In: Wasson, B., Zörgő, S. (eds.) Advances in Quantitative Ethnography, pp. 3–16. Springer International Publishing, Cham (2022)

A Case for (Inter)Action: The Role of Log Data in QE

Jennifer Scianna[1]([⊠]) [iD], Xiner Liu[2] [iD], Stefan Slater[2] [iD], and Ryan S. Baker[2] [iD]

[1] University of Wisconsin, Madison, WI 53711, USA
jscianna@wisc.edu
[2] University of Pennsylvania, Philadelphia, PA 19102, USA

Abstract. Digital tools have the ability to log the fine-grained details of user experiences within and across the system. These digital experiences can lend valuable contextualization to other ethnographic insights. In this paper, we discuss the potential for using interaction logs as a data source and the pipeline considerations that can facilitate and enhance quantitative ethnographic research using this type of data. We draw on previous QE work and examples from QE adjacent fields such as educational data mining, learning analytics, and human-computer interaction to provide evidence for this approach.

Keywords: Interaction Data · Ethno-Mining · Automated Codes

1 Introduction

Personal and handheld computing has increased the ubiquity of technology as an element in many daily interactions. It is not uncommon to see people engaging in person while simultaneously also sharing media through their devices. This new level of engagement indicates that there may be social elements unaccounted for when conducting ethnographic work that does not include the technical elements of the sociotechnical system. In addition, an increasing amount of deep interaction occurs between humans and computers, particularly as people interact in new – increasingly social and relational – fashions with technologies [1].

Quantitative ethnography (QE) research has engaged fields where these forms of interaction are commonplace. Medical simulations [2], educational platforms [3–5], entertainment games [6], and social media [7, 8] have all been utilized as both site and object for QE studies. As researchers have moved into these more technology-mediated domains, there has been a call for techniques that can better incorporate the accompanying data streams that are available.

Interaction logs have been used to a greater degree in QE-adjacent communities, such as educational data mining (EDM), learning analytic (LA), and human-computer interaction, for many years. These areas draw from the rich, facilitated user interactions with both the system and other users, to explore the emergence of a highly contextualized digital world that operates in parallel to the "real" embodied and internal worlds of participant and researcher [9]. Fortunately, log files generated from these interactions

© The Author(s), under exclusive license to Springer Nature Switzerland AG 2023
G. Arastoopour Irgens and S. Knight (Eds.): ICQE 2023, CCIS 1895, pp. 395–408, 2023.
https://doi.org/10.1007/978-3-031-47014-1_27

provide valuable insights into the nature of this world and how users navigate it. Take for example previous QE work exploring user identity development as discussed through discussion forums. This work made inference solely from players' posts about their gameplay, work that could have been augmented by an analysis of the gameplay between posts [6]. Connections to in-game experiences might enhance the analysis by allowing for more grounded exploration of player behavior alongside their meta-reflections. This type of grounded exploration of player behavior in the context of their interaction with a game is seen in [4], which relates player strategies, identified through qualitative coding, to the implicit feedback the game provided.

Beyond the QE community (and prior to its advent among scholars now active in QE), interaction logs have been shown to provide valuable insights into the situational context that impacts user behavior [10], enabling the identification of patterns and anomalies in decision-making processes [11], and offering a window into the user's affective states and reactions to the system or environment [12, 13]. In these projects, the work of interpreting interaction logs can be seen as ethnographic in that it involves analyzing data to uncover insights about how individuals interact within cultures using digital tools. Thus, a thorough examination of interaction log data in relevant contexts may provide more insights for QE research.

The considerable uptake of interaction logs within QE-adjacent communities provides an additional opportunity for interaction log data – the possibility of extending on what can easily be accomplished through human coding, to scale across much larger corpuses of data. Like the work on extending human coding of text through tools like nCoder [14], automated detectors of user interaction developed through machine learning can enable the analysis of patterns of interest across contexts, using tools like epistemic network analysis [e.g. 3, 4].

In this paper, we first situate our work in relation to other thinking on digital data and ethnography. We then follow with a discussion of the ways in which interaction data has been utilized in QE and how expanded inclusion of this data may further augment prior QE research. We discuss two ways to develop qualitative codes on interaction data: through evidence-centered approaches and extending upon them using machine learning. Ultimately, through comparing each of these approaches to more established paradigms for QE, we discuss why machine learning codes are particularly useful for understanding interaction, and we conclude with a discussion of the compromises inherent to the use of this practice in QE.

2   Digital Data and Ethnography

Shaffer & Hod [15] reiterated the importance of ethnography as the focal point of QE research during the 2022 conference in Copenhagen, stating that the tools and methods being used were directly a response to the need for ethnographers to be able to capture the interactions of culture. As part of exploring the many ways interaction logs may be utilized for QE research, it may be valuable to first step back and consider the role that digital data has had in ethnography itself.

Haines [9] identifies a trajectory of ethnographic work that begins with research that considers digital as the subject of inquiry, which involves studying how digital technologies shape people's behaviors and experiences, such as through netnography (online ethnography of digital communities) [16] and analyzing social media platforms like Twitter [8]. From there, Haines suggests that the next iteration for digital ethnographic work is the move to considering digital spaces as a site [9]. QE researchers have historically engaged in this way, using Twitter as a "place" to explore Covid discussions [8] and discussion forums as a site for game communities that support user identity change relevant to the gaming participatory culture [6].

The next step for digital ethnographic work as advocated by Haines is to move beyond the digital as the sole object of study and to consider it as a dimension of social life, embedded within the broader context of social and cultural practices. Viewing digital as a dimension surfaces new possibilities for understanding the interplay between online and offline worlds and is supported by the inclusion of interaction data. If the research around Twitter had included interaction logs, greater insight into the role of social media for isolated people may have been evident alongside the conversation content. Gameplay data may have allowed researchers to connect game-based achievements and events to the trajectory of community member identities. These added dimensions can support QE research by supporting interpretation of the phenomena at hand, and that interpretation begins with coding.

2.1 Relationship of Data to Codes

Data itself can be thought of as the recording of some observation. With digital data, the recording is the manifestation of an implicit conversation between the humans -- the designer and the user -- and the computer messenger. In order for these observations to be developed into a more comprehensive understanding of user activity, a stage of description must take place that allows for interpretation of the many events present within the logs. That a sensor tripped or a button clicked can only tell exactly *what* has happened [17]; codes encapsulate the meaning of a series of logged interaction events within the physical and digital context of the users.

The difficulty in digital data coding is that there is relatively little support to move beyond the *what*. In discourse coding, language plays a role in enabling interpretation by those who were outside of the initial conversation. While coding discourse transcripts gives primacy to certain elements (the literal words) over others (such as body language), language itself can generally be understood by the researchers as it was by the participants. This may not be the case when researchers seek to interpret raw logged events. Instead, there may be a process of transforming the data from the raw event logs, which are typically a form of shorthand developed by a programmer to represent user and system behavior, into something comprehensible by humans. There are several approaches being used to make meaning of this data through coding including participant co-examination of visualizations [18], video replay [19], and text replays [20]. In each case, researchers make sense of the logged events in aggregate by narrativizing the actions as a larger unit. While being able to watch the series of actions or read through them like a story is useful in exploring the data, this only provides the first step towards coding the data. The next step is determining how to operationalize a system for coding (a step taken in each of these approaches). It is with this in mind that we consider the question: How should codes be operationalized for interaction log data from a quantitative ethnographic paradigm? To address this question, we examine the methods used by

QE adjacent communities to operationalize their descriptive codes on data, both through the liberal use of evidence-centered definitions and increasing use of machine learning after an initial human interpretation step. We provide examples of these processes before discussing implications for broadening the QE toolkit to include machine learning in this way.

3   Codes from Evidence

Digital systems which have been designed using evidence-centered design principles [21] support the interpretation of user interactions into meaning. In such systems, interactions are intentionally tied to constructs, so each task a user partakes in can be directly connected to the component behaviors as individual pieces of evidence for or against a larger construct. In this way, the design of the system begins with the codes as the behaviors that designers wish to see from their users.

In Physics Playground, Karumbaiah et al. [3] use codes that describe simple machines to translate user behaviors -- drawing lines with varying lengths, curves, slopes, and connections -- into evidence for whether a player understood the challenge of a given puzzle. Similarly, user relationships to aggregate features (e.g. relative time spent on a puzzle compared with other players) were used as codes in discussing fairness of Shadowspect, a spatial reasoning game-based assessment [22]. The aggregate features connected theoretical understandings of persistence to the behavior observed across players within the digital, game-based context, thus demonstrating interaction codes' fairness to theory.

However, this approach also raises questions around the need to be fair to data and community [23]. Evidence-centered codes may not be enough to fully capture the variety of behaviors present in a system which manifest in the interaction data. In Physics Playground, questions arose around why players were quitting certain levels. The system was not intentionally designed to evoke quitting behavior as a means of gathering evidence on student learning; rather, instances of quitting were identified and observed during the examination of interaction logs [3]. Connecting the emergent quitting behavior to behaviors that the game was intentionally designed to elicit allowed researchers to better understand when students had shortcomings in their understanding of the utility of certain simple machines. However, quitting is a fairly straightforward behavior to code for on the basis of one event in the interaction log – players left a level without completing it successfully. Other behaviors may not be as straightforward to interpret from the events themselves. Thus, additional techniques may be necessary to map the emergent behaviors backwards to the interaction events and data features which characterize them.

4   Developing Emergent Codes from Interaction

Qualitative codes of interaction data can be used in two ways: as objects of analysis in and of themselves, or as the basis (training set) for a machine learning approach, much as qualitative codes of text are used to train tools such as nCoder [14]. The first task in either of these research paradigms is the same: generating human-coded data labels. In this step, researchers code video and text replays of interaction data to generate labeled datasets which can be analyzed directly or used as training data for machine learning classification tasks [24]. Recent work has attempted to partially automate this step as well, using artificial intelligence to suggest coding categories or conduct mixed-initiative coding [25], but this work is outside the scope of this paper.

In order to apply machine learning after the human coding step, it is necessary to distill features of the data that can support computer detection of the differences between code examples and nonexamples. This process typically involves human design of the features which are aggregates of elements of the captured interactions [26]. It is an iterative process to determine which features will be most effective at describing the codes as developed by the researcher [27], a process similar to the iterative code development described by Shaffer and Ruiz [23]. In this section, we elaborate on the processes used to both interpret and label interaction data as well as means by which researchers identify features that can be used to automate coding.

4.1 Creating a Dataset of Qualitative Codes

The coding process within and beyond QE relies on being able to create descriptions that are meaningful and interpretable beyond one person familiar with the data. This is the role of agreement metrics like kappa and Shaffer's rho for the QE community [28]. Working towards agreement through triangulation between human coders and machines allows for a minimization of uncertainty for the reliability of a description of a phenomena [23]. The trouble with interaction logs is that each event can be likened to a word in a sentence. There is potential for meaningful codes when the words come together, but it can be challenging to find complex meaning in a single word. Thus, when researchers seek to identify labels for the phenomena in interaction logs, they often utilize alternative representations (e.g. text, video, or visualizations) to assist human interpretation of the logged events.

Take, for example, text replays, used in many papers within EDM [20]. Text replays turn the events registered by the computer system (such as clicks) into textual descriptions of the event that can be read narratively. The process of translation does not require additional interpretation by the researcher as the descriptions provided can be taken directly from the data schema of the system designers. Using this method, the "observations" being recorded take the perspective of the data logging designers who may give primacy to certain types of user events and computer feedback. The strength of text replay is that it transforms the event stream into a story which can be segmented into different sized utterances. For example, in order to identify whether students struggle on a given task, it may be necessary to see the task from beginning to end; however, to identify productive use of guide text, it may only be necessary to see the first few actions after a user receives help. Decisions about clip size, the EDM term for utterance, are therefore iteratively grounded in the behavior being identified and the data itself.

Video replays [19] are somewhat more removed from the interaction log itself, but they allow behavior to be situated within the context of the digital tool (as seen by the user). Video replays typically reconstruct logs into a movie rendition of the user interactions. Therefore, observation is less from the perspective of the designer and more from that of the user or traditional researcher lens. During coding, this allows the researcher to consider the state of the technical system, a particularly important element in games and other dynamic technologies, without the cognitive load of trying to track the state between system events because it is all viewable on the screen. Thus, coding can proceed more naturally with researchers considering the contextual game state as part of the determining factors for a given code.

Visualizations are one of the less transparent methods of coding interaction logs because there is less direct translation from the log itself to something observable by the researcher. Instead, actions are considered in aggregate as rates of change or quantified comparisons. For example, in their mapping of player activity in Plant Wars, researchers created metrics for the amount of fertilizer players were applying in game and plotted it based on the time the activity took place [29]. This mapping allowed them to easily answer questions around what and when behaviors were taking place, but it was harder to answer the question of why. Ultimately, a shift in when player activity was occurring encouraged researchers to dig deeper by interviewing players whose data was particularly representative of the anomaly of interest; these interviews elicited new-found understandings by identifying key context: some players were recent graduates whose sleep schedules had changed. Without the mappings to help surface questions, the researchers may never have been able to understand that element of gameplay behavior and misattributed the behavior to unrelated factors.

The ability to question the nature of the data beyond summary statistics is valuable because it allows research teams to ground the interpretation in cultural analysis, acknowledging the uniqueness of individual experience instead of normalizing assumptions about populations [18]. Visualizations can also be used to support participatory research which increases agency for participants in data collection and interpretation. Previously, QE researchers have utilized visualizations of a researcher-developed model to engage participants in participatory research [30], but participants may also be able to identify how trends connect with overarching codes from the initial stages of research as well. When HCI researchers were interested in understanding trends of device usage within the home, they used interaction logs alongside location data to help frame conversations with participants [17], an example of data-driven retrospective interviewing [31]. Engaging the participants in their own data allowed for the trends to be interrogated and framed by participants themselves (e.g. participants could define what family dinner looked like in their own data) [18].

Regardless of the method used to identify the codes and understand what is happening within the technical elements of the system, the plentiful nature of interaction logs necessitates automated coding if researchers desire to examine interactions beyond a few cases. Thus, we need a means for taking the insights and labels on our dataset and creating interpretable features that computers can utilize for automating the detection of the codes within the larger corpus of data.

4.2 Determining Relevant Features

In discourse-centered QE research, many researchers have chosen to use the tool nCoder to assist in the automation of codes [14]. The tool supports human coders in calculating agreement (in service of validating codes) with a computer based on textual features of each utterance. The human coders provide the desired features for the computer in the form of regular expressions. For example, if a researcher is trying to capture people talking about symptoms, they may choose to include regular expressions like "headach*" and "feel" to try and capture the discussion. These expression-based features must be developed in relation to the corpus as a whole to avoid unintentionally indicating positive cases to the computer. The more data the researcher sees, the more refined they can make their features.

Similar approaches are used by EDM/LA researchers when working with interaction logs (see discussion in [11, 13, 32]). Once the labels have been established for positive and negative cases, they can be used to inform the feature generation process. However, features of interaction logs are not as straightforward as identifying a word that occurs in a sentence. Instead, aggregate features are calculated at the level of clip size to provide characteristics of the utterance that are interpretable by the computer. These features can then be used in a variety of algorithms to attempt to delineate between examples and nonexamples of the behavior.

One method to determine which features are relevant is to consider the human perspective of expertise. For example, Paquette et al. [33] considered the ways that experts thought through whether students were gaming the system in an intelligent tutoring system (ITS). The experts noted the importance of pause length for identifying the behavior within the interaction logs. When students in the ITS rapidly submitted answers over and over with little pause, experts deduced that the students were not taking time to try alternative strategies and were thus, likely gaming. These features may not be enough to support computer interpretation on their own. For example, Paquette and colleagues noted that the usefulness of the pause-based features is amplified by considering the edit distance (a metric that shows how different two submissions are) of each subsequent submission by the student. Gaming behavior could include rapid, formulaic answers (e.g. increasing subsequent answers by 10), thus the two features together assist computers in identifying the behavior.

Similar tactics could be utilized for code labels that originate from video replay or data visualization. Analogous to the identification of keywords as regex features, researchers need to consider what is leading them to code a given case positively. There are also general guidelines regarding what kinds of features can provide enough information for description of system interaction behavior [34]. Baker & Owen [34] describe the importance of including user behavior, system feedback, and user progression when generating feature sets. In the Plant Wars example [29], researchers designed features about how much fertilizer was being used, whether the game system indicated needing fertilizer, and player progress metrics.

Concerns may arise in thinking about features as aggregates (i.e. time between actions, number of clicks, etc.) that seem far removed from the phenomena of interest (i.e. whether a user is scanning for information or persisting in gameplay). This is why it is important to consider how each feature is relevant to the phenomena being observed. Grounding both label and feature generation in theory (see examples in [10, 35]) can be beneficial to addressing questions of validity. Feature selection techniques such as correlation and checking for collinearity may also allow researchers to filter out less meaningful features. Striking a balance between useful features that correlate with the phenomena and features based on a more traditional view of construct validity may be helpful in increasing transparency of the resultant model for stakeholders while maintaining the ability to computationally differentiate examples and nonexamples. To once again draw a comparison to textual data, it may be useful to incorporate a keyword "black box" in automating a code for "trust" in the context of AI discussions, but the keyword on its own may oversimplify the discussion. QE relies on being able to point back at the evidence for why an utterance is coded in a particular way and contextualize that decision [23]. Therefore, understanding the relationship between feature selection and the phenomena of interest, while providing explanations for their relevance, is crucial for ensuring fairness and contextually-grounded decisions in QE research with interaction data.

4.3 Making Models

Explainability is equally as important in model selection to detect code presence as it is in feature generation. Some ML models are more explainable or transparent than others in the way they present results, although recent work has attempted to increase the explainability of more inscrutable algorithms such as neural networks [36, 37].

There are potential challenges for QE researchers in trying to utilize AI models, even the more interpretable or explainable ones. For example, the degree to which explanations are interpretable to someone who is not an ML expert varies considerably [37]. The potential to automate the coding of identified behaviors offers a strong incentive to explore machine learning models for QE, enabling deeper exploration of these behaviors in connection with other behaviors and participant groups.

5 Why ML Codes are Useful for Understanding Interaction

In this section, we provide examples of ML codes and their utility for QE research to understand interaction data. We draw connections between the details that QE allows researchers to "get right" and the ways that the ML model would support those goals.

5.1 Situatedness Matters

Interactions emerge from "conversation" between participants and the digital system [4]. These sociotechnical systems are complicated, and the interactions are nuanced in a way that a click may not be just a click -- it may communicate a great deal more. To understand the subtleties of interactions, researchers must be able to use their codes to "generalize within" the context to consistently describe interactions where the patterns of both user and computer system behavior remain consistent [38].

Take for example, the user behavior called Wheel-Spinning [39]. Students in digital learning environments may exhibit this behavior when they are stuck, thus continuing to try to solve a problem without making progress. Given just user actions, one may see a number of clicks and blank submissions, changes to strategy (such as asking the system for help), and even breaks between actions where users are considering new approaches. The system actions would likely be almost wholly consisting of negative feedback. Contextualizing the actions and negative feedback in light of a lack of forward progress allows for the existence of a Wheel-Spinning code, but so what?

QE and the focus on behaviors within context would allow exploration of this behavior within the classroom. Many educators would likely agree that wheel-spinning is an intervention-worthy behavior. Do the teachers successfully intervene? Do they even notice? Do other students notice? How does a student's Wheel-Spinning behavior manifest in discourse or collaboration? These are all questions that rely on a deeper understanding of the behavior in context. To answer these questions, we need to be able to connect the behaviors, not just clicks or feedback, that cross the digital boundaries to the situational context they exist within. It isn't just about being able to detect the behavior and tag it for interactions, but using QE, we may be able to uncover the nature of the system and its implications.

Furthermore, the use of detectors to code the interaction log may be a methodological necessity in this case. When participant behaviors cross over into digital spaces and spill into other physical spaces (either via transience in their own position or interaction with other participants who are not collocated), local observation by the ethnographer may not adequately capture the phenomena under observation [27]. In other words, if a researcher is watching a student in one classroom who is playing a collaborative game with students in another classroom, they may miss the potential downstream interactions happening with the other students as a result of the digital interactions because they are focused on the individual in front of them. The choices we make as researchers in what we choose to include and attend to as data impacts the way we return to the observations for analysis [40]. In an effort to not lose the metaphorical forest for the trees, tools (like SPACLE [41]) have been developed to assist researchers in extending their observations to position individual interaction logs alongside whole class data and observations in a replay system. By employing the use of logged interactions, we can consider a perspective that incorporates more elements of the sociotechnical system in situ.

5.2 Perspectives Matter

We must also consider whether the codes themselves consider the user in order to achieve the QE principle of fairness to the community [23]. Development of emic codes (those which are community generated) may come directly from the user during open-ended experience sampling [42], for instance. Users may participate in surveys where questions attempt to uncover latent constructs such as affective states; however, these self-report measures can be unreliable when moving to interpersonal ratings and are weakly correlated to external behavioral measures [43]. Furthermore, self-report may be distorted by the user's ability to accurately describe their state, a potential problem for children, and in cases where the affect/behavior is not socially acceptable. An alternate approach, in-the-moment interviews driven by detectors, creates some potential to probe deeper than a survey can [44]. For example, being able to detect frustration or other negative affect through interaction logs can provide a way to ground conversations around how design choices impact user experience [44]. Similar to visualization exploration, interviews where users revisit their experience with the technical system allow for redefinition of codes. For instance, as users discuss their experience in interviews, their responses may lead the researcher to uncover nuances between feelings of frustration and challenge, prompting a need to revise the code model for a more accurate representation.

Why rely on ML models to begin these conversations? Tacit knowledge is often left out of conversations and interviews with participants; researchers don't know to ask the questions, and the actions are so intuitive to users that they may not be readily articulated to an observer [27]. Assigning labels to moments of interest from the perspective of the researcher allows for more in-depth questioning about the perspective of the participant.

6   Unknown Compromises in Using Machine Learning

Although there are several potential benefits to the use of machine learning coding of interaction data, there are several compromises that are inherent in incorporating this practice into the QE workflow. Principally, there is a need for discussions centered on the ideas of triangulation and transparency. We begin the discussion here, raising questions and providing guidance for QE researchers looking to join this trajectory.

6.1   Triangulation

Interaction logs are not the only form of "big data," and automated coding outside of detectors has been heavily leveraged by the QE community through tools like nCoder [14]. These tools require not only agreement between the human coders on training data, but also agreement between the automated classifier and both human coders in order to minimize uncertainty [23]. This is also a standard practice when developing detectors in digital environments. In almost all cases, a machine-learned model's performance is evaluated on whether its inferences agree with human coders for data not used to develop the models. In exemplary cases, when generalizability beyond the initial data and context is imperative, after a machine-learned model has been fully completed, entirely new data is obtained, coded by humans, and tested for agreement.

When models underperform, researchers often return to the data in attempts to improve them by both inspecting areas where models mislabeled the data and creating new features to help capture previously missing elements [45]. Each subsequent return to the data allows researchers to refine their understanding of the relationship between features of the data and the code. The developers of Aeonium, an ML tool that supports qualitative coding, recommend embracing this practice and especially the ambiguity that arises from disagreement as a part of the process, bringing forth subjectivity and data inconsistencies for interrogation leading to better codes [46].

Additionally, discussions for acceptable kappa thresholds will be required within the QE community. Traditionally, kappa values above .61 have been seen as acceptable in other communities [47]. In QE community tools, kappa levels of .9 are the expectation [14]. In EDM and LA, much lower levels of kappa -- as low as .2 -- are sometimes seen as acceptable, depending on the way a model will be used. For example, even slightly better than chance performance may be valuable if the potential benefit of an intervention is high and the cost of an incorrectly-delivered intervention is low. These differences require that researchers are explicit about the strengths and weaknesses of their ML code models and the models that the codes are introduced into, such as network analyses. For machine-learned models, whether developed using nCoder or on interaction data, careful consideration is needed of whether the model's accuracy is sufficient for its intended use, and what the risks to interpretation and fairness are of using an imperfect model.

6.2 Transparency

A component of the detailed explanation expected of QE researchers is the transparency with which they can tell the story of their data. Transparent models are essential for closing the interpretive loop [28] by connecting the final model to the codes and back to the data features that labeled the interaction with that code. Different ML models have different levels of explicability and transparency. Recent work has attempted to increase the explainability of even inscrutable models such as neural networks [37], but these attempts remain imperfect, and explainability methods often disagree with each other [48]. This reifies the trade-off within machine learning between accuracy and explainability -- more accurate models are often harder to understand than simpler, less accurate models. This challenge is not unique to interaction data; contemporary NLP approaches involving large language models can often produce much better performance (particularly for unseen data) but are much harder to explain or interpret. Algorithm selection may come down to weighing the cost of poorer accuracy against the cost of less transparency and interpretability.

7 Conclusions

Qualitative interpretations of a phenomena are deeply personal to the position of the researcher, the participants, and the context within which the observations take place [49]. Digital tools are now pervasive in the spaces we work in, and many phenomena of interest to QE researchers also involve digital data. These tools offer potential insights that may help to reframe participant actions and behaviors that cannot be fully understood from place-based observation or even participant interviews. Leveraging data as a talking point with participants may allow researchers to identify novel behaviors and better understand how those behaviors are situated within the context of study (e.g. life changes for young gamers [29]). Machine-learned models developed using interaction data may provide insights into fine-grained aspects of user activity that are emergent and hard to otherwise study. Interaction logs provide valuable information to the QE researcher; the challenge for the community will be to continue finding and refining methods that allow for transparent description of this data and to continue pursuing development and alignment of QE paradigms for research involving this data, while maintaining the principles and research values of the QE community more broadly.

References

1. Pentina, I., Hancock, T., Xie, T.: Exploring relationship development with social chatbots: a mixed-method study of replika. Comput. Hum. Behav. **140**, 107600 (2023). https://doi.org/10.1016/j.chb.2022.107600
2. Shah, M., Siebert-Evenstone, A., Moots, H., Eagan, B.: Quality and safety education for nursing (QSEN) in virtual reality simulations: a quantitative ethnographic examination. In: Wasson, B., Zörgő, S. (eds.) Advances in Quantitative Ethnography. ICQE 2021. CCIS, vol. 1522, pp. 237–252. Springer, Cham (2022). https://doi.org/10.1007/978-3-030-93859-8_16

3. Karumbaiah, S., Baker, R.S., Barany, A., Shute, V.: Using epistemic networks with automated codes to understand why players quit levels in a learning game. In: Eagan, B., Misfeldt, M., Siebert-Evenstone, A. (eds.) Advances in Quantitative Ethnography. ICQE 2019. CCIS, vol. 1112, pp. 106–116. Springer, Cham (2019). https://doi.org/10.1007/978-3-030-33232-7_9

4. Scianna, J., Gagnon, D., Knowles, B.: Counting the game: visualizing changes in play by incorporating game events. In: Ruis, A.R., Lee, S.B. (eds.) Advances in Quantitative Ethnography. ICQE 2021. CCIS, vol. 1312, pp. 218–231. Springer, Cham (2021). https://doi.org/10.1007/978-3-030-67788-6_15

5. Scianna, J., Kaliisa, R., Boisvenue, J.J., Zörgő, S.: Approaching structured debate with quantitative ethnography in mind. In: Wasson, B., Zörgő, S. (eds.) Advances in Quantitative Ethnography. ICQE 2021. CCIS, vol. 1522, pp. 33–58. Springer, Cham (2022). https://doi.org/10.1007/978-3-030-93859-8_3

6. Barany, A., Foster, A.: Examining identity exploration in a video game participatory culture. In: Eagan, B., Misfeldt, M., Siebert-Evenstone, A. (eds.) Advances in Quantitative Ethnography. ICQE 2019. CCIS, vol. 1112, pp. 3–13. Springer, Cham (2019). https://doi.org/10.1007/978-3-030-33232-7_1

7. Arastoopour Irgens, G.: Using knowledgeable agents of the digital and data feminism to uncover social identities in the #blackgirlmagic twitter community. Learn. Media Technol. **47**, 79–94 (2022)

8. Hobbs, W., et al.: Challenges and solutions to examining twitter data: reflections from QE-COVID19 data challenge. In: Second International Conference on Quantitative Ethnography: Conference Proceedings Supplement, p. 84. Online (2021)

9. Haines, J.K.: Towards multi-dimensional ethnography. In: Ethnographic Praxis in Industry Conference Proceedings. 2017, pp. 127–141 (2017). https://doi.org/10.1111/1559-8918.2017.01143

10. Gašević, D., Dawson, S., Siemens, G.: Let's not forget: learning analytics are about learning. TechTrends **59**, 64–71 (2015)

11. Reimann, P., Frerejean, J., Thompson, K.: Using process mining to identify models of group decision making in chat data. In: O'Malley, C., Suthers, D., Reimann, P., Dimitracopoulou, A. (eds.) Computer Supported Collaborative Learning Practices: CSCL2009 Conference Proceedings, pp. 98–107. International Society of the Learning Sciences, Rhodes, Greece (2009). https://doi.org/10.22318/cscl2009.1.98

12. Baker, R.S.J., Ocumpaugh, J.: 16 Interaction-Based Affect Detection in Educational Software. The Oxford Handbook of Affective Computing, p. 233 (2014)

13. Bruckman, A.: Analysis of log file data to understand behavior and learning in an online community. In: Weiss, J., Nolan, J., Hunsinger, J., Trifonas, P. (eds.) The International Handbook of Virtual Learning Environments, pp. 1449–1465. Springer, Dordrecht (2006). https://doi.org/10.1007/978-1-4020-3803-7_58

14. Marquart, C., Swiecki, Z., Eagan, B., Shaffer, D.W.: ncodeR: techniques for automated classifiers [R package] (2019). https://cran.r-project.org/web/packages/ncodeR/index.html

15. Shaffer, D.W., Hod, Y.: The role of ethnography in quantitative ethnography. In: Fourth International Conference on Quantitative Ethnography: Conference Proceedings Supplement (2022)

16. Kozinets, R.V., Gretzel, U.: Netnography. In: Encyclopedia of Tourism Management and Marketing, pp. 316–319. Edward Elgar Publishing (2022)

17. Aipperspach, R., Rattenbury, T., Woodruff, A., Anderson, K., Canny, J., Aoki, P.: Ethno-Mining: Integrating Numbers and Words from the Ground Up, p. 13 (2006)

18. Anderson, K., Nafus, D., Rattenbury, T., Aipperspach, R.: Numbers have qualities too: experiences with ethno-mining. In: Ethnographic Praxis in Industry Conference Proceedings 2009, pp. 123–140 (2009). https://doi.org/10.1111/j.1559-8918.2009.tb00133.x

19. Harpstead, E., MacLellan, C.J., Aleven, V., Myers, B.A.: Replay analysis in open-ended educational games. Serious games analytics: Methodologies for performance measurement, assessment, and improvement, pp. 381–399 (2015)
20. Baker, R., de Carvalho, A.: Labeling student behavior faster and more precisely with text replays. In: Educational Data Mining 2008 (2008)
21. Mislevy, R.J., Almond, R.G., Lukas, J.F.: A brief introduction to evidence-centered design. ETS Res. Rep. Ser. **2003**, i–29 (2003). https://doi.org/10.1002/j.2333-8504.2003.tb01908.x
22. Kim, Y., Choi, J.: Expanding fairness in game-based assessment with quantitative ethnography. Presented at the International Conference on Quantitative Ethnography 2022, Copenhagen, Denmark (2022)
23. Shaffer, D.W., Ruis, A.R.: How we code. In: Ruis, A.R., Lee, S.B. (eds.) Advances in Quantitative Ethnography. ICQE 2021. CCIS, vol. 1312, pp. 62–77. Springer, Cham (2021). https://doi.org/10.1007/978-3-030-67788-6_5
24. Zhang, J., et al.: Detecting SMART model cognitive operations in mathematical problem-solving process. International Educational Data Mining Society. (2022)
25. Choi, J., Ruis, A.R., Cai, Z., Eagan, B., Shaffer, D.W.: Does active learning reduce human coding?: A systematic comparison of neural network with nCoder. In: Damşa, C., Barany, A. (eds.) Advances in Quantitative Ethnography. ICQE 2022. CCIS, vol. 1785, pp. 30–42. Springer, Cham (2023). https://doi.org/10.1007/978-3-031-31726-2_3
26. Jiang, Y., et al.: Expert feature-engineering vs. deep neural networks: which is better for sensor-free affect detection? In: Penstein Rosé, C., et al. (eds.) Artificial Intelligence in Education. AIED 2018. LNCS, vol. 10947, pp. 198–211. Springer, Cham (2018). https://doi.org/10.1007/978-3-319-93843-1_15
27. Hsu, W.F.: Digital ethnography toward augmented empiricism: a new methodological framework. J. Digit. Humanit. **3**, 3–1 (2014)
28. Shaffer, D.W.: Quantitative Ethnography. Cathcart Press (2017)
29. Shadoan, R., Dudek, A.: Plant Wars Player Patterns: Visualization as Scaffolding for Ethnographic Insight. http://ethnographymatters.net/blog/2013/04/11/visualizing-plant-wars-player-patterns-to-aid-ethnography/. Accessed 23 Apr 2023
30. Vega, H., Irgens, G.A.: Constructing interpretations with participants through epistemic network analysis: towards participatory approaches in quantitative ethnography. In: Wasson, B., Zörgő, S. (eds.) Advances in Quantitative Ethnography. ICQE 2021. CCIS, vol. 1522, pp. 3–16. Springer, Cham (2022). https://doi.org/10.1007/978-3-030-93859-8_1
31. El-Nasr, M.S., Durga, S., Shiyko, M., Sceppa, C.: Data-driven retrospective interviewing (DDRI): a proposed methodology for formative evaluation of pervasive games. Entertain. Comput. **11**, 1–19 (2015)
32. Baker, R.S.J., Corbett, A.T., Wagner, A.Z.: Human classification of low-fidelity replays of student actions. In: Proceedings of the Educational Data Mining Workshop at the 8th International Conference on Intelligent Tutoring Systems, pp. 29–36 (2006)
33. Paquette, L., de Carvalho, A.M., Baker, R.S.: Towards understanding expert coding of student disengagement in online learning. In: CogSci (2014)
34. Owen, V.E., Baker, R.S.: Fueling prediction of player decisions: foundations of feature engineering for optimized behavior modeling in serious games. Technol. Knowl. Learn. **25**, 225–250 (2020). https://doi.org/10.1007/s10758-018-9393-9
35. Beigi, G., Tang, J., Liu, H.: Social science guided feature engineering: a novel approach to signed link analysis. ACM Trans. Intell. Syst. Technol. **11**, 1–27 (2020). https://doi.org/10.1145/3364222
36. Xu, F., Uszkoreit, H., Du, Y., Fan, W., Zhao, D., Zhu, J.: Explainable AI: a brief survey on history, research areas, approaches and challenges. In: Tang, J., Kan, M.Y., Zhao, D., Li, S., Zan, H. (eds.) Natural Language Processing and Chinese Computing. NLPCC 2019. LNCS,

vol. 11839, pp. 563–574. Springer, Cham (2019). https://doi.org/10.1007/978-3-030-32236-6_51

37. Angelov, P., Soares, E.: Towards explainable deep neural networks (xDNN). Neural Netw. **130**, 185–194 (2020)

38. Munk, A.K., Olesen, A.G., Jacomy, M.: The thick machine: anthropological AI between explanation and explication. Big Data Soc. **9**, 1–14 (2022). https://doi.org/10.1177/205395 17211069891

39. Beck, J.E., Gong, Y.: Wheel-spinning: students who fail to master a skill. In: Lane, H.C., Yacef, K., Mostow, J., Pavlik, P. (eds.) Artificial Intelligence in Education. AIED 2013. LNCS, vol. 7926, pp. 431–440. Springer, Berlin, Heidelberg (2013). https://doi.org/10.1007/978-3-642-39112-5_44

40. Hall, R.: Videorecording as theory. In: Handbook of Research Design in Mathematics and Science Education, pp. 647–64. Lawrence Erlbaum, Mahwah, NJ (2000)

41. Holstein, K., McLaren, B.M., Aleven, V.: SPACLE: investigating learning across virtual and physical spaces using spatial replays. In: Proceedings of the Seventh International Learning Analytics & Knowledge Conference, pp. 358–367 (2017)

42. Zirkel, S., Garcia, J.A., Murphy, M.C.: Experience-sampling research methods and their potential for education research. Educ. Res. **44**, 7–16 (2015). https://doi.org/10.3102/001318 9X14566879

43. Dang, J., King, K.M., Inzlicht, M.: Why are self-report and behavioral measures weakly correlated? Trends Cogn. Sci. **24**, 267–269 (2020). https://doi.org/10.1016/j.tics.2020.01.007

44. Baker, R.S., et al.: Affect-targeted interviews for understanding student frustration. In: Roll, I., McNamara, D., Sosnovsky, S., Luckin, R., Dimitrova, V. (eds.) Artificial Intelligence in Education. AIED 2021. LNCS, vol. 12748, pp. 52–63. Springer, Cham (2021). https://doi.org/10.1007/978-3-030-78292-4_5

45. Slater, S., Baker, R.S., Wang, Y.: Iterative feature engineering through text replays of model errors. International Educational Data Mining Society (2020)

46. Chen, N.-C., Drouhard, M., Kocielnik, R., Suh, J., Aragon, C.R.: Using machine learning to support qualitative coding in social science: shifting the focus to ambiguity. ACM Trans. Interact. Intell. Syst. **8**, 1–20 (2018). https://doi.org/10.1145/3185515

47. McHugh, M.L.: Interrater reliability: the kappa statistic. Biochem. Med. **22**, 276–282 (2012)

48. Swamy, V., Radmehr, B., Krco, N., Marras, M., Käser, T.: Evaluating the explainers: black-box explainable machine learning for student success prediction in MOOCs. arXiv preprint arXiv:2207.00551. (2022)

49. O'Connor, C., Joffe, H.: Intercoder reliability in qualitative research: debates and practical guidelines. Int J Qual Methods **19**, 1609406919899220 (2020). https://doi.org/10.1177/160 9406919899220

Approaches to Code Selection for Epistemic Networks

Dorottya Árva[1]([✉]) [iD], Anna Jeney[2] [iD], Diána Dunai[3] [iD], David Major[1] [iD], Annamária Cseh[1] [iD], and Szilvia Zörgő[4] [iD]

[1] Semmelweis University, Budapest 1089, Hungary
arva.dorottya@med.semmelweis-univ.hu
[2] The Academy of Korean Studies, Seongnam 13455, Republic of Korea
[3] Eötvös Loránd University, Budapest 1117, Hungary
[4] Maastricht University, 6200 MD Maastricht, The Netherlands

Abstract. When employing unified, quantitative-qualitative methods such as Epistemic Network Analysis (ENA), the relative frequency of codes and their co-occurrence is of interest. However, in projects utilizing a large number of codes, if all codes are included, the interpretation of these models becomes challenging. In this paper, we provide three potential approaches to code selection. In the theory-based approach, code clustering and selection was founded on relevant literature or theory. In the insight-based approach, clusters of codes were defined by the grounded observations of researchers. Lastly, in the model-based approach, fully inclusive ENA models were generated to select codes for future models. We illustrated these approaches using data from our ongoing project that aims to measure the effects of a health education intervention on near-peer educators' understanding regarding the biopsychosocial model of health. All three approaches may be useful in guiding code selection for final ENA models or in providing a baseline for further refinement of model parameters. By outlining these approaches, this work contributes to discourse on making conscious and transparent decisions regarding ENA parameterization.

Keywords: Code Selection · Epistemic Network Analysis · Model Parameterization

1 Introduction

1.1 Background

If aligned with ontological and epistemological assumptions, as well as research objectives, researchers may decide to transcribe and code qualitative data to identify patterns therein. Codes represent sets of concepts, gestures, expressions that capture relevant aspects of data (as defined by the research questions) and help researchers systematically categorize phenomena in their data [1, 2]. Provided a dataset has been coded systematically, the frequency, position, and interaction of codes can be subjected to further scrutiny, and quantitative models of the coded data can be generated [3]. Quantitative models may inform qualitative insight and offer additional warrants to qualitative findings.

G. Arastoopour Irgens and S. Knight (Eds.): ICQE 2023, CCIS 1895, pp. 409–425, 2023.
https://doi.org/10.1007/978-3-031-47014-1_28

Models of quantified qualitative data can, for example, display the strength of association between codes, generally operationalized as co-occurrence frequencies. One way to model code co-occurrences is via Epistemic Network Analysis (ENA), which depicts the relative co-occurrence frequency of unique pairs of codes in designated segments of qualitative data [4, 5]. ENA models display two coordinated representations of the data in a two-dimensional space: (1) network graphs, where the nodes in the model correspond to the codes, and the edges represent the strength of association between codes, and (2) ENA scores, showing the relative position of each network as points. The position of nodes and the location of ENA scores in the constructed space are not arbitrary; network graphs can be used to interpret the meaning of ENA scores in terms of the network structures they represent [6]. For this reason, if a model parameter is altered, for example, by adding or removing a code, one alters the ENA model as well, which may have marked effects on its interpretation [7, 8].

ENA was originally designed to model a small set of codes [9] developed under the aegis of epistemic frames theory [10], but as it became applied to other theories in various fields, the scope and number of potential codes began to vary. Lefstein emphasizes the importance of "contextualization, performativity, co-construction, multi-modality and ideology in how we mean" and that these meaning-making processes constitute the foundation of hermeneutics [11]. He suggests these be most actively involved in the "precoding" or code development stage, but also subsequent to final coding, as the micro-analytic investigation of "select events" can not only validate our quantitative models, but also help discover novel topics and ideas that require further investigation [11]. Such iterative coding processes may generate a large number of codes, which, when placed into a single model, can present an overwhelming complexity.

The question of code selection has been addressed by Wang et al. as "parsimony": including the fewest number of codes that sufficiently explains the phenomenon of interest and retains interpretive alignment between the qualitative interpretation and the quantitative model [6]. The authors developed Parsimonious Removal with Interpretive Alignment (PRIA) to answer this challenge [6]. Yet, this technique entails having a 'gold standard model' to which more parsimonious (deflated) models are compared using statistical significance, goodness of fit, and interpretive alignment [6].

Especially if codes are developed inductively (grounded in or emerging from the data, as opposed to codes adopted from theory or a previous coding scheme), researchers may not have a clear 'gold standard model' prior to parameterization and analysis. Even with well-formulated research questions and goals, initial ENA models may serve solely exploratory purposes to identify salient themes and patterns within the data, which are subsequently examined in more detail [11]. In the following we discuss: what are some possible approaches to selecting codes to include in ENA models?

1.2 Epistemic Networks

Describing in detail how networks are generated does not fall within the scope of this paper (cf.: [1, 3, 5, 12]). Succinctly, in the process of wrangling, qualitative data is segmented into lines (smallest meaningful pieces of data) and coded. Once in tabular form, ENA can process this coded data and produces a matrix with code co-occurrences, calculating the frequency of each unique pair of codes within given segments of data with a form of accumulation specified as a "stanza window". ENA aggregates the cumulative frequencies for each unit of analysis per "conversation" (a form of data segmentation); units are the totality of lines of data associated with a network within a model, and are usually defined as data providers or groups of data providers. The cumulative co-occurrence matrix for each unit is represented as a vector and forms an n-dimensional space. Vectors are normalized to account for varying amounts of data, which captures the relative frequency of code co-occurrences and also converts frequencies to fall between 0 and 1.

Subsequently, ENA applies a dimensional reduction procedure (singular value decomposition, SVD, or means rotation, MR) to reduce the n dimensions to just two. These two dimensions form the axes along which the unit vectors are then projected as points (ENA scores) into the two-dimensional space. The coordination of network graphs and plotted points means that the positions of the nodes can be used to interpret the dimensions forming the space and explain the positions of ENA scores. The x axis represents the dimension that explains the most variation in the co-occurrences, while the y axis represents the dimension that explains the most variance in the co-occurrences after the variance explained by the first dimension has been partialled out.

Thus, characteristics of the coded and segmented data, along with decisions in model parameterization, define epistemic networks and the space into which they are projected. Consequently, deciding on which codes to include in the model not only affects what relationships the networks display (i.e., which codes become nodes), but also determines the projection space and affects the interpretation of dimensions.

Precisely because ENA is sensitive to parameterization regarding codes, and because interpretive alignment with the qualitative data was paramount in its design as a visualization tool, we employ ENA to demonstrate approaches to selecting codes for co-occurrence frequency modeling and discuss potential implications for these choices.

1.3   Approaches to Selecting Codes

Theory-Based.   Some qualitative analytical frameworks that prescribe the researcher's stance to be as atheoretical as possible, such as Grounded Theory, where the aim of analysis is to generate a theory from the data [13]. Yet, most analytical procedures involve a dialectical relationship between theory and data, and advocate using theory to state preliminary assumptions and generate (sets of) codes. ENA can, in turn, be employed to explore assumptions about the relationships among codes [6]. Relevant literature and theory are most frequently employed at research design and code development, but can also scaffold methodological choices in modeling.

Insight-Based.   Once data has been collected (or even during data collection itself), researchers often engage with their data and gain qualitative insights. These observations (e.g., constructs of interest, perceived patterns, inconsistencies or atypical examples) may contribute to code development, especially if codes are created inductively. As researchers develop and test the applicability of their codes, they may formulate "favorite theories" about their data [11], a grounded understanding leading to preconceptions about critical relationships (or their absence) among certain codes [14]. A more mature set of observations (e.g., based on initial coding or hermeneutic analysis) may be referred to as a theme: a constellation of codes the researcher identifies as meaningful and significant [15]. Such grounded assumptions, "favorite theories", or themes may serve as the basis for selecting codes to include in an ENA model.

Model-Based. Provided the use of theory was not justified or possible, and qualitative engagement with the data was not warranted or did not yield any observations (or yielded too many), another, more quantitative approach to selecting codes may be appropriate. Since epistemic networks are projected into a meaningful space, the position of nodes can be employed to formulate assumptions about relationships among codes. All codes can be included in a single model to inspect this space, albeit this may create a highly dense network, and nodes may even eclipse each other. Yet, the clustering of certain codes, or code positions relative to the axes (dimensions) creating this space, may offer insight into how codes relate to each other within the entire dataset. These insights can then be mobilized to create subsets of codes and their respective models.

In the following, we use data from our ongoing project to elaborate examples for all three suggested approaches and to discuss their implications regarding model construction and interpretation. First, we introduce the context of our research, our goals, employed methods, and disclose our codes. Next, each example will reflect a viable means of selecting codes for model construction and a brief discussion of the generated results. Subsequently, we discuss the implications of these approaches.

2   Data in Use

2.1   Project Overview

Several models of health and illness share the understanding that health is determined by a number of factors and their interactions [16, 17]. Bircher [18] states that health emerges from interactions among individual, social, and environmental factors. A widely known model capturing the interplay of such factors is referred to as the *biopsychosocial model* of health [16]. Effective health promotion, prevention, and health care leverage this model, and congruently, so do successful health education programs.

The Balassagyarmat Health Education Program (BEP) was a school-based health education intervention, run between 2018–2021, aiming to improve the health behavior of high school students in Balassagyarmat, a city in a socioeconomically disadvantaged region in Hungary [19]. Interactive offline and online sessions were designed using gamification and peer education, a commonly employed method in school health education [20]. Students of medicine, as near-peer educators, taught high schoolers for a year. The program, developed by a multidisciplinary team at Semmelweis University, covered a wide range of health-related topics in nine modules: healthy nutrition and physical activity, smoking, alcohol, drugs, reproductive and mental health, infection control, and basic life support. Educators received 18 h of training each semester, which focused on the material they delivered to high school students and the biopsychosocial model of health.

Upon completion of the BEP intervention, we not only wanted to explore the effects it had on high school students as the primary target group, but also on the educators themselves. To achieve the latter, we are currently comparing the educators' understanding of the biopsychosocial model to those of medical students' who did not participate in the intervention. We assumed there is a correlation between exposure to the intervention and knowledge on the biopsychosocial model of health.

3 Methods

Both subsamples were recruited from Semmelweis University, Budapest, Hungary: 1) BEP educators (who learnt all modules and taught in-person; n = 9), 2) controls (medical students pair-matched for academic year and sex; n = 9). We conducted simulation interviews (a form of knowledge elicitation, cf.: [21]) where cognitive task analysis [22] was performed on visual stimuli. Interviewees were probed via a standardized protocol on declarative and procedural knowledge on the determinants of health and their interplay. We also administered a survey to collect sociodemographic data and self-reported health behavior. Data were collected online by pairs of seven trained interviewers between December 2021 and February 2023; interviews lasted 99 min on average.

Codes were developed in several stages in a guided inductive process based on the eight[1] modules of the intervention constituting parent codes. For a more detailed description of code development, see our preregistration (https://osf.io/hjs5b). The final codebook contained two code clusters: substantive codes reflecting the intervention modules and "metacodes" capturing aspects of our data that spanned across substantive codes. Substantive codes were hierarchical, comprising two levels of abstraction; metacodes were clustered in a flat structure. Table 1 contains the simplified version of our final codebook; the more detailed version is available online: https://osf.io/t8xh5.

Table 1. Simplified version of our codebook.

Parent code	Child code	Code definition
Nutrition	Unhealthy nutrition	Malnutrition, bad eating habits, bad food choices
	Healthy nutrition	Healthy eating habits, good food choices
	Unhealthy weight	Overweight or underweight, energy imbalance
	Healthy weight	Healthy weight, energy balance
Physical activity	Healthy exercise	Healthy quality and quantity of exercise
	Unhealthy exercise	Inactivity or too much exercise
	Adequate sleep	Right hours and quality of sleep, no disturbances
	Inadequate sleep	Too little/much sleep; bad quality, disturbances
Smoking	Active smoking	Using tobacco or nicotine products

(continued)

---

[1] We decided not to include the topic of basic life support in code development because it pertained to health achieved by proxy in emergency situations.

Table 1. (*continued*)

Parent code	Child code	Code definition
	Passive smoking	Exposure to someone else's smoking
Alcohol	Alcohol unhealthy	Dysfunctional, chronic, uncontrolled drinking
	Alcohol acceptable	Moderate, controlled, or occasional drinking
Drugs	Drugs unhealthy	Unhealthy and serious effects of drugs
	Drugs acceptable	Less harmful drugs and experimentation
Sex	Healthy sex	Physical and mental health promoting sex life
	Unhealthy sex	Physical or mental health harms of sex life
Mental health	Social support	Good relationships, positive social influences
	Social negative ·	Bad relationships, negative social influences
	Mental well-being	Personal mental health and self-understanding
	Mental ill-being	Mental health problems, lack of self-acceptance
Infection control	Hygiene	Basic hygiene and cleanliness
	Lack of hygiene	Lack of hygiene and cleanliness
Metacodes	Addiction	Addiction to any substance or behavior
	Abstinence	Refraining from exhibiting a certain behavior
	Finance	Money as a factor in health or ill-health
	Regulations	Laws and regulations on alcohol and drugs
	Access	In/availability of services and products
	Preventive health care	Non/use of healthcare for preventive purposes
	Adherence	Use of medication according to prescription
	Ability	Knowledge, skills and responsibility for health
	Physical environment	Health effects of housing conditions, physical environment, geographical location

Interviews were transcribed verbatim and anonymized. Sentences comprised our lowest level of segmentation; we employed the Reproducible Open Coding Kit (ROCK) R package[2] to place sentences on separate lines and designate a unique utterance identifier to each. We used the Interface for the Reproducible Open Coding Kit (iROCK)[3] to code and segment our data. Five researchers in our team "specialized" in a set of codes each (5–7 codes from the total 31), and one researcher was responsible for segmenting transcripts according to visual stimuli (three pictures used during the simulation interviews) and health determinants (elaboration of determinants by interviewees).

---

[2] https://rock.opens.science/.
[3] https://i.rock.science/.

Coding was performed on the level of sentences. The six coded versions of each interview were merged with the ROCK R package and exported into tabular format where sentences comprised rows, and columns were designated for each of our codes and types of segmentation. If a code was present in a line of data, it was indicated with a 1, the absence of a code with a 0. Stimuli-based segmentation was categorical, determinant-based segmentation received ordinal numbering within each interview. The interview protocol, visual stimuli, comprehensive codebook, coded dataset, and other materials are available in our repository: https://osf.io/ynjv4.

In the following, we explore three approaches to selecting codes for our ENA models. Our coding is currently in progress, hence we utilize only the intervention group data for our examples. Code names and quotes (translated by the authors), marked with the case ID [cid] of participants, are in italic.

4   Results

4.1   Selecting Codes Based on Theory

In the theory-based approach, we selected codes founded on relevant literature and theory. Our intervention aimed to improve the health status of adolescents, hence theory was aligned with this target group. Substance use behaviors often begin during adolescence [23] and are associated with both short-, and long-term health problems [24]. The smoking, alcohol, and drug use-related disease burden is significant in the European Union, especially in Hungary [25], therefore the prevention of adolescent substance use and addictions are relevant targets for public health interventions. Planning such preventive measures can build on the growing literature of *risk and protective factors* for substance use. Numerous risk factors have been identified, such as 1) substance use among friends, peers, and family, 2) high perceived accessibility of drugs, and 3) mental health problems, such as depressive symptoms and anxiety [26, 27]. Protective factors have also been identified, for example: 1) psychosocial competencies (e.g., assertiveness, coping, mindfulness, and optimism), 2) secure attachment and family cohesion, 3) successful integration in school, and 4) anti-substance policies [26–29]. BEP covered both risk and protective factors in its modules on alcohol, smoking, and drugs [19]. To explore the associations between substance use and its risk and protective factors in BEP educator narratives, we generated an ENA model by selecting all children of parent codes: *Smoking, Alcohol, Drugs, Mental health* as well as metacodes *Ability, Addiction, Abstinence, Access,* and *Regulation.*

Table 2 contains ENA model parameterization. Units were specified in a nested structure which allowed us to create a mean network for the intervention subsample (Group), participants (cid), and stimuli. Conversation was defined as determinants, which were subsections within narratives on specific stimuli. Code co-occurrences were accumulated with a weighted whole conversation stanza window, which was justified by theory regarding the meaning of co-occurrences in the text and by iteration between qualitative insights and quantitative models.

Table 2. Parameters of the Epistemic Network Analysis (ENA) model generated for illustrating the theory-based approach to selecting codes.

Unit	Group > cid > stimuli
Conversation	Determinants
Stanza window	Weighted whole conversation
Codes	Active smoking, Passive smoking, Alcohol unhealthy, Alcohol acceptable, Drugs unhealthy, Drugs acceptable, Social support, Social negative, Mental well-being, Mental ill-being, Addiction, Abstinence, Finance, Regulations, Access, Ability
Minimum edge weight	0.04
Projection	SVD1 (12.7%); SVD2 (11.6%)

Figure 1 displays the network reflecting participants' understanding of risk and protective factors regarding substance use. In terms of risk factors, there was a strong emphasis on substance use in social situations, as reflected in the connection between *Social support* and *Active smoking*: *"These gatherings are essential to build relationships among teenagers, and alcohol is part of these, even if smoking should not be"* (cid 101). Peer-pressure, manifesting in the connection between *Social negative* and *Active smoking* and *Drugs unhealthy*, also appeared as a related risk factor. This signified that peers and culture have a powerful negative influence on an individual's substance use: *"Well, unfortunately we're susceptible to influence and we like to be alike, and that includes if it's drug use or even just smoking"* (cid 101). Risk associated with mental health issues was also present in our network via its connection to dangerous drug use (*Drugs unhealthy*), reflecting the view that psychological distress may lead to drug use as a coping mechanism and drug use may result in mental health issues. High perceived accessibility of substances, however, was not present in the narratives as a risk factor: no connections were exhibited between the substance use codes and *Access* or *Regulations*.

Considering protective factors, *Mental well-being* and *Regulations* did not have connections with substance use codes, but the role of assertiveness appeared in the connection between *Ability* and *Addiction*: *"[It is healthy] if someone is aware of the addictiveness of substances and of his/her proneness to addictions [...] and can draw a line and keep it, when facing these things"* (cid 109). Thus, participants related substance use to both risk and protective factors, however, representation of the latter was less pronounced.

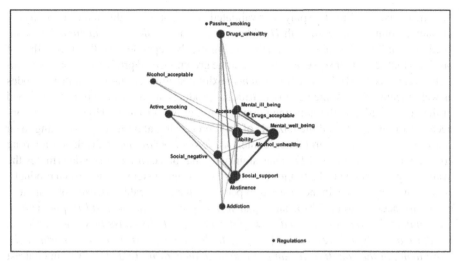

Fig. 1. Mean epistemic network of the educators of the Balassagyarmat Health Education Program (intervention group) on risk and protective factors of substance use, illustrating the theory-based approach to selecting codes. Codes are represented by nodes (circles); node size and edge thickness indicate the relative frequency of code co-occurrence.

4.2 Selecting Codes Based on Insight

Employing the insight-based approach to code selection, we leveraged the grounded assumptions of researchers from the stages of data collection, codebook development, and final, deductive coding. One observation was that, according to participants, healthy nutrition was dependent on the availability of healthy food in shops (e.g., whole grain products), and the latter was said to be determined by the size of the municipality of residence and the financial situation of individuals. To systematically explore this theme, we constructed a model including children of the parent code *Nutrition* and metacodes *Access, Finance* and *Physical environment*. Table 3 summarizes ENA model parameterization. The stanza window designation was changed compared to the previous model to optimize the model's ability to fit with qualitative insights.

Table 3. Parameters of the Epistemic Network Analysis (ENA) model generated for illustrating the insight-based approach to selecting codes.

Unit	Group > cid
Conversation	Determinants
Stanza window	Moving stanza of 4 lines
Codes	Unhealthy nutrition, Healthy nutrition, Unhealthy weight, Healthy weight, Access, Finance, Physical environment
Minimum edge weight	0.04
Projection	SVD1 (45.8%); SVD2 (25.7%)

The network in Fig. 2 displays our validated preliminary insight on nutrition. *Access* displayed connections with both *Healthy nutrition* and *Unhealthy nutrition.* The connections manifested as nutritional habits being highly dependent on the availability of products that can either serve health (e.g., home grown/farmed products) or be detrimental to it (e.g., fast food). *Physical environment* exhibited connections to the nutrition codes as well, meaning that some healthy nutritional products are more commonly consumed in the countryside, as the abovementioned home grown products. However, this connection also encompassed the hazards of food processing at home (e.g., smoking meat can result in increased carcinogen content). *Physical environment* displayed a strong connection with *Access* and *Finance*, signifying that place of residence determines the availability of certain products and services (e.g., sewage system, home-grown products, education) and that the financial status of people influences health. An exemplar of these co-occurrences is captured by a participant as follows: *"We can suggest [people living in the countryside] to buy processed meat of a better quality [because they are healthier], but those are way more expensive [...] Vegetables are expensive too. [...] Fortunately, those living in the countryside can grow some of their own"* (cid 108). Yet, in contrast with our preliminary insight, it was *Physical environment*, not *Access*, that showed the most marked connections with nutrition codes.

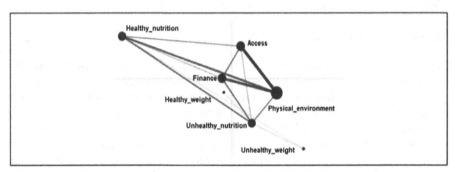

Fig. 2. Mean epistemic network of the educators of the Balassagyarmat Health Education Program (intervention group) on determinants of healthy nutrition, illustrating the insight-based approach to selecting codes. Codes are represented by nodes (circles); node size and edge thickness indicate the relative frequency of code co-occurrence.

4.3 Selecting Codes Based on a Full Model

When applying the model-based approach, we generated an ENA model with all codes, observed the ENA projection space, and made selection decisions for future models based on node positioning. Table 4 contains the parameters of this ENA model. The stanza window designation in this model was chosen arbitrarily, as no theory or qualitative insight could guide this decision.

Table 4. Parameters of the Epistemic Network Analysis (ENA) model generated for illustrating the model-based approach to selecting codes.

Unit	Group > cid > determinants
Conversation	Determinants
Stanza window	Moving stanza of 4 lines
Codes	All 31
Minimum edge weight	0.00
Projection	SVD1 (6.1%); SVD2 (4.5%)

The x axis, explaining the most variance in our data, was constituted by *Access, Physical environment,* and *Finance* on the one hand, and *Ability, Mental well-being,* and *Social support* on the other. This dimension, shown in Fig. 3, can be interpreted as contrasting environmental and socioeconomic determinants with individual ones; the former characterized by lower individual control and greater determination by the broad societal and environmental systems, the latter by personal and interpersonal aspects of health over which the individual may have more control. Defining this dimension could thus help form a grounded theory on how code clusters can be created; the two poles of the dimension and associated codes are potentially separate models (e.g., an ENA model displaying individual factors in health). Congruently, the y axis can be used to enrich the theory built from the first dimension or to construct a novel grounded theory.

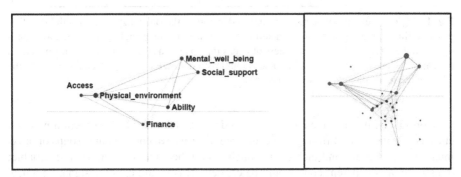

Fig. 3. *Right:* A full epistemic network of the educators of Balassagyarmat Health Education Program (intervention group) on the determinants of health. Nodes highlighted in red are represented in the left plot. *Left:* Specific codes that drive the x axis. Codes are represented by nodes (circles); node size and edge thickness indicate the relative frequency of code co-occurrence.

Viewing the ENA projection space in terms of quadrants (upper right, upper left, lower right, lower left) may also inform code selection. Codes taking on a proximal position in the space exhibit similar connections to all other codes in the dataset. By this logic, using quadrants (or node placement in general) can be employed to define code clusters based on co-occurrence patterns. Depending on analytical goals, we may want to investigate connections among codes that exhibit similar co-occurrence patterns in the data or codes that differ in how they connect to other codes.

If we wanted to delve deeper into connections among codes that exhibit a similar co-occurrence pattern in the dataset, we could select codes that are proximal in the ENA space and generate a separate model for them. For example, as shown in Fig. 4, we may choose codes *Mental ill-being, Active smoking, Ability, Social negative, Alcohol unhealthy,* and *Drugs unhealthy* to examine their interactions more closely (purple cluster, Fig. 4, left). A separate model could be created for codes *Healthy nutrition, Unhealthy nutrition, Unhealthy exercise,* and *Passive smoking* for the same purpose (teal cluster, Fig. 4, left). This would contribute to conclusions such as individual decisions are key to substance use behaviors, and peer pressure and mental health issues make healthy choices more difficult.

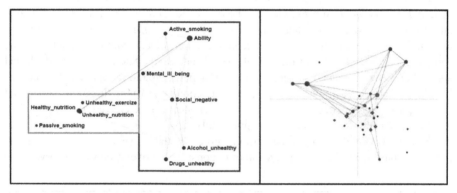

Fig. 4. *Right:* A full epistemic network of the educators of the Balassagyarmat Health Education Program (intervention group) on the determinants of health. Nodes highlighted in red are represented in the left plot. *Left:* Two clusters of codes that exhibit a similar co-occurrence pattern in the dataset. Codes are represented by nodes (circles); node size and edge thickness indicate the relative frequency of code co-occurrence.

Conversely, if we wanted to create a model that elaborates the connection between clusters of codes with differing co-occurrence patterns, we could create groups of proximally situated codes and dichotomize their occurrence into a novel, derived variable; in essence, a new parent code would be created. This would entail designating a new column in the dataset that is coded line-by-line as other code columns.

Code proximity, as the basis for derived parent codes, can be inspected in the default ENA space or with an alternative plot called a unit circle[4] shown in Fig. 5. Codes can be grouped in several ways, for example, based on quadrant or proximity to an axis (e.g., *Hygiene, Lack of Hygiene, Regulations* and *Alcohol acceptable* in Fig. 5).

---

[4] The unit circle node layout positions the network nodes where a line drawn from the origin to each node in the default ENA layout intersects a unit circle. This places the nodes such that they are all equidistant from the origin.

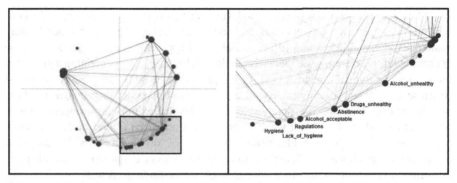

Fig. 5. *Left:* Unit circle node layout of a full epistemic network of the educators of the Balassagyarmat Health Education Program (intervention group) on the determinants of health. *Right:* A closer view of its highlighted area in the right plot. Codes are represented by nodes (circles); node size and edge thickness indicate the relative frequency of code co-occurrence.

5 Discussion

In this paper, we aimed to demonstrate viable approaches to selecting codes for ENA models. The theory-based approach entailed using literature or theory to formulate assumptions and code clusters that affirm or challenge those. The insight-based approach relied on the researchers' grounded observations as the basis of code selection. Lastly, in the model-based approach, an ENA projection space was created that included all possible codes; selection relied on inspecting the position of codes in this space.

Theory is an integral and inherent element of research [30]. Yet, guided inductive code development (basing codes/codebook on theory or literature) or deductive code development (adopting codes/codebook from others) is not without challenges. Often, codebooks may not be made public by researchers or may not reach the level of specificity needed to adopt and apply codes reliably [31]. Furthermore, constructs may differ in how they are defined even among authors using the same theoretical framework. Thus, use of identical construct labels does not necessarily imply that they are measuring the same phenomenon [32, 33].

The effects of researcher biases and preferences are ubiquitous throughout research, and are even embedded in analytical tools [34, 35]. One might argue that constructing a model of the data that reflects qualitative insights only generates findings prone to the confirmation bias [36][5]. Preregistering research and employing credibility strategies, such as reflexivity, iterative codebook construction, and social moderation during the code development phase, or respondent validation and peer debriefing during the analysis phase, may prove to be effective in reducing researcher bias [37]. The coded dataset should already be a scrutinizable output of transparent and systematic processes. Thus, basing code selection on insights gained during various phases of research does not necessarily increase the effects of bias, in fact, the iteration between qualitative understanding and quantitative model may even disprove initial researcher assumptions.

---

[5] We are intentionally sidestepping the crucial epistemological and ontological question of whether biases should be minimized in scientific outputs or employed as an analytical tool.

When working with many codes, the level of difficulty in interpreting pairwise connections in an epistemic network rises, and nodes may start to eclipse each other, lending challenges to visual inspection [9]. A model-based approach to code selection may be appropriate if, for example, no theory is employed (because, e.g., generating a grounded theory is an analytical objective [13]) or no qualitative insights can reliably be gained (because, e.g., insights of interest depend on multiple attributes of data providers). Albeit, one should exercise caution in solely selecting codes that exhibit the strongest connections and excluding those with weak or no connections from future models, as some crucial connections may be hidden behind the effects of "dominant codes" [9] and weak connections may play a significant role in explaining variance. Furthermore, code pairs exhibiting no connection may be a critical aspect of the findings as well.

The most notable limitation of this study is that in order to elaborate the three approaches to code selection, we did not address other questions in model parameterization, and did not discuss how those decisions affect networks and their interpretation. Choices pertaining to co-occurrence accumulation and aggregation (e.g., operationalization of unit, conversation, and stanza window) are especially crucial [1, 14]. A further limitation is that the specification of our units was primarily guided by the number of codes we wanted to include in our model. Aiming to keep the number of units higher than the number of codes to ensure statistical validity [12] resulted in varying unit designations across the demonstrated approaches.

6 Conclusions

The presented approaches to code selection offer strategies for addressing a large number of codes in analysis, both to uncover fine details and to outline broader associations. The networks that are produced in any of these approaches can be considered initial, exploratory models aiding a dialectic with the researcher's qualitative understanding of the data, or can constitute the final models included in the write-up of results. Our paper aims to spark further discussion on modeling interaction among many codes, a common challenge in conveying qualitative research findings.

Acknowledgements. We wish to thank our interviewees for their participation and sacrificing their time. This study was supported by the ÚNKP-22-3-I-SE-11 New National Excellence Program of the Ministry for Culture and Innovation from the Source of the National Research, Development and Innovation Fund and by the European Union and the Hungarian State (grant number: EFOP-3.4.3-16-2016-00007). This project also received funding from the European Union's Horizon 2020 research and innovation program under the Marie Sklodowska-Curie grant agreement No. 101028644, as well as from University Fund Limburg/SWOL. The opinions, findings, and conclusions do not reflect the views of the funding agency, cooperating institutions, or other individuals.

References

1. Zörgő, S.: Segmentation and code co-occurrence accumulation: operationalizing relational context with stanza windows. In: Damşa, C., Barany, A. (eds.) Advances in Quantitative Ethnography. ICQE 2022. CCIS, vol. 1785, pp 146–162. Springer, Cham (2023). https://doi.org/10.1007/978-3-031-31726-2_11

2. Cai, Z., Siebert-Evenstone, A., Eagan, B., et al.: nCoder+: a semantic tool for improving recall of nCoder coding. In: Eagan, B., Misfeldt, M., Siebert-Evenstone, A. (eds.) Advances in Quantitative Ethnography. ICQE 2019. CCIS, vol. 1112, pp. 41–54. Springer, Cham (2019). https://doi.org/10.1007/978-3-030-33232-7_4

3. Shaffer, D.: Quantitative Ethnography. Cathcart Press, Austin (2017)

4. Shaffer, D.W., Collier, W., Ruis, A.R.: A tutorial on epistemic network analysis: analyzing the structure of connections in cognitive, social, and interaction data. J. Learn. Anal. 3, 9–45 (2016)

5. Zörgő, S., Peters, G.-J.: Using the reproducible open coding kit & epistemic network analysis to model qualitative data. Health Psychol. Behav. Med. 11, 2119144 (2023). https://doi.org/10.1080/21642850.2022.2119144

6. Wang, Y., Swiecki, Z., Ruis, A., Shaffer, D.W.: Simplification of epistemic networks using parsimonious removal with interpretive alignment. In: Ruis, A.R., Lee, S.B. (eds.) Advances in Quantitative Ethnography. ICQE 2021. CCIS, vol. 1312, pp. 137–151. Springer, Cham (2021). https://doi.org/10.1007/978-3-030-67788-6_10

7. Siebert-Evenstone, A.L., Arastoopour, G., Collier, W., et al.: In search of conversational grain size: modelling semantic structure using moving stanza windows. J. Learn. Anal. 4, 123–139 (2017)

8. Zörgő, S., Swiecki, Z., Ruis, A.R.: Exploring the effects of segmentation on semi-structured interview data with epistemic network analysis. In: Ruis, A.R., Lee, S.B. (eds.) Advances in Quantitative Ethnography. ICQE 2021. CCIS, vol. 1312, pp. 78–90. Springer, Cham (2021). https://doi.org/10.1007/978-3-030-67788-6_6

9. Mello, R.F., Gašević, D.: What is the effect of a dominant code in an epistemic network analysis? In: Eagan, B., Misfeldt, M., Siebert-Evenstone, A. (eds.) Advances in Quantitative Ethnography. ICQE 2019. CCIS, vol. 1112, pp. 66–76. Springer, Cham (2019). https://doi.org/10.1007/978-3-030-33232-7_6

10. Shaffer, D.W.: Epistemic frames for epistemic games. Comput. Educ. 46, 223–234 (2006)

11. Lefstein, A.: Interpretation in Linguistic Ethnography: Some Comments for Quantitative Ethnographers. Work Pap Urban Lang Literacies, p. 297 (2022)

12. Bowman, D., Swiecki, Z., Cai, Z., et al.: The mathematical foundations of epistemic network analysis. In: Ruis, A.R., Lee, S.B. (eds.) Advances in Quantitative Ethnography. ICQE 2021. CCIS, vol. 1312, pp 91–105. Springer, Cham (2021). https://doi.org/10.1007/978-3-030-67788-6_7

13. Glaser, B.G., Strauss, A.L.: The Discovery of Grounded Theory: Strategies for Qualitative Research. Aldine Publishing, Chicago (1967)

14. Zörgő, S., Brohinsky, J.: Parsing the continuum: manual segmentation of monologic data. In: Damşa, C., Barany, A. (eds.) Advances in Quantitative Ethnography. ICQE 2022. CCIS, vol. 1785, pp. 163–181. Springer, Cham (2023). https://doi.org/10.1007/978-3-031-31726-2_12

15. Braun, V., Clarke, V.: Thematic analysis. In: Cooper, H., Camic, P.M., Long, D.L., Panter, A.T., Rindskopf, D., Sher K.J. (eds.) APA Handbook of Research Methods in Psychology, Vol. 2. Research Designs: Quantitative, Qualitative, Neuropsychological, and Biological, pp. 57–71. American Psychological Association (2012). https://doi.org/10.1037/13620-004

16. Engel, G.L.: The need for a new medical model: a challenge for biomedicine. Science 196, 129–136 (1977). https://doi.org/10.1126/science.847460

424   D. Árva et al.

17. Dahlgren, G., Whitehead, M.: Policies and strategies to promote social equity in health. Background document to WHO - Strategy paper for Europe. Inst. Futur. Stud. Arbetsrapport **14** (1991)
18. Bircher, J., Kuruvilla, S.: Defining health by addressing individual, social, and environmental determinants: new opportunities for health care and public health. J. Public Health Policy **35**, 363–386 (2014). https://doi.org/10.1057/jphp.2014.19
19. Eörsi, D., Árva, D., Herzeg, V., Terebessy, A.: Komplex iskolai egészségfejlesztő program a COM-B modell tükrében [Introduction to a complex school-based health education program from the COM-B model's perspective]. Egészségfejlesztés **61**, 36–47 (2020). http://folyoirat.nefi.hu/index.php?journal=Egeszsegfejlesztes&page=article&op=view&path%5B%5D=540
20. Mellanby, A.R., Rees, J.B., Tripp, J.H.: Peer-led and adult-led school health education: a critical review of available comparative research. Health Educ. Res. **15**, 533–545 (2000). https://doi.org/10.1093/her/15.5.533
21. Cooke, N.J.: Varieties of knowledge elicitation techniques. Int. J. Hum.-Comput. Stud. **41**, 801–849 (1994). https://doi.org/10.1006/ijhc.1994.1083
22. Crandall, B., Klein, G., Hoffman, R.: Working Minds: A Practitioner's Guide to Cognitive Task Analysis (2006)
23. Inchley, J., Currie, D., Budisavljević, S., et al.: Findings From The 2017/2018 Health Behaviour In School-Aged Children (Hbsc) Survey In Europe And Canada International Report, Volume 1. Key Findings Spotlight on adolescent health and well-being Spotlight on adolescent health and well-being (2020)
24. Lee, H., Henry, K.L.: Adolescent substance use prevention: long-term benefits of school engagement. J. Sch. Health **92**, 337–344 (2022). https://doi.org/10.1111/josh.13133
25. OECD/European Observatory on Health Systems and Policies: Hungary: Country Health Profile 2021, State of Health in the EU. OECD Publishing, Paris (2021). https://doi.org/10.1787/482f3633-en
26. Bozzini, A.B., Bauer, A., Maruyama, J., et al.: Factors associated with risk behaviors in adolescence: a systematic review. Rev Bras Psiquiatr **43**, 210–221 (2021). https://doi.org/10.1590/1516-4446-2019-0835
27. Nawi, A.M., Ismail, R., Ibrahim, F., et al.: Risk and protective factors of drug abuse among adolescents: a systematic review. BMC Public Health **21**, 2088 (2021). https://doi.org/10.1186/s12889-021-11906-2
28. Das, J.K., Salam, R.A., Arshad, A., et al.: Interventions for adolescent substance abuse: an overview of systematic reviews. J. Adolesc. Health. **59**, S61–S75 (2016). https://doi.org/10.1016/j.jadohealth.2016.06.021
29. Evren, C., Dalbudak, E., Evren, B., Demirci, A.C.: High risk of Internet addiction and its relationship with lifetime substance use, psychological and behavioral problems among 10(th) grade adolescents. Psychiatr. Danub. **26**, 330–339 (2014)
30. Collins, C.S., Stockton, C.M.: The central role of theory in qualitative research. Int J Qual Methods **17**, 1609406918797475 (2018). https://doi.org/10.1177/1609406918797475
31. Zörgő, S., Peters, G.-J.Y., Porter, C., et al.: Methodology in the mirror: a living, systematic review of works in quantitative ethnography. In: Wasson, B., Zörgő, S. (eds.) Advances in Quantitative Ethnography. ICQE 2021. CCIS, vol. 1522, pp. 144–159. Springer, Cham (2022). https://doi.org/10.1007/978-3-030-93859-8_10
32. Peters, G.-J.Y., Crutzen, R.: Pragmatic nihilism: how a theory of nothing can help health psychology progress. Health Psychol. Rev. **11**, 103–121 (2017). https://doi.org/10.1080/17437199.2017.1284015
33. West, R., Godinho, C.A., Bohlen, L.C., et al.: Development of a formal system for representing behaviour-change theories. Nat. Hum. Behav. **3**, 526–536 (2019). https://doi.org/10.1038/s41562-019-0561-2

34. Arastoopour Irgens, G., Eagan, B.: The foundations and fundamentals of quantitative ethnography. In: Damşa, C., Barany, A. (eds.) Advances in Quantitative Ethnography. ICQE 2022. CCIS, vol. 1785, pp. 3–16. Springer, Cham (2023). https://doi.org/10.1007/978-3-031-317 26-2_1
35. Vaandering, D., Reimer, K.E.: Relational critical discourse analysis: a methodology to challenge researcher assumptions. Int J Qual Methods **20**, 16094069211020904 (2021)
36. Nickerson, R.: Confirmation bias: a ubiquitous phenomenon in many guises. Rev. Gen. Psychol. **2**, 175–220 (1998)
37. Zörgő, S.: Preregistration template for qualitative and quantitative ethnographic studies (2021). https://doi.org/10.17605/OSF.IO/TGK49

Negative Reversion: Toward Intelligent Co-raters for Coding Qualitative Data in Quantitative Ethnography

Zhiqiang Cai$^{(\boxtimes)}$ [ID], Brendan Eagan [ID], and David Williamson Shaffer [ID]

University of Wisconsin, Madison, WI 53703, USA
{zhiqiang.cai,beagan}@wisc.edu, dws@education.wisc.edu

Abstract. Artificial intelligence has been applied to simulate many human activities in Quantitative Ethnography(QE). This paper evaluates the creation of an intelligent co-rater for coding qualitative (text) data in QE research. The intelligent task for a computer agent in this study is helping human researchers identify patterns by smartly sampling items that contain patterns of interest the researcher has yet to identify. This study compares the performance of an existing bidirectional LSTM model, *bLSTM*, a new nearest neighbor model, *weNN*, and a newly proposed combination of the two. The study focuses on learning data collected from implementations of an epistemic game and associated qualitative coding data coded by regexes. The contributions of this paper include: 1) a newly proposed combination of *bLSTM* and *weNN*, referred to as *bwInter*, which was identified to have the best performance among the three models, with efficiency from approximately 5.8 (lower recall band) to 10.3 (upper recall band) times greater than random searching, compared to the existing *bLSTM* which had 4.8 (lower recall band) to 5.8 (upper recall band); 2) an examination of the effectiveness of *bwInter* at five different phases of automated classifier development, which showed, when compared to random searching, increasingly better performance from earlier to later phases in classifier development; and 3) an investigation of performance across different qualitative codes, which showed that, while the effectiveness varies from code to code, the model *bwInter* always performed significantly better than others, with a minimum efficiency 3.20 times that of random searching. Overall, this paper suggests that, the newly identified model *bwInter* could be used to create highly effective intelligent co-raters that help identify missing text patterns in coding qualitative data in QE research.

Keywords: intelligent co-rater · negative reversion · qualitative coding · bidirectional LSTM, · neural network · word embedding · nearest neighbor

1 Introduction

The advance of artificial intelligence has made computers able to simulate human intelligence in solving complicated problems in QE research. For example, intelligent tutoring systems (ITSs) simulate the performance of human tutors in helping students to learn

© The Author(s), under exclusive license to Springer Nature Switzerland AG 2023
G. Arastoopour Irgens and S. Knight (Eds.): ICQE 2023, CCIS 1895, pp. 426–437, 2023.
https://doi.org/10.1007/978-3-031-47014-1_29

through natural language conversation [15]; teachable agents simulate human students to provide learning-by-teaching experiences [2]; intelligent mentors simulate human mentors to guide learning process in epistemic games [22], intelligent essay assessors simulate teachers' assessment by automatically grading student essays [12], and more. Yet, there are important tasks that AI has not been able to replicate to acceptable levels of performance in comparison to human performance. One such task is coding text data in QE research [7, 14, 21].

Coding is a complicated process that is difficult for machines to simulate [18]. For example, a typical "bottom up" coding process involves a cycle consisting of three coding levels – open coding, axial coding and selective coding [23]. The first level, *open coding*, aims at identifying basic concepts and related text pattern (concept-indicator model) emerged in the data. The second level coding, *axial coding*, refines the concepts and their corresponding patterns and organizes the basic concepts into key categories. The last level, *selective coding*, further refines these key categories and indicators and merges the key categories into themes which could be used to form a theoretical framework. Taking such approaches, a researcher tries to answer two basic questions: "What is the code I am interested in?" and "What are the text patterns (indicator(s)) that count as evidence for the occurrence or presence of the code?". In the words of Shaffer and Ruis, coding is a process in which researchers "defining concepts and identifying where they occur in data" [21]. Unlike "black-box" machine learning classification, transparent coding approaches require that the researcher could "point" to specific parts of the texts as evidence of the code occurrences [21].

Thus, an intelligent agent needs to simulate human intelligence by 1) identifying key concepts as they appear in the data; and 2) identifying text patterns that accurately represent a specific concept.

There are machine learning algorithms that can simulate human coding to some degree. Topic modeling [3, 11] represents underline topics by topic proportions in each document (text segment) and topic probability distributions on vocabulary words. The topics can be taken as codes. The meaning of a code can be approximately interpreted by the words with highest topic probabilities and the occurrence of a code in a segment can be determined by the topic proportion score. A binary classifier can be constructed using the topic proportion score: if and only if the topic proportion score exceeds a certain threshold, say, 0.5, the code is considered to be present. While this method is fully automatic, it simulates human intelligence in a very limited way. First, interpreting the meaning of a topic is often ambiguous, inconclusive, or inaccurate. While the topic distributions may show some impressive patterns that seem to make sense, they often do not cleanly represent specific concepts. For example, a topic may have the words "education", "school", "student" at the top of the topic probability distribution. However, a researcher may not feel comfortable to interpret the topic as "education" because there could be other words irrelevant to education that have probabilities close to these words. Second, proportion scores fail to provide specific text pattern(s) that can be shown as evidence of code occurrence, resulting in non-transparent coding [6, 21].

Another approach, supervised machine learning, are based on models that are trained from human coded data and then be applied to data without human coding [8, 10, 19]. When working with large data sets, such algorithms can reduce the amount of human effort required to classify the data. However, supervised machine learning approaches do not have the intelligence to automatically identify concepts and text patterns and require large amounts of human coded data to achieve acceptable levels of performance.

A more promising method is active learning, in which the machine acts as a co-rater that works with a human rater [5, 21]. In such a system, a human rater is responsible for defining a code, identifying some of the text patterns, and providing coded items. The machine co-rater takes the identified text patterns and coded items as input to train a learning model. The trained model then identifies new items that most likely contain missing or inaccurate text patterns. These items are provided to the human rater along with possible patterns that can be revised or added to the set of text patterns the researcher believes represent an occurrence of the code. The human rater codes these new items and refines the definition of the codes and corresponding text patterns. The iteration continues until the text patterns are accurate and complete, or the automated classifier has achieved a desired level of performance. In such a process, The machine corater needs to simulate human's intelligence in 1) identifying items that contain inaccurate or missing text patterns; and 2) generating and revising text patterns. In this paper, we focus on the algorithms that helps the machine to intelligently identify items that contain missing text patterns. We call these items "False Negative Items" (FNI). In the sections below, we first describe these algorithms. We then apply the algorithms to a real education data with 6 automated codes over 10 recall bands. Finally, we compare the algorithms and show that the combination of a bidirectional LSTM(Long Short Term Memory) model and word embedding based nearest neighbor model most efficiently identify FNI.

2   Negative Reversion Set and Research Questions

2.1   Negative Reversion Set

Cai and colleagues introduced the *Negative Reversion Set* (NRS) to improve the low recall performance of rule based coding methods [4, 5]. Coding rules are usually created through text patterns: "if a text item contains any of the text patterns in the collection, the code occurs in the item". Thus, when a collection of text patterns is identified, the data can be automatically coded using those rules. Items in which a code occurs are coded as *positive*; otherwise the item is considered *negative*. Coding errors from such method are of two types. One is from *inaccurate* text patterns. A text pattern is inaccurate, if there are items that contain this pattern but the code does not occur in said item. Such inaccurate patterns cause *false positives*. A second type of coding error is rooted in missing text patterns. A text pattern is missing if it is contained in an item that a human expert would code as positive but is coded as negative by the current collection of text patterns. Missing patterns cause *false negatives*.

Missing text patterns can only be identified from examining false negative items (FNIs). However, finding FNIs is often difficult. Codes of interest often have low frequencies in the dataset of interest. Thus, even if the number of FNIs is a small proportion of the coded negative set, they could easily out number the positive occurrences of the code in the data. For example, consider a set with 11000 items, with 1000 coded as positive and 10000 as negative. If 10% of the negative items are FNIs, they are equivalent to

100% of the coded positives, which is often too high an error rate to tolerate. However, to identify the missing text patterns present in the FNIs, a researcher would have to search among the 10000 coded negative items of which only 10% are false negatives.

The *negative reversion set* is a subset of the items that are coded as negative by identified text patterns but reversely coded as positive by another "intelligent co-rater". The intelligent co-rater may correctly or incorrectly reverse the items. However, a co-rater with high "intelligence" can identify a negative reversion set with dense FNIs. Cai and colleagues created a co-rater using a bidirectional LSTM neural network and applied to a real data set collected from an epistemic game. They showed that, at about the half way point of the coding rule development phase, the density of FNIs in the negative reversion set could be from 3 to 12 times higher than in the entire negative set coded by the under-development text patterns [5]. In another study, Cai et al. simulated the use of the negative reversion set in real coding process and found that their algorithm could reduce required manual coding items by 50% to 63%, compared with random sampling [4].

In this paper, we investigate possible further improvement of the co-rater's "intelligence" by combining the bidirectional LSTM model with a word-embedding based nearest neighbor model. The models are compared using the same data set used by Cai and colleagues. In addition, we investigate the FNI densities as functions of rule completeness and explore the effectiveness of negative reversion sets across the whole rule development process. To get some idea about how the model could be applied to new data and new codes, we investigated the performance differences across the existing six codes. Specifically, our research questions are:

1. Does a certain combination of a bidirectional LSTM neural network model and a nearest neighbor model yield better negative reversion sets?
2. How does the effectiveness of the negative reversion sets change in the rule development process?
3. How does the effectiveness of the negative reversion sets change with different codes?

3 Mathematical Definitions and Algorithms

3.1 Mathematical Definitions

Following the work of Cai and colleagues [4, 5], we give mathematical definition of the notions we use in the rest of the paper. All these definitions are relative to a given code.

- **data set** D: a data set containing segmented text items;
- **ideal rater** R_i: a rater that correctly classifies every item in D as positive or negative;
- **rule based classifier** C_r: a rule based classifier based on identified text patterns;
- **intelligent co-rater** R_c: a machine rater that learns from the result of the rule based classifier C_r and identifies possible wrong ratings of C_r;
- **ideal positive set** P: the set of items in D classified as positive by the ideal rater R_i;
- **ideal negative set** N: the set of items in D classified as negative by R_i;
- **classified positive set** $P^\sim$: the set of items in D classified as positive by the rule based classifier C_r;
- **classified negative set** $N^\sim$: the set of items in D classified as negative by C_r;

- **co-rater positive set** $\tilde{P}$: the set of items in D classified as positive by the co-rater R_c;
- **co-rater negative set** $\tilde{N}$: the set of items in D classified as negative by R_c;
- **negative reversion set** $N\tilde{P}$: set of the items classified as negative by C_r but reversed as positive by R_c.

In the formulas above, "XY" denotes the intersection of two sets "X" and "Y". The following metrics are used in this paper to measure the error and accuracy of the rule based classifier:

- **proportion of true positives:** $tp = |P\tilde{P}|/|D|$;
- **proportion of false positives:** $fp = |N\tilde{P}|/|D|$;
- **proportion of false negatives:** $fn = |P\tilde{N}|/|D|$;
- **proportion of true negatives:** $tn = |N\tilde{N}|/|D|$;
- **precision:** $precision = tp/|\tilde{P}| = tp/(tp + fp)$; and
- **recall:** $recall = tp/|P| = tp/(tp + fn)$.

3.2 Algorithms Pattern

The algorithms used in this study include a bidirectional LSTM neural network model, referred to as *bLSTM*, a word embedding based nearest neighbor model, referred to as *weNN*, and a combined model, referred to as *bwInter*. Every model is implemented as an "intelligent mind" of a negative reversion co-rater. That is, each model is able to learn from coded data and then find possible positive items from the negative item set of the rule based classifier. We use these models in their simplest way without considering any possible fine tuning. Therefore, the performance of our models can be considered as their baseline performance. In addition to the three intelligent models, we add another non-intelligent model, labelled as *random*. The details of these four models are given below.

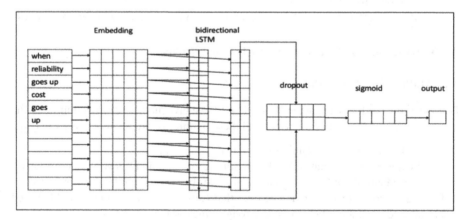

Fig. 1. Bidirectional LSTM neural network model for text classification

Bidirectional LSTM Neural Network Model. Figure 1 shows the bidirectional LSTM model, *bLSTM*. This model assumes 1) the text data has been segmented as a collection of documents; 2) each document has been tokenized; and 3) each unique token has been indexed. The input layer takes a document index vector and passes it to the embedding layer, which creates a unique vector representation for each unique token. The ordered token vectors are passed to a bidirectional LSTM layer that creates two vector representations, one forward and the other backward. The two vectors are merged into a single vector representation. The dropout layer randomly removes 50% of elements in the vector to control for over-fitting. The remainder of the vector elements are passed to the sigmoid layer which computes a probability that indicates how likely the input document should be coded as a positive. The probability value is then converted to a binary coding value using a cutoff threshold 0.5 [17]. This algorithm is used to create an "intelligent" negative reversion co-rater that reverses a negative item $x \in N^-$ if the predicted probability value is greater than 0.5.

Word Embedding Based Nearest Neighbor Model. The package *text2vec* [20] is used to train the word embedding model, which learns from segmented and tokenized text data and generates a unique vector representation for each document. The cosine values between all pairs of documents are then computed to form a document similarity matrix. For two subsets $X \subset D$ and $Y \subset D$, the nearest neighbor of a document $y \in Y$ in the subset X is a document $x \in X$ that has the highest similarity to y. Namely, there is no document in X that has similarity to y higher than the similarity between x and y. This model, referred to as *weNN*, is used to create a co-rater that reverses an item $x \in N^-$ if it is a nearest neighbor of an item $y \in P^-$.

Combined Model. The combined model, referred to as *bwInter*, creates a corater by intersecting the negative reversion sets from a bLSTM model and a weNN model. That is, *bwInter* creates a co-rater that works by reversing an item's classification $x \in N^-$, if a model bLSTM and a model weNN both reverse x.

Random Model. The random model, referred to as *random*, is not considered intelligent. It doesn't have any information about which items may be false negatives. Thus, it presents all items in N^- to the researcher who has to randomly search in the whole set N^- in order to find FNIs. This model is included for comparison purpose.

4 Method

4.1 Data

In this study, we used the same *Nephrotex* data set used by Cai and colleagues [4, 5]. This *Nephrotex* data was collected from an epistemic game [1, 9, 13], in which participants worked as interns at a fictitious company that designs and manufactures ultra-filtration membranes for hemodialysis machinery used to treat end-stage renal failure. The epistemic game implementations were divided into two phases utilizing a classic jig-saw approach. In the first phase, participants were grouped into teams of five, with each team working on a specific task. In the second phase, participants were regrouped, into new teams of five members from different teams in the first phase. The task in the second phase was to reflect the work each member did in the first phase to collaborate with their new team with varied expertise each participant brought from their first group. The utterances in all online team chat conversations were collected, resulting in a data set with 50,888 utterances. After filtering out the 70 longest utterances, 50,818 utterances were used, each with a length under 100 words.

4.2 Codes

Previous researchers created six codes, including *Tech Constraints, Performance, Collaboration, Design, Data* and *Requests.* The automatic classifier of each code was developed as a collection of regular expressions [16], representing the identified text patterns. The classifications were validated by two raters. The code descriptions, regex examples and the validation statistics can be found in Cai and colleagues [5].

4.3 Simulation Procedure

To answer our research questions, we simulated the co-rating process using four different models on the *Nephrotex* data set. For each of the six codes, we took the classifier with the complete regex list as the ideal rater R_i, a partial regex list randomly sampled from the full list as the under-development rule based classifier C_r. To get robust statistical results, we ran 100 iterations for each code. In each iteration, we randomly sampled 10 partial regex lists from the full regex list of the code so that the recall of classifiers are equally distributed in 5 "recall bands": [0–0.2), [0.2, 0.4), [0.4–0.6), [0.6–0.8), and [0.8–1]. We assumed that every regex was correctly composed, namely, the precision for every partial classifier was 1. For each given partial classifier C_r, the negative reversion set was identified by each of the four co-raters. We then computed FNI density in each negative reversion set and statistically compared the co-raters on the densities, as well as the ratio to the random model.

5 Results

The 100 iterations on 6 codes and 10 partial classifiers was expected to result in 6000 data points. However 664 items were missing because the regex list for some required recall intervals were not found; and 287 items were invalid because the process returned empty negative reversion set. The final results included 5049 valid data items.

Overall. Figure 2 shows that the overall FNI density of each model (upper figure) and ratio to random model (lower figure) across all codes and recall bands. The random model established the base line of the overall average FNI density, which was $(5.94 \pm 0.12)\%$. The FNI density of the nearest neighbor model, *weNN*, was $(25.37 \pm 0.61)\%$, which was 4.27 times the density of the random model. The bidirectional LSTM neural network model, *bLSTM*, was $(30.28 \pm 0.71)\%$, which was 5.09 times the density of the random model. The combined model *bwInter* was $(41.10 \pm 0.90)\%$, which was 6.92 times the density of the random model. The averages were computed on 5049 items and the confidence intervals were computed at 95% confidence level.

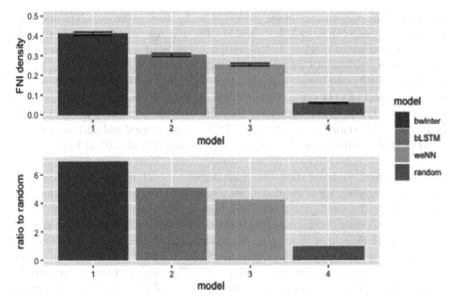

Fig. 2. Average FNI density (upper) and ratio to random (lower) across five recall bands and six codes over 100 iterations.

As Functions of Recall. Figure 3 shows mean FNI density as functions of recall. As recall increased, the FNI density for all models decreased. However, the ratio of the densities of each intelligent model to the random model increased. On all recall bands, the

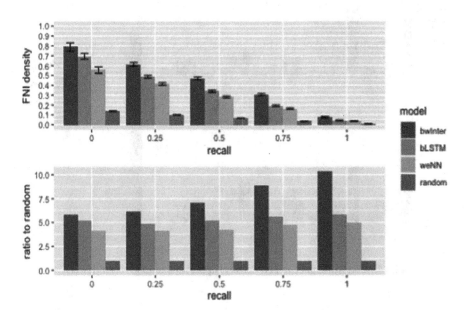

Fig. 3. FNI density (upper) and ratio to random (lower) as functions to recall

rank order of the performance of the models were the same as the overall performance, i.e., *bwInter > bLSTM > weNN > random*. The average density of the best model, *bwInter*, started with (78.92 ± 4.19)% at low recall band and decreased to (7.35 ± 0.74)% at high recall band. Compared to the random model, the density ratio of *bwInter* to *random* is 5.82 at the lowest recall band and increased to 10.30 at the highest recall band. The model *bLSTM* started from (69.56 ± 2.96)% at lowest band and decreased to (4.08 ± 0.71)% at the highest band. The ratio to *random* ranged from 4.83 to 5.83. The model *weNN* started from (55.48 ± 3.25)% at lowest band and decreased to (3.51 ± 0.31)% at the highest band. The ratio to *random* ranged from 4.08 to 4.94.

Code Difference. Figure 4 shows the mean density of each model on each code. The rank order of performance of the models were again the same as the overall performance on every code. The intelligent models had highest performance on the code "performance". For this code, the average FNI density of the best model, *bwInter*, was (73.13 ± 1.82)%, 8.31 times that of *random*; the model *bLSTM* was (54.95 ± 1.81)%, 6.25 times of *random*; and the model *weNN* was (52.62 ± 1.57)%, 5.98 times of *random*. The average density of *random* was (8.80 ± 0.32). The worst performance occurred on the code "data". The average density of *bwInter* was (17.02 ± 1.15)%, 3.20 times of *random*; *bLSTM* (16.02 ± 0.94)%,3.01 times of *random*; and *weNN* (8.97 ± 0.39), 1.69 times of *random*. The average density of *random* was (5.32 ± 0.21)%. The highest ratio to *random* occurred on the code "request": *bwInter* 14.52, *bLSTM* 7.95, and *weNN* 6.84.

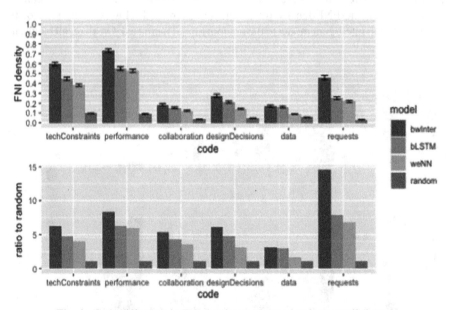

Fig. 4. Code difference in FNI density (upper) and ratio to recall (lower)

6 Conclusions

In this study we aimed to create an intelligent co-rater to help code qualitative data. In service of this goal, we investigated three models, an existing bidirectional LSTM model, *bLSTM*, a newly proposed nearest neighbor model, *weNN*, and a novel combined model, *bwInter*. Our simulation suggested the following. While the nearest neighbor model *weNN* is not as good as *bLSTM*, combining *weNN* and *bLSTM* yields a significantly better model (*bwInter*). On the simulated data, the average FNI density over all recall bands and all six codes was 41.10% for *bwInter*, in contrast to 30.28% for *bLSTM*. Since the cost in identifying text patterns is inversely proportional to FNI density [5], the overall cost of the combined model *bwInter* is about 74% of the cost of *bLSTM*. 2) The combining model, *bwInter*, works especially well in later development of text patterns. Our simulation showed that the FNI density in the negative reversion sets decreased when the text pattern completeness increased. However, the ratio of density of the intelligent models to *random* increased. The ratio for *bwInter* increased from 5.82 at the lowest recall band to 10.30 to the highest band, while *bLSTM* went from 5.13 to is 5.83. 3) The combining model *bwInter* could possibly be a better choice for other data and codes. Our simulation showed that, although the performance varied from code to code for all three models, *bwInter* consistently worked better than *bLSTM* and *weNN*. That is, we believe that *bwInter* is a useful automated co-rating tool that can assist human researchers to more efficiently create transparent automated coding algorithms of qualitative textual data in education research and practice.

Limitations and Future Work. The first limitation of this paper is that the proposed algorithms are all in their simplest form and may have room for further improvement and optimization. For example, the nearest neighbor model may be constructed using other semantic representations; and the combination could be in other forms. The second limitation is that we didn't identify the source of code differences, although we see that the performance of all three intelligent models differed from code to code. The third, whether or not the reversion sets would introduce systematic bias to coding is yet to be explored. These are directions we will continue to pursue in future work.

Acknowledgment. This work was funded in part by the National Science Foundation (DRL-2100320, DRL-2201723, DRL-2225240), the Wisconsin Alumni Research Foundation, and the Office of the Vice Chancellor for Research and Graduate Education at the University of Wisconsin-Madison. The opinions, findings, and conclusions do not reflect the views of the funding agencies, cooperating institutions, or other individuals.

References

1. Arastoopour, G., et al.: Nephrotex: measuring first-year students' ways of professional thinking in a virtual internship. In: 2012 ASEE Annual Conference & Exposition, pp. 25–971 (2012)
2. Blair, K., Schwartz, D.L., Biswas, G., Leelawong, K.: Pedagogical agents for learning by teaching: teachable agents. Educ. Technol., 56–61 (2007)

3. Blei, D.M., Ng, A.Y.: Latent dirichlet allocation. J. Mach. Learn. Res. **3**(4–5), 993–1022 (2003)
4. Cai, Z., Eagan, B., Marquart, C., Shaffer, D.W.: LSTM neural network assisted regex development for qualitative coding. In: Damşa, C., Barany, A. (eds.) Advances in Quantitative Ethnography, ICQE 2022. Communications in Computer and Information Science, vol. 1785, pp. 17–29. Springer, Cham (2023). https://doi.org/10.1007/978-3-031-31726-2_2
5. Cai, Z., Marquart, C., Shaffer, D.: Neural recall network: a neural network solution to low recall problem in regex-based qualitative coding. In: Mitrovic, A., Bosch, N. (eds.) Proceedings of the 15th International Conference on Educational Data Mining, pp. 228–238. International Educational Data Mining Society, Durham, United Kingdom (2022).https://doi.org/10.5281/zenodo.6853047
6. Cai, Z., Siebert-Evenstone, A., Eagan, B., Shaffer, D.W.: Using topic modeling for code discovery in large scale text data. In: Ruis, A.R., Lee, S.B. (eds.) ICQE 2021. CCIS, vol. 1312, pp. 18–31. Springer, Cham (2021). https://doi.org/10.1007/978-3-030-67788-6_2
7. Charmaz, K.: Constructing Grounded Theory. Sage, London (2006)
8. Chen, N.C., Drouhard, M., Kocielnik, R., Suh, J., Aragon, C.R.: Using machine learning to support qualitative coding in social science: shifting the focus to ambiguity. ACM Trans. Interact. Intell. Syst. **8**(2), 9:1-9:20 (2018). https://doi.org/10.1145/3185515,10.1145/3185515
9. Chesler, N., Ruis, A., Collier, W., Swiecki, Z., Arastoopour, G., Shaffer, D.: A novel paradigm for engineering education: virtual internships with individualized mentoring and assessment of engineering thinking. J. Biomech. Eng.ng. **137**(2), 1–8 (2015)
10. Crowston, K., Liu, X., Allen, E.E.: Machine learning and rule-based automated coding of qualitative data. Proc. Am. Soc. Inf. Sci. Technol. **47**(1), 1–2 (2010)
11. Darling, W.M.: A theoretical and practical implementation tutorial on topic modeling and gibbs sampling. In: Proceedings of the 49th Annual Meeting of the Association for Computational Linguistics: Human Language Technologies, pp. 642–647 (2011)
12. Foltz, P.W., Laham, D., Landauer, T.K.: The intelligent essay assessor: applications to educational technology. Interact. Multimed. Electron. J. Comput.-Enhanced Learn. **1**(2), 939–944 (1999)
13. Gautam, D., Swiecki, Z., Shaffer, D.W., Graesser, A.C., Rus, V.: Modeling classifiers for virtual internships without participant data. In: Proceedings of the 10th International Conference on Educational Data Mining, pp. 278–283 (2017)
14. Glaser, B., Strauss, A.: The Discovery of Grounded Theory: Stretegies for Qualitative Research. Aldine, Chicago (1967)
15. Graeser, A.C., Hu, X., Rus, V., Cai, Z.: Conversation-based learning and assessment environments. In: Yan, D., Rupp, A.A., Foltz, P.W. (eds.) Handbook of Automated Scoring, pp. 383–402. Chapman and Hall/CRC, New York (2020)
16. Kaur, G.: Usage of regular expressions in NLP. Int. J. Res. Eng. Technol. IJERT **3**(01), 7 (2014)
17. Li, G., Jiabao, G.: Bidirectional lstm with attention mechanism and convolutional layer for text classification. Neurocomputing **337**, 325–338 (2019)
18. Longo, L.: Empowering qualitative research methods in education with artificial intelligence. In: Costa, A.P., Reis, L.P., Moreira, A. (eds.) WCQR 2019. AISC, vol. 1068, pp. 1–21. Springer, Cham (2020). https://doi.org/10.1007/978-3-030-31787-4_1
19. Rietz, T., Maedche, A.: Towards the design of an interactive machine learning system for qualitative coding. In: ICIS (2020)
20. Selivanov, D., Bickel, M., Wang, Q.: Package 'text2vec' (2020)
21. Shaffer, D.W., Ruis, A.R.: How we code. In: Advances in Quantitative Ethnography: ICQE Conference Proceedings, pp. 62–77 (2021)

22. Wang, J., Li, H., Cai, Z., Keshtkar, F., Graesser, A., Shaffer, D.W.: Automentor: artificial intelligent mentor in educational game. In: Lane, H.C., Yacef, K., Mostow, J., Pavlik, P. (eds.) AIED 2013. LNCS (LNAI), vol. 7926, pp. 940–941. Springer, Heidelberg (2013). https://doi.org/10.1007/978-3-642-39112-5_154
23. Williams, M., Moser, T.: The art of coding and thematic exploration in qualitative research. Int. Manage. Rev. 15(1), 45–55 (2019)

Automated Code Discovery via Graph Neural Networks and Generative AI

Zheng Fang$^{(\boxtimes)}$, Ying Yang, and Zachari Swiecki

Monash University, Clayton, VIC 3800, Australia
zheng.fang@monash.edu

Abstract. Quantitative Ethnographic researchers sometimes use machine learning to help them discover codes in discourse. Commonly used techniques, such as topic modelling via Latent Dirichlet Allocation (LDA), are computationally limited and may produce results that are difficult to interpret. We present a novel approach for automated code discovery using graph neural networks (GNNs) and generative artificial intelligence (GAI) that identifies and interprets topics in discourse. Using data collected from a collaborative sensemaking task, we compare the results of our method to the outputs of a similar approach using LDA, as well as manually derived codes. We found that for these data (a) GAI can produce reasonable interpretations of topics; (b) the LDA-based approach discovered content-related codes; (c) the GNN-based approach discovered process-related codes; and (d) the outputs of both approaches had little overlap with manually derived codes.

Keywords: qualitative coding · graph neural networks · topic modelling · generative artificial intelligence

1 Introduction

The process of *coding*—assigning labels to pieces of data—is central to quantitative ethnographic (QE) research. When determining what to code their data for, QE researchers may apply a variety of approaches. One such approach is data-driven in which they use quantitative techniques to search for patterns in their data that are suggestive of [C]odes[1]. For example, researchers might use natural language processing (NLP) techniques to count the most frequent terms of varying lengths. More sophisticated techniques include *topic modelling*, which examines the co-occurrence of terms in the data to identify clusters of related terms called *topics*. Using the terms in these topics, researchers can provide summaries or interpretations of the topics to help decide on which [C]odes to investigate with their data.

---

[1] In QE, we often distinguish between [C]odes—culturally relevant meanings of actions—and [c]odes—features of data that we use to indicate the presence or absence of [C]odes [22]. [C]odes are the big idea we are interested in; [c]odes are things in the data that signify the big idea is happening.

G. Arastoopour Irgens and S. Knight (Eds.): ICQE 2023, CCIS 1895, pp. 438–454, 2023.
https://doi.org/10.1007/978-3-031-47014-1_30

While quantitative approaches to [C]ode discovery are potentially useful and time-saving, they are relatively under-explored in the context of QE. One reason may be that techniques like topic modelling can quickly suggest collections of related terms, but the process of interpreting these collections of terms into meaningful [C]odes may be difficult and, once interpreted, the [C]odes they suggest may not be useful for the later steps of the QE analysis [2, 6].

To address these issues, we present a preliminary study that tests a new method for automatically discovering [C]odes in discourse. The method adds two novel components to prior quantitative approaches. First, we apply graph neural networks (GNNs) to the data for topic modelling, rather than standard techniques. GNNs are computationally more powerful and sensitive to both global features of the data and the interdependencies that exist between segments of the data–e.g., turns of talk. Second, we pass the output of the GNN model to a generative AI—here, *ChatGPT* [15]—to automatically provide an interpretation of each topic and thus suggest [C]odes for further analysis.

To evaluate our method, we compared it to an approach that uses standard topic modelling via Latent Dirichlet Allocation (LDA) and the same generative AI for interpretation. We qualitatively compared the collections of terms and [C]odes suggested by both approaches to identify meaningful differences and compared these outputs to actual [C]odes applied to the data in an ongoing QE analysis. Our results show that (a) generative AI can produce reasonable interpretations of topics; (b) the LDA-based approach discovered content-related [C]odes; (c) the GNN-based approach discovered process-related [C]odes; and (d) the outputs of both approaches overlapped only slightly with manually derived [C]odes.

2   Background

2.1   Identifying [C]odes

QE researchers are interested in developing an understanding of some culture or community of practice. After collecting some record of the activities of this culture as data, one of the first steps in the QE process is to code the data. [C]odes are significant concepts or actions in the culture being examined and the process of coding refers to the act of associating pieces of data with those concepts or actions [22].

In general, there are two approaches that QE researchers take to determine the [C]odes for their data. One is a "top-down" or "deductive" approach in which researchers adapt an existing coding scheme from the literature to their own purposes. For example, this was the approach taken by Sun and Barany [24] when they applied a coding scheme adapted from Nadal's work [14] on Asian American categorisation.

The second approach, which is the main concern of this study, is often referred to as "bottom-up" or "inductive". Here, researchers come to the data without an explicit conceptualisation of a coding scheme. Instead, they examine the data in order to suggest appropriate [C]odes. Researchers might do this examination qualitatively, taking what is know as a "grounded" approach in which they read their data until they identify a suitable set of [C]odes. This was the approach taken by Swiecki and colleagues [25] in their study of the conversations of air defense warfare teams in training.

It is also possible to conduct the bottom up approach quantitatively, for example by using NLP and machine learning approaches to find patterns of terms in the data that may be suggestive of [C]odes. Such an approach was adopted by Cai and colleagues [5], who used topic modelling to discover [C]odes for a dataset of collaborative conversations between students.[2]

Once a suitable set of [C]odes has been identified, QE researchers create a *codebook* that maps the [C]odes to their instantiations in the data (i.e., [c]odes) [21]. Generally, codebooks contain three pieces of information: (a) the name of the [C]ode; (b) the definition—that is, a description or explanation of—the [C]ode; and (c) examples of the [C]ode as they appear in the data. In this paper, we operationalise the (tentative) discovery of a [C]ode as determining an initial name and definition for a potential [C]ode. This leaves out a crucial step of finding examples; however, because the process of determining names, definitions, and examples can plausibly happen in tandem, sequentially, or cyclically, separating out naming and defining from finding examples can be useful during the coding process. Moreover, such a processes (at least initially) can free the researcher from concerns about reliably coding the data and instead allow them to focus on plausible ideas to investigate further. Of course, reliably coding data is a vital step in the coding process, but it is not the focus of this paper.

2.2   Topic Modelling via LDA

As the work by Cai and colleagues [5] demonstrates, topic modelling can be a powerful method for [C]ode suggestion. Topic modelling is a widely used technique outside of QE for determining the content of text and developing classifiers. Several approaches have been applied for topic modelling, but the most common is Latent Dirichlet Allocation (LDA)—a generative probabilistic model that utilizes Dirichlet distributions to model document-topic and topic-word distributions [4]. LDA functions by iteratively updating topic and word distributions based on the co-occurrence of words within documents, assuming that documents are mixtures of topics and topics are mixtures of words. A document can be any pre-defined collection of terms, such as web-pages or turns of talk.

While it is widely used, the LDA approach to topic modelling has several computational limitations. First, LDA does not explicitly model relationships between documents, focusing only on the distribution of topics in each document. Second, LDA is a linear generative model, which might miss certain non-linear relationships in the data [4]. Finally, vanilla versions of LDA rely on probability distributions over a given number of topics and a list of words and

---

[2] Of course, these approaches need not be mutually exclusive. It is possible to combine them, for example, by beginning with an existing coding scheme and then examining the data in a bottom up way to add to or change that coding scheme.

does not consider other features that might bear on potential [C]odes, such as sub-populations within the data.

2.3 Topic Modelling via GNNs

One approach that address the limitations of LDA is the application of graph neural networks (GNNs). GNNs are deep learning models specifically designed to operate on network-structured data. In the case of textual analyses, nodes of the GNN represent terms and edges represent relationships between them, such as co-occurrence or semantic similarity. The primary output of GNNs are *node embeddings*—vector representations that capture local and global structural information.

As graph-based models, GNNs have several potential advantages as a topic modelling technique. First, GNNs are able to capture non-linear—and thus more complex—relationships between nodes (i.e., terms) [29]. Second, GNNs leverage the capabilities of neural networks to easily incorporate vast amounts of information in the form of node and edge features [9]. This leads to richer representations and the ability to capture relationships based on diverse types of information [20,30]. Third, a fundamental component of GNNs are *message passing* schemes, which define how information is exchanged between nodes in the graph during construction [29]. Message passing works by aggregating information from a node's neighbors and using this information to update the node's embedding. Message passing means that each node's embedding contains information not just about itself but also information about its neighbor's in the graph, thus, unlike LDA-based approaches, GNN-based approaches attend to the *interdependencies* that may exist between terms in discourse that go beyond simply co-occurring within the same "document".

While GNNs are applicable to a variety of downstream tasks, they have also been used as an alternative approach to LDA for topic modelling. For example, Zhu proposed the GraphBTM method [33], which calculates word co-occurrences within documents and extracts topics using Graph Convolutional Networks (GCNs) [11], a specific type of GNN. Relatedly, Yang [31] developed a topic modeling approach known as GATON, which utilises another variant of GNNs, graph attention networks (GATs), [27] to integrate word similarity and word co-occurrence structures. This work (see also, [23] and [32]) has begun to demonstrate the utility of GNNs for topic modelling, but remains limited due to its reliance on word-level node representations. In contrast, we propose a GNN approach to topic modelling that models each *turn of talk* as a separate node in the graph. This provides a more data-rich representation while preserving the coherence of the original segments of discourse.

2.4 Topic Interpretation

Topic modelling (via LDA or GNNs) has two primary outputs—topic proportion scores which show the distribution of topics within each document—and the topics themselves, which are represented as groups of terms ranked by highest probability of association with the topic. Typically, the top N terms from the latter are used for interpretation. However, prior work in the QE field has suggested that interpreting topics can be difficult. For example, Bakharia [2] found that specific domain-knowledge is critical to identifying fine-grained topics. Relatedly, Cai and colleagues [6] found that the top terms of a single topic can contain terms from multiple human-generated [C]odes and terms from human-generated [C]odes can appear as high-probability terms in multiple topics. This mixing can make interpretation difficult.

To address this issue, our method supplies topic modelling output to *generative AI* (GAI) to produce natural language interpretations. GAI are deep learning models that can produce human-like art, computer code, and text. Arguably the most well know GAI, ChatGPT, allows users to interact with the model via a simple chat interface—users *prompt* ChatGPT with natural language text and the tool responds in a conversational way [15]. Our method integrates the list of top terms for each topic into a *contextualised prompt* that asks ChatGPT for interpretations in the form of a short title and descriptive summary—in other words a potential name and definition for a [C]ode.

2.5   Research Question

Three prior studies have explored topic modelling via LDA for [C]ode discovery in the context of QE [2, 6, 19]. Each study compared [C]odes discovered by LDA-based models to [C]odes derived by human researchers. We extend this work by (a) proposing a novel method for [C]ode discovery that leverages GNNs and GAI and (b) comparing the results of this approach to those of an LDA-based method, as well as manually derived [C]odes. The following research question guided our work:

> How does a GNN-based topic modelling approach compare to an LDA-based approach for suggesting [C]odes in the context of a QE analysis?

The goal of the present study was to compare the [C]odes discovered by the LDA and GNN approaches in terms of the names and definitions suggested by applying generative AI to their outputs. As a check on the plausibility of these names and definitions, we compared them to the names and definitions of manually derived [C]odes for the same dataset. The goal was not check whether the LDA or GNN based methods could *reproduce* the manually derived [C]odes, but instead to use the manual [C]odes as another data point from which to qualitatively understand the plausibility of the automatically discovered [C]odes.

3   Methods

3.1   Dataset

We trained topic models using a dataset consisting of the transcribed conversations of teams participating in a collaborative sensemaking task. These data are representative of typical data used in QE analyses that contain turns of talk from a collaborative setting. Participant teams were divided into two conditions: one in which they completed the task using a novel virtual-reality (VR) environment and another in which they completed the task using a standard web interface.

Teams completed two sensemaking tasks as part of the study. Both tasks involved solving a mystery in which each participant was provided with a separate set of clues that they needed to share with their teammates. One task focused on solving a murder; the other focused on identifying who robbed a bank. Participants used their unique clues to create virtual concepts to help them solve the mysteries.

Data was collected by recording and transcribing participants speech during the tasks. For analysis, the data was segmented by turn of talk. The dataset includes 6,180 turns of talk, from eight teams and ten individuals. As part of an ongoing analysis, these data were coded for topics based in part on Toulmin's classification scheme for arguments [26]. This scheme comprises seven distinct [C]odes: INFORMATION, STRATEGY, QUERY, CLAIM, GROUNDS, ORGANISATION, AND SOCIAL. Definitions and examples for these codes are provided in the codebook below (Table 1).

Table 1. Table of manually derived [C]odes, definitions, and examples from an ongoing QE analysis. Participant names have been replaced with [name] to maintain anonymity.

Name	Definition	Example
Information	Sharing information provided in the clues	After the murder and she frequently left the building
Strategy	Proposing methods for solving the mystery	Let's try to find some common stuff
Query	Asking question	OK, can you explain your rationale?
Claim	Making conclusions	So this Mr. Jones shot Mr. Kelley then. At 12 midnight
Grounds	Providing evidence for conclusions	Like it would have had to take the 7:00 AM flight up to the town at the bank town if you wanted to go back right? Which means he probably didn't do the robbery
Organisation	Structural features of the concept map	I'll put it on the top
Social	Asking for help or referring to teammates by name	OK, so [name] you have put in quite a few new things you wanna walk us through

3.2   Pre-processing

We pre-processed the transcripts by tokenising them into words using the *nltk* package in Python [3].[3] In many NLP tasks, it is typical to remove *stopwords* from the text prior to further analysis. The goal is to remove words—typically commonly used words like articles—that are likely to be unimportant to the analysis. However, as we were conducting our analysis from the perspective of researchers who are coming to the data without a specific coding scheme in mind, we opted to not remove stopwords as this could remove potentially important words for this specific dataset.

3.3   Topic Modelling (LDA)

Topic modelling via LDA assumes a generative model that represents documents as mixtures of topics and topics as mixtures of terms. For example[4], we might obtain the following representations from the model:

- Sentences 1 and 2: 100% Topic A
- Sentence 5: 60% Topic A, 40% Topic B
- Topic A: 30% broccoli, 15% bananas, 10% breakfast, 10% munching, ...
- Topic B: 20% chinchillas, 20% kittens, 20% cute, 15% hamster, ...

Topics are interpreted by looking for commonalities in their associated terms. For example, Topic A above may be interpreted as being about food, while Topic B may be interpreted as being about cute animals.

To produce these kinds of results, LDA uses an iterative process that begins by randomly assigning each term in each document to one of K topics, producing an initial distribution of topics and terms like the example above. Next, the method goes through each term in each document for each topic and updates its current topic assignment based on (a) the proportion of terms in the document currently assigned to the topic and (b) the proportion of assignments to the topic that come from that term. This process is repeated a large number of times until stable topic and term distributions are obtained.

To implement topic modelling via LDA, we used the *LatentDirichletAllocation* function from the *sklearn* package in Python [17]. We selected seven topics—to align with the number of manually derived [C]odes described above—and used the ten terms with the highest probabilities to represent each topic. Rather than considering individual words as terms, we used bigrams and trigrams (combinations of two or three words) to provide a richer topic representation.

---

[3] We conducted all experiments using a Mac computer equipped with an M1 Pro chip, a 10-core CPU, 32-core GPU, and 64GB of unified memory and GPU acceleration powered by Nvidia RTX 3090Ti.

[4] Example adapted from Edwin Chen's blog [7].

3.4   Topic Modelling (GNN)

A full account of GNN training is beyond the scope of this paper. However, we briefly outline the steps below. For a more detailed description of GNN implementation, see [11, 27].

Training a GNN requires defining the nodes and edges of the graph. Here, we defined each turn of talk in the data as a separate node. One advantage of the GNN method is that it affords the inclusion additional features for each node of the graph. For our GNN approach, we included two kinds of features. The first was a vector that contained the TF-IDF scores for each word in the turn of talk. TF-IDF is a commonly used NLP metric that multiplies the term frequency—defined as the number of times the term appears in the turn of talk—by the inverse document frequency, a value that represents the number of turns of talk that word appears in [1, 18].[5]

The second kind of node feature we used was a binary value that distinguished between turns of talk from participants in the web-interface condition vs. the VR condition. We scaled this binary feature, assigning a value of 0 to web-interface participants users and a value of 10 to VR participants, to increase the importance of the condition variable, prompting the GNN to pay greater attention to it. By integrating this information, the GNN is able to learn node embeddings that capture not only the relationships between nodes and graph structure, but also the context of the experimental conditions.[6]

To define the edges of the graph structure, we computed the semantic similarity between turns of talk using cosine similarity between their TF-IDF vectors. After applying a threshold to the results, we created an adjacency matrix whose cell values were 0 if the corresponding turns of talk had a cosine similarity less than 0.1 and 1 if the cosine similarity was greater than 0.1.

Next, we specified our particular GNN architecture, which defines the message passing scheme, the number of layers in the GNN, and the various activation functions that introduce non-linearity into the model. We used both a GCN and GAT message passing scheme, along with 32 layers. For more details, see our analysis code here.

To train the GNN model, we used the *PyTorch* package in Python [16]. The GNN model was trained over 1000 epochs, or runs, in an unsupervised manner using a modified version of Velickovic's graph contrastive loss function [28]. The goal of this process is to learn similar embeddings for connected pairs of nodes and dissimilar embeddings for unconnected pairs of nodes.

The upshot of the above process is an embedding vector for each node in the graph—that is, each turn of talk in the data. These node embeddings contain

---

[5] Frequent terms in a turn of talk that are rare in the dataset overall will have higher TF-IDF scores. This feature vector thus describes the "originality" of the words in each turn of talk.

[6] In our study, the VR/Desktop condition was excluded from the LDA approach to highlight the flexibility of the GNN approach—which naturally accommodates the inclusion of contextual information—over the vanilla LDA approach.

the information about the node itself, neighboring nodes, graph structure, and the experimental condition from which the turns of talk were produced.

To identify topics based on these node embeddings, we used the k-means algorithm implemented in the Python package *sklearn* [17] to group the node embeddings into seven clusters. k-means is an unsupervised learning algorithm used to cluster data points into k distinct groups based on their similarity in the feature space [8,10]. We extracted the top ten terms from each cluster by averaging the the TF-IDF vectors associated with the cluster and taking the ten elements (which correspond to particular terms) with the largest magnitude. In other words, this process produced a list of the 10 most "original" words in each of the clusters that were identified via the combination of GNN embedding and k-means clustering.

3.5   Generative AI Prompting

The outcome of both the LDA and GNN-based topic modelling approaches was a set of seven topics and their top 10 associated terms (14 total topics and 70 total terms). We engineered a prompt that provided contextual information on the data source and the list of topic key-terms and asked *ChatGPT* to summarise the theme for each topic in one to two sentences and give the theme a short descriptive title. Specifically, the prompt was as follows:

> The keywords and phrases provided below were generated from the transcripts of people participating in two mystery games. Their goal was to solve the mystery and justify their decisions. Some people tried to solve the mystery in a desktop environment, while others used a virtual reality environment. People constructed virtual concept maps to help them solve the mysteries. One mystery focused on the murder of Mr. Kelley. Possible suspects include Mr. Kelley's wife, Mr. Scott, Mr. Jones, the elevator man, and Miss Smith. Possible weapons included a knife or a gun. Important locations included Mr. Scott's apartment, Mr. Jones' apartment, Mr. Scott's car, a park, and Miss Smith's yard. The other mystery focused on the robbery of the First National Bank of Minnetonka. Suspects included Margaret Ellington, Albert Greenbags, the janitor, Elwood Smith, Howard Ellington, a hippie, Dirsey Flowers, Anastasia Wallflower, and the bank president. Important items included the key to the bank vault and dynamite. Important locations included a construction company, the airport, Mexico City, Dogwalk, Birdwatch, and Minnetonka.
> Given the following keywords and phrases:
>
> *[insert keywords & phrases]*
>
> summarize the key theme for each topic they suggest in 1 to 2 sentences and give the theme a short descriptive title.

We manually entered the prompts into the subscription version *ChatGPT* powered by GPT-4 [15], replacing the topics and key-terms as needed. Each prompted was entered as a separate conversation to avoid cross contamination with ChatGPT's "memory" of prior promps. We repeated this process several times to ensure that the outputs were consistent.

3.6 Qualitative Analysis

We qualitatively compared the key-terms and topic interpretations discovered [C]odes produced by the LDA and GNN methods, looking for similarities and differences between the two. In addition, we compared the names and definitions of the discovered [C]odes to the actual qualitative [C]odes developed for these data to determine whether there was any overlap between the automated and manual methods.

4 Results

4.1 Data Context

As described above, the dataset contained turns of talk from two sub-populations, those who solved the task in the VR condition and those who solved the task in the web-interface condition. In the VR condition, teams operated avatars within a confined virtual space and could collaboratively create a 3-D concept map of clues by placing notes in the space and connecting them via edges. In the web-interface condition, teams used an online collaborative platform, similar in functionality to *Miro* boards [13], to make 2-D concept maps of the clues.

The two mysteries—murder and robbery—had distinct sets of clues and each team member was given a unique set of clues that they needed to share with their teammates. Clues in the murder mystery included information about the murder victim, Mr. Kelley, suspects—e.g., Mr. Jones, Miss Smith, Mr. Scott— important locations and times—e.g., Miss Smith's yard, a park, Mr. Scott's apartment, 1:30 am—actions—e.g., the body had been dragged a long distance—and material evidence—e.g., a knife, a bullet. Clues in the robbery mystery included information about suspects—e.g, Margaret Ellington, Elwood Smith, Albert Greenbags, a hippie—locations and times—e.g., Minnetonka, 5 pm on Thursday, flight arrival times—actions—e.g., borrowing a key, stealing dynamite—and objects— e.g., key to the bank door, key to the vault, dynamite.

4.2 LDA [C]odes

The second column in Table 2 shows the ten highest probability terms for each topic from LDA; the last two columns show the [C]ode names and definitions generated by ChatGPT. Across the topics, the top terms identified by LDA relate to clue-specific content from the two mysteries. For example, Topic 0 includes the terms "howard ellington" and "bank" and Topic 1 references terms related to Mr. Scott, his apartment, and Mr. Kelley's wife. The majority of the topics (0, 1, 3, 5, and 6) refer to a mix of suspects in the two mysteries, their roles, and particular locations. Topic 2 refers exclusively to Margaret Ellington and the key to the front door. Topic 4 refers to the knife—a potential murder weapon—and an "arrival time"—presumably referring to the arrival time of flights mentioned in the bank robbery clues. With the exception of Topics 4—which references a

Table 2. Table of terms, [C]odes and definitions identified by LDA + ChatGPT.

Topic	Top Terms	Name	Definition
0	i have, howard ellington, i think, went to, the bank, and then, i see, at the, in the, it a	Bank Visit and Howard Ellington	This topic is focused on a visit to the bank and the presence of Howard Ellington. The speaker mentions seeing something in the bank
1	scott apartment, went to, to scott, kelley wife, went to scott, to scott apartment, kelley went to, kelley went, so what, jones apartment	Kelley's Visit to Scott's Apartment	This topic is focused on Mr. Kelley's visit to Mr. Scott's apartment and his wife's presence. Mr. Jones' apartment is also mentioned
2	the front, front door, the front door, the key, key to, key to the, to the, the key to, to the front, margaret ellington	Key to the Front Door	This topic is focused on the key to the front door of a location, possibly the bank. Margaret Ellington is also mentioned
3	elwood smith, i do, no, is the, in charge, we can, the janitor, no i, in charge of, charge of	Elwood Smith and Janitorial Duties	This topic is focused on Elwood Smith and his role as a janitor. The speaker mentions not knowing something and the possibility of someone else being in charge
4	this is, so it, thank you, the knife, so the, is it, i have, the murder, arrival time, but then	The Murder Weapon and Arrival Time	This topic is focused on the murder weapon, possibly a knife, and the arrival time of someone. The speaker mentions having information
5	this one, wa found, albert greenbags, the president, the park, in the, wednesday afternoon, anything else, i think, is the	Albert Greenbags and the Park	This topic is focused on the discovery of something in the park, possibly a body. Albert Greenbags and the bank president are also mentioned
6	miss smith, i think, hold on, the building, left the, left the building, i have, so jones, out of, frequently left the	Miss Smith and Frequent Departures	This topic is focused on Miss Smith and her frequent departures from a building. Mr. Jones is also mentioned

weapon from the murder mystery and the arrival time of a plane—and Topic 5, which mentions a suspect from the robbery (Albert Greenbags) and a location from the murder mystery (the park)—all of the topics refer to clues exclusive to either mystery.

Examining the [C]ode names and descriptions derived from ChatGPT, they appear to be consistent with the key terms suggested by LDA; each topic name and description references elements corresponding directly to terms in the topic. For example, for Topic 1, "Bank Visit and Howard Ellington" corresponds directly to the "howard ellington", "went to", and "the bank". However, the interpretations provided by ChatGPT are piece-meal in the sense that they do not offer an overarching summary of the terms in the topic—instead they interpret specific pieces and then paste them together. For example, Topic 3, which includes terms related to the front door, a key, and Margaret Ellington is defined as "This topic is focused on the key to the front door of a location, possibly the bank. Margaret Ellington is also mentioned". Here, there is no attempt to link Margaret Ellington to the key to the front door—for example, by suggesting that she is the one who had it or used it. Together, these results suggest that the combination LDA and ChatGPT suggested [C]odes focused on *mystery-specific content*.

4.3   GNN [C]odes

Table 3. Table of terms, [C]odes and definitions identified by GNN + ChatGPT. Participant names have been replaced with [name] to protect their privacy.

Topic	Top Terms	Name	Definition
0	i think, miss smith, i have, elwood smith, the key, this one, to the, i do, is the, this is	Sharing Opinions and Suspicions	This theme revolves around participants expressing their thoughts and suspicions about the mysteries, focusing on key suspects like Miss Smith and Elwood Smith
1	crime analyst, it am, no hello, the unit, uhm so, i gone, so apartment, appeared once, sorry [name], wordsmith and	Analyzing Clues and Seeking Assistance	The theme involves participants discussing the role of crime analysts, searching for clues, and seeking assistance to better understand the mysteries
2	he inaudible, look there, eleven pm, when sorry, i bullet, and paper, there was nothing, was nothing, just keep together, keep together	Investigating Details and Uncertainty	This theme focuses on participants examining specific details, such as timestamps and evidence, while expressing uncertainty about various aspects of the mysteries
3	scott, wait i, shui yuwei, bird watch, seeing examiner, smith wait, margarita please, another extension, who jone, jones outside	Deliberating on Suspects and Connections	Participants discuss key suspects like Scott and Jones, as well as exploring connections and possible motives in the mysteries
4	it went, [name] please, without making, remove program, something made, another connection, kelley hmmm, or should, look fine, hippie definitely	Problem Solving and Evidence Evaluation	The theme revolves around participants working through the mysteries, evaluating evidence, and considering various connections and possibilities
5	spritz is, change size up, up your panel, up your, spritz is to, inform same, your panel, same size, this spritz is, this spritz	Adjusting Visual Tools and Strategies	This theme involves participants discussing ways to adjust and manipulate their virtual concept maps, using tools like "spritz" to change the size of their panels
6	cut [name], this card, make this card, you take margaret, you take, cheating business there, name silent, silent anything, greenberg green greenberg, with blood	Uncovering Hidden Information and Relationships	The focus is on participants uncovering hidden information, such as secret relationships, and connecting it to the mysteries, while discussing potential motives and actions of key suspects

The second column of Table 3 shows the ten most significant terms for each topic as identified by GNN; the [C]ode names and definitions provided by Chat-GPT are in the second two columns. Compared to the key terms identified by

LDA method, the terms suggested by GNN are less straightforward to interpret. Across topics, there is comparatively less of a focus on mystery-specific clues, though they do appear throughout the topics—for example, Topic 0 references Miss Smith, Elwood Smith, and the key; Topic 3 references Mr. Scott, Birdwatch park, Miss Smith, and Mr. Jones. Instead, there is more of a focus on action-oriented words and phrases—for example, "i think" (Topic 1), "look here" (Topic 2), "wait i", (Topic 3), "something made" (Topic 4), "change size up" (Topic 5), and "make this card" (Topic 6).

The [C]ode names and descriptions provided by ChatGPT support this distinction between clues and actions—each [C]ode name includes an action oriented word or phrase—sharing, analysing, investigating, deliberating, problem solving and evaluation, adjusting, uncovering. The relationship between the interpretations and the key terms is straight forward in some cases. Topic 0, for example includes the terms "i think" and "i have" which correspond to "Sharing Opinions". Similarly, Topic 5, includes the terms "change size up", "up your panel", and "same size" which refer to the panels participants used in their respective interfaces to group clues and correspond to "Adjusting Visual Tools and Strategies". However, the relationships between the terms if less clear in other cases. For example, it is not clear which terms are related to "Seeking Assistance" in Topic 1 or which terms suggest "motives" in Topic 3. Taken together, the results suggested by the combination of GNN and ChatGPT do not appear focused on particular clues or classes of clues, but instead they focus on *mystery-solving processes*.

4.4   Comparison to Manually Derived [C]odes

Section 3.1 includes the manually derived [C]odes applied to this dataset as part of an ongoing analysis. Broadly, these codes focus on elements of argument as defined in Toulmin's framework [26]—CLAIM, GROUNDS—process-related concepts—INFORMATION, STRATEGY, QUERY, ORGANISATION—and social references—SOCIAL.

Compared to the [C]odes discovered via LDA, there is little conceptual overlap. All of the [C]odes suggested by LDA refer to mystery-specific content. The only manually derived [C]ode related explicitly to the content of the clues is INFORMATION, which has to do with sharing information provided in the clues. There is slightly more conceptual overlap compared to the [C]odes discovered via GNN. "Sharing Opinions and Suspicions" corresponds closely with INFORMATION and "Adjusting Visual Tools and Strategies" aligns with ORGANISATION, which has to do with organising and refining their virtual concept maps. The rest of the manually derived [C]odes have no obvious corollaries with the automatically discovered [C]odes.

5   Discussion and Conclusions

In this paper, we presented a novel automated method for [C]ode discovery in the context of a QE analysis. Our data came from a representative QE study that examined the conversations of teams solving mysteries in different virtual environments. Our method combines topic modelling via GNNs with interpretation via ChatGPT. Comparing our method to an approach that combines topic modelling via LDA and ChatGPT, we found that the GNN-based approach discovered [C]odes—more specifically, the names and definitions of [C]odes—related to mystery-solving *processes* while the LDA approach discovered [C]odes related to mystery-specific *content*. The LDA approach produced one [C]ode that overlapped clearly with manually derived [C]odes, while the GNN approach produced two.

Our results suggest that the computational differences between LDA and GNNs—namely that GNNs (a) capture non-linear relationships; (b) accommodate denser information via node features; and (c) account for interdependencies between terms—are related to a content vs. process distinction. Further exploration is needed to understand why this might be the case; however, this task will likely remain difficult given the opaque nature of deep learning techniques. It may be though, that for the purpose of [C]ode discovery, explainability is not a necessary condition. When trying to determine a reasonable starting place for coding the data, the plausibility of the suggested [C]ode—which can be readily verified with a suitable understanding of the context of the data at hand—seems more important than explainability. However, when the researcher transitions to *applying* the [C]ode to the data explainability increases in importance because they need to verify whether the [C]ode has been applied reliably and make well-informed decisions to improve that reliability. The question of the reliability of the coding process is beyond the scope of this paper.

For now, we can say that our results align with previous findings from Bakharia [2], which found that domain knowledge was crucial to interpreting [C]odes suggested by LDA-based topic models. In this study, the [C]odes suggested by LDA were highly domain specific. In contrast, the [C]odes suggested by GNNs were less domain-specific, focusing instead on broader actions and processes related to the context. These findings suggest that the GNN approach may be more desirable when researchers want to move beyond highly domain-specific content. Furthermore, our results suggest that GAI like ChatGPT are a useful tool for interpreting the output of topic models. Given a relatively small amount of context about the data and input about the topics (only ten terms), ChatGPT was able to produce sensible [C]ode names and definitions in most cases. Future work should explore other applications of GAI to automated coding given these encouraging results.

Our study has several limitations. First, it is not possible, in general, to say whether the LDA or the GNN-based approach discovered "better" [C]odes. Indeed, neither the automatically discovered [C]odes nor the manually derived [C]odes can be said to be the "best" [C]odes for the data. There is no such thing as a best set of [C]odes, only those that are more useful for some purposes rather than others. Our results suggest that if one is interested in content-related ideas, the LDA approach may suggest some useful options. Similarly, if one is interested in process-related ideas, then the GNN approach may be the way to go. More generally, the results suggest that the combination of topic-modelling and generative AI can discover plausible [C]ode names and definitions that could jump-start a QE analysis. This plausibility is supported by the face validity of the names and definitions suggested in relation to the context of the data and that some (albeit few) of the names and definitions conceptually overlap with the [C]odes identified by human researchers.

Second—although not reported above—we found that the GNN approach, being more computationally intensive, took longer to complete model training compared to the LDA approach. In our experiments, the GNN model took roughly six minutes to complete, while the LDA model took roughly 30 s. Using more sophisticated hardware, we were able to reduce the GNN training time to approximately 15 s. This highlights the tradeoff between computational complexity and training time. Future work should explore whether the difference in [C]odes produced is worth the increased computational time.

Third, our method is not a complete end-to-end automated system. Currently, it requires the contextualised prompt to be manually entered into the ChatGPT online interface. Future work will explore extending the method to communicate with ChatGPT or similar GAI automatically via existing APIs. It may also be possible to integrate the method into tools for automated coding such as current and future versions of the *nCoder* [12].

Fourth, we only tested our method with one dataset. Future work will need to test the generalisability of findings using data from other contexts.

Finally, GAI like ChatGPT are inherently stochastic meaning that they may generate different outputs given the same inputs. To mitigate this issue, we provided a fixed contextualised prompt and repeated the prompting process several times to verify consistency. However, future work will be needed to more systematically verify the consistency of [C]ode discovery dependent on GAI. Potential approaches include repeating the prompting phase a large number of times and verifying that the outputs are semantically similar within some tolerance threshold before providing the results to human users.

Despite these limitations, this preliminary study suggests that the combination of GNNs and GAI is a potentially useful tool for [C]ode discovery in the context of QE. The method addresses several computational limitations of LDA for text analysis, while providing a solution to the well known problem of topic interpretation. Our results suggest that the method may be particularly useful in situations where process related [C]odes are desired over content-related [C]odes.

References

1. Aizawa, A.: An information-theoretic perspective of TF-IDF measures. Inf. Process. Manage. **39**(1), 45–65 (2003)
2. Bakharia, A.: On the equivalence of inductive content analysis and topic modeling. In: Eagan, B., Misfeldt, M., Siebert-Evenstone, A. (eds.) ICQE 2019. CCIS, vol. 1112, pp. 291–298. Springer, Cham (2019). https://doi.org/10.1007/978-3-030-33232-7_25

3. Bird, S., Klein, E., Loper, E.: Natural Language Processing with Python: Analyzing Text with the Natural Language Toolkit. O'Reilly Media, Inc. (2009)
4. Blei, D.M., Ng, A.Y., Jordan, M.I.: Latent Dirichlet allocation. J. Mach. Learn. Res. **3**(Jan), 993–1022 (2003)
5. Cai, Z., Eagan, B., Dowell, N., Pennebaker, J., Shaffer, D., Graesser, A.: Epistemic network analysis and topic modeling for chat data from collaborative learning environment. In: Proceedings of the 10th International Conference on Educational Data Mining (2017)
6. Cai, Z., Siebert-Evenstone, A., Eagan, B., Shaffer, D.W.: Using topic modeling for code discovery in large scale text data. In: Ruis, A.R., Lee, S.B. (eds.) ICQE 2021. CCIS, vol. 1312, pp. 18–31. Springer, Cham (2021). https://doi.org/10.1007/978-3-030-67788-6_2
7. Chen, E.: Introduction to latent Dirichlet allocation (2011). http://blog.echen.me/2011/08/22/introduction-to-latent-dirichlet-allocation/. Accessed 8 May 2023
8. Hamerly, G., Elkan, C.: Learning the k in k-means. In: Advances in Neural Information Processing Systems, vol. 16 (2003)
9. Hamilton, W., Ying, Z., Leskovec, J.: Inductive representation learning on large graphs. In: Advances in Neural Information Processing Systems, vol. 30 (2017)
10. Hartigan, J.A., Wong, M.A.: Algorithm as 136: a k-means clustering algorithm. J. Roy. Stat. Soc. Ser. C (Appl. Stat.) **28**(1), 100–108 (1979
11. Kipf, T.N., Welling, M.: Semi-supervised classification with graph convolutional networks. arXiv preprint arXiv:1609.02907 (2016)
12. Marquart, C.L., Swiecki, Z., Eagan, B., Shaffer, D.W.:. ncodeR: techniques for automated classifiers. R package version 0.1. 2 (2018)
13. Miro (2023). https://miro.com/
14. Nadal, K.L.: The brown Asian American movement: advocating for south Asian, southeast Asian, and Filipino American communities. Studies **9**(10), 11 (2019)
15. OpenAI. GPT-4 technical report (2023)
16. Paszke, A., et al.: PyTorch: an imperative style, high-performance deep learning library. In: Advances in Neural Information Processing Systems, vol. 32 (2019)
17. Pedregosa, F., et al.: Scikit-learn: machine learning in python. J. Mach. Learn. Res. **12**, 2825–2830 (2011)
18. Ramos, J, et al.: Using TF-IDF to determine word relevance in document queries. In: Proceedings of the First Instructional Conference on Machine Learning, vol. 242, pp. 29–48. Citeseer (2003)
19. Saravani, S.M., Ghaffari, S., Luther, Y., Folkestad, J., Moraes, M.: Automated code extraction from discussion board text dataset. In: Damşa, C., Barany, A. (eds.) ICQE 2022. CCIS, vol. 1785, pp. 227–238. Springer, Cham (2023). https://doi.org/10.1007/978-3-031-31726-2_16
20. Scarselli, F., Gori, M., Tsoi, A.C., Hagenbuchner, M., Monfardini, G.: The graph neural network model. IEEE Trans. Neural Netw. **20**(1), 61–80 (2008)
21. Shaffer, D.W.: Quantitative ethnography (2017). Lulu.com
22. Shaffer, D.W., Ruis, A.R.: How we code. In: Ruis, A.R., Lee, S.B. (eds.) ICQE 2021. CCIS, vol. 1312, pp. 62–77. Springer, Cham (2021). https://doi.org/10.1007/978-3-030-67788-6_5
23. Shen, D., Qin, C., Wang, C., Dong, Z., Zhu, H., Xiong, H.: Topic modeling revisited: a document graph-based neural network perspective. In: Advances in Neural Information Processing Systems, vol. 34, pp. 14681–14693 (2021)
24. Sun, J., Barany, A.: Epistemic network analysis on Asian American college access literature. In: Fourth International Conference on Quantitative Ethnography: Conference Proceedings Supplement, pp. 133–136 (2022)

25. Swiecki, Z., Ruis, A.R., Farrell, C., Shaffer, D.W.: Assessing individual contributions to collaborative problem solving: a network analysis approach. Comput. Hum. Behav. **104**, 105876 (2020)
26. Toulmin, S.E.: The Uses of Argument. Cambridge University Press, Cambridge (2003)
27. Velickovic, P., et al.: Graph attention networks. Stat **1050**(20), 10–48550 (2017)
28. Veličković, P., Fedus, W., Hamilton, W.L., Liò, P., Bengio, Y., Hjelm, R.D.: Deep graph infomax. arXiv preprint arXiv:1809.10341 (2018)
29. Wu, L., et al.: Graph neural networks for natural language processing: a survey. Found. Trends® Mach. Learn. **16**(2), 119–328 (2023)
30. Xu, K., Hu, W., Leskovec, J., Jegelka, S.: How powerful are graph neural networks? arXiv preprint arXiv:1810.00826 (2018)
31. Yang, L., et al.: Graph attention topic modeling network. In: 2020 Proceedings of The Web Conference, pp. 144–154 (2020)
32. Zhou, D., Hu, X., Wang, R.: Neural topic modeling by incorporating document relationship graph. arXiv preprint arXiv:2009.13972 (2020)
33. Zhu, Q., Feng, Z., Li, X.: GraphBTM: graph enhanced autoencoded variational inference for biterm topic model. In: Proceedings of the 2018 Conference on Empirical Methods in Natural Language Processing, pp. 4663–4672 (2018)

A Lightweight Interactive Regular Expression Generator for Qualitative Coding in Quantitative Ethnography

Zhiqiang Cai(✉) ⓘ, Cody Marquart ⓘ, Brendan Eagan ⓘ, Yaxuan Xiao ⓘ,
and David Williamson Shaffer ⓘ

University of Wisconsin-Madison, Madison, USA
{zhiqiang.cai,cody.marquart,beagan,xiao97}@wisc.edu,
dws@education.wisc.edu

Abstract. Quantitative ethnography approaches are often used to analyze large scale qualitative data. Manually coding such data is expensive and time consuming, if not impractical or impossible. In contrast, machine learning algorithms can code virtually unlimited amounts of data once a model has been created. However, machine learning approaches lack transparency and rely on large amount of training data. An alternative automated coding approach using regular expressions has the advantage of minimizing required training data while providing transparency. However, manually creating regular expressions during the coding process can be a very challenging task for many researchers. One potential solution to this challenge is automatic regular expression generation. Unfortunately, existing algorithms are all based on large pre-coded training data which is often unavailable in quantitative ethnography tasks. In this paper, we present a lightweight and interactive algorithm that actively constructs regular expression-based coding classifiers with the researcher. We use a simulation on an education data to show that the proposed algorithm is promising.

Keywords: Regular expression generation · Active learning · Qualitative coding · Automatic coding tool

1 Introduction

As Shaffer and Ruis explained, qualitative coding is a process of "defining concepts and identifying where they occur" [12, 13]. Traditionally, coding has been a manual process that is time consuming and often inaccurate when used on large scale qualitative data because humans have difficulty maintaining coding consistency [5, 6, 10]. Machine learning based coding is fast but often requires a large number of training items and the processes lack transparency [7].

© The Author(s), under exclusive license to Springer Nature Switzerland AG 2023
G. Arastoopour Irgens and S. Knight (Eds.): ICQE 2023, CCIS 1895, pp. 455–469, 2023.
https://doi.org/10.1007/978-3-031-47014-1_31

Regular expressions (Regexes) are widely used in representing text patterns. A regex is a sequence of characters that represents a text pattern. For example, we may use the regex, "\S+@\S+" to approximately represent an email address, where "\S" means "any nonwhitespace character; "+" means "to repeat the previous item (nonwhitespace character, in this example) one or more times". Thus, this regex refers to a string that contains the character "@", preceded and followed by one or more nonwhitespace characters.

When used for qualitative coding, most regexes can be thought of as compact representations of keywords or key phrases. For example, "\beducat" represents any word starting with "educat", where "\b" means "word boundary". Thus, "\beducat" represents the word "educate" and its derived forms, such as "educates", "educating", "educated", "education", and "educations". Similarly, the regex "\bmath teach" may represent the phrases such as "math teaching", "math teacher" or "math teachers". Of course, more complicated keyword combinations can be composed. For example, "\bcould.{0,5}\bmeet\b" represents the word "could" before the word "meet" separated by any character string with length from 0 to 5. In this case, it matches phrases like "could meet", "couldn't meet" and "could not meet".

Regex-based coding has several advantages over manual and machine learning approaches. First, it is more efficient than manual coding, because once a valid regex-based classifier is constructed, all data can be coded automatically. Second, humans can more easily maintain coding consistency by building regexes. Third, regex coding provides transparency because it can indicate exactly where a code is being identified in a given segment of text data [3–5]. There are some situations that a code cannot be fully represented by a regex. For example, when a pronoun refers to different antecedents or keywords, the regex may fail. Also, when coding is heavily context-dependent or relies on context from other segments of data, it is often more complicated to capture with regex-based coding. The degree to which all qualitative coding of text data can be accomplished using a regex-based approach is an interesting topic but beyond the scope of this paper. This paper tries to solve a simpler problem: suppose that a code can be identified by regex, can the regex be automatically generated with acceptable efficiency and accuracy? While regexes could be in very complicated forms, we only consider a few very basic forms so that the computation is fast enough for quick interaction with the researcher. It is in this sense we call our method "lightweight". Also, we don't assume that our generator can work alone. It is supposed to be used in an "interactive" process to co-generate regexes with the researcher.

2   Related Work

There have been various approaches to automated regex generation and two of these are relevant to our study. Bartoli et al. proposed an active learning algorithm [1] to generate regexes for entity extraction tasks (e.g., identifying email, author, user name, date, time, etc.). Entity extraction is to identify whether or not a text string is of a specific form. For example, an email is a text string with one or more characters before and after the symbol "@", roughly speaking. In coding, regexes are mainly constructed at word level, or more technically speaking, "token" level, although specific entities may be involved sometimes.

For example, "clean water" may be used to construct a regex for the code "environment issues". So, while regexes represent specific "forms" in entity extraction, they represent specific "meanings" in coding.

In a different approach, Li et al. used regexes as attentive rules in combination with a neural network model to provide a transparent classification of medical texts. They used a bi-directional Long Short-Term Memory (LSTM) neural network model with an attention layer that allows the network to identify keywords for regex construction. The regexes generated by Li et al. include positive keywords and negative keywords, "and" (represented by ".*"), "or" (represented by "|"), and adjacency (represented by ".a, b", where a and b are the minimum (a) and maximum (b) number of characters that may occur between two tokens). Their algorithm could be used to construct coding regexes in the general domain. However, their work is a heavy supervised learning algorithm, which relies on large amount of pre-coded data [11].

3 Our Approach

We are taking a different approach to automatically generating token based regexes using an active learning model. In this section, we first describe four basic regex forms used in our algorithm, followed by the types of user input allowed in our process. We then describe our algorithm, mostly as a conflict resolution process or a way of addressing coding disagreements between the human and the classifier, and present our research questions used to assess the performance of our approach.

3.1 Four Basic Forms of Regex

In this paper, we only consider four basic types of regexes that take the following forms: 1) n-gram; 2) ordered pair; 3) token with negation; and 4) pair with negation. In this paper, we use "positive" to indicate an item that a code occurs and "negative" to indicate an item that the code doesn't occur.

n-gram. A regex representing an n-gram is in the form "\b$A_1$ A_2 ... A_n\b", where "A_i" is a token, and "\b" represents token boundary. We can consider removing the boundary at the end of the regex so that it can automatically include word derivatives. However, doing so may also introduce false positives in our coding – the classifier may match on words it should not. For example, "\bwe" is supposed to match the word "we". Without the end boundary, it also matches words like "wet", "weat", "weather", and more. It requires more complex natural language processing to correctly represent word derivatives. Since our purpose is to build a "lightweight" regex generator, we included the boundary on both sides of the n-gram so that heavier language processing approach is not needed.

Ordered Pair. A regex representing an ordered pair with a specific range of adjacency is in the form "\b$A_1$\b.{a, b}\b$A_2$\b", where $a \leq b$ represents the range of the number of characters between tokens A_1 and A_2. In our algorithm, we always set $a = 0$ and optimally choose b to be 5, 10, 15, or 20. While other values are certainly possible, we only use these numbers of characters to avoid a long optimization time.

Token with Negation. This form is used to match a token A under the condition that another token B is absent. The regex is in the form "^(?!.*(\bB\b)).*(\bA\b)". For example, if we want to match the word "bank" only when "river" is absent, we use the regex "^(?!.*(\briver\b)).*(\bbank\b)".

Pair with Negation. This last form is used to match an ordered pair of tokens A_1 and A_2 with any adjacency, under the condition that another token B is absent. It is in the form "^(?!.*(\bB\b)).*(\bA_1\b.*\bA_2\b)". For example, if we want to match the word pair "fire" and "gun" under the condition that "game" is absent, we may use the regex "^(?!.*(\bgame\b)).*(\bfire\b.*\bgun\b)"

These four basic forms can be combined using the alternation operator "|" to represent more complex regexes. For clarity, in this paper, we always use regex lists to represent a regex-based code classifier, instead of a single combined regex. That is, when we talk about a regex list of a code, we mean that items in the list will be combined by "|" when it is used for coding data.

3.2 User's Input

To construct our active learning algorithms, we assume that the regexes are co-generated by a human user and a computer in an iterative process, in which the user provides input using the following actions in each iteration:

1. rating a given excerpt (positive or negative);
2. accepting or rejecting a basic form of regex suggested by the computer;
3. revising an existing regex in the list if it is not accurate;
4. removing an existing regex from the list if it is not needed;
5. adding a regex in any complicated form to the list when the user sees a new pattern in a excerpt.

3.3 Active Learning Algorithm

Figure 1 shows the flowchart of our active learning algorithm. Notice that the algorithm is for a single code. That is, we don't consider the situation of generating regex lists for multiple codes simultaneously. The process starts from a list of training excerpts and an empty regex list and proceeds with one excerpt at a time. The user and the computer interactively revise the regex list until all training items are used, or the user believes the classifier is good enough for testing. In the following, we describe the algorithm based on three procedures, namely, the active learning procedure, the false negative conflict resolution procedure, and the false positive conflict resolution procedure.

Active Learning Procedure. This is the main procedure, which calls the following two as sub-procedures.

1. The computer samples a new excerpt from the training list. The excerpt could be drawn randomly or by some smart sampling method that could accelerate the process.
2. The computer rates the excerpt using the current regex list. If the excerpt has a match to the regex list, then the computer's rating of the current excerpt is positive; otherwise it is negative.

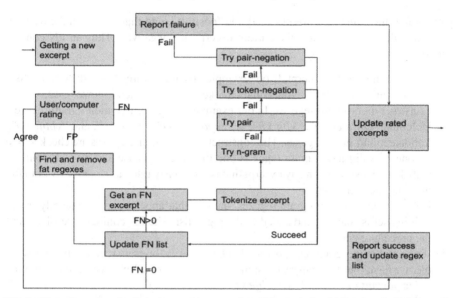

Fig. 1. Flowchart of active learning regex generation. FN stands for "false negative"; FP stands for "false positive"; and "fat-regexes" are regexes that wrongly match the newly presented excerpt.

3. The computer presents the excerpt to the user.
4. The user revises the regex list.
5. The user rates the current excerpt as positive or negative.
6. The computer compares its rating to the user's rating of the current excerpt.
7. If the user's rating is the same as the computer's, go to step 10.
8. If the user's rating is positive but the computer's rating is negative, a false negative (FN) conflict occurs and an FN conflict resolution procedure is started to resolve the conflict. The regex list is revised if the resolution succeeds, otherwise the regex list is unchanged.
9. If the user's rating is negative but the computer's rating is positive, a false positive (FP) conflict occurs. An FP conflict resolution procedure is started to resolve the conflict. The regex list is revised if the resolution succeeds, otherwise the regex list is unchanged.
10. The computer saves the ratings of the current excerpt, update the regex list and goes back to the top of the procedure for a new iteration.

FN Conflict Resolution Procedure. FN conflicts occur when the current excerpt is rated as "negative" by the computer but "positive" by the user. That signals that some regex is missing. To resolve this FN conflict, a new regex that matches the current excerpt needs to be added to the regex list. Notice that, when a new regex is added, other "negative" excerpts may become "positive" and thus cause new FP conflicts. The following FN conflict resolution procedure generates a regex that resolves the current FN conflict without causing any new FP conflicts. For example, consider the excerpt "Water is important to life" to illustrate what happens in each step, assuming that the user is rating a code "Environment" and thinks that "water" before "life" is a meaningful pattern and thus rates the current excerpt as "positive", and that, based on the existing regex list, the computer rates the current excerpt as "negative". Thus an FN conflict occurs.

1. Tokenize the current excerpt. In our example, five tokens are obtained: "water", "is", "important", "to", "life". Notice that all tokens are converted to lower case.
2. Construct mono-gram regexes. In our example, there are five mono-gram regexes, including "\ bwater \ b", "\ bis \ b", "\ bimportant \ b", "\ bto \ b", and "\ blife \ b".
3. Validate mono-gram regexes. The constructed mono-gram regexes are checked one by one. A valid mono-gram regex is one that doesn't cause any new FP conflict, namely, it doesn't match any excerpt that is previously rated as negative by both the user and the computer.
4. If there are valid mono-gram regexes, the one that appears most frequently in the training set is selected and added to the regex list. The FN conflict is resolved and the procedure ends.
5. If no valid mono-gram regex is found, then construct bi-gram regexes. In our example, we have four bi-gram regexes, including "\ bwater is \ b", "\ bis important \ b", "\ bimportant to \ b", and "\ bto life \ b".
6. Validate bi-gram regexes. The constructed bi-gram regexes are validated one by one, the same way as validating mono-gram regexes.
7. If there are valid bi-gram regexes, the one that most frequently appears in training set is selected and added to the regex list. The procedure ends.
8. If bi-gram fails, then try n-gram for n = 3, 4 and 5, constructing, validating and selecting a regex in the same way as in mono-gram and bi-gram. The procedure ends if any of the n-gram succeeds.
9. If n-gram fails, then construct ordered pair regexes. In our example, there are $4 + 3 + 2 + 1 = 10$ ordered pair regexes with 4 possible adjacency ranges, such as "\bwater.{0, 5}is\b", "\bwater.{0, 10}important\b", "\bwater.{0, 20}life\b", etc.
10. The ordered pair regexes are validated and the one mostly appears in training set is selected. The procedure ends if one valid regex is found.
11. If all of the above fails, then construct "token with negation" regexes. Every token A in the current excerpt is used to pair with a negation token B. For a given token A, a valid negation token B satisfies: 1) it doesn't appear in the current excerpt; and 2) it is a common token of all excerpts that contain the token A and previously rated as "negative" by the user and the computer. If B exists, then construct regex "^(?!. * (\bB \ b)). * (\bA \ b)". For example, suppose there is a previously rated negative excerpt "Any food that makes my mouth water is a threat to my life.". We want a regex that matches our current excerpt but not this previous negative excerpt. The token "water" paired with the negative token "mouth" can do the job. The regex "^(?!. * (\bmouth \ b)). * (\bwater \ b)" can then resolve the conflict. If there are more than one such regexes, the one appears in the training set most frequently is selected. The procedure ends if such a regex is found.
12. If the regex is still not found, then regexes in the form of ordered pair with negation are constructed. If a valid negation token B (not matching the current excerpt and common to all FP conflict excerpts) is found for an ordered pair A_1 and A_2, then the regex "^(?!. * (\bB\b)). * (\bA_1\b. * \bA_2\b)" is constructed and added to the regex

list. In our example, the regex could be "^(?!. * (\bmouth\ b)). * (\bwater\ b. * \blife\ b)". If such a regex is found, the conflict is resolved and the procedure ends.
13. If all above fails, report failure and ends the procedure.

FP Conflict Resolution Procedure. FP conflict occurs when the current excerpt is rated as "positive" by the computer but "negative" by the user. Since the computer rates the item as "positive", some of the regexes in the list "wrongly" match the current excerpt. We call such regexes "fat regexes", meaning, they match too many excerpts. These regexes need to be removed from the list in order to resolve the current FP conflict. However, removing the "fat" regexes may cause new FN conflicts, because previously rated "positive" (by both the user and the computer) may become "negative" to the computer. Thus, this procedure tries to remove the fat regexes and resolve all new FN conflicts that are caused by removing the "fat" regexes.

1. Find all "fat" regexes in the regex list.
2. Find all new FN conflict items due to the removing of the fat regexes.
3. For each new FN conflict excerpt, start an FN conflict resolution procedure to resolve the FN conflict. New regexes are generated in each FN conflict resolution.
4. If all new FN conflicts are resolved, then the regexes generated in the FN conflict resolutions are added to the regex list, and the fat regexes are removed. The procedure ends with success.
5. If any of the new FN conflicts is not successfully resolved, report failure and keep the regex list unchanged.

3.4 Research Questions

Broadly, our goal was to create a lightweight regex generator algorithm that is both accurate and fast. In order to test our proposed active learning algorithm for regex generation, this study aimed to answer three research questions, focusing on both accuracy and efficiency.

RQ1: How accurately can the four simple forms of the regexes represent human-created complex regexes? We were especially concerned with two issues:

1) the proportion of conflicts that can be successfully resolved by the generator;
2) the performance of generated regex on unseen data.

RQ2: How much time does the generator take for each iteration? Since this is an interactive algorithm, we expect the system to respond to the user within a few seconds.
RQ3: How many iterations are needed to generate highly accurate regexes? Since the user needs to rate an excerpt in each iteration, we hope the number of iterations is within the range that a human user can reasonably handle.

4 Simulation

To answer our research questions, we ran a simulation on an education data. In this section, we describe the data, method, and results of the simulation.

4.1 Data

We used an educational data set, called *Nephrotex*. It was collected by previous researchers from an engineering virtual internship [8, 9]. Participants interned at a fictional company that produces ultrafiltration membranes for hemodialysis machines used in the treatment of end-stage renal failure. Participants worked in teams of five. The dataset contained 50,888 items from chat conversations of those teams. Each item contained an excerpt and six associated ratings from the validated regex-based classifiers.

Codes. Six regex-based text classifiers were created and validated in previous research for six discourse codes, including *Tech Constraints, Performance, Collaboration, Design, Data* and *Requests*. Details about the code definition and validation results can be found in Cai et al., 2022 [2, 3].

4.2 Method

The answers to our research questions are sensitive to four factors, 1) the length of the excerpts, 2) the complexity of the codes, 3) the consistency of the user's rating, and 4) the quality of the user-created regexes. In this simulation, we only explored our RQs under limited conditions. Firstly, we only simulated one data set with relatively short excerpts. As a result, the impact of excerpt length was not considered. Secondly, in order to simulate the performance of our algorithm we used previously validated regexes to simulate human rating in the active learning process, which implies that the codes are simple enough to be represented by regexes. Thirdly, since the "user's ratings" were actually the classifier ratings, there was no inconsistency in the "user's ratings". And lastly, we restricted the user's input to excerpt rating only. In other words, our simulation assumed that the user did not have fluency in creating or modifying regexes.

The 50,888 items were randomly divided into a training set with 3,000 items and a test set with 47,888 items. For each of the six codes, a new regex list was generated using the active learning algorithm described above. When the generation process started the initial regex list of a code was assumed to be empty and therefore did not match on any excerpt. The regex generation process went through all 3000 randomly sampled training items, one at a time. For each item, the only input from the simulated "user" was the "human" rating of the excerpt for the specific code. The regex list was modified when a conflict occurred (i.e., the new regex rating and the "human" rating were not the same for the excerpt), and the process for generating a code finished when all training items were checked. At each "conflict" iteration, the regex generation time was recorded, and the Cohen's kappa between "human rating" and "regex rating" (using the regex generated up to the conflict iteration) was computed on both training set (3,000 items) and test set (47,888 items).

4.3   Result

Table 1. Code name, number of conflicts iterations occurred in training, average generation time at each conflict iteration in training, training and test kappa after 3000 iterations.

Code	Conflicts	Average Time (second)	Training κ	Test κ
TECH CONSTRAINTS	57	0.018	1	0.987
PERFORMANCE	44	0.020	1	0.979
COLLABORATION	53	0.017	1	0.983
DESIGN	173	0.023	1	0.859
DATA	146	0.026	1	0.896
REQUESTS	88	0.024	1	0.957

We implemented the simulation in R and ran the simulation on a MacBook Air with macOS Monterey 12.2.1, Apple M1 chip 8 core CPU, 8 GB memory. Table 1 shows the total conflicts that occurred, average generation time in each conflict iteration, final training kappa, and final test kappa after 3,000 iterations. The number of conflicts for the six codes ranged from 44 to 173. The average generation time per conflict ranged from 0.017 to 0.026 seconds. The final training kappa were all 1, indicating that all false negative conflicts and false positive conflicts were resolved. The final test kappa ranged from 0.859 to 0.987.

Figure 2 shows the training kappa (blue) and the test kappa (red) at each iteration for each code. The generation process for the codes "Tech Constraints" and "Performance" converged most quickly. They reached a high test kappa value of $\kappa = 0.9$ in less than 500 iterations. The process for the code "Collaboration" was slightly slower, it reached test kappa $\kappa = 0.9$ in about 800 iterations. The generator took about 2000 iterations to reach the same test kappa for the code "Request", about 3000 iterations for the code "Data". For the code "Design", the test kappa never reached 0.9 in the 3000 iterations. The number of conflicts encountered in the 3000 iterations negatively correlated to the test kappa and the convergence speed. That is, codes with a smaller number of conflicts converged more quickly and reached higher final test kappa.

Table 2 shows a comparison of the original human-created regexes and the generated regexes for the code "Tech Constraints". Except for the regex "\bchemical", all original regexes were retrieved. Among all generated regexes, only three (at the bottom row of the table) did not have corresponding items in the original regex list.

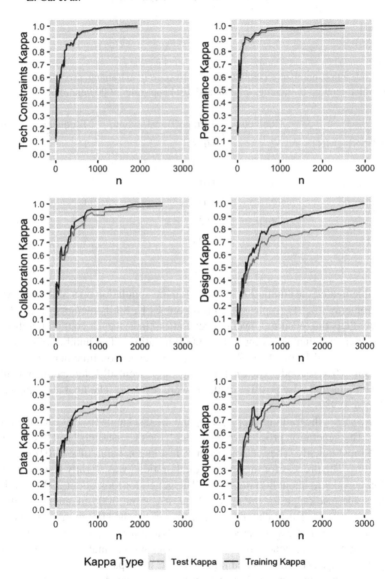

Fig. 2. Training kappa and test kappa at each conflict iteration for each code. Some curves ended before 3000 iterations because no more later conflict iteration occurred. (Color figure online)

The basic regex forms in our generation cannot represent all practically possible regexes. For example, in our simulation, the original regex list for the code "data" included a regex that represents any numeric values greater than 10, with some exceptions, including those with "player", "min", "am", "pm", and the percentage symbol "%". The original regex was in the form "\b(?<!player)(?<!player)(?<![V])(?<!:)[1-9][0-9](?!%)(?! %) (?!min)(?! min)(?!:)(?!pm)(?!am)", which can-not be constructed

Table 2. Original and generated regex lists for code "Tech Constraints"

Original Regexes	Generated Regexes
\bpespvp, \bdry-jet, \bjet, \bnegative charge, \bsurfactant, \bvapor, \bvapor deposition polymerization, \bpmma, \bprnlt, \bmanufacturing process, \bmaterials, \bphase inversion, \bsteric, \bpolyamide, \bnano, \bcarbon nanotube, \bbiological, \bprocesses, \bpolysulfone, \bhydro, \bcnt	\bpespvp\, \bjet\b, \bcharge\b, \bsurfactant\b, \bsurfactants\b, \bvapor\b, \bpmma\b, \bpmma_batch2\b, \bprnlt\b, \bi agree with prnlt2\b, \bmanufacturing process\b, \bmaterials\b, \bphase inversion\b, \bsteric\b, \bpolyamide\b, \bnanotube\b, \bnanotubes\b, \bbiological\b, \bprocesses\b, \bpolysulfone\b, \bhydro\b, \bhydrophilic\b, \bhydrophillic\b, \bcnt\b
\bchemical	
	\b2.4\b, \bso then thats\b, \blisted\b

by our four basic forms. To match such numeric tokens, our generator had to generate regexes that represent each specific number, such as "\b120\b", "\b900000\b", "\b32.22\b", etc. (see Table 3). Since our generator is designed for an interactive process, in which the user has the opportunity to supply good regexes, we may assume that, after seeing regexes representing specific numbers, the user could realize that a regex representing such numeric values is needed and add a valid one to the regex list. How helpful would that be? We ran a follow-up simulation in which we added the numeric value regex when the first excerpt with the specified numeric number appeared. The result showed that the total number of conflicts dropped from 146 to 58 in the 3000 iterations. The number of regexes in the list dropped from 82 to 26, and the test kappa increased from 0.896 to 0.990. The required number of items for the test kappa to reach $\kappa = 0.9$ dropped from about 3000 to less than 560. Table 4 shows the generated regex list (right column) with the numeric regex added by the user.

Table 3. Original and generated regex list for code "Data"

Original Regexes	Generated Regexes
\bperformed well, \bmaximizes, \bresult, \brates, \bscore, \bworst, \bpoor, \bchart, \btoo high, \baverage, \btests, \bgraph, textbackslash bdata, \breading	\bperformed well\b, \bmaximizes\b, \bresults\b, \bresult\b, \bresulted\b, \brates\b, \bscore\b, \bscores\b, \bscored\b, \bworst\b, textbackslash bpoor\b, \bpoorly\b, \bchart\b, \bcharts\b, \btoo high\b, \baverage\b, \btests\b, \bgraph\b, \bgraphs\b, \bgraphing\b, \bdata\b, \breading\b
\b(?<!player)(?<!player)(?<![V])(?<!:)[1-9][0-9](?!%)(?!%)(?!min)(?! min)(?!:)(?!pm)(?!am)	\b110\b, \b29\b, \b319\b, \b11\b, \b130\b, \b900000\b, \b65.56\b, \b120\b, \b13\b, \b100\b, \b20.0\b, \b17\b, \b230\b, \b40\b, \b18\b, \b105\b, \b140\b, \b500000\b, \b21\b, \b32.22\b, \b1000000\b, \b70\b, \b14\b, \b80\b, \b50.00\b, \b65\b, \b90\b, \b724\b, \b133\b, \b353\b, \b613\b, \b23\b, \b800,000\b, \b43.33\b, \b12\b, \b10.0\b
(.*?\blowest.*?\bcheapest.*?), (.*?\bcheapest.*?\blowest.*?), \bcost more, \bwas good in, \bequal value, \bwas found to be, \bhad the lowest reliability, (.*?\bseems to be.*?\bcostly.*?), (.*?\bcostly.*?\bseems to be.*?), (.*?\bperformed.*?\buniformly.*?), (.*?\buniformly.*?\bperformed.*?), \bperform well, \bperforms.*?\breliability, (.*?\boverall.*?\bperformed.*?), (.*?\bperformed.*?\boverall.*?)	
	\bphase 20\b, \bbar\b, \bfail\b, \bincome\b, \b400k\b, \band prnlt\b, \b31st\b, \bvdp\b, \bcar\b, \bevaluation\b, \bprnlt\b.{0,5}\bdry\b, \breplaced\b, \beach aspect\b, \b7 of\b, \btables\b, \b5pm\b, \bflux of\b, \b28th\b, \bmean we\b, \bfr\b, \bdramatic\b, \binsignificant\b, \b1 had\b, \bnmg\b, \bhave 0\b, \bmatters\b, \bresolve\b, \b1;31\b, \b10 is\b

Table 4. Original generated regex lists for code "Data" with user creation

Original Regexes	Generated Regexes
\bperformed well, \bmaximizes, \bresult, \brates, \bscore, \bworst, \bpoor, \bchart, \btoo high, \baverage, \btests, \bgraph, \bdata	\bperformed well\b, \bmaximizes\b, \bresults\b, \bresult\b, \bresulted\b, \brates\b, \bscore\b, \bscores\b, \bscored\b, \bworst\b, \bpoor\b, \bpoorly\b, \bchart\b, \bcharts\b, \btoo high\b, \baverage\b, \btests\b, \bgraph\b, \bgraphs\b, \bgraphing\b, \bdata\b, \breading\b
\b(?<!player)(?<!player)(?<![V])(?<!:)[1-9][0-9](?!%)(?!%)(?!min)(?! min)(?!:)(?!pm)(?!am)	\b(?<!player)(?<!player)(?<![V])(?<!:)[1-9][0-9](?!%)(?!%)(?!min)(?! min)(?!:)(?!pm)(?!am)
(.*?\blowest.*?\bcheapest.*?), (.*?\bcheapest.*?\blowest.*?), \bhad great reliability, \bhad the lowest reliability, (.*?\bseems to be.*?\bcostly.*?), (.*?\bcostly.*?\bseems to be.*?), \bequal value, \bwas found to be, (.*?\bperformed.*?\buniformly.*?), (.*?\buniformly.*?\bperformed.*?), \bperform well, \bcost more, \bwas good in, \bperforms.*?\breliability, (.*?\boverall.*?\bperformed.*?), (.*?\bperformed.*?\boverall.*?)	
	\bfail\b, \bincome\b, \beach aspect\b, \b1 had\b, \bresolve\b

5   Conclusions and Discussions

In this study, we proposed a lightweight interactive regex generator for qualitative coding. The simulation partially answered our research questions, constrained by our simulation conditions. We had hoped that the generator could respond to the user in a few seconds. The simulation showed that the average generation time was about 0.02 seconds per conflict. Therefore, we conclude that the algorithm is fast enough for an interactive system. All six codes we simulated accurately retrieved the original regexes. Therefore, we conclude that, for codes that can be accurately represented by regexes, the algorithm can converge to the right regexes. Finally, we conclude that it may take 500 to 3000 items to train a high-accuracy regex for data with similar excerpt length and code complexity to ours.

Limitations. Our findings are limited in several ways. First, although our data was relatively large and we tried six different codes, the lengths of the excerpts were relatively small (12.04 tokens by average) and the codes were relatively simple, in the sense that they could be represented by a relatively small set of basic regexes. For data with longer excerpts and more complex codes, it may take more iterations to generate high accuracy regexes. The time on each iteration may also be longer. Second, the replacement of "human" user by validated regex lists limits the input a human user gives. How much the performance of the generator could be improved by human user's regex creation has not been systematically evaluated. Third, we did not provide a way to dynamically estimate the quality of generated regexes. The kappa values in this study were computed based on the known validated regex lists which won't be available in real regex development process. The process of estimating the quality of the regexes is called "validation" , which is an important topic but beyond the scope of this paper. Last but not least, regex for coding are generating patterns for meaning, which implies that advanced natural language process (NLP) techniques may help. We were cautious on integrating NLP techniques due to the concern with computation complexity. However, it is possible that some "heavy" computation may be done only once at the beginning of the coding. For example, training a Latent Semantic Analysis (LSA) space [5] may take several minutes but that is a computation for only one time per data set. Once an LSA space is trained, it could be used to find tokens that are similar in meaning. That could potentially be used to greatly accelerate the generation process. For example, once some candidate n-grams are found, instead of selecting the most frequent one, the one that are most similar in meaning with existing selected n-grams could be a much better choice. As a final note, the proposed regex generator has been integrated in our coding tool named "Codey". Readers who are interested in seeing how the algorithm works in Codey may contact authors.

Acknowledgements. This work was funded in part by the National Science Foundation (DRL-2100320, DRL-2201723, DRL-2225240), the Wisconsin Alumni Research Foundation, and the Office of the Vice Chancellor for Research and Graduate Education at the University of Wisconsin-Madison. The opinions, findings, and conclusions do not reflect the views of the funding agencies, cooperating institutions, or other individuals.

References

1. Bartoli, A., De Lorenzo, A., Medvet, E., Tarlao, F.: Active learning of regular expressions for entity extraction. IEEE Trans. Cybern. **48**(3), 1067–1080 (2018). https://doi.org/10.1109/TCYB.2017.2680466. http://ieeexplore.ieee.org/document/7886274/
2. Cai, Z., Eagan, B., Marquart, C., Shaffer, D.W.: LSTM neural network assisted regex development for qualitative coding. In: Damşa, C., Barany, A. (eds.) ICQE 2022. CCIS, vol. 1785, pp. 17–29. Springer, Cham (2023). https://doi.org/10.1007/978-3-031-31726-2_2
3. Cai, Z., Marquart, C., Shaffer, D.: Neural recall network: a neural network solution to low recall problem in regex-based qualitative coding. In: Mitrovic, A., Bosch, N. (eds.) Proceedings of the 15th International Conference on Educational Data Mining, Durham, United Kingdom, pp. 228–238. International Educational Data Mining Society (2022). https://doi.org/10.5281/zenodo.6853047
4. Cai, Z., Siebert-Evenstone, A., Eagan, B., Shaffer, D.W.: Using topic modeling for code discovery in large scale text data. In: Ruis, A.R., Lee, S.B. (eds.) ICQE 2020. CCIS, vol. 1312, pp. 18–31. Springer, Cham (2021). https://doi.org/10.1007/978-3-030-67788-6_2

5. Cai, Z., Siebert-Evenstone, A., Eagan, B., Shaffer, D.W., Xiangen, Hu., Graesser, A.C.: nCoder+: a semantic tool for improving recall of ncoder coding. In: Eagan, B., Misfeldt, M., Siebert-Evenstone, A. (eds.) ICQE 2019. CCIS, vol. 1112, pp. 41–54. Springer, Cham (2019). https://doi.org/10.1007/978-3-030-33232-7_4

6. Charmaz, K.: Constructing Grounded Theory. Sage, London (2006)

7. Chen, N.C., Drouhard, M., Kocielnik, R., Suh, J., Aragon, C.R.: Using machine learning to support qualitative coding in social science: shifting the focus to ambiguity. ACM Trans. Interact. Intell. Syst. 8(2), 9:1–9:20 (2018). https://doi.org/10.1145/3185515

8. Chesler, N., Ruis, A., Collier, W., Swiecki, Z., Arastoopour, G., Shaffer, D.: A novel paradigm for engineering education: virtual internships with individualized mentoring and assessment of engineering thinking. J. Biomech. Eng. 137(2), 1–8 (2015)

9. Gautam, D., Swiecki, Z., Shaffer, D.W., Graesser, A.C., Rus, V.: Modeling classifiers for virtual internships without participant data. In: Proceedings of the 10th International Conference on Educational Data Mining, pp. 278–283 (2017)

10. Glaser, B., Strauss, A.: The discovery of grounded theory: stretegies for qualitative research. Aldine, Chicago (1967)

11. Li, X., Cui, M., Li, J., Bai, R., Lu, Z., Aickelin, U.: A hybrid medical text classification framework: integrating attentive rule construction and neural network. Neurocomputing 443, 345–355 (2021). https://doi.org/10.1016/j.neucom.2021.02.069. https://linkinghub.elsevier.com/retrieve/pii/S0925231221003258

12. Shaffer, D.: Quantitative Ethnography. Cathcart Press, Madison (2017)

13. Shaffer, D.W., Ruis, A.R.: How we code. In: Ruis, A.R., Lee, S.B. (eds.) ICQE 2020. CCIS, vol. 1312, pp. 62–77. Springer, Cham (2021). https://doi.org/10.1007/978-3-030-67788-6_5

From nCoder to ChatGPT: From Automated Coding to Refining Human Coding

Andres Felipe Zambrano$^{(\boxtimes)}$, Xiner Liu, Amanda Barany, Ryan S. Baker, Juhan Kim, and Nidhi Nasiar

University of Pennsylvania, Philadelphia, USA
azamb13@upenn.edu

Abstract. This paper investigates the potential of utilizing ChatGPT (GPT-4) as a tool for supporting coding processes for Quantitative Ethnography research. We compare the use of ChatGPT and nCoder, the most widely used automated coding tool in the QE community, on a dataset of press releases and public addresses delivered by governmental leaders from seven countries from late February to late March 2020. The study assesses the accuracy of the automated coding procedures between the two tools, and the role that ChatGPT's explanations of its coding decisions can play in improving the consistency and construct validity of human-generated codes. Results suggest that both ChatGPT and nCoder have advantages and disadvantages depending on the context, nature of the data, and researchers' goals. While nCoder is useful for straightforward coding schemes represented through regular expressions, ChatGPT can better capture a variety of language structures. ChatGPT's ability to provide explanations for its decisions can also help enhance construct validity, identify ambiguity in code definitions, and assist human coders in achieving high interrater reliability. Although we identify limitations of ChatGPT in coding constructs open to human interpretations and encompassing multiple concepts, we highlight opportunities and potential benefits provided by ChatGPT as a tool to support human researchers in their coding process.

Keywords: Automated Coding · ChatGPT · nCoder · Coding Process · Reliability

1 Introduction

One of the key components of qualitative analysis of textual data is the process of defining themes and patterns and identifying where they appear in the data, to derive meaningful insights. This is especially true in quantitative ethnographic (QE) research, where theoretical and practical attention has been paid to the concept of *fairness* to ensure interpretations are consistently agreed upon by relevant stakeholders and that different manifestations of the same concept are comparable [1, 2]. This process of assigning valid codes in a reliable manner often proves both tedious and complex. While manual coding techniques remain popular in both QE and broader research [3], such approaches remain infeasible for larger datasets, and the potential for human error remains.

G. Arastoopour Irgens and S. Knight (Eds.): ICQE 2023, CCIS 1895, pp. 470–485, 2023.
https://doi.org/10.1007/978-3-031-47014-1_32

Recent efforts to offload the burden of coding while maintaining or maximizing fairness have drawn on the affordances of computer science and natural language processing technologies. The development of automated coding tools such as nCoder [4], for example, has assisted researchers in coding data that would otherwise necessitate an extensive and time-consuming manual process. This freely accessible online tool (https://app.ncoder.org/), enables users to define codes and automate the coding process based on regular expressions provided by the researchers [5]. A regular expression is a sequence of characters or other text constructs, with the option of including gaps in the sequence. nCoder categorizes each line of data based on the presence or absence of regular expressions pre-defined by human researchers. nCoder also allows for the assessment of coding agreement between and across humans and machines and supports the review of any disagreements to support a human analyst in the refinement of regular expressions used in these classifiers. Through this iterative process, the classifiers become more capable and proficient at discerning language structures that signify the presence of each code on each line. Once researchers deem the agreement between themselves and the detector to be sufficiently high, based on indicators such as Kappa, precision, recall, and Shaffer's rho [1, 6, 7], researchers can then generalize these classifiers to code the entire dataset. While nCoder has proved useful in QE research [3], there are still concerns that nCoder may be unable to capture all cases where a human would identify a code (recall), as regular expressions may not match human coders' capacity to consider contextual features or semantic nuance.

A similar iterative process could be conducted with other algorithms as well. There is an extensive history of machine learning methods being used to code textual data [8–10], with neural networks emerging as a particularly effective algorithm for this application in the last few years [11–13]. Very recent work has suggested that the use of neural networks may speed the process of qualitative coding by automating it, though this requires more samples of human coding than nCoder [14]. Other very recent work has demonstrated the potential of Large Language Models (LLM) such as ChatGPT [15] to perform automated coding of textual data [16]. LLMs can discern semantic relationships between words and concepts rather than searching for a specific sequence of characters or elements, capturing complex linguistic patterns that are often difficult for human coders to identify rationally through regular expressions.

Furthermore, ChatGPT's ability to interact with human analysts allows them to query it to better understand the conceptual reasons for discrepancies between human and machine coding. This interaction could potentially furnish valuable insights to enhance human coding practices, particularly in identifying inconsistencies in coding, which is important even when interrater reliability is high overall. Similarly, the explanations provided by ChatGPT can offer insights into construct validity, the extent to which the constructs used in coding accurately represent the intended elements or themes being studied. Due to its capacity to interact with human researchers, LLM chatbots such as ChatGPT hold potential utility as a coding instrument that can facilitate not only automated coding but also improve the consistency and validity of human coding with less effort than the methods currently most-widely used in quantitative ethnography.

Given these possibilities, this work is an exploratory look at the potential of Chat-GPT for supporting data coding processes in Quantitative Ethnography. We evaluate the interrater reliability of ChatGPT and nCoder with human coders within the context of a dataset consisting of press releases and public addresses delivered by governmental leaders from seven countries during the period of late February to late March 2020 [17]. Moreover, we examine how the explanations provided by ChatGPT for its coding decisions can support humans in refining both their coding scheme and individual codes, ultimately aiming to improve consistency and construct validity.

2 Methods

2.1 Study Contexts

In this study, we examine the potential advantages of utilizing ChatGPT (GPT-4 model; see [15]) in the coding process. We first focus on improving the accuracy of the automated coding procedure, using nCoder as a reference for comparison. Then, we assess the consistency and construct validity among human-generated codes using ChatGPT's explanations of its coding decisions.

For this purpose, we employ a dataset that comprises transcripts of press releases and public addresses delivered by governmental leaders from seven countries from late February to late March 2020 [17]. The authors used a codebook incorporating seven categories: *Medical Positive, Medical Negative, Economic Positive, Economic Negative, Social Positive, Social Negative,* and *Political Positive*. One of the authors that originally used this dataset contributed to this analysis to reduce any potential risk of misinterpretation of the original codebook. The average inter-rater agreement, measured by Cohen's Kappa, was 0.94. For a more comprehensive discussion of the codebook, refer to [17].

We selected this dataset because the categorization of the content of leaders' discourse in the seven constructs defined by the authors is complex. In this dataset, similar information can be conveyed using a wide variety of vocabulary, and subtle differences between some constructs, such as social and political, or between positive and negative sentiment within the same construct, may prove difficult to distinguish reliably using automated classifiers. Therefore, we hypothesize that automated coding based on semantic similarity (closeness in meaning between two pieces of text) could be more effective than relying on exact wording for this dataset, making this a case where ChatGPT might demonstrate advantages relative to nCoder.

2.2 Coding Process with nCoder and ChatGPT

For both nCoder and ChatGPT, we randomly selected a training set of 100 lines from the original dataset. We tested both nCoder and ChatGPT's performance using an additional set of 100 unobserved lines from the dataset. We used the same training set and test set for both nCoder and ChatGPT.

Following the process outlined by Cai et al. [5], we used an iterative approach to craft regular expressions in nCoder that maximized agreement between the classifier and human coders for each code category. We first established a set of regular expressions based on the construct definitions provided by [17], using the examples provided in the original codebook, and applied them to code the training set. We then analyzed any instances where nCoder and human coders disagreed and evaluated the effect of adding or deleting regular expressions on the overall kappa value. In this step, verbs, substantives, adjectives, and adverbs, including their linguistic roots (e.g., the linguistic root 'hope' in the word 'hopeful') were considered as potential regular expressions that could be added or deleted to enhance kappa value. Next, we fine-tuned each classifier incorporating those regular expressions that increased the agreement between nCoder and humans for the training set. Finally, we tested the optimized regular expressions on an additional set of 100 unobserved lines for each construct.

We adopted a similar approach for ChatGPT. For each construct, we provided Chat-GPT with the construct name and original definition that was used by the authors [17]. It is essential to provide ChatGPT with a straightforward, specific, and clearly stated prompt to obtain optimal results. Therefore, we coded only one construct at a time and requested a binary vector as the response to avoid overloading ChatGPT with excessive information, which could reduce the accuracy of the coding. We then addressed each disagreement between ChatGPT and human coders by requesting explanations from ChatGPT regarding its decisions. We incorporated these explanations to enhance the code definitions used in the prompts for ChatGPT, refining, clarifying, or supplementing the definitions where needed, and including clarifying statements and examples of appropriate and inappropriate phrases to help define the constructs. It is important to note that the definitions given to ChatGPT were revised, but we did not subsequently have the human coders re-code the data based using this modified codebook (we discuss this possibility below). We also asked ChatGPT for suggestions for updating the definitions to gain insights about how we could reframe the definitions of each construct. Any definitions or supplements suggested by ChatGPT were reviewed and fine-tuned by human researchers. If a revised code definition negatively impacted the agreement between ChatGPT and human coders, we disregarded that new definition and proceeded to the next disagreement until we had reviewed the entire training set once. The flowchart of this process is presented in Fig. 1.

An example of this process is shown in the results section. To avoid confusing ChatGPT due to information overload, we limited each definition to a maximum of five sentences. The coding process with ChatGPT was conducted in subsets of 25 lines, repeating the process four times, due to the maximum prompt length currently allowed by ChatGPT. After completing all coding, review, and refinement, we compared ChatGPT's performance to nCoder, using 100 additional unobserved lines from the dataset. This test set was the same for both coding strategies. Kappa, precision, recall, and Shaffer's rho [6, 7] were then calculated for the comparison between nCoder and ChatGPT using [18]. We employed Shaffer's rho to reduce the potential risk of Type 1 error of Kappa [7]. We also calculated precision and recall to understand how the automated and human codes differ.

3   Results

3.1   Prompt Creation

In this section, we illustrate an example of the ChatGPT prompt creation process using the code category labeled as *Social Positive*. According to [17], this construct is associated with concepts such as empathy, community, unity, and public education. Based on this original definition, we tasked ChatGPT with coding the training set of 100 randomly

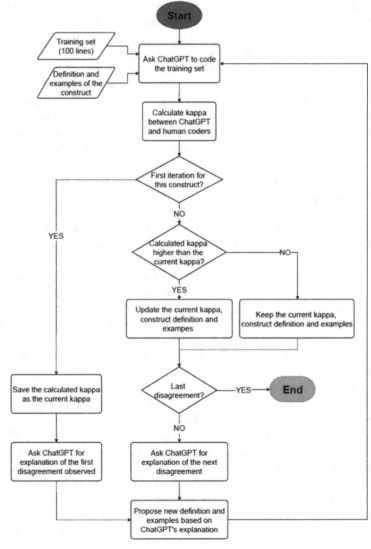

Fig. 1. Flowchart of the proposed process for developing the coding prompt of one construct using ChatGPT.

selected lines (in sets of 25 lines, as mentioned above). The first disagreement observed between ChatGPT and human coders occurs in Line 280, which.

states: "*Let us never despair*". ChatGPT justified its choice of coding this line under the construct of *Social Positive* by explaining that:

This line conveys a message of hope and unity, encouraging people to remain hopeful and resilient in the face of challenges. It promotes a positive attitude and urges community members to support each other, which aligns with the concept of Social Positive.

Human coders, on the other hand, determined that this line should be coded as *Social Negative*, as they viewed it as a warning rather than a message of hope. We provided ChatGPT with this clarification and requested a revised definition of the code as follows:

I consider this line a warning rather than a message of hope. It should not be categorized as Social Positive. How can I modify the original definition of the code to state it clearer?

Based on this prompt, ChatGPT responded with a more precise definition of the construct addressing the misunderstanding:

I apologize for the misunderstanding. To modify the original definition of Social Positive, you may want to emphasize the explicit demonstration of beneficial impact, and provide clearer examples. Here's an updated definition:

*The concept of "social positive" refers to **actions, attitudes, or behaviors that explicitly demonstrate a beneficial impact on society or** positive perceptions of the community, through promoting activities or initiatives that directly support the community. Some examples of this concept are: volunteering, community-building events, promoting unity and collaboration, educational programs, or clear expressions of empathy and support for fellow community members.*

Based on this new definition, we ask ChatGPT to code the training set again and continue to the next disagreement, which occurred in Line 71, which states: "*My dear fellow citizens.*" According to ChatGPT:

This line is a simple salutation or greeting addressed to the citizens. Although it demonstrates a level of empathy and connection, it does not explicitly promote activities or initiatives directly supporting the community, unity, collaboration, or educational programs as described in the revised definition of Social Positive.

Based on this explanation, we clarified to ChatGPT that greetings that show empathy and camaraderie should also be considered under the category *Social Positive*. After offering ChatGPT this clarification, ChatGPT developed the following definition of the code:

The concept of "social positive" refers to actions, attitudes, or behaviors that explicitly demonstrate a beneficial impact on society or positive perceptions of the community, through promoting activities or initiatives that directly support the community **or by expressing empathy and connection.** *Some examples of this concept are: volunteering, community-building events, promoting unity and collaboration, educational programs, clear expressions of empathy and support for fellow community members,* **or heartfelt greetings that display a sense of camaraderie and connection.**

This process was replicated for all disagreements in the training set of each code category. In nCoder, code and coding refinement requires that researchers examine inconsistencies, diagnose validity or consistency issues independently from the tool, and alter regular expressions accordingly. Through the use of ChatGPT, the process becomes more interactive and embedded in the study context (code and data features), serving as a scaffolded support for identifying and addressing issues related to construct validity (code definitions) or consistency (code applications).

3.2 Agreement Metrics

Table 1 shows the degree of agreement between machine and human codes. During training, nCoder shows higher agreement with human coders (average Kappa = 0.77) than ChatGPT (average Kappa = 0.54), which is likely due to the use of regular expressions that explicitly define the words and language structures considered by humans when categorizing the examples. For the test data, nCoder also shows a higher level of agreement with human coders (Kappa = 0.53) compared to ChatGPT (Kappa = 0.46). In terms of precision, which assesses the machine's ability to accurately identify the presence of a construct in each line while minimizing false positives, nCoder (Precision = 0.79) outperforms ChatGPT (Precision = 0.52). However, for recall, which evaluates the proportion of true positive categorizations made by the machine over all the actual positives coded by humans, ChatGPT (Recall = 0.8) surpasses nCoder (Recall = 0.6).

Table 1. Training and testing agreement between human and machine coding.

Code	Machine Coder	Train	Test			
		Kappa	Kappa	Precision	Recall	Shaffer's rho
Medical/ Positive	nCoder	0.85	0.5	0.88	0.54	1
	ChatGPT	0.59	0.47	0.59	0.69	1
Medical/ Negative	nCoder	0.73	0.39	0.65	0.5	1
	ChatGPT	0.54	0.50	0.60	0.69	1
Economic/ Positive	nCoder	0.83	0.64	0.76	0.7	0.5
	ChatGPT	0.87	0.83	0.90	0.87	0.04
Economic/ Negative	nCoder	0.82	0.47	1	0.43	1
	ChatGPT	0.56	0.51	0.42	0.89	1

(continued)

Table 1. (*continued*)

Code	Machine Coder	Train	Test			
		Kappa	Kappa	Precision	Recall	Shaffer's rho
Social/ Positive	nCoder	0.78	0.66	0.83	0.8	0.47
	ChatGPT	0.46	0.38	0.5	0.81	1
Social/ Negative	nCoder	0.86	0.67	0.82	0.69	0.46
	ChatGPT	0.31	0.2	0.27	0.83	1
Political/ Positive	nCoder	0.55	0.41	0.58	0.54	1
	ChatGPT	0.46	0.32	0.36	0.84	1
Average	nCoder	0.77	0.53	0.79	0.60	0.78
	ChatGPT	0.54	0.46	0.52	0.80	0.86

In looking at these differences, one of the key factors is whether specific words are sufficient to recognize a category. Take, for example, the *Medical Positive* code, which exhibits a precision of 0.88 but a recall of 0.54 for nCoder. For this code, the presence of words such as "*vaccines*" or "*hospitals*" allows nCoder to easily recognize this construct. Consequently, each time a new unobserved line contains either of these words, if there is no language structure indicating a reduction or absence, the nCoder classifier can categorize it as *Medical Positive* with a low risk of error. However, nCoder may struggle to generalize to all the names of medical institutions or devices that were not observed during training. In other words, although nCoder's precision can be relatively high because it received specific examples for each code category, it may face low recall when generalized to broader data, since regular expressions require exact words. As Cai et al. [5] note, it is impossible to provide nCoder with all possible examples.

As ChatGPT is a pre-trained LLM, recall issues can be mitigated by the vocabulary and semantic structures that ChatGPT has already learned. For example, for the *Medical Positive* code, ChatGPT has previously learned a broad range of medical vocabulary, under the semantic field of medicine or health, which can enable it to recognize organizations, devices, or other concepts that are not observed during the training process but that would be related to the code category. This capability of ChatGPT is also evident in the examples provided when defining the prompt of the category *Social Positive* in Sect. 3.1. ChatGPT identified a greeting even without being given an example or the explicit language structure of a greeting in the prompt.

In general, ChatGPT can offer high performance in code categories where the range of possible interpretations is limited, and the semantic field is concrete. For instance, for the construct Economic Positive, which the authors originally defined as any concept related to commerce, trade, and marketplace, ChatGPT achieves precision and recall greater than 0.85 and a Shaffer's rho of 0.04, indicating it can accurately code the entire dataset for this construct according to the standards suggested by [1, 6]. However, for constructs that are more open to interpretation or less thematically discrete, ChatGPT's pre-established semantic connections may result in overgeneralization, leading to the incorrect categorization of some lines as belonging to those constructs. This issue is apparent in the lower precision shown by ChatGPT for code categories about social or political actions compared to nCoder. For example, Line 1 of Emmanuel Macron's speech states:

"Thursday evening, I spoke to you to discuss the health crisis that our country is going through. Until then, the epidemic may have been a distant idea for some, it has become an immediate, pressing reality."

This line was categorized as *Medical Negative* by human coders, who identified the concept of a health crisis in this line exclusively as a medical issue, recognizing that its social and economic consequences are not mentioned within the line. However, Chat-GPT interpreted this line as belonging to both *Medical* and *Social Negative* categories, providing the following rationale for the *Social Negative* construct:

This line is coded as Social Negative because it refers to the negative consequences of the ongoing crisis, which likely includes social issues such as close contact restrictions, lockdowns, or other related social issues. The statement implies that the implemented measures are a response to the crisis, and the deepening of the crisis suggests that the population is facing challenges and difficulties.

Even after instructing ChatGPT not to categorize lines that exclusively refer to the health issues of the pandemic as Social or Economic Negative, its semantic structures continue to classify such lines as Social Negative. This overgeneralization is the main reason for the relatively low precision ChatGPT achieves.

3.3   ChatGPT Explanations for Consistency Checks and Construct Validity

When we consider nCoder and ChatGPT's properties for replicating human coding on this task, it is worth noting that human coding can also be fallible. A low precision or recall can indicate that ChatGPT or nCoder perform poorly in the coding task, but it also can represent fuzziness in the construct being coded by humans. Disagreements between human coders and ChatGPT or nCoder can arise from inconsistencies or idiosyncrasies in how a construct is conceived or coded. Therefore, although the semantic structures developed by ChatGPT as described in the previous sections may be imperfect at capturing the codes, the tool's capacity to offer explanations grounded in those previous structures can be valuable for detecting possible inconsistencies and idiosyncrasies in human understanding. This provides an additional perspective for some decisions in the coding process, supporting the humans who make decisions about codes in a critical examination of their interpretations and assumptions.

ChatGPT's grounded and detailed explanations offer an opportunity for human coders to identify and critically reexamine any inconsistencies that may exist between any code they apply and their working understandings of the code categories. ChatGPT can support human coders to think through their own rationales (and any underlying assumptions) while coding, especially when a code definition is more subjective or leaves room for interpretation. It can offer peer-like support (a thought partner) to help human coders be reflective on their own decision process in a more systematic fashion.

An exploration of repetitive inconsistencies may also further highlight issues in construct validity, including when the coding scheme is not clearly defined or fails to capture the underlying construct [19–21].

These types of inconsistencies can occur in almost any coding scheme attempting to capture complex, rich constructs. Though we explore them in [17] work, it is important to note that these inconsistencies only manifest in a small proportion of the data codes. We highlight them with the purpose of showing the potential benefits of using ChatGPT as an additional tool for revising the inconsistencies that can be present in the human coding process -- even for coding schemes and codes that are generally high-quality -- and for enhancing construct validity and interrater reliability.

We can illustrate this process by studying the construct with the lowest agreement between humans and ChatGPT, *Social Negative*. This code category was originally defined to include "nationalism, xenophobia, racism, lockdown, and closed schools" [17], a broad range of topics. However, on two occasions, human coders agreed not to categorize lines related to school closures and lockdowns under the *Social Negative* construct. For example, Line 136 from the speech by Yoshihide Suga states:

"We ask private companies to take into consideration the situation of employees with children. In particular, the closure of schools will be a very significant burden for micro-, small- and medium-sized business operators, who already routinely face a shortage of workers, as well as medical professionals and nursing and childcare workers."

Although human coders did not consider this to be within *Social Negative* category, ChatGPT categorized this line as *Social Negative* arguing that:

It [Line 136] addresses the negative consequences faced by employees with children due to the closure of schools, which is a social issue. The line highlights the challenges and difficulties that micro-, small-, and medium-sized business operators, medical professionals, and childcare workers experience as a result of this situation.

In this example, ChatGPT clearly associated the school closure mentioned in this line with the original definition of the code category *Social Negative*. Similarly, for Line 196 in the speech by Cyril Ramaphosa, which mentioned:

"As a consequence, the National Coronavirus Command Council has decided to enforce a nation-wide lockdown for 21 days with effect from midnight on Thursday 26 March,"

ChatGPT coded this as *Social Negative* due to the inclusion of the concept of lockdown, disagreeing with the human coders, who coded this as *Political Positive*. Although human coders included lockdown as one of the examples of the *Social Negative* code, they agreed not to code Line 196 as *Social Negative*. The explanation provided by ChatGPT was:

This line is associated with the concept of "Social Negative" because it discusses a nation-wide lockdown, which is a direct response to a social issue (the pandemic).

Lockdowns lead to negative consequences and difficulties faced by the population, such as restrictions on movement, closures of businesses, and potential economic repercussions.

This explanation reveals again that ChatGPT was not fully successful in differentiating between medical and social issues, which aligns with COVID-19 emerging in 2020 as a global medical concern with a high level of social impact. As mentioned earlier, this limitation is a primary cause of the low precision (but high recall) exhibited by ChatGPT when identifying the *Social Positive* and *Social Negative* constructs. Despite this limitation, ChatGPT proved helpful, detecting that human coders were not classifying this line adhering to the predetermined definition of *Social Negative*.

Furthermore, ChatGPT also provided the opportunity to continue consideration of these disagreements. For instance, after reviewing its explanation for the coding of Line 196, we clarified to ChatGPT that, under the original coding scheme, *the pandemic is considered a medical issue rather than a social issue.* ChatGPT's response to this explanation was:

You're right that the pandemic is primarily a medical issue. However, the consequences of the pandemic, such as lockdowns and restrictions, have significant social impacts as well. These social impacts include disruptions to daily life, economic challenges, and mental health issues, among others. In this context, line 196 touches upon a "social negative" aspect since it refers to the implementation of a lockdown, which affects the social life and well-being of the population.

This response serves as evidence that ChatGPT can present valid justifications for its coding decisions and maintain consistency in those decisions, providing similar argumentation to the one previously observed in the example shown in Sect. 3.2 for Line 1. While it may not necessarily persuade human researchers to modify their own coding schemes, it can prompt them to engage in more critical reflection, in this case on the discreteness of coding categories.

In addition to discrepancies between construct definitions and coding, ChatGPT can also assist in uncovering inconsistencies between two lines that have similar semantic meanings but were coded differently by humans. For instance, human coders agreed to categorize the following lines in the speech by Cyril Ramaphosa as *Social Positive* but not as *Medical Positive*:

- *Wash hands frequently with hand sanitisers or soap and water for at least 20 s;*
- *Cover our nose and mouth when coughing and sneezing with tissue or flexed elbow;*
- *Avoid close contact with anyone with cold or flu-like symptoms.*

This categorization suggests that, for these human coders, all instructions aimed at citizens for reducing contagion risk, without any negative connotation in the message, should be coded exclusively as *Social Positive*. However, Line 174 in the speech by Cyril Ramaphosa, which states, "*We reiterate that the most effective way to prevent infection is through basic changes in individual behavior and hygiene,*" was coded as both *Medical* and *Social* by human coders. ChatGPT therefore argues that this set of lines should be categorized consistently. It categorizes all the abovementioned lines as *Medical Positive* and provided the following rationale for each of them regarding the *Social Negative* construct:

> *This line provides a recommendation for a hygienic practice to help prevent the spread of illness. It does not explicitly discuss any of the social issues mentioned in the definition of "social negative" (nationalism, xenophobia, racism, stockpiling, basic necessities unsatisfied, lockdowns, and closed schools) nor does it highlight the negative aspect of these issues. Therefore, it was coded as 0, meaning it is not associated with the concept of Social Negative.*

ChatGPT's primary contribution is not to correct human coding on these lines, but to emphasize that all of these lines should be categorized consistently. Consequently, ChatGPT may also be employed as an additional means of reviewing the application of codes across the dataset, reducing potential inconsistencies even after agreement has been reached between the two human coders.

However, ChatGPT's reasoning is still imperfect in many cases. For instance, Line 163 in Cyril Ramaphosa's speech - *"The response of the South African people to this crisis has been remarkable. Millions of our people have understood the gravity of the situation"* - was coded by ChatGPT as *Social Negative* rather than *Social Positive*, with the following rationale:

> *It [Line 163] refers to the crisis and the gravity of the situation being faced by the South African people, highlighting the challenges and difficulties they are experiencing due to the crisis. While it doesn't mention a specific social issue, it implies that there are negative consequences faced by the population in a broader context.*

This example illustrates that ChatGPT can sometimes overlook valuable nuances within lines, such as the word *"remarkable"*, which gives this line a positive connotation that caused humans to categorize it under the *Social Positive* construct instead of *Social Negative*. Therefore, although ChatGPT's explanations can be valuable for detecting possible inconsistencies in human coding, it can also neglect relevant information, focusing on other words or concepts that it considers more relevant, leading to errors in ChatGPT's coding. Despite these limitations, the examples discussed in this section demonstrate how ChatGPT has the potential to support human coders by providing explanations and warnings about possible issues in their codes and/or coding schemes. These explanations can assist human coders in becoming not only more aware of their own decision-making process, but also more systematic. Repetitive inconsistencies may also highlight issues with construct validity, alerting human researchers to aspects of the coding scheme that are not clearly defined or fail to capture the intended construct.

4   Discussion and Conclusions

In this paper, we have discussed how ChatGPT can be a useful tool for improving the coding process for qualitative data. We first explored the use of ChatGPT as a tool for automated coding. We compared ChatGPT with nCoder, the current most common tool for automated coding within the quantitative ethnography community, in terms of each approach's performance for unseen data. We observed that the tools had different affordances and constraints, suggesting that the decision to use one or the other depends on the context and the nature of the data, as well as the researcher's goals. The use of the regular expressions in nCoder led to higher precision but lower recall, as it could capture exactly what the human coder intended but often could not capture ways to phrase the construct that were not seen in the training data. By contrast, ChatGPT can achieve better recall because it can capture the same semantic meaning represented with different words and phrases, but in some cases, it can miss nuances or misinterpret information, leading to lower precision for some constructs.

Based on these results, nCoder might be more helpful than ChatGPT in contexts and codebooks in which a code can be represented through a small set of regular expressions. However, even in those situations, ChatGPT's prompts can be fine-tuned to recognize specific language structures. Although we did not explore the use of regular expressions in ChatGPT's prompts, if the definitions on those prompts specifically include the set of regular expressions that ChatGPT should use during the coding process, it might be able to emulate nCoder functioning. Future research could therefore examine this possibility to determine whether ChatGPT can mimic nCoder and achieve the best of both approaches. Nevertheless, for this type of more concrete constructs, the semantic structures previously learned by ChatGPT can also be enough for reaching a higher agreement. For example, the agreement between ChatGPT and human coders was the highest for the construct *Economic Positive*, outperforming nCoder without needing to include any regular expression in the prompt.

On the other hand, ChatGPT's agreement with human coders diminished for constructs with less concrete definitions and constructs open to human interpretation. Consider, for example, the *Social Positive* and *Social Negative* constructs, for which ChatGPT had the lowest agreement. Firstly, these two codes are prone to subjective interpretation regarding what constitutes positivity or negativity; this also holds true for social, political, and economic aspects to a lesser extent. In addition, the *Social* constructs emerged in inductive coding as a broader, catch-all code that covers a wider spectrum of concepts from more diverse semantic domains, such as healthcare guidelines, education, empathy, lockdowns, and xenophobia, which may not fall under a single discrete thematic construct in many cases. In fact, ChatGPT was more likely to relate health care instructions with medical concepts (*Medical Positive*) than with community empathy or unity (*Social Positive*). Therefore, we hypothesize that ChatGPT may be most successful with constructs that are mutually exclusive and collectively exhaustive [19]. However, this does not indicate that ChatGPT does not provide valuable insights about constructs that are less thematically discrete.

As previously mentioned, the indicators presented in this study evaluate the (dis-) agreement between human and machine coding, but they do not necessarily establish which one is accurate or erroneous. Consequently, a reduced Kappa, precision, or recall for ChatGPT (or nCoder) only indicates that the automated method has a different understanding of the code definitions provided by the human researchers. Therefore, even with constructs where the agreement between ChatGPT and human beings is low, the main benefit offered by ChatGPT, as we demonstrate in Sect. 3, is that ChatGPT can explain its reasoning. These explanations help the human using ChatGPT to gain more insight into these disagreements and review whether any inconsistencies in human coding have gone undetected during the earlier interrater reliability checking with another human. Ultimately, even if ChatGPT's insight into its own decisions is not fully correct, human coders may find the explanations it provides valuable for supporting reflexivity around the coding process.

Moreover, ChatGPT's ability to provide explanations can also be valuable for enhancing construct validity by identifying potential ambiguity in the definition of a coding category and illustrating when and how a code may not appropriately capture the phenomenon/construct. Human-developed code definitions, even after substantial attempts to reach clarity, still often leave room for interpretation [19]. ChatGPT can help to tackle this issue by providing elaborate explanations for the reasons for each of its codes, enabling humans to develop richer, more contextualized, and more concrete code definitions. This may make it easier to get high inter-rater reliability amongst human coders, and eventually to achieve better human-computer agreement. This approach may also prove useful for checking and improving consistency across longer human-coded datasets, as coders often refine construct definitions and code applications over time (drift, see [20]). If we train ChatGPT with definitions and examples of constructs at the end of the coding process, it could help coders detect and resolve inconsistencies in earlier coding stages without needing us to check or recode the entire dataset, enhancing the efficiency of the process. Future work might also examine the potential for ChatGPT, and LLMs in general, to support thematic analysis of qualitative data as part of the inductive development of codes and coding schemes. Each of these directions for future research (construct validity, drift, and inductive code development) could yield valuable insights into the potential of ChatGPT as a responsive resource for qualitative data analysis beyond its benefits for automation of the coding process.

This paper has explored the potential of ChatGPT as a tool for supporting the coding process. ChatGPT has specific affordances and limitations for coding certain constructs in specific contexts as compared to other automated tools such as nCoder. Beyond this, ChatGPT can also provide justifications for coding decisions that can help researchers to develop richer and more concrete or complete construct definitions. This feature also offers an extra layer of verification of the accuracy and consistency of codes and constructs, ultimately improving the current approach of assessing consistency and construct validity through assessing inter-rater reliability. The application of language models such as ChatGPT in qualitative research is quite new. Further exploration of their potential is necessary, particularly in terms of their ability to enhance fairness and reliability in coding and analysis. Therefore, we encourage our colleagues to continue exploring the possibilities and constraints of large language models to facilitate their effective utilization in research. Our hope is that this work opens new avenues in quantitative ethnography to explore the potential of GPT and other language models to refine the coding process and enhance our understanding of complex data.

Acknowledgments. We extend our sincere gratitude to the members of the 2020 and 2021 ICQE data challenges who collected, processed, and coded the dataset used in this study. Special thanks go to Michael Phillips, Anthony J. Taiki Kawakubo, and Jun Oshima for their vital contributions to coding, project conceptualization, and research dissemination. We would also like to acknowledge the assistance provided by ChatGPT in improving the grammar and writing clarity of our initial drafts. All content was thoroughly reviewed and edited by human authors prior to submission. Andres Felipe Zambrano thanks the Ministerio de Ciencia, Tecnología e Innovación and the Fulbright-Colombia commission for supporting his doctoral studies through the Fulbright-MinCiencias 2022 scholarship.

References

1. Shaffer, D.W., Ruis, A.R.: How we code. In: Advances in Quantitative Ethnography: Second International Conference, ICQE 2020, Malibu, CA, USA, 1–3 February 2021, Proceedings 2, pp. 62–77. Springer, Berlin (2021)
2. Kim, Y.J., Choi, J.: Expanding fairness in game-based assessment with quantitative ethnography. In: Damşa, C., Barany, A. (eds.) Fourth International Conference on Quantitative Ethnography: Conference Proceedings Supplement, pp. 49–54. The International Society for Quantitative Ethnography (ICQE) (2023)
3. Zörgő, S., Peters, GJY., Porter, C., Moraes, M., Donegan, S., Eagan, B.: Methodology in the mirror: a living, systematic review of works in quantitative ethnography. In: Wasson, B., Zörgő, S. (eds.) Advances in Quantitative Ethnography. Communications in Computer and Information Science, vol. 1522, pp. 144–159. Springer, Switzerland (2022). https://doi.org/10.1007/978-3-030-93859-8_10
4. Marquart, C.L., Swiecki, Z., Eagan, B., Shaffer, D.W.: ncodeR (Version 0.1.2) (2018)
5. Cai, Z., Siebert-Evenstone, A., Eagan, B., Shaffer, D.W., Hu, X., Graesser, A.C.: NCoder+: a semantic tool for improving recall of nCoder coding. In: Eagan, B., Misfeldt, M., Siebert-Evenstone, A. (eds.) ICQE 2019. CCIS, vol. 1112, pp. 41–54. Springer, Cham (2019). https://doi.org/10.1007/978-3-030-33232-7_4
6. Shaffer, D.W.: Quantitative Ethnography. Cathcart Press (2017)
7. Eagan, B., Brohinsky, J., Wang, J., Shaffer, D.W.: Testing the reliability of inter-rater reliability. In: Proceedings of the Tenth International Conference on Learning Analytics & Knowledge, pp. 454–461 (2020)
8. Grimmer, J., Roberts, M.E., Stewart, B.M.: Text as Data: A New Framework for Machine Learning and the Social Sciences. Princeton University Press, Princeton (2022)
9. Chang, T., DeJonckheere, M., Vydiswaran, V.V., Li, J., Buis, L.R., Guetterman, T.C.: Accelerating mixed methods research with natural language processing of big text data. J. Mixed Methods Res. **15**(3), 398–412 (2021)
10. González Canché, M. S. Latent code identification (LACOID): a machine learning-based integrative framework [and Open-Source Software] to classify big textual data, rebuild contextualized/unaltered meanings, and avoid aggregation bias. Int. J. Qual. Methods **22** (2023)
11. Yao, L., Mao, C., Luo, Y.: Graph convolutional networks for text classification. In: Proceedings of the AAAI Conference on Artificial Intelligence, vol. 33(1), pp. 7370–7377 (2019)
12. Wang, J., Wang, Z., Zhang, D., Yan, J.: Combining knowledge with deep convolutional neural networks for short text classification. In: Proceedings of the Twenty-Sixth International Joint Conference on Artificial Intelligence (2017)
13. Sagha, H., Cummins, N., Schuller, B.: Stacked denoising autoencoders for sentiment analysis: a review. Wiley Interdisc. Rev. Data Min. Knowl. Discovery **7**(5), e1212 (2017)
14. Choi, J., Ruis, A.R., Cai, Z., Eagan, B., Shaffer, D.W.: Does active learning reduce human coding? A systematic comparison of neural network with nCoder. In: Advances in Quantitative Ethnography: 4th International Conference, ICQE 2022, Copenhagen, Denmark, 15–19 October 2022, Proceedings, pp. 30–42. Springer, Switzerland (2023). https://doi.org/10.1007/978-3-031-31726-2_3

15. OpenAI. GPT-4 Technical Report (2023). ArXiv, abs/2303.08774
16. Gilardi, F., Alizadeh, M., Kubli, M.: ChatGPT outperforms crowd-workers for text-annotation tasks (2023). arXiv preprint arXiv:2303.15056
17. Barany, A., Philips, M., Kawakubo, A.J.T., Oshima, J.: Choosing units of analysis in temporal discourse. In: Wasson, B., Zörgő, S. (eds.) Advances in Quantitative Ethnography. ICQE 2021. Communications in Computer and Information Science, vol. 1522, pp. 80–94. Springer, Cham (2021). https://doi.org/10.1007/978-3-030-93859-8_6
18. Eagan, B., Rogers, B., Pozen, R., Marquart, C., Shaffer, D.W.: rhoR: Rho for inter rater reliability (2016). https://app.calcrho.org/
19. Saldaña, J.: The Coding Manual for Qualitative Researchers, pp. 1–440 (2021)
20. Miles, M.B., Huberman, A.M.: Qualitative data analysis: an expanded sourcebook. Sage, Newcastle upon Tyne (1994)
21. Charmaz, K.: Constructing Grounded Theory: A Practical Guide Through Qualitative Analysis. Sage, Newcastle upon Tyne (2006)

Teaching Quantitative Ethnography as Data Science Education: How Novices Learned in Using Epistemic Network Analysis

Ayano Ohsaki$^{(\boxtimes)}$ (iD)

Shinshu University, 4-17-1, Wakasato, Nagano 3808553, Japan
aohsaki@ohsaki-lab.net

Abstract. This study aims to bridge teaching quantitative ethnography (QE) and data science education. For this purpose, this study proposed and conducted the educational program using epistemic network analysis (ENA) and analyzed students' reports. The research questions were (1) What do novices learn in introductory QE education? and (2) How do students learn in the proposed educational program? Recently, education for data science and data literacy has been discussed in many countries because data science knowledge and skills have become essential in the 21st century. It is required to develop the educational program in literacy level as well as growing data scientists. Moreover, teaching QE has become a high-profile topic in the QE community. Consequently, I examined the potential of an experiential education program in which novices analyze data by ENA. As a result, the students understood the operation and usefulness of ENA through the course. Besides, they enjoyed interpreting the data with diverse team members. This study discusses the course design and educational materials as the first step to QE democratization.

Keywords: Teaching Quantitative Ethnography · Data Science Education · Epistemic Network Analysis · Higher Education

1 Background and Research Questions

This study proposes an educational program with a quantitative ethnography (QE) tool for data science education and examines what and how students learned using it. The QE community has been expanding since the first textbook on it was published in 2017 [1]. To improve the quality of research and practices, educational programs on QE are essential, but previous discussions have focused on specialized education for the researchers. Hence, this study examines the potential of QE in general data science education.

This study bridges data science education for literacy and teaching QE. Data science knowledge and skills have become essential in the 21st century and are no longer reserved for data scientists. With the promotion of the concepts of *data democratization* [2] and *AI democratization* [3], meaning situations in which everybody can access and use data and AI, respectively, opportunities to study data analysis and AI are expanding. Hence,

G. Arastoopour Irgens and S. Knight (Eds.): ICQE 2023, CCIS 1895, pp. 486–500, 2023.
https://doi.org/10.1007/978-3-031-47014-1_33

education in data science and data literacy is actively discussed in many countries. For example, the National Academies of Sciences, Engineering, and Medicine in the U.S. published their visionary report on data science for undergraduates [4]. They named the core concept of data science skills *data acumen*, which refers to the correct conduct for data collection, analysis, presentation, and decision-making and dataset creation. This report not only defined data science knowledge but also provided social impacts, educational materials, and case studies. Moreover, the Association for Computing Machinery (ACM), a U.S.-based international learning society for computing, created a standard curriculum for data science education [5]. Despite being developed for a data science degree, the curriculum's fundamental interdisciplinary content means it can also be used as a reference for the development of educational programs for novices. Similarly, in Japan, discussions on data science education are ongoing. The Japanese government [6] has set the following goals to be achieved by 2025: (1) teach all high-school students basic mathematics, data science, and AI knowledge; (2) train approximately 250,000 people each year in mathematics, data science, and AI so they can apply the knowledge in their field; (3) discover or develop human resources (approximately 2,000 people/year including approximately 100 top-level people/year) who can create innovations using data science and AI and play an active role in the world; and (4) create opportunities to study statistics, data science, and AI as recurrent education for approximately 1 million people per year. Based on this four-part policy, discussions on data science education have become active as several universities have collaborated to build a consortium to develop and provide educational materials [7].

In the learning sciences, there is discussion about students learning data literacy through a data analysis process like that of data scientists. For example, Wise [8] defined data science as the process of connecting subjects to audiences and mapped the research for data science education as follows: Generation, Storage, Transformation, Interpretation, and Presentation. This study described that data are related to situations and understanding relationships and that *Data Acumen* includes critical elements not only for data scientists but also citizens with data literacy. However, many practical educational materials focus on processing data such as creating histograms and machine learning [7, 9]. Consequently, setting up an educational program that can teach the importance of *Data Acumen* throughout the entire data science process in an interesting way for complete novices is necessary.

In the last couple of years, educational programs have become a high-profile topic within the QE community. For example, a webinar [10] was set up and a specialized meeting, "Teaching with QE Meetup," was held at the ICQE22 conference [11]. The QE community has published many resources on how to use epistemic network analysis (ENA), which is a tool for QE [12], and has started graduate-school level courses for specialized education for QE [13]. However, there have been no studies on teaching QE for an introductory level of data literacy, even though QE is an essential approach in the age of big data to capture phenomena that are not revealed by statistical analysis or misleading numbers.

Consequently, this study discusses the potential of a data science educational program using the QE tool for literacy. The research questions are as follows: (1) What do novices learn in introductory QE education? (2) How do students learn in the proposed educational program? This study endeavor will enhance QE educational prospects while also significantly contributing to the instruction of both QE and data science.

2 Methods

2.1 Course Design

The course was designed as an introductory QE education program as part of literacy-level data science education programs. A fundamental program to learn basic QE concepts, an intermediate program to enable learners to analyze their own data based on QE, and an advanced program to allow students to work on QE as researchers have previously been discussed. However, this proposed program introduces QE, including the interpretation of unquantified data, in a more elementary approach. The expected learners are students who are unfamiliar with data analysis and programming and who are aware that data analysis is the mathematical processing of already obtained quantitative data. For example, in Japan, high school students who struggle with mathematics tend to choose to study the humanities and social sciences, such as psychology, literature, education, and economics, and often find data science challenging.

Hence, as an introductory QE program part of data science education for literacy, the course contains the following three goals for students: (1) to enjoy data analysis; (2) to appreciate the usefulness of interpreting data with team members; and (3) to understand the characteristics of ENA. The first two relate to the fundamentals of data science, and the third is related to teaching QE. Furthermore, as an introduction to QE, students experience coding and interpretation in the course. However, it does not require students to understand the difference between QE and ENA, the meaning of ethnography, or the details of ENA's functions, such as stanzas, mean points, and statistical tests [12, 14, 15]. Moreover, students use web ENA [16] instead of rENA [17] in this course because it is for novices in data analysis, including programming. However, the teacher supports students' consideration of the emotions, cognitions, and cultures of the people associated with the data they analyze.

The course was constructed as seven 100-min online lessons (Table 1). Five lessons were real-time online sessions using Microsoft Teams (MS Teams) [18], and two of the lessons were held as on-demand lessons. In the real-time online sessions, students gathered in the online meeting room, listened to the teacher's short lecture for about 20 min, and discussed the theme, which was given by the teacher, with the team members. The teams were created during Lessons 1, 4, and 7 because students could be exposed to various opinions. On-demand lessons were set so that students could conduct independent trial-and-error investigations with the data. During the on-demand lesson, the teacher set up an online Q&A session with teaching assistants. All students could ask the graduate students questions in the real-time online meeting.

The course was designed based on the Attention, Relevance, Confidence, and Satisfaction (ARCS) model in instructional design [19] and psychological safety in organization science [20]. The ARCS model is a well-known model for motivation. In this theory, learner motivation is constructed of the four elements within the model's name. Hence, instructional designers must design small challenges and scaffolding to achieve goals. Meanwhile, psychological safety facilitates team learning by creating an environment in which members can ask each other questions honestly. Hence, for psychological safety in the classroom, the teacher set the codes of conduct for the classroom as follows: (1) contribute to the class (such as asking questions and writing notes), (2) enjoy thinking and focus on finding the questions instead of answers, and (3) keep in mind the goodness of collaborations. Additionally, students were required to evaluate their contribution in the group or classroom in every lesson based on criteria such as tasks required by their roles, discussions, and assistance for their group outcomes. These evaluations were not graded so that students could reflect on their activities authentically.

Table 1. Course schedule.

Lesson	Content	Learning objective	Data science process
1	Overview of the course and preparation for the team discussion	To be able to explain the outline of the course (objectives, grading methods, outline of the content in the course, etc.)	---
2	Outline of the ENA	To be able to explain the outline of ENA	---
3	Practice of using ENA (on-demand lesson)	To know how to use web ENA tool	Interpretation
4	Preparation for the project work	To be able to explain their ideas of what can be visualized using ENA	---
5	Analyzing data by oneself for the project work (on-demand lesson)	To complete coding data and analyze the coded data in web ENA tool	Generation, Storage
6	Create presentation of project work	To be able to explain the advantages of interpreting the results of ENA with team members	Transformation, Interpretation
7	Final presentation and wrap up	To be able to describe the learning results of the 7-week lessons	Presentation

2.2 Course Schedule

This section describes the details of the course schedule in this study (Table 1). The first lesson showed students the outline of the course and the codes of conduct, and the learning objective was "to be able to explain the outline of the course (objectives, grading methods, outline of the content in the course, etc.)." Moreover, the teacher set a team discussion about unfamiliar words with students to prepare for the data analysis as a complex problem-solving activity.

In the second lesson, students tried to operate a web ENA. The learning objective was "to be able to explain the outline of ENA." At the first, the teacher announced the task of the third lesson and that all students needed to operate ENA in the third lesson. Additionally, students listened to a short introduction of ENA's characteristics, which are the ability to quantify qualitative data, visualize connections in data, and compare among some groups. Moreover, the teacher showed a short video about a TV program that was analyzed by ENA to attract students' attention [21]. After that, due to the limited number of simultaneous access to the web ENA server, the teacher set one of the team members to be in charge of the demonstration of using ENA so that the whole group could see how to operate the system. The demonstration used a sample dataset in web ENA. In the lesson, students logged into the web ENA, selected the project, folder, and dataset, and created a subtracted graph by clicking the mean points of the first and second games. The instruction manual (which was provided in the lesson) showed the way to sign-up, log in, upload the dataset, set the model, and create graphs. The manual was created with reference to QE educational materials [22–27].

Lesson 3, as an on-demand lesson, was a tutorial on how to use ENA. The teacher provided the coded dataset of the Japanese play *Shin-Hamlet* [28] written by Osamu Dazai, a famous Japanese novelist. Students were required to compare two scenes of the play and report their results and ideas on how to use ENA. The teacher expected students to understand the operation of the web ENA, understand the advantage of the tool, and think about the relationship between their life and data analysis through practice.

Students started the project with new team members in Lesson 4. Their team members were decided by the teacher based on the students' answers to the preliminary questionnaire. The teacher chose three to four team members so that students from different departments with similar interests were on the same teams. In this lesson, students had to choose the data to analyze in the project. The three possible datasets for analysis were dialogues from the movie *Fantastic Beasts and Where to Find Them* [29], data from interviews with university students [30], and the minutes of the city council for the city in which the college students lived [31]. The teacher prepared these data because the students selected fiction data as that which they most wanted to analyze in the preliminary questionnaire. Moreover, the teacher thought that the data would be of interest to the students because it involved elements familiar to them such as the city in which they lived and the discourse of the university students. Through discussing with team members what data to choose, the students aimed to achieve the goal of being able to explain their ideas of what can be visualized using ENA.

The task of Lesson 5, which was an on-demand lesson, was coding the data they had chosen themselves. The task procedures were as follows: (1) code the data and create a dataset for ENA, (2) upload the dataset to ENA for error checking, and (3) paste their own dataset into the team's shared spreadsheet for submission. The students' progress in this work greatly depended on their information and communication technology (ICT) skills and characteristics. Therefore, the teacher designed this activity as an on-demand lesson so that students could work at their own pace.

Lesson 6 was the last opportunity for students to work on this project. Students uploaded the dataset of all team members' coded data to ENA and interpreted the analysis results. Moreover, they created presentation slides by pasting the graphs and filling in their interpretation in the template slides file the teacher provided. Sometimes, collaborative learning causes issues of social loafing and free riding, especially for large-scale classes of compulsory subjects. In this course, to prevent these issues and support the active participation of all students in the activity, the teacher designed the lesson with reference to the jigsaw instruction method [32]. Specifically, at the beginning of the lesson, the teacher explained that the students needed to be prepared to present their team's project in that week's lesson because all students would present their team's project in a new group for evaluation in the final lesson. Furthermore, the teacher shared the questions of the final report and told them that the evaluation in the final lesson would affect the team members' individual reports. The learning objective of Lesson 6 was to be able to explain the advantages of interpreting the results of ENA with team members.

In the final lesson, students shared their teams' presentations in a new group, and the teacher wrapped up the course. The groups had four or five members who came from different teams. The learning objective of the lesson was "to be able to describe the learning results of the 7-week lessons." Students conducted short presentations and evaluated each other and confirmed what they studied throughout the whole course.

2.3 Data Analysis

This study analyzed the data collected in a course for general education as a compulsory subject in a Japanese private university. Regarding this subject, several faculty members held courses in parallel, and they needed to design their courses based on their respective specialties. In other words, even though the subject name was the same, students learned different topics depending on the course they took. Moreover, students could not choose a course according to their own departments or interests; rather, they were automatically assigned to one of the courses. In the data collection course, all students were in their first year and from several departments, such as Japanese Literature, Social Welfare, Architecture, Pharmacy, and Economics. Many students had not studied basic programming or data analysis. There were 106 students enrolled in the course, but some students did not fully participate, i.e., some did not attend classes or did not submit the assignment. Therefore, this study focused on the 90 students who submitted their final reports, which had a significant impact on their grades, so that only the data of students who worked through the course to the end for credit were analyzed. Therefore, the number of data units (students' descriptions) analyzed was 420.

The data from the short reflection reports in Lessons 2 ($N = 87$), 4 ($N = 80$), 6 ($N = 79$), and 7 ($N = 84$) and the description of ENA in the final report ($N = 90$) were analyzed. Lessons 3 and 5 did not require students to write short reflection reports because they were on-demand lessons. In addition, Lesson 1 did not include ENA or data analysis; instead, it concentrated on team discussions because it was the first time many students from other departments had engaged in discussions using MS Teams. The reflection report prompt was "Please explain what you learned in the class regarding today's learning objectives and what you would like to know more about." On the other hand, the final report prompt about ENA was "Please explain Epistemic Network Analysis (ENA) to the juniors participating in the first week of next year's class."

The coding table (Table 2) includes 14 codes divided into two categories: learning content and students' emotions. The learning content category covers the characteristics of ENA and data science and includes the codes Connection, Comparison, Qualitative Data, Quantification, Visualization, Data Analysis, Others' Presence, and Interpretation created through the inductive process. The students' emotion category includes the viewpoint of the ARCS model [19, 33] for motivation theory and includes the codes Attention, Relevance, Confidence, and Satisfaction defined in a form more specifically corresponding to the data handled in this study, referring to previous research definitions. According to the research [33], those four words are specialized terms: Attention is related to learners' interest and curiosity; Relevance is required for a positive attitude, including personal needs and goals; Confidence refers to learners' belief that they will be successful; and Satisfaction is related to internal and external rewards. Furthermore, to determine the students' emotional transition related to the ARCS model and course learning content, the codes Concern and Difficulty were created by the inductive process.

The coded data were analyzed by web ENA. The settings of web ENA were as follows: report type and student's ID were used in Units and Conversations; Stanza size was Whole Conversation; the Codes were the 14 listed in Table 2. The reason for using Whole Conversation for the stanza size was that the description unit was independently based on the reports and students.

Table 2. Coding Table.

Category	Code	Definition	Example
Content	Connection	Expressing connection as a feature of ENA	ENA is an analysis method that focuses on connections
	Comparison	Comparison as a feature of ENA	[ENA] can visualize changes in connections
	Qualitative Data	Handling of qualitative data	[ENA] can do qualitative and quantitative analysis
	Quantification	Quantification from qualitative data	[ENA analyze data] using quantified data on what was said and the intensity of emotions, etc
	Visualization	Visualization as a feature of ENA	I was surprised that data was visualized
	Data Analysis	Data analysis or data science	Many groups were analyzing the data of Fantabi [Fantastic Beast]

(continued)

Table 2. *(continued)*

Category	Code	Definition	Example
	Others' Presence	Members in team, group, or class	I was curious to see how the others in the group would analyze it
	Interpretation	Viewpoints of analysis or interpretation of data analysis	I learned that even though the results were the same, the interpretation varied
Emotion	Attention	Fun, interest, or enjoyment	It's interesting to have the data appear in an easy-to-understand diagram just by having it upload [to ENA], and it's pretty addicting!
	Relevance	Own ideas of what can be visualized using ENA	Based on that [the characteristics of my favorite writers] understanding [by ENA], make it easier to find books to my like
	Confidence	Confidence for operation ENA or data analysis	Reaffirming operation [on ENA] has helped me to explain them with confidence
	Satisfaction	Resolution of their concerns or the positive aspects of the data analysis process	I was happy to hear how great it was that I had written in detail from members in the group
	Concern	Concern for operation ENA or data analysis	When I was listening to how to operate the system, I honestly felt a little uneasy whether I could understand it and operate [ENA]
	Difficulty	Difficulty or lack of understanding of ENA	I still don't fully understand how to use ENA

3 Results

3.1 ENA Graphs

Figure 1 shows the mean points of each report and the subtracted graph of Lesson 7 and the final reports about ENA. Overall, the mapping codes shape a large triangle with the nodes Interpretation, Satisfaction, and Visualization at its vertices. The left side of the triangle includes three codes of Interpretation, Attention, and Others' Presence. The top of the triangle has the five codes of Satisfaction, Difficulty, Confidence, Qualitative Data, and Concern. The right side of the triangle has the four codes of Visualization, Quantification, Connection, and Relevance. Then, the two codes of Data Analysis and Comparison are in the middle between the top and right edges of the triangle.

Regarding the mean points, the final report and the short reflection report of Lesson 7 are the furthest apart. According to the statistical test of web ENA, along the X axis, the Mann–Whitney test showed that the Lesson 7 (Mdn = −0.46, N = 84) was statistically significantly different at the alpha = 0.05 level from Final report (Mdn = 0.54, N = 90 U = 67.00, p = 0.00, r = 0.98). In contrast, along the Y axis, the Mann–Whitney test showed that Lesson 7 (Mdn = -0.12, N = 84) was not statistically significantly different at the alpha = 0.05 level from Final report (Mdn = −0.21, N = 90 U = 3772.00, p = 0.98, r = 0.00). In the subtracted graph, the characteristic of the final report is the connection between Visualization, Connection, and Relevance, and the characteristic of Lesson 7 is the connection between Attention, Interpretation, and Others' Presence. The results indicate that students enjoyed interpreting data with others. Students learned that the advantage of ENA was to visualize connections and they were able to imagine how to apply ENA to their lives.

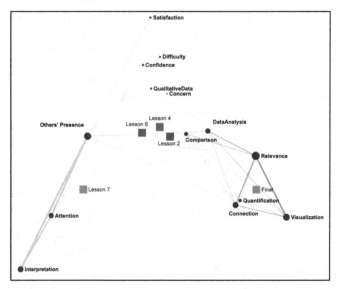

Fig. 1. The mean points' transitions of the students' description and subtracted ENA graph between the 7th lesson's reflection report and the final report

On the other hand, the mean points of Lessons 2, 4, and 6 are mapped to nearby locations. Hence, I created the single graphs of Lessons 2, 4, and 6 to evaluate each lesson design, which are shown in Fig. 2.

In Lesson 2 (Fig. 2a), the most characteristic connections are between Difficulty and Data Analysis, Difficulty and Satisfaction, and Difficulty and Concern. Students felt difficulty throughout the demonstration. The data confirmed that the students felt that their understanding of ENA was not sufficient and that they found it difficult to read the graphs. One student also described the difficulty he experienced because the data for the demonstration was in English. Figure 2a shows the strong connection between Attention and Difficulty. Hence, difficulty was not a major problem in the class and may have contributed to amplifying the students' interest.

Figure 2b visualizes that the connections in Lesson 4 are between Satisfaction and Others' Presence and Others' Presence and Attention. This result suggests that the students enjoyed knowing other members' opinions in Lesson 4, which helped them overcome their anxiety. In practice, many of the students' descriptions of Lesson 4 indicated that they could get answers to the questions they had in the on-demand lessons. They also wrote that they were exposed to new perspectives through discussions in their new teams.

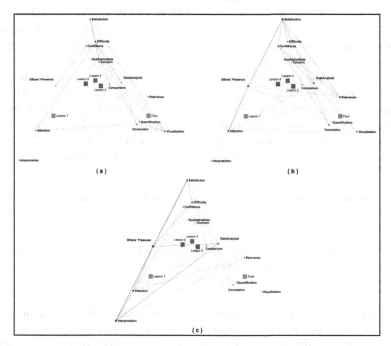

Fig. 2. Single ENA graphs of (a) Lesson 2, (b) Lesson 4, and (c) Lesson 6.

The characteristics of Lesson 6 (Fig. 2c) are the connections between Satisfaction and Others' Presence, Others' Presence and Attention, and Attention and Interpretation. In this lesson, students combined their own data and needed to interpret the graphs. Hence, it seems that they enjoyed sharing their own opinions and interacting with each other. Furthermore, the graph shows the connection between Data Analysis and Interpretation. This expresses that the students in Lesson 6, unlike Lesson 7, still were aware of data analysis because they practiced with the dataset, such as maintaining and uploading it.

3.2 Qualitative Examples

This section shows qualitative examples to describe how the ENA graphs indicate students' learning and thoughts. For example, a student from the Japanese Literature Department transitioned from (Lesson 2) not knowing about IT or computers to (Lesson 6) overcoming the anxiety of analyzing data using computers and eventually (Lesson 7) learning that the same data can be interpreted differently by a person. In another example, a student from the Department of Social Welfare, who wanted to become a social worker, struggled to understand how to interpret ENA graphs (Lesson 4). However, eventually, she/he realized that analyzing relationships between clients and environments with ENAs helps social workers provide better support to clients (Final report). In addition, the student learned how to use spreadsheet software as well as ENA in the activity in Lesson 4, confirming that this course served as an opportunity for the student to learn data analysis from a broad perspective.

Furthermore, to confirm precisely how ENA graphs show the course situation, the students' descriptions of Lesson 7 and the final report based on the ENA graph were reviewed again (Fig. 1). Then, the examples with the characteristic codes in each report were chosen (Table 3). The report of Lesson 7 was chosen based on the codes of Others' Presence, Interpretation, and Attention. This example shows that the students were interested in interpreting the data with other members as a group or class. On the other hand, the final report example was chosen because this description was coded with Connection and Visualization. Additionally, this part of the report had Comparison and Quantification codes. This example shows that the student understood the advantage of ENA because she/he wrote it in their own words instead of using the teacher's expressions.

Table 3. Example description of the seventh reflection and the final report.

Report type	Description
Lesson 7	Through previous classes, I have learned that ENA analysis is more interesting when multiple people examine it from various viewpoints rather than when one person does so alone, and the information gained is overwhelmingly more interesting
Final report	Network analysis is a tool for analyzing human relationships such as in organizations by visualization and finding important points (codes). ENA can analyze [data] by visualizing and quantifying how connections are strong and the episteme of the targets. The advantage of ENA is that, as mentioned above, the connections and codes are simply presented in a diagram, so they can be easily compared by placing them side-by-side or overlapping them, and the differences can be easily identified

4 Discussion

This study asked two research questions: (1) What do novices learn in introductory QE education? (2) How do students learn in the proposed educational program? To answer these questions, this study proposed a data science education program with ENA for literacy and analyzed the data of students' descriptions. Of course, QE is not completely identical to ENA, but the course was designed to study QE and data science through data analysis using ENA. This is because the proposed course was short and for students who are unfamiliar with mathematics, programming, computer use, and data analysis.

However, as a discussion on QE, the teacher supported students to analyze the culture and community in the qualitative data during the course.

As a result, this study confirmed that students learned the analysis method and the tool and updated their interpretations. First, the proposed course could teach novices the usefulness of ENA for the visualization of connecting elements, as shown in the final reports (Table 3), even though the students were randomly assigned to the course and did not have a prior interest in data science and QE. Second, Fig. 1 shows students could imagine the relevance between data analysis with ENA and their lives including their personal interests. For example, a student wrote that ENA would help them understand the characteristics of their favorite writer's works and could more easily find books they like based on that understanding. Furthermore, ENA graphs in Figs. 1 and 2 indicate students learned diverse interpretations and the importance of interpreting data with others. In summary, these results suggest that the proposed course can teach *Data Acumen*, which is discussed in previous studies [4, 8].

Regarding the second research question, the result suggests that the presentation in Lesson 7 had the most impact on students and that conflicts were related to Satisfaction and Confidence. Specifically, Fig. 1 shows the differences among Lessons 2, 4, 6, and 7 by the positions of the mean points. The mean points of Lessons 2, 4, and 6 are located near each other, and the networks in the graphs illustrate that students wrote about their concerns and difficulties in the early phase. With each lesson, the mean points of students' descriptions became closer to the code Attention. In other words, they solved the problems they faced during learning and increased their interest in the subject matter.

Additionally, this study contributes to the creation of design principles for a novice educational program with ENA. First, the course design of demonstration, tutorial, practice, and presentation is effective. In this study, the teacher prepared coded Japanese data for the tutorial so that students could perform trial and error. Then, the teacher confirmed students' progress in achieving their learning activities, including the usage of ENA. However, example data must be prepared in multiple languages to improve the course. In Lesson 2, a student wrote that he/she could not understand what the analysis was about because the data for the demonstration was in English, despite the student's strong interest in ENA, as shown in their writing. When we approach data with QE and ENA, we must read between the lines and understand the background of the data. Therefore, creating coded data using the native languages of various countries and increasing opportunities for analysis in such languages will help create more chances for learning as well as facilitate learner understanding.

The second finding for the design principles is the importance of choosing what data students analyze. To enhance students' motivation, the proposed course had three datasets that students could choose from to analyze. In Fig. 2b, the mean point of Lesson 4 moved closer to Attention and there were strong connections between Satisfaction and Others' Presence and Others' Presence and Attention. According to the students' reports in Lesson 4, they enjoyed the discussion on deciding what data they would analyze in the new group. Some groups reported that they discussed selecting data that other groups would not choose. Moreover, a student reported that they were satisfied with the teacher's choice of teams because they found that during the discussion, the interests of the other members were similar to their own. Therefore, choosing data worked as an icebreaker and improved students' motivation.

5   Conclusion

This study proposed a data science educational program using ENA and examined its potential with the aim of bridging teaching QE and data science education. Based on analysis of students' lesson reports and final report, this study confirmed that students learned how to operate ENA and updated their interpretations with other group members through demonstrations, tutorials, practice, and presentations. In addition, the study highlighted the importance of using non-English datasets and allowing learners to choose data independently.

Despite the significance of its findings, this study still has some limitations. First, the data that could be analyzed to capture the students' learning process was limited to class reflection reports. Although the reflection report prompts were designed to capture a broad range of learning experiences and outcomes, teachers could gain further insight by creating prompts that help students to describe their situation in more detail. Second, this study did not analyze the relationship between students' backgrounds and learning process. Accordingly, to contribute to the development of more effective educational programs, future studies should ask the following research questions: (1) Are there differences in what students learn in different departments? (2) How does students' pre-existing data science knowledge affect their learning process? Third, the proposed course did not cover the difference between QE and ENA, and the best way to connect the course to higher levels of QE education was unclear. The introductory QE education program is expected to be included in the overall curriculum so that students and educators can more explicitly see the connection to higher levels of QE education.

However, this study shows that the students in this course experienced a data science journey that went from dataset creation by coding to presentation. The introductory QE education activities in this study were organized based on the data science education process in the previous study and show the potential of QE education as data science literacy education. Based on the results of the present study, a short educational program introducing QE education as a type of data science education has already been developed. This study expands opportunities for QE education and contributes to both teaching QE and education data science literacy.

Acknowledgment. I would like to thank Yuanru Tan and the QE researchers for their advice in creating the course. Also, three graduate students supported to create the course materials and work as teaching assistants in the course. The present research was supported by JSPS KAKENHI Grant Numbers JP18K13238, JP19H01715, JP20K03066, JP22H01043, and JP 23K11357. This work was funded in part by the National Science Foundation (DRL-1661036, DRL-1713110, DRL-2100320), the Wisconsin Alumni Research Foundation, and the Office of the Vice Chancellor for Research and Graduate Education at the University of Wisconsin-Madison. The opinions, findings, and conclusions do not reflect the views of the funding agencies, cooperating institutions, or other individuals.

References

1. Shaffer, D.W.: Quantitative Ethnography. Cathcart, Madison (2017)
2. Marr, B.: What is Data Democratization? A Super Simple Explanation and the Key Pros and Cons, Forbs (2017). https://www.forbes.com/sites/bernardmarr/2017/07/24/what-is-data-democratization-a-super-simple-explanation-and-the-key-pros-and-cons/?sh=6de8efcc6013
3. Goasduff, L.: 2 Megatrends Dominate the Gartner Hype Cycle for Artificial Intelligence, Gartner (2020). https://www.gartner.com/smarterwithgartner/2-megatrends-dominate-the-gartner-hype-cycle-for-artificial-intelligence-2020. Accessed 25 Aug 2023
4. National Academies of Sciences, Engineering, and Medicine: Data Science for Undergraduates. https://nap.nationalacademies.org/catalog/25104/data-science-for-undergraduates-opportunities-and-options. Accessed 30 Apr 2023
5. ACM Data Science Task Force: Computing Competencies for Undergraduate Data Science Curricula. https://dstf.acm.org/DSTF_Final_Report.pdf. Accessed 30 Apr 2023
6. Cabinet Office, Government of Japan: AI strategy. https://www8.cao.go.jp/cstp/ai/aistrategy2022en.pdf. Accessed 30 Apr 2023
7. Japan Inter-University Consortium for Mathematics, Data Science and AI Education: Model Curriculum Compatible Materials for Literacy Level. http://www.mi.u-tokyo.ac.jp/consortium/e-learning.html. Accessed 30 Apr 2023
8. Wise, A.F.: Educating data scientists and data literate citizens for a new generation of data. J. Learn. Sci. 29(1), 165–181 (2020). https://doi.org/10.1080/10508406.2019.1705678
9. O'Neil, C., Schutt, R.: Doing Data Science: Straight Talk from the Frontline. O'Reilly Media, Inc., Sebastopol: CA (2013)
10. International society for quantitative ethnography: Teaching a QE Course: Triumphs and Tensions. https://www.qesoc.org/webinar-archives/. Accessed 29 Apr 2023
11. ICQE22 schedule. https://www.icqe22.org/schedule/. Accessed 29 Apr 2023
12. International society for quantitative ethnography: Epistemic Network Analysis. https://www.qesoc.org/epistemic-network-analysis/. Accessed 29 Apr 2023
13. University of Wisconsin-Madison: EdPsych 551: Quantitative Ethnography, https://learninganalytics.education.wisc.edu/edpsych-551-quantitative-ethnography/, last accessed 2023/4/29
14. Shaffer, D.W., Ruis, A.R.: Is QE Just ENA? In: Damşa, C., Barany, A. (eds.) Advances in Quantitative Ethnography, ICQE 2022, Communications in Computer and Information Science, vol. 1785, pp. 71–86. Springer, Cham (2023). https://doi.org/10.1007/978-3-031-31726-2_6
15. Arastoopour Irgens, G., Eagan, B.: The foundations and fundamentals of quantitative ethnography. In: Damşa, C., Barany, A. (eds.) Advances in Quantitative Ethnography. ICQE 2022. Communications in Computer and Information Science, vol. 1785, pp. 3–16. Springer, Cham (2023). https://doi.org/10.1007/978-3-031-31726-2_1
16. Epistemic Network Analysis (ENA). https://www.epistemicnetwork.org/. Accessed 29 Apr 2023
17. Marquart, L.C, Swiecki, Z., Collier, W., Eagan, B., Woodward, R., Shaffer, W.D.: rENA: Epistemic Network Analysis
18. Microsoft Teams. https://www.microsoft.com/en-us/microsoft-teams/group-chat-software. Accessed 29 Apr 2023
19. Keller, J.M.: Development and use of the ARCS model of instructional design. J. Instr. Dev. 10(3), 2 (1987)
20. Edmondson, A.: Psychological safety and learning behavior in work teams. Adm. Sci. Q. 44(2), 350–383 (1999)
21. Epistemicanalytics, Analyzing Conversations Using Epistemic Network Analysis (ENA). https://youtu.be/wrTiXNIeHZA. Accessed 7 May 2023

22. Tutorial video on uploading a data set to the ENA webtool, Uploading a dataset to ENA. https://mediaspace.wisc.edu/media/Uploading+a+dataset+to+ENA/0_hr2687ro. Accessed 29 Apr 2023

23. Tutorial video on manually creating ENA models, Using manual mode to create an ENA model, https://mediaspace.wisc.edu/media/Using+manual+mode+to+create+an+ENA+model/0_5ai6qbnb. Accessed 29 Apr 2023

24. Tutorial video on running statistics in the ENA webtool, Running stats in ENA. https://mediaspace.wisc.edu/media/Running+stats+in+ENA/0_tbjiaup6. Accessed 29 Apr 2023

25. Tutorial video on using the data view to see what data led to a specific connection in an ENA model., Clicking connections: data view. https://mediaspace.wisc.edu/media/Clicking+connectionsA+data+view/0_fzw4nidc. Accessed 29 Apr 2023

26. Tutorial video on creating samples or groups of ENA units, Creating samples in ENA. https://mediaspace.wisc.edu/media/Creating+samples+in+ENA/0_ika2mdvg. Accessed 29 Apr 2023

27. Epistemic Network Analysis Web Tool User Guide. https://bookdown.org/tan78/intro_to_ena/. Accessed 29 Apr 2023

28. Dazai, O.: Shin-Hamlet. https://www.aozora.gr.jp/cards/000035/card1576.html. Accessed 29 Apr 2023

29. IMDb: Fantastic Beasts and Where to Find Them. https://www.imdb.com/title/tt3183660/. Accessed 29 Apr 2023

30. Hokkaido University: SDGs Interviews. https://sdgs.hokudai.ac.jp/approach-to-sdgs/interview/. Accessed 29 Apr 2023

31. Tokyo Metropolitan Assembly: Minutes/ Stenographic Records. https://www.gikai.metro.tokyo.lg.jp/record/. Accessed 29 Apr 2023

32. Miyake, N., Kirschner, P.A.: The social and interactive dimensions of collaborative learning. In: Sawyer, R.K. (ed.) The Cambridge Handbook of the Learning Sciences (Second edition), pp. 418–438. Cambridge University Press, New York (2014)

33. Keller, J.M.: The arcs model of motivational design. In: Motivational Design for Learning and Performance. Springer, Boston, MA (2010). https://doi.org/10.1007/978-1-4419-1250-3_3

Author Index

A

Adisa, Ibrahim Oluwajoba 140
Akumbu, Ruth Vitsemmo 96, 244
Andres-Bray, Tyler 155
Árva, Dorottya 409
Ashiq, Muhammad 365

B

Baker, Ryan S. 34, 395, 470
Barany, Amanda 18, 34, 155, 261, 304, 470
Brohinsky, Jais 349

C

Cai, Zhiqiang 49, 349, 426, 455
Chen, Bodong 34
Cheng, Fanshuo 49
Condon, Lara 316
Cseh, Annamária 409

D

Damsa, Crina 81
Dane, Jai Oni 81
Dunai, Diána 409

E

Eagan, Brendan 365, 426, 455
Espino, Danielle 96
Espino, Danielle P. 112, 290

F

Famaye, Tolulope 140
Fan, Aysa Xuemo 125
Fan, Yizhou 3
Fang, Zheng 438
Folkesdtad, James 381

G

Gašević, Dragan 3, 66
Ghaffari, Sadaf 381
Goldstein, Adina 230

Gonder, Mary Katherine 155
Goslen, Alex 18
Green, Samuel 290

H

Hamilton, Eric 96, 112, 275
Hurford, Andrew 275
Hussein, Basel 34
Hutt, Stephen 18

I

Iqbal, Sehrish 3
Irgens, Golnaz Arastoopour 140, 187

J

Jeney, Anna 409
Jimenez, Francisco A. 365

K

Kaliisa, Rogers 81
Keene, Bryan C. 290
Kim, Juhan 261, 470
Koncz, Zsuzsa 316
Kovács, Szilárd Dávid 316

L

Lee, Seung B. 112
Lester, James 18
Li, Haiying 49
Li, Tongguang 3
Li, Xinyu 66
Lin, Jionghao 3
Liu, Qianhui 125
Liu, Xiner 34, 261, 395, 470
Luther, Yanye 381
Lux, Kristina 96, 112

M

Mackey, Sheri L. 330
Mahmud, Usama 215

G. Arastoopour Irgens and S. Knight (Eds.): ICQE 2023, CCIS 1895, pp. 501–502, 2023.
https://doi.org/10.1007/978-3-031-47014-1

Major, David   409
Mallikaarjun, Vinay R.   215
Marquart, Cody   49, 455
Martinez-Maldonado, Roberto   66
Moraes, Marcia   381
Mott, Bradford   18
Mulholland, Katherine   187, 316

N
Nasiar, Nidhi   18, 470
Nguyen, Chi   202

O
Ocumpaugh, Jaclyn   18
Ohsaki, Ayano   486

P
Paquette, Luc   125
Pinto, Juan D.   125
Pratt, Jade   81

R
Ravitch, Sharon M.   215
Remillard, Janine   230
Rivera-Kumar, Stephanie   304
Rowe, Jonathan   18
Ruis, A. R.   349

S
Sanchez, Daniel   81
Schulz, Dante   96
Scianna, Jennifer   81, 395
Seol, Yujung   173

Shah, Mamta   365
Slater, Stefan   395
Sun, Jonathon   202
Swiecki, Zachari   3, 66, 438

T
Tan, Yuanru   66, 349
Tsai, Yi-Shan   3

W
Wang, Grace   49
Wang, Yeyu   349, 365
Werbowsky, Payten   290
Wiebe, Eric   18
Williamson, Marguerite   275
Williamson Shaffer, David   66, 349, 365,
         426, 455
Wilson, Cheryl   365

X
Xiao, Yaxuan   455

Y
Yan, Lixiang   66
Yang, Binrui   349
Yang, Ying   438

Z
Zambrano, Andres Felipe   18, 261, 470
Zambrano, Andres   304
Zhang, Yingbin   125
Zhao, Linxuan   66
Zörgő, Szilvia   316, 409

Printed in the United States
by Baker & Taylor Publisher Services